# A COMMON COUNTENANCE

Stability and Change
in the Canadian Curriculum

George S. Tomkins

Prentice-Hall Canada Inc., Scarborough, Ontario

*... there is throughout Canada a common countenance of education with features sufficiently well marked ... to hide its own wrinkles of administrative division.*

*(Fred Clarke, 1935)*

**Canadian Cataloguing in Publication Data**

Tomkins, George S., 1920-1985
  A common countenance: stability and change
in the Canadian curriculum

ISBN 0-13-152661-8

1. Education – Canada – Curricula – History
I. Title

LB1564.C3T65 1986      375'.00971      C85-099969-3

©1986 Prentice-Hall Canada Inc.,
  Scarborough, Ontario

Prentice-Hall Inc., Englewood Cliffs, New Jersey
Prentice-Hall International, Inc., London
Prentice-Hall of Australia, Pty., Sydney
Prentice-Hall of India Pvt., Ltd., New Delhi
Prentice-Hall of Japan, Inc., Tokyo
Prentice-Hall of Southeast Asia (Pte.) Ltd., Singapore
Editora Prentice-Hall do Brasil Ltda., Rio de Janeiro
Prentice-Hall Hispanoamericana, S.A., Mexico
Whitehall Books Limited, Wellington, New Zealand

Production Editors: Heather Strongitharm/Chelsea Donaldson
Designer: Jo-Ann Jordan
Typesetting: PrimeType Inc.

Printed and bound in Canada by Alger Press

ISBN 0-13-152661-8

1  2  3  4  5  6  AP  91  90  89  88  87  86

# CONTENTS

# ABBREVIATIONS

With the exception of occasional variations noted in the text, annual reports for provincial boards, councils, departments or ministries of education are cited AR preceded by the abbreviated name or initials of the relevant province, e.g. Sask. AR or N.S. AR. Prior to 1868 when Ontario was known as Upper Canada, reports for that province are cited U.C. AR. Other abbreviations are as follows:

| | |
|---|---|
| AUCC | Association of Universities and Colleges of Canada |
| CEA | Canadian Education Association |
| CHA | Canadian Historical Association |
| CMEC | Canadian Ministers of Education, Canada |
| CNCMH | Canadian National Committee on Mental Health |
| CNEA | Canada and Newfoundland Education Association |
| CSSE | Canadian Society for the Study of Education |
| CTF | Canadian Teachers Federation |
| CRCPE | Canadian Research Committee on Practical Education |
| DBS | Dominion Bureau of Statistics |
| DEA | Dominion Education Association |
| NCCU | National Conference of Canadian Universities |
| OEA | Ontario Educational Association |
| OECD | Organization for Economic Co-operation and Development |
| OISE | Ontario Institute for Studies in Education |
| RCITTE | Royal Commission on Industrial Training and Technical Education |

# ACKNOWLEDGEMENTS

During the five years spent on researching and writing this book I have benefited from the assistance of individuals and organizations too numerous to mention. The assistance of colleagues at the University of British Columbia in the Department of Social and Educational Studies and of scholars in other institutions across Canada is acknowledged in the notes, mostly by way of citation of the many studies without which this work would not have been possible. Many discussions, written exchanges, comments, criticism and advice greatly enhanced my efforts. For "outside" counsel, I found the encouragement of Professor R.J.W. Selleck of Monash University, Australia especially helpful.

The staffs of university, legislative and other libraries across Canada greatly lightened my task. I particularly wish to acknowledge the assistance of Joan Gagne of the library of the Faculty of Education, McGill University, the staffs at the Killam Library, Dalhousie University, the Toronto Reference Library, the Robarts Library, University of Toronto, the libraries of the Ontario Institute for Studies in Education, the education libraries of the University of Saskatchewan and the University of Alberta and the library of the University of British Columbia.

I am indebted to the Committee on Research of the University of British Columbia and to the Social Science and Humanities Research Council of Canada for generous grants in support of research expenses. The Council also provided a leave fellowship and two research stipends which enabled me to devote fulltime periods to research and writing. This assistance was supplemented by a short period of paid leave provided in 1980 through the office of the Acting Dean of Education, T.R. Bentley, of the University of British Columbia.

Jean Mann served as my able research assistant throughout most of the project. I also benefitted from the assistance of Judith Stringer, Barbara Rowland and Debbie Markland. I had the unfailing help through numerous drafts of the manuscript of the stenographic and computer skills, and the patience, of Morrie Cringle, Margaret Sakon, Sandra Tomkins and Joerg Messer. As always my wife Doreen provided tangible assistance and moral support, taking time from her own writing and other tasks.

In this work I have drawn on various papers of my own. These are listed in the bibliography.

December 1984                                              George S. Tomkins

# FOREWORD

What must children learn so that they can function appropriately as adults in their society? Who is responsible for teaching them what they need to know? What role does formal schooling play in making children into adults? At the most abstract level, one can argue that the answer to the first question has not changed over the whole range of time covered in George Tomkins' *A Common Countenance*. From the very beginnings of settlement in Canada until the present, parents and society have agreed that children need to learn how to do the essential tasks of what would become their lifetime work, they must learn enough cultural skills to function within their society, and they must learn the norms that will govern their behaviour towards each other and in society as a whole.

Less stability and more change characterizes the history of the responses of Canadians to the last two questions. Tomkins shows us that, until well into the nineteenth century, families, churches, and the state combined in a variety of mostly informal ways to prepare the young for adulthood. Most children in New France, for example, mastered essential domestic and agricultural skills in the family setting, learned their catechism and perhaps some letters from the curé, and became enfolded in the community that structured most of its life around the calendars of seasons and faith. In the early part of the nineteenth century, however, Canadians came to more complex notions of what their children should learn. In turn, the state began to take an increasingly active role in ensuring that children reached an acceptable minimum level of learning, and together with parents, called on schools to increase their role in socializing children. Over the next century and a half parents and state together ensured that most children received some elementary education. Over the last quarter of a century they have added secondary education to the fare of virtually all young people.

This brief summary conceals, of course, an extremely complex history. Indeed, over the last couple of decades a considerable band of historians has clarified much of the story for us. Somewhat surprisingly, few of these historians have tried to give detailed and systematic answers to the particular questions with which I opened this introduction. Now, with *A Common Countenance*, George Tomkins has filled in that substantial gap in our knowledge. In doing so, Tomkins has written what is obviously one of the seminal books in the history of Canadian education. His work will broaden the understanding of those interested in Canadian intellectual and social history, and unlike much of the recent and important monographic work in the history of education, Tomkins' book will be widely read within academic fields in education as well.

Traditionally, history of education served a professional and often inspirational role. Its task was to help initiate novice teachers into their role in the educational system. If it included elements from the history of curriculum, it did so primarily to contrast past practices unfavourably with present ones. At its best, such history provided a context for the essentially presentist and practical nature of teacher education and graduate programs.

The practitioners of the new history of education that I mentioned above have directed their writings towards a much more diffuse audience. Together with those investigating other forms of the new social and intellectual history, they shared in the effort that extended mainstream history in Canada outward from its primary concerns with the political and economic development of the nation. One perhaps inevitable result of these changes is that many historians of education have distanced themselves from the notion that their field has any special claim for a place in the professional development of teachers. Indeed, many working in the field have no connection with either teacher education or graduate studies in education.

If traditional undergraduate and graduate programs in education gave little or no attention to its history, they certainly included much on other aspects of the curriculum. As Tomkins shows us, however, most of the time this focus tended to be discrete – usually on a subject-by-subject basis. Normal school and university instructors, and prospective and practicing teachers gave their attention to such questions as: Is arithmetic a necessary part of the education of all pupils? If the answer to this question is yes, then what arithmetic should elementary pupils learn? What secondary and advanced mathematics must prospective teachers take in order to prepare themselves to teach elementary school arithmetic? What method or methods should teachers employ to teach this arithmetic to their pupils? Until recently much of the effort put into reforming the curriculum involved intervening at one or more stages of this relatively simple process.

In the 1960s and 1970s, most western societies embarked on major efforts to transform their curricula. Those embarking on this task employed a methodology far more sophisticated than earlier efforts at transforming schooling. The work of curriculum reformers, as well, included a major effort to construct a theory of curriculum and of curriculum implementation. Employing notions from philosophy together with methodologies characteristic of sociology, anthropology, and the social sciences generally, the curriculum makers devised new ways of articulating the goals of the curriculum, new ways of introducing new curricula to pupils and teachers, and new ways of evaluating how effectively the changes had been carried out.

As had their predecessors, this new generation of curriculum theorists customarily excluded history from the reform process. There are perhaps two reasons for this exclusion. First, the new educational historians were not as interested in this dimension of the educational past as they were in many other things and thus did provide much that could be used by curriculum theorists. Second, while curriculum theorists were coming to see more clearly than other reformers how deeply traditional practices were woven into the fabric of education, they still perceived that their professional goal was to root them out.

In the late 1970s and early 1980s, enthusiasm for curriculum innovation waned. Many of the new curricula has not delivered all or even much of what they had promised. Certain traditional practices – never altogether banished from classrooms – again became fashionable. At this point history began to assume a more important place in the study of curriculum. On the one hand, curriculum theorists wanted to examine the recent past to discover what had really happened over the last couple of decades. What innovations had been successful? What innovations had been failures? Why had some succeeded and others failed? History also began to enter curriculum theory at a more fundamental level. Historians of education began to see that they had not given the attention it deserved to the history of curriculum in both the recent and more distant past. Curriculum theorists began to see that history formed an essential element of their field.

*A Common Countenance*, then, appears at a particularly auspicious time. It will interest both professional and academic audiences. Prospective and practicing teachers will find in it a context into which they can place the classroom practices of their profession. Unlike traditional histories of education, it does not try to convince teachers that they are members of a great crusade that, with a little more push, will break through to a final victory over ignorance. On the other hand, and unlike some recent works in the field, it does not leave teachers or anyone else concerned with the state of education with a sense of despair, a feeling that all attempts at change are at best failures or at worst that they leave children less well off than when they began. To both teachers and curriculum makers, it provides enough of the broad sweep of the history of Canadian education to show how deeply the curriculum is rooted in Canadian culture.

Above all, in the book's very considerable emphasis on the recent past, it provides a realistic perspective on present prescriptions and practices, on the constraints that the Canadian context places on change, and on the not unworthy tradition of which contemporary teachers and other educational professions are a part. In so doing it avoids over-emphasizing the stability and continuity that people are prone to idealize in the past. Instead, it shows us the tensions that persist between a society increasingly characterized by considerable change and educational institutions called upon to meet perennial needs such as basic literacy, as well as the need for skills demanded by a transformed economic and social environment. *A Common Countenance* shows us that those changes in the Canadian curriculum that have taken in the distant and the recent past, have done so because they have been in rough harmony both with the Canadian tradition and with changes in the wider society. To historians, Tomkins provides a curriculum-focussed synthesis of much of the substantial body of monographic work in the history of Canadian education completed over the last two decades. In conducting this task, Tomkins transcends the great historiographic debates that accompanied the production of that rich literature. His text shows that he clearly understands the theoretical perspectives involved — feminist, neo-Marxist, social control theory, and so on — but that each produced much that could be usefully employed through his conceptual investigation.

The closer an historian gets to the present the closer he comes to topics on which his readers may hold strong views. Many teachers and historians joined with members of the general public in taking part in the vigorous debates over curricular issues of the post-1945 era. One of the great merits of *A Common Countenance* is that Tomkins gives a fair account of the conflicting points of view, lets us feel the passions they arouse, but stands clearly if sympathetically above the battles. Such distancing is essential in a book that is not a work of advocacy but a scholarly account of recent as well as distant events. It is, however, rarely achieved by someone who more often than not was actively and even passionately involved in the events he describes.

Born and educated in Montreal, George Tomkins began there a career that eventually came to encompass teaching at all levels from elementary classroom to graduate seminar. He grew from being a fine geography teacher to a pre-eminent theoretician and a central figure in the development of both Canadian studies and the history of Canadian curriculum. Tomkins began by studying and applying to the Canadian scene the pedagogy of school geography that had been developed by such British geographers as James Fairgrieve, Neville Scarfe, and R.C. Honeybone. In *A Regional Geography of North America* and other texts, Tomkins provided materials and activities on the British model which helped youngsters begin to sense the "personality" of regions. In contrast to their counterparts elsewhere, these texts also included elements drawn from systematic geography in such a way as to enable youngsters to put their regional work together into a coherent whole. Tomkins was the first to show how the psychological constructs of Jerome Bruner provided a powerful rationale for the new school geography. These notions in turn came to provide the intellectual structure for the major curricular reforms of the late 1960s and 1970s in geographic education, in both Canada and the United States.

Tomkins conducted much of this work at the University of British Columbia, where he joined the faculty in 1960. It was there that his interests in geography gradually evolved into a major concern for the broader field of Canadian studies. In 1971, Tomkins took a leave from the University of British Columbia and worked for five years with Birnie Hodgetts as Co-director of the Canada Studies Foundation. Under Tomkins' skillful guidance, teams of enthusiastic teachers became competent at developing materials and methods of teaching about Canada in Canadian elementary and secondary schools. One can see the effects of Tomkins' teaching in both the content and modes of instruction of social studies in nearly all the provinces.

When Tomkins returned to the University of British Columbia, he began a decade's work on curriculum — including a term as Director of the

Centre for the Study of Curriculum and Instruction — that culminated in the writing of *A Common Countenance*. In it, readers will find, he has brought together his long experience with the practical, day-to-day concerns of teachers with his wide-ranging reading and research in curriculum and in history. In one sense, it both explains and marks the end of one of the most turbulent periods in the history of Canadian education. In another, it transforms the writing of the whole of that history. With *A Common Countenance*, the history of curriculum in Canada takes its place as a new and important field of academic inquiry. As his bibliography clearly shows, many other scholars helped Tomkins in this task. Nevertheless, it is not an exaggeration to say that he has put the field together into a coherent whole for the first time, and that later work will be written in his very long shadow.

Neil Sutherland
*University of British Columbia*

# PROLOGUE

The major objective of this study is to provide a tentative interpretation and preliminary synthesis of the course of Canadian curriculum development from its beginning in early French and English Canada until 1980. Although before Confederation the term "curriculum" seems to have been rarely used officially, during the nineteenth century curriculum development, as such, gradually became a more or less systematic process by which courses of study and school programs were conceived and implemented. It is the study of this process, of the contexts in which it occurred, of the principles that guided it and of the curricula which emerged from it that constitute the major themes of this book.

In pursuing these themes, the curriculum will be defined as the ostensible or official course of study, typically made up in our era of a series of documents covering various subject areas and grade levels together with statements of "aims and objectives" and sets of syllabi, the whole constituting, as it were, a set of rules, regulations and principles to guide what should be taught. However, both in the past and today, this tidy definition may obscure (and be obscured by) the reality of the curriculum actually taught by the teacher and experienced by the pupil in the classroom. This fact underscores the importance of understanding what modern policy-makers call "curriculum implementation." Although contemporary educators are aware of the complexities and difficulties of change, they tend to assume that curricular and other intended outcomes of schooling proclaimed by their predecessors in legislation, regulations and cascades of official rhetoric were attained. Yet there is abundant evidence that, in being forced to respond to public demands, earlier school promoters faced problems of implementation comparable to our own.

Some will ask if it is appropriate to speak of Canadian curriculum development or of a Canadian curriculum in a "system" of education which, since 1867, has constitutionally consisted of a series of provincial and territorial public school jurisdictions, most of which, under various legislative arrangements, also include several types of separate religiously-based school systems. Despite these circumstances and despite the absence of a formal federal presence in education, the following phenomena emerged: with industrialization after 1867 came national initiatives in technical and scientific education, with immigration came demands for "Canadianization" of the curriculum, with concern about national sobriety came temperance education, with "rural decline" came agricultural education, and with francophone nationalism and Quebec separatism came bilingual education.

Those developments suggest the national perspective that will be taken in this book, with Canadian education viewed as more than the sum of its parts, even as constitutional constraints and inveterate regionalism will require attention to particular provincial jurisdictions. In taking this view we shall see that to many educators, Canadian and non-Canadian alike, it has long been evident that a distinctive Canadian education and curriculum clearly exist. Thus, Fred Clarke, a British observer during the 1930s, in coining a felicitous phrase (which has been borrowed for the title of this book), had no difficulty in perceiving "a common countenance" of education, at least throughout anglophone Canada. French Quebec, he implied, had a significantly different countenance.[1] In making the latter point Clarke was probably exaggerating, even at that time, the separateness in educational and other matters of two deeply conservative societies which shared more common values than their obvious linguistic, religious and other cultural differences implied. In recent decades, as I shall argue, educational and other disparities between the two solitudes have narrowed, a reflection of the closer sharing of a common North American way of life; paradoxically, political differences have at times increased to the point of endangering the very fabric of Confederation itself.

In seeking to promote socialization to approved religious, social and cultural norms, school promoters in both solitudes were inevitably caught up in conflict. Such conflict arose out of the desire for cultural survival that animated all groups that made up an increasingly diverse Canadian mosaic after the mid-nineteenth century. Cultural survival entailed the retention of group characteristics expressed by social, ethnic, linguistic, religious and other distinctive forms of cultural identity. For the dominant Anglo-Celtic majority, survival meant socialization to Protestant Christian and British patriotic norms, and resistance to external, mainly American, cultural hegemony; secondarily it meant resistance to the claims of the various minorities, especially the francophone minority within the Canadian "mosaic." For the minorities, cultural survival meant resistance to the cultural leadership of the dominant majority. Francophones in particular sought to preserve their language, cultural traditions and Catholic morality.

Cultural conflict, cultural survival and related controversies have become pervasive themes in much of the "new" social and educational history. Unfortunately, the curriculum dimension of these themes and the degree to which each has played a major role in Canadian curriculum development has been underplayed. Thus in discussing the often bitter controversies over language and religion ranging from the famous Manitoba schools question of the 1890s to that of Quebec's Bill 101 in the 1970s, scholars have tended to focus on legal, constitutional and political issues to the neglect of curriculum issues. Yet cultural conflict in Canadian education has characteristically been curriculum conflict, focussed on the basic curriculum question of what the schools should teach, that is, on the objectives and content, including often the materials used in the classroom. In few nations has the course of study prescribed for schools engendered more conflict in the wider society.

Despite the neglect of curriculum issues *per se* by scholars, their work has been of considerable value to contemporary policy-makers who have increasingly come to realize the importance of understanding the historical roots of modern controversies. A comparative boom in social, cultural and intellectual history has revealed the contexts within which past curriculum development took place, and has made the course of that development more explicable. Thus, although we have as yet no intellectual history of Canadian education, no interpretations or syntheses of indigenous educational theory, the recent work of such scholars as Berger, Armour and Trott, McKillop, Smith and others has proved invaluable in this study in suggesting the philosophical traditions and contexts in and out of which curriculum policy and practice grew and developed.[2] As a consequence, the relationship between theory and practice has been illuminated, and an enhanced understanding has been gained of those ideas and ideologies that have guided the actions and deliberations of Canadian curriculum policy-makers and helped them to define their purposes and goals.

In seeking to trace the development of curriculum as policy we need, beyond better contextual and theoretical understanding, much more detailed knowledge about the origins and course of the process *per se* and about the characteristics of the curricula that resulted from it. For such knowledge, we must turn to policy statements and debates in journals and in proceedings of official and unofficial bodies that sought to influence curriculum policy; to commissioned studies; to general statements of goals found in annual reports, curriculum guides and similar documents; and to the minutiae of curricula revealed in courses of study, textbooks and examinations, among other sources. A great deal of such information is to be found in the growing body of monographic studies, dissertation research and similar recent scholarly works, many of them in unpublished form, without which this study could not have been carried out. When related to earlier research (most of which was directed by policy-makers to their own pressing practical and theoretical concerns), this recent work and my own investigations provide, it is hoped, a valuable sketch map for guiding future graduate studies and research, for meeting the needs of contemporary students, and for responding to public interest in the evolution of the modern curriculum. Much of my own work here takes the form of conceptual investigation, which has been described as a mode of research that organizes facts already on hand or critically appraises existing concepts.[3]

That this study must be preliminary is suggested by a consideration of the work that remains to be done on topics that have direct or indirect salience for understanding the course of curriculum development. Thus, we have no significant studies of textbooks and their impact comparable to that by Elson in the United States.[4] Although my work has benefited from studies of the subject areas of the curriculum, for example, English, art, music, science and physical education, we need updated research on these from a national perspective. As yet, we have nothing comparable to Goodson's social history of the British curriculum based on his studies of the origins and evolution of the subjects that comprise it.[5] There are no national studies of the development of teacher training. School administration has been notably ahistorical. There is a serious need for competent studies of the testing and guidance movements and of special education. Valuable studies of school finance have been undertaken but we need to know much more about how assessment, taxation and other policies affected curriculum provision and contributed to or mitigated disparities in such provision.[6] There is a crying need for biographies of influential policy-makers such as Alexander MacKay, George M. Weir, Gédéon Ouimet and Peter Sandiford to supplement the few competent studies that have appeared to date.[7]

Although the emphasis in this study is on schools and on the official curriculum as the central focus of formal educational endeavours, consideration will be given to the influence of other institutions, notably universities, which have long had a profound influence on curriculum development. An emphasis on schooling does not deny the existence and powerful influence on teaching and learning of the so-called "hidden curriculum," including the structures, rules and regulations of the school itself, as well as what has been called the cultural baggage that children bring into the classroom. Canadians have long viewed education as much broader than schooling. This perspective underscores the fact that the school can only be understood in its relation to other educative institutions and to society itself. This fact is equally true of curriculum development. For the United States, Lawrence Cremin has written of educational configurations made up of associations of institutions and informal agencies interacting together and with society. These have included schools, families, churches, museums, libraries and the mass media.[8] On the early North American frontier the prevailing configuration was dominated by family and church, with the school playing a secondary role whereas with the coming of industrialism and urbanization, the nineteenth century became "the century of schooling." In our own time, a new configuration has given prominence to the mass media, notably television. In the view of some critics it has relegated schools and teachers to a lesser, if not minor, educational role.

An emphasis on schools reminds us that the neglect of curriculum history noted earlier has left us with little knowledge of school processes, or of the details of life in Canadian classrooms. A full- blown history of the curriculum or schooling must await studies drawn from such sources as school registers, student record cards and reports, teachers' day books, minutes of curriculum committees and school board meetings and oral accounts.[9] Unfortunately, few Canadian school boards or organizations such as teachers' federations maintain proper archives. Provincial and federal archives have until very recently given little priority to educational collections. Where contemporary studies are concerned, we have nothing in Canada of the scope of Rutter's study of London inner city schools, or of Goodlad's nationwide study in the United States.[10]

Earlier references to contexts remind us that most studies have had, and still have, international as well as national and local dimensions. Beginning with the Jesuits and their famous *Ratio Studiorum* (plan of studies), the course of study was part of an international mainstream from the start, as Canadian educators, like their counterparts in other nations, were influenced by developments beyond their own borders. Various theories of education associated with particular thinkers such as Pestalozzi, Froebel, Herbart, Spencer, Dewey and Thorndike attracted attention in Canada. However, in looking at the Canadian curriculum experience we shall be wise to heed Michael Katz's admonition that "simple notions of direct borrowing will not suffice any more adequately than have assumptions about cultural isolation."[11] What seems certain is that common social currents were flowing from the mid-nineteenth century onward in all western nations, emphatically including Canada, a fact which requires an emphasis on the broad social context in which schooling developed. That context influenced school structures and organization, and forced a reappraisal of the nature and goals of the curriculum. The numbers, diversity and changing nature of the schools' clients were alone sufficient to promote change. The so-called factory model of the graded school was one such change; the development of mechanisms of curriculum control by means of uniform textbooks, examinations, teacher training and supervisory or inspection systems, and the establishment of compulsory attendance laws were other examples.

Part I of this book deals with the origin and growth of the Canadian curriculum, from its beginnings in New France and early English Canada to 1892. In a brief survey of what I have called the pre-industrial curriculum that existed before 1840, I discuss Canadian schooling as an informal, intermittent experience not yet sharply separated from work in parent-church-controlled systems that aimed at teaching basic literacy, religious precepts and loyalty to the reigning monarch. These goals represented social and political imperatives that arose out of the need for cultural survival in both founding societies. However, although such goals would animate schooling for generations to come, we can hardly speak of curriculum development during this period as a systematic process in any modern sense.

With the emergence after 1840 of "responsible government," the era of state-controlled schools and curricula began. Over the following half century school promoters established administrative structures that enabled them to sort children into classes and grades, to create a hierarchically organized teaching force and to devise a common curriculum for a whole province. It was during this era that official courses of study embodied in legislation and official documents began to appear. Simultaneously the mechanisms of curriculum control already referred to were developed as a means of implementing this curriculum.[12] As educators in an emerging industrial society confronted conflicting demands for liberal and practical schooling and for curricula that would serve moral, intellectual and civic purposes — this last reflected in nascent concerns for developing a distinctive Canadian identity — there emerged themes that would remain pervasive in curriculum development into our own time.

Part II of this study begins in 1892, with the founding of the Dominion Educational Association, an event that conveniently marks the beginning of a nationalizing era in Canadian education. In it I trace the development of a *de facto* national curriculum across anglophone Canada at a time when, under the impact of the forces of modernity, traditional education was being called into question in all western nations. Francophone development proceeded separately, but was not unaffected by reform impulses. In the absence, until recently, of research similar to that undertaken in anglophone Canada since 1945, discussion of these must necessarily be limited. It was in this era that, in order to meet pressing social needs generated by rapid industrial and technological change, Canadians cautiously developed new policies based on a new consensus about childhood.[13] In schools, this took the form of the New Education or "progressivism." As educators rationalized and professionalized their school systems, now familiar structures of schooling were put into place and more efficient methods of curriculum control were established.

In Part III I have attempted to trace curriculum development during the post-1945 decades when affluence, the baby boom, new demands for mass schooling and the gradual breakdown of the long established consensus based on Judeo-Christian and Anglo-conformist imperatives led to conflicting demands for curriculum change. Rapid social change, was reflected in rapid oscillations between subject-centred, work-centred and child-centred reform after 1960. New knowledge, new demands for more practical schooling, larger and more diverse school populations and new social tensions were reflected in a questioning of traditional values, renewed fears of Americanization, the rise of Quebec separatism and the demands for equality of Native peoples, other minorities and women. All these trends were reflected in widespread curriculum innovation and in a temporary relaxation of centralized control. These developments, together with a conservative resurgence in the late 1970s, the emergence of a new social consensus based on a new ethic of respect for cultural diversity and the persistence of nationalizing imperatives are discussed in a concluding epilogue.

## Notes to Prologue

1 F. Clarke, "Education in Canada," 313.

2 The reference here is to Carl Berger, Leslie Armour and Elizabeth Trott, A.B. McKillop and Allan Smith whose works, to be cited later, are included in the bibliography.

3 Brauner, 3 citing Cowley.

4 Elson.

5 Goodson.

6 For examples of useful extant studies, see bibliographical references to Maxwell A. Cameron, H.B. King, K.F. Argue, David Cameron, W.J. Brown.

7 See studies by Chernefsky and Oviatt and the recent study of J.H. Putman by B. Anne Wood.

8 Cremin, *Public Education*, 30-31.

9 The beginning of this type of research has been made by such scholars as Michael Katz, Neil Sutherland and Robert Patterson. Useful data about past school life, mainly in urban settings, will be found in the accounts provided by Calnan, Charyk, H. Cochrane, Cummings and MacSkimming, Disbrowe, Dukhan, Fair, Flynn, Lapp, Londerville, Nesbitt, Shutt, R. Stamp's "School Days", Vernon, Waites and W. Wilson. Novels and autobiographies are other useful sources several of which are cited in the text. See also Oster, "The Image of the Teacher in Canadian Prairie Fiction".

10 Rutter; Goodlad.

11 Mattingly and Katz, vii.

12 Sutherland, "The New Education," 49-50.

13 Sutherland, *Children*.

# PART I

## THE ORIGIN AND GROWTH
## OF THE
## CANADIAN CURRICULUM
## TO 1892

# CHAPTER 1

# THE PRE-INDUSTRIAL CURRICULUM

*The residents ... of Montreal ... have recourse to you begging ... that you will record their good intentions in obtaining for them such teachers as may be most capable of exercising a proper control over the young and inspiring them with those sentiments of submission necessary to render them good servants of the king and at the same time good servants of God.*
*(Petition to the King of France, 1727)*

*Good Schoolmasters imbued with doctrinal soundness and a regard for British institutions [are] much wanted, [the] chief hope [of the Colony] being among the rising generation.*
*(Society for the Propagation of the Gospel, Nova Scotia, 1749)*

Canada before 1840 was a pre-industrial, rural society. As such it was not purely agricultural having had its initial economic origins in the trading staples of fish, furs and lumber. Iron smelting, established in 1736 at the Forges de St. Maurice, the building of canals and, in 1836, the opening of Canada's first railway together with flour milling, saw milling and rudimentary paper making were small harbingers of an industrial future. In New France, settlement and economy focussed on the St. Lawrence, the great river of Canada which would eventually serve as the highway to a transcontinental dominion. By the time of the British Conquest in 1763, New France was a community in its own right, its people, *les Canadiens*, distinctive from those of Old France. In the post-Conquest period this people would assert its distinctiveness in the interest of cultural survival *(la survivance)*, using church-controlled schools as a major means to that end. In English Canada, early settlements of "pre-Loyalists" in Nova Scotia combined with Loyalist settlement after 1783 to establish the basis of a distinctive society based on British values. Here, too, schools would serve as a major instrument of cultural survival. However, in both founding societies they were initially but one element and often the least important one, in the educational configurations of the period. Although the concept of systematic curriculum development was little understood in either New France or early English Canada, the rudiments of formal studies were nevertheless well established by 1840.

## New France: Piety, Practicality and Cultural Conflict in the Curriculum

### Early Society and Schooling

Moogk observes that in modern French Canada little children are some-times called *les petits sauvages*. This unflattering designation would have been accepted in New France, where children were widely regarded as will-ful, disobedient and disrespectful. In fact, the picture is much exaggerated, if only because children were kept in a prolonged state of legal dependence, so that majority was not attained until age twenty-five. Socially, childhood extended to age fifteen or sixteen. With an average of 5.65 living children for parents surviving to age fifty, families were large, a consequence of phenomenally high birthrates. Mortality rates were also high, and it is esti-mated that 45 per cent of children did not survive beyond the age of ten. The population was a youthful one with no less than 44 per cent under the age of fifteen in 1734. Most children were put to work before that age, their labour being essential to the family.[1]

As a sacramental religion, Catholicism, unlike Protestantism, did not hold Bible reading to be essential to salvation. As a result there was less zeal for popular education than in the adjacent British colonies. Moogk has identified three aspects of education in New France: religious instruction, essentially the learning of the catechism; occupational training, mainly in the form of apprenticeship which constituted the chief form of education in the colony; and academic education, the provision of which was meagre, with schooling for most children brief and intermittent. The major aims of schooling were to train the clergy and to evangelize the Indians. Much teaching was informal and, as in all pioneer societies, the separation be-tween schooling and work was not sharply defined, as children at any given age might alternate between both. Illiteracy was widespread and ap-pears to have increased in the later years of the colony.[2]

Contrary to myth, New France was not a static feudal society trans-planted from France. In part this was because the seigneurs had relatively limited power. Settlements initially based on fur trading posts and forts rather than on farming suggest that for a long period this society was in a real sense urban and commercial, despite a small population and slow growth that gave New France hardly 10 000 people by 1700. It was only after the British Conquest in 1763 that French-Canadians turned back to the soil as a folk culture emerged. A business (middle) class together with military and civil officers and the clergy dominated the small society by 1750.[3]

Concern for cultural survival was an imperative in a precarious colony, where to the threat of a hostile wilderness was added conflict between the stable rural values of agriculture and the disorganizing social ethos of the fur trade. Although modern scholars now question the economic significance of the trade after 1700, the famous nomadic *coureurs de bois* — those stock characters of Canadian social studies curricula — did undermine moral constraints. Social instability was marked by drunkenness, prostitution, occasional violence and disrespect for law and authority.[4]

Cultural survival rested on the inculcation of loyalty to the monarch and Christian virtue, designed to make children "good servants of the King . . . and of God." To counter instability, settlers were fairly carefully screened to ensure that only those of sound moral and religious character were admitted. After 1627, only Roman Catholics were permitted entry, a policy that would contribute greatly to the ultimate social and cultural homogeneity of French Canada. Cultural survival meant more than teaching patriotism, morals and religion or even letters. Economic needs dictated a practical curriculum in a colony that needed navigators, fishers, sailors, mechanics and farmers, trained in part through apprenticeship.

## Formal Studies

No school system as such developed in New France, since the state, although offering spasmodic financial support, left initiatives to the church and church-related private effort. Although a few schools were established before 1630, the *petites écoles* established after that date may be regarded as the first organized schools in Canada. Offering an elementary education to only a minority of children, the basic curriculum of the *petites écoles* consisted of the catechism and the three Rs, supplemented for the more gifted students by the rudiments of Latin as a preparation for secondary studies. The parish served as the basic unit for the forty-seven *petites écoles* known to have been established in New France by 1763, but probably no more than half the parishes possessed such schools. Itinerants often served as both priests and teachers. As noted earlier, informal schooling was common, often provided by notaries or other laypersons. In 1703, Bishop St. Vallier of Quebec established rules to ensure "that the children do not read evil books and that the boys and girls never attend the same school."[5] In 1727, an intendant's ordinance forbade anyone to teach reading and writing or "to keep schools" without the written permission of the Bishop of Quebec "by whom they shall be subject to be examined both at the time of receiving a license and afterwards in the course of his visitations . . . "[6] Here were the origins of the concept of teacher certification and inspection in Canada.

The arrival of the Jesuits in 1625 and the appointment of Laval in 1658 as the first bishop of New France ensured the dominance of a conservative faith — "enthusiastic, serious, moral, evangelical, mystical" — that would characterize French Canadian society and schooling for the next three centuries. As a result, the church controlled education and determined the curriculum of French-Canadian schools until 1960. As the first Canadian teachers, the Jesuits represented a powerful organized international elite;

they established the tradition of highly centralized curriculum control in the form of the *Ratio Studiorum*, arguably the most systematic course of study ever devised. This carefully graded curriculum organized into classes foreshadowed the "standards" or grades that later became a basic organizing principle for schools in all western systems of education.

The famous Jesuit College established at Quebec in 1635, a year before Harvard College in Massachusetts, marked the beginning of Canadian secondary schooling and foreshadowed the later development of higher education. Significantly, French was introduced as the language of instruction at a time when Latin was still used in Jesuit schools in Europe. Greek, Latin, the teaching of grammar, rhetoric and philosophy, as well as history, geography and mathematics were included in a secondary curriculum as broad as most found in France. In addition to the training of priests, the college met the needs of upper and middle class laypersons.[8] Laval University, the premier institution of higher education in French Canada, grew out of Laval's Petit Seminaire, founded in 1668.

The education of girls formally began with the arrival of the Ursulines at Quebec in 1639. In 1657, Marguerite Bourgeoys opened her famous school at Montreal, beginning the work of the Congregation of Notre-Dame, which became the leading female teaching order. To the curriculum of the catechism and the three Rs was added the teaching of domestic skills and "female accomplishments" such as needlework and etiquette. French visitors noted the purity of accent and ease of speech that gave many Canadian girls a social bearing equal to girls in France itself.[9] By the 1740s, the Congregation was also teaching about one hundred girls at Louisbourg in Ile-Royale (Cape Breton). There, as in Quebec, female literacy rates, measured by the ability of girls to sign their names, were much higher than in the homeland.[10]

## Native Education and Cultural Conflict

Jaenen has described French efforts to Christianize and "francise" the Native peoples. "Francisation" was designed "to make French; to affect with French characteristics ... in manners, tastes and expressions." While considered culturally inferior, Indian children were regarded as intellectually equal to French children. Attempts were made to educate Indian children and youth through mission schools and boarding schools, by sending an elite minority of boys (and a few girls) to be educated in France and through *petites écoles* set up on reserves or in French settlements.[11] All these efforts to turn Indian into French failed. Herding a nomadic people on to reserves and attempting to convert them to a sedentary farming and Christian life posed particular difficulties. Efforts to induct Indian girls into religious vocations also failed, although more success was achieved with the general education of Indian girls. Language became a basic instrument of social control through the introduction of alphabetical writing by the Jesuits who prepared Native translations of basic biblical texts.[12]

The failure of the French missionary effort was in educational terms a consequence of the first cultural conflict and the first curriculum conflict in Canadian history. The Indians had an informal curriculum based on their own survival needs, one in which teaching was culturally diffused rather than institutionalized. By contrast, the missionary curriculum was a rigid learning experience, most of it irrelevant to Native needs and imposing alien concepts of time, order, competitiveness and punishments for misdemeanors. The objectives of French policy as cited by a contemporary source foreshadowed problems that have bedevilled Caucasian-Native relations in education and other matters throughout Canada down to our own day:

> To assemble a people made up of French and Indians who will be converted so as to render them sedentary, to train them to practise the mechanical arts and farming, to unite them under a common discipline in the exercise of the Christian life .... and if once reason obtains the advantage over their old customs, with the examples of the French ... inciting them to work, it seems that they will set themselves straight ..."[13]

## Curriculum for "La Survivance" — The Post-Conquest Struggle for Control

### Society, Schooling and Early Cultural Conflict in Post-Conquest Quebec

With the assumption of political and economic power by the conquerors in 1763, the way was open for the church to assert its spiritual and cultural authority in a closely knit rural society of 60 000 souls, based on the values of farm, faith and family *(la ferme, la foi, la famille)*. Over the following century, this small community from which most of today's francophone Canadians are descended gave rise to one of the most phenomenal population explosions in Western history. That explosion would place enormous strains on the social fabric, not least on the inherited fragile educational structure. By 1840, the population had multiplied tenfold, bursting beyond the bounds of the St. Lawrence Valley into harsh lands where church-going, school attendance, family cohesion and godly behaviour among a poverty-stricken, illiterate peasantry were likely to be the exception rather than the rule.[14] Well before the Conquest, concern had been expressed about increasing illiteracy and a decline in intellectual life and educational standards, a trend attributed by the French to Canadianization which they equated with barbarization.[15] In the absence of priests and teachers after the Conquest, illiteracy increased to the point that by 1800 only a quarter of the population could read, and no more than one tenth could write their names. At this time, there was no institution for preparing teachers, few textbooks and no standard curriculum.[16]

For the French-Canadians, cultural survival meant the preservation of their land and language, their customs and laws and their religion. In 1763, the conquerors provided a civil court in which French civil law was recognized and in which the French language could be used. The Quebec Act of 1774 confirmed these rights and recognized the church's right to control schooling. In 1791, the Canada (Constitutional) Act established the separate provinces of Lower Canada (Quebec) and Upper Canada (Ontario) and provided limited representative government.* For French-Canadians, the following decades marked the development of an instinctive sense of community and self-conscious nationalism which became a basis for *la survivance.*[17] A century and a half of history was coming to life. They were beginning to remember their martyrs, their heroes and their battles, future grist for history curricula that would later become central to French-Canadian education. The masthead of *Le Canadien*, "the first genuinely French-Canadian newspaper," established in 1806, proclaimed French Canada's aspirations, *notre langue, nos institutions, nos lois;* it also featured those later symbols of Canadian nationhood, the beaver and the maple leaf.[18]

Cultural conflict between conquerors and conquered focussed largely on education. The French-Canadians resisted English attempts to establish a comprehensive state system of elementary and secondary schools and a provincial secular university, seeing the plan as a blueprint for anglicization and secularization. The short-lived Royal Institution for the Advancement of Learning, established in 1801, provided for locally established schools but faced similar opposition. The plan did lead to the establishment of an anglophone Protestant school system including a university, McGill.[19] Meanwhile, the French-Canadians, stung by accusations of neglect of education, had by 1832 established a quasi-system of schools that numbered 872 in that year. Nationalism and the challenge of illiteracy were the basis of a short-lived period of state intervention (1801-1836) preceding a new assertion of church authority that was maintained until the 1960s.[20]

## The Origins of the Dual System

Following the rebellions of 1837-1838, Lord Durham was sent to Canada to recommend solutions to the problems that had led to revolt in Ontario and Quebec. He devoted most of his attention to Quebec where he declared, in the most famous statement in his report, "I found two nations warring in the bosom of a single state . . . ." Canada must be "nationalized and anglified," a process for which schools would be "at once the most convenient and powerful instrument."[21]

---

*Here and in subsequent chapters, these provinces or colonies as they were usually described before 1867 will be called by their modern names. Lower Canada and Upper Canada were separate colonies from 1791 until 1840. From 1841 to 1867 they were the United Province of Canada, the two parts of which were designated Canada East (Quebec) and Canada West (Ontario).

The report was highly critical of the low quality and status of teachers, the lack of textbooks and the extent of illiteracy, even among children who attended school regularly and used books. Durham reported that "they hold the catechism book in their hand as if they were reading, while they only repeat its contents which they know by rote." On the other hand, too many bright young men, selected for seminary training, ended up in the overstocked professions of advocate, notary and surgeon. The education of girls in nunneries was of high quality and inexpensive.[22]

Durham realized that the anglicization of the French Canadians would be a long-term process and that meanwhile their rights must be respected. The granting of responsible government to both Ontario and Quebec and the reuniting of both provinces were the main outcomes of the report. Educationally, Durham's proposals led after 1841 to the establishment of the famous dual system in Quebec, which would remain virtually undisturbed for more than a century, providing a basis for the the autonomous schooling of the francophone majority and of the anglophone minority. Nowhere would the two solitudes be more firmly established, a fact illustrated in later times by the crucifix as, in Magnuson's words, "the dominant symbol of the Catholic school" and by "a portrait of the King or Queen" in the Protestant classroom.[23] F.X. Garneau's monumental *Histoire du Canada* appeared in the 1840s as a response to Durham's cutting observation that the French-Canadians lacked a history or a literature. By celebrating the achievements of *les Canadiens*, Garneau created a nationalist ideology in history teaching that remains influential in Quebec curricula to this day.

## Cultural Survival and Curriculum Beginnings in Early English Canada

### Early Society and Schooling

As compared with early French Canada, English Canada was from the beginning marked by cultural and religious diversity. As a consequence, sectarian strife and cultural conflict were widespread in the evolution of religion and education in all the English colonies of British North America. In each, survival was a keynote. To the Anglican elite, survival required a hierarchical social order based on the principles of an established church and on a distinctive British social, religious and cultural identity. The place of schooling and the nature of the curriculum were in the forefront of concern of all groups. Despite differences, general acceptance of the over-riding imperative of cultural survival based on Christian morality, British patriotism and resistance to American hegemony led to the establishment after 1840 of unified public school systems on a non-denominational, essentially Protestant basis. The notable exception was found in the special rights accorded Roman Catholics, but this sizeable, vocal, largely Irish-born minority, despite frequent imputations of its disloyalty, was to prove no less accepting of the general consensus that gradually developed.

By the 1770s, the earliest English-Canadian settlements, those of Nova Scotia, were already remarkably diverse and included Tory Anglicans, New England Baptists, Protestant and Roman Catholic Gaelic-speaking Scots, Lunenburg Germans, English Methodists and French-speaking Acadians. New England and Scottish elements dominated this colony of 20 000 souls and were soon reinforced by 15 000 Loyalists from the Thirteen Colonies. A transatlantic orientation would later cause a weak sense of Canadian identity reflected in a strong imperial sentiment in curricula and textbooks. Even after 1867, London rather than Ottawa continued to serve as Nova Scotia's spiritual capital.

While the citizens of New France were seeking a schooling that would make their children godly and loyal, those of Nova Scotia were simultaneously pursuing a similar conservative aim, albeit one resting on Protestant and British rather than on Catholic and French values. To the Society for the Propagation of the Gospel which spearheaded the colony's first educational efforts, the goals of schooling encompassed "doctrinal soundness and a regard for British institutions." Established in London in 1701, the Anglican SPG played a role similar to that of the Catholic Jesuits in New France, establishing its first school at Annapolis in 1728 and later evangelizing the Indians through a Micmac translation of the Prayer Book and a Micmac Grammar. The SPG curriculum included reading of the scriptures and the catechism and writing "in a plain and legible hand" in order to prepare children "for useful employments and arithmetic for the same purpose."[24] In 1766, an "Act Concerning Schools and School-masters" recognized some state responsibility for education in Nova Scotia but this precedent was weakened by the provision that teachers must be examined and approved by members of the Anglican clergy, a policy that sowed the seeds of future conflict. Like earlier Quebec policy, the Act also foreshadowed future notions of teacher certification and school inspection.[25]

The Loyalist migrations to the British North American colonies, totalling 35 000 to 49 000 by one estimate, led to the establishment of two new colonies, New Brunswick and Upper Canada (Ontario). The Loyalist immigrants were far more diverse than stereotypes often suggest and included a minority of the well-born and educated and a majority of "plain people;" ethnically they included those of German, Dutch and Highland Catholic origin and the Black Loyalists of Nova Scotia, in addition to those of Scottish and English Protestant origin. The Tory Anglican minority sought to create a new British society on Canadian soil that as a monarchy with a conservative social-cultural tone would be different from the new American republic. In this endeavour it gave English Canada "a body of sentiments and traditions that cause it to differ from the United States." Canadians would acquire a mental reservation about things American, providing them with a common bond of anti-Americanism and "strong sentiments of loyalty to the conception 'British.'"[26]

What has been called the Loyalist cult developed after the mid-nineteenth century and was manifested in curricula that featured textbook accounts of early wilderness hardships (the Hungry Year) and of the War of 1812. These have remained staples of social studies curricula into our own time. The initial emphasis in formal schooling before 1840 was on secondary education in order to prevent some of the elite "from rushing to . . . seminaries . . . in the United States."[27] Attempts in Nova Scotia to prohibit student attendance at "the Romish mass or the meeting house of Presbyterians, Baptists or Methodists" did nothing to reduce cultural conflict in a culturally diverse colony. Sectarian controversy in Nova Scotia manifested itself most strongly in higher education where most denominations established their own colleges. Only Dalhousie University, established in 1818, was non-sectarian.

The establishment of boards of school commissioners or education in the Atlantic colonies provided for the superintendence and inspection of schools and the examination and licensing of teachers; in New Brunswick in 1827, for example, teachers were examined "as to morals, character, literary attainments and loyal principles." Here was the dim outline of a nascent public school system.[28] In Newfoundland, education remained a charitable, missionary private venture catering to the children of the poor, initially under the aegis of the SPG, and after 1823 under that of the Newfoundland School Society. Nowhere in Canada would denominationalism be carried so far as when, after 1836, the colony acquired a system of a half dozen or more separated sectarian school jurisdictions that have endured until our own time.

It was in Upper Canada that the special mission that the Loyalists sought to fulfil was most strongly expressed. Men such as Bishop Strachan, the founding father of schooling in the colony, and John Graves Simcoe, the Eton and Oxford graduate who became the first governor, saw the mission as upholding tradition and properly constituted authority. The church must oversee education if "enthusiastic and fanatic teachers" and "the levelling spirit" emanating from the United States were to be kept in check. Immediate provision must be made for the education of the "superior classes;" that of the "lower degrees of life" could be left to chance and local initiative.[29] In 1807, a District Public (Grammar) School Act provided for denominational, Anglican district schools for the "sons of gentlemen." Non-Anglican groups, who by 1840 constituted a majority of the colony's half a million people, were forced to establish their own institutions. The huge Irish Catholic famine migrations shortly began, adding to a cultural diversity that would lead to conflict focussed primarily on education. .

Unlike Simcoe, Bishop Strachan was concerned about the lack of elementary schooling. In 1816, a Common Schools Act provided the first state support for elementary schools to be administered by locally elected boards of trustees and staffed by teachers who had to be natural-born British subjects or to have taken an oath of allegiance. The three-member boards provided legislative sanction for the pre-existing informal, voluntary, parent-controlled schools and were given responsibility for virtually the whole range of local educational policy. The 1816 Act thus established two fundamental principles for the development of nineteenth century schooling in Ontario: first, the primary responsibility of the school board was owed to the local community; second, the territorial extent of the unit of local educational government was to be the attendance area of a single school. The one-room school in the township "section" later reached its peak as an institution in the 1920s, surviving in Ontario into the 1960s. The section school board gave effective political voice to the dominant values of the small rural community and ensured the socialization of children to those values. Here was the basis for local resistance to the establishment of true state education, which was seen as undermining the relationship between the school and the local community.[30] However, a short-lived provincial General Board of Education headed by Strachan was established in 1823 with the authority to appoint teachers and choose texts. As in the eastern colonies, this precedent foreshadowed the eventual establishment of a public school system and a uniform curriculum.

In 1839, a legislative committee recommended a common school system for Upper Canada. By this time, what Gidney has termed the early Victorian obsession with education was established. This obsession, evident most strongly in the press, reflected a consensus among Ontario's elite about the importance of mass schooling and helps to explain the rapid development of state education after 1840. As Gidney comments:

> From the mid-twenties, Upper Canadian newspapers reprinted increasingly large amounts of material from British and American newspapers on the progress of popular education. Foreign educational ideas were discussed in editorials, letters to the editor, and in assembly debates, while proposals for improving the local schools were increasingly judged against the standards set in Scotland or New York or Germany.[31]

Thus were new ideas about education such as the pedagogical innovations of Pestalozzi introduced to Canada. Conservatives, liberals and radicals alike agreed that popular education was the surest means of realizing their differing social aims. Schooling would be a bulwark against democratic excesses, a weapon against oppression, a means of improving farming, expanding trade, eliminating crime and spreading the gospel, utopian aims that have a remarkably modern ring. As the *Kingston Chronicle* put it in 1842, education was "the young man's capital, the best assurance of further competency and happiness." This argument, together with that which saw schooling as essential to industrial prosperity, extended to the view that education could become the prime moral agent in reducing social ills.[32]

## An Informal Curriculum of School and Work

While the ferment described was underway, pioneer schooling remained a largely voluntary parent-controlled enterprise before 1840. Although such visitors as Anna Jameson, an acerbic British bluestocking, were sharply critical of widespread illiteracy that even extended to the legislative assembly, many of whose members, she claimed, could not read or spell, Gidney's careful research points to a more positive picture. Schooling was widely available in Upper Canada before 1840 and most children probably attained literacy. As in New France, school and work were not sharply separated; being a pupil was only part of growing up. From the beginnings of settlement, rudimentary provision had been made for schooling, frequently in the home, for which the earliest formal schools were often a supplement. The purpose of the latter was relatively clear, simple and practical, as illustrated in a teacher's contract drawn up in 1826 by subscribers to a school in Norfolk county. Desirous that their children should "be able to read the word of God and transact their own business," they hired a teacher "to teach the different branches of reading, writing, arithmetic and English grammar ..."[33]

Under the Common School Act of 1816, upwards of 800 grant-aided schools had been established by the mid 1820s, each in theory required to be open for six months annually. Gidney has shown, however, that there were probably an equal number of "non-aided" schools of great variety. The village or rural dame school, conducted by a woman in her own home, represented, as Prentice terms it, the "domestic phase" of teaching, which would later become a public phase as the occupation became increasingly feminized. The dame school evolved into a public (common) school, often still conducted in the teacher's home by a woman who in time became a certificated public rather than an uncertificated private teacher.[34] The first school buildings were often log shanties, thirty feet by twenty-two, cornered but not hewed, the chinks between the logs being filled with moss, the whole plastered over with clay, with but one small window in each side. Pupils worked on their slates, seated on rough basswood planks built around the walls. The teacher's desk was built on four upright wooden pillars and contained a small drawer in which the dominie's switch, ruler and other "official equipments" were kept. Such buildings might be erected by the settlers by means of "bees."[35] Teaching, still a mainly male preserve during these early decades, was a transient occupation, taken up temporarily by immigrants or semi-literate retired soldiers with no training and a common school education at best, but adept at wielding the switch or birchrod.

An interesting pioneer innovation included the "moving" school, authorized in New Brunswick in 1805 as an adaptation from New England that entailed the "keeping" of school by a teacher in each of several parishes in turn.[36] Private venture, Latin schools, special schools for girls and academies were other innovations. In most schools, the three Rs were the basic curriculum and the Protestant Bible was a basic text. In the growing towns, this curriculum might be supplemented by commercial mathematics, bookkeeping and penmanship.

Although most children attended school and acquired literacy, impediments to schooling that would bedevil reformers for another century

were already familiar, in the form of inadequate teachers, irregular attendance and inaccessible schools. Few children were enrolled for more than
three or four years of intermittent attendance. Many were in attendance for
but a few months in a period when child labour was essential. Large
families, too poor to pay the full subscription, might send their children to
school a week in turn, so that all might learn a little.[37]

Reformers were critical of an inadequate badly taught curriculum
which failed to improve the children's morals.[38] From a modern perspective it is paradoxical that conservative reformers demanded centralized
control, while liberal reformers upheld what Michael Katz has called decentralized "voluntary localism."[39] Both groups saw the need for education as
a means of creating a stable community in a society in which most people
lived in isolated rural communities and where the Methodist camp meeting
was often the only alternative to the spree or fight induced by the
omnipresence of whiskey.[40] It is easy to see why the leaders of such a society, facing, as they saw it, a perpetual crisis of survival, would turn to
education as a panacea.

Early concern about American influences on the Canadian curriculum
would prove to be a persisting one to our own time. Fears were expressed
that American teachers "used their own schoolbooks ... and tinctured the
minds of their pupils with their own political views," instilling republicanism "into the tender minds of the youth of the province."[41] In 1843 the
legislature imposed citizenship requirements on American teachers.[42] A
year earlier, Dr. Thomas Rolph, a British visitor to Upper Canada, recorded
his dismay over American influence in the following words:

> It is really melancholy to traverse the province and go into many of the
> common schools; you find a herd of children instructed by some anti-
> British adventurer instilling into the young ... mind sentiments hostile
> to the parent state; false accounts of the late war ... geographies setting
> forth [American cities] as the largest and finest in the world; historical
> reading books describing the American populations as the most free
> and enlightened under heaven and American spelling-books, diction-
> aries, and grammar teaching them an anti-British dialect and idiom.[43]

Another source of curriculum conflict arose out of debates over the
use of the Bible as a textbook in schools. Such conflicts, illustrated in
acrimonious discussions in Newfoundland's new House of Assembly in
1833, pointed up a policy issue that persisted in all the British North
American colonies for many decades. Such controversy illustrated how
differences over the values and knowledge deemed to be of most worth
in schools have been rooted in differing cultural perceptions held
by Canadians.

West of Ontario, education began, as in eastern Canada, under the
private auspices of churches and their missionaries, with the support of the
Hudson's Bay Company. Company regulations issued in 1823 and 1835
required traders to teach their Metis progeny their letters and catechism

"and such elementary instruction as time and circumstances permit," utilizing the father's first language. When the first school was opened at Red River in 1815, its patron, Lord Selkirk, suggested a curriculum consisting of the three Rs taught in the settlers' native Gaelic, adding "and I care not how little the children are taught the language of the Yankies" — a first expressed suspicion of things American in education west of Ontario.[44] The "genteel tradition" was introduced to the West in the form of a girls' school for daughters of the Hudson's Bay families. Conducted on the model of a European finishing school, it taught social usage, music, modern languages and embroidery.[45] Similar schools were established on the Pacific Coast after 1840. School development in the West replicated the eastern transition from informal private schooling to state control in a remarkably short time, based on legislative arrangements that were contemporaneous with those of the older colonies.

## Early Curriculum Theory and Teaching Method

Despite the inadequacy of schooling and the lack of a system of education, some attention was being paid to what we might today call "curriculum theory." Thus Richard Cockrell, an English-born Upper Canadian schoolmaster with experience in the United States, has been credited with the authorship in 1795 of the first book in English on educational theory and practice in North America.[46] Entitled *Thoughts on the Education of Youth*, it was advanced for its day in its treatment of discipline and teaching methods. Cockrell commented that "The master who does not observe method in teaching will find himself continually in confusion, and the business of the school not half done."[47] He recommended the American practice of examining teachers before appointment. Cockrell's advocacy of object-lesson teaching was well ahead of his time. He also advocated the use of spellers in reading instead of the Bible. Wilson observes that Cockrell's commendation of American practices in education helped to establish a Canadian precedent that has endured to the present day.[48]

In Nova Scotia in 1819 Thomas McCulloch adumbrated the first full blown English-Canadian curriculum theory in the form of a statement on liberal education that antedated by a generation that of Egerton Ryerson in Ontario. At Pictou Academy, McCulloch equated liberal education with "literary studies" defined, however, in broader terms than the traditional classics. A literary curriculum should include philosophy, mathematics and the natural sciences. McCulloch was Canada's first great teacher of natural philosophy; (botany, zoology and geology), and achieved international recognition.[49] His broad conception of liberal education was both classical and utilitarian at the same time that it was non-sectarian, a concept advanced for the time.

McCulloch's interest in the psychological and philosophical principles underlying learning was revealed in his assertion that the original tendency of the human mind in its operations indicated "a susceptibility of necessary impressions and also a desire to receive them, and to supply its original want of intelligence and qualify itself for a course of activity and happiness ..." McCulloch added that "In the structure of mind a principle of curiosity constitutes a prominent feature ..." Such curiosity is gratified by the acquisition of knowledge. But the individual cannot "acquire that intellectual and moral improvement for which man is designed" without guidance, (education). "Wherever society has existed," averred McCulloch, "the education of youth has been viewed as involving in it alike the improvement of the individual and the prosperity of the whole ..."[50]

McCulloch observed that the invention of letters and the art of printing tended to the diffusion of knowledge with the consequence that "their influence upon the intellectual and moral character of man must have been great ..." Teachers had come to communicate "not only the principles of knowledge but also those qualifications which might afford [their students] access to the sources of intelligence ..." Liberal education had as its primary object "knowledge which could not be easily acquired in any other way [than formal instruction] ..." It was a prerequisite to the learned professions, law, medicine and theology, "which are so important in the preservation of health and the moral excellence and happiness of man ..." Finally, McCulloch made the case for science and the ancient languages. Science for him was more than knowledge of facts: it formulated general principles and abstract truths.[51]

In Upper Canada in 1829, the General Board of Education introduced Mavor's already widely used *English Spelling Book* in the form of large cardboard sheets around which large groups of children could gather. This pedagogical device had been pioneered by an English educator, Andrew Bell.[52] Also shortly authorized in New Brunswick, Mavor's 167-page book was intended as a comprehensive text, "the whole library of a poor child" and contained, besides spelling lists, reading lessons, measurement tables, moral exhortations, worldly advice in getting good interest, a few pages of encyclopedic facts, some poetry, a little grammar, French and Latin and catechisms on the duties of loyal subjects.[53] The emphasis on rote and rule in teaching arithmetic and on parsing in grammar were examples of formalistic, mechanical methods that would persist over most of the following century. Problems of systematic, consistent instruction were exacerbated by the lack of teacher training, of any organization of pupils into classes or grades and of uniform textbooks. An 1831 school register recorded the use of seven different arithmetic textbooks in a single pioneer school.[54] All these problems would likewise persist for many years.

In terms of teaching method, attempts to provide basic literacy took their most interesting form in the establishment of British-style monitorial or pupil teacher schools which Phillips terms "the last major effort of philanthropy."[55] The system of Madras schools, pioneered by Andrew Bell in a school for British orphan children in Madras, India had its Canadian origins in Halifax in 1816 under the sponsorship of the SPG. By 1820 Madras monitorial schools had spread to New Brunswick and Quebec.

Organized according to Church of England tenets, the schools were intended as institutions for "the gratuitous education of the lower orders" but the larger ones attracted fee-paying "children of the first respectability" and from all denominations. In New Brunswick, the need for the systematic training of monitorial teachers paved the way for normal school instruction.[56] The Madras System employed definite and distinctive if mechanical methods of instruction. To combine efficiency and economy and to enable one teacher to instruct many children, the older and brighter pupils acted as monitors, instructing groups of pupils, usually ten in number, at assigned classroom stations in lessons previously taught to them by the master teacher.

In Upper and Lower Canada, the Madras System was promoted as a device for Anglican control of schools and met with predictable opposition. In these provinces, monitorial schools with a "non- conformist" Protestant bias were introduced by Joseph Lancaster, an Englishman who established a school in Montreal during the 1830s. Lancaster's dictum that "every child [should] have for every minute of his school time something to do and a motive for doing it" epitomized the philosophy of monitorial teaching.[57] The rote memorization of biblical passages and poems, together with spelling drill, also promoted obedience and provided moral training. The curriculum basically consisted of the three Rs, sometimes supplemented by grammar, geography and French. A teaching innovation in monitorial schools was the use of dictation in spelling, which had formerly been solely an oral exercise. The later expansion of common school curricula probably hastened the demise of the system, a condition enhanced by the acceptance of more child-centred Pestallozian methods of instruction after 1840. Nevertheless, in its cheapness, efficiency, stern discipline and the lack of a need for large numbers of adult teachers, the monitorial method helped to meet incipient early demands for mass schooling.

## Notes to Chapter I

Note: The quotation from the SPG at the head of this chapter is a verbatim combination of quotations from two archival sources respectively cited by W.B. Hamilton, "Society and Schools in Nova Scotia," p. 91 and by C.F. Pascoe, *Two Hundred Years of the SPG*, Vol. I, p. 110.

1 Moogk, "Les Petites Sauvages," 17, 20, 24, 35.

2 Ibid, 38. Sée also Moogk, "Manual Education," 125-168.

3 Fregault, 15; Rioux and Martin, I, 17.

4 S.D. Clark, *Developing Canadian Community*, 20-40; Eccles, 419-441.

5 Audet, "Society and Education in New France," 73.

6 Gosselin, 349.

7 Lower, Colony to Nation, 25.

8 Fregault, 15.

9 Audet, "Society and Education," 72.

10 Johnston, 48-66.

11 Jaenen, "Education for Francisation," 1, 2, 11.

12 Jaenen, *Role of the Church*, 11, 33-4, 105.

13 Ibid., 26-7.

14 R.C. Harris, 23-50.

15 Jaenen, *Role of the Church*, 108.

16 Audet, "Attempts to Develop a School System," 148.

17 Neatby, *Quebec*, 25, 262.

18 Lower, *Colony*, 155.

19 Boulianne.

20 Ouellet, 246.

21 C. Lucas, II, 16, 36.

22 Ibid. 31-2.

23 Magnuson, 95.

24 SPG, *Classified Digest*, 844.

25 Hamilton, "Society and Schools in Nova Scotia," 92.

26 Lower, *Colony*, 118-9.

27 Hamilton, "Society and Schools in Nova Scotia," 93.

28 Hamilton, "Society and Schools in New Brunswick," 113.

29 Landon, 59.

30 D. Cameron, 10-12.

31 Gidney, "Upper Canadian Public Opinion," 48-9.

32 Ibid., 49-50.

33 Gidney, "Elementary Education," 17, 18, 34-5.

34 Alison Prentice, informal presentation, Simon Fraser University, January, 1982.

35 Hodgins, *Documentary*, VII, 292-3.

36 K. MacNaughton, 15.

37 Hodgins, *Documentary*, VII, 292.

38 Gidney, "Elementary Education," 15.

39 M. Katz, "Class, Bureaucracy and Schools," 21.

40 Lower, *Colony*, 163-4, 181.

41 Hodgins, *Schools and Colleges*, I, 1; *Documentary*, III, 34.

42 Hodgins, *Schools and Colleges*, I, 153.

43 Hodgins, *Documentary*, III, 3.

44 Cited in Lupul, "Education in Western Canada," 245-48.

45 Ibid. 249

46 J.D. Wilson, "Education in Upper Canada," 198-9.

47 Cited in Prentice and Houston, *Family and Schooling,* 29.

48 J.D. Wilson, "Richard Cockrell," 2.

49 W. Hamilton, "Thomas McCulloch," 32-3.

50 McCulloch cited in Lawr and Gidney, *Educating Canadians,* 18.

51 Ibid. 19, 21.

52 Curtis, "The Speller Expelled," 12.

53 C.E. Phillips, *Development,* 142-3.

54 Hodgins, *Documentary,* VII, 290.

55 C.E. Phillips, *Development,* 116.

56 K. MacNaughton, 67-69. See also H.P. Thompson, 134.

57 Cited in K. MacNaughton, 69.

# CHAPTER 2

## THE BEGINNINGS OF
## THE PUBLIC CURRICULUM:
## FOUNDATIONS OF POLICY IN
## VICTORIAN CANADA, 1841-1892

*... the present time ... is pre-eminently with us an ocean of change, the waves of which are obliterating so many ancient landmarks ...*
*(Egerton Ryerson, 1849)*

*Popular education on sound principles is the handmaiden of religion and the best safeguard of public order ...*
*(Egerton Ryerson, 1847)*

### The Social Context of Curriculum Policy

#### Society in an "Ocean of Change"

Following the ascension of Queen Victoria to the British throne in 1837, the British North American colonies began an evolution that transformed them into a self-governing nation under Confederation by 1867. This political evolution reflected an equally important economic, social and cultural evolution that marked the beginning of what historians call "modernization." The term describes a society undergoing extensive social change because of the application of industrial technology to extend an individual's control over the environment.[1] Technologically, modernization was signalled most strongly by the coming of the railway. Socially, it was evident in rapid urbanization and population growth and by institutional development. The age of improvement was marked by a rapid growth of public institutions, notably the public or common school. Ontario set the pace for "the century of schooling" as a formal, centralized, state-controlled public system gradually replaced the informal, decentralized, local, parent-controlled system that had existed before 1841. Later, this public system served as a prototype for school organization in much of the rest of Canada.

By the 1850s, Ontario was entering the horse and buggy age as rural roads connected with a growing rail network reduced the isolation of the countryside and exposed it to urban influences. Better communication and denser settlement made it easier to centralize control of schools and curricula and to expand school facilities. High school classrooms were now sometimes housed in separate buildings. By this time, many school houses were of frame construction and had blackboards, maps and desks instead of benches for the pupils.[2] A few were solid two-storey stone buildings, serving both common and grammar school classes. In 1879, Farmersville High School in eastern Ontario was built in handsome modified cruciform with a gabled roof topped by a flat-roofed wooden tower. In his novel *A New Athens*, Hugh Hood has described this building, which led the people of Farmersville to rename their town after the ancient Greek seat of learning. They meant no presumption but only wished to recognize that their school, two generations removed from the Canadian wilderness, was in the tradition of the Academy of Athens.[3]

In Quebec, the St. Lawrence Valley was similarly transformed. Rural destitution beyond the valley, as described earlier, was exacerbated under population pressure. On one seigneury it has been estimated that in 1851 not a single habitant was literate.[4] By 1867, many habitants were migrating to Montreal, eventually forming a dispossessed urban proletariat that withal retained rural values. Atlantic Canada remained a rural and sea-based society during the period. Nova Scotia, the fourth maritime shipping "nation" in the world, enjoyed a golden age; New Brunswick's prosperity was based on a growing timber trade. But this golden age would soon end with the decline of the wooden ship. Canadian regional disparities were already evident; in 1862 New Brunswick's Lieutenant-Governor, A.H. Gordon, was struck by "the startling contrast" between the poverty-stricken, stagnant province and more prosperous, vigorous Upper Canada.[5]

Between 1821 and 1871 the population of British North America multiplied nearly five-fold, a faster rate of growth than that of any subsequent half century in Canadian history. The first Dominion census in the latter year recorded nearly 3 700 000 people, about 70 per cent of them native-born. Half the population was under the age of twenty, a proportion that explains the demand for schooling. Transiency was a marked feature of an age when geographical mobility was comparable to that of our own foot-loose century. Gagan and Mays have described "perpetual motion" in one Ontario township where less than one quarter of the households listed in the 1851 census were still present in 1871.[6] Such transiency affected school attendance patterns and contributed to a haphazard learning experience for children. Much movement was to the United States. The number of emigrants exceeded arrivals between 1851 and 1871. During the 1871-1891 decades out-migration by one estimate constituted about 40 per cent of the total population in the former year, a movement hardly designed to ensure a stable society with a secure national identity.[7] Internally, the movement to cities accelerated after 1867 as the number of urban dwellers tripled by 1891.

Culturally, the population was increasingly diverse. Persons of British and French origin constituted 90 per cent of the total in 1871 but the former included three ethnic groups, one of which, the Irish, outnumbered both Scots and English, constituting the largest group after the French-Canadians. The Irish Protestants organized themselves into the Orange Order; it was strongly concentrated in Ontario, where their lodges often served as the first schools, churches or town halls. In that province they outnumbered their Catholic compatriots and through their control of many school boards and city councils gained wide scope for the practice of their religious intolerance. By the end of the century, Canada had more Orange Lodges than any nation, including Ireland.[8] Roman Catholics made up 42 per cent of the population, a proportion roughly comparable to that today. Anglicans, Baptists, Methodists and Presbyterians were, again as now, the largest Protestant denominations. To ethnic and religious differences were added linguistic differences: 31 per cent of Canadians were French-speaking in 1871, a somewhat higher proportion than today. Cultural diversity was reflected in endemic educational policy controversy and curriculum conflict that often arose from denominational strife. In Ontario's divided Protestant community Anglican claims to preferment continued, as before, to arouse hostility.

The Gross National Product, per capita income and consumer expenditures, increased at rates of 60 per cent or more between 1867 and 1892. Per capita expenditure on education rose from $1.00 to $2.50.[9] Manufacturing growth especially in Ontario was spurred by the adoption of the National Policy in 1878, a system of protective tariffs aimed at developing an industrial base. A call ensued for a more practical curriculum to meet demands for a more skilled labour force. The lack of any relationship between formal schooling and industrial development was widely deplored.

Some Victorian observers such as Goldwin Smith, the Toronto sage and expatriate former Oxford historian, and George Grant, the nationalistic principal of Queen's University, feared social anarchy as they contemplated class conflict, the destitution in Canada's growing cities and the decline of old virtues. Such fears were real enough and suggest that "Victorian," however useful as an historical label, is an inappropriate stereotype to describe the social attitudes and behaviour of the age. Victorian attitudes in the work ethic and in social restraint took hold only slowly, coming to focus on the ravages of alcohol which, by the 1870s, was being viewed as an economic as well as a social problem. Until then, efforts to promote temperance or prohibition — the terms were often synonymous — met with little success. Street drunkenness was common and often served as a catalyst for boisterous public behaviour. In the long run the local option prohibition promoted by the Canada Temperance Act of 1878 was a failure, but as the problem of "booze" attracted the attention of educators, temperance teaching became a prime curriculum issue.[10]

As Canada moved from an oral to a print culture, the press became a pervasive institution. As early as 1853, Susannah Moodie had noted that

"The Canadian cannot get along without his newspaper any more than an American without his tobacco." By the 1890s, more than 400 newspapers were being published and total circulation exceeded the number of families — proof that Canada's first mass medium had arrived. Such popularity attested to the growth of mass literacy in which the school played the most essential part. Despite the sensationalism of the press, apparent in the space devoted to football matches, prize fights and murder trials, the major newspapers were models of Victorian rectitude and Canada had no counterpart to the American "yellow press." Religion and politics dominated the serious side of the press, with racial and linguistic controversies, often focussed strongly on education, especially prominent. [11]

Urban growth was seen as a serious menace to the future of the nation, even as cities were paradoxically regarded as the physical embodiment of progress and culture. To overcome civic apathy and political corruption and to promote economy and efficiency, reformers created bureaucracies of expert professional managers to administer police, public health, utility, recreational and public welfare services. [12] Scientific management came more slowly to school systems, although professionals such as James L. Hughes in Toronto and Alexander McKay in Halifax foreshadowed the modern school administrator.

The obverse of the need for urban reform was the need for rural reform to arrest population decline and moral decay. The dilemma of using education to stem rural decline was evident in the autobiography of Andrew MacPhail, later a distinguished Canadian scholar and champion of lost rural virtues. MacPhail, with unconscious irony, entitled his nostalgic account of his Prince Edward Island schooling *The Escape*. [13] The attempt to improve rural schooling and thereby to regenerate the countryside would be among the most persistent themes and frustrations of reformers over the greater part of the first century of Confederation. Their nostalgia stemmed from recollections of their own experience when the school had been a community, the chief focus of life outside the home, a centre of social, musical, dramatic, political, religious and other events. As one of the few social institutions that many rural people encountered daily, the school integrated the community even though it was sometimes the source of fierce conflict over the location of the schoolhouse itself, the selection of the teacher and the form of religious instruction.

## Childhood, Family and Reform

Deep moral concern, arising from fears of urban growth, focussed largely on children who were numerous and highly visible, especially before they were swept off the streets and into schools. Fears centred on American immigrants and especially on the "famine Irish" who arrived during the 1840s. Egerton Ryerson, who had been appointed Chief Superintendent of Schools for Upper Canada in 1846, expressed widespread concerns when he observed:

The physical disease and death which has accompanied their influx among us may be the precursor of the worse pestilence of social insubordination and disorder. It is therefore of the last importance that every possible effort should be employed to bring the facilities of education within the means of the families of these unfortunate people that they may grow up in ... industry and intelligence ... and not in the idleness and pauperism, not to say mendacity and vice of their forefathers.[14]

Ryerson's statement was an early example of anti-immigrant attitudes that would be reflected in practices and policies towards New Canadians for most of the following century. Schooling was viewed as the prime means of uplifting them and their children from iniquity to Canadian levels of morality and industry.[15]

Increasingly, children came to be viewed as a class that should, as far as possible, be segregated from society. This was to be achieved by keeping more of them in school for longer periods. Segregation of pupils by sex, age and achievement was intended to improve economy, efficiency and morality; it also permitted grading and classification. A system of classes and grades required larger schools. As enrolments burgeoned after 1850, small urban schools were consolidated into larger central schools. Age segregation eliminated the educational anomaly and moral danger of eighteen- and seven-year-olds sharing common classrooms. By the 1870s, segregation by sex was the norm in urban common schools, even to the separation of school libraries into shelves marked "male" and "female."[16] Although sexual segregation at this level was eventually abandoned, it remained the practice at the secondary level for decades.

By 1880, as the child increasingly became the focus of efforts to improve society, child welfare policy became the most important catalyst of general social policy. As the family changed from a work-centred economic unit in which parents and children functioned as producers on farms or in village cottage industries to a love-centred nurturing unit, much of its training and educational function was lost.[17] A major consequence of the new factory system was the separation of work and residence that took fathers away from home and thereby increased the influence of mothers. Thus, as the family's role in the education and training of its children diminished, its influence on their development, prospects and life chances increased; here was the genesis of the role of the modern nuclear family.

Sutherland suggests that, until the 1880s, English-Canadians showed little awareness of children as individuals and had little insight into their inner emotional life. Changing perceptions were revealed by the "child saving" movement which arose in Great Britain and led to the migration to Canada of 80 000 British orphan children, "waifs and strays" and street urchins between 1868 and 1923. Whereas in the 1870s there were no complaints in Canada about the morals of the children, by the 1890s they were seen as threats to the well-being of society. Although many of the children suffered tragic emotional neglect in Canadian foster homes, the child saving movement reflected a new humanitarian impulse. This impulse was evident in new infant care and child-rearing practices, child psychology, temperance education and prohibition, workmen's compensation, control of immigration, elimination of "pernicious books," censorship of music hall and later of movie performances, improved housing, nursery schools, supervised playgrounds, neighbourhood houses, and sex and family education in home and school.[18]

The greatest success was achieved in child and family health improvement. Reforms such as school medical and dental inspection would, when finally implemented after 1900, have significant implications for the school curriculum, as teachers were drawn into a wider socializing role that gradually extended significantly beyond their traditional instructional role. Thus, daily health inspection became a routine task for the elementary teacher, associated with the teaching of "physiology and hygiene" and temperance.[19]

Canadians were increasingly looking beyond their own borders and "were integral parts of a series of developing professional international communities in public health, in education and in social welfare."[20] Among the new reform organizations was the International Women's Christian Temperance Union, the first branch of which was formed in Canada in 1874 at Owen Sound, Ontario. The union took the lead in promoting the teaching of temperance and hygiene and in actively combatting the circulation of "pernicious literature." In education, many Canadians belonged to such organizations as the National Education Association of the United States, which met in Toronto in 1891 and served as a model for the Dominion Education Association founded a year later. Toronto itself was becoming a model in North America for new approaches to social reform. Individuals such as James L. Hughes, a leading Froebelian and a pioneer of the kindergarten in North America, were proof that Canadians were at the cutting edge of curriculum change. The kindergarten was part of a movement soon to be known as the New Education, which sought to make the school the major focus of social reform.

## The Cultural and Intellectual Background to Curriculum Policy

### The Culture of Science, Liberal Education and Disciplined Intelligence

If Canadians were avid readers of newspapers, they were not notable readers of books. Nevertheless, the desire for self- improvement among the small but growing middle class was evident in the great popularity of literary, historical and scientific societies and in attendance at museums, exhibitions and conferences. This interest reflected an emerging culture of science in a period when the new scientific discoveries and writings and an interest in nature were regarded as essential for every educated person.

Canadians belonged to the American Association for the Advancement of Science and to the British Association, both of which met in Canada a number of times between 1850 and 1900. Some belonged to both groups and J.W. Dawson, the principal of McGill University, served as president of each.[21] Dawson's leadership and his role as a world figure in geology underscore W.L. Morton's claim that science was the most substantial intellectual achievement of Victorian Canada.[22] In a pre-Darwinian scientific age when science was still regarded as the accumulation of information, the work of such organizations as the Geological Survey of Canada (1842) and the Royal Society of Canada (1882) had cultural, scholarly and utilitarian value. All these values eventually became significant in justifying science and technical education in curricula.[23]

Before Confederation the study of nature was associated with aesthetic appreciation and religious feeling. What was called natural theology taught that nature was the handiwork of God, whose divine plan was revealed, for example, in the structures of plants. With religion occupying a central place in college and university curricula, nearly every subject was taught for the "Christian evidences" that it provided. At the same time, scientists had quite sophisticated concepts of natural development. The great age of the earth was well understood by the 1830s as was Lamarck's argument for evolution. Human beings, however, were viewed as a special creation who had existed for but a few thousand years.[24]

Natural theology paved the way for Darwin's theory of natural selection by familiarizing students with the idea of adaptation in nature. Acceptance of evolutionary theory was more restrained and muted in Canada than elsewhere but, by 1900, Darwinism was generally recognized in the universities. The loss of any religious points of reference for scientific investigation and the emergence of a "critical spirit" were the legacies of Darwin that caused the most concern to Canadian intellectuals. Canadian educators seem to have avoided the religious implications of Darwinism while accepting it as a scientific principle that integrated disciplines such as botany and zoology. Alexander MacKay in Nova Scotia, a botanical enthusiast, spread Darwinian ideas among teachers. A similar approach was taken by R.R. Wright in his introductory textbook on zoology for schools, published in Toronto in 1889. By this time, the natural history societies, having lost their former scientific status, turned to the promotion of nature study in schools.[25]

School promotion in Canada may be likened, as Tyack and his colleagues have described it for the United States, to a widely based decentralized social movement unified by a basic system of similar beliefs and a common vision.[26] Such a system implied a theory of education that could be implemented in the form of curricula. Canadian school promotion involved a relatively small number of key mutually acquainted reformers whose similar beliefs and common visions derived from their common British and Protestant backgrounds. Operating typically under more centralized direction and with a seeming bureaucratic tidiness that later excited the envy of American educators, these leaders were influential in determining policies and in defining what would now be called their aims and objectives for schooling. The ideas of Ontario's Egerton Ryerson served as the prototype for such men as S.P. Robins in Protestant Quebec, David J. Goggin on the Prairies and John Jessop in British Columbia, all of whom were either his former students or graduates of his system. Ryerson's concept of education was succinctly expressed in his 1846 report which set forth a plan for a school system for Ontario:

> By Education I mean not the mere acquisition of certain arts or of certain branches of knowledge, but that instruction and discipline which qualify and dispose the subjects of it for their appropriate duties and employments of life as Christians, as persons of business and also as members of the civic community.[27]

Ryerson devoted more than thirty pages of his report to the teaching of non-sectarian religion and morality, which he defined as "the general system of truth and morals taught in the Holy Scriptures." Such teaching would be in contrast with godless American schooling, for Ryerson believed that "without a Christian education, there will not long be a Christian country."[28] Moral education could not be separated from Christian education. Complementing his Christian bias was a stress on patriotism intended to make Ontario "the brightest gem in the crown of Her Britannic Majesty."[29] As Curtis has suggested, this emphasis on religious and moral aims belies the view that Ryerson aimed at repressing the consciousness of the masses in the interests of "social control." On the contrary, it can be argued that he hoped to heighten mass consciousness in the interest of creating the loyal informed public required by the emerging state. By improving moral behaviour, the need for physical discipline and coercion would be replaced by self-discipline that would lead to the abolition of vice and crime. A "common Christianity" was a kind of political behaviour that would enable people to act in accordance with Christian principles. A common school would unite civil society by creating social harmony.[30]

Like Thomas McCulloch in Nova Scotia who was an ordained Presbyterian minister, Ryerson, an ordained Methodist minister, based his concept of liberal education on the Christian intellectual orthodoxy of the time. That orthodoxy found its home in universities and colleges such as Dalhousie University in Halifax, and Victoria College, later a federated college of the University of Toronto, of which McCulloch and Ryerson were respectively appointed first principals in 1838 and 1842. As public school systems developed, the ideas and moral imperatives that underlay university curricula influenced school curricula, especially in secondary schools that were for so long downward extensions of the universities.[31]

Early colonial leaders sought to preserve their inherited cultural tradition and to maintain a common purpose by means of what McKillop has termed "disciplined intelligence."[32] The intellect must be disciplined by the will, by the moral sense, in the interest of cultivating the whole being.

Knowledge might be power, as Francis Bacon had said long before, but only if used to carry out the will of God. Knowledge "for its own sake" was a threat to a proper education. Initially, disciplined intelligence drew on so-called Scottish Common Sense philosophy for its justification. This philosophy rested on the assumption that human beings, as reasonable entities, could use their understanding to grasp directly certain fundamental moral intuitions about the world. Scottish Common Sense dominated philosophical thought in the English-speaking world during much of the nineteenth century, and strongly influenced American college curricula.[33] Its influence was even stronger and more long lasting in Canada. Complementing Common Sense in both countries was natural theology, noted earlier, with its teaching of God's design as revealed in nature.

No Canadian educator was a greater advocate of disciplined intelligence than Egerton Ryerson, a fact that assumes special significance in the light of his role as the age's greatest school promoter. His 1842 inaugural address as principal of Victoria College has been described as "probably the most important statement of the nature and object of a liberal education made in Canada during the nineteenth century." The statement "set forth certain assumptions which governed the structure of arts and science curricula for many years."[34]

For Ryerson, liberal education required two types of curricula. The first of these was a preparatory level, "requisite for the ordinary duties of life," for those not planning to attend college. This curriculum stressed the study of English language and literature as well as "mathematics and natural science ... the outlines of mental and moral philosophy, evidences of Christianity, geography and history." Ryerson's second curriculum was intended for those planning to enter "professional pursuits," such as the ministry, law, politics and business. It was taught through five departments at Victoria: classics, mathematics and the physical sciences, moral science, rhetoric and *belles lettres* and theology.

At the centre of Ryerson's curricula were moral science and theology, the former intended to cultivate a sense of obligation or duty and a pious disposition, and the latter viewed as "the most extensive and important science in the world." All other subjects were to be subordinated to these, the ultimate purpose being to help the student discern the will of God. Moral philosophy was a required undergraduate course in the University of Toronto curriculum until as late as 1877. School textbooks in such subjects as zoology and geology treated content as proof of God's handiwork well into the 1890s.[35] With the emphasis on "a well-balanced and varied culture," and the distrust of specialization, Ryerson's curricula reflected the prevailing Scottish influence.[36] However, it was in the formalism of teaching methods based on lectures, catechetical questioning and examination preparation that Scottish influence had its greatest long-range impact on Canadian practice.

Ryerson combined classical, liberal and practical elements in his vision of schooling. Education was a means to an end, for instance, to make youth "good men" and diligent, useful members of civil society.[37] In 1848 in an article significantly entitled "The Importance of Education to a Manufacturing and Free People," he described the importance of preparing the rising generation for an era of "sharp and skillful competition" that was marked by "sleepless activity."[38] Ryerson failed to see that the utilitarianism he promoted as a practical educator would contribute to the gradual process of secularization of the curriculum.[39] He and other Canadian intellectuals became increasingly agitated as they sought to reconcile religion and science and thus maintain a disciplined intelligence. By the 1870s, the university curriculum could no longer remain free of "the din of controversy" and Scottish Common Sense, based on "the mere opinion of ordinary intelligence," was no longer adequate to meet the challenges of Darwinism and the "critical spirit." What was required was a new philosophy based on rigorous reasoning which would still permit the cultivation of a pious disposition.

A new rational idealist philosophy was at hand which drew heavily on the work of Hegel and other German philosphers and, like earlier Scottish Common Sense, became pervasive throughout the English-speaking world. The leading North American Hegelian was William Torrey Harris who as Superintendent of St. Louis schools and later United States Commissioner of Education represented a unique combination of idealism and practicality.[40] In Canada, Hegelian philosophy was best represented by John Watson at Queen's University and George Paxton Young at Toronto. Watson, who had come to Canada from Scotland in 1872 at the age of twenty-five, later gained recognition as one of the world's greatest idealist philosophers. Such men represented a new breed of Canadian academics who emphasized a scholarly rather than a pastoral role.[41]

Armour and Trott, in their 1981 history of Canadian philosophy, have argued that the use of reason in preference to emotion and intuition has served a unique function in maintaining harmony in Canadian society. Reasoning together has served as a social tool enabling people fairly unlike one another to come together to build institutions. Thus, Canadians have combined opposing ideas, such as tax support for both public and separate schools.[42]

Watson, Young and other idealist philosophers held strong views about the school curriculum. Young had earlier served for some years as Ryerson's inspector of grammar schools. Like Harris in the United States, Watson emphasized the moral and intellectual function of schooling, favouring a common compulsory humanistic curriculum for all, with students going as far as their various abilities could carry them. During the post-Confederation era, secularized Christian morality and British classical ideals, rooted in imperial nationalist sentiment, underlay secondary school and college curricula and the content of common school readers and textbooks. To such eminent Canadian Victorians as George Monro Grant, the principal of Queen's University, and George Parkin, the headmaster of Upper Canada College, schooling was the prime means of promoting ideals.[43] At Upper Canada College, Parkin sought to promote character development through discipline, service and work and thereby to make the college, as an exemplar of the English public school, an explicit model for the development of the Ontario high school.[44] Selectivity, academic values and a curriculum pervaded by imperial nationalism would long serve as hallmarks of the province's secondary schooling.

## What Knowledge Is of Most Worth?

International debate over the purposes of schooling revolved largely around the relative merits of a liberal or classical vis-à-vis a practical or scientific curriculum. In 1859, Herbert Spencer, the English social philosopher, asked "What knowledge is of most worth?" thereby posing the question that would dominate curriculum policy-making for generations to come.[45] Spencer's short answer was science, which could best prepare for what he called "complete living" in an industrial age. Ranged on the other side of the debate was Matthew Arnold, the famous poet and elementary school inspector. For Arnold, as an exponent of classical learning, the great purpose of education was to learn "to know the best which has been taught and said in the world."[46]

For Spencer, the problem with the traditional curriculum was that it was determined by "mere custom, or liking or prejudice." No criteria were available to decide among the conflicting claims of various subjects on the educator's attention. "Before there can be a rational curriculum," he concluded, "we must settle which things it most concerns us to know ..." and "we must determine the relative values of knowledge." No longer should mere custom set priorities and allow the ornamental to override the useful. Anticipating John Dewey and later progressives, Spencer observed that "that which our school courses leave almost entirely out, we find to be that which most nearly concerns the business of life."[47] Adapting Darwin's theory of biological evolution to social development — a concept later known as Social Darwinism — Spencer argued that history is the progressive adjustment of human character to the circumstances of living. The main purpose of education was to enable people to make that adjustment. This emphasis on adjustment, and on utilitarianism and practical education, notably science, constituted Spencer's most notable legacy to future curriculum policy-making.

For Spencer, curriculum priorities should be determined by (1) those activities ministering directly to self-preservation; (2) those that secure the necessities of life; (3) those concerned with the rearing and disciplining of offspring; (4) those that maintain proper social and political relations; and (5) those devoted to the gratification of tastes and feelings. This list portended later statements of "aims and objectives" that would characterize scientific curriculum making in North America. In the United States, where he was lionized during his 1882 visit, Spencer's ideas were probably best exemplified later in the statement of "the cardinal principles of education" adopted by the National Education Association in 1918.[48]

In Canada, the Arnold-Spencer curriculum debate rested largely on arguments developed elsewhere. Before 1900, the issue of a liberal vis-à-vis a practical emphasis was largely theoretical as Canadians continued to uphold traditional academic values in a period when only a miniscule minority of young people proceeded to secondary education, and even fewer proceeded further. Social Darwinism gained limited acceptance and few Canadians were Spencerians.[49] However, both Arnold and Spencer were fairly widely read and their works, particularly those of Spencer, eventually appeared on normal school reading lists. Examinations in the principles of education at the University of Toronto gave strong emphasis to Spencer's theories. Thus in 1909, students were asked to criticize his five-fold classification of knowledge summarized above.[50] Spencerian ideas were evident in the 1913 national study of industrial training and technical education that will be discussed later.

Debates over the relative merits of liberal and practical studies had a remarkably modern ring. Traditionalists upheld mental discipline theory, emphasizing the cultivation of general intelligence as the best basis for developing practical skill. Reformers attributed unemployment to an impractical curriculum. To David Boyle, pioneer archaeologist, museum educator and Pestalozzian, students were over-educated academically to the neglect of scientific, technical and agricultural training.[51] A recurring theme in international debate was the relation of education to national industrial prosperity. British and American leaders blamed inadequate schooling for the alleged failure of their nations to keep up with their commercial rivals, especially with Germany. Thus it was that at the United States Centennial Exposition held in Philadelphia in 1876, pedagogical innovation associated directly with industrial development came under close scrutiny. Lawrence Cremin has described how in the end "a few displays of tools from Russian schools literally stole the show . . . [by demonstrating] that Russian educators had finally scored a breakthrough on the thorny problem of how to organize meaningful, instructive shop training as an essential adjunct of technical education." Dismay over their technical inferiority shortly led the Americans to introduce manual training into their schools. As a result, asserts Cremin, American education "was never the same thereafter."[52]

The Ontario Department of Education mounted a large display covering 2750 square feet of floor space at Philadelphia. The exhibit of more than 2000 articles won several major awards and attracted highly favourable press comments.[53] Yet despite their success, Ontario educators such as J.G. Hodgins were as discomfited as the Americans, for it was plain that European systems surpassed their own in practical education, and that Canada was lagging behind other nations in industrialization. "Even in our best schools," Hodgins noted, "the teaching of drawing is the rare exception, not to speak of higher industrial arts training."[54]

Similar concerns were expressed in the Atlantic provinces. In 1877,

Principal Crocket of the Fredericton Normal School summed up the Arnold-Spencer debate for Canadian educators when he observed:

> With respect to curriculum for secondary or superior instruction, the battle has waxed not between the two great classes — the partizans (sic) of the old classical studies and the partizans of what are known as the real or useful studies."[55]

In 1887, *The Educational Review* noted that the province's high schools and colleges trained students only for the overcrowded professions and "mercantile pursuits." The international praise that had been lavished on New Brunswick's exhibit at the 1886 Colonial Exhibition in London failed to allay the same concerns that had discomfited Ontario educators at Philadelphia a decade before. To the Review's editor there was but one remedy: "greater attention to industrial education."[56]

In Nova Scotia, when Alexander MacKay urged the establishment of manual training, he found himself at odds with David Allison, the province's classically oriented Superintendent of Education. Allison was opposed to the idea of converting the schools into institutions "furnishing special training for special pursuits." He resisted politicians who demanded that scientific training replace the study of dead languages. Unwilling to compromise, Allison gave up his position and was succeeded by MacKay in 1891.[57]

On the national scene, issues related to practical education were joined most strongly in the report of the 1889 Royal Commission on the Relations of Capital and Labour in Canada. The decline of the old apprenticeship system meant that the means "by which a young man was taught his trade [have] disappeared and we have nothing in our industrial system to take its place." Apart from this argument, the commissioners demanded that "children . . . deal chiefly with real things during the first years of school life" as "the most certain way" of exercising their intellectual faculties.[58]

Industrial education for Indian boys, vagrant children and delinquents emphasized moral redemption. This aim provided one impetus for the manual training movement which educators such as James L. Hughes began to promote in Ontario in the 1880s.[59] The emphasis on manual training for low status, non-academic students helped to reinforce prejudices against practical education that still persist and belied arguments for its liberal socially elevating value. In Canada as elsewhere, arguments revolved in part around the respective claims of what the British sociologist Eggleston has called high status versus low status knowledge. The former, based predominantly on vicarious experience acquired through books and received wisdom, served as the basis of a selective secondary school curriculum. Low status vocational, utilitarian knowledge was purveyed in the common school. Both types of curriculum aimed at developing character; the secondary type also embodied the concept of an intellectual who would form the small elite needed to lead society.[60]

In training leaders, the elite curriculum itself assumed a vocational function. Examination systems designed to provide entry to universities and the professions illustrated that however much Canadians might pay homage to liberal ideals, they were no less committed to utilitarian schooling. Allan Smith in discussing what he terms "the myth of the self-made man" in Victorian Canada cites the anonymous writer who in 1866 described the academic course he had received "as a toolchest — as something to work with ..."[61] Egerton Ryerson counted training for the ministry and the law as technical education.[62]

Later, the initial entry into the curriculum of such practical subjects as manual training, agriculture and commercial studies will be noted. Science as a new subject was valued for both its cultural and practical worth as we have seen. "Pure" science would shortly vie with the classics, mathematics and modern languages as a liberal subject that some critics claimed lost practical relevance. Applied science, established at McGill as early as 1855, and practical science, established at Toronto in 1877, ultimately paved the way for modern engineering faculties.

## Society, Schooling and a National Frame of Mind

Allan Smith has described the early evolution in Ontario of "a national frame of mind" or sense of Canadianism. Later, textbook policy led to a modest Canadianization of curriculum content; as Ontario textbooks came to dominate the national market in anglophone Canada a *de facto* national curriculum was created. As early as the 1840s, Ontarians were becoming increasingly preoccupied with creating cultural agencies that would expand their knowledge of themselves.[63] Carl Berger has described the Geological Survey of Canada, organized in 1842, as the most important scientific institution in Victorian Canada.[64] In 1864 the *Canadian Illustrated News* commended a 900 page twenty-year summary of the Survey's work by noting its national relevance in giving Canadians a better idea of the land they lived in.[65] Later, naturalists such as John Macoun, a botanist who was appointed Dominion Naturalist in 1887, began to make vast catalogues of plants, animals, birds and fossils that helped to establish a preliminary outline of Canada's natural features. To these catalogues, they also began to add information on the customs, arts, burial sites and specimens of early human beings, thus contributing to the ultimate establishment of the human sciences.[66]

Canadian achievements in the arts were modest. However, in 1880, the Royal Canadian Academy of Art and the National Gallery of Canada were established. These developments inaugurated a tradition of government encouragement of cultural life that has been extended by the establishment of the CBC and the Canada Council in our own time. Canadian writers made much effort to identify what was distinctive about Canada as a community. Its British heritage and northern location — the latter providing a morally purifying climate — were among the prime claimed attributes. These attributes and a related heritage of northern races were said to have bred self-reliance, strength and hardihood. Such qualities were contrasted with those imputed to the degenerate "southern," i.e. American character. The absence of slavery was cited as an especially positive moral distinction that made Canada a better and more perfect society than its neighbour.[67] The need for racial unity was stressed, although some noted that heterogeneity and the problem of harmonizing national and imperial sentiment made it much more difficult than in the United States to identify a national character. It was during this period that the maple leaf emerged as the most appropriate symbol embodying Canadian identity in a single striking image.[68]

In spite of the emphasis on Canadian distinctiveness in North America, Smith argues that many of the basic myths in terms of which Canadians attempted to make their experience intelligible — the myths of the land, of progress, of mission and of individualism — were cast largely in terms of ideas drawn from the south. Then, as now, the exposure of Canadians to American news played a particularly important role in creating a continental frame of reference which caused them to view such issues as slavery as though they were their own. The arrival of refugee slaves in Canada before the American Civil War had made necessary some alterations in Ontario's social institutions, notably education, causing the province to introduce segregated schools.[69] Canadians also imbibed American cultural and political ideas which led them to feel that they shared a dramatic past with their neighbours. One journal described Francis Parkman, the American historian, as "our best chronicler" for his scholarly accounts of the French and Indian Wars. Henry Wadsworth Longfellow's *Evangeline* made him "our national poet."[70] Significantly, both writers early found their way into Canadian school readers and textbooks, Longfellow's *Hiawatha* being the best known example.

Nowhere was concern about American influence more evident than in education, where Canadian policy-makers were often accused, sometimes correctly, of accepting American fads uncritically and of viewing their educational system and its problems in American terms. At this time, critics began to follow the still common unscholarly practice of using descriptions by Americans of their own schools as surrogate descriptions of Canadian schools. Moreover, American criticisms of American schools were sometimes used as surrogate criticisms of Canadian schools. At the same time, Canadian educators envied a school system that emphasized the flag, citizenship and loyalty. It was said that whereas American students learned to think of themselves as primarily Americans, developing a wonderful homogeneity, Canadians were taught to see themselves as different from one another.[71] Later, American style homogeneity was promoted through Anglo-conformist "national schools."

After 1867 the informal intellectual nationalist movement known as Canada First served to counter continental influences. In promoting British ideals as an antidote to republican ideals, the movement emphasized Canada's status within the British Empire. Canada was seen as a first among equals, her nationality enhanced through loyalty to an empire the imperial unity of which provided a larger arena for nationalism.[72] Over most of the next century, the ideology of imperialism would be promoted in school curricula through an emphasis on the Loyalist legacy and on the greatness of British institutions.

The exuberant nationalism and optimism of Canada Firsters was by no means universally shared, for Confederation had not been the intense spiritual experience of the American Revolution.[73] The emotional contrast was evident in the emphasis in the British North America Act on "peace, order and good government" while the American Constitution guaranteed "life, liberty and the pursuit of happiness." Few groups or provinces in the new nation displayed much attachment to it. The primary loyalties or sentiments of most were directed elsewhere. Many, probably most, Nova Scotians were anxious to withdraw from Confederation. Quebec and Ontario were badly divided by the execution of Louis Riel in 1885, an event that reopened the deepest racial and religious cleavages soon to be reflected in fierce conflicts over the question of minority school rights in western Canada. Although many after Confederation saw the schools as a major means of creating a new nationality, the fact that the British North America Act had assigned education to the provinces militated against such a role.

This was the period when what came to be called "the Canadian question" was first posed. As Goldwin Smith put it in his pessimistic book about Canada's future, the question was whether the separate regions could ever achieve unity.[74] Smith thought not, for Canada's inevitable destiny was continental. Expressing a frustration that would bedevil generations of textbook writers, Smith commented that it was impossible to write a decent history of the country because of "the difficulty of running histories of several provinces abreast and imparting anything like unity to the whole."[75]

Despite the difficulties cited by Smith, Canadians had long seen history as an instrument of cultural survival. "La survivance" was the principal theme of Francis Xavier Garneau's famous *Histoire du Canada*, noted in Chapter 1, which recalled francophones to their glorious past. History served a similar purpose for anglophone Canadians of Loyalist descent. For both groups, the past was in Carl Berger's words "shot through with nostalgia" as each "sought to assuage the memory of conquest or disaster by invoking the images of some golden age in the past ... "[76] Garneau's work inspired a number of popular English-Canadian histories, among them John McMullen's 1855 work that became a standard guide for the rest of the century. McMullen's aim was "to inspire a spirit of Canadian nationality into the people generally — to mould the native-born citizen, the Scotch, the English and the Irish emigrant into a complete whole."[77]

Teaching the Canadian identity was a recurrent concern in the curriculum. As Ottawa's school superintendent lamented in 1849, "It is a matter of regret that while we can learn from our textbooks something of almost every other country, we can learn nothing of our own ..."[78] To meet this concern, J.G. Hodgins published his *Geography and History of British North America* in 1857. Anticipating Confederation, Hodgins sought to provide "a fuller acquaintance with the mutual history, conditions and capabilities of each of the colonies."[79]

During the 1860s, growing nationalism, the onset of Confederation, economic uncertainties, fears of annexation engendered by the American Civil War and prospective westward expansion combined to accelerate the concern for "Canadianizing" the curriculum. By this time, the Irish National Readers which had replaced American readers after 1846 were under attack as being insufficiently Canadian in content. In 1868, the Canadian National Series of Readers or so-called Ryerson Readers, were formally authorized. However, many selections were retained from the Irish Readers and selections from the American McGuffey Readers were even added. In 1874, the New Canadian Readers were authorized, the first indigenous series to be used across Canada generally. An obvious attempt was made to inculcate national pride in some selections through comments like, "Canadian boys and girls love the maple leaf and the beaver."[80]

What Berger has called the Loyalist cult culminated in the 1884 celebrations of the centennial of Loyalist settlement. On June 3rd of that year, "Loyalist Day" was marked by parades, orations, recitations and songs. Among the songs was "The Maple Leaf Forever" which later became a quasi-national anthem in Canadian classrooms. As such, it celebrated Canadian victories in the War of 1812, interest in which has been called a barometer of Canadian nationalism. Victories in the war had included the Battle of Queenston Heights, that "classic of the Canadian classroom" which represented a kind of Thermopylae for English-Canadians.[81] Also celebrated was the victory at Chateauguay where the militia of both races had stood together, exemplifying a unified Canadian nationality.[82]

This emphasis on French-Canadian valour reflected the attempt by textbook authors such as Hodgins to reconcile the heritages of the two races in the new land and to present a romantic view of New France in textbooks. For the descendants of the Loyalists, the great French-Canadian explorers could take a legitimate place as heroes with their own ancestors. William Kirby's portrayal of the French-Canadian pioneers in his famous novel, *The Golden Dog* became a standard reading in school literature courses for generations, into the 1950s.

In a curriculum that primarily celebrated a British conservative tradition, Canadian history *per se* was a poor relation, subordinated to British and to ancient history in the schools and the universities alike. At the University of Toronto in 1888, a writer protesting the policy of hiring British academics insisted that "Our university must be a national one, not a colonial one ... We must have our professors in touch with Canadianism."[83] By this time Canadian history was gaining more prominence in Ontario school curricula, a fact that caused imputations of disloyalty to be directed at the Minister of Education, George Ross. In 1892, Ross, as first president of the Dominion Educational Association, made a comment reflecting views familiar to Canadian teachers since:

> I have perused with great care the various histories in all the provinces of this Dominion, and I have found them all to be merely provincial histories, without reference to our common country ... Can't we agree upon certain broad features common to the whole of this Dominion with which we can indoctrinate our pupils, so that when a child takes up the history of Canada, he feels that he is not simply taking up the history of Canada, such as the old Canada was, but that he is taking up the history of a great country?[84]

In Quebec, national sentiment meant French-Canadian sentiment. Canadian history unrelated to Quebec was all but ignored, being reduced to the category of foreign history.[85] Nova Scotians exhibited evidence of an ambiguous Canadian patriotic sentiment. When a Halifax school inspector urged in 1877 that Nova Scotia children should, like American children, be taught to revere their country, it was not clear what country he meant. Thus he praised freedom of speech and the press as "nowhere greater than in London."[86]

## The Legislative Background to Curriculum Policy

### Central Authority, Incipient Bureaucracy and Denominational Conflict

Few educational developments are more striking than the remarkable concurrence during the latter half of the nineteenth century of legislation and curriculum policies that began to give the British North American colonies a common countenance of schooling. As the structures of public education were put together, the issues and terms of the accompanying debate were also strikingly similar, especially where religious and language issues were concerned. All systems drew on external sources, notably on New England, Ireland, Scotland and Prussia.

In the Maritime provinces, provincial boards of education were established between 1847 and 1852. Eventually, all gained the power to regulate local school boards, to license teachers, to inspect schools and to authorize textbooks. In Nova Scotia, J.W. Dawson became the first Superintendent of Education. Before leaving to assume his duties as principal of McGill University, Dawson established a Journal of Education and founded the Provincial Normal School. Widespread illiteracy and non-attendance revealed by the 1861 census led to the Free School Act of 1864, the enactment of compulsory school taxation, and later of compulsory attendance.[87] New Brunswick drew widely on outside influences in fashioning its system. In 1844 advice was received from Dr. James Kay-Shuttleworth, the first secretary of England's new Board of Education. In 1854, Egerton Ryerson and J.W. Dawson were commissioned to advise on educational policy. The first superintendent, Marshall d'Avray, had studied at London's

Battersea Normal Training College and had trained elementary teachers in Mauritius.[88]

Sectarian controversy and denominational conflict engulfed schooling in all the Atlantic provinces, although both were comparatively muted in Nova Scotia. There Roman Catholic separate schools followed the prescribed curriculum, but were permitted to offer religious instruction after school hours.[89] A similar *de facto* dual system was established in New Brunswick under the Common Schools Act of 1871.[90] Conflict was particularly severe in Prince Edward Island where an eventual settlement provided for optional attendance at opening exercises where the teacher read from the scriptures without comment.[91] In Newfoundland, where the use of the Bible was an equally divisive issue, separate Protestant and Roman Catholic school boards were established in each district in 1836. With the acceptance in 1874 of the principle of the division of the school grant among the Protestant groups, the basis of Newfoundland's unique denominational school system was established.[92]

In Quebec, where church control gained ascendancy after 1841, the School Act of that year established the dual system by providing that "dissident persons" could "establish schools which satisfy their needs." Between 1841 and 1875, various measures formalized the dual system by establishing separate denominational publicly-supported school systems under a Council of Public Instruction with autonomous Roman Catholic and Protestant committees. This arrangement gave each group effective control over teacher training and certification and over inspection, curricula and textbooks, with the result that, in Audet's words, students of the two faiths progressed "side by side for almost a century, ignoring each other almost completely."[93]

In Ontario the principle of dissidence was likewise recognized after 1841. The School Act of 1843 used the term "separate schools" for the first time.[94] As a result of Roman Catholic political pressure, separate schools soon became eligible for municipal as well as for provincial grants. In addition, a common school teacher was no longer required to be a Protestant. After 1863, these concessions were balanced by the requirement of provincial inspection of separate schools, government control of teacher training and centralized control of curriculum and textbooks, though not of religious instruction.[95]

The passage of the Common School Act of 1841 reflected a growing Ontario consensus that the state should assume greater responsibility for the supervision and inspection of schools. The more effective 1843 Act paved the way for better supervision by creating a corps of local supervisory field officers or inspectors who gained powers that for the first time limited local autonomy. Their reports, based on standardized record keeping, provided the first useful statistics available in the province. Data on teachers, textbooks and pupil progress constituted a first systematic view of the curriculum in practice.[96] However, the Act formalized a system of thousands of section boards, with the result that Ontario later lagged behind most other provinces in developing consolidated schools and in broadening rural school curricula.

The 1843 Act was followed by those of 1846 and 1850, which were masterminded by Egerton Ryerson. By this time he had become Chief Superintendent of Schools and also served as chairman of an appointed General Board of Education, later known as the Council of Public Instruction. Together, the three acts became the prototype for Ontario's centralized system and later systems in other provinces. In framing the 1846 Act on the basis of his great report prepared in that year and published in 1847, Ryerson drew many ideas from his visits to the United States, the British Isles and the Continent in a period when "the schoolmaster was abroad." The first principle upon which he felt popular education must rest was that of "universality" or elementary education for all. This principle implied free and compulsory education, although, having regard for the controversy that compulsion aroused, Ryerson hedged his advocacy of the idea. A second principle was "practicality," for the mere acquisition of knowledge without the requisite qualities to apply it "does not merit the name of education ..." The remaining principles embraced three dimensions: religion and morality, "the development to a certain extent of all our faculties" and "an acquaintance with several branches of elementary knowledge."[97] Elementary knowledge embraced a broad curriculum of fifteen subjects which Ryerson set out in more than eighty pages of detail.

The 1846 Act and subsequent legislation gave Ryerson broad powers of curriculum control, based on the central authority's ability to withhold the annual legislative grant. By establishing criteria for hiring teachers and approving texts and by requiring superintendents to follow departmental regulations, the central authority for the first time gained a voice in determining what actually happened in the schools. Uniformity was further promoted by a graded system of instruction and by supervision and inspection. To improve teaching, a normal school was opened in 1847. A year later, the *Journal of Education* was established. Further measures included property assessment to support schools and the provision of free schools, both on a "local option" basis, as a prelude to later province-wide compulsion. In 1850 the grammer schools became subject to public supervision for the first time. The Grammar School Act of 1853 provided for regulation of the course of study and textbooks and the appointment of inspectors. Two years later, the union of common and grammar schools was permitted. For decades in many rural districts the secondary program would be a department added to a common school, with both taught by a single teacher.[98]

In summary, Ryerson as a quintessential bureaucrat imposed a degree of order, uniformity and effectiveness in administration unknown before. However, local resistance, political obstacles and the sheer problem of administering a far flung, dispersed, rural-based system in an age of poor communications combined with Ryerson's own cautious administrative style to give him a degree of control rather less than is often assumed. Essentially, he created an administrative and legal framework which facilitated the efforts of the many school boards that were willing to raise taxes beyond the minimum, establish school libraries and graded classes, hire the most qualified teachers available and build better schools.[99]

Although some scholars have argued that the bureaucratic structures created by Ryerson and school promoters in other provinces reflected a desire to impose centralized state control, Gidney and Lawr suggest that in Ontario bureaucratization was in large measure a response to local demands. The resolution of endless disputes over taxes, voting, school location, textbook policy and other curricular arrangements required uniform rational decision-making, rules, routines and procedures that were essential if justice and equity were to be assured.[100] Without a buffer between himself and trustees, parents and other taxpayers, the teacher was at the mercy of the local community. The power of "democratic localism," to use Katz's term,[101] was illustrated in Ontario in the 1860s by Ryerson's unsuccessful attempt to convert the grammar schools into true classical academies instead of maintaining them as the all-purpose general secondary institutions that they had become. He sought to limit grammar schools to larger centres, thus denying to boys elsewhere the classical instruction needed for university entrance. Girls were to be restricted to an "English only" program and denied the chance to study Latin. Commercial subjects were to be excluded from the curriculum of the new academies. These proposals stirred unprecedented opposition from local rural elites determined to maintain their children's opportunities for further education.[102] Ryerson's eventual abandonment of his policy serves as an early illustration of the perils of curriculum implementation.

The Common School Act of 1871, which capped Ryerson's long career, made schooling free, universal and compulsory province-wide, requiring attendance for four months per year for children aged seven to twelve. It proclaimed that "Every child ... shall have the right to attend school ... " The common school had become a public school with publicly defined goals, part of a highly articulated system of schools.[103] The 1871 Act conveniently marks the emergence of the modern concept of a formal course or program of studies on a province-wide basis. In 1876, following Ryerson's retirement, an official Department of Education was created.

Legislative policy and curriculum development in western Canada after 1867 were strikingly similar in structure and issues to those of the eastern provinces, in particular to that of Ryerson in Ontario. The Free School Act of 1865 on Vancouver Island — the first public school law in western Canada — followed that of Nova Scotia by only a year. Though abortive, the Act established the principle of government financed, non-sectarian schools under a General Board of Education. Following the entry of British Columbia into Confederation in 1872, a second act reasserted the non-sectarian principle, giving the province the only fully secular school system in Canada, a feature that lasted until 1977. In opposing state aid to denominational schools, and in warning against school textbooks which purveyed "the very essence of American teaching," such political leaders as

Amor De Cosmos, a Nova Scotian by birth, were alive to the same issues that had long concerned eastern school promoters.[104]

Manitoba's first Education Act was passed in 1871, a year after the province entered Confederation and in the same year as Ryerson's crowning legislation in Ontario. It set up a Quebec style dual school system, with Roman Catholic and Protestant superintendents. But, contrary to the hopes of French-Canadian and Metis Roman Catholics, no "little Quebec" would develop on the Prairies. By the 1880s, Manitoba was a western projection of Ontario, its majority having the settled conviction that Canada was a "British" country. In 1890, the Manitoba legislature abolished the dual system and eliminated the official status of French. The *de facto* rights of other language minorities were also eliminated. As a result of these actions, the school question became a national issue. Involving Section 93 of the British North America Act, it became the only educational controversy in Canadian history that figured prominently in a federal election, that of 1896. Later, Sir Wilfred Laurier was able to negotiate a compromise which provided for a limited restoration of minority rights, but this lasted only until the upsurge of unilingual Anglo-conformity during World War I.

In the Northwest Territories, out of which the future provinces of Saskatchewan and Alberta would be carved, the school system resembled that of Manitoba. A dual system was established in 1875 and confirmed in the first School Ordinance of 1884. But, as in Manitoba, duality was abolished in 1892. The School Ordinance of 1892 established Ryersonian state control over curriculum and textbooks and provided for school inspection. This system was confirmed in 1905 when the three territories became the new provinces of Saskatchewan and Alberta. Later, national schools that emphasized common patriotic and Protestant religious goals attempted to maintain Anglo-conformity. A major federal initiative was the Dominion Lands Policy of 1872, which set aside two sections [1280 acres or 520 hectares] in every Prairie township as a school endowment. By 1930, when the lands were ceded to the provinces, they had yielded revenues from sales, rentals and taxes in excess of $77 000 000.[105]

The separate school question and denominational conflict that concerned school promoters before 1867 and that continued after that date, especially in western Canada, were central issues in the framing of the British North America Act of 1867.[106] John A. Macdonald appears to have preferred federal control of education, in the hope that schools would replace local loyalties with national loyalties.[107] In the event, education was made a provincial matter, with provision for the maintenance of the rights and privileges "which the Protestant or Catholic minority in both Canadas may possess as to their Denominational Schools at the time when the Union goes into operation." This proviso, which became the basis of the famous Section 93 of the BNA Act, was intended to safeguard minority denominational (but not linguistic) rights in the central provinces, particularly those of the Anglo-Protestant minority in Quebec, which demanded the same treatment that had been accorded Roman Catholics in Ontario.

As the Confederation debates heated up, the question of education became so central that Sir Charles Tupper, one of the leading supporters of union, later declared that, without the inclusion of Section 93, "the measure of Confederation would not have been accomplished."[108] The statement that only provincial legislatures may, in the words of the Section, "exclusively make laws in relation to Education" has occasioned much controversy regarding the federal role in education. Some authorities have contended that this provision bars any federal intervention in education, while others contend that it permits Ottawa to legislate matters that go beyond a particular province's jurisdiction. We shall note later that in practice the federal government now engages in a vast range of educational activities, including the promotion of curriculum development.

Although there were considerable divergences in the patterns of denominationalism that emerged after 1867, there were also striking similarities. The effective public control of separate school curricula achieved by Ryerson in Ontario became the norm in most other provinces. In public schools religious instruction and religious exercises in the form of the Lord's Prayer and Bible readings were mandated everywhere.[109] Most provinces permitted denominational instruction by clergy on school premises after school hours, but in time this policy was abandoned. Quebec and Newfoundland were the major exceptions to Ryersonian uniformity. In the latter province, this can be explained by extreme denominationalism and the long delayed entry into Confederation. In Quebec, two quasi-public systems of schooling effectively left curriculum control in the hands of the two religious-linguistic communities, denying the government any significant role in education for most of the next century.

## The Problem of School Attendance

Securing the regular and punctual attendance of all children at school has been called the central educational problem of the nineteenth century.[110] Gradually the definition of "neglected" and "vagrant" children came to be equated with "not being in school." It was a short step from regarding this condition as a misfortune to treating it as an offence when compulsory attendance laws were established.[111]

The failure of children to attend school and the enormous daily and seasonal variation in attendance stemmed from parental indifference, sheer poverty, the preference of children to work, and the desperate need for their labour on farms. Schools with their inadequate teachers, overcrowding, lack of ventilation and general unhealthy conditions were themselves a cause of non-attendance. Brutal corporal punishment and school time wasted in "listless activity and stupor," with the pupil required only to recite his or her ABCs twice a day were "methods" hardly conducive to learning.[112]

In these circumstances, Prentice comments that it is perhaps a wonder that the common schools attracted as many children as they did. Overcrowding was itself evidence of the desire of many to educate their children. Roman Catholic and black parents insisted on sending their children to school even in the face of the refusal of Protestant and white teachers to instruct their offspring.[113] Gaffield has shown that, despite rural poverty in eastern Ontario, a network of common schools developed in Prescott County before the mid-century effort to construct a uniform province-wide system.[114] This spontaneous development confirms for Canada Meyer and Tyack's assertion for the United States that compulsory attendance laws followed the increase in enrolment.[115]

During "the century of schooling" the number of school-age children in Ontario considerably outpaced the general population increase, while the nearly fivefold increase in the numbers actually registered in schools far surpassed both. The number of common schools nearly doubled during the period, while the number of teachers more than doubled. Neither rate of growth, however, was adequate to demand: in Ontario the pupil teacher ratio rose from 34.8 in 1846 to 75.2 in 1876.[116]

Phillips has observed that, whereas before 1860 the length of schooling in Canada increased by virtue of getting more children into school, after that the gains were made by keeping them in school for a longer time. Between 1850 and 1890 the enrolment period per child tripled from twenty months to sixty months, an improvement that was enhanced by the extension of the school year by about two months. However, enrolment must not be confused with attendance, measured in terms of what Phillips terms "the child's bodily presence in school." Attendance increased from ten months in 1850 to thirty-five months in 1890, but this still represented "bodily presence" for only about half the time. Irregularity of attendance and the large size of classes were crucial factors that reduced the individual child's exposure to the curriculum.[117]

Compulsory attendance was instituted first in Ontario in 1871, and by the end of the century had been introduced in various forms in most provinces. Grants came to be tied to attendance. At first, compulsion was on a local option rather than on a province-wide basis, with enforcement by attendance and truant officers. Ontario's 1891 legislation gave truant officers the authority to enter shops and factories where children were employed and to take legal action against parents who did not send their children to school.[118] However, in a still largely rural, dispersed population, these procedures would have been ineffective without a strong parental demand for schooling.

## Notes to Chapter 2

1 Rutherford, *Victorian Authority*, 242.

2 Royal Commission on Education in Ontario (The Hope Report, 1950), 12. Hereinafter, this royal commission study will be cited as The Hope Report.

3 Hood, 58-9.

4 C. Harris, 44.

5 MacNaughton, 177-8.

6 Gagan and Mays, 106, 113.

7 Urquhart and Buckley, 22.

8 Houston and Smyth.

9 Firestone, 239-41, 261.

10 Waite, 12-13, 16-21, 26-8.

11 Rutherford, *Victorian Authority*, 3, 5, 26, 200.

12 Rutherford, "Tomorrow's," 203, 213-14.

13 Lower, *Canadians*, 340.

14 *Journal of Education for Upper Canada*, 1848 (1), 299-300.

15 McLeod, "A Short History," 20-1.

16 Prentice, *School Promoters*, 153.

17 Sutherland, *Children*, 23.

18 For discussions of the child-saving movement see N. Sutherland, *Children*, 6-7, 28-36. Other works include Parr; Rooke and Schnell, *Studies* and "The King's Children."

19 All these developments are discussed in Sutherland, *Children*.

20 Ibid. 26-7.

21 Jarrell, 10; Berger, *Science*, 23.

22 Cited in Berger, *Science*, xiii.

23 C. Berger, *Science*, 9, 17.

24 Ibid, xii, 38-43.

25 Ibid., 56-60, 70-77.

26 Tyack, et al, "Educational Reform," 254-257.

27 Ryerson, *Report on a System*, 9.

28 Ibid., 22, 31.

29 Cited in McDonald, "Egerton Ryerson," 84.

30 Curtis, "Preconditions," 100, 110-12.

31 See J. Scarfe, "Letters."

32 McKillop, *Disciplined*.

33 See Cremin, *National Experience*, 25-8.

34 McKillop, *Disciplined*, 16-17. The following references to Ryerson's address are drawn from McKillop.

35 Van Brummelen, "Shifting."

36 McKillop, *Disciplined*, 34.

37 Fiorino, "Moral Education," 67.

38 Ryerson, "The Importance," 300.

39 Fiorino, "Philosophical," 244-5.

40 Cremin, *Transformation*, 15-16.

41 See J. Scarfe, "Letters."

42 Armour and Trott, 3, 22.

43 For a discussion of Grant and Parkin and their ideas see C. Berger, *Sense*, especially Chapters 1 and 8.

44 Ketchum, 10, 68-72.

45 Spencer, *Education*.

46 Arnold, 5.

47 Spencer, 27-29, 43, 54.

48 For an excellent discussion of Spencer's influence on American educational thought see Cremin, *Transformation*, 91-4.

49 Armour and Trott, 183.

50 Annual Examinations, General Course, Faculty of Education, University of Toronto, 1909.

51 Boyle, 36-45.

52 Cremin, *Transformation*, 25.

53 Stamp, "Ontario at Philadelphia," 305-6.

54 Hodgins, *Documentary*, XVII, 220.

55 Cited in Phillips, *Development*, 437.

56 *The Educational Review*, 1, 1 (June, 1887), 1-2.

57 N.S. AR, 1881, xvii-xx. See also Henley, 22.

58 G. Kealey, 57.

59 See Morrison, "Reform."

60 Eggleston.

61 A. Smith, "The Myth," 194-5.

62 Cited in Brewin, 7.

63 A. Smith, "Old Ontario."

64 C. Berger, *Science*, 5.

65 A. Smith, "Old Ontario," 202.

66 C. Berger, *Science*, 17, 18, 26, 41.

67 C. Berger, *Sense*, 128-31, 155-8, 162.

68 Smith, "Old Ontario," 206-8.

69 A. Smith, "Continental Dimension," 444, 446. On school segregation see Winks, "Negro School," 164-91.

70 A. Smith, ibid., 457-8.

71 Rutherford, "The New Nationality," 462-3, citing the London *Free Press*, September 28, 1889.

72 C. Berger, *Sense*, 5.

73 Lower, *Canadians*, 289.

74 G. Smith.

75 Cited in Klinck, I, 247.

76 Berger, *Sense*, 90.

77 Cited in Klinck, I, 229-30.

78 A. Smith, "Old Ontario," 195.

79 Hodgins, *Geography and History*, 111.

80 Craddock, 3.

81 Lower, *Colony*, 172. The popularity of Pierre Berton's volumes on the War published in the early 1980s, attests to its continuing salience for nationalistically minded Canadians.

82 Berger, *Sense*, 105.

83 Cited in Symons and Page, *A Question*, 33-4.

84 DEA, *Proceedings*, 1892, 52.

85 Jain, 52-3.

86 Henley, "Canadianization," 10.

87 W. Hamilton, "Society and Schools in Nova Scotia," 100-2.

88 MacNaughton, 84, 112, 112.

89 W. Hamilton, "Society and Schools in Nova Scotia," 104.

90 Sealy, 308.

91 W. Hamilton, "Society and Schools in New Brunswick and Prince Edward Island," 125.

92 W. Hamilton, "Society and Schools in Newfoundland," 138.

93 Audet, "Education," 172, 187.

94 J.D. Wilson, "Education in Upper Canada," 212.

95 J.D. Wilson, "The Ryerson Years," 237.

96 Gidney and Lawr, "Development," 168.

97 Ryerson, *Report on a System*, 20, 22.

98 Gidney and Lawr, "Development," 172-8.

99 Ibid., 178-9.

100 Gidney and Lawr, "Bureaucracy," 439.

101 See M. Katz, in Myers, *The Failure*, 21.

102 For an account of the dispute see Gidney and Lawr, "Egerton Ryerson." See also Royce for an interesting discussion of mid-century arguments over the education of girls.

103 Prentice, *School Promoters*, 17.

104 Cited in Prentice and Houston, *Family*, 106. For an account of the origins of the British Columbia School system see F.H. Johnson, *A History*.

105 See Lupul, "Education in Western Canada" and "Educational Crisis" for accounts of early developments in Manitoba and the Northwest Territories. On Dominion Lands policy, see Morton and Martin, 227-9, 336-56.

106 Except where otherwise indicated, most of this discussion is based on Marvin Lazerson and J. Donald Wilson, "Historical and Constitutional Perspectives on Family Choice in Schooling: The Canadian Case" in M. Manley – Casimir (ed.). *Family Choice in Schooling: Issues and Dilemmas*, Lexington, Mass, Lexington Books 1982, which traces the historical and constitutional aspects of denominational and related linguistic and other cultural issues prior to Confederation down to the present day.

107 Lupul, "Educational Crisis," 267.

108 Cited in Tomkins, "Education and the Canadian Constitution," 7.

109 Lazerson and J.D. Wilson, "Historical," 12.

110 M. Katz, "Who Went," 432.

111 S. Houston, "Victorian," 85, 90, 95.

112 Cited in Prentice, *School Promoters*, 158-60.

113 Ibid., 160-1.

114 Gaffield.

115 Meyer and Tyack, 596.

116 Prentice, *School Promoters*, 19.

117 Phillips, *Development*, 184-5.

118 R. Stamp, *Schools*, 38.

# CHAPTER 3

## IMPLEMENTING THE
## PUBLIC CURRICULUM:
## THEORY, METHOD AND
## THE SEARCH FOR ORDER

*Thus the harmonious and proper development of all the faculties of the mind is involved in the very method of teaching, as well as in the books used and even irrespectively, to a great extent, of the subjects taught.*

(*Egerton Ryerson, 1847*)

*... the same principles and spirit would pervade the entire system, from the Primary Schools up to the University.*

(*Egerton Ryerson, 1847*)

The educational structures and policies established after 1840 by legislation resulted in a rudimentary, primitive, informal curriculum comprised at first of a course of study made up of a permissive list of subjects with no coherent program. Ryerson's concept of an elementary curriculum that would be moral, liberal and practical as set forth in his 1846 report was analogous to that which he had outlined for higher levels in his Victoria lecture of 1842. For Ryerson, reading (including spelling), writing and arithmetic (the three Rs) were "the roots of the tree of knowledge and the primary elements of intellectual power." As "practical arts" they provided skill rather than knowledge, enabling the means of acquiring knowledge to be "indefinitely multiplied."[1] The 1846 report also listed the following subjects: grammar, geography, linear drawing, music, history, natural history, natural philosophy (science), agriculture, human physiology, civil government, political economy and biblical instruction and morality.

Ryerson's 1846 plan is best viewed as an expression of his ultimate ideal at a time when the bare bones of the three Rs were the best achievable curriculum in all but a few schools. He himself recognized this in observing that the completion of the structure he proposed "must be the work of years — perhaps of an age."[2] The introduction of the Irish National Readers after 1846 was a major step in the direction of a prescribed uniform curriculum based on graded, integrated textbooks embodying a systematic pedagogy and a *de facto* curriculum. The term "curriculum" was itself rarely used during the period, although as early as 1852-1853 the Superintendent of Schools for the Town of London observed that "as a necessary consequence of the progressive advancement of pupils regularly attending school, a demand arises for a higher order of studies and a more extended *curriculum.*"[3] (Emphasis in original.)

As a statement of aims and objectives, of detailed content and method for each subject and as a plan for implementing a curriculum through school organization, textbooks, examinations, teacher training and inspection, Ryerson's 1846 plan is the single most important policy document in Canadian curriculum history. Ryerson also pioneered what we now call implementation and in-service education through correspondence and articles and by means of speaking tours across Ontario. *The Journal of Education,* inaugurated in 1848, included articles about new apparatus and methods employed in American and European schools and articles encouraging new ideas such as those of Pestalozzi. An Educational Depository made approved textbooks and apparatus available to schools at half price; an Educational Museum was established in Toronto in 1855 in conjunction with the Normal School which had been opened eight years earlier.

Ryerson's efforts were paralleled in Nova Scotia by J.W. Dawson and his successor, Alexander Forrester. The latter's detailed treatise, *The Teacher's Text-Book* was later highly recommended by Ryerson in his journal, an indication that diffusion of ideas and materials among the colonies was developing during the nineteenth century.[4] In New Brunswick reformers promoted a similar curriculum to that of Upper Canada, introducing the Irish readers in 1846-7.[5]

## Theory and Method in an Embryonic Course of Study

### A Rudimentary Science of Education

The decades preceding 1867 saw the development of what came to be called "a science of education." Mental discipline theory was based on metaphors of the learner's mind as a machine or a muscle, viewed, in either case, "as a tool to be sharpened, honed and polished by the application of certain kinds of subjects to it ..."[6] Here was one rationale for the continued emphasis on the classics in the curriculum. The related theory of faculty psychology conceived of the mind as subdivided into numerous individual capacities or faculties, such as memory, imagination, reasoning and, of course, the conscience or moral faculty, all to be developed or trained. Training involved dividing material to be learned into small bits, sequentially organized as the elements of subjects such as reading, spelling and grammar were analyzed relentlessly, often in violation of both sense and utility.[7]

Nineteenth century educators were greatly concerned that too much use of the young mind might wear out rather than strengthen it. Parents of bright children were especially exhorted not to overwork their supposedly physically weak offspring. An enriched curriculum for the gifted would have been considered dangerous. Questions about the nature of the child and how children learn were not seriously asked. Attention focussed on which kind of textbooks, which methods of instruction and which techniques and devices worked best. "There was little analysis of what happened in the child, but much concern about how to put the material to him."[8] To keep the brain in good working order, frequent changes of subject matter and type of work were advocated, and recesses and diversions like marching to music were suggested. Alexander Forrester's comment in *The Teacher's Textbook* that lack of proper lighting might adversely affect the abstract and reasoning faculties demonstrated a new concern for the physical environment of the classroom.[9] This concern did not extend to textbooks which, with their small type, dull covers and lack of illustrations, remained unattractive.

Competition was universally used as a motivating device, as it long had been. Discipline was harsh and severe and corporal punishment was the norm. A pupil, recalling later that the strap "was ever in sight," remembered a poor weak-minded boy who, unable to spell "laugh," was required to stand on one leg and be strapped on the bare ankle to improve his intellectual powers.[10] Nevertheless, by mid-century some educators were beginning to question the conventional view of children as machines and education as a mechanical, punitive process. Henry Esson, Calvinist preacher, schoolmaster and professor of mental and moral philosophy at Toronto, advocated more enlightened teaching methods. He stressed the importance of the early childhood years for there was no stage of education "more important or more universally influential." In arguing that the newborn child's mind consisted of an "innate alphabet" that observed the world and from which all things grew, Esson was expressing a belief in natural development which implied that the teacher should look to the child rather than the reverse.[11] This concept, like that of developing "the faculties," was an advance over monitorial rote learning. To Ryerson, a more humanistic pedagogy would use the child's emotions and interests to improve teaching. Unlike monitorial instruction, the new pedagogy made the teacher-pupil relationship important. Subjects such as music, if properly taught, would "refine and humanize the pupils."[12]

## Promoting Literacy: Spelling and Reading as Basics

A widespread fear that society was sinking into a state of barbarism from which children, especially, had to be redeemed, led educators to equate ignorance and illiteracy with crime, poverty and immorality. Egerton Ryerson described ignorance itself as a crime.[13] Literacy was equated with "correctness" and high culture was intended to promote English and Protestant "respectability" in manners, appearance and speech, in an age when religion, education and status all went together. The unfortunate brogue of Irish children must be eliminated, along with the "anti-British dialect and idiom" of American textbooks.[14]

Walker suggests that language transformation in individual speech and writing was the major *raison d'être* for the establishment of nineteenth century school systems. School promoters had no faith in the vernacular. With the ordinary language of children viewed as a social and moral threat, literate English had to be treated as a second or new form of language, with texts and readers as far removed from everyday patterns of speech as possible.[15] Reading skills and comprehension *per se* were subordinated to a Platonic idealist theory of knowledge that emphasized imitation as the basis for mental development. Codes of conduct, social values and cultural knowledge were to be absorbed from exemplary, authoritative texts that embodied in Matthew Arnold's words "the best that has been thought and said in the world." The emphasis on style, on correct pronunciation, modulation and clarity of diction confused oral performance with cognitive skill, with the result that comprehension was often wrongly assumed to have been achieved.[16]

Spelling was at first looked upon as a necessary preparation for reading through the learning of letters and the combination of them into syllables and words. Jeremiah Willoughby, recalling his early schooling in Nova Scotia, remembered that "at first only two of our number could read without spelling out the words and most of us had to begin at the letter A." The primers taught letters followed by easy syllables in the form of consonant-vowel pairs (ba, be, bi, bo, bu) to be sounded.[17] Then words of one, two and more syllables were pronounced and spelled. Words in spellers were classified by length. Before beginning to read, children were expected to master the spelling of long words. Rote learning resulted in children being able to spell complicated words while still being unable to spell monosyllabic ones.[18]

The archaic alphabet or ABC "letters to words" method and the overemphasis on spelling was denounced by Egerton Ryerson as "irrational drudgery" that encouraged mechanical reading and low levels of literacy. Such an unnatural process should be replaced by teaching spelling as part of reading, with spelling words taken from reading lessons.[19] Yet because, as Cobb's widely used spelling book put it, "there is no branch of education by which the learned and unlearned are so readily and so generally distinguished," an inordinate amount of instructional time — as much as a half or more — continued to be put on spelling.[20] One reason for the hold of the subject was the popularity of the spelling bee, a major community social activity in isolated pioneer settlements.

Although Alexander Davidson's *The Canadian Spelling Book*, following the example of Noah Webster's famous American speller, used familiar Canadian words, Ryerson refused to adopt it because it employed the alphabet method. The Irish National Readers were aimed at reforming the teaching of spelling and at the abolition of the spelling book. Each reader included an introduction devoted to discussions of teaching methods. Gradually, the alphabet method was replaced by the Prussian whole word method. Pupils learned words as whole units, instead of as aggregations of letters. The first few lessons in the First Reader proceeded by the "Look and Say" method, using sight rather than sound. Names of objects were associated with pictures of objects. The remaining lessons were taught by the phonic method, which had been part of the old alphabet method.[21] Thus, after mid-century, modern arguments over the relative merits of the "Look and Say" and phonic methods were familiar to teachers, confirming Phillips' view that by 1871 everything that could be said about learning to read then and since had been written and published.[22] By this time "interrogation" or constant questioning of pupils on the meaning of words had been adopted as a means of assisting the recall or recognition of information in the readers, and of requiring pupils to find out and remember what the author said.[23]

Reforms in teaching spelling were promoted in a manual, *The Spelling Book Superseded*, written by Robert Sullivan of the Dublin Normal School. Spelling was to be taught by general rules. Through rules of orthography and pronunciation, homonyms, antonyms, synonyms, prefixes, suffixes, Latin and Greek roots, etymologies and especially difficult words would be taught. Sullivan's book also included nonsense phrases for practice and a section on proverbs.[24] The following lesson from the First Reader of the Irish series illustrated how pupils were to learn to spell and acquire the meanings of words in context:[25]

**Lesson I (2)**

| | | | |
|---|---|---|---|
| can | cap | lap | mat |
| had | hat | flap | sat |

Can it be Sam or Pat? It is Sam. Pat had on a hat as he sat on the mat. Has Sam a hat? No, he has a cap. Has the cap a lap or a flap?

Pupils now pronounced words before spelling them rather than the reverse as before. Following the reading, words were chosen at random and spelled with books closed.

A related aspect of teaching literacy was the teaching of writing or penmanship. This was based on "scientific" principles embodied in manuals and teachers' textbooks. Forrester's famous textbook explicated in detail the principles and concepts of penmanship. The mechanical or practical aspects related to the muscular movements required to develop a good hand were then treated.[26] Probably no subject better exemplified uniformity: Miller cites one textbook which urged that pupils, using goose quill pens, write in unison so that they not only made the same letter but the same part of the letter at the same time. Teaching procedures prescribed nine steps ("signals") in starting a writing lesson, for instance, "Place the right hand upon the inkstand" and ten steps in closing it, such as "Close inkstands." Such methodology had a military precision.[27]

## Values Education in the Victorian Curriculum

As noted earlier, disciplined intelligence based on the teaching of religion and morality was the central goal of the Victorian curriculum. What was called "moral education" constituted a form of indoctrination similar to that espoused today by some Christian educators through "values schools." It was quite different from the moral reasoning approach used in much modern values education. In Ryerson's 1846 report, more than thirty pages were devoted to the teaching of religion and morality, including biblical instruction. Ryerson emphasized the "absolute necessity of making Christianity the basis and cement of the structure of public education." No truly wise legislator, he asserted, could think for a moment of separating Christianity from moral education.[28]

Victorian educators understood the moral and aesthetic importance of the school environment. Good thoughts, they believed, could only occur in beautiful surroundings. Increasing attention was given to the appearance and form of school buildings as aspects of what some modern educators call the hidden curriculum.[29] Textbooks were seen as a prime instrument of moral education. In an increasingly centralized school system the small, closely-knit anglophone cultural elite was able to exert a direct influence on the writing and choice of textbooks. Academics such as Goldwin Smith and J.W. Dawson wrote widely used texts. The religious dimension of textbooks was explicit well into the later decades of the century. Thus, textbooks used in the new British Columbia school system all assumed a literal interpretation of the Bible, and a belief in orthodox Christian doctrines. Collier's *Outlines of General History* taught that the world was created in 4004 B.C. and treated Adam's fall, Noah's Flood and the Tower of Babel as literal historical events. Grammar texts, readers, geography books and chemistry books included scriptural references.[30]

Reformers sought to transmit moral precepts and standards of conduct by building moral education into all subjects. Temperance education was an example of the attempt to control conduct by means of an organized course of instruction. There was heated debate over the relative merits of direct moral instruction through such subjects and through courses in "manners and morals" as contrasted with indirect, incidental teaching through standard subjects such as history. Considerable attention was given to "character formation" and "habit training," terms that were often used interchangeably. Bruneau has noted how after 1870 public school officials in one county after another proclaimed a new public curriculum of civic virtues: thrift, orderliness, family responsibility, time-work discipline and respect for property and godliness. In Canada, the notion of a civic curriculum had been explicit in Ryerson's 1846 report. His *First Lessons in Christian Morals for Canadian Families and Schools*, published in 1871, although unsuccessful as a textbook, was illustrative of the new international movement in moral education. More successful was J.B. Calkin's *Notes on Education*, published by Truro Teachers' College in 1888, which became a widely used normal school manual over the next two decades. Such manuals in the form of school management textbooks typically included treatments of "moral instruction," usually in association with discussions of discipline and punishment.[31]

Some educators doubted the efficacy of the school's moral influence. In 1873, Goldwin Smith warned Ontario teachers that "it is only to a limited extent that the school can be expected to contend against the bent and bias of society."[32] Many deplored the inculcation of dogmatic ethical precepts as part of teaching Christian morals while systematic instruction in morals was neglected. During the 1870s, Smith assisted in the removal of religiously-offensive passages from the Collier's histories.[33] Nevertheless, critics of religion in the curriculum unhesitatingly accepted the school's responsibility for teaching general moral precepts. Traditionalists argued that morality could not be taught in the absence of religion.

While the formal teaching of religion declined, religious and patriotic exercises gradually became a mandatory part of the curriculum everywhere. Thus, in Quebec Protestant schools devoted the first half hour of each day to Scripture knowledge, including Scripture reading, hymn singing and prayers while Roman Catholic schools stressed the catechism and sacred history. Patriotism, taught through history and literature, remained an important dimension of moral education.

## Practical Education and the Schooling of Girls and "Ladies"

As noted earlier, the initial debate over practical education was couched largely in economic terms rather than in cultural and educational terms. Following the Philadelphia Exposition of 1876, Canadian efforts followed American examples, with trans-Atlantic influence filtered through American experience. By the 1880s, the educational argument was being given more weight. James L. Hughes, as a Froebelian, saw manual training as a natural outgrowth of the play activities of the kindergarten. This broader perspective made the debate over manual training more complex and confused. It could no longer be dismissed as mere "trades training," out of place in public schools. Proponents began to argue from either a practical or cultural position or, more commonly, from a combination of both.[34] By 1890, manual training as a term gradually began to replace what had previously been called "industrial" or "practical" education. Initially critics opposed manual training. Teachers claimed that it added to an already overcrowded curriculum. Trade unionists feared that it would undercut the apprenticeship system and lead to the production of second-rate "botch carpenters." They also feared that manual training would restrict the upward mobility of working class children by denying them a liberal education.[35]

During the post-Confederation period increasing attention was given to teaching agriculture and commercial subjects, although these continued to find only a marginal place in the curriculum. In 1870 in Ontario, Ryerson himself prepared a text, "First Lessons on Agriculture for Canadian Farmers and Their Families." Agriculture became part of the elementary course of study the following year and was made compulsory in rural senior grades during the 1890s.[36] Nova Scotia appointed a lecturer in agriculture at the provincial normal school in 1885. Five years later the subject was added to the curriculum of the Northwest Territories. An overly academic approach that emphasized chemistry and detailed technical treatment of "The Principles of Feeding," together with rote teaching methods, contributed nothing to the popularity of agriculture and led to derisive criticisms of "book farming." Like manual training, agriculture did not come into its own until after 1900, although even then it was a less than successful innovation, as we shall see. As nature study, agriculture later became the basis of general science.

The education of girls can properly be discussed in conjunction with practical education, in the light of the increasing criticism of the restriction of schooling for middle class females to such "polite accomplishments" as music, singing, drawing, needlework and a smattering of foreign languages. In preparation for a sheltered life of dependency, before 1870, middle class girls were educated separately, as far as possible, sometimes in different schools located at safe distances from those for boys. Gradually, a more intellectually demanding and practical education for middle class girls was advocated. In 1879, Principal Grant of Queen's University denounced the false ideals set before girls in good society that condemned them to a "dreary, aimless, brainless round of exhausting frivolity . . ."[37] Grant's own institution and others, inspired by British and American examples, were beginning to offer serious "regular courses of lectures" to "ladies" through extension programs. In 1874, Mount Allison University in New Brunswick became the first university in the British Empire to confer a bachelor's degree on a woman. Educators now felt a moral obligation to train women as proper mothers and as fit companions, counsellors and helpmates to men. Such training would improve the moral and social quality of the larger community.[38]

Attendance at normal school, a form of quasi-higher studies, was the chief type of further education for girls in a period when teaching was becoming a feminized mass occupation. By this time, the realities of rural and small town life made coeducation the norm for all girls, as it had long been for working class females. For the latter group, employment in an increasing range of usually unrenumerative occupations was often a necessity. In 1868, 5000 Toronto girls and women — more than 20 per cent of the city's female inhabitants — were forced to work to support themselves.[39] For most girls, schooling was still a training for domestic life. One of the first textbook references to "Household Economy" appeared as a chapter in Ryerson's 1870 textbook on agriculture. The chapter aimed at assisting farm women to acquire home management skills in the interest of health, piety and ultimate salvation.[40] In 1884, James L. Hughes advocated a more practical education for girls through the teaching of knitting, sewing and weaving.[41] Here was the beginning of later domestic science or home economics. Bookkeeping was linked to household economy and was taught to provide a domestic rather than a vocational asset at a time when office employment was still not acceptable for girls. In 1872, Quebec's Superintendent of Education asked how, without bookkeeping "can you expect a girl when married ... [to] keep an account of her practical household affairs ...?"[42]

For boys, bookkeeping, first taught spasmodically, became a recognized optional commercial subject, important for record-keeping in an expanding business and commercial society that required an ability to cast accounts. In Quebec, reformers such as Gédéon Ouimet, who served briefly as premier and Minister of Public Instruction during the short period (1867-1875) when Quebec had a separate education ministry, demanded a more practical curriculum that would permit French Canada to modernize and compete successfully with English Canada. Following his appointment as Superintendent of Public Instruction in 1876, Ouimet attended the Philadelphia Exposition. On his return he pressed for a greater emphasis on commercial subjects and English, in preference to classical, clerically dominated education. Although the clergy saw such innovations as a threat to the spiritual character of French Canada, some were accepted and, in time, the commercial training offered to girls in convent schools by the Grey Nuns and other orders even attracted the admiration and patronage of Protestant parents.[43]

The general neglect of commercial subjects by Canadian schools led, by the 1860s, to the growth of private business colleges. The colleges flourished over the next half century or so until the public secondary schools overcame their prejudice against practical training and began to offer efficient commercial instruction.

### Child-centred Pedagogy: Foreshadowing the New Education

The reforms in the pedagogy of reading and spelling sketched earlier and the new interest in practical education reflected a shift towards more progressive views of teaching and learning after 1860. The editor of *The Educationalist* anticipated modern "discovery learning" with the assertion that "children should be led to make their own inferences. They should be *told* as *little* as possible, and induced to *discover* as *much* as possible."[44] But such views were as yet prophetic rather than widely accepted, and discipline remained harsh.

The post-Confederation period can properly be considered as a transitional one between what came to be known as the Old Education and the New, from education viewed as knowledge acquired through memorization of content to education viewed as mental development. "New Education" as a term had come into use in the United States as early as 1869, in an article by Charles W. Eliot, the new president of Harvard.[45] John Dewey attributed the popularization of the term to Frances W. Parker, who christened and launched the New Education in 1882.[46] Later, Parker visited Nova Scotia and Ontario and became a close friend of James L. Hughes.

In 1886, an Ontario collegiate principal, J.E. Wetherell, criticized the Old Education for its emphasis on storing the mind with knowledge through memorization and the study of books. By contrast, the New Education was "devoted more to things than books" and minimized "parrotry." The Old Education dealt with abstractions, with the unseen and the unfamiliar and was dominated by teacher talk, "the didactic disease." The new methods emphasized "the presentation of truth in the concrete," leaving learning initiatives largely to the pupil. Above all, as contrasted with the one-sided Old Education, the New sought to develop "the whole being, the mental, the moral, the physical."[47]

Wetherell's remarks showed the influence of the ideas of Pestalozzi and Froebel, two earlier nineteenth century European reformers whose ideas had long been familiar to Canadian educators. Pestalozzi's ideas were best exemplified in "object teaching," a major innovation which influenced elementary instruction for more than a half century. Object teaching was essentially an oral question and answer method that was intended to stress sense perception and to challenge the dominance of the textbook. The method was based on Pestalozzi's dictum that stressed "things, not words," utilizing his principle of proceeding from the known to the unknown, from the simple to the complex. The teacher held up an object or a picture of an object, asking questions about it to elicit information from the pupils before providing more information about its qualities.[48] In 1867, Alexander Forrester gave the following illustration of the object method to teachers in Nova Scotia:

> You all know what this is. A piece of coal. Who can tell me some of its properties or qualities? It is pure black. Anything else? It is glistening bright. Can you see through it? No. Then it is not transparent, and if so, it must be . . . opaque. John, bring a hammer, I apply it and it breaks into a thousand pieces. You call this property . . . brittle. I am going to throw one of these pieces into the fire, watch what becomes of it. It burns with a bright flame, and gradually becomes . . . red hot, and then . . . a cinder, or ashes. This shows it to be . . . .You don't know the term . . . combustible . . . like wood, or peat, or turf. It is then one . . . of the inflammables. Do you know any other quality this coal possesses? Yes — some kinds of coal have a great deal of gas. This is extracted and lights . . . cities and dwelling-houses. Will you now repeat the qualities of coal? It is black and glistening - brittle - opaque - combustible and gaseous.[49]

By 1871, Ryerson was urging a greater emphasis on sense perception and object teaching in Ontario schools.[50] The oral-object method undoubtedly increased teacher-pupil interaction and encouraged classroom discussion through what came to be called the "conversational method." However, as Forrester's example above suggests, it may be doubted that the system reduced "word mongery." Too often, as abstract mental discipline theories continued to dominate, Pestalozzi's methods were formalized and their vitality was lost.[51] We have little data on how widespread object teaching became but, given the lack of teacher training, large classes and often primitive ill-equipped school rooms, it seems unlikely that the method was very widely adopted. Like most curriculum innovations then and since, it made heavy demands on the teacher, particularly because it required an extensive knowledge of many varied topics.

The new child-centred regime was most closely associated with the writings of Froebel, of whom James L. Hughes became the leading Canadian disciple. In 1874, the year of his appointment as inspector in Toronto, an epoch-making visit to a Boston kindergarten confirmed Hughes' view that "schools could never give a real education so long as the work done in them was confined to learning from books." Froebelian theory advanced a concept of child growth through stages using the metaphor of a plant — thus kindergarten or children's garden — based on a harmonious development of the mental, moral and physical attributes of the child. The acorn as a familiar metaphor was used by Alexander Forrester.[52] Froebel's theory emphasized interconnection or the unity of things as a means of fully developing the child's right relationships with God, human beings and nature.[53] Selleck has suggested that in England, the basis of Froebel's mystical, intellectually confused philosophy was ignored and that educators, accepting his principles of play and self-activity, "reduced the kindergarten to practice."[54] This also happened in Canada, where the freedom and creativity of the kindergarten often ended in uniformity and control. Canadian Froebelians, influenced by John Watson's idealist concept of an organic Christian community, sought to subordinate the individual to the group. Opposed to teaching reading in the kindergarten because it required a premature introduction to abstract ideas, they also opposed free play, which could undermine self-control and discipline. Through carefully controlled games and other structured play activities, an ideal could be created in which childhood spontaneity could be channeled into acceptable social and moral behaviour.[55]

The kindergarten movement grew rapidly in Ontario after Hughes' future wife, Ada Marean, opened the first public kindergarten in Toronto in 1883. By 1900, more than 11 000 Ontario children under six years of age were enrolled in 120 kindergartens.[56] The movement spread rapidly to other provinces. Large classes of fifty to seventy-five pupils often attenuated Froebelian aims. The idea if not the practice of a socializing curriculum was epitomized by Hughes' declared view that "the kindergarten values the child more than the knowledge to be communicated to it or acquired by it."[57] Hughes' book, *Froebel's Educational Laws for All Teachers* became the leading treatise on the German master for many North American educators, and established its author as one of the leading Froebelians on the continent. Kindergarten theories provided a rationale for more progressive methods at other levels.

A more scientific child study movement, arising from the work of the

American psychologist, G. Stanley Hall, became an academic interest for some Canadians after 1880. The new ideas, to be examined in some detail in Chapter 5, reflected an increasing interest in teaching method and classroom psychology. Phillips notes that more attention was being given to questioning techniques. Elliptical questions, requiring pupils to complete statements in unison, "yes" or "no" answers and repetition of answers were avoided by better teachers. Some teachers made a fetish of insisting that students answer in complete sentences. Various methods of distributing questions were advocated, including what was called "the promiscuous method" by which questions were thrown out to pupils indiscriminately or to any selected pupils, even during the exposition of the lesson.[58]

## Controlling the Curriculum

### The Textbook Question

During an era when the textbook was the *de facto* curriculum, there was hardly a dimension of policy that textbooks did not touch. What came, in Ontario especially, to be called "the textbook question," had many aspects — religious, political, social, economic — including issues of American influence, denominational conflict, patronage and the demand for a Canadian publishing industry.

Until 1846 there was little distinction between school books and other classes of literature. Textbooks often served as recreational reading for adults. After 1846 they became a special class of literature for schools. Formal textbook policies in Upper Canada had been recommended by a legislative committee in 1839. The committee was especially distressed by the "evils arising from the want of a uniform system of instruction" and suggested that schools be provided with cheap textbooks from Great Britain, or with British books reprinted in Canada.[59] In 1843 the Reverend Robert Murray, Ryerson's predecessor, gave top priority to curriculum uniformity by means of uniform textbooks, stressing the need for a more carefully organized course of study rather than one where the pupil might "commence his studies whenever he has a mind, and prosecute them in whatever order he pleases."[60]

In the absence of uniform textbooks, the classification of pupils was impossible. Children came from home with a variety of books, such that in 1845 one teacher remembered that he had to use two different readers, three spellers, three grammars and five arithmetic books.[61] As a result, inefficient "individual teaching" was the rule. Uniform texts permitted group instruction in classes, using the "simultaneous mode" of teaching. They became the basis of school organization with each book in the Irish series constituting a "standard" or class, such as "the Second Book class." Later the first four standards were converted into eight grades, on the basis of two grades per standard, thus forming the eight years of elementary schooling that became a common pattern across Canada. Uniform texts also influenced method in a period when most teachers lacked training and could best learn pedagogy from textbooks. In normal school training, texts ensured that teachers could be trained in the books and according to the methods they would use in their future classrooms. Textbooks also facilitated school inspection and common examinations.

Uniform texts eased the problem of pupil mobility from school to school, a widespread phenomenon in a population so much on the move. Ryerson, ever mindful of local sensitivities, gave a very moderate interpretation of the "principle of uniformity." As he put it in 1846, the principle was "not so much that one set of books should be used in a State but that only one uniform set ... should be used in the same school ... and next in a district or city." Provincial uniformity was a long range aim, but local uniformity was popular with parents, trustees and teachers alike, for it was economical and efficient.[62]

In 1850 Ryerson authorized the establishment of school libraries. He issued a catalogue of books from which trustees could select and purchase with the aid of a grant matched by local funds.[63] The catalogue was a precursor to Circular 14, first issued in 1888, which still serves as the list of authorized books for Ontario schools. Within twenty years, 1146 common school libraries had been established, containing a total of 240 000 books, a considerable achievement for a still rural society.[64] Ryerson's policy excluded "fictitious reading" such as "trashy" novels, "works of a licentious, vicious or immoral tendency, or hostile to the Christian religion" as well as those dealing with controversial topics in theology and politics.[65] The Irish Readers were designed to ensure that while learning to read, the pupil was "at the same time acquiring a knowledge of sound moral principles, and of a vast number of important facts in History, Literature and Science."[66] Their scope was indicated by the fourth and fifth books in the series which included Physical Geography and Geology, Jewish History, Political Economy, General History, Vegetable and Animal Physiology, Natural Philosophy including Mechanics, Astronomy, Hydrostatics, Pneumatics, Optics, Electricity and Chemistry.

Patriotic education was closely linked with moral education in the Irish Readers. Used in Scotland and England as well as in Ireland, Australia and New Zealand, the Readers had a pan-imperial appeal without being stridently nationalistic. In Canada, they countered American influence at a time of rapidly increasing enrolments when, despite prohibitions, there was a need to use textbooks and to hire teachers from the United States. Although Ryerson has been accused of using anti-Americanism as a means of gaining support for uniformity, in the wake of the War of 1812 and the 1837-1838 troubles, Canadian fears were real enough. Even if American books were not as widely used as he claimed, their popularity in such sensitive subjects as geography pointed to concerns that still arouse the apprehension of Canadians.[67]

Paradoxically, Ryerson was sometimes accused of favouring American textbooks. Like many Canadian educators since, he often had little choice. Realizing that total exclusion was impractical, he aimed "at making a safe and proper selection of them ..."[68] To counter the low cost of foreign textbooks Ryerson arranged for cheap reprints of the Irish Readers. As early as 1847, the question of Canadianizing foreign textbooks arose. In that year, Ryerson observed with pleasure that Morse's *New Geography*, published in New York, contained substantial Canadian content. Moreover, the publisher had agreed to prepare a special edition containing statistics and other material on Canada.[69]

Ryerson pinned much hope on the religious and moral content of the Irish National Readers, which aroused little criticism even from Roman Catholics. However, neutral religious content so readily complemented the literary content that a teacher of any denomination could easily interpret the selections in the light of his or her own beliefs, thus undermining Ryerson's aim of inculcating a non-sectarian Christian morality. Moreover, while Catholics had few objections to the Readers, to Ryerson's disappointment they still insisted on separate schools.

The adoption of the Irish National Readers overcame the necessity of dealing with the many Canadian authors and publishers seeking authorization of their books. Thus, Ryerson's policy solved the patronage problem. However, the policy undoubtedly inhibited a burgeoning Canadian textbook writing and publishing industry.[70] In opposing Ryerson's policy, publishers found allies among those such as "true grit," fiercely Protestant George Brown who demanded the use of Canadian textbooks.[71] No doubt Brown's ire was aroused by such statements in the Irish Readers as "The country where you, children, live in (sic) is called Ireland." In 1870, a New Brunswick school inspector reported that a teacher had discussed this statement as though it were true and that on subsequent examination the pupils believed they really did live in Ireland.[72] As noted in Chapter 2, the first Canadian readers were introduced at this time. "Canadian" came to mean not only concern for Canadian content, but included a policy of encouraging the publication and manufacture of books in Canada.

How successful was Ryerson's policy and what long-range effects did it have? Undoubtedly it greatly reduced the number of American textbooks, although many continued in use. Uniformity was greatly enhanced although, even as late as 1879, thirty unauthorized series remained in use. For a variety of reasons related to cost, availability and local preference, school boards were permitted to adopt unauthorized books as "exceptions." In the long run Ryerson's policy prevailed, for eventually a system of province-wide adoption of uniform texts was implemented; with minor changes it lasted for seventy-five years.[73]

During the Ryerson years, separate textbooks in such subjects as geography and history began to supplement the readers. Later, George Ross required that each subject in the course of study be covered as far as possible by a single textbook. Uniformity was promoted by regulations that forbade teachers to use unauthorized textbooks, and witheld the legislative grant from any school board that permitted such use. Gradually, province-wide adoption was established. Ross maintained a policy of rigid control of textbooks "as to authorship, matter, arrangement, sentiment, workmanship, price, distribution, manufacture and copyright."[74]

During this period, the principle of free textbooks was established on a local option basis, as provided in the Ontario Public Schools Act of 1891. By now, the most objectionable American textbooks, mainly those in history and literature with their "aggravated national vanity," had been effectively excluded. In other subject areas, the advantages of American books were recognized. Ross promoted the use of Canadian content by requiring the use of suitable local references or quotations. He was criticized for requiring children to learn from their textbooks trivial information and unheard of places, merely because they were Canadian.[75]

During the post-Confederation years, extensive discussion of textbooks and their proper use foreshadowed later interest in formal curriculum planning. S.S. Herner, addressing the Ontario Educational Association in 1881, thought that, while no textbook could replace the teacher, it had the advantage of presenting knowledge in a proper form and order available to all pupils. At the same time, a textbook could not be complete in itself. It should present "a complete outline of the subject of which it treats" but much must be left "for the teacher to add and for the pupil to find out."[76]

The ultimate success of Ryerson's textbook policy was momentous, not only for the Ontario curriculum, but for that of other provinces as well. In 1870 New Brunswick mandated uniform texts, and a year later replaced the Irish readers with Ontario readers.[77] Most other provinces also used uniform Ontario texts which, with their large home market, were relatively cheap. Most textbooks used in Manitoba and the first books authorized in the Northwest Territories in 1885 were from Ontario.[78] In British Columbia under the Public School Act of 1872, Superintendent John Jessop, a former student of Ryerson, authorized a full list of prescribed books from Ontario.[79] British Columbia's progress toward uniformity was achieved in a much shorter time span than in Ontario, in a vast new province where a public school system was created from scratch to serve a widely dispersed population that had few prior or alternative sources of books.[80] Everywhere the use of Ontario textbooks contributed strongly to a *de facto* national curriculum for decades. The curriculum centralization and uniformity promoted by Ryerson became a hallmark of Canadian education.

## Examinations, Inspection and Accountability

School examinations were well established in Ontario by the mid nineteenth century. Initially, these were conducted by "visitors" such as clergy and other local notables, in the presence of trustees and parents. Children gave previously memorized recitations, chanted multiplication tables or read aloud. Work and deportment were evaluated, and criticism or praise was offered the teacher and perhaps the trustees as well. In due course, every school was legally required to hold "a public and quarterly examination."[81]

The position of inspector evolved from that of visitor. We have seen that early legislation had created a corps of local superintendents who were required to follow Ryerson's instructions, to maintain standardized records and to implement regulations governing teacher certification and textbook selection. Before long, Ryerson had 300 officials who formed a chain of command between his office and thousands of section boards throughout the province. By the 1870s inspectors were regularly employed officials required to have professional qualifications in the form of a teaching certificate and evidence of teaching experience and ability. By the 1890s "they were professionally qualified agents of the central authority."[82] The professionalization of inspection was an illustration of the trend towards the bureaucratization of all public administration in an age when centralization and a cult of uniformity developed that stressed selection by merit and evaluation by impartial purportedly objective means.[83]

Examinations, together with textbooks, became the prime means of grading and classifying pupils. They served as the major source of inspectoral power through the inspector's authority to issue regulations for conducting them, and to set standards of achievement. In Ontario after 1860 university entrance examinations included junior matriculation written after three years (or forms) of high school for entry to first year; senior matriculation written after four years, permitted entry to the second year. After 1870, Ontario instituted the dreaded high school entrance examination which, in due course, became the major hurdle and chief sorting device for the entire system.[84]

The entrance examination allayed much of the criticism of declining standards. It promoted curriculum uniformity by ensuring that the curriculum laid down by the department of education was taught as prescribed in all common schools. The examination also reinforced the hierarchical nature of the school system by maintaining the sharp distinction between common (elementary) and high schooling. It served indirectly as a selection method for university as well as for secondary education, and helped to ensure university dominance of the curriculum. During this period, Ontario and New Brunswick instituted short-lived "payment by results" schemes, emulating one that had been adopted earlier in England. The system tied the high school grant to pupil success in passing an intermediate examination written a year or two after admission. The emphasis on cramming and on teaching for the examination shortly led to an abandonment of this early accountability procedure. In 1890, a New Brunswick entrance examination invited pupils to define Voice, Mood, and Tense and to write out a scheme of the tenses of the Indicative Mood, Active Voice, using the verb "take." In arithmetic they were asked: I have 10 bbls. of potatoes, each bbl. weighing 180 lbs; there are three potatoes in each lb.; how many square yards of land can I plant if I plant 20 potatoes in each sq. yd.?[85]

## Teacher Training and the Rise of the Normal School

During the mid-century decades, when content was considered more important than method, many, and probably most, Canadian teachers were untrained. Although the Toronto Normal School was established in 1847, most training in Ontario was conducted in county model schools, fifty of which flourished after 1877. These were elementary schools with normal-trained principals and teachers. The novice could qualify for a Third Class Certifcate, renewable by examination, following three months of apprenticeship and a modicum of instruction by the local inspector. Second and First Class Certificates could be obtained by attending normal school, but only a minority did so before the 1890s.[86]

Admission requirements to both model and normal schools were extremely low for many decades. Before 1875, the main requirements were proficiency in the three Rs and a certificate of good moral character signed by a member of the clergy. Shortly, a year or two of secondary education became mandatory, a measure which Phillips believes helped to reduce the distinction between the two levels of education, and left the normal schools free to give more time to professional education and teaching methods. The demand for teachers became a major impetus for the growth of the high school.[87]

Then, as now, there were controversies over the relative importance of content and method. In 1875, in Nova Scotia, the fact that literary attainments and teaching ability as qualifications were often "widely sundered" was deplored, for both were said to be essential to success. A "natural talent" for teaching was not an acceptable offset "to the want of proper literary qualifications" while possession of the latter, however advanced, was no guarantee of success in the absence of an ability to impart instruction.[88] By this time more attention was being given to method. J.H. Sangster, the principal of the Toronto Normal School, commented in 1869 that every lecture was designed not only to impart knowledge of content, but "to serve as a model of the method in which the same subject is to be discussed before a class of children."[89] The term "normal," derived from the *école normale* in France in 1834, had its root meaning in method viewed as "the norm" or as normative, i.e. "the right way." Egerton Ryerson defined normal as significant "according to rule or principle," a normal school being one "in which the principles and practices of teaching according to rule are taught and exemplified."[90]

Between 1847 and 1857, normal schools were opened in all the eastern provinces except Newfoundland. The Stow Method of Training, imported from Glasgow into Prince Edward Island, was based on progressive Pestalozzian ideas. In Nova Scotia, Alexander Forrester, who became the chief Stow advocate in Canada, disseminated these ideas in *The Teacher's Textbook*, one of the first normal school manuals. In Ontario, Ryerson argued for the "elevation of school-teaching into a profession," an aim that could only be achieved by proper training.[91] Again he drew on the Irish system, sending his assistant, Hodgins, to study at the Dublin Normal School, and appointing T.R. Robertson, an Irish school inspector, as the first master of the Toronto Normal School.

From the beginning, normal school curricula featured an overcrowding which has continued to plague teacher training into our own time. In the 1850s, at the training school in Saint John, New Brunswick, would-be teachers covered a curriculum of nineteen subjects in twelve weeks, in a program that put a premium on rote learning and memorization. Phillips aptly observes that the normal school must be charged with some of the blame for slave-driving teachers who made life miserable for their pupils and themselves during the decades following Confederation.[92] In essence, training was a lockstep process similar to that endured by common school children. Student teachers were examined on the minutiae of the elementary school curriculum, learned through a close study of textbooks.

In western Canada, the need for elementary teachers became the *raison d'être* for establishing union schools (elementary schools with continuation classes added) and high schools. The so-called non-professional subjects, those with the content needed to teach the elementary course of study, formed the core of early high school curricula. The professional subjects were taught in some high schools or in normal departments attached to them by means of lectures on pedagogy given by the principal. Gradually, school inspectors took over this task.[93]

Calam has described examinations in British Columbia which certificated teachers before the province acquired a training institution. As evidence of their broad liberal education, candidates might be asked to state all cases in which Euclid proved two triangles to be equal to one another, to spell "catastrophe," to identify the source of animal heat, to describe the use of the eccentric fly-wheel and governor of a steam engine, to give the exact location of Bangkok, to locate the Irrawaddy River and to name the islands and capitals of the British West Indies. They also required a broad knowledge of British history, and might be asked to write on the Edict of Nantes and Catholic Emancipation; a knowledge of literary works ranging from Shakespeare through Thackeray was also expected.[94]

If the high expectations of such examinations were attenuated by rote memorization and formulated answers, they nevertheless betokened a perceptible improvement in standards. By the 1890s, Ontario women were required to reach the age of eighteen instead of sixteen before being eligible for a certificate, and three times as many teachers were normal school graduates as compared with a generation earlier. Toronto teachers have been described as young women of good morals who were prepared to take their profession seriously.[95] Just as the Ryersonian common school and high school became models for other provinces, so did the normal school. S.P. Robins, the principal of Montreal's McGill Normal School, had been a protegé of Ryerson. David Goggin, the founder of the Winnipeg and Regina normal schools, was an Ontario man.

Teacher training was closely tied to certification, the responsibility for which was shifting from the local to the provincial authority by 1867. Eventually all provinces established provincial boards to conduct uniform examinations and to issue certificates valid throughout each.

## Notes to Chapter 3

1 Ryerson, *Report on a System,* 106-7.

2 Ibid. 190.

3 Cited by Bruce Curtis, letter to the author, December 12, 1882 from U.C.AR, 1851.

4 Ryerson, *Journal of Education for Upper Canada,* XXI, August 1868, 117.

5 MacNaughton, 115-119.

6 A. Miller, 190. This discussion of mid-nineteenth century teaching methods and practices draws heavily on Miller's study.

7 Ibid. 138-9.

8 Ibid. 133, 136, 141-2.

9 Forrester, 433, 69.

10 Birchard, 94.

11 Esson, 9-10.

12 Ryerson, *Report on a System,* 131; B. Curtis, "Preconditions," 108-110.

13 U.C.AR, 1857, Part 1, 47.

14 Prentice, *School Promoters,* 75-6.

15 L. Walker, 75-6.

16 de Castell and Luke, "Defining Literacy," 378-9.

17 Willoughby, 10-11.

18 A. Miller, 342.

19 Ryerson, *Report on a System,* 63-5, 82.

20 E.T. White, 26.

21 Ibid, 21.

22 C.E. Phillips, "The Teaching of English," 59.

23 L. Walker, 80.

24 Curtis, "The Speller Expelled," 9; A. Miller, 342-3.

25 Cited in E.T. White, 17.

26 Forrester, 416.

27 A. Miller, 347-8.

28 Ryerson, *Report on a System,* 32-4.

29 Prentice, *School Promoters,* 47.

30 Van Brummelen, "Shifting," 6-7.

31 Bruneau, 1-2, 8-9.

32 Cited in C.E. Phillips, *Development*, 527.

33 E.T. White, 62.

34 W. Mackenzie, 4-5.

35 R. Stamp, *Schools of Ontario*, 57-8.

36 E.T. White, 68-9.

37 C.E. Phillips, *Development*, 376, 379.

38 Ronish, "Canadian Universities."

39 Light and Prentice, 200.

40 Ryerson, *First Lessons*.

41 Guillet, 109.

42 Quebec AR, 1872-3, 7.

43 Jain, "Nationalism" 49-50; Audet, "Education," 167, 184.

44 Editorial, *The Educationalist*, I, Sept. 15, 1960, 4.

45 Krug, 121.

46 R. Stamp, *Schools of Ontario*, 258.

47 Wetherell, "Conservatism and Reform."

48 A. Miller, 326. Miller and C.E. Phillips provide good accounts of Pestalozzian methods and object teaching.

49 Forrester, 434.

50 C.E. Phillips, *Development*, 413.

51 Ibid.

52 Ibid., 424. For good discussions of the Froebelian movement in Canada see N. Sutherland, *Children*, 17-18 and R. Stamp, *Schools of Ontario*, 54-7.

53 Corbett, "Public School Kindergarten," 5.

54 Selleck, *New Education*, 198, 201.

55 See R. Stamp, *Schools of Ontario*, 55 and Wood, "Ontario's Kindergarten-Primary Movement," 99-100.

56 C.E. Phillips, *Development*, 423.

57 J. Hughes, "The Kindergarten," 266-7.

58 C.E. Phillips, *Development*, 416, 457.

59 Hodgins, *Documentary*, III, 215.

60 Gidney, "Robert Murray, " 201-2.

61 Hodgins, *Documentary*, V, 275-6.

62 Ibid., VI, 267. See also Lawr and Gidney, "Who Ran . . .?", 134.

63 E.T. White, 10. See also Stubbs.

64 The Hope Report, 12.

65 A. Miller, 40-1 citing Stubbs and Emery.

66 Hodgins, *Documentary,* VI, 276.

67 This last point is relevant to Curtis' argument in "The Myth of Curricular Republicanism" that Ryerson deliberately exaggerated the problem of American textbooks.

68 Cited in Love, "Cultural Survival," 376.

69 Hodgins, *Documentary,* VII, 164.

70 Love, "Cultural Survival," 371. 375.

71 Stamp, "Canadian Education," 31.

72 MacNaughton, 176 citing *Journals of the New Brunswick House of Assembly.*

73 Lawr and Gidney, "Who Ran . . .?", 134.

74 parvin, 58, 62.

75 Ibid, 52, 59.

76 Herner, 103-4.

77 MacNaughton, 182.

78 Langley, 13-15.

79 Johnson, *A History,* 82.

80 Van Brummelen, "Textbook Policies," 17.

81 Mainwaring, 6; Ontario AR, 1875, 1.

82 C.E. Phillips, *Development,* 145.

83 Mainwaring, 23.

84 Ibid., 19.

85 *Educational Review,* December 1890, 123.

86 J. Hardy.

87 C.E. Phillips, *Development,* 576.

88 *Journal of Proceedings of Her Majesty's Legislative Council for Nova Scotia,* Annual Report, Appendix 14, 1875, 9.

89 C.E. Phillips, *Development,* 575.

90 Boylen *et al,* 5.

91 Ryerson, *Report on a System,* 157-9.

92 C.E. Phillips, *Development,* 574-5.

93 B. Walker, "High School Program," 213.

94 Calam, "Culture," 12-15.

95 H. Cochrane, *Centennial Story,* 72-3.

# CHAPTER 4

## EXPANDING
## THE COURSE OF STUDY:
## CURRICULUM DEVELOPMENT
## BY ACCRETION

*By forcing this extensive programme upon our youth we are inflicting an injury which will soon show itself in the abundant production of useless book-worms and intellectual abortions.*

(The Ontario Teacher, 1874)

*The high school must be the people's junior university and as such must give the keys of knowledge to the principles which underlie generally every line of human activity.*

(Alexander MacKay, 1892)

## Emerging Elementary and High School Curricula

### The Elements of the Elementary Curriculum

The Victorian common school was intended to provide an elementary education, that is, to teach the "elements" of learning. The graded curriculum and group instruction made possible by uniform textbooks, together with the organization of the new city schools into separate classrooms, resembled the factory model of the emerging industrial system. Grading permitted better supervision of pupils and encouraged "emulation" or competition. Knowledge was broken into pieces, reduced to its elements and compartmentalized; pupils themselves were viewed as raw material to be processed. School rituals such as recitation in unison, the practice of "penmanship" noted earlier and the precise division of the day into periods likewise stressed the order, obedience and uniformity characteristic of the factory system.[1]

To be sure, crowded classrooms in which the maximum of seventy-five pupils per teacher established for Toronto schools in 1869 was often exceeded were hardly conducive to reflective learning or to the orderliness cherished by the school promoters.[2] These facts help to explain why the core elements were long restricted to the three Rs and a modicum of grammar and geography; to these might be added Bible lessons, object lessons as a form of science teaching, a little drawing and music and possibly needlework for girls.[3] Gradually this curriculum was broadened. The first formal province-wide course of studies in Ontario promulgated by Ryerson in 1871 for common schools (henceforth called public schools) contained upwards of fifteen subjects. In addition to the traditional core, to which composition was added as a separate subject, other subjects besides those noted above included bookkeeping, nature study, agriculture, physical drill and hygiene, this last including physiology and temperance. In New Brunswick, the Common Schools Bill of 1871 promulgated a similar broad curriculum.[4]

Already in the emerging era of differentiation, critics were complaining of an overcrowded curriculum. One high school teacher in the 1870s claimed that twenty-seven subjects now demanded the time of pupils. He argued that since most would, like their parents, become farming men and women, they needed little education. Defenders of a broader curriculum argued for its practical and disciplinary value and its value in overcoming the "drudgery of barbarous routine," a reference to the overemphasis on the three Rs. Improved methods would enable the basics to be taught more efficiently in half the time.[5]

As Sutherland's description of Albert School in Saint John illustrates, the New Education was taking hold in urban schools by the late 1880s. Temperance, "Minerals Plants and Animals," Printing and Print-Script and what we now call environmental studies were taught. At the University of New Brunswick, science professor Loring Bailey, a Harvard graduate and ex-student of Louis Agassiz, the famous naturalist, encouraged practical activities in geography and nature study, showing teachers how to conduct field trips. In object lessons pupils made their own objects of clay. Withal, they continued to do traditional classwork, learning by traditional methods.[6]

In ungraded crowded rural elementary schools, the story was different. In Ontario in 1890, all public school pupils studied the three Rs and nearly all engaged in drawing; two thirds studied geography, grammar and composition. However, only a minority learned some Canadian history, drill and calisthenics, music and hygiene and English history. In some rural schools none of these subjects was taught.[7] In the 1880s, Superintendent David Allison of Nova Scotia deplored the absence of a definite program of studies which resulted in school work lacking a common basis or aim, and producing results that as a consequence were "not fairly comparable." He laid out a "Conspectus of Studies" sanctioned by the Council of Public Instruction, but, significantly, commented that such sanction "does not include the provision of machinery for its compulsory introduction into the schools." Allison's program was designed "to impart fundamental instruction of universal utility" using object teaching to provide elements of scientific and technical knowledge of "general application." However, untrained teachers with but a year or two of high school themselves were in no position to realize such an ambitious aim.[8]

The seriousness of Canadian classrooms in the post-Confederation era was vividly portrayed by a British visitor who had previously visited schools in the United States.

> Entering a Canadian school, with American impressions fresh upon the mind, the first feeling is one of disappointment. One misses the life, the motion, the vivacity, the precision — in a word, the brilliancy. But as you stay, and pass both teacher and pupils in review, the feeling of disappointment gives way to a feeling of surprise. You find that this plain, unpretending teacher has the power, and has successfully used the power, of communicating real solid knowledge and good sense to those youthful minds, which, if they do not move rapidly, at least grasp, when they do take hold, firmly ... The knowledge is stowed away compactly enough in its proper compartments, and is at hand, not perhaps very promptly, but pretty surely, when wanted. To set off against their quickness, I heard many random answers in American schools; while, per contra to the slowness of the Canadian scholar, I seldom got a reply very wide of the mark. The whole teaching was homely; but it was sound.[9]

Not all Canadians would have agreed that the teaching was sound. There was much criticism of pupil achievement, bearing out Phillips' contention that "there was never a time when critics did not complain that educational standards had fallen." In 1884, the Bishop of Niagara looking back thirty years asserted nostalgically that "I can testify that the pupils in our common schools of those days could spell, read, write, cipher and understand geography better than they do now."[10]

## The High School and an Emerging Curriculum Dilemma

Phillips has aptly identified the origin of issues that would make secondary education the most contentious level of schooling over the next century and more. As he states, "...when the grammar schools were inserted between the common schools and the universities as an intermediate stage in the new educational ladder, they acquired the pupil population characteristics of the former and a curriculum adapted to the latter." Pupils who sought further education for a better life in a workaday world among ordinary people "were introduced suddenly to a curriculum distinguished by precisely the opposite characteristic."[11] The modern dilemma of the high school, whereby it was viewed by some as a downward extension of the university and by others as a continuation of the elementary school, had emerged. Elementary and secondary schooling constituted different separated *kinds* of education rather than the different continuing *stages* of education that would characterize them in our own time. Fees and entrance examinations were used to restrict entry to secondary schools.

The entrance examination was established in Ontario to arrest the alleged decline in classical learning and mathematics. By the late 1850s the complaints of university people were legion. Colleges were forced either to lengthen their introductory courses or to organize special preparatory classes, the forerunners of modern remedial instruction. Many rural "union schools" had tiny high school departments where one teacher might offer a heterogeneous curriculum to a heterogeneous group of pupils. Although a jumble of options, the curriculum did meet the vocational and pre-vocational needs of middle class families, of prosperous farmers, small merchants, independent artisans and small town professionals. While in 1860 matriculants numbered but 53 out of 4546 grammar school pupils — others were educated privately — a modicum of classical instruction met the matriculations needs of boys and prepared them for the entrance examinations of the law and medical societies. Others took higher mathematics and English needed for surveying or engineering apprenticeships and learned advanced commercial skills such as bookkeeping or penmanship and related English subjects. Girls prepared for the teachers' examinations of the County Board of Examiners.[12]

The serious weaknesses of grammar school instruction were noted by George Paxton Young, the energetic inspector and later academic philosopher whom Ryerson had appointed in 1864. A preoccupation with ineffective classical instruction led to an equally low level of English teaching. To meet these problems and changing social needs, Young recommended that the grammar schools be replaced by two new institutions. High schools were established to provide training in English, commercial subjects and natural science, especially agriculture; the better funded collegiate institutes prepared students for university entrance.[13] In Nova Scotia, collegiate institutes were called county academies and, as in Ontario, eventually became free to all who passed the entrance examinations. A similar secondary institution developed later in western Canada. Gradually, the distinction between the two types of institution was narrowed.

Under the Ontario School Act of 1871, secondary education was irrevocably made a public responsibility but remained highly selective, designed to provide a "liberal culture" and to train an elite who would be "the advisors and guides of the future."[14] As high schools and collegiate institutes replaced "union" schools, the separation between elementary and secondary education became in some respects sharper than before. The continuing selectivity of the high school was revealed by the fact that in 1891, of the minority who reached the "senior fourth" (the eighth or highest elementary grade) slightly more than half wrote the entrance examination, and about half of those students passed. Ninety-five per cent of the 160 pupils enrolled in the average size high school did not proceed beyond the second form. Three students wrote for junior matriculation and one wrote senior matriculation.[15] The well-equipped and well-staffed urban schools that developed in Ontario after 1871, while multi-purpose in function, retained a strong classical orientation as a result of their continuing dominance by the universities. Science and commercial subjects were only grudgingly incorporated into their curricula as concessions to industrial demands and scientific advances.

By the 1890s Ontario secondary students were studying English, history, geography, arithmetic and algebra. Two thirds studied geometry, drawing and bookkeeping. More than one third studied French, less than one third Latin, about one quarter physics and about one sixth chemistry.[16] Enrolment in Latin and the sciences seems surprisingly low, until it is recalled that only 20 per cent of the pupils attended beyond the first year (Form I) and less than 5 per cent beyond the second year (Form II). The proportions enrolled in the "hard" subjects later increased markedly with the increase in the holding power of the high school.

The high school curriculum gradually broadened and secondary enrolments increased outside Ontario. In the western provinces and territories development, like other aspects of education, occurred in remarkable tandem with that of the eastern provinces. By 1880, British Columbia had opened its first high school at Victoria and had established an official course of study as broad as any established or proposed in the eastern provinces.[17] On the Prairies, the high school, as noted, developed very much on the Ontario model; Winnipeg's first collegiate institute opened in 1882. The opening of union schools at Regina and Calgary in 1889 and the establishment in the latter city of public and Roman Catholic Separate high schools marked the beginning of secondary schooling in the future provinces of Saskatchewan and Alberta. As noted earlier, all these schools initially functioned primarily as *de facto* normal schools to meet the burgeoning demand for elementary teachers.[18] The broad curricula prescribed in most provinces were typically restricted to urban high schools.

Before Confederation, matriculation had often been obtained in preparatory classes attached to the universities. Gradually, the high schools were permitted to do all the university preparatory work. In some provinces, junior matriculation could be attained by completion of Grade XI, while in others the standard North American pattern of Grade 12 was required. In 1892 the Dominion Educational Association considered a proposal for a joint examination board "for the whole dominion," with a common standard of junior matriculation.[19] However, despite their passion for uniformity, Canadians then and later were unable to agree, as the Americans soon did, on a standard twelve year eight-four pattern for elementary and secondary schooling.

By 1892 the Ontario view of the high school as an elite institution modelled on the English public school ideal derived from Upper Canada College remained powerful.[20] At the same time, reformers such as Alexander MacKay in Nova Scotia were beginning to speak of "the true scope and function of the high school" as being much broader than conservatives would admit. In 1892 MacKay told the Dominion Educational Association that secondary education, like common schooling, should be free, for it was "even more valuable for the general good." The high school "must be the people's junior university and as such must give the keys of knowledge to the principles which underlie generally every line of human activity." But it should not specialize as a university does. "The function of a high school is not to make the student a chemist, it is to enable him to understand what chemistry is." He suggested that while smaller high schools might house "a large nucleus of imperative subjects" with a few options, a larger school might offer two courses, "one articulating with the University; the other general, perhaps, with options and alternates." Thus did MacKay anticipate the later comprehensive or composite high school.[21]

MacKay was more elitist and selective than he sounded, as revealed in his advocacy of strict entrance requirements and a uniform course of study. The high school should be "the natural channel" through which should rise university, professional, industrial and political leaders. His meritocratic rather than democratic view was revealed in his comment that "some of the most remarkable leaders of thought and action arise from the humbler ranks of the poor and middle classes."[22]

MacKay's specific curriculum proposals are of interest, the more so since he was addressing a national audience and clearly had a *de facto* national curriculum in view. As the most comprehensive such statement of the period, his proposals are especially important in giving us a hint of the kind of high school curriculum that would emerge across Canada during the coming half century of nationalizing educational imperatives. MacKay implied that the same textbooks could be used nationally in most subjects, although in the study of local government in civics a special book would probably be needed for each province. The course of study "should have a wide range" but English, mathematics, history and geography (including civics), drawing, calisthenics and military drill, music and the natural sciences should all be compulsory. Manual training, classical and modern languages should be optional, although MacKay did not intend that languages be restricted to a few students, for prospective teachers especially needed Latin to improve their ability in English. Drawing, "a relief from general study," should be both "freehand and mathematical" not only for its practical value but for manual and mental training. Besides their intrinsic value, music, calisthenics and military drill served valuable "general discipline" purposes.[23]

English and mathematics were the core of MacKay's high school curriculum. English grammar and analysis should be mastered together, with at "least a sketch of the history of the language." Prose and poetry should be studied critically in relation to "grammatical language development and other theories" so that students could "cultivate their own powers of expression by reading and writing under criticism." Literature should also be "a source of pleasurable if not profitable contemplation." Mathematics included "advanced arithmetic" in which MacKay included the principles of bookkeeping, algebra, and geometry together with "their practical applications to a limited extent." Special mathematics options should be allowed in the senior years.[24]

MacKay devoted the most attention to the natural sciences which he ranked next to English and mathematics. As noted, general principles should be stressed: the high school should not produce botanists and chemists *per se*. The sciences had moral value to MacKay, for not even theologians possessed a "firmer morality than (that found) among the truth-seekers of Nature." The persistence of earlier concepts of science was suggested by MacKay's statement that "God ... reveals Himself most plainly to those who study the works of His hand." Science also expanded the imagination. But "utility" was its greatest value as a high school subject.[25]

## The Subjects of the Course of Study

MacKay's comments on the various subjects in his ideal curriculum reflected his knowledge of developments in content and method that had been in progress since Ryerson had set out "the several branches of knowledge" in detail nearly half a century earlier. In Canada, traditional subjects appear to have maintained themselves and new subjects to have become established much in the manner described by Goodson for Great Britain. Goodson argues that the hierarchy of subjects in the curriculum results from conflicts over status, resources and territory. Such conflicts go far toward explaining curriculum stability and change.[26] In Canada the continuing requirement of Latin was the best example of how a traditional subject could maintain its status long after it ceased to serve a relevant need. University graduates in Latin, unable to obtain other gainful employment, turned to teaching and became staunch advocates of the subject.[27]

Goodson argues that conflicts about subjects result from alternative definitions and versions of each. New subjects are first justified in terms of pedagogic and utilitarian objectives. In the search for status, they gradually become defined academically and come under the influence of specialist scholars who influence the selection of content. University status is achieved as teaching and examinations fall under the control of specialist teachers and their university mentors. New resources such as science laboratories become available, a process enhanced by the fact that high status academic subjects attract the ablest students to whom more resources are typically devoted. The status and career paths of the teachers of these subjects are likewise enhanced.[28]

In Canada by the 1880s, several new subjects had achieved high status. Mathematics which, like classics, had long had such status, evolved out of arithmetic into the examination subjects of algebra, geometry and trigonometry. English literature and composition grew out of reading, spelling and grammar. British and Canadian history gained equal status with ancient history. Modern languages and science gained acceptance despite the resistance of classicists.[29] The growth of science in particular bears out Goodson's thesis. The subject gradually moved from object teaching and nature study, with their pedagogical and utilitarian objectives, toward academic pure science that had high status by 1900. Traditionalists tried to contain the expansion of science and other new subjects by weighting examination marks in favour of their own subjects. Thus Latin counted for 200 marks for matriculation as compared with 100 marks allotted to science. Music, art and the practical subjects faced the greatest difficulty, as they still do, in gaining academic status.

As noted earlier, the practical subjects (commercial studies, agriculture, manual training) still existed in only rudimentary form. The following discussion will focus on six groupings of academic subjects: English and other languages, arithmetic and mathematics, science, geography and history, the arts, and physical culture and physical training.

## English and Other Languages

Initially, grammar together with reading and spelling was closely associated with "correctness" and respectable patterns of speech. In Ontario and Nova Scotia, Lindley Murray's English Grammar with its emphasis on propriety and Lennie's *Principles* were widely used for decades.[30] By the 1870s, the ability to speak and write English correctly became the primary criteria for admission to Ontario high schools and collegiate institutes. An "acquaintance" with English grammar was added to the formal requirements for admission to the Normal School.[31]

As grammar came into its own during the 1860s with its own textbooks, it became a very formal subject, viewed increasingly as a science rather than an art.[32] Methods were a direct heritage from the teaching of Latin grammar. Pupils began with the study of vowels and consonants, diphthongs and syllables, and it was not until they were nearly ready to leave school that the study of a complete sentence was introduced. Great emphasis was placed on parsing and analysis and on the correction of errors in false syntax. Kirkham's text began an abstract discussion of these topics by asking, "Do you recollect the meaning of the word analysis? If you do not I will explain it [but] first I wish you to remember that analysis is the reverse of synthesis."[33] With the introduction of new textbooks in 1868, somewhat less emphasis was given to the mechanical learning of arbitrary rules taught with little explanation or understanding. Miller's textbook was designed to teach grammar "by practice and habit rather than by study of rules and definitions."[34] Teaching became more inductive. The pupils were expected to determine the part of speech of a word by observing the duty it performed in the sentence. A complex scheme for parsing each part of speech was illustrated in the "Order of Parsing the Noun:"

| Proper | | Masculine | | Singular | | Nominative | |
|--------|------|-----------|--------|----------|--------|------------|------|
| Common | Noun | Feminine | Gender | Plural | Number | Possessive | Case |
| Abstract | | Neuter | | | | Objective | |
| | | Common | | | | | |

Phillips describes the period after 1880 as "the age of supremacy" for

English grammar. Its status and nature would remain substantially unchanged for the following seventy-five years. Controversies over its value also persisted. Critics argued that no reliance could be placed on grammar to improve ability in English: children might study it for years and be unable either to speak or write correctly. Composition began with the writing of short sentences and simple descriptions of familiar objects but for older children teaching was inhibited by the belief that they had no thoughts worthy or permissible of expression.[35] Nevertheless, in the Ontario *Public School Grammar* authorized in 1886, a serious effort was made to correlate grammar with composition.[36]

In literature, the emphasis on "correct reading," on the dangers of "fictitious reading" and on "improving literature" or "useful knowledge" have been noted. By the 1880s, as teachers took to heart Arnold's admonition about teaching "the best that has been thought and said in the world," a broader view of literature developed, with appreciation increasingly a primary aim. However, its study often entailed memorizing details of the history of literature and detailed analyses of authors' works. Although less stress was given to parsing in the form of crucifying Milton's poetry on the blackboard, an emphasis on minute literary analysis complemented detailed grammatical analysis. Poems were analyzed stanza by stanza, line by line, phrase by phrase and word by word to disclose the technique of their artistry.[37] By the 1890s, whole works of authors instead of parts were prescribed for the junior matriculation examination in Ontario. Such works as Scott's "Lay of the Last Minstrel" could be found in the syllabi of most provinces where they often endured for the next half century, contributing to a national curriculum, albeit one based on Old World culture.

Where other languages were concerned, Latin remained dominant during the period, a status it retained for decades to come, causing later British observers to comment that in few nations was the subject stressed more than in Canada. Inspector George Paxton Young found the study of the classics to be often "nominal," unsuitable for the multitudes of children who would never become classical scholars in any proper sense. The content of Latin remained stable. Caesar and Virgil held sway with Latin grammar in matriculation examinations from the 1870s until World War II.[38] Opposition to the compulsory requirement of Latin peaked in Ontario's "great Latin debate" after 1900. Even its staunch advocates admitted that its earlier growth had been "forced and unnatural."[39] The mental disciplinary value of Latin was regularly proclaimed, but some critics argued that the greater difficulty of Chinese and Russian would justify those languages more fully.[40]

Latin, although declining as an oral language in Europe after 1700, became enormously influential in the teaching of modern languages, with methods modelled on the rigid grammar-translation system used in the study of the dead ancient languages. As in teaching English, an emphasis on rules, parsing and analysis became an end in itself, quite apart from the acquisition of language competence.[41] During the nineteenth century this approach, with its emphasis on application to study and on memorization, ideally suited the prevailing educational theories of mental discipline and faculty psychology.[42]

In 1854, French appeared in the Ontario grammar school program of studies for the first time. Many educators believed that girls were not adapted for learning classics but that French, "a graceful and elegant language ... [was] peculiarly a woman's study and accomplishment ..."[43] A broader view was taken by Dr. Daniel Wilson of the University of Toronto, who thought that "...every educated man in this country ought to know at least French — which here is a spoken language — and German also."[44] Wilson's statement recognized the growing importance of modern languages in a scientific world; they were becoming as important for utility as for culture.

During the decade 1855-1865, when French became accepted as a matriculation subject, grammar school enrolments increased from 365 to 1733, a faster rate than that of any other subject. However, in the universities conservatives remained bitterly opposed to modern languages. A Queen's University professor averred in 1860 that their study was "injurious to the acquirement of classical and mathematical learning which it is the main purpose of university education to communicate."[45]

University graduates in French and specialist teachers were few. Inspectors emphasized the importance of "purity of accent" to overcome the lamentable pronunciation of teachers but the emphasis on grammar and on written examinations precluded attention to oral French. The Modern Language Association of Ontario — the formation of which in 1886 was a notable event in the growth of language teaching — urged that oral tests be used as part of the matriculation examination, but this proposal was rejected by the University of Toronto.[46] However, some improvement occurred with the introduction of dictation (*dictée*) and a modicum of conversation. The moral value of French was expressed by one school inspector who thought that the study of Corneille's tragedy *Horace* would "fortify the minds of our young women" against questionable publications that were designed to undermine the Christian home.[47]

The Ontario Public School Act of 1871 gave status to the modern languages by specifying them as secondary school studies for the first time. Later, a modern language became obligatory for matriculation purposes; Latin became optional for pupils not proceeding to matriculation. French enrolments in Ontario exceeded those of Latin for the first time, although the classics retained high prestige as a result of the force of tradition and a greater mark weighting in examinations.[48] French also gained headway in other provinces. In 1892, the subject was made obligatory for college and normal school entrance in Prince Edward Island.[49]

German had been taught as early as the 1840s but only gained a place in the Ontario Programme of Studies in 1871. Germany's rise to preeminence in science and industry, German immigration and the growing popularity of German in British and American schools enhanced its acceptance in Canada.[50]

## From Arithmetic to Mathematics

Walkingame's text, introduced in the 1830s, was one of the first to be widely used in Upper Canada, and remained popular even after the Irish National Arithmetics were introduced in 1847.[51] The exercises set for pupils were not always practical, however, as this example illustrated:

> A gentleman meeting with some ladies said to them, 'Good morning to you, ten fair maids.' 'Sir, you mistake,' answered one of them, 'we are not ten, but if we were three 147 times as many as we are, we should be as many above ten as we are now under.' How many were they? Answer: 5[52]

Mental discipline and and faculty psychology dominated arithmetic methodology prior to 1890.[53] Textbooks used a method based on rule, whereby definitions of terms were given first for pupils to memorize, the rule was provided, the teacher worked out an example on the blackboard illustrating it and the pupils were then set to solving problems with no effort at explanation or at teaching understanding. Charles Gordon (Ralph Connor) remembered memorizing the Rule of Cube Root which "consisted of at least six paragraphs of small print . . ."[54]

In 1836 Casimir Ladryet's French language text, one of the century's outstanding Canadian arithmetic books, attempted to rationalize arithmetic concepts and processes through solving problems by analysis instead of by rule.[55] In Ontario, John Herbert Sangster of the Toronto Normal School later pioneered a similar approach and also introduced mental arithmetic. Problems such as "What principal will in 37 years at 7 per cent amount to $555.55?" were read by the teacher once and were to be solved by the class in perfect silence in their heads, without the use of paper, slate or pencil.[56] Mental arithmetic, claims Cochrane, produced a generation of rapid reckoners who have never been equalled since.[57]

Gary Phillips' analysis of four Canadian published arithmetic textbooks used between 1850 and 1870 reveals a high proportion of British content early in the period.[58] According to Crawford, the adoption of decimal currency resulting from increased trade with the United States following the Reciprocity Treaty of 1854 was a significant influence on the arithmetic syllabus. In 1859, John Sangster "decimalized" the Irish National Arithmetic.[59]

The "unitary method," by making rules unnecessary and by replacing rote methods, made arithmetic a process of step-by-step reasoning. A pupil asked to find out the cost of a dozen oranges from the cost of five could work out the cost of one orange as a logical step to finding the correct answer. The approach was embodied in Hamblin Smith's English classic, *A Treatise on Arithmetic on the Unitary System*, introduced in Ontario in 1877. Although criticized by conservatives, Smith's text went through two editions, and by 1895 was being used in every province and in the Northwest Territories.[60] The work was an early example of a process whereby foreign textbooks were "Canadianized" for Ontario use and then authorized in other provinces.

Bookkeeping or "the knowledge of accounts" was a practical application of arithmetical skills needed in business in the days before calculating machines. Algebra and geometry became widely taught in all provinces in the post-Confederation era, their supremacy justified by their purported capacity to "cultivate and develop the powers of memory, abstraction and generalization," to teach "strict logical inference" and to give "power and continuity of thought."[61] This mental discipline view increased the status of mathematics in the curriculum, particularly as the classics declined. Some critics felt that mathematics was given a prominence "altogether out of proportion," as one writer put it in 1881. It was too often taught "as the art of a conjuror rather than the mental exercise of a sober logician."[62]

Weinstein observes that arithmetic textbooks, like readers, were increasingly used by their authors as agents of community consciousness, reflecting prevailing ethics, morals and values. The subject matter content of story problems deliberately included dates of historical and religious significance, geographical data and population statistics and dealt with such topics as alcohol, tobacco and crime.[63]

## Science

Early science teaching encompassed "natural history," i.e., the simplest elements of botany and zoology, including human physiology taught by means of object lessons. "Natural philosophy" chiefly meant the rudiments of physics and chemistry. By the 1880s effective, if factual, teaching of chemistry was well established in most provinces. The subject had obvious practical applications and lent itself to the new experimental methods. By this time modern textbooks emphasizing "the individual experiment" as opposed to the old "teacher demonstrator" method of teaching were being written, although little laboratory work was done by pupils before 1890.[64] Croal claims that the introduction of scientific method into the classroom was more important than the growth of science *per se*.[65] By 1890, science had gained acceptance at Toronto as both a pass and honours matriculation subject.[66] Ontario high schools were now required to have laboratories in order to gain collegiate status. The "pure" science of the university disciplines meant, as it would continue to, that applied aspects received short shrift in the curriculum. Biology teaching stressed the structure of the subject.[67] Botany became very popular.

Science teaching sometimes subsumed the teaching of health and "scientific temperance," subjects which had both practical and moral implications. During the 1880s, agitation in Nova Scotia and Ontario led to the introduction of temperance teaching in schools.[68] Ontario teachers were expected to give "familiar lectures" on hygiene to common school pupils. In 1887, "temperance" was added to the course of study and a textbook,

*Public School Temperance* was authorized. Shortly, temperance became compulsory for the High School Entrance Examination. Weekly one hour "familiar conversations" on the "degrading tendencies" of the habitual use of alcohol and narcotics were required.[69]

Temperance education strongly resembled modern anti-smoking and anti-drug campaigns. Hygiene as "the science of health" illustrated the tendency of educators to formalize and academicize every subject. Although temperance and hygiene were intended to meet a real social problem, subject matter was presented in small-type textbooks lacking illustrations and often taught as a combination of dogmatic dry-as-dust factuality and frightening propaganda with little regard for accuracy.[70]

## Geography and History

Ryerson's 1846 report devoted considerable space to these subjects, which he urged be taught "in close alliance," a view that presaged modern social studies. He also urged the teaching of civil government ("a branch of moral science") and political economy ("the science of national wealth"). History should begin with Biblical history, the best guide to the study of the ancient world.[71] In geography an American text by Olney was very popular but its limited and "false and slanderous" treatment of Canada led to its exclusion. Morse's famous text was much less objectionable and a slightly Canadianized version remained in use for many years. The Irish geography texts were hardly more suitable than American books. As a result, Ryerson commissioned one of the earliest Canadian textbooks, J.G. Hodgins' *Geography and History of British North America*, published in 1857. As we have seen, Hodgins' work anticipated Confederation by attempting to provide interrelated accounts of the development of the colonies. Significantly, it devoted an equal number of pages to sketches of French and British rule in Canada, and emphasized the common elements in the heritages of both groups. By downplaying conflict and spreading "social harmony" Hodgins' book helped to establish a tradition of blandness and uniformity which Hodgetts more than a century later would find still prevalent in Canadian social studies classrooms.[72]

In geography, the approach was encyclopedic, stressing rote memory overlain by an attitude and method illustrated in Hodgins' *Easy Lessons in General Geography* published in Montreal in 1865:

Q: Are all nations equally civilized?
A: No, Some are uncivilized, others are half-civilized.
Q: How do nations become fully civilized?
A: By means of the religion of the Bible, aided by education.[73]

Pestalozzian methods were exemplified in the stress on the study of the local area before proceeding to studies of the country and the world and on object teaching, utilizing visual aids. Besides objects, Ryerson's Depository stocked printed object lessons. In 1860 alone, 12 746 sheets of such lessons were distributed.[74] In addition to maps, globes and models, one of the most popular aids was the magic lantern, the precursor of our whole modern range of audio-visual apparatus.[75] Rural schools lacked the most elementary aids, however.

A methodology for teaching later developed, based on such devices as "Formula for Describing a State or Country" in geography and "Questions for the Analysis of Any Reign" in history. Such formulations, despite their memoriter character, did represent a methodological advance. The precision of knowledge that was demanded was sometimes stated in terms similar to modern behavioural objectives as the pupil might be expected "to be able to point out on a map of the world each Contintent and Ocean and to know which part of the map is North, South, East or West."[76]

History textbooks took the form of summaries or condensed outlines packed with information, as in Hodgins' work, with moralistic homilies interspersed. Collier's *School History of the British Empire,* authorized in 1867 was more readable and included social history, illustrated by detailed descriptions of houses and hovels in medieval England. A *Public School History of England and Canada,* authorized in Ontario in 1886,[77] indicated the growing demand for Canadian content.

## The Arts

Ryerson's 1846 report urged the importance of linear drawing, "a delightful amusement," with aesthetic and practical value that assisted writing skill and contributed to geography and geometry.[78] After 1871, drawing was a regular subject in Ontario. Pupils made copies of the exercises in their drawing books and occasionally did a little work in designing. An 1884 drawing book suggested: "Having chosen a design for a lesson, the teacher should place a copy of it on the blackboard and aid the pupil to analyze its form and to understand the plan of its construction."[79]

By 1900, "drawing," now an examination subject, had become "art." The new theories of education made drawing of considerable significance for "hand and eye" training. By the early 1880s, art schools existed at Toronto, Saint John and other centres and helped to meet the growing demand for art teachers. The elementary course in the Toronto school included "freehand outline," "freehand shaded, ornamental design" and "painting in water and oil colours." A typical Normal School examination question in 1878 was "Sketch a doorway with a door half open."[80]

Music began with vocal music which took the form of rote-singing and instruction in the rudiments.[81] According to Trowsdale, the acceptance of music in Ontario revolved around the question of whether all children could learn to sing. It was argued successfully that if all could learn to read and write, all could sing. Trowsdale credits Ryerson with giving the subject status for the first time by making it the responsibility of the classroom teacher and by introducing it into the normal school in 1848. The 1871 Act required boards to teach music although lack of books, of trained teachers and of a sound methodology, and the view that it was a subject for the talented few made implementation difficult, especially in rural schools.[82] In other provinces, vocal music was introduced in Nova Scotia in 1855, in Quebec in 1871 and in New Brunswick in 1872.[83]

The aims of music were justified in terms of its extrinsic values. To Ryerson music was "a powerful agent of moral culture." Church music encouraged religious participation. Singing "national airs" promoted patriotism. "Fireside melodies," including "moral songs" had leisure value in displacing questionable social amusements such as drinking. For some educators, music reinforced classroom discipline and had positive physiological effects that assisted all teaching. Music gained its strongest acceptance as a mental discipline; where it was promoted for "relaxation" it was accepted merely as an "auxiliary" subject.[85]

Sight reading, by training the mind and providing technical skills for future enjoyment, was an attempt to realize simultaneously the academic, ceremonial and leisure values of music. Using Pestalozzian principles of simplification, music was taught in terms of three elements: rhythm, melody and dynamics, taught separately at first and then in combination. Rote singing gave the child a wealth of singing experience through a "reading readiness" which prepared him for later reading.[86]

The introduction of the tonic sol-fah system which had revolutionized music teaching in England led to a heated methodological controversy. The substitution of syllables for notes on a conventional musical stave assisted the teaching of simple musical understanding and made effective choral work possible. Pioneered by A.T. Cringan, Ontario's first music supervisor appointed in 1886, the sol-fah system was soon widely adopted in the province and quickly spread to other provinces. One of the most successful singing plans ever devised, sol-fah could be taught in the regular classroom by a teacher with little training.[87] Although instrumentalists opposed a system which was useless for their needs, the practical success of the sol-fah system in teaching far more children to sing ultimately made it one of the most successful innovations of the New Education.

## A Note on "Physical Culture"

Ryerson thought that any system of instruction that neglected physical education must necessarily be imperfect. "Physical culture" was conducive to school discipline and morale. It cultivated habits of obedience while serving, as he put it, as "a powerful antidote to inattention or absence of mind."[88] Although gaining little formal place in Canadian curricula before 1900, such forms of physical culture as team games, military drill, gymnastics and calisthenics were early valued for their contribution to moral and general character development and their fostering of Christianity and patriotism. These objectives stemmed from the ideas of Thomas Arnold, the influential headmaster of England's Rugby School (and father of Matthew Arnold) whose ideal of "godliness and good learning" emphasized a "manliness" that connoted moral courage and maturity. This ideal became transmuted into "muscular Christianity" in such novels as Thomas Hughes' *Tom Brown's School Days* wherein manliness became equated with masculinity. "Manly sports" designed to counter effeminacy became central to the English Public School tradition and encouraged anti-intellectual attitudes.[89]

According to Redmond, manliness in both its original form and as muscular Christianity gained influence in such Canadian private boys' schools as Upper Canada College, from where it spread to public secondary schools. Cricket and rugby football, imported from England, were the most popular sports in Canada by 1867, but were shortly supplanted by lacrosse and hockey and later by North American football. Winter sports were promoted by the rigorous climate, which nationalists were fond of invoking as a character-building factor.[90]

Team games helped to promote "physical culture" in the curriculum, mainly in the form of physical and military drill which emerged during the 1860s. Exercises in the form of calisthenics taught by the regular classroom teacher were regarded as a "corrective," a routine that "would correct faulty posture, provide mental relief and bring health and vigour to the body." Physical culture was also intended to overcome the lack of fitness induced by fast living. By 1892, military drill was the dominant mode of physical education. Its main objectives were to promote patriotism and military preparedness, which persisted as objectives over most of the following century. Preparedness stemmed from threats of American invasion manifested in the hit and run Fenian raids that occurred from the New Brunswick to the Manitoba borders following the Civil War. In 1878, the ability to drill a company and conduct a class in calisthenics became a requirement for a first class Ontario teaching certificate for males.[91]

## Conclusion

What had been accomplished in Canadian curriculum development during the half century that ended in 1892? Ontario had clearly set the pace, with adult illiteracy reduced to less than 10 per cent; among persons between ten and twenty years of age it was less than 6 per cent. In a generation, educational expenditure had increased by 50 per cent per capita on a total population basis.[92] Phillips comments that Ontario had shown what could be done "by getting every child in school for a few years," by obtaining as teachers minimally trained "docile young men and women," "by prescribing exactly what should be taught and how it should be taught" in a system where the whole process of education was subjected to the pressure of external examinations. He summed up the achievement:

> Ontario pupils in the elementary schools of 1890 were able to reproduce accurately an exceptionally large number of prescribed facts, to repeat

from memory an unusual quantity of approved verbal content in prose and poetry, and to make a good showing in the performance of mechanical skills in spelling, reading, arithmetic, and grammar. Those who survived the grind and the selective examinations and went on to do advanced work under better educated teachers showed equal proficiency in content requiring more intellectual ability, although power to memorize was still the greatest asset.[93]

At higher levels, Ontario secondary education, deliberately and sharply separated from elementary schooling, offered a sound academic education and a modicum of commercial training to a tiny but growing minority of the age group. In rural areas, separate well equipped full high schools were still the rare exception. At the post-secondary level, the University of Toronto and Queen's University were establishing the sound base that would make them national institutions in later decades. Despite many gaps and serious limitations, the Ryersonian system projected a sense of order and efficiency that aroused the envy of American educators. At the World's Columbian Exposition held in Chicago in 1893, the Ontario Department of Education received a special award for "a system of public instruction almost ideal in the perfection of its details and [for] the unity which binds together in one great whole all the schools from the kindergarten to the university."[94]

For the nation as a whole, Phillips sums up development at the end of the period by commenting that everywhere:

> Provincial departments of education trained teachers, issued courses of study, authorized textbooks and conducted an impressive number of examinations ... School boards ... built enduring plants for local branches of the education industry ... Elementary education was free and virtually universal if not everywhere compulsory. Secondary education was cheap, if not everywhere free.[95]

These comments were far from applicable to most of Quebec and the Atlantic provinces, which were struggling with longstanding problems of poverty and illiteracy. Western Canada with nascent systems that were on paper the closest replicas of Ontario's, was only at the beginning of a development that was already rapidly bringing all the problems — in particular the ubiquitous "rural school problem" — that the eastern provinces had been trying to work through for decades. Everywhere in rural Canada, meagre resources, limited inspection, the meagre backgrounds and sheer lack of teachers, their transiency and that of their students meant that the curriculum as experienced by the individual child was probably idiosyncratic to a degree that belied bureaucratically imposed uniformity.

## Notes to Chapter 4

1 Prentice, *School Promoters*, 146-54.

2 Ibid., 160.

3 C.E. Phillips, *Development*, 433.

4 MacNaughton, 197.

5 C.E. Phillips, *Development*, 434, citing *The Ontario Teacher*, 1873-75.

6 N. Sutherland, *Children*, 155-163.

7 The Hope Report, 17.

8 *Journals, Nova Scotia House of Assembly*, Appendix 5, 1882, xiii-xxi.

9 Cited H. Cochrane, 61.

10 C.E. Phillips, *Development*, 505, citing *The Toronto Globe*, February 9, 1884.

11 Ibid., 442.

12 Lawr and Gidney "Egerton Ryerson," 454. Ryerson's unsuccessful attempt to limit the scope of the curriculum in small rural grammar schools was described in Chapter 2.

13 Hodgins, *Documentary*, XX, 116.

14 Ont. AR, 1873, Part III, 8-10.

15 Heyman and Stamp, 14-15. See also The Hope Report, 18.

16 G. Ross, "Policy," 14.

17 Johnson, *A History*, 59-63.

18 B. Walker, "High School Program."

19 *DEA Proceedings* (1892), 168-72.

20 Ketchum, 76.

21 A. MacKay, "True Purpose," 68, 71, 75.

22 Ibid., 69.

23 Ibid., 68-9.

24 Ibid., 68.

25 Ibid., 72-3.

26 Goodson, 394.

27 C.E. Phillips, *Development*, 501-2.

28 Goodson, 394, 397.

29 Stratton.

30 E.T. White, 40-1. See also L. Walker, "More a Torment."

31 Martyn, 23-4.

32 Ibid., 13, 24.

33 E.T. White, 42.

34 Martyn, 42.

35 C.E. Philliips, *Development*, 476, 479-80.

36 Martyn, 45.

37 C.E. Phillips, *Development*, 421.

38 Ibid., 500.

39 Stratton, 180.

40 C.E. Phillips, *Development*, 500-1.

41 Goldstick, 88.

42 Cipolla, 11.

43 Goldstick, 81-2, 111.

44 Cited by Stock, 5.

45 Goldstick, 98, 103-4.

46 Ibid., 194-5.

47 Stock, 7.

48 Goldstick, 146, 148, 162, 168, 178.

49 American and Canadian Committees on Modern Languages, 20.

50 Goldstick, 177-8.

51 E.T. White, 30.

52 Ibid., 32.

53 Weinstein, 443-4.

54 C.W. Gordon, *Postscript*, 18.

55 Weinstein, 48.

56 Sangster, 187-199.

57 H. Cochrane, 199.

58 G. Phillips.

59 D. Crawford, "School Mathematics in Ontario, 1763-1894," 377.

60 C.E. Phillips, *Development*, 484.

61 Ibid., 485.

62 *Canada Educational Monthly*, 1, 1881, 39-40.

63 Weinstein, 455.

64 Warrington and Newbold, 158-161.

65 Croal, 2.

66 Phillips, *Development*, 489-90.

67 S. Taylor.

68 Sheehan, "External Input."

69 E.T. White, 70-1.

70 Phillips, *Development*, 495.

71 Ryerson, *Report on a System*, 60-1, 132.

72 See Prentice, *School Promoters*, 128; and Hodgetts, *What Culture?*

73 Hodgins, *Easy Lessons*, 22.

74 U.C.AR, 1861, 16.

75 A. Miller, 330.

76 Quick, 73-4.

77 E.T. White, 61, 63.

78 Ryerson, *Report on a System*, 122.

79 E.T. White, 74-5.

80 Gaitskell, 4, 12-13.

81 Kalman, 853.

82 Trowsdale, 70, 483.

83 Kalman *et al*, 853.

84 Ryerson, *Report on a System*, 126.

85 Trowsdale, 72.

86 Ibid., 109, 119, 206.

87 Ibid., 255, 278.

88 Ryerson, *Report on a System*, 58-9.

89 Redmond; Judge, 516.

90 Redmond, 12-14.

91 Gear, 4, 7, 9, 11.

92 Heyman and Stamp, 14-15.

93 C.E. Phillips, *Development*, 508.

94 Ontario A.R., 1893, 1.

95 C.E. Phillips, *Development*, 180.

# PART II

## CURRICULUM CHANGE IN A NATION-BUILDING ERA, 1892-1945

# CHAPTER 5

## CONTEXTS
## OF CURRICULUM CHANGE,
## 1892-1920

*... the unity of our people ... can alone be secured by the training of our children not as sectionalists but as Canadians and beyond this as integral parts of the great empire to which we belong.*

(J.W. Dawson, 1892)

*The history of our educational system for the last quarter of a century has been a history of crazes — the method craze, the object lesson craze, the story-telling craze, the phonic craze, the vertical writing craze, the examination madness.*

(A. Kirk Cameron, 1904)

### The Social Context

#### Social Change, 1892-1920

Between the census of 1891 and that of 1921, Canada's population increased by about four million, or more than 80 per cent. The new provinces of Saskatchewan and Alberta were formed in 1905 and new mining and energy resources were developed in northern Quebec and Ontario and in eastern British Columbia. Federal immigration policy was aimed primarily at settling the newly opened West. Non-British European immigrants or "New Canadians" added a new ethnic dimension to national life, extending cultural pluralism on a major scale by raising the proportion of the population that was neither Canadian born nor British born from 3 to 10 per cent.[1] This large influx put enormous pressure on provincial school systems, especially in the Prairie provinces. American and British immigrants who, significantly, were not regarded as New Canadians added to the pressures. Indeed, British immigrants constituted the largest single group of newcomers.[2]

Foreign trade, foreign investment, the economic growth stimulated by wheat, the building of two new transcontinental railways, and the coming of the automobile were among the major features of a rapidly urbanizing age.[3] Yet Canadians were much less willing than Americans to expand education to meet the new economic demands, preferring to import skilled labour and professionals. By 1921, when American investment exceeded that from Britain for the first time, fears of foreign economic domination were added to traditional fears of cultural domination. The Canadian Manufacturers' Association urged the teaching of Made-in-Canada principles in schools as an aspect of promoting loyalty and patriotism.[4]

American cultural penetration was revealed by the fact that in 1907 a single American weekly newspaper sold more copies in Canada than all domestic periodicals combined. The *Ottawa Free Press* commented that such newspapers were moulding Canadian speech, shaping the character of the young and serving as a source of national ideals.[5] A 1913 editorial in *The School* described new distractions that had led to a decline in Bible reading:

> A half century ago there was less travel than today; people had fewer amusements and perhaps more leisure time. The newspaper, the theatre, professional sports and the excitement of rapid travel did not engage the time and attention of the average boy and girl as they do today. Above all there was not the same abundance of reading material within ready reach of those who were inclined to find their pleasure in reading as there is today. The public library and the all-story magazine had not yet begun to fill a place in the life of the reader.[6]

Americanization was but one source of tension in a period when eastern domination of the west, conflict between capital and labour and discontent among farmers became acute problems. Catholic-Protestant conflict and related French-English conflict were exacerbated, reaching levels during World War I that exceeded even those of the earlier Riel troubles. As with immigration, conflict focussed largely on school issues that, as noted in Chapter 2, came to the fore with the autonomy bills that established Alberta and Saskatchewan as provinces in 1905. The most acrimonious educational conflict of all focussed on the issue of bilingual schools in Ontario. The province's Regulation 17, promulgated in 1912, restricted the use of French as a language of instruction in separate and public schools to the first two grades. The resulting controversy, which brought anglophone and francophone Roman Catholics into conflict, led to unsuccessful legal appeals by the francophone minority under the BNA Act. Inflamed after 1914 by wartime passions, the dispute remained a live one, punctuated by bitter parliamentary debates, fierce press exchanges and public demonstrations, riots and strikes involving francophone parents, teachers and students in Ottawa, the main focus of conflict.[7]

Immigration and French-English linguistic and religious conflict were closely conjoined. French-Canadians saw their precarious rights outside Quebec further eroded by the influx of the "New Canadians" and by the perception that English-Canadians did not see francophones as having any special status as regards language, religion and culture. Here were the seeds of modern francophone skepticism towards multiculturalism as a policy in education and other matters.

English-Canadian responses to immigration were ambivalent. On the one hand, immigrants were badly needed, especially in the rural west. On the other hand "alien" stocks were seen as indigestible elements, especially if they were of Slavic origin. The Canadianization of the newcomers through assimilation to Anglo-Celtic institutions and norms was seen as a task primarily for the schools, making that institution a major focus of cultural tensions. With the schools expected to provide a "genetic correction" that would enable immigrants and their children to acquire majority norms, there was no place in the curriculum for any positive treatment of cultural pluralism.[8] Anglo-conformism came to a peak during World War I, a conflict which proved to be a major catalyst of Canadian nationalism and of further industrialization, urbanization and other social change.

## New Views of Childhood

In Chapter 2 we noted that the attitudes of Canadians toward their children were slowly beginning to change by the 1880s. After 1892, efforts to improve home and family life through improving child welfare accelerated. As family size steadily declined, families increasingly became child-rearing, love-centred units, although work remained an equally important function for many rural parents and their children into the 1930s. In a modernizing society, family influence over the development, prospects and life chances of the young, focussed largely on schooling, gradually increased.[9]

Institutional efforts to implement the new consensus about childhood were evident in the formation of Children's Aid Societies in the major Canadian cities and in the organization of the Social Service Council of Canada. In 1920, the first conference on child welfare, organized with federal assistance, agreed to establish a broadly based Canadian Council on Child Welfare.[10] This new national body promoted the professionalization of child welfare, in the process acquiring the ever-expanding functions described by Rooke and Schnell:

> As the council implemented its programs and policies by aggressively attempting to influence or absorb the country's important charity organizations and child care services, it also expanded its functions. Diverse social problems were assimilated. Movie censorship, school attendance laws, youth employment, mental hygiene, "social" diseases, unwed parenthood, mothers and family allowances, child legislation, delinquency, moral reform, drug and liquor traffic, birth control, immigration, housing, playgrounds, handicapped persons, and divorce all fell under its purview. The council acted as the moral watchdog over all aspects of child and family life.[11]

All the efforts described had a strongly nationalistic flavour. In 1920, to reduce dependence on American child health and welfare materials,

Dr. Helen MacMurchy, a fervent nationalist and first chief of the new federal Division of Child Welfare, set about preparing materials that emphasized the rearing of the Canadian child by Canadian parents in the Canadian home in the Canadian way. The result was the publication in 1921 of the first edition of *The Canadian Mother's Book*, a free practical guide to every major aspect of motherhood and child rearing which, over the next sixty years, achieved a distribution of more than six million copies in both official languages and in several other languages as well. Government sponsorship of the publication illustrated the growing trend of state policy aimed at control over child and family life.[12]

The new professional cadre of public health physicians, nurses and sanitary inspectors succeeded in making the health of Canadian children a national issue during World War I. Like most reformers, their highly successful efforts focussed strongly on the schools where health campaigns played a major role in socializing the curriculum. The classroom provided a captive audience of children who could be easily examined, treated and propagandized. The school nurse was by now "clearly moving into the central position in school health programs" frequently assuming an informal instructional role. By World War I the health professionals had succeeded in making the teaching of health (hygiene) and physical education compulsory.[13] Lewis has described concern for the health of the child during the period as a matter of promoting "physical perfection for spiritual welfare."[14]

By this time, mental health was finding a place on the agenda of school reformers, to the consternation of some conservatives. Later, we shall see how this movement became reciprocally related to the testing movement, to the development of special education and guidance, and to early childhood education, with significant curricular consequences. For conservatives, the new emphasis on physical and mental health, quite apart from its questionable educational value, contributed to curriculum overload and diverted precious time and energy away from the traditional subjects. The reaction of many teachers had been expressed as early as 1904 by Agnes Dean Cameron when she complained that

> The progressive doctor, the preacher, the moral reformer, the specialist of varieties manifold demand . . . that his particular fad shall be accorded . . . a place of prominence on our already much 'enriched' school programme . . . The truth is the large numbers of children gathered daily into schoolrooms form tempting fields of easy access to every hobby horse rider for the introduction of what each considers the *sine qua non* for reforming the world.[15]

The more scientific approach to child-rearing revealed two somewhat contradictory trends after 1920. While improved physical care greatly enhanced infant survival, a systematic, regimented scientific approach, exemplified by breast feeding at set times, superseded traditional maternal instinct and child rearing, turning the infant, as both advocates and critics noted, into a "little machine."[16] This metaphor, reflecting the new relativistic social sciences, replaced the earlier idealistic, Froebelian image of the child as a flower or plant.[17] In his 1961 analysis of various editions of *The Canadian Mother's Book*, Naegele noted a second trend in child rearing, reflected in an increasing emphasis on psychological security and greater personal happiness for the child as parenthood became more self-conscious and uncertain.[18] The shift was apparent by 1930 in the work of a young psychologist/psychiatrist, Dr. W.E. Blatz, who directed the University of Toronto's Institute of Child Study, established four years earlier. In 1930, Blatz became director of Windy Ridge Day School, which had been organized by a group of upper-middle-class Toronto parents along the lines of similar progressive schools in New York's Greenwich Village.[19]

## The Educational Context

### Changing Educational Theory: From Rational Pedagogy to Experimentalism

After 1892, as Canadian intellectuals sought new ways of explaining nature and society and criticized the evils of a business civilization, their educational concerns focussed on the perceived erosion of moral and academic standards in a changing curriculum. Besides the further growth of a "critical spirit," the longstanding moral imperative was threatened by the continuing explosion of knowledge. In their "search for an ideal," intellectuals sought to adjust to the new age in different ways based on different views of what constituted truth and how knowledge was acquired.[20] As before, philosophical idealists exalted pastoralism, classical education, Christian ethics, and a cultural imperialism that assumed the moral superiority of British values. They were pessimistic about "the spirit of the age" in which a questioning outlook and a doubt of absolute truth meant that, as Stephen Leacock put it, "We have long since discovered that we cannot know anything."[21] Idealists continued to pin their faith on a rational pedagogy which emphasized the cultivation of morality and character. For them the teacher was essentially a moral tutor purveying a curriculum based on eternal moral principles and absolute standards of culture.[22]

Positivists or realists sought to meet social chaos and disintegrating conviction through empirical methods which foreshadowed modern social science with its emphasis on technique and "value free" scholarship. Where idealists saw pedagogy as a rational science, realists saw it as experimental. For idealists education was an expression of primary values rather than a means to an end; realists emphasized means. Idealists tended to see schooling as educative, pursuing intrinsic objectives that promoted mental development, while realists prized extrinsic socializing objectives. We shall see that both groups shared a good deal of typically Canadian progressive conservatism in educational matters. Talk about practical teaching problems introduced many longstanding philosophical questions into public discussion, imparting a quality to turn of the century educational theorizing that would rarely be equalled in the future.

Rational pedagogy made the curriculum rather than the student the first consideration in planning the course of study. When in 1898 J.G. Hume, one of the very few German-trained Canadian professors of philosophy, asserted that intellectual training would enable the child to gain "a glimpse of the ideal," he was expressing a typically Hegelian view.[23] To Hegelians the chief goal of the curriculum was to transform children into civilized human beings by having them study and master subjects representative of their cultural heritage. Their own natural tastes and inclinations could be ignored. Under the guidance of teachers who knew what was right and whose authority was unquestioned, children would eventually learn to think and act for themselves.[24]

Hegelian pedagogy was illustrated in the detailed analysis of poetry in disregard of the pupil's taste for and opinion of prescribed works. Some teachers were introduced to Hegelian theory, as in Manitoba where those preparing for first class certificates in 1897 were required to read Rosenkranz's *Philosophy of Education*. In his *School Management,* John Millar, Deputy Minister of Education in Ontario, recommended the writings of W.T. Harris and Rosenkranz, the chief North American exponents of Hegelian theory.[25] Proponents of the New Education such as J.H. Putman and others, took degrees in pedagogy at Queen's University and the University of Toronto, where they were exposed to the Hegelian world views of such philosophers as Watson and Hume. Anne Wood has shown how the New Education was underlain by common moral and spiritual values based on British ideals of citizenship and mutual social obligations. Such values and ideals served as a justification for utilitarian goals. At times, this resulted in a diversified curriculum of which Watson did not approve.[26] On the other hand, idealist educational theory, with its emphasis on the deliberate transmission of a coherent body of knowledge and belief, may help to explain the limited influence in Canada of John Dewey's experimentalist ideas.[27]

A perusal of requirements, reading lists and examinations for degrees in pedagogy at the University of Toronto reveals the important place accorded philosophy and psychology in advanced educational studies at the time. Readings ranged across the whole gamut of scholars, from the ancients through later thinkers such as Descartes, Hobbes, Locke, Kant, Bentham, and Mill to moderns including Spencer, William James, G. Stanley Hall and Dewey. A 1907 examination on ethics set by J.G. Hume asked candidates to discuss the value of studying ethics in training teachers. Another paper, apparently set by John Watson, was entirely devoted to the philosophy of Immanuel Kant, rigorously avoiding any consideration of possible educational applications of Kant's ideas. Other examinations called for critiques and explications of Spencer's theories; further questions asked candidates to elaborate their understanding of the term "training for citizenship," to explain the implications of evolutionary theory for education and to compare various ethical perspectives on the growth of moral consciousness. An ultimate test was a request to elaborate a theory of knowledge in terms of its implications for a theory of education.[28]

Numerous examination questions on Herbartianism provide evidence of the attention that some Canadian educators were giving to another form of rational pedagogy. This was largely a result of the influence of American educators who, after 1870, had come to know the work of the philosopher Johann Herbart by sitting at the feet of his German disciples. Brauner has described the American Herbartians as "the first group in American educational history with a well-developed theoretical structure . . ."[29] Unlike their American counterparts, few Canadian educators appear to have undertaken any sustained study of Herbartian theories. However, in 1892, James Seth of Dalhousie University addressed the Dominion Educational Association on the Herbartian theory of apperception which he described as an essential process in "the organization or assimilation of the materials offered to the mind . . ."[30] The Herbartian emphasis on the power of ideas to influence behaviour and on education as the development of moral character was no doubt appealing to Canadian educators.[31]

Like the ideas of Froebel noted earlier, it was the practical applications of the Herbartians that interested Canadians. Herbartian practice was based on concrete methods, and thus had some affinity with the principles of Pestalozzi. As a popularized rational pedagogy, Herbartianism posited the mind as a unity through which learning could be mediated by means of "the five formal steps." The five steps included recollection (of what was already known and had been learned previously), presentation (of new ideas), comparison (of the percepts of the new material, separating out the main essentials in order to apprehend the new concepts), generalization (deriving rules and general principles from what had been learned) and application (of what had been learned).

According to Quick, this method of lesson planning became a widely used formula in Ontario normal schools, influencing teacher training from the turn of the century until the 1950s.[32] Peter Sandiford, writing in 1913, thought that the five formal steps had been worked to excess and that "Herbartianism run mad" was seen when even music, writing and gymnastic lessons were planned according to them.[33] As in England, the Herbartian system aroused interest at a time when Canadian teachers were being assailed by conflicting methods and theories.[34] The Herbartian emphasis on subject-centred verbal learning, largely through history and literature, was likewise probably very appealing. Quick claims that correlation of these subjects was promoted by Herbartianism in Ontario and that the Herbartian emphasis on virtue as the purpose of education made history an important subject in the elementary school.[35]

By 1915, Ontario was producing its own teachers' manuals which had a strong Herbartian flavour. Manuals such as *The Science of Education* (1915) and *Principles of Methods* (1930) and others that dealt with the pedagogy of almost every elementary school subject have been described as the first significant indigenous Canadian attempt to clothe the dry bones of theory with the flesh and blood of practice.[36] Written largely by normal school masters, the manuals dominated Ontario normal school instruction for a generation and were also used in some other provinces, appearing for example on the reading lists of both the British Columbia normal schools.[37]

Although the formalism and moralism of rational science had obvious appeal for Canadian educators, the experimental ideas of William James, G. Stanley Hall, John Dewey and other American educators attracted increasing attention. Hall, a student of James and a mentor of Dewey, had published his influential "The Content of Children's Minds Upon Entering School" in 1883. Based on questionnaire data, the study concluded that with the coming of urban life schools could no longer assume children brought with them the same concepts as in the older farm days. Hall was advancing the radical notion that the content of the curriculum itself could be determined from the data of child development.[38]

As a pioneer of child study Hall drew on the Pestalozzian tradition of object teaching. Unfortunately, descriptive observational studies of child behaviour with their tendency to hasty generalization and speculation about child nature discredited the scientific pretensions of child study. However, when incorporated into American normal school curricula they had value in turning the attention of students of education to the study of children, rather than to theories about children.[39] Later, Hall published *Adolescence*, which became possibly his most famous work, creating an awareness among educators of the problems of educating an age group which was beginning to stay in school in significant numbers. In 1894, Hall brought his child study message to Canada through a series of lectures delivered in Toronto. In 1895, a child study section was formed in the Ontario Educational Association. Shortly, Frederick Tracy, Hall's ex-student and professor of philosophy at the University of Toronto, published his own work on adolescent psychology which was eventually translated into several languages. Hall's observational method was explicit in the 1902 syllabus of the Ontario normal schools, as revealed in a detailed outline entitled "The Study of Children."[40]

By this time, Tracy and other Canadian educators were acknowledging John Dewey for his leadership in the scientific child study movement. In 1889, J.A. McLellan of the Ontario Normal School adapted and published Dewey's *Applied Psychology,* a work which attempted to incorporate the newer science into the Hegelian idealism in which Dewey had been reared. In 1895 the two men co-authored *The Psychology of Number.* For Dewey, no studies were intrinsically endowed with liberating or cultural powers *per se,* for any subject, according to how it was taught and learned, could have cultural value. Dewey's response to Spencer's question, "What knowledge is of most worth?" was that knowledge was essentially social. Like Hall, Dewey thought that education must be transformed to meet the needs of a new urban industrial society and to enable the school to assume the educative functions of traditional agrarian life. These ideas owed much to the work of Francis W. Parker, whose work was already known in Canada.[41]

Quite apart from his collaboration with McLellan, Dewey seems to have been well known in Canada, apparently having made his first visit in 1901 when he spoke in St. Thomas, Ontario, on "Education and Everyday Experience."[42] However, although his ideas were disseminated quite widely before 1920, they appear to have had little practical impact before the progressive period of the 1930s, and even then their effect was limited. Dewey's works, notably *Democracy and Education*, were cited on normal school reading lists. In 1915, the Ontario history of education manual described "the ideal school of the future" in Deweyan terms. In such a school it was claimed, "the passive reception of knowledge will disappear" with self-discipline and self-reliance "arising out of the child's self-activity (serving) as the order of the day." Significantly, however, these words appeared in a chapter entitled "Education for Social Efficiency" which espoused a conservative philosophy at odds with Dewey's liberal progressive views.[43]

Among Canadian educators, J.W. Robertson and Loran de Wolfe in Nova Scotia may have come closest to an intuitive grasp of Deweyan theory, and agricultural education may have been, at its best, the most successful application of Dewey's ideas before 1920. Robertson's essentially Deweyan perspective had been expressed as early as 1903 when he declared that "There has been in our schools a most unhappy separation between the word and the deed."[44] In 1917, in Ottawa, Robertson arranged for Dewey to be made an honorary member of the Dominion Educational Association. Dewey addressed the group on the topic "Socializing the Schools".[45]

William James, another American theorist, advocated scientific psychology as a theoretical guide to school practice. His *Talks to Teachers* became widely used in Canadian normal schools. More influential in Canada than either Dewey or James was Edward Lee Thorndike, another scientific psychologist. While Dewey represented the liberal side of American progressivism, Thorndike and other "pedagogical scientists" represented the conservative side. Thorndike's view of education as a scientific means of social improvement marked him as a true progressive even as his social philosophy marked him as a conservative.[46] His social conservatism and scientific progressivism was consistent with a Canadian educational tradition that could be traced to Ryerson's time.

Viewing mind as a product of the organism's response to its environment rather than as a separate entity, Thorndike aimed to make psychology and pedagogy true experimental sciences, based on the study of observable, measureable human behaviour. "Whatever exists at all exists in some amount" he declared in one of his most oft quoted statements.[47] Thorndike's stimulus/response psychology and his famous "laws of learning" with their concept of positive reinforcement revolutionized pedagogical theory. By undermining existing theories of the transfer of training, Thorndike shattered time-honoured assumptions about the mental disciplinary value of traditional school subjects. If transfer of training was non-existent or limited, then the justification for teaching Latin or geometry on the grounds that they enhanced the general mental faculties could not be sustained. This view also served to justify the new subjects and their equivalence to traditional studies.

Thorndike's theories were being cited in the Ontario *Teachers' Manuals* by 1915. Later they were cited in British Columbia's *Putman-Weir Survey* to discredit the mental discipline theory that dominated the province's schools. However, Canadian educators proved typically cautious in abandoning the old psychology and were slow to broaden the curriculum, especially at the high school level, according to the dictates of Thorndike's findings. They also overlooked the moral and theological implications of Thorndike's theories which discarded the Biblical notion of original sin and treated human nature as infinitely plastic, capable of being exploited for good or ill.[48] Such ideas were hardly consistent with Canadian concepts of disciplined intelligence, but it was the practical aspects of Thorndike's scientific pedagogy that interested educators.

Thorndike's major impact in Canada arose out of his pioneer studies of individual differences and his related work on human intelligence, mental testing, classroom grouping and retardation. In Canada, the leading exponent of experimentalism and testing was Peter Sandiford of the University of Toronto who had originally come from the University of Manchester to do his doctorate under Thorndike at Columbia in 1910. In 1912, C.K. Clarke, a psychiatrist at the University of Toronto, made one of the earliest uses of intelligence tests. Both men became closely associated with the mental hygiene movement.

Elsewhere in Canada, Sinclair Laird of McGill University's School for Teachers, Quebec's Protestant normal school, thought that medicine, social science and psychology had much to contribute "if considered from an educational standpoint."[49] In 1912, S.B. Silcox, the principal of Ontario's Stratford Normal School, cited Thorndike in an article "The Time Factor and the Course of Study" that foreshadowed modern "time on task" research. Silcox's article appeared only a year after the establishment in the United States of a Committee on Economy of Time in Education, a move which signalled the growing interest in applying industrial management methods to the improvement of school effectiveness.[50] Silcox noted that one of Thorndike's students had demonstrated that in arithmetic "a large amount of time expended is no guarantee of a high degree of efficiency." Yet one hour a day, and forty minutes a day were devoted to arithmetic and spelling respectively in Ontario. It was suggested that pupils should work faster and should be grouped by ability.[51]

The survey methods of research championed by the scientific educators were carried over into Canada in a limited way. W.L. Richardson and J.C. Miller used such methods in their respective national surveys of urban and rural schools, as did Putman and Weir in their provincial survey in British Columbia.[52] Individual studies of city school systems were carried out in Ottawa, Vancouver and Winnipeg. All these surveys will be discussed in Chapter 12. However, the school survey movement was much more limited in Canada than in the United States. The conservative Canadian attitude towards scientific education was summed up in 1920 by J.H. Putman who, in decrying the application of business methods to schools, revealed his idealist background. Education could not be treated as a science or "machine system" when it "[dealt] with the human will" and was "largely a spiritual process." Putman thought that scientism ignored the natural powers of the child in planning the curriculum and made the course of study "the deciding factor."[53]

Despite these views, Putman had expressed great admiration for American social efficiency in education during his United States tour seven years earlier.[54] He took great pride in his efficient administration of Ottawa's schools, and in 1918 encouraged one of the first scientific surveys of a city school system in Canada. Later, he advocated scientific management methods as a means of reforming the British Columbia system. Like other Canadian educators, Putman saw no problem in using social efficiency methods to serve traditional curriculum goals. He ignored the fact that, in basing their curricula on traditional textbook subject matter, Canadian educators also made the course of study the deciding factor. Their past-oriented curricula were no more child-centred than the adult-centred, future-oriented school program advocated by American pedagogical scientists such as Franklin W. Bobbitt.

## Voluntary Initiatives, Federal Intervention and Legislative Change

The wider varied and overlapping goals of the new school promoters reflected an equally wide and varied range of interest groups that sought to influence and control the curriculum after 1892. Reform initiatives were undertaken simultaneously by leaders such as James W. Robertson who came from outside the school system, and by a new generation of school promoters from within such as Alexander MacKay in Nova Scotia, John Seath and J.H. Putman in Ontario and David Goggin in western Canada. Soon these leaders began to implement the Ryersonian principles they had inherited.

Many new initiatives were promoted by or through various national voluntary organizations, such as the Dominion Educational Association, formed in 1892. In addressing words of welcome to the new body's first meeting in Montreal, Sir William Dawson asserted the necessity for "a general plan of education" to be promoted by "a union of educators." Such a plan would enable young Canadians "to grow up as members of one common country with a sentiment for Canada common to all." This could only be secured "by the training of our children not as sectionalists but as Canadians and beyond this as integral parts of the great empire to which we belong."[55] Dawson's call for "a general plan of education" had overtones of a call for a national curriculum that reflected a new self-conscious sense of national purpose. Under George W. Ross' leadership the Association adopted a bilingual constitution and quickly organized itself on the NEA model into four departments, viz., Elementary Education, Higher Education, Industrial Education and Inspection and Training.

The early years of the Association revealed an interest in various perennial issues that have persisted to our own day. Thus, a resolution adopted in 1892 affirmed that "elementary instruction in all [university] subjects ... should be given in the secondary schools and not in the university." Nor should the work of the elementary schools "materially overlap that of the high schools ..."[56] A common national standard of university matriculation was proposed. The provinces were urged to establish a common classification of schools to deal more effectively "with the attainment of pupils who have changed their residence from one province to another." Dominion-wide recognition of provincial teaching certificates was also recommended. Other resolutions touched on the need to improve the teaching of Canadian history in the interests of national unity, on better inspection of schools, problems of attendance and on better teacher training.[57] In later years, the Association urged more attention to technical education and advocated uniform textbooks among the provinces. It also assisted in the establishment in 1919 of the Education Division of the Dominion Bureau of Statistics, which provided for a pooling of provincial statistics and other basic information.

After 1918, the Association, by then known as the Canadian Education Association, became moribund for more than a decade. On its revival in the 1930s it again became a significant nationalizing force, initially by promoting development in such fields as health and vocational education. Over the decades the organization has played a catalytic role in encouraging or promoting the curricular concerns of other national groups.

In 1907 J.W. Robertson had commented to a Charlottetown audience that "The whole child goes to school — body, mind and spirit and the training of hand, head and heart should go on harmoniously." Eight years earlier, Robertson, then federal Commissioner of Agriculture, had sought to realize this Deweyan vision of education by organizing a seed contest for youngsters, an event which Sutherland associates with the beginning of the New Education as an organized movement.[58] The contest entailed the selection of choice heads of grain from one year's crop to be used as seed in the next, a process that Robertson hoped would not only improve Canadian crops, but would also train children in "habits of observation and thought and study [that] would remain with them."[59]

Sir William Macdonald, a tobacco merchant and philanthropist, agreed to fund the contest for a three-year period. At the same time, he provided support for the Macdonald Manual Training Fund. In 1901, the Macdonald Rural School Fund was established. Together, these benefactions and others provided the financial basis for the Macdonald-Robertson movement, the first and one of the most influential national curriculum reform endeavours in Canadian history. In addition to supporting the seed contest and manual training, Macdonald funding supported school gardens, nature study, domestic science (later called home economics) and school consolidation. These developments will be discussed in detail in Chapter 6.

The Macdonald-Robertson Movement stimulated a federal interest in education. Although Sir Wilfred Laurier refused for constitutional reasons to set up a Ministry of Industrial Education, he did agree, at the persuasion of his Minister of Labour, William Lyon Mackenzie King, to establish the first federal Royal Commission on Education. Established in 1910 with the unanimous concurrence of the provinces, the Royal Commission on Industrial Training and Technical Education, as it was called, was said to be within Ottawa's jurisdiction because vocational education was "a matter of economics rather than scholarship."[60]

The Commission was chaired by Robertson, who had meanwhile become the principal of Macdonald College of McGill University, a new institution designed for instruction in the three "fundamental mothering occupations" of farming, home-making and teaching.[61] Robertson's agricultural experience and work with the manual training movement had convinced him of the need to upgrade rural and technical education. However, the commission's 1913 report was much more than a narrow study of these and other related areas of practical training. It served as a blueprint for implementing the New Education, drew national attention to the economic aims of the curriculum, and suggested curriculum changes to educators in all provinces.[62] Through visits to more than 100 centres, the solicitation of 1650 oral and written briefs and meetings with premiers, cabinet ministers and government officials in each province, the Commission stimulated a nation-wide debate over issues that became central to the formulation of Canadian curriculum policy over the next generation. The members also made extensive visits to the United States, Great Britain and several continental nations.

In addition to promulgating vocational aims for the curriculum, Robertson urged that attention be given to health, "the harmonious growth of the powers of the body, mind and spirit," the training of the senses, the formation of "habits of obedience, courtesy, diligence and thoroughness" and the cultivation of high ideals and proper standards of conduct and character. These objectives anticipated a number of those that would later be promulgated in the United States in the form of the "cardinal principles of education" enunciated in 1918 by the NEA's Commission on the Reorganization of Secondary Education.[63]

Robertson's proposal for a complete system of vocational education for Canada under federal auspices was never implemented, for both constitutional reasons and for reasons of cost. However, even before Robertson completed his report the federal government was taking major initiatives that would have a direct impact on the school curriculum. These included legislation supporting the teaching of military drill, agriculture and technical education, three innovations to be discussed subsequently. The Agricultural Aid Act of 1912 and the Agricultural Instruction Act of 1913 were designed to improve rural economic, social and educational conditions and, in the case of the latter, explicitly to promote the teaching of agriculture in schools. In 1919, the Technical Education Act committed a total of ten million dollars over a ten-year period to enable Ottawa to assist in the building of provincial facilities for vocational education. The 1913 and 1919 acts distributed the funds among the provinces according to population but out of deference to provincial autonomy left the responsibility for the administration of the resulting programs with the appropriate provincial departments. Later, in examining the impact of both acts on school curricula, we shall see that these provisions proved limiting.

## Illiteracy, School Attendance and "Retardation"

Compulsory attendance laws assisted an improvement in attendance that was the major factor in the growth of Canadian school systems during the half century following 1892. Between the 1891 and 1921 censuses, total enrolments doubled. A 250 per cent increase in the teaching force greatly improved the teacher-pupil ratio. Secondary school expansion led the way; in some provinces the ratio of high school to elementary pupils tripled or quadrupled.[64] Contrary to the expectations of school officials, increased enrolments increased the regularity of attendance. By 1921, the average daily attendance of pupils enrolled in the upper elementary grades exceeded 90 per cent. More regular attendance meant that children stayed in school longer and completed more grades.

All provinces but Quebec had compulsory attendance laws by the end of World War I. Upper ages ranged from twelve in New Brunswick and Nova Scotia to fifteen in Alberta.[65] As before, the laws reflected rather than led public opinion for, in Sutherland's words, "as a rising standard of living reduced the need of many families for the income of their youngsters, a greater proportion of Canadians made a deeper commitment to the education of their children."[66] Improved attendance and population growth put tremendous pressure on school facilities, especially in the new western provinces. Alberta had 600 schools in 1905, about 1750 in 1911 and about 3000 in 1918. In the whole of Canada, the number of classrooms increased from 27000 to 51000 between 1901 and 1919.[67]

Another consequence of improvement in attendance was a sharp decline in illiteracy. In 1921 the Dominion Bureau of Statistics, paid a tribute that would have gladdened the hearts of earlier school promoters:

> On the whole, therefore, the progress made since 1911 and especially the very marked progress since 1891, may be said to have been brought about solely by the schools of Canada, and that in spite of increasing difficulties, the advantages of improved settlement being more than counterbalanced by the disadvantages of the immigration of illiterate persons. The active instruments of progress in educational status may, therefore .... be reduced to one — the school ...[68]

Between 1891 and 1921, the proportion of the population unable to read and write fell from 13.8 per cent to 5.1 per cent.[69] The Bureau study found "a decided connection" between the illiteracy of a community and poor school attendance. Extreme rural conditions such as severe climate and sparseness of population were related to illiteracy, but in general urban-rural differences were attributed to psychological or social, i.e. to mental, social and racial factors, rather than to physical conditions.[70] The foreign-born had a significantly higher degree of illiteracy than the British or the native born.[71] The element of "race" was defined as "the strongest factor in illiteracy in Canada." This naive view ignored an earlier nation-wide analysis carried out in 1897-8 by a Quebec scholar, Leon Gerin, one of the founding fathers of Canadian sociology, who attributed differences in illiteracy to cultural and familial factors rather than to "race."[72]

Related to the problems of compulsory attendance and illiteracy was what educators called "retardation" which was a major cause of low high school enrolments. The term referred to grade (and age) retardation rather than mental retardation *per se*, at a time when, to be sure, there was little hesitation in hanging a "defective" label on children unable to meet arbitrary standards. "Repeating the grade" was the standard prescription for dealing with learning problems. W.L. Richardson's 1918-19 nationwide survey of the administration of schools in Canadian cities concluded that "Of every 100 children in Canadian city schools, 30 to 50 were [grade] retarded." The "failure to do the prescribed work" resulted in "repetition of work, then monotony and then loss of interest." Richardson reported that according to an "admittedly unscientific" Toronto study, causes of failure were curricular and could be reduced to one: "the maladjustment of pupils with materials of instruction."[73]

During the 1920s, the Putman-Weir Survey in British Columbia recommended promotion from grade to grade by subject, as a means of combatting age and grade retardation. The system of "subject promotion" eventually spread from British Columbia to other provinces, with significant consequences for curriculum organization; it also hastened the adoption of the unit or credit system. Retardation everywhere was related to the problem of drop-outs. Although by 1921 Canadian school promoters had succeeded in getting most children into elementary school, as late as 1959 the majority of Canadian adolescents still dropped out before completing high school.

## Notes to Chapter 5

1 Urquhart and Buckley, 19.
2 The impact of British immigration was particularly dramatic in British Columbia. Whereas in 1901 the province had been demographically Canadian, by 1911 it had been transformed into a British one, with one third of the white population born in Great Britain and Ireland. This proportion held into the 1920s with the British

group outnumbering those born in British Columbia, elsewhere in Canada and in other countries. See Barman, 16, 176.

3 R.C. Brown and Cook, 1.
4 Angus, 213.
5 Moffett, 96-7, 108.
6 *The School* I, no. 6 (February 1913), editorial, 373.
7 Stamp, *Schools of Ontario*, 84-92.
8 Palmer and Troper, 19.
9 N. Sutherland, *Children*, 14. On the growth of family influence, Sutherland cites the British sociologist Frank Musgrove, *The Family, Education and Society*, London: Routledge and Kegan Paul, 1966, 1-15.
10 R. Allen, 12-13; N. Sutherland, *Children*, 229.
11 Rooke and Schnell, "Child Welfare," 491.
12 Lewis, "No Baby," 2-5, 9-10.
13 N. Sutherland, *Children*, 39-55.
14 Lewis, "Physical Perfection."
15 A.D. Cameron, 243.
16 Lewis, "Creating," 44-5.
17 Strong-Boag, "Intruders," 166.
18 Naegele, 29-30.
19 See Northway, *Twenty-five Years* and "Child Study."
20 S. Shortt, 8.
21 Leacock, "Apology," 186. See also S. Shortt, 75.
22 S. Shortt, 8.
23 Hume, "Moral Training," 233-4.
24 C.E. Phillips, *Development*, 420-1.
25 Ibid.
26 Wood, "Hegelian Resolutions," 262-3, 268.
27 See L. Armour and E. Trott, 513.
28 See University of Toronto Annual Examinations for Degrees in Pedagogy, 1907, 1909, 1910.
29 Brauner, 51.
30 Seth, 149.
31 For more on Herbartian theories see Brauner, 53-5; Selleck, *New Education*, 227.
32 Quick, 202-220.
33 Sandiford, "Lesson Plans," 129.
34 See Selleck, *New Education* for a discussion of Herbartian influence in England, 202.
35 Quick, 187.
36 Newcombe, 58.
37 Putman and Weir, *Survey*, 200.
38 Cremin, *Transformation*, 101-3.
39 Brauner, 81.
40 Provincial Normal Schools, *Syllabus* (1902) 7.
41 Cremin, *Transformation*, 117, 125, 129.
42 Binkley, 6.
43 Ontario Teachers' Manuals, *History*, 184.
44 Cited in O.E. White, 50.
45 N. Sutherland, *Children*, 215.
46 Cremin, *Transformation*, 369.

47 Cited in ibid., 185.

48 Ibid., 112.

49 Laird, 294.

50 Cremin, *Transformation,*193.

51 Silcox, 31-34.

52 W. Richardson; J.C. Miller, *Rural Schools*; Putman and Weir, *Survey.*

53 Putman. "Shortening," 450-6.

54 Wood, "Putman's American Tour."

55 J.W. Dawson, *DEA Proceedings* (1892), 37.

56 *DEA Proceedings* (1892), 29.

57 Ibid., 29-31.

58 N. Sutherland, *Children,*181-3

59 RCITTE, 153.

60 Ottawa, House of Commons Debates (1908), 2861.

61 RCITTE, 157.

62 N. Sutherland, *Children,*199.

63 RCITTE, 9. For a discussion of the cardinal principles see Krug, 378-425. The seven principles included health, command of fundamental processes, worthy home membership, vocation, citizenship, worthy use of leisure time and ethical character.

64 Urquhart and Buckley, 587-91.

65 Ibid.

66 N. Sutherland, *Children,* 165.

67 C.E. Phillips, *Development, 189-90.*

68 Dominion Bureau of Statistics, *Illiteracy,* 84.

69 Ibid. 8.

70 Ibid. 124-5.

71 Ibid. 8.

72 Falardeau, 59-75; W. Martin and Macdonnell, 248.

73 W. Richardson, 206, 227-8.

# CHAPTER 6

## NEW SUBJECTS
## FOR A NEW EDUCATION

*The work of the school day should gradually be arranged less and less on subjects as such, and more and more on occupations, projects and interests [forming] ... a centre for the correlated study of ... reading, composition, number work, writing and drawing.*
(Royal Commission on Industrial Training and
Technical Education, 1913)

*... manual training has become a fetish in our primary education .... It is doubtful if the manufacture of hat-racks and towel-rollers has much more bearing on the average man's life than a course in history.*
(Vincent Massey, 1911)

The specific curriculum innovations of the New Education took the form of various new subjects, of which manual training, domestic science, agriculture (including "nature study") and health and physical education were the most important. Most of these innovations overlapped in various ways. J.W. Robertson thought that nature study "should be central, with manual training and domestic science on either side of it."[1] Manual training included a variety of components that together cut across most of the new subjects. Long established but peripheral subjects such as art and music achieved new status or assumed new forms. Temperance education, one of the less successful innovations, was associated variously with health, domestic science and general science. The emphasis given to primary ducation, which saw possibly the most longstanding improvement, gave new impetus to the kindergarten movement.

The overlapping, disparate objectives of the new subjects, reflecting the general aim of the New Education to educate "the whole child," were expressed by Robertson in his 1913 report, as noted earlier. In 1915 an official Ontario teachers' manual expressed four purposes for education under the significant rubric, "Education for Social Efficiency." These included social control, for instance, an appreciation of liberty, respect for institutions and the need to vote intelligently; the dissemination of knowledge upon which depended "intelligence, social progress and happiness;" social improvement, the enhancement of the welfare of society which was much more important than enhancing "the individual advantage of pupils;" industrial efficiency to be promoted by means of practical subjects which would "make each individual a productive social unit."[2]

Robertson's strategy of disseminating the new subjects through demonstration had mixed success, largely because it depended in the long run on the willingness of local educators and in particular, local ratepayers, to assume responsibility for maintaining innovation after Macdonald Fund support ceased. Failure to understand or accept the philosophy behind the new subjects and unwillingness to assume the costs were major impediments, illustrated by the attempt to promote school consolidation, probably the most conspicuous failure of the Macdonald-Robertson movement. Yet, the facilities and better trained teachers that consolidation promised were essential to the success of the new subjects.

Too often manual training, domestic science and other innovations were merely tacked on to an overcrowded curriculum, despite the intent of reformers who viewed them less as subjects than as sources of projects and activities through which the three Rs could be enriched and correlated in order to make learning more interesting and efficient, more "educative." While this ambitious goal was rarely achieved, and while innovations often suffered from formalization, many elements of them were tried out and incorporated into the curriculum. If by 1920 the Canadian curriculum had not been transformed, the school experience of the Canadian child — at least of the urban child — was nevertheless significantly different from what it had been a few decades before.

Like their anglophone counterparts, many Quebec educators were interested in trying to reform their school system. In that province, efforts were spearheaded by a group of business people, professionals, civic leaders and rural reformers led by Godfroy Langlois, a journalist, who founded La Ligue de l'Enseignement in 1902. One of its members, Gaspard de Serres, later became a member of the Robertson Royal Commission of 1910. Like their anglophone counterparts, the Quebec reformers drew inspiration from several European countries and from the United States. American ideas especially influenced the Ligue's demands for the full panoply of New Education reforms.[3] A lack of resources that was even more serious in Quebec than in other provinces made it difficult to promote educational innovation, even though many Catholic teachers and trustees favoured change.[4] The New Education could take little hold when schools lacked manual training rooms and gymnasia. As we shall see, more success was achieved in agricultural education.

## Manual Training

The North American debate over the virtues and place of manual training in the curriculum that had peaked following the interest aroused by the Russian exhibit at the Philadelphia Exposition in 1876 continued after 1892. The Russian plan entailed the group training of students in "instruction shops" instead of through the individual training provided by the old apprenticeship system. In 1879, Calvin Woodward had adopted Russian methods as the basis for the first manual training school in the United States at St. Louis. Woodward's school paved the way for secondary vocational education everywhere and the idea soon spread to Canada. In 1889 an early program was established in Woodstock, Ontario.[5] Two years later, Nova Scotia established a program called "mechanic science" to distinguish manual training from domestic science for girls. "Mechanic science" included drawing, benchwork, science and agriculture or "rural science."

Confusion over the nature and purposes of manual training continued. With more global objectives than any other innovation, the subject was seen by many reformers as a virtual curriculum panacea. Motives for introducing manual training were mixed. As before, a basic issue was whether goals should be cultural or vocational. According to Stamp, goals in Ontario included Froebelian personal development, the need to develop useful skills to counter a bookish curriculum and to combat unemployment, rural depopulation and "dropping out;" and the need for skilled labour to meet industrial competition in a period when traditional apprenticeship was in sharp decline.[6] James L. Hughes thought that boys needed manual training because they were "all thumbs" as compared with girls who gained dexterity from needlework and playing the piano. Yet, for him the very term was narrowing, directing attention to external instead of internal development, to producing things instead of character.[7]

Hughes' view underscored the value ascribed to manual training in promoting what was called "hand and eye" training. Ontario Inspector John Seath applauded a mental discipline approach that could train every faculty.[8] Selleck has explicated the theory as it came to be accepted in Britain. Educators assumed that particular muscles of the body are connected with particular brain centres and that both must be co-ordinated for the proper functioning of each. It was claimed that the brain centre, connected with the hand, developed during the first fourteen years of life. Manual training would develop both. The theory was appealing to practical and liberal educators alike on both utilitarian and moral grounds. It also appealed to those concerned with the child's personal development.[9]

The hand and eye theory may have reached Canada indirectly via St. Louis through the first manual training teachers recruited by Robertson overseas. During visits to Great Britain in 1899 and 1900, when he advertised for and selected most of the approximately twenty-five manual training teachers he eventually hired, Robertson drew on the ideas of the Royal Commission on National Education in Ireland which had reported in 1898.

Aimed at making Irish education more practical, the commission had derived its own ideas in part from the Russian plan which British educators had seen in operation on a visit to Woodward's school in St. Louis. Their practice was also influenced by the Swedish system of manual training or "educative handwork" called sloyd.[10] Several of Robertson's recruits had been trained in Sweden and Germany. Here was an interesting example of the international diffusion of innovations to which Canadians gained access by a respectable British route.[11]

Robertson showed considerable enterprise in using his recruits as change agents, employing a dissemination and demonstration strategy that resulted in the quite rapid creation of an informal national network as they moved across the country. Collectively, the group worked in nearly all provinces, from Nova Scotia to British Columbia, and at least one instructor, Kidner, a graduate of the City and Guilds Institute of London, served as an official in three provinces.[12] By the end of 1902 there were Macdonald schools in 21 centres across Canada, enrolling 7000 pupils. Seven years later 20 000 boys and girls were studying manual training and domestic science. Most urban school boards maintained the centres after Macdonald demonstration funding ended. Although the emphasis in the program was on rural regeneration, Robertson promoted manual training in cities and towns to which the country, as he said, looked for guidance.[13] This was a strategy that he had noted in the work of the British royal commission. However, the Canadian movement had very limited success in rural areas.[14]

Sutherland notes that it took some years to come to a rough consensus about the nature of manual training. By 1910, the term referred essentially to work with wood and metal and was more clearly differentiated from domestic science. By the 1930s, the two subjects had become known as industrial arts and household science; the latter term was later replaced by home economics. Manual arts as pre-vocational activities for young children accorded with the practices of the kindergarten and child study movements. For this reason and because teachers required little special training or equipment, Sutherland observes that by the 1920s they had secured a permanent position in the practices of many Canadian elementary classrooms. In the upper elementary grades, sloyd became a sterile, mechanical routine that failed to play its promised role as integrator of the curriculum and became simply an added subject.[15]

Nor did manual training serve the purpose of directly training Canadian workers as proponents of vocational education had hoped. As a result, attention at the secondary level shifted to what came to be called industrial education, later known as industrial arts. In Ontario, British-born John Seath, who served between 1906 and 1919 in the revived position of Chief Superintendent, was the main promoter of industrial education. Seath worked closely with Albert Leake, one of Robertson's British recruits who had become Ontario's Inspector (later Director) of Technical Education in 1902. Both men became increasingly attracted to developments in the

United States at a time when a greater vocational emphasis in manual training was being promoted in that country through such bodies as the National Society for the Promotion of Industrial Education and the Committee on the Place of Industries in Public Education. In 1911, following several American visits that included attendance at conferences of these bodies, Seath produced a major report entitled *Education for Industrial Purposes* which led to the landmark Industrial Education Act of that year. He distinguished manual training and domestic science which he called "cultural and practical" from industrial and technical education. Industrial education prepared students for trades; technical education prepared them for "higher directive positions" in industry.[16] Although Seath advocated industrial education in separate schools it eventually became more firmly established in "regular" schools. However, "industrial arts" rarely became part of general education for all students.

During and following World War I, industrial arts grew modestly in secondary schools. British Columbia had established its first technical high school courses in 1916-1917. The Vancouver Technical High School was opened in 1921. Junior high school programs were launched in the province during this decade. The nation-wide curriculum revisions of the 1930s gave a new impetus to manual training and domestic science. White notes that, whereas British Columbia had twenty-two industrial arts centres with seventeen teachers in 1911-12, a generation later, in 1938-39, the numbers had increased to 141 centres with 112 teachers.[17]

## Domestic Science

The innovation of domestic science was linked with manual training, if only because girls had to be provided for while boys were in shop. To Adelaide Hoodless, a Hamilton homemaker who was the prime mover of domestic science, the objectives of the subject were clear. In her pioneering textbook, *Public School Domestic Science* published in 1897, Hoodless defined her purpose as being "to assist the pupil in acquiring knowledge of the fundamental principles of correct living."[18] A knowledge of such principles was essential to strengthening the values of family which Hoodless, like other middle class reformers, assumed were in decline.

Arguing from the perspective of what some modern scholars have called "maternal feminism," Hoodless claimed that with the loss of the economic functions of the home, mothers had lost many opportunities to teach character building and related practical elements. Future mothers and domestic servants must learn to apply scientific methods to household practices. Objectives included the teaching of Christian morality and citizenship, the training of youthful character among the poor in the interests of "national thrift;" temperance, and the Canadianization of immigrant girls. It was blithely assumed that the poor generally were morally wanting, and that New Canadians especially were of doubtful loyalty. Domestic science was seen as a major means of remedying these defects. Like manual training, the subject also had a mental discipline "hand and eye" function. Beyond its domestic function, it was also seen as serving the needs of girls entering the labour force. Hoodless cited the need for trades training for girls, but apart from commercial studies this injunction was not taken seriously in Canadian schools.[19]

Hoodless' text, which had been commissioned by George Ross, constituted the curriculum of Ontario's first domestic science course. The book stressed the importance of the family and was a practical compendium of advice regarding all types of domestic activities and potential problems. The moral dimension was the dominant theme; for this reason too much scientific detail (for instance, the "chemistry of food") was to be avoided because it tended "to cause confusion in the mind of the average school girl."[20]

Domestic science helped to diversify the curriculum and to make the classroom more socially relevant and less restrictive. However, despite the wider claims advocated for it, the subject remained pre-eminently practical and avoided the bookish fate of some other new subjects such as health. Somewhat paradoxically, the fact that domestic science became a university subject — which boys' manual training never did — may have made it more relevant and lively, rescuing it from mere craft training.[21] Like manual training, domestic science was part of an international movement. Several of Robertson's British recruits such as H. Dunnell in British Columbia, became provincial supervisors of manual training and included domestic science in their responsibilities. In that province, Alice Ravenhill, who had been a University of London lecturer on hygiene, public health and household science, brought new prestige to efforts by the Vancouver Local Council of Women to promote the subject when she took up residence in the city in 1911. Canadian leaders such as Adelaide Hoodless participated in the Lake Placid, New York conferences on home economics during the period and thereby gleaned many American ideas.[22]

Domestic science was effectively disseminated nationally. It was accepted as an option in the Ontario curriculum revision of 1904 and was incorporated in the first Alberta course of study in 1912. By 1920, twenty-nine domestic science centres had been established in British Columbia.[23] In most provinces the subject became linked with agriculture as a means of improving rural life, and qualified for assistance under the Agricultural Instruction Act. During the 1920s, domestic science seems to have grown only slowly. In Ontario in 1937 the establishment of Grade 9 as an exploratory year with practical education and career options made domestic science compulsory for girls. Shortly nearly one third of all female high school students were enrolled in the subject, mainly in urban collegiate institutes since rural continuation schools were not equipped to offer it. The new program aimed "to develop a sound standard of living and an appreciation of the functions of family and community life." In practice this meant further apprenticeship in cooking, sewing and cleaning, building on skills acquired in elementary school. This stress on practical skills included competence in family relations and correct attitudes towards motherhood and marriage.[24] In British Columbia, the number of domestic science centres quadrupled in a generation to 113 by 1939.[25] In that year the Canadian Home Economics Association was formed, the name reflecting a more comprehensive progressive view of the subject. In the Roman Catholic schools of Quebec, where the subject had been made compulsory in 1921, home economics retained a purely domestic emphasis.[26] In the Protestant schools some attention was given to its wider applications. To some critics, there was a danger that home economics would raise unrealistic expectations among working class girls by introducing them to foods and domestic equipment such as electric refrigerators beyond their station and pocketbooks as future wives and mothers.[27]

## Agriculture

Agriculture had long been taught perfunctorily as a bookish subject. The reformers attempted to make it more active, vital and relevant. Sutherland describes the "object lesson" gardens set up in the Maritime provinces by J.W. Robertson through the Macdonald Rural School Fund. Similar efforts were promoted in the western provinces by David Goggin on the Prairies and by J.W. Gibson in British Columbia.[28] Ontario added school gardening to its curriculum in 1904.

The objectives of school agriculture encompassed the same global scope as those of manual training and domestic science. The moral dimension was based on the concept of "spiritualizing" agriculture which J.W. Gibson in British Columbia had derived from the work of Liberty Hyde Bailey, the leader of the American Country Life Movement. The subject was to be taught scientifically but paradoxically, like "manual arts" it was thought to be simple enough to be taught by minimally trained teachers. Gibson and his idealistic district school supervisors — half-time high school teachers who also served as agricultural representatives — saw agriculture as a subject that would solve the rural school problem by creating "rural-mindedness" in teachers, making them community teachers; it would also reduce transiency, make schooling "relevant" and alleviate parent and trustee apathy.[29] Other utopian objectives included the creation of a set of health giving principles, a positive viewpoint concerning country life, the recognition of virtues immanent in the work of the soil and the acknowledgement and application of the individual's power over nature.[30]

The Agricultural Instruction Act of 1913 constituted a ten-year program entailing a federal outlay of ten million dollars distributed among the provinces on the basis of population, as noted earlier. The teaching of agriculture developed particularly strongly in British Columbia, Alberta, Ontario and Nova Scotia, all of which adopted texts, courses and manuals for the subject. In these provinces texts such as McCaig's *Elementary Agriculture of Alberta,* Ontario's course of study and Nova Scotia's 1911 teachers' manual stressed such topics as soil, plants, tillage and crops, forest conservation, arbor day, orchard work, farm arithmetic and rural road improvement. Methods included observation, active investigation and correlation of agriculture, geography and physiology, all aimed at "spiritualizing" agriculture and building character.[31]

While other innovations of the New Education made limited impact in Quebec, agriculture, inspired by fears of rural decline and influenced in part by the Macdonald-Robertson movement, was an exception. Quebec's first agricultural representatives appointed in 1913 and a superintendent of school gardens appointed two years later extended the movement through in-service and pre-service teacher training, home gardens and agricultural school fairs. A few experimental urban gardens were even established to teach city children to appreciate rural life. Teachers were exhorted to fill their pupils' minds with the "poetic breeze of an earthy scent" by using agricultural examples in arithmetic, grammar and other lessons.[32] The agriculture course included "object lessons and familiar science," drawing on programs developed in France, Belgium and Sweden.[33] School gardens in the province grew in number from 188 in 1910 to 1468 in 1920.[34]

Despite the efforts noted, school agriculture faced serious problems. Robertson's 1913 report presented a discouraging view of the impact of the innovation. He quoted a Prince Edward Island inspector to the effect that "School gardening is almost a thing of the past."[35] Robertson's report and the Agriculture Instruction Act represented the major new attempt to promote the subject. Yet, as David Jones' account of problems in western Canada after 1913 demonstrates, school agriculture was an early example of the perils of curriculum implementation. Failure stemmed not only from poorly prepared transient teachers who lacked enthusiasm and leadership ability, but also from local opposition based on fears that children would be educated "off the farm." At the same time, there was a paradoxical resentment of a rural curriculum that deprived children of the benefits of an urban-oriented education.[36]

Critics of "frills" believed that the curriculum should be restricted to the dispensing of knowledge i.e., the three Rs and the teaching of theories. As a result, nature study, as agriculture was often called, was frequently reduced to formalism, taught second hand from books without the use of real life specimens. When, at Gibson's request, examinations in the subject were eliminated in British Columbia, interest in and time spent on the subject declined even further.[37] However, according to Sutherland, the school gardening aspect of nature study was the one element of the New Education that had some impact on rural schools.[38] In the eastern provinces, such creative educators as Loran De Wolfe in Nova Scotia used nature study as a basis for the initial development of elementary school science and general science. In that province it was linked as "rural science" with "mechanic science" (manual training) and domestic science.

After 1920, farm production in Canada increased, belying the argument that school agriculture was necessary to increase agricultural efficiency. The new scientific agriculture was far beyond the understanding of the average teacher. School agriculture "was too insubstantial, too ethereal and too general, too character oriented and too impractical to be significant to lean and desperate farmers" caught up in post-war agricultural depression.[39] The Agricultural Instruction Act died in 1923. The problem and the fate of agricultural education, together with opposition to it, were remarkably similar from coast to coast. Curriculum innovators such as J.W. Gibson in British Columbia and Loran De Wolfe in Nova Scotia shared similar frustrations.

## Physical and Health Education

Like other innovations, physical education and health (hygiene), including temperance, encompassed a wide range of objectives and included disparate elements. We have seen that physical education had had at least a perfunctory place in the curriculum before 1892 in the form of physical culture. After that date physical training, to use the significant term that educators increasingly preferred, became compulsory in most provinces in the form of military drill and gymnastics for boys and calisthenics for girls, as the subject gradually became one of the three or four required elements of the Canadian curriculum. In some respects, physical training became the most pervasive and certainly the most uniform of any innovation associated with the New Education. It emphasized a formalism compounded of the above-named elements supplemented by extra-curricular games, to the virtual exclusion of play-oriented activity. Mott has described how "manly games" were introduced in Winnipeg before 1910 in order to promote "British manliness."[40]

The major goals of physical training encompassed discipline, moral and social self-control, military preparedness and patriotism, this last including the Canadianization of immigrant children. As with manly games, therapeutic values were ascribed to calisthenics and military drill as a means of combatting physical, mental and moral decline resulting from urban life and the debilitating influences of materialism. Carl Berger has described how Maurice Hutton, the pre-eminent classicist at the University of Toronto, saw drill as promoting law and order, punctuality, obedience, subordination and loyalty. It was needed as an "offset to democracy and liberty" and their abuses. Drill conducted by male instructors was also a counter to the influence of female teachers on boys.[41]

Squad drill and cadet corps were established features of Ontario and Quebec schools by 1900, but it was the intervention of the Dominion Militia Department in 1907 that most clearly marks the shift from physical culture to physical training. In that year, the department began to assist provincial departments of education by providing some drill instruction in schools and courses for interested teachers. Supporters justified this federal initiative by referring to Section 91 of the B.N.A. Act which gave Parliament the right to make laws necessary for the maintenance of peace.[42] Following the establishment of the first program of cadet training and physical and military drill in Nova Scotia in 1908, Frederick Borden, the Minister of Militia, persuaded Lord Strathcona, who had long had an interest in military preparedness, to establish a fund to support military and physical training. As a result the Strathcona Trust was established with an endowment of $500 000, the annual income from which was to be divided among the provinces in proportion to the number of school age children in each.[43] By 1911, all provinces had agreed to participate. Within two years, 759 cadet corps existed across Canada.

Eventually, the Militia Department's instructional certificates in physical training and military drill were adopted in every province as part of every teacher's license. Uniform programs to provide the required training were adopted in normal schools across the country. By 1912, Parliament was voting funds annually for cadet programs and had appointed a national director for them. Federal involvement in provincial school curricula had become nation-wide. Like some other innovations of the New Education, the Strathcona program entailed minimal costs, since the physical training aspect could be easily implemented by a minimally trained teacher through daily exercises conducted right in the classroom. Teachers followed the prescribed *Syllabus of Physical Exercises for Schools*, a Canadian edition of a British syllabus that was itself based on a Swedish system of gymnastics.

The syllabus was intended to promote the harmonious development of all parts of the body and included "games and dancing steps" to ensure some "freedom of movement and a certain degree of exhilaration." As implemented in Canada in the form of military-style calisthenics, the system was notably unexhilarating. Vancouver's supervisor of drill, Sergeant-Major A.C. Bundy, boasted in 1910 that "daily movements of the pupils" were uniform across the city.[44] In Nova Scotia, Alexander MacKay entertained much grander visions of uniformity. As he told the Dominion Educational Association in 1909,the Strathcona system had the advantage of:

> a uniform language of movement which will prove to be enormously valuable when it is the language of every school, of every boy and girl in the provinces, in the dominion, within the Empire, as the basis for the orderly management of any crowds for any purpose, as a preparation for the cadet instruction in the High Schools and as a fundamental training for the defenders of our Empire and our homes should the contingency ever arise.[45]

Some Canadians, including labour groups and pacifists, objected to the militaristic nature of the new program. Nor were all educators in favour of it. A Saskatchewan school inspector deplored a warlike spirit that was inimical to a spirit of justice, fairness and kindliness towards others. True patriotism could be better taught through literature, history, civics and geography.[46] Other educators advocated a broad view of physical education that would include studies of personal health, simple classroom and playground exercises and non-competitive athletics and games. While World War I stimulated enthusiasm for military drill, Gear notes that non-military aspects of physical training were stressed by many of the female instructors who replaced men away at the front. As a result of wartime disenchantment with military drill, the Strathcona Syllabus was revised in 1919 and an emphasis placed on gymnastics and games. In practice, however, calisthenics remained dominant as a paramilitary form of physical education.[47]

During World War II cadets corps and military drill, which had been largely abolished during the anti-militaristic, progressive 1930s, were restored to schools. By 1948, the emphasis gradually shifted to game skills, recreational activities, athletics and physical fitness, an emphasis that has since continued. The National Physical Fitness Act passed in 1943, and the establishment the following year of a National Council on Physical Fitness helped to stimulate more interest in physical education in the schools and in university programs.[48]

Apart from calisthenics, physical education remained essentially a male preserve throughout the period, with the terms of female participation dictated and mostly controlled by male educators and doctors. The notion of the "feminine woman," unlike that of "manliness," ignored character building and emphasized the "reproductive health" of middle class females through special ladylike versions of "manly games," "light gymnastics" and other physical activities. However, by 1900 some medical men, assuming the role of "moral physiologists," expressed concern about inactivity among women which militated against the development of healthy "pure" mothers. Methods which served as a means of refrigerating the passions and creating spartan habits among boys were surely of equal value to girls.[49] Between the wars, only a minor share of physical education and athletics budgets were allocated to girls' activities — the girls' gymnasium in a large high school was likely to be half the size of the boys' facility, for example — and males continued to control most policy decisions.

Temperance education was now often taught as part of health. When taught from graded textbooks as an examination subject, temperance easily fell prey to academic formalism.[50] Temperance education had ambitious objectives of which the most prominent was to reduce, if not to prohibit or eliminate, alcohol consumption. Physical, moral and patriotic objectives were concerned with maintaining health, promoting good habits, preserving home and family life, protecting women and children, and shoring up social stability. Social and industrial efficiency would also be promoted by temperance which, it was argued, was essential to a disciplined work force.

Temperance as a national issue was reflected in curricula in almost identical programs, using uniform textbooks and similar examinations across the nation. Programs were promoted by the Women's Christian Temperance Union which, through its provincial and local branches, lobbied every department of education.[51] Despite such efforts, Scientific Temperance Instruction (STI) became a low priority in most provincial curricula following the adoption of prohibition during World War I. During the war it was promoted in schools as a patriotic duty, but Sheehan suggests that the real impact of the schools may have been through enhancing imperial sentiment which influenced voting in prohibition elections and referenda.[52]

Like agricultural education, temperance was an example of the problems faced by groups external to the schools seeking curriculum reform.[53] Like the agricultural reformers, the temperance educators had a messianic faith in education. They failed in part because teachers were poorly prepared; inadequate textbooks with their pictures of organs diseased by alcohol fostered a negative approach. In addition, the curriculum was overcrowded and educators faced too many other pressing problems. In time, temperance education became the responsibility of Sunday schools and other child and youth groups.[54]

The impact of the public health movement on the curriculum through the teaching of hygiene has already been noted. As a formal subject, hygiene was restricted to the elementary grades; in urban classrooms it was frequently taught by the school nurse. In 1911, a Winnipeg doctor collaborated in the writing of a textbook for Manitoba schools that was eventually adopted in seven provinces. The book emphasized "the life of the body" and the means "by which it can be preserved in a state of high efficiency." The authors suggested a number of health experiments the children could perform.[55] However, such innovative ideas did not prevent hygiene from becoming a bookish, memoriter subject, epitomized in examinations by questions requiring the pupils to state the length of their small intestines or to name the parts of the ear. In British Columbia by 1929, classroom teachers had replaced school nurses in teaching health, in conducting handkerchief and toothbrush drills and in making daily cleanliness inspections.[56]

Sex education was part of hygiene and physical education, although the topic generally had little formal place in the curriculum. In British Columbia, controversy centred on who should teach sex education and whether, if taught at all, it should not be a parental responsibility, even though parents themselves needed to be educated. It was agreed that if taught in schools, "sex hygiene" should be taught by school health workers or specially trained persons and not by classroom teachers. By the 1920s, Harold White was giving annual talks on hygiene and sex to Vancouver high school boys and Nurse M. Campbell was instructing girls. Students of the time recalled later that the emphasis was on personal hygiene and physical development with only extremely oblique references to sex *per se*.[57] In the later curriculum revisions of the 1930s in British Columbia, the subject found a modest, optional place in health and guidance courses as part of character training. Teachers were enjoined not to accelerate development by raising problems too soon. Yet instruction should be provided "sufficiently early to prevent unfortunate habits and mental attitudes."[58]

Elsewhere, "purity lectures," later called "eugenics lectures," were introduced into Ontario schools by the WCTU in 1905 and taken over by the Ontario Department of Education in 1911. Given to elementary school boys by a former overseas missionary named Beall who toured the province's schools for a generation, the lectures were eventually published verbatim as a manual for parents and teachers. The main theme of these special talks was the danger involved in young boys bleeding away the "life fluid" from the "male part." One lesson ended with the boys all repeating after Beall, "The more you use the penis muscle, the weaker it becomes; but the less you use the penis muscle the stronger it becomes." No doubt such lessons, as Bliss comments, interested young boys in masturbation for the first time in their lives.[59] According to Lenskyj, veiled warnings against "the secret indulgence" found a place in hygiene textbooks for girls. However, the emphasis on "bust development" in some textbooks suggests that the cultivation of sexual attractiveness was an acceptable goal of female hygiene.[60]

## Commercial Training and the Education of Girls

Commercial subjects, with their narrow, utilitarian objectives, benefited especially from the vocational imperatives of curriculum reform that resulted from the demands of new occupations. The need of business and industry for armies of girls in offices as, in McLuhan's words "the typewriter replaced the spitoon," led to the expansion of commercial education beyond bookkeeping to include typing, shorthand and office practice. The training in discipline, system and order that these subjects provided was fully consistent with the moral and social efficiency objectives of the New Education. They became vocationalism's most firmly rooted subjects, providing marketable skills that made commercial studies the most conspicuous success of practical education.

In 1913, expanding job opportunities for girls were underscored in a brief to Robertson's Commission entitled "Offices Rob the Schools." The Quebec authors of the brief expressed concern that "many hundreds of persons who used naturally to become teachers now become typists and stenographers."[61] Before World War II stenographers were often paid significantly better than teachers. Office work also provided an alternative to domestic service and nursing. Its higher levels demanded advanced training, a fact that, together with the training needs of teaching and nursing, helps to explain why the high school retention rate for girls was significantly higher than that for boys throughout the period and later. Commercial education led to genteel occupations for middle class girls awaiting marriage.

Commercial education became established quite rapidly across the country.[62] In 1891, commercial departments were authorized in Ontario high schools.[63] In that year 2000 commercial certificates were issued in the province. By this time, Quebec's classical colleges and a few schools in the

Maritime provinces and western Canada were offering, besides bookkeeping, such subjects as stenography, commercial arithmetic, and commercial correspondence. In 1910, J.H. Putman in Ottawa pushed for the establishment of technical and commercial classes for "concrete-minded" adolescents. He succeeded in establishing a School for Higher English and Applied Arts for students who had failed their high school entrance examinations. A commercial course was combined with a sound English education.[64] Toronto's Central High School of Commerce, opened in 1916, was possibly the leading example of a special school. The demand for marketable skills during British Columbia's post-1900 economic boom led to the establishment of a three-year high school commercial course by 1914. There as elsewhere a shortage of properly trained teachers and a continuing tendency to regard commercial programs as inferior and to overemphasize the academic components were serious problems.[65] After 1920, commercial education in most provinces was established on a stronger footing in academic, vocational and composite high schools, a development assisted in part by federal grants under the 1919 Technical Education Act.

Arguments over the academic education of girls continued as they had earlier. These ranged from fears that academic study would impair girls' health or "defeminize" them to the stout defence of "collegiate education for women" on the grounds that due to "an essential unity of human nature" female capacities and needs differed from those of males less than was supposed.[66] Although most girls finishing high school who went on to further education entered non-university programs in normal, nursing or commercial schools, by 1911-12 women made up one fifth of the university student body, a proportion that had increased twelvefold in thirty years.[67] The growth of domestic science teaching had led to the opening of schools of household science in some universities which provided new opportunities for higher education for young women. After 1920, an increasing demand for university graduates to teach the high school academic subjects provided another incentive. Despite further modest increases in undergraduate female enrolments, the tendency toward sex segregation in both high school and university courses and programs still found today and the virtual exclusion of women from science, professional and graduate programs continued to restrict educational and vocational opportunities for girls.

## Notes to Chapter 6

1 Cited in W. Mackenzie, 8. For the best account of the innovations and their impact see Neil Sutherland, *Children in English-Canadian Society*, 155-224.

2 Ontario Ministry of Education, *History of Education, Ontario Teachers' Manual*.

3 Heap, "New Patterns."

4 Copp, *Anatomy*, 69.

5 See G. Sutherland; O.E. White, 237.

6 R. Stamp, "John Seath," 237.

7 Ontario AR, 1882-3, 329; W. Mackenzie, 6.

8 Ontario AR, 1889-90, 208.

9 Selleck, *New Education,* 117-120.

10 O.E. White, 30-1.

11 W. Mackenzie, 10-12. Mackenzie notes some disagreement among various authorities regarding the actual number of teachers Robertson recruited. The total was approximately 25, with the great majority from England, one from Sweden and one or possibly two from the United States.

12 Ibid., 12.

13 N. Sutherland, *Children,* 183-4, 296.

14 W. Mackenzie, 10.

15 N. Sutherland, *Children,* 179, 185.

16 Seath, 3.

17 O.E. White, 70, 72-3, 97.

18 Hoodless, *Public School,* v.

19 Hoodless, *Report,* 4-5.

20 Hoodless, *Public School,* vi.

21 N. Sutherland, *Children,* 190.

22 See S. Wilson, J. Thomas.

23 N. Sutherland, *Children,* 190.

24 Danylewycz *et al,* 96-9.

25 O.E. White, 97.

26 Heap, "Rural School," 18.

27 Danylewycz *et al.*

28 N. Sutherland, *Children,* 187.

29 D. Jones, "The Little Mound," 87-8.

30 D. Jones, "Strategy," 138.

31 D. Jones, "The Little Mound," 89.

32 Heap, "Rural School."

33 J.C. Miller, *Rural Schools,* 71.

34 Heap, "New Patterns."

35 RCITTE, 1757.

36 D. Jones, "Strategy," 146.

37 D. Jones, "Creating," 160-5. Jones' other numerous publications on agricultural education as listed in the bibliography give the fullest available account of the movement, especially in Western Canada.

38 N. Sutherland, *Children*, 187.

39 D. Jones, "The Little Mound," 91.

40 Mott, 2.

41 C. Berger, *Sense of Power*, 254-7.

42 Gear, 11-12.

43 Borden, *House of Commons Debates*, XC(1909), 3199.

44 N. Sutherland, *Children*, 192-3.

45 A. MacKay, "What Is Aimed At," 167.

46 N. Sutherland, *Children*, 192.

47 Gear, 14-15.

48 West, 42.

49 See Lenskyj; Vertinsky.

50 N. Sutherland, *Children*, 177-8.

51 Sheehan, "National Pressure," 84-5.

52 Sheehan, "Temperance, Education and the WCTU," 120.

53 Ibid., 119.

54 Sheehan, "The WCTU and Education," 2-5.

55 Halpenny and Ireland, iii-v; see also Sutherland, *Children*, 53.

56 Lewis, "Physical Perfection," 152-3.

57 Ibid. 155-6.

58 *B.C. Junior High School Program of Studies*, (1936), 261.

59 Bliss, "Pure Books," 107.

60 Lenskyj, 6.

61 RCITTE, 1884.

62 C.E. Phillips, *Development*, 299.

63 Brewin, 13.

64 Wood, "American Tour," 36.

65 Dunn, "Teaching the Meaning," 239-43. See other works by Dunn for further discussions of commercial education in British Columbia.

66 Ritchie, 120.

67 R. Harris, A History, 624-8.

# CHAPTER 7

## PROBLEMS OF
## FOCUS AND PURPOSE,
## 1892-1920

*...The secondary school has been organized and conducted chiefly to prepare for college and the learned professions and does not give good preparatory training for the life and occupation of those who have had to leave school at about 16 or 18 years of age."*
*(Royal Commission on Industrial Training and Technical Education, 1913)*

*My main line is the kiddies ... make them good Christians and good Canadians which is the same thing ....*          *(Ralph Connor, 1909)*


## The Educative Elementary Curriculum:
## An Unfulfilled Promise

Both before and after 1920, the major efforts of curriculum reformers were directed to the elementary level, which was also probably where they achieved most of whatever success they had. Then as now the child-centred nature of the elementary school — as contrasted with the subject-centred high school — together with the lesser need to be as responsive to the demands of the labour market and to those of higher educational institutions provided a greater degree of freedom. Even so, the new subjects were not uniformly successful in gaining incorporation into the curriculum. Progress was everywhere hindered by meagre material resources and by a minimally trained teaching force.

From the beginning of the New Education reformers had been concerned about the need to develop the curriculum beyond the three Rs and to strengthen the correlation between the old and new subjects. The elementary school, they insisted, must try to free itself of the dominance of the high school just as the latter must be freed of university domination. In rural areas where typically a year or two of high school work was tacked on to ungraded continuation, central or union elementary schools, parents, trustees and others often complained that the work of the lower years was neglected. With the growing demand for the relegation of high school work to the elementary grades, particularly in the "tool subjects," such as the three Rs, the possibilities reformers saw for a more "educative" curriculum were rendered more difficult. A tradition of curriculum development by accretion remained as the overcrowding of subjects exacerbated difficulties.

The notion of an educative elementary curriculum as the single most creative idea of the New Education was possibly best expressed by J.W. Robertson in his 1913 report, when he called for the activities and projects of the new subjects to serve "as a centre for the correlated study of ... reading, composition, number work, writing and drawing."[1] Or, as Alexander MacKay in Nova Scotia put it, "in schools where only the three Rs are taught the childmind starves." The new subjects would provide intellectual content from which exercises in reading, writing and arithmetic could be drawn.[2] The possibilities Robertson and MacKay alluded to had already been made apparent in such cases as Saint John's Albert School, described by Sutherland.[3] However, such schools were hardly typical even in the larger urban centres. Most continued to stress a curriculum based on the "fundamentals," with the new subjects treated as extras or frills.

The continuing hold of the traditional curriculum before 1920 was revealed by Sandiford's listing of the 1915 elementary school course of study which devoted an average of 205 minutes daily to the three Rs. Sixty-five minutes of this time was devoted to reading alone, almost as high a proportion as the 25 per cent of time that had required twenty years earlier near the beginning of the New Education. Sixty minutes per day were being devoted to arithmetic, not including bookkeeping. Too much time, said Sandiford, was devoted to these tool subjects which were of little educational value in themselves, "but educative only in their applications."[4]

Sandiford described the course of study in any province as "remarkably uniform" with a syllabus that was "seldom suggestive," "almost invariably prescriptive" and "frequently restrictive ... " Rarely was the curriculum fitted to local conditions. "Thus the Jew in the Ghetto of the city is taught the same subjects, in the same way and from the same textbooks as the Gentile on the farm." Such uniformity had much to commend it but educators failed to recognize "how little of certain common branches we really need to know in order to make a success in life." Not everyone, suggested Sandiford, needed to learn square and cube root in arithmetic. Such material was retained, he thought, because of the continuing belief in "the formal discipline theory of studies," which, although discredited everywhere else, was adhered to in Canada "with mid Victorian tenacity."[5]

Although there was an overemphasis on the tool subjects to the corresponding neglect of practical skills and cultural enrichment, Sandiford was optimistic about the future. In a prediction that would prove to be very wide of the mark, he thought Canada would move to greater local control. The elementary school would give less attention to the tool subjects and more to content, particularly in literature, history, arts and crafts. It would, he thought, "seek to ally itself with the native interests of the young." It would "tend to become more of a place for doing things rather than memorizing facts about them." It was sure to become "a more joyous and healthier place."[6] This prediction likewise would not easily come to pass.

Increasing attention was given to the more efficient teaching of the traditional curriculum after 1900. James L. Hughes' *Public School Methods* was a comprehensive systematic manual for teaching based on scientific child study that devoted 123 detailed pages to a prescription for teaching reading. Language, including grammar, merited sixty-four pages. Similar treatises were provided for every major subject, together with prescriptions for every aspect of the school environment, of hygiene, discipline, morals, teaching methods (these stressing "mental powers"), school management and questioning. The earlier Froebelian child-centred rhetoric of the chief Canadian advocate of the kindergarten was muted. Admirable in its thoroughness, the book illustrated the formalism that so often belied the theory of the New Education.[7] Wood suggests that adherence to formalism was one reason why Ontario educators rejected Maria Montessori's famous experiental curriculum in 1913. They agreed that her use of plants, animals and materials was praiseworthy in producing pupils avid to learn, but thought that her approach was too unstructured. H.T.J. Coleman, arguing from the experimentalist premises of Thorndike, thought that play should be taught.[8] Not until the 1930s would Montessori's ideas become acceptable in Ontario.

Two events that sparked renewed interest in progressive ideas were the publication of Dewey's *Democracy and Education* in 1916 and W.H. Kilpatrick's *The Project Method* in 1918. The latter was in essence a plan for implementing Dewey's ideas in the classroom. After 1920, Dewey's work became a bible for many progressives, many of whom misinterpreted the master's ideas. A generation later, in *Experience and Education* (1938), Dewey made clear that he did not approve of the excessive individualism and unorganized curricula that some reformers promoted in his name.

## The High School Debate and the Vocational Controversy

The growing realization of the need to improve articulation between the elementary and secondary levels and to treat the curriculum as continuous was accompanied by an effort to differentiate the high school curriculum *per se* in a more systematic way. By the turn of the century, reform rhetoric was already stressing the role of the high school as more than university preparation. All these ideas were inherent in the 1893 report of the Committee of Ten in the United States. The Committee was chaired by President C.W. Eliot of Harvard and had been set up by the National Education Association to bring order into the American high school curriculum and to improve articulation with college and university programs. While taking a mental disciplinary stance, the Committee insisted that there should be no distinction between the curricula of students preparing for college and those preparing for occupations.[9]

The Committee of Ten report set the terms of debate about the direction of American secondary education for the following generation and became fairly well known in Canada. It did become required reading for Manitoba students seeking first class teaching certificates and also influenced the revision of the high school mathematics curriculum.[10] In general however, the report had limited relevance in the Canadian milieu with its higher dropout rates and more selective high school population, its greater uniformity of curricula and college entrance requirments, its smaller number of local jurisdictions and universities and its more acute rural problem. With nearly all of the miniscule number of senior high students enrolled in single track matriculation programs, Canadian educators did not share American concerns about a lack of school-university articulation. The famous elective system introduced by Eliot at Harvard, which encouraged subject and course options at both the college and school levels, had little appeal in Canada. With strong English, Scottish and Roman Catholic traditions, Canadians were prepared to defend a prescribed curriculum on philosophic grounds.[11]

Despite basic curriculum stability, differentiation had been apparent in Canada as in the United States even before the Committee of Ten report. Thus, the growing interest in modern languages and the sciences anticipated one of the major thrusts of the report. Later, in 1897, four years after the report appeared, George Ross affirmed that the chief purpose of the Ontario high school was no longer university preparation *per se*. For every student thus enrolled, six were preparing for teaching and many others for farming, business and the professions.[12] Ross reported that secondary school enrolments had doubled in twenty years. Later, Ross boasted with typical Ontario complacency that both administrative uniformity and curricular diversity had been achieved as a result of "more perfect classification of pupils and more perfect division of labour among the teachers" in an organization that could be "not unfairly regarded as the most perfect system of secondary schools in any English-speaking country."[13]

A broadened curriculum was evident in Ontario, where Ross reported increased enrolments in physics from 2880 students in 1882 to 9887 in 1895. Chemistry had increased from 2522 to 5671 and botany, a new subject, enrolled 14 593 students. A more practical orientation was evident in the spectacular growth of commercial subjects in which 12 242 pupils had been examined in the previous four years.[14] The commercial and the normal or model school entrance courses required only a year or two of secondary preparation. Thus, increased enrolments in them did not mean that more students were completing high school, for very few matriculated. However, the retention rate for girls increased as compared with that of boys.

The changes described led to "the great high school debate" in Ontario which was launched in 1901 at a Queen's University conference. According to Stamp, the debate provided a public forum where the different purposes of the high school were discussed and where for the first time in Ontario's history "the traditional academic and literary subjects were ... forced to justify their entrenched positions."[15] Much of the debate centred on the place of Latin in the high school curriculum. For this reason it was also referred to as the Latin debate. In 1904 in a report to the Minister of Education, the senate of Victoria University, an affiliate of the University of Toronto, took issue with a proposal to substitute science for Latin in the teacher's examination, as a preparation for teaching nature study. The report argued that even the rudiments of Latin were useful in order to teach English effectively. Science, particularly advanced zoology and physics, was a poor substitute, "distasteful and repellent" to many who would make admirable teachers and might, under the new program, be deterred from entering the profession.[16] Hostility to science naturally aroused the concern of such proponents of the new university applied sciences as Nathan Dupuis of Queen's. They became ready advocates of a broader school curriculum.[17]

The Latin debate also waxed in other provinces. In 1900, Alexander MacKay in Nova Scotia, while acknowledging the value of Latin, asked if "in the face of common sense and the trend of education all over the world," the province could justifiably divert its energies to the study of foreign languages "so remote from their inherent and most pressing needs."[18] In the event, Latin retained its high place in the high school curriculum everywhere for several more decades. Its prestige as a university matriculation subject in Ontario was probably related to the continuing influence of the English public school classical ideal in that province. As late as World War II nearly all pupils in Grade 12 were enrolled in the subject. However, Latin was much less popular in other provinces by that time.[19]

Proponents of liberalization in Ontario welcomed the high school regulations for 1904 which provided for seven different courses of study: general, matriculation, teachers, non-professional, commercial, manual training, household science and agriculture. Three years later, Saskatchewan instituted four courses: general, teachers, matriculation and commercial and agriculture. In 1919, Alberta began a curriculum revision that was implemented in 1922, with six high school courses. In practice in all cases, however, it was the matriculation and teachers' courses that predominated.[20] One reason why academic courses persisted was that they were the cheapest to offer, which did not require special equipment, small classes or specially trained teachers. It was a special paradox, still evident in Canadian schools, that the most intellectually demanding courses were often assigned to the least qualified teachers. Anyone could be assigned to teach mathematics, for example, while manual training could only be entrusted to the teacher with special knowledge and skill.

Despite proposals to relegate some rudimentary studies to the elementary school, Canadian high schools continued to teach the three Rs. Harold Foght saw a need "of earlier entrance upon high school work" in Saskatchewan where he had found fifty teaching periods a week not unusual at that level.[21] In 1920, J.H. Putman in Ontario in a *Queen's Quarterly* article entitled "Shortening the Elementary School Course" advocated the junior high school (6-3-3) system which Winnipeg had already begun to experiment with a year earlier.[22] Peter Sandiford advanced the same proposal as a means of easing the transition from elementary to secondary education. He thought that the age of fourteen was too late for high school entrance, which should occur before "the storm and stress of adolescence." Sandiford claimed that Canada was "the only country in the world where formal reading, writing, spelling and arithmetic are carried into the high school and taught to pupils fifteen and sixteen years of age.[23]

University control was evident in the continuing predominance of Latin and, as noted earlier, in the increasing control of examination systems by higher institutions. Harris observes that as early as 1890 matriculation requirements were essentially the same for all universities. Conservatism was reflected in continuing criticisms of declining high school standards and in nostalgia for past achievements.[24] John Seath noted in 1903 that university people asked, "What is the matter with the high school? We are all the time getting matriculants ignorant of the elements of English."[25] A.R.M. Lower, who was a high school student at the time, captured what academic conservatives have ever since sought to retain from the old Ontario high school system:

> The collegiate institute which catered only for fairly bright children gave to those who wanted it a good education, with enough elements of culture about it to make it more or less complete in itself without the necessity of going on to university. The high school teacher ... though seldom an original scholar, had often been an old-fashioned 'learned man'.[26]

A less romantic view of the high school was taken by Thomas Kirkconnell, who served as a headmaster — the title was significant — in eastern Ontario early in the century. Kirkconnell felt that the high schools were too rigid in aim and method and too dominated by external requirements to meet the needs of the majority who did not go beyond secondary school. He was against "the Prussian system" that Ryerson had imposed, which was now being "reinforced ... by American pedagogical theory of the Behaviourist type." The high school should classify pupils according to their abilities, training the majority for future employment with the scholastic minority "winnowed out" and prepared for university.[27]

Problems of status and standards for secondary education persisted during the period at a time when there was a great variety of institutions offering high school instruction ranging, as in Nova Scotia, from work added on to ungraded elementary schools to work in graded high school classrooms. In 1913, only 8 per cent of Nova Scotia's students were enrolled in high school grades, half of them in the lowest one, Grade 9. As late as 1940 more than 80 per cent of the province's schools offering high school work were one-room institutions.[28]

In the West, Saskatchewan's "union schools," continuation schools and regular high schools followed a similar pattern to that of Nova Scotia. In Manitoba, secondary education began with the teachers in small schools simply teaching additional grades to students who requested instruction because they were intending to enter normal school to become teachers themselves.[29] At first, the Prairie high school itself functioned as a teacher training institution, teaching "non-professional" subjects, the content needed to teach elementary school and professional subjects such as pedagogy.[30]

Controversies over the nature and purpose of the high school curriculum that focussed on the place of Latin vis-à-vis that of manual training pointed up the old dilemma over the balance between liberal and practical studies that had come to the fore internationally in the writings of Arnold and Spencer. In Great Britain later, philosopher Alfred North Whitehead wrote of the fallacious antithesis between the two types of education. Nevertheless, the antithesis gained popular acceptance as a useful distinction which took root in practice. As such it persisted into the twentieth century although, as Silver notes, little is known about popular attitudes toward it and disputes among educators over the issue have often revealed confusion.[31]

Grubb and Lazerson have shown how American educators such as Franklin Bobbitt embraced a social efficiency model which stressed the economic, job training function of the school. Manual training was used to defuse opposition to vocationalism by legitimating curriculum differentiation. A social efficiency emphasis that appealed to labour and business interests was also appealing to educators concerned with making the curriculum more relevant to an expanding high school population. While vocational enrolments were not high, the American manual training movement helped to redefine the concept of equality of educational opportunity. Students were channeled into school programs according to predicted job roles, as determined by their social class backgrounds. Such channelling and the ability grouping which accompanied it were made possible by scientific testing and guidance, two interrelated developments that gained impetus from the vocational movement. Ability grouping encouraged curriculum differentiation.[32]

Vocationalism had similar though less widespread effects in Canada. As elsewhere, educational controversy often revealed confusion. In the wake of the great high school debate, James Cappon, a literary scholar at Queen's, followed John Watson in arguing for a common curriculum based on the three Rs supplemented by a modicum of the new subjects. At the high school level, a common curriculum for Cappon meant an education for a select elite in an institution that had quite different purposes and offered a different kind of education to a different clientele from that of the elementary school. He was critical of "Spencerian fallacies" that glorified "concrete methods" and undermined the "literary and abstract methods" that constituted true education.[33] In response, J.W. Robertson argued for an educative curriculum that would offer all children an introduction to culture. He claimed that it was the very bookishness of schooling that "hindered the turning out of pupils with the ability to read and write well, to speak correctly and to compute accurately and quickly." The methods of the new subjects, he asserted, could "supplement books in helping the children to express themselves in clear, correct and beautiful language ... ."[34]

As noted earlier, John Seath in Ontario drew a distinction between manual training as a cultural and practical subject and industrial education as a form of advanced vocational studies. With Albert Leake he took an ambivalent view of practical education. On the one hand, he praised its mental discipline value, urging it as a common cultural experience for all high school students. On the other hand, he took an increasingly utilitarian view of practical education. His ambivalence was illustrated in his defence of "intellectual culture" when he observed that, despite "all that can be said on behalf of the practical, the claims of the academic must always be paramount."[35] Yet, in his 1911 report, Seath declared, "We are going to make the boy a workman, not necessarily a scholar."[36]

For his part, Albert Leake frequently argued that the difference between liberal and vocational studies was subjective and relative for "a subject that is cultural for one is vocational for the other." Leake thought that chemistry was a good example, for it was vocational for the scientist or technician and cultural for the minister or lawyer. He had no patience with "culturalists" who held that the formal aim of education was more important than the material aim. School and work were not synonomous terms but should be. Yet Leake seemed to contradict these Deweyan views when he stated, "It is high time we ceased worshipping the fetish of equality ... we have at least two castes, those who are of the elect and those who are not, those who can absorb the printed page and pass the prescribed examinations and those who, for both mental and financial reasons are not able to do so."[37] For the lower caste, Leake saw the need to keep students in school in order, as he put it in 1913, "to reduce the supply of adolescent labour." This view reflected a growing concern about an overcrowded labour market with its numerous dead-end jobs. By giving the curriculum "a direct industrial trend," Leake hoped that schooling would minimize "the physical and moral degeneration caused by work which provides neither education in the present nor economic prospects in the future."[38]

Leake and Seath both assumed that the higher the social class the greater the academic ability. In their view, most students lacked the desire and the ability to complete a regular secondary education.[39] In expressing these views, both men were reflecting their British background, while also drawing on their knowledge of American developments gleaned during their extensive travels across the border. Albert Leake, in downplaying the importance of social unification, was possibly the best example of a Canadian social efficiency educator. He thought that education should be placed "on a purely business basis so that the greatest possible return both in a material and moral sense may be secured from the investment."[40]

Unlike their United States counterparts, both Seath and Leake argued that vocational students should be educated in separate specialized secondary schools, with curricula retaining, however, a strong academic emphasis. Thus, commercial students in Ontario took the same required academic core as matriculants, with commercial subjects simply replacing some of the options taken by the latter. An elitist perspective that was heavily influenced by British attitudes enabled Canadian educators to justify separate types of secondary education conducted in separate institutions. This policy was facilitated by a more centralized system than that of the United States. The high school entrance examination was used to sort students into the two types of school. Consequently, there was less need in Canada for vocational testing programs. This fact and high dropout rates also made guidance programs less necessary. As a result, the testing and guidance movements developed more slowly in Canada although, as will be noted later, the former took strong hold during the 1920s.

The vocational controversy spilled over into the universities, where it focussed on the place of the sciences in curricula. Stephen Leacock and other traditionalists feared that technical education might shatter the old classical curriculum and threaten the prestige of the liberal arts.[41] When N.F. Dupuis, as Dean of Applied Science at Queen's University, insisted that the sciences were equal to the classics as a means of education, he was making a plea for a broader university curriculum very similar to that made for the schools by J.W. Robertson.[42] At both levels, *de facto* national curricula were already emerging by 1920. Although a utilitarian trend was neither rapid nor pervasive, the vocationalization of higher education probably contributed to a sense of national community during an era of expansion as engineers, agricultural scientists and other professionals moved among the provinces and contributed to a growing economy.

Businesspeople were another group who sought practical educational reform. Not all were as hostile to traditional learning as Stephen Leacock and some other academic critics implied. The self-made man or woman could be transformed by liberal studies into a less bumptious and more humane person with a mental discipline that would also contribute to commercial success.[43] At the same time some businesspeople deplored topsy-turvy social and educational priorities that filled students with sciences and arts and "ologies," causing them to disdain manual labour, and training them to despise commercial and business life. In addition, it was charged that too much time was wasted in the indiscriminate study of algebra and mathematics and the dead languages.[44] Similar concerns were expressed in Quebec, where many members of the small French-Canadian business community were convinced that the dominance of the traditional professions explained the lack of French-Canadian commercial success. It was charged that the professions sought to perpetuate themselves by controlling a school curriculum based on *les langues mortes* which rendered students unfit for a business career. The primary school must be radically changed, even though this would necessarily involve ending the church's control of education.[45]

Yet, as Copp observes, French-Canadian secondary education was at least as practical or vocational as that in English Canada. One third of the students registered in the classical colleges were in the commercial course. Ironically, Quebec Protestant education was no less classical and non-scientific in its own way, and thus resembled the stereotype of Roman Catholic education."[46] Curriculum policy conflict in Quebec, muted by the overwhelming, monolithic influence of the church, was paralleled by moralistic, conservative anglophone Protestant attitudes in other provinces. Magnuson points out that on both sides of the two solitudes, business success depended less on education than on experience.[47] In anglophone Canada, bankers — those prototypical members of the establishment — rarely held university degrees until recently. They were classic examples of upward mobility unsullied by academic training.

## Systematic Curriculum Making

By the turn of the century, in Phillips' words, "The choice of content for the school curriculum was determined by tradition, by the views people held, by the knowledge teachers possessed and by the possibility of testing what the pupil learned."[48] Nevertheless, "curriculum making" as a term was coming into its own, and new concepts of curriculum organization were being advanced. Demands for a broader curriculum arising from the controversies over vocationalism noted above led to more systematic attention to educational goals.

James Cappon observed, as early as 1893, that the curriculum was no longer simple. Not only were there new optional subjects — notably the sciences — but the traditional ones had been upgraded "by the introduction of higher methods or more specific matter." This multifarious curriculum was "being more and more modified into a preparatory training ... likely to be directly useful ... in the actual business of the world ..." One consequence, thought Cappon, was that "we are constantly making and remaking our courses ...." A more systematic approach was laudable but there was serious danger "of neglecting what is sound and profitable because it is old, and of embracing what is merely superficial because it is novel and ... progressive." The old educational ideal was the scholar, while "the new ideal is the citizen ..."[49]

Many of the issues to which Cappon referred arose at the 1901 Queen's University conference which, as noted, had launched the high school debate. John Watson argued against any concession to practicality in the curriculum. The student entering public (elementary) school must be presumed to be a scholar until his or her ability and vocational fitness "has been established by trial." Consequently, with minor variations, all students should receive the same schooling up to the leaving age of thirteen or fourteen. Watson deplored the inefficient teaching of the three Rs and a public school curriculum that left a student "with no feeling for the literature of his ancestors ..."[50] N.F. Dupuis as an applied scientist shared educators' concerns over the tendency of the curriculum of the higher institutions to dominate that of the lower levels. He charged that conservatives sought to maintain a curriculum that had prevailed for nearly a thousand years. The advance of science was retarded by the claim that classical education alone gave culture "What any other line gives," he observed sarcastically, "I do not know; possibly knowledge."[51]

W.S. Ellis, principal of Kingston Collegiate Institute and future education dean at Queen's, spoke on "The Making of a Curriculum." Ellis argued that curriculum revision was "a very different thing from the rearrangement of certain subjects of study." There were three main concerns in curriculum making: the balance between liberal and practical studies, "the proper relationship between the stage of mental advancement [of] the pupil ... and the kind of exercise that the studies afford," and the matter of interest. He urged that public and high school courses of study be continuous.[52] In a later paper, Ellis, like Dupuis, was critical of university dominance of school offerings and of the lack of any sound curriculum design. He thought that the course of study should be a scientific whole made up of interrelated parts, rather than a mere fortuitous grouping of subjects. Ellis recommended that the curriculum be grouped into four areas: language (for communication and thought expression), quantity studies (space, number, computation), nature studies (matter, life and the laws of the universe), and human studies (history, aesthetics, morality and religion). "The proper grouping of these at any one period of the student's life constitutes a curriculum which gradually passes from simple to complex as the unfolding powers of mind become capable of dealing with the more abstract and generalized forms of knowledge."[53]

The terminology of curriculum making became more precise during the period. In 1914, Alexander MacKay in Nova Scotia defined a program as all the studies in a given school. A curriculum was defined as "a group of studies schematically arranged for a pupil or set of pupils." A course of study referred to the "quantity, quality and method of the work in any given subject of instruction." The multiplicity of subjects could be explained by the need to subdivide the main ones so that the leading features of each would not be overlooked by inexperienced teachers. Thus, English was subdivided into grammar, composition, spelling, reading and literature. An orderly development of each subject was designed to "keep pace with the child's mental growth ..." and "to render possible the orderly and systematic organization of knowledge ..."[54]

Nova Scotia syllabi were now being published annually in the *Journal of Education*. An accompanying handbook for teachers had expanded to 110 pages by 1914.[55] A year earlier, J.C. Miller had noted a national trend towards making curriculum outlines "fuller and more suggestive" and including helpful source-material references for both pupils and teachers.[56] But generally, Miller felt, the provinces had failed "to realize the possibilities of properly prepared courses of study as educational instruments." Rural teachers especially needed more help than could be provided by an "unmodified outline" that left them alone "to do as well or ill as they can." A properly prepared course of study with a special bulletin in each subject would make it easier "to secure, select, evaluate and organize the needed materials" and would offer suggestions as to how they might best be utilized and taught. In declaring that the fundamental idea governing course organization should be "what is considered to be the minimum body of common knowledge, appreciation and abilities which every child should possess" Miller anticipated the modern curriculum guideline.[57]

In 1918, Peter Sandiford described the making of Canadian high school curricula. He saw two distinct theories or plans regarding curriculum construction. The "extensive plan," used in eastern Canada, entailed a large number of uniform, rigidly prescribed courses "carried [on] at the same time and continued over a number of years ... " The "intensive plan" found in Western Canada was more flexible because it entailed a greater variety of courses, only a few of which were studied at one time, each in depth until the syllabus was covered and the subject dropped.[58] The two plans continued to distinguish Eastern and Western Canadian approaches to curriculum organization until the 1970s. The American inspired intensive plan used a credit system to recognize work successfully completed.

Another concept that gained currency in Western Canada during these years was that of the spiral or concentric curriculum. Calgary superintendent Melville Scott argued that by introducing sophisticated concepts early and building on them spirally through repetition and review, the pupil would no longer leave school "without a grasp of what more advanced subjects mean."[59] Systematic curriculum making also included the organization of the course of study around projects. The project method, adumbrated in 1918 in the book of that title by William Heard Kilpatrick of Columbia University, became the basis for so-called enterprise teaching, whereby the curriculum was organized around units of study, or enterprises. The method took firmest hold in Alberta during the 1930s, and became widely advocated across Canada. The Carnegie credit system was another approach to curriculum organization that had considerable influence in Western Canada during the interwar years. Enterprise teaching and the Carnegie system will be discussed in Chapter 10.

By 1918, curriculum making in the United States was beginning to follow an industrial or scientific management model. By applying principles of management drawn from time and motion studies in industry, individuals such as Franklin Bobbitt and W.W. Charters argued that the efficiency of schools could be vastly improved. Vague statements of curriculum objectives must be replaced by particularized objectives based on the activities, especially the occupations, of humanity. These ideas were set out by Bobbitt in two influential books, *The Curriculum* (1918) and *How to Make A Curriculum* (1924). Through his most famous student, Ralph Tyler, Bobbitt influenced later curriculum making and anticipated modern behavioural objectives and competency-based approaches.

The industrial model of curriculum making seems to have had limited impact on Canadian practice, although technocratic rhetoric sometimes crept into the language of policy documents. In 1913 Albert Leake in Ontario denounced the inefficiency of schools, asking with reference to the high drop-out rate "What would be thought of [a] business organization that concentrated its attention on 20 per cent of its product."[60] Foght's Saskatchewan report of 1918 provided a detailed list of industrial, commercial and service occupations in Regina and Saskatoon, implying that such data should be used as a basis for curriculum making.[61]

Later, British Columbia's curriculum revisions of the 1930s represented possibly the most comprehensive, self-conscious effort to apply scientific principles. No curriculum making efforts before and few since have equalled a program that totalled 2700 pages and covered all grade levels. Bobbitt's system of curriculum making was specifically recommended to the revision committees. Careful attention was paid to formulating aims and objectives. In his 1935 report on school finance which appeared on the eve of the revision work, H.B. King observed that the curriculum "has not been adequately studied in this country at least from a scientific point of view.", Instead of curriculum being determined by what university professors would like students to know, sound principles of curriculum construction should be used, so that the course of study would be "subject to continual revision under scientific direction." King praised the American cardinal principles of education as a modern formulation of objectives that expanded on traditional aims and helped curriculum planners to think of objectives in terms wider than the accumulation of information.[62]

## Making Good Christians and Good Canadians

Patriotism and morality as the oldest goals of the Canadian curriculum remained central aims during the era of the New Education. When Ralph Connor demanded in *The Foreigner* (1909) that the schools produce good Christians and good Canadians, he was expressing a longstanding anglo-conformist viewpoint. Seventeen years earlier, George Ross had asked the members of the Dominion Educational Association in 1892, "Are we going to be provincial in our education or are we going to be national?" Ross was voicing a growing national sentiment that was as forceful as it was unclear. He hoped that educators could "agree upon certain broad features common to the whole of this Dominion with which we can indoctrinate our pupils" leading to an appreciation "that the sentiments of the provinces are united into one harmonious whole."[63] Like his predecessors and successors, Ross was assuming that Canadian nationalism was his own Ontario regionalism writ large. The problem was that even in Ontario there was profound disagreement about what Canadianism meant and what the goals of civic education should be. Ross himself, although a classic liberal imperial nationalist, faced imputations of disloyalty for allegedly favouring Canadian over British history in the Ontario course of study.[64] In Nova Scotia the ambiguity of Canadianism and the lack of consensus on the meaning of loyalty and patriotism was illustrated in 1896 when the provincial assembly voted against declaring July 1 a school holiday. One speaker observed that Nova Scotians remained loyal to Great Britain but that the province's coerced entry into Confederation had been "a dark page in its history."[65]

McDonald suggests that anglophone Canadians attempted to accommodate to the new Canadian political community by espousing a generalized abstract patriotism that was equated with leading a virtuous life and with allegiance to monarch and Empire rather than to the polyglot political community of Canada. As in Ryerson's time, imperial allegiance and nonsectarian Christian morality were seen as safer, more effective and less divisive means of cultivating civic loyalty. The assumption was that a morally upright person was automatically a good citizen who would always support the "right" side in any controversy or conflict.[66]

Ross' plea for a more national history led the Dominion Educational Association, the provincial teachers' associations and the provincial governments to sponsor a Dominion-wide competition for the writing of a history of Canada that would reflect a Dominion viewpoint. A two thousand dollar prize was offered. The book selected was W.H.P. Clement's *The History of the Dominion of Canada*. Published in 1897 and intended, as the preface stated, "[to] unite the various currents of provincial history into the broader channel of the Dominion,"[67] Clement's book was immediately authorized for use in Nova Scotia, Quebec, Ontario and Manitoba. Its success was short-lived, however. Nevertheless, the competition presaged a half century of various initiatives aimed at the Canadianization of curriculum materials, as well as efforts to achieve maximum national uniformity in textbooks in all subjects.

In 1898, Alexander MacKay, encouraged by George Ross, persuaded the Dominion Educational Association to endorse the celebration of "Empire Day" as a means of cultivating "the larger British sentiment" to which Canada had contributed so much; as well, such a celebration should lead to "the cultivation of feelings of loyalty and attachment to our country and to its institutions."[68] The statement was an apt illustration of Carl Berger's argument that, for many Canadians after Confederation, imperialism was a legitimate form of nationalism. The two concepts were inextricably intertwined.[69]

On May 23, 1899, the day before the birthday of Queen Victoria, Nova Scotia and Ontario became the first provinces to observe Empire Day. The idea quickly spread to the other provinces, becoming an element of school programs that contributed to the growth of a national patriotic curriculum. With its overt political socialization by means of recitations, songs, readings, classroom displays, sports and parades, Empire Day reflected an over-whelming imperialist orientation that was paradoxically American in form but British in content.[70]

Reinforcement of imperial nationalism and anglo-conformity in the schools was promoted by the Imperial Order of the Daughters of the Empire (IODE), an elite group of women mostly of middle class British origin, united under the motto "One Flag, One Throne, One Empire."[71] Organized in 1900-01 during the height of the imperial fervour engendered by the South African (Boer) War, the IODE through an education committee that included ministers of education, academics and military representatives embarked in 1904 on an extensive program of political socialization conducted largely through the schools. By means of essay contests, school-to-school links and "pen pal" programs among Empire countries and through donations of teaching aids (Union Jacks, photographs of royalty, library books and picture collections) the committee reinforced the imperial curriculum particularly in the teaching of geography, history and literature. Special efforts were directed to schools with large numbers of foreign-born children, especially in the Prairie provinces where IODE chapters some-times adopted such schools. Teaching materials were also distributed to normal schools across the country. During the interwar years growing nationalism forced the IODE to modify its imperialist perspective even to the point of encouraging the singing of "O Canada" along with "God Save the King" in patriotic exercises.

Schools needed little encouragement to promote imperialist senti-ment. Stamp has described the *Ontario Fourth Reader* issued in 1910 which surpassed all others in its imperial message. Written for the two senior elementary years (Grades 7 and 8), the book's flyleaf proclaimed the motto "One Flag/One Fleet/One Throne" under a coloured Union Jack. Poetry and prose selections glorified militarism and imperialism.[72] The theme of Empire likewise permeated the Manitoba curriculum. In physical education the teacher was admonished to remember, as the children were marched around the school yard, that he or she was building a strong empire. Literature was to be taught as "a consummate expression of the spirit of the British people." Geography served a similar purpose.[73] It was such a cur-riculum that caused Arthur Lower, in reflecting on his Ontario childhood, later to observe that it was no wonder that "the Canadian public school was not making young Canadians but young Englishmen" who in 1914 would be prepared to rush off across the seas "to fight for a country they had never seen ..."[74] Concern about Americanization continued. In 1909, Calgary school superintendent Melville Scott complained that some Alberta children believed that President Theodore Roosevelt was the King's representative in their province.[75]

Not all Canadians, even those of British origin, accepted the imperial dimension of nationalism. The South African War proved to be highly divi-sive. Anglo-conformist imperialism led to cultural conflict which no abstract patriotism could allay. Conflict peaked in Ontario after 1910 as a result of the bilingual schools controversy noted in Chapter 5. In neighbouring Quebec national sentiment was promoted among the francophone Roman Catholic majority, but in 1904 an article in *L'Enseignement primaire*, an official teachers' journal published by the government, made clear that a Canadian conscience meant a French Canadian and Catholic conscience. Religious morality served as the chief component of patriotism, for the Catholic faith was the most precious treasure of French-Canadians, the surest guarantee of their survival.[76] "National" history in schools essentially meant French-Canadian history. The political socialization dilemma for Canadian educators as revealed in religious and linguistic duality was well expressed in 1907 by an astute foreign observer from France, Andre Siegfried:

> In a country like Canada the school must sooner or later become to a greater degree than elsewhere the principal stake to be struggled for by the opposing forces, national and religious ... Catholics and Protestants, French and English ask themselves with anxiety what is being made of their children. Hence the intense fierceness of the discussions bearing upon this subject: what is at stake is not merely the lot of a ministry, a party, a method of government, but the very destiny of two peoples and two civilizations ...[77]

Apart from traditional Protestant-Catholic and francophone-anglophone conflict, political socialization took on its most significant and ominous dimensions for English-speaking Canadians as a result of the vast influx of European "third force" immigrants before 1914. By that year, Toronto had established a few special classes for "pupils of foreign tongue." Others were placed in "slow learners" classes. The total emphasis was on Canadianization.[78] At this time, textbooks were openly racist. In the *Ontario School Geography* of 1910 Caucasians were described as "the most active, enterprising and intelligent race in the world" while, by contrast, the Yellow race included "some of the most backward tribes of the world." The Red race was "but little civilized" and the Black race, while capable of faithfulness and affection, was said to be "somewhat indolent" and "often impulsive ..." Not that all Caucasians were equally progressive, even when of British stock, for while the Scots and the English had exemplary qualities, the Irish, it was implied, lacked energy, intelligence and high ideals. As for other Caucasians, the French included excitable urban dwellers and backward rural dwellers.[79]

In Western Canada, school reform, including compulsory schooling, was linked, as in Saskatchewan, with the resistance to ethnic schools and the creation of unilingual public schools.[80] Language controversy was particularly fierce. New Canadian immigrants saw bilingualism as a desirable end for schooling, leading to Canadianism, whereas anglophones insisted on unilingual schools as a basis for an anglo-conformist English-speaking society.[81] Pedagogical and other issues related to teaching English as a second language will be considered in Chapter 11. In Alberta, the desire of the newcomers for integration rather than assimilation into society was indicated by the response of a group of Ukrainian settlers to the declaration of an educational official that the province was English. The settlers replied that Alberta was Canadian.[82]

Not all Canadian educators were uncompromising anglo-conformists. One Manitoba educator supported bilingualism and opposed "Drag[ging] the New Canadians to a dead-level, even type of Canadian ..." J.T.M. Anderson, who had described the education of the New Canadians as Canada's greatest educational problem, nevertheless insisted that the "foreigners" were actually Canadians and entitled to fair play. Racial fusion would occur naturally when the school had done its job well.[83] The school would thus become "the great national unifier," as George Bryce put it in his 1911 presidential address to the Royal Society of Canada. In calling for a national patriotic curriculum, Bryce implied that such a curriculum already existed for, as he said, "The reading books in all the provinces are full of patriotic selections."[84]

Some years later, Manitoba's Minister of Education expressed similar sentiments in words that echoed George Ross' comments in Ontario a generation earlier: "A teacher should be a teacher, not for one province only but for all Canada. Our schools should not be Manitoba schools, but Canadian schools situated in Manitoba."[85] A problem in making each teacher "a teacher for all Canada" was the inveterate parochialism of so many. As S.P. Robins of McGill University's normal school remarked to the DEA in 1901 in terms remarkably similar to those employed by A.B. Hodgetts sixty-seven years later:

> Our Dominion stretches in a narrow line of settlements from the Atlantic to the Pacific. It threatens to break into a series of detached communities, each sufficient for itself, thinking its own thoughts and speaking its own dialect. Already provincial peculiarities obtrude on the traveller, and these peculiarities are emphasized in the case of teachers, whose pronunciation, manner and style formed in the narrow circle of their homes, their local public school, and their local training school, are not corrected by the larger intercourse with many men that corrects local tendencies in men of affairs. If the best of teachers moved more readily from Province to Province, they themselves, would grow broader and would help to counteract the petty parochial feeling and aims of narrow-minded people.[86]

Robins was speaking at the beginning of large-scale western settlement and failed to anticipate the many teachers from all the eastern provinces who would accompany the newcomers and contribute a national ambience to the schools.

Issues related to the goals, content and method of moral education in the new industrial age became an increasing international concern after 1880. New secular movements that were undermining the old religious values were no less concerned than were the churches about the alleged decline in personal and public morality and about the need for the school to put more emphasis on the teaching of morals. Thus, a Moral Instruction League was established in Great Britain and a National Institution for Moral Education in the United States. The Ethical Culture movement founded in the United States by Felix Adler became recognized on both sides of the Atlantic as the guiding light of the new trend. Adler's influential book, *The Moral Instruction of Children,* published in 1895 and widely used in Canadian normal schools promoted an indirect approach whereby morality would permeate the entire curriculum and the whole atmosphere of the school.[87]

Internationally, the new interest in civic moral education was expressed in an inquiry conducted under British and American auspices that resulted in a report, *Moral Instruction and Training in Schools,* published in 1908. Edited by Michael Sadler, a leading British educator, the report contained contributions from many countries, including a detailed survey by Alexander MacKay of moral education in Canadian schools. MacKay proudly cited arrangements in rural Ontario for the transportation of children to and from school. To forestall "evil and corrupting communications" school van drivers had been instructed to watch carefully over the words and actions of their charges. "No other sort of school," said MacKay, "can claim such control over their pupils at these hours."[88] The report covered a wide range of issues dealing with the philosophy and pedagogy of moral education, including discussions of what would now be called "stage theories" of children's moral development.[89] In 1896, Professor Walter Murray of Dalhousie University, later the founding president of the University of Saskatchewan, had familiarized Canadian educators with such theories in a paper entitled "Public Schools and Ethical Culture."[90]

Despite the trend towards a secular, state-based morality, the evidence is that well into the interwar period the moral outlook of Canadian educators remained strongly religious. Conceptions of moral education were indistinguishable from those of Egerton Ryerson earlier. Thus, in 1905, Nathaniel Burwash, Chancellor of Victoria College at the University of Toronto, described National Education — the capitalization was noteworthy — as moral, thorough, truthful, practical and patriotic. The atmosphere of the school "should be that of the fear and love of God, of reverence and piety and of justice and charity towards man." Instruction by a virtuous teacher who taught by example was much superior to "an hour a week of outside teaching by a clergyman."[91] Burwash's comments indicated that nineteenth century notions of disciplined intelligence persisted as Anglo-Canadians sought to preserve their central Christian ideals of unity and order.[92]

The same Ryersonian moral outlook was evident at the 1919 Winnipeg Conference on Character Education in Relation to Canadian Citizenship. Faith in the power of education was expressed by one of the conference organizers, a businessperson, who observed, "The character of this country could be modelled in the public schools of this country."[93] The Winnipeg meeting revealed an interesting contrast between the outlook of the

American and Canadian speakers. To the former, morality was conceived in secular terms, whereas to Canadians it was still conceived fundamentally in Christian terms. In the keynote address entitled "Moral and Spiritual Lessons of the War," the Reverend C.W. Gordon (Ralph Connor), a leading Presbyterian cleric, expressed the essential spirit of the conference:

> ... the War has asserted *The Supreme Place* of Religion in Character-making and Nation-building ... I hope the day is coming to Canada when we still think that religion is not the business particularly of a preacher but that it is the business of man. [Applause] ... A nation's religion informs it, makes its ideals, supports those ideals, fortifies the courage of man in making these ideals and shows the way to finer and higher ideals.[94]

The planning group for the Winnipeg conference, dominated by an anglo-conformist elite, including Protestant church leaders, also included remarkably tolerant representatives of the Jewish and Roman Catholic communities. All agreed on the need to improve ethical aspects of Canadian schooling by conveying Christian principles through "the whole content of subjects of instruction," especially by infusing textbooks "inferentially" with the spirit of Christian ethics.[95] An important aim was declared to be "to give the foreign-speaking people of the West the proper ideals of truth and integrity" in disregard of the possibility that New Canadians might already possess these qualities.

The notion of inculcating Christian ethics "inferentially" pointed up the chief controversy about teaching morality, for instance, whether it should be direct and didactic or indirect and incidental. E.P. Hurley, a member of the Halifax Anglican clergy, advocated teaching a "science of ethics," as opposed to mere habit training. Through moral reasoning children should learn to understand *why* they should be good.[96] Explicit instruction took the form of formal moral and religious teaching and in what was often called "morals and mannners," the latter foreshadowing the later emergence of a secular "personal guidance." A common pattern across the provinces was the opening of school with prayers and scriptures reading; the latter was typically presented without comment. In Protestant Quebec, Scripture was a didactic examination subject like any other. Catholic Quebec had the most complete program of direct and indirect moral education, including regular and frequent religious observance, the formal teaching of religion, and the deliberate infusion of the curriculum and life of the school with a religious spirit.[97]

As befitted the Ryersonian system, policies and procedures regarding moral instruction were particularly comprehensive and thorough in Ontario. In 1896, George Ross had declared that "No course of moral instruction is prescribed." However, teachers were expected, by personal example and instruction as well as by the exercise of their authority, to "imbue every pupil with respect for those moral obligations which underlie a well-formed character." Ross pointed to the detailed regulations on religious exercises, noting that such exercises were to be non-denominational, conducted "with the utmost reverence and decorum." Parents or guardians had the right to withdraw their children from them at their discretion. Teachers objecting to the reading of the Scriptures and the opening and closing of the school by prayer were "discharged from the performance of this duty." On the other hand care must be taken to prevent teachers from propagating dogmas "inconsistent with a popular system of education." The regulations remained substantially in force in Ontario over the next half century. Variations of them were adopted across anglophone Canada.[98]

Despite the emphasis on explicit moral and religious instruction, "manners and morals" increasingly came to be taught incidentally, in theory permeating the entire course of study. Nova Scotia's Education Act was explicit in defining the moral duties of teachers. They were expected " . . . to inculcate by precept and example a respect for religion and the principles of Christian morality, and for truth, justice, love of country, loyalty, humanity, sobriety, industry, frugality, chastity, temperance and all other virtues."[99] In Nova Scotia, "moral and patriotic duties" were taught together with hygiene and temperance and were classified as "recreative subjects" as opposed to "the nerve-exhausting subjects" of the academic curriculum.[100] In 1914, Alexander MacKay reported that moral and civic instruction in the province was "mainly incidental" with only five minutes per day devoted to "moral and patriotic duties." These duties were taught formally through civics, using a textbook that was shortly authorized in most provinces. For morals, the syllabus and publications of the British Moral Instruction League and the Duty and Discipline Movement were recommended as aids to the teacher.[101]

Moral education during the early Prairie period was almost a replica of that in Nova Scotia, as revealed by an examination of annual reports, curriculum guides, teacher requirements, inspectors' reports, examination questions and textbooks.[102] Saskatchewan used the same British syllabus and instruction guides.[103] Because formal moral instruction was a non-examination subject, it lacked prestige in an examination-ridden curriculum, and thus fared poorly. Gradually it was dropped as a separate subject as a moral perspective came to pervade the entire curriculum and all school activities from student organizations and social events to recess and noon hour activities. As in Nova Scotia, history and literature lessons were expected "to form moral notions in children" and "to teach patriotism and civic duty."[104] Sheehan notes that the Alexandra readers, modeled on the Ontario readers and introduced in Alberta and Saskatchewan in 1908, covertly taught political moral and social concepts derived from Judeo-Christian teaching. Stories taught that idleness and laziness were particularly sinful. In "The Sentinel's Pouch" the child learned that if you followed orders you were doing your duty and would be rewarded.[105] Examinations were used to promote moral education. Thus, pupils were asked to write about the "moral tone" of "The Tempest." One examination struck a modern note in 1913 when reference to "value choices" was made, but it was moral indoctrination rather than reflective discussion that was typically prized.[106] In Manitoba, the Department of Education's Advisory Board, which included the Anglican archbishop of the province, a Roman Catholic priest and a Presbyterian minister, expected teachers " . . . to inculcate in the minds of all children in the school, (a) Love and fear of God, (b) Reverence for the name of God, (c) Keeping His Commandments."[107] The Manitoba curriculum aimed at "a methodical, systematic and active implementation of morals in everyday life."[108]

Increasing attention was given to the pedagogy of moral education during the period. Normal school curricula stressed content and method related to moral and religious instruction, to temperance and hygiene, and to other subjects that would prepare teachers to be moral overseers of their charges. School management textbooks in the form of teachers' manuals included sections on discipline and punishment which typically dealt directly with "moral instruction," "habit training," "character formation" and religious teaching. Among the most widely used was J.B. Calkin's *Notes on Education,* which was listed in normal school curricula for two decades following its first publication by Truro Teachers' College in 1888. The 1915 Ontario Teachers' Manual entitled *School Management* was also popular.[109]

In addressing the Winnipeg Conference in 1919, J.F. White, the principal of the Ottawa Normal School, was critical of the "fitful and unsystematic" methodology of moral education and of the lack of proper teacher training. In a wide-ranging address entitled "The Function of the Public School in Character Formation" White anticipated Lawrence Kohlberg and modern theories of the child's moral-psychological development by forty years in commenting that, "It is important for the teacher to have a definite idea of the various stages of moral development in children, of the different forces which influence their moral life and of the progressive standard of conduct and morality for each stage." He also explained the importance of play, medical inspection and attractive surroundings for the effective pursuit of the goals of moral education.[110]

## Notes to Chapter 7

1 RCITTE, 10.

2 *N.S. Journal of Education,* April, 1913, 34-5.

3 N. Sutherland, *Children,* 155-62.

4 Sandiford, *Comparative,* 367.

5 Ibid., 304-5, 367.

6 Ibid., 434-5.

7 Hughes *et al, Public.*

8 Wood, "In Defence," 1-4.

9 See Sizer.

10 C.E. Phillips, *Development*; D. Crawford, "School Mathematics in Ontario, 1894-1959," 388.

11 R. Harris, *History*, 120.

12 G. Ross, "The Policy," 13.

13 G. Ross, "Education in Ontario," 176-7.

14 G. Ross, "The Policy," 14-15.

15 R. Stamp, "John Seath," 241.

16 "Report of the Senate of Victoria University on the Draft of the Proposed Changes in the Public and High School Courses of Study and Organisation and in the Departmental Examination System," *Educational Monthly of Canada*, (April 1904), 169, 174.

17 Dupuis.

18 N.S.AR, 1900-1, vvii.

19 For accounts of changes in Alberta in particular see Chalmers, *Schools*, 191-4 and B. Walker, "Public Secondary Education."

20 B. Walker, "Public Secondary Education."

21 Foght, *Survey*.

22 Putman, "Shortening."

23 Sandiford, *Comparative*, 403, 367.

24 R. Harris, *History*, 120.

25 Cited in C.E. Phillips, *Development*, 523.

26 Lower, *Canadians*, 355.

27 W. Kirkconnell, *A Canadian*, 27, 128-30.

28 DBS, *Elementary*, 1938-40, 50.

29 Gonick, 71.

30 See B. Walker, "The High School."

31 Silver, 151-2.

32 Grubb and Lazerson, 6-9.

33 Cappon, "Macdonald," 320.

34 J. Robertson, "Professor," 422.

35 Semple, 106 citing Ontario Sessional Papers, 1901, 266.

36 Seath, 286.

37 Leake, *Industrial*, 19-21, 50, 136.

38 Ibid., 19, 44-5.

39 See Brewin, 38, 43.

40 Leake, *Industrial*, 38.

41 See for example Leacock, "Apology," "Literature," "The University" and James Cappon, "Is Ontario to Abandon Classical Education?"

42 Dupuis.

43 A. Smith, "The Myth," 196-7.

44 Bliss, *A Living Profit,* 117-8.

45 Ibid., 118-9.

46 Copp, *Anatomy,* 58.

47 Magnuson, 71.

48 C.E. Phillips, *Development,* 431.

49 Cappon, "Literature," 28-9

50 Watson, "The University," 328-9.

51 Dupuis, 120-122.

52 Ellis, "The Making," 296, 298.

53 Ellis, "The University," 62-65.

54 MacKay, *Monograph,* 6.

55 Ibid., 8.

56 J. Miller, *Rural Schools,* 70.

57 Ibid., 76-78, 69.

58 Sandiford, *Comparative,* 405.

59 M. Scott, "What Is Aimed At," 181.

60 Leake, *Industrial,* 8, 15.

61 Foght, *Survey,* 132.

62 H. King, 28, 30-33.

63 G. Ross in *DEA Proceedings* (1892), 50-2.

64 See Jain, 43. As a result, Ross felt forced to introduce a note of imperialism into his reports and to introduce imperialist "patriotic programs" into the schools of Ontario, a policy that culminated in his sponsorship of Empire Day a few years later.

65 Nova Scotia House of Assembly, *Proceedings,* 1896, 124-6.

66 McDonald, "Political Socialization," 12, 17.

67 Clement, v-vi.

68 MacKay, *DEA Proceedings,* 1898, xxxvi.

69 C. Berger, *Sense of Power,* 70.

70 For a thorough account of Empire Day in Ontario schools see R. Stamp, "Empire Day."

71 This discussion of the IODE in the schools draws on Sheehan, "The IODE."

72 See R. Stamp, *Schools of Ontario,* 93.

73 Gonick, 89-90.

74 Lower, *Canadians,* 352-3.

75 M. Scott, "What Is Aimed At," 182.

76 *L'Enseignement primaire*, 1903-4, 134-5.

77 Siegfried, 59.

78 McLeod, "A Short History," 26.

79 See R. Stamp, *Schools of Ontario*, 92.

80 McLeod, "Education and the Assimilation of the New Canadians," 252.

81 N. Sutherland, *Children*, 210-11.

82 Potrebenko, 90.

83 J. McKay; J. Anderson. Both cited in National Council of Education *Report of the National Conference*, 64; 96-7.

84 Bryce, "The Canadianization," lii.

85 *Western School Journal*, (May, 1920), 177.

86 Robins, "The Desirability," 56.

87 Berard, 2, 9. See also Bruneau, 12.

88 A. MacKay in Sadler, Vol. II, 298.

89 Ibid. 22.

90 W.C. Murray, "Public Schools."

91 Burwash, 47-48.

92 McKillop, *Disciplined*, 3-5.

93 Lyons, "In Pursuit." 75.

94 National Council of Education, *Report of the Winnipeg Conference*, 6.

95 Lyons, "In Pursuit,"

96 Cited in Berard, 13 from *The Educational Review*, 6 (1892-3), 173-5, 197-8, 232-4.

97 See Jain, "Nationalism," 50-53.

98 G. Ross, *School System*, 65, 136-8.

99 Nova Scotia Council of Public Instruction, *Manual to the Public Instruction Act and Regulations*, 1900, 29.

100 Nova Scotia, *Journal of Education*, 1896, xvi.

101 MacKay, *Monograph*, 9.

102 See Sheehan, "Indoctrination."

103 Saskatchewan Educational Commission, *Report*, 1915, 203-4.

104 Sheehan, "Indoctrination," 225-6, citing the Northwest Territories AR for 1896, 231.

105 See Sheehan, "Character Training," citing the Alexander Reader, Third Book, 1909.

106 Sheehan, "Indoctrination," 229-30.

107 Cited in Gonick, 113.

108 Ibid.

109 Calkin; *Ministry of Education, Ontario, School Management*. See also Bruneau, 9-10.

110 J. White, 61-63.

# CHAPTER 8

## CONTINUING MODERNIZATION AND PERSISTING CURRICULUM ISSUES AFTER 1920

*The position taken in this report regarding school curricula is that all public education must combine the general and the specific, the cultural and the practical.*

(Canada and Newfoundland Education Association, 1943)

*From the point of view of society, the schools in any state exist to develop citizens, or subjects, according to the prevailing or dominating ideals of the state or society ....*

(Programme of Studies for the Elementary Schools of British Columbia, 1936-37)

### Inter-war and War-time Social Trends

Granatstein has described the 1920s as the first modern decade as we would understand the term today. "Airplanes were a frequent sight in the sky, the movies were everywhere and entertainment was cheap, radio was becoming increasingly popular and the era of the automobile had begun." These developments and new dress styles epitomized the new youth culture of the "roaring twenties." The automobile was "the decisive factor in [the] transition to modernism" for it changed life in the city and reduced rural isolation.[1] By making school consolidation possible, automotive transport helped to give rural children access to a broader curriculum. Because parents expected the school to shield their adolescent children from the new moral and social temptations, the high school took on an expanding custodial role analogous to that which the elementary school had assumed earlier.[2]

What has been called the discovery of adolescence, its recognition as a stage or way of life, had become apparent before 1920. Adolescence seems to have been closely associated with the establishment of compulsory attendance, the prolongation of schooling and the withdrawal of youth from the labour market. G. Stanley Hall's famous work, published in 1904, crowned a generation of concern about an age group that was seen as especially vulnerable to the demoralizing forces of an urban-industrial society. A propensity for delinquency was no longer seen as restricted to working class youth.

A marked phenomenon of the period after 1910 was the growth of youth organizations such as the YMCA and the YWCA, which actually had had their origins more than a generation before. By 1920 both groups were operating structured programs influenced by progressive ideas and aimed at both working adolescents and students. The YMCA had a particular influence on schools through the school-based Hi-Y clubs that it sponsored for boys after 1920. By this time, the British-inspired Boy Scouts and Girl Guides were also well established in Canada. Led by adults, these groups were designed to counter the perils and exploit the character building possibilities of the adolescent years.[3]

More nationalistic were such church-based groups as the Canadian Girls in Training (CGIT), organized in 1917 with YWCA assistance to promote liberal Christian ideals and a positive Canadian citizenship. Over the following generation, the CGIT gave upwards of 250 000 Canadian girls their first opportunities to develop leadership and discussion skills based on activity-centred, progressive pedagogy derived from William Heard Kilpatrick's project method. Prang argues that the many teachers among CGIT leaders gained better opportunities to put into practice the progressive theories they had learned in normal school than they could find in their classrooms.[4]

The new social and moral custodial role of the high school provided one impetus for the growth of supervised extra-curricular activities. Toronto trustees complained that "boys are too frequently seen escorting the girls to and from school" but could find no legal means of stopping the practice.[5] Although a majority of youth reached high school by the mid-1920s, only a minority graduated, as economic deprivation at home forced most to enter the labour market early. Marsh's study of employment in Canada showed that the child of an artisan might face a choice between school and work at fourteen, but the child of a professional man could delay this decision up to the age of twenty.[6]

Familiar problems of economic recession, political confusion, sectional conflict, French-English antagonism and fears of Americanization continued in the 1920s. The resumption of immigration after World War I was marked by a new wave of British newcomers. Among the foreign-born, immigrants from the United States were the largest single group. "New Canadians" also continued to arrive but, as before, they remained mostly invisible in the curriculum. Racism was rampant during the inter-war decades. Terms such as "drunken Indian," "wop," "sheeny," "frog," "kike" and "hunky" were in common use even among the better educated. The Ku Klux Klan, aimed mostly at Jews and Catholics, became well established, especially in Saskatchewan and Ontario. Deportation of immigrants considered subversive was common. No fewer than 7647 were deported in 1933 alone. Labour unrest was rife after World War I, peaking in the most famous strike in Canadian history, that at Winnipeg in 1919. Rural based protest movements led to the formation of new political parties, of which the most enduring, formed in the 1930s, would prove to be Social Credit and the Co-operative Commonwealth Federation (CCF), the latter the predecessor of today's New Democratic Party (NDP).

The 1920s were an era of nationalism as young English-Canadian intellectuals and artists such as Vincent Massey sought to promote unity through the creation of national symbols, myths and heroes.[8] As before, nationalism was typically ambivalent, imbued with a strong sense of Canadianism admixed with imperial patriotism. A kind of rebirth of the earlier Canada First movement occured during the inter-war period through the revitalization of the Canadian Clubs, originally organized in 1893, and through new national organizations such as the Native Sons of Canada, the Canadian Legion and the Canadian Council of Child Welfare. The 1930s saw the founding of the CBC, the Bank of Canada, Trans Canada Airlines (now Air Canada) and the Dominion Drama Festival. By this time, the United Church, formed in 1926, as a union of Methodists, Congregationalists and some Presbyterians, was nearing the peak of its influence in Canadian life. In the world of art, the Group of Seven was educating Canadians to a continuing vision of "the true north strong and free."[9] Despite growing nationalism, however, the cultural content of anglophone school curricula remained basically imperial.

Canada's first radio station began programming in 1920. In 1923, the Canadian National Railway formed a network to provide Canadian programming as a counter to American radio. The inauguration of school broadcasts at this time marked a recognition of the educational potential of radio. A 1929 royal commission whose members included the Deputy Ministers of Education recommended a national government broadcasting system and the regulation of private broadcasting. As a result, the CBC was formed in 1932 with a mandate to educate, to entertain and to foster Canadian nationalism.

Renewed "moral protectionism" was also aimed at the movies and mass circulation magazines. The moral and cultural dangers posed to Canadian youth by both media were of concern to the National Council of Education, a voluntary body organized in 1919. At Victoria a decade later, the Council dealt with the issue of "the foreign film" and its sex and violence through a resolution approving "some measure of limitation of the freedom of children in attending moving picture theatres." A more positive proposal urging governments to undertake the production and distribution of educational and other types of film suitable for children was realized when the National Film Board, formed in 1939, began to produce films directly related to school curricula.[10]

The Victoria meeting was told that the alleged low moral tone and un-

British attitudes of "the foreign magazine" were exemplified by American magazines that were said to deride marriage as an institution and to lower respect for womanhood by pictures exhibiting the female form "in an astonishing variety of poses and postures, graceful, ungraceful and disgraceful." The "confident tone" of publications extolling the American way of life made it small wonder that to many Canadians Abraham Lincoln was probably a more familiar figure than Sir John A. Macdonald.[11] In 1931, restrictions imposed on American publications entering Canada were extended.

The period was one of heavy southward migration: 325 000 Canadians, many well educated and ambitious, left for the United States during the years 1920-23 alone. There was a reverse migration, a continuation of the pre-1914 northward migration by Americans in search of cheap western land. A major 1943 study concluded that the remarkable intermingling of the two peoples through migration, tourism, business and other means made the average Canadian as familiar with an American as with a Canadian of another province.[12] Canadian-American educational contacts greatly increased during the inter-war period. By one estimate, more than one thousand Canadians enrolled for graduate studies at Columbia University alone between 1923 and 1938.[13]

After 1929, the Depression, arguably the most traumatic mass experience in Canadian history, preoccupied most Canadians, whether those still fortunate enough to work at low-paying jobs or those forced to subsist in soup kitchens, in relief camps or on drought-stricken Prairie farms. Population growth slowed under the impact of reduced immigration, heavy emigration and the lowest birthrates recorded to that time. When the provinces were forced to curtail their educational expenditures, various federal initiatives were launched to combat youth unemployment, culminating in the Youth Training Act of 1939.

During World War II, educators began to turn their attention to long-term post-war needs and planning. A concern for general social reform was signalled by the establishment of the federal Committee on Reconstruction headed by F. Cyril James, the principal of McGill University. The most notable outcome of the James Committee was the so-called Marsh Report which proposed a comprehensive national program of social security including health insurance, family allowances and unemployment insurance. These proposals foreshadowed the emergence of the post-war Canadian welfare state. Earlier, the Rowell Sirois Commission on Dominion-Provincial Relations had noted in its 1940 report that the quality of education and welfare services was no longer a matter of purely provincial or local concern. In arguing the need for minimum national standards in these areas, the Commission foreshadowed wartime centralization and provided a justification for future federal intervention in education.[14]

S.D. Clark has characterized Canadian society on the eve of World War II as bureaucratically structured, offering few opportunities for upward mobility. Social stability was maintained by the draining off of surplus populations to the United States. The society had a narrow middle-class base in 1939, resting on a sub-stratum of what Clark terms "cultural islands," for example, French-Canadians, Native peoples, women, rural New Canadians on the Prairies, those living in marginal farming and fishing areas from coast to coast, and unskilled workers. All these groups lacked the capacity — largely due to lack of education — for meaningful public participation in the society.[15]

## Governmental and Voluntary Educational Initiatives

After 1920 legislative and other initiatives at both provincial and federal levels, like those of the preceding period, often had national curriculum significance. At the former level, reforms adopted in one province, such as school consolidation, the reorganization of school finance and the establishment of the junior high school sometimes served as catalysts for similar action in other provinces. Such was the case with school broadcasting. which had begun experimentally in Nova Scotia in 1923 and in Manitoba in 1925. By the 1940s, with the co-operation of the provinces and the support of the Canadian Teachers' Federation, the CBC had arranged the first national school broadcasts. The planning and content of the programs were the responsibility of the provincial authorities and the time, facilities and production capability were provided by the CBC. In 1943, an Advisory Council on School Broadcasting was set up that included representatives from every province, from the universities and from organizations of parents, school trustees and teachers.

The national school broadcasts were specifically designed "to strengthen national unity and increase Canadian consciousness among students."[16] Efforts were made to tie broadcasts directly to specific subject areas of the curriculum. The great popularity of broadcasts of Shakespeare plays caused several provinces to align their English courses with the radio presentations. Regional broadcasters also used CBC facilities as local programs became tied even more directly to provincial curricula. By 1943 it was estimated that about 4000 schools were using school broadcasts. By 1951 the number had doubled[17]

In the area of technical and vocational education the effects of the Technical Education Act of 1919 and various adaptations to it during the inter-war and war-time periods will be considered below. Ottawa's establishment during the war years of family allowances had an impact on provincial school systems. Since payments to mothers were conditional upon school attendance of children, the immediate effect of the measure was to improve attendance, particularly among the disadvantaged.[18]

The Junior Red Cross was a voluntary organization that, in contrast with such groups as the CGIT, was school-oriented and attempted to have an impact on the curriculum. Established in 1914 to encourage the war-time humanitarian work of the International Red Cross, the Junior Red Cross was retained after 1918 as a children's peace-time organization designed to promote good health, humanitarian ideals, good citizenship and international amity. The essential element in the success of the organization was the classroom-based club operated voluntarily by the teacher in class time. Using progressive techniques based on the project teaching method, the organization gave major emphasis to health education by means of a monthly magazine, wall posters, discussions and classroom plays. It also provided supplementary materials in Canadian history and civics, geography and nature study. By the 1930s, the Junior Red Cross had enrolled more than 100 000 children across Canada and was a fixture in Canadian schools.[19] The organization serves as an interesting example of how an external agency could supplement the formal curriculum.

The Canadian National Federation of Home and School Associations, formed in 1927, had its origins in provincial and local groups organized during World War I. Inspired by "maternal feminism" the home and school movement, as the first large formal organization to involve non-professionals in school systems, sought to assert the influence of women in education, to improve the physical environment of schools and the health of children and to promote progressive innovations such as play-oriented physical education. While reformist in thrust, the movement never seriously challenged the centralized school systems in place by the 1920s. By 1945, the Federation had 60 000 members in 1300 local associations.[20]

The National Council of Education was a unique inter-war organization that, with the temporary eclipse of the CEA during the 1920s, became a kind of unofficial voice for many Canadian educators. The Council grew out of a national conference on character education in relation to Canadian citizenship convened in Winnipeg in 1919 which has been described as the first attempt to focus the attention of all Canadians on the problems facing Canadian education. With 1504 registered delegates from all provinces, it was the largest national educational gathering held in Canada to that time.[21] Funded by private and government sources and made up of fifty members representative of educational, business and women's groups from across Canada, the Council sought to arrest the nation's alleged moral decline by means of school programs in character education. It also sought to promote more Canadian content in school textbooks.[22] The Council's own series of textbooks included the successful civics primer, *This Canada of Ours*, and Sir Ernest Macmillan's *Canadian Song Book*.

Despite its emphasis on Canadianism, the thrust of the Council's ideology was imperialist in tone. Its executive director, Major Frederick Ney, a former British army officer and chief secretary of the Manitoba Department of Education, aimed to develop imperial sentiment through "the greatest factor of Empire — the schoolroom." Addresses at the Winnipeg conference were a strange mixture of Christian idealism, Canadian patriotism, imperial jingoism and New Education doctrine. Later conferences held in Toronto (1923), Montreal (1926) and Victoria (1929) featured generalized, moralistic, idealistic speeches that ignored controversial issues and the pressing problems of Canadian education.[23] As we have seen, the Victoria meeting deplored the unBritish, immoral influence of American films and magazines. With the revival of the Canadian Education Association and a serious diminution of the Council's financial support, the organization became defunct in the 1940s.

An important organizational trend during the inter-war period was the growth of provincial teachers' associations, which led to the formation of the Canadian Teachers' Federation in 1919. The Federation's interest in school broadcasting noted earlier, its efforts to promote federal aid to education, national standards in the education, certification and salaries of teachers, to reduce educational inequality and to expand Canadian content reflected concern for matters that all had clear national curriculum implications. By facilitating interprovincial dialogue among teachers on curriculum matters the Federation and its interprovincial affiliates exerted indirect influence on policy.

The National Conference of Canadian Universities (later renamed the Association of Universities and Colleges of Canada), organized in 1911, became increasingly active after 1920.[24] The growing sense of national self-consciousness among Canadian university educators was exemplified in McGill principal Sir Arthur Currie's 1927 presidential address to the NCCU. He asked, "Is Canadian Education Fulfilling its Purpose?" Currie related this to another question, "Is there any such thing as Canadian education as a whole?" He wondered if Canadian education consisted of "merely several provincial systems." His answer was that, despite differences, there was much in common: "Common interchange of teachers, the employment of superintendents educated in other provinces, a general similarity among Canadians, co-operation between universities," all these, he claimed, "have made our provincial systems so similar that they might almost be regional districts under one authority."[25]

The NCCU regularly discussed curriculum problems, frequently as an aspect of university-school relations. A Carnegie funded 1922 study of education in the Maritime provinces conducted by Learned and Sills threw considerable light on curriculum problems in that region.[26] Admission (matriculation) standards and examinations and the need for national uniformity regarding them were recurring NCCU concerns. Some academics deplored the democratization of education evident in increased enrolments and vocational emphases at the high school level. As a McGill classicist put it in 1927, "We have banished illiteracy but in so doing we have banished scholarship."[27]

Despite its moribund state during the 1920s the Canadian Education Association urged the expansion of vocational and agricultural education, school consolidation, and the standardization of teaching certificates. The training of teachers was also studied. After 1930, the organization was revitalized. Requirements for high school graduation and the problem of better articulation between the schools and universities were explored. The Association had some success in urging more flexible university admission requirements, reflected in the decision by several institutions to recognize art and music as matriculation subjects. In 1938, Newfoundland was admitted and the body was renamed The Canada and Newfoundland Education Association. In 1941, the Canadian Council for Educational Research was established by the CNEA under a grant from New York's Carnegie Foundation.[28] A year later, the CNEA launched a national survey of educational needs in Canada. The survey and a number of ensuing studies of practical education will be discussed subsequently.

During the war years, the Canadian Youth Commission, a private independent body established in 1943 out of concerns regarding youth (defined as the fifteen to twenty-four age group) and its place in postwar society, provided the first comprehensive view of what Canadian young people thought about their schooling. The 1467 young people who responded to a questionnaire prepared by the Commission's education committee gave a generally positive evaluation of their school experience. They urged more emphasis on teaching an understanding of modern society and of citizenship responsibilities through greater attention to politics and public affairs in the curriculum, but flatly rejected traditional modes of indoctrination. Providing assistance in getting jobs and in developing abilities and interests was rated as more important than preparation for university entrance. Despite their support for utilitarian school objectives, the respondents rated the traditional school subjects — English, French (among those of that first language) mathematics, science and history — as the most valuable.[29]

Adult education became a major growth area during the inter-war period. The movement could be traced to Mechanics' Institutes and similar organizations in the nineteenth century. With twentieth century children, youth and adults now segregrated by age and grade and no longer mixed indiscriminately in classrooms, schools were less appropriate places for mature learners. Adult education was promoted by university extension services after 1920.[30] In 1936, the Canadian Association for Adult Education was formed, assisted by generous funding from the Carnegie Foundation of New York.

The increasing inter-war Canadian-American educational contacts noted earlier led to the professionalization and to a degree of Americanization of Canadian leadership in education. Canadian branches of American organizations such as the Modern Language Association and the National Committee for Mental Health were formed. In 1938, H.F. Angus, a leading social scientist, published *Canada and Her Great Neighbour,* a study which included the first national survey of the reading, radio listening and related activities of Canadian children. Conducted in order to determine children's attitudes to, contacts with and knowledge of the United States and things American, the survey confirmed other findings and reinforced longstanding concerns regarding the pervasive influence of foreign media.[31] At the same time, Angus found that formal instruction about the United States in Canadian curricula was "extraordinarily slight." He reported that in no province "does the curriculum comprise systematic instruction designed to develop a balanced and comprehensive understanding of the United States..."[32] These findings were confirmed by later complementary studies of the place of each country in the school curricula of the other that were conducted by C.E. Phillips and A.A. Hauck, the respective Canadian and American heads of the Canada-United States Committee on Education that was formed during the 1940s.[33]

## Rural-Urban and Other Educational Disparities

Disparities between urban and rural areas, between provinces and regions and between ethnic groups reflected comparable disparities in school provision, expenditure, teacher qualifications and experience and related variables. Before 1920, many reformers tried to cope with an expanding urban milieu, while others such as J.W. Robertson were more concerned about what came to be known as "the rural school problem." For them, the regeneration of what was seen as a decaying countryside that was losing people to the city was the central purpose of the New Education. Ironically, concern about rural decline developed during the unprecedented agricultural prosperity of the Laurier boom before 1914. At the turn of the century the rural problem has provided the impetus for the Macdonald-Robertson movement. It was also a central concern of Robertson's 1910 Royal Commission.

After 1914, concern accelerated. In that year, John MacDougall, a member of the Presbyterian clergy, published *Rural Life in Canada — Its Trends and Tasks*. To MacDougall the rural problem was a moral problem, for the old simple, pure and creative country life had been undermined by the character defects of the people.[34] MacDougall blamed the schools for diverting young people from the farm into teaching or other professions or business; those who did stay in the country saw "no connection between their studies and life ..." In Quebec French-Canadian Catholic farm leaders were expressing similar concerns. The author of a Quebec normal school textbook *(manuel de pedagogie)* first published in 1901 observed that to teach rural children in the same manner as urban children *"c'est favoriser une agglomeration excessive dans les villes et depeupler les campagnes."*[35] In this province, proposals for compulsory attendance and a Ministry of Education met opposition from the clergy and the nationalist elite who feared the imposition of godless non-confessional schools.[36] In Nova Scotia, Alexander MacKay's longstanding concern about the rural problem was based on different circumstances than those in central Canada. In that province the rural exodus was not to cities within the province, but to other parts of Canada, mainly to Ontario and the West.[37]

In no part of Canada was the rural school problem more stark than in Northern (or new) Ontario. Abbott has written of "hostile landscapes" and "the spectre of illiteracy" as it applied to what one Ontario school inspector called the "sequestered" child in a milieu where as many as one third of the children escaped the educational net. Rural was not the most appropriate term to describe a broken Laurentian landscape of scattered, often ephemeral bush settlements based on mining and forest industries. The most successful attempts to solve the problem took the form of correspondence courses and the famous railway-car "schools on wheels" instituted in the 1920s. The former proved more effective, reaching many more children and being much cheaper to provide. By the 1930s correspondence students were more than holding their own in high school entrance and other departmental examinations.[38]

If the Maritime provinces suffered from an exodus, New Ontario and the western provinces faced the problem of a vast influx of people. Rapid settlement placed an enormous burden on school facilities. In Saskatchewan, rural school reform was spurred in part by the feeling that the province had in the past "too slavishly followed the school system of Ontario and eastern Canada" with the result that education did not "effectively fit into our present western Prairie conditions."[39] Change was closely linked to the temperance and conservation movements as well as to concern about the influx of European immigrants.

The organization of the Saskatchewan Public Education League in 1916 led to the commissioning of a survey by Dr. Harold W. Foght, an American specialist in rural education. As the first province-wide survey conducted by an American educator in Canada, Foght's report provided a lucid and insightful analysis that has rarely been surpassed in Canadian education. Foght was particularly critical of the rigidity, formalism and mechanical methods of teaching in Saskatchewan classrooms. The textbook was "enthroned" and grammar was overdone. The lecture method was "ever present" with questions answered by the instructor "before opportunity can be given for answer by the pupil."[40]

Foght reported that grade retardation (repeating the grade) affected 68.7 per cent of Saskatchewan pupils, a fact that partly explained why only 17.4 per cent of the high school age group was enrolled in high school studies.[41] He was particularly critical of a course of study in which "practically nothing was being done to meet local community needs." The curriculum should be "shot through and through with occupational information." By this, Foght did not mean a narrow vocational education since "the best preparation for life is a good general education for all the children." He meant an education "rooted in the soil" in rural schools and "welded to industry" in city schools.

Many of Foght's proposals, notably school consolidation, had already been anticipated from a national perspective five years earlier by J.C. Miller, a Canadian educator trained at Teachers' College, Columbia University. His *Rural Schools in Canada*, was another fine example of curriculum criticism. In promoting nation-building objectives, Miller deplored the lack of "any aspect of educational work considered from the viewpoint of the Dominion as a whole." In surveying the inspection and supervision needs of Canadian rural schools, he touched on ideas of scientific management that would lead in later decades to a common national pattern of school administration. For Miller the only immediate solution to acute rural problems of transiency and attendance and uneducated teachers was uniformity imposed by a strong central authority.[42]

Teacher mobility had some positive results, arising from the fact that, as teachers moved among the provinces, a national perspective was promoted. Those native-born Nova Scotia teachers whom one school inspector complained had gone west, no doubt taught their own brand of Canadianism to their foreign-born charges.[43] Of British Columbia's eighteen inspectors in 1925, none had been born in the province, but fifteen were Canadian-born: five in Ontario, six in Nova Scotia, two in New Brunswick and two in Prince Edward Island.[44] During the inter-war years, common prescribed courses of study and new administrative structures such as the larger rural school unit and its concomitant, the consolidated school, together with similar policies regarding textbooks, examinations and teacher training contributed to a high degree of curricular uniformity among the provinces.

On the other hand, uniformity was attenuated by significant disparities in actual curriculum provision that resulted from disparities in available resources within and among the provinces. During the inter-war years uneven economic growth and a slower rate of increase in educational expenditures increased disparities. After 1930, as provincial Depression budgets shrank, municipalities were forced to assume 80 per cent of the burden and school revenues actually declined. Urban-rural disparities were revealed in 1936 in Ontario: city teachers earned two to three times more than their rural colleagues; 355 of the former had university degrees as compared with only 54 of the latter.[45] Nova Scotia inspectors' reports in 1940 described "coloured," i.e., segregated, schools as so dilapidated as to be uninsurable, and other schools with uncomfortable homemade desks, few library books and little equipment except tattered maps that could have been written in 1875 or 1910.[46]

On the Prairies, disparities were intensified due to depressed conditions resulting from earlier overexpansion into dry marginal areas. Population decline and farm abandonment in the Alberta Dry Belt during the 1920s led to social and educational disintegration. During the 1930s, a similar process in Saskatchewan reached the proportions of a national catastrophe. In his examination of the Alberta school district of Berry Creek, Jones has described the problems of maintaining schools in circumstances where two thirds of the population had moved out. Problems were exacerbated by teacher training programs that offered normal school students no opportunity to observe or practise in rural schools. Such conditions helped to provide the justification for larger school districts. After 1930, Berry Creek became the first major rural consolidation in Alberta.[47] In urging consolidation, a 1935 legislative report noted that half the students in ungraded rural schools had no access to high school instruction. Although high school enrolment had quadrupled, only a minority of students advanced far and an undifferentiated academic curriculum prevailed.[48]

A comprehensive and sophisticated national survey conducted in the 1940s by K.F. Argue on behalf of the Canadian Teachers' Federation revealed striking provincial disparities ranging from $550 annual expenditures per classroom in one province to $1297 in another. These disparities resulted in differences among the provinces in the quality of the teaching force, median teacher experience, pupil drop-out rates and attendance patterns. Argue asked "Is an educational system which excludes 17 per cent of Canada's fourteen year olds, 34 per cent of her fifteen year olds, 54 per cent of her sixteen year olds, 71 per cent of her seventeen year olds and 81 per cent of her eighteen year olds adequate for the education-demanding decades ahead?" To improve efficiency and in the interest of democratic fairness, Argue advocated the concept of equalization which would ultimately become a principle of Canadian federal-provincial financial relationships.[49] At the local level, the need for consolidation to overcome inefficient administration was revealed by another study which showed that in 1939 Canada had 22 659 school boards with almost 100 000 trustees to supervise 50 000 teachers.[50] In rural Nova Scotia during the 1930s there was one school board for every 1.3 teachers.[51]

During and after World War II, educational expenditures in Canada increased significantly, tripling between 1941 and 1951. By the latter, the provinces were bearing more than one third of school costs, a proportion which assisted better and more uniform curriculum provision within each.[52] Maxwell Cameron, in his masterful 1945 study of school finance in Canada, concluded that the provincial share of school costs could exceed 50 per cent without endangering local autonomy.[53]

## New Vocational Imperatives and Needs Assessment

By the mid-1920s, vocational education had been accepted as a legitimate function of secondary schooling in most provinces. Ontario led the way, enrolling half of all vocational students throughout Canada, its schools the beneficiaries of large provincial and federal grants, the latter resulting from the Technical Education Act of 1919. By 1925, there were facilities for vocational education in most sizeable Ontario cities. Stamp claims that the Act helped to break the academic monopoly of the traditional curriculum in secondary schools where about one quarter of all pupils were enrolled in vocational programs by 1928.[54] Despite Seath's advocacy of separate institutions, the trend by this time was towards the composite school model. Vocational wings were established in many collegiate institutes. However, unlike American composite high schools where university- and work-bound students took common core subjects together and separated for electives, Ontario schools retained a curricular and administrative split between academic and vocational classes. Links between the groups were maintained informally through extra-curricular activities and similar means but disparity of status remained the norm.[55]

A weakness of the 1919 federal legislation was that it failed to encourage vocational education in those provinces which had not already established such systems.[56] The shared fifty-fifty cost arrangement benefited the wealthier provinces. The poorer provinces feared that they might be required to assume the full costs of any programs established under the Act following its statutory expiry in 1929. Provinces where the economy was basically agricultural saw no need for technical education. The interests of the provinces were so diverse that no voluntary arrangements could be made to standardize the program. Funds were sometimes put to unintended uses and skill training was often sacrificed to the demands of cultural and academic subjects. In 1929, the Act was extended for another ten years to encourage all provinces to draw their full allotment. Yet most of the minority of Canadian adolescents who attended high schools continued to follow academic, matriculation-oriented curricula.[57] Few of the stop-gap measures taken by Ottawa to combat youthful unemployment during the Depression years had much impact on schools.[58]

During a period of declining school revenues, outcries against frills caused a decline in vocational education, particularly in rural communities. In Alberta in 1935, it was reported that vocational training was unavailable to rural youth due to a lack of facilities in small high schools or to a lack of high schools *per se*.[59] As the Depression wore on, some Canadians became interested in the relationship between education and unemployment. In 1940, L.C. Marsh, in a pioneer study, *Canadians In and Out of Work*, attempted to analyze this and other relationships, including those involving ethnicity, social class and opportunity. He concluded that "deficiencies in education and vocational planning affect two thirds of the annual crop of school leavers and [that] these deficiencies are cumulative." Marsh recommended a much greater vocational orientation in the schools through the diversification of secondary curricula. But education must be much more than a "vocational instrument." It should also be a means of creating a more democratic citizenship. Marsh noted the dearth of higher education facilities and the difficulty of access to them. In calling attention to the lack of an educational "middle ground" between courses intended for the specialized technician and practical craft training, he was one of the first to note a deficiency in the Canadian curriculum that would persist for another generation. Canada lacked non-university intermediate post-secondary institutions of the later community, regional or junior college type.[60]

As wartime demands revealed serious deficiencies in schooling, members of the Canadian educational establishment became much more aware of the underdeveloped state of their systems and of the need for long range policies to deal with the resulting problems. In 1942, at the behest of the federal James Committee on Reconstruction noted earlier, the CNEA established a survey committee to study Canadian post-war educational needs. At the Victoria meeting of the Association that year, James observed that

Canada was lagging far behind Britain in thinking about post-war educational policy. Provincial disparities and differences in educational standards were major problems. A more practical curriculum was needed in the form of more carefully integrated cultural and vocational courses for the majority who would never attend university. James also advocated larger administrative units, observing that the typical unit, controlled by a local school board, was "a little area delimited, a century or more ago, on the basis of the pupil's ability to walk to school ... on the assumption that a little elementary instruction in the three Rs ... was all that was needed."[61]

James concluded his insightful analysis by specifically calling on the Association to make a comprehensive survey of education throughout the Dominion of Canada and to present its report directly to his committee.[62] His suggestion was quickly taken up and the survey was completed within six months. Ten thousand copies of the report were distributed, including nearly 1000 copies to members of the House of Commons, provincial legislatures "and to other people of influence in Canada and Newfoundland."[63]

In modern curriculum jargon, the report constituted a "needs assessment," focussing on the need for a greater degree of educational opportunity. Striking tribute to the uniformity of Canadian schooling was paid in the disclosure that "the resemblances in the present curricula of the nine provinces ... [was shown] to be much more striking than the differences," particularly in the traditional academic subjects. The report supported a traditional academic orientation based on general curricula termed "cultural" in character, as opposed to a specific vocational orientation termed "practical" or "utilitarian." Nevertheless, the committee felt that curriculum differentiation had become a necessity, for schools in a democracy "must break away from their former single track and ... afford cultural, vocational and avocational, social and character-forming educational experiences suitable to the demands of individual lives." In a more practical curriculum students need not all pursue the same course of study, academic subjects need not be the sole criterion of educational worth, college entrance need not be the sole aim of secondary education, and standard entrance requirements to higher education would be broadened. In other words "The curricula should be made to fit the individual, not the individual the curricula."[64]

The new curricular dispensation — which in actuality was a restatement of the principles of the earlier New Education — aroused little immediate controversy. It echoed wartime educational policy debated in the United States, a fact suggested by the survey committee's statement that "it is probably true that if as large a percentage of pupils is to remain in school as in the United States, the old emphasis on certain compulsory academic requirements for all must be relaxed as it has been there."[65] South of the border, "life adjustment" education was gathering force as a vocationally-oriented conservative version of progressivism in contrast to the liberal social progressivism of the 1920s and 1930s. This reaction was much more limited in Canada, if only because liberal progressivism itself remained more muted in a curriculum that continued to stress academic over vocational goals.

## Cultural Pluralism, Patriotism and Morality in the Inter-war Curriculum

After 1920, all three Prairie provinces continued to follow an aggressive assimilation policy in their schools. So-called missionary teachers of Anglo-Protestant Canadian or British birth were recruited by the Fellowship of the Maple Leaf, an Anglican Church society and by the Masonic order, to serve in Saskatchewan's immigrant bloc settlements.[66] Teachers faced serious tactical and moral dilemmas in seeking to transmit the desired British Protestant values. Those who were British-born usually had as little Canadian background as the "foreign" settlers themselves. No teachers could appear to be superior or intolerant, even though they firmly believed that their values were far superior to the customs and behaviour of the community.

The missionary teachers, like most rural Prairie teachers, continued to meet sometimes desparate problems of educational deprivation in the form of one-room schools with fifty or more pupils, meagre supplies, low salaries and teacherages that, advertised as "furnished residences," were often dilapidated shacks.[67] In the post-1945 period, however, these conditions would slowly improve as educational authorities pursued Canadianization most effectively by improving the quality of the school experience of all rural Canadian children. Sutherland observes that by raising teacher qualifications, improving attendance, re-making the curriculum, building modern schools and teacherages, raising salaries and turning schools into community centres, the Prairie provinces gradually brought virtually all children into schools where English was the sole language.[68]

The first and oldest Canadians of all represented a special case of a cultural minority. As such, they made up a great diversity of Indians, Metis and Inuit peoples. Eleven Amerindian languages and seventy dialects were spoken among the first two of these groups. Peter Sandiford naively thought in 1918 that through federal day, boarding and industrial schools "The Indians have had a 'squarer deal' in Canada than elsewhere." The unconscious irony of his factually accurate account was illustrative of prevailing attitudes towards Canada's Native peoples — a mirror image, in fact, of similar attitudes revealed by Sandiford in discussing policy toward the feeble-minded.[69]

Federal Indian educational policy, based on an acknowledged goal of "civilizing and Christianizing savages" similar to that originally established in New France, was administered through the Department of Indian Affairs set up in 1880. In 1909, Duncan Campbell Scott, poet and man of letters, became the first Superintendent of Education, responsible for the schooling of Registered Indians through reserve-based residential schools, city-based industrial schools located far from reserves, and a few day schools, all operated as joint ventures with the major churches. Industrial schools, first established in Western Canada in the 1880s, proved expensive failures. They completely separated children from their environment and were ineffective in providing promised advanced training. After 1920, when compulsory attendance of all Indian children between the ages of seven and fifteen was established, the emphasis was on residential and, increasingly, on day schools. When Scott retired in 1930, enrolments, retention and attendance had all improved. The curriculum offered boys "a plain English education adapted to the needs of the working farmer and mechanic" while girls gained domestic skills leavened in each case with games and calisthenics. On balance, aculturalization and the transformation of the Indians into an unskilled and semi-skilled workforce remained cornerstones of policy. By the late 1940s, a new policy of educating children in regular day provincial public schools was being mooted.[70]

At this time, R.A. Hoey, writing, like Sandiford, for an international audience, revealed that there were 10 000 Indian pupils between the ages of seven and sixteen for whom no educational facilities had been provided.[71] The fact that non-status Indians, Metis, Inuit and other non-reserve Indians were excluded meant that no coherent educational policy respecting Native schooling could be established. Even for registered Indians, the problems were exacerbated by the inability of government officials and educators to agree on a satisfactory curriculum for those who still led a nomadic life. As Hoey commented, in words that could have been repeated in any decade before or since;

> A feeling persists that the residential school, enrolment in which removes the Indian child from his environment, unfits him for the tasks that await him on his return to the band. Indeed, there are those who contend that the pupil frequently returns a dissatisfied and frustrated individual, unable to compete with the white man on the one hand, and unable to adjust himself to Indian life on the other.[72]

Hoey concluded that "The education of the Indian assuredly cannot be undertaken with any hope of success, if indeed it can be undertaken at all, unless scientific consideration is given to his physical and economic needs ... and ... related matters."[73] By the mid-1940s, about 20 000 Native students — or about two thirds of the relevant age group — were enrolled in school. Of these, only 490 or about 2.5 per cent were receiving a secondary education. In commenting on Inuit education, Hoey noted that since 1939, the Inuits had been legally classified with non-status Indians. However, compulsory schooling did not apply to them. As a more nomadic people with strong family bonds, parents seemed reluctant to live apart from their children during the regular school period. In any case, Hoey thought that the Inuit "are essentially content with their lot in life ..."

Other "visible minorities" included Japanese Canadians who had come to British Columbia in the 1880s. By heroic efforts in the face of severe prejudice they sought to Canadianize their children through the public schools and to maintain their culture through their own institutions, including Japanese language schools. These efforts were severely set back during World War II when their community, including their schools, was destroyed as a result of their enforced dispersal to interior British Columbia and other parts of Canada.[75] Canadian blacks were an older minority, some of whom had been in Canada as long as most Anglo-Canadians. Robin Winks has documented racial segregation in Canadian schools. Legislation permitting "coloured schools" was not finally repealed in Nova Scotia and Ontario until the 1960s.[76] The fate of the blacks in education, like that of other minorities, was an illustration of majority attitudes and policies in an era when cultural diversity, if recognized at all, was actively opposed.

Throughout the 1892-1945 period the curriculum continued to reflect an anglo-conformist ethnocentrism, revealed in the literature in frequent references to national schools, that left no room for any positive treatment of ethnicity or cultural pluralism.[77] Yet, as Jaenen has noted, anglo-conformity failed in its most radical manifestations, in part because the host society was unprepared and unable to absorb so large and so diverse a segment of the population. As a result, "the other ethnic groups" were able to survive to our own time, and, reinforced by a further vast post-World War II migration, to assert demands for the inclusion of positive multicultural content in the modern curriculum.[78]

The ambiguities of an indigenous Canadian nationalism that was admixed with imperialism continued during the inter-war years. Some native-born Canadians questioned the Canadianism of British immigrants who, they felt, needed to be Canadianized no less than "foreigners." British newcomers outnumbered those of other origins even in the polyglot Prairie provinces. In British Columbia the private schools they founded as putative exemplars of the late nineteenth century English public school ideal perpetuated a British ethos that was consciously separate from a Canadian ethos.[79] According to Putman and Weir in 1925, a similar separateness existed in the province's public schools where "a sane Canadian outlook" was inhibited by English-born pupils who, having lived in Canada most of their lives, nevertheless expected at the insistence of their parents to be called "English" rather than Canadian.[80] A few years earlier, British Columbia's Superintendent of Education had felt forced to withdraw a history of Canada that he admitted was the best on the market because the Orange Order had objected to its supposedly un-British tone. Its author, W.L. Grant, although headmaster of Upper Canada College and a decorated World War I officer, was accused of disloyalty because he had stated that Louis Riel "was no coward," and had used unflattering but accurate adjectives to describe various British personages. Totally lacking any sense of Canadian history, critics focussed entirely on the British dimension of the book.[81]

The foregoing account makes clear that, despite fears of Americanization, the cultural content of the curriculum during the inter-war period remained essentially imperial and British. The Putman-Weir Survey found a remarkable ignorance of "some of the most elementary facts about British Columbia and Canada." Pupils often knew more about Asia and Africa.[82] The Americanization of Canadian children probably derived mostly from the media, although during the 1930s American textbooks became more popular.[83] The earlier practice of "Canadianizing" foreign textbooks continued.

In 1943 the Canada and Newfoundland Education Association, renewing the concern that its parent body had expressed half a century earlier, established a committee to study Canadian history textbooks in relation to the problem of national unity. However, the Committee reported that criticism "in one section of the press" — presumably in Quebec — and letters to historians on "certain controversial questions" had led, embarrassingly, to the sudden resignation of the French-language secretary of the project.[84] Nevertheless, the Committee recommended a more balanced and comprehensive treatment of Canadian history, but its limited success in achieving the acceptance of history textbooks emphasizing "the common heritage of the Canadian people" became evident in such later reports as that of Hodgetts (1968) and the study by Trudel and Jain (1970) conducted by the Royal Commission on Bilingualism and Biculturalism.[85]

After 1920, the emphasis in moral education gradually shifted towards character and citizenship and away from pietistic indoctrination in textbooks. However, a strong Christian moral imperative remained, as revealed in the adoption, in many elementary curricula, of Hurlburt's famous volume of Bible stories for young children. To an observer of Nova Scotia schools, class reading of the Bible each morning by pupils in turn without teacher comment or explanation was impressive, for no one could leave school after a few years without having the doctrines, imagery and phraseology of the Scriptures firmly imprinted on the mind. There was no danger in future adult life of anyone missing an apposite reference to Scripture characters.[86] However, in British Columbia, by 1925 the connection between religion and morality had become less direct.[87] The new emphasis became evident in curriculum changes in various provinces between 1927 and 1937. Thus, in the former year, British Columbia's program of studies for the new junior high school explicitly set out character development and citizenship objectives. The emphasis in all subjects was on social rather than on individual objectives. Individual improvement was to be explicitly directed towards "national improvement and race-betterment."[88]

The 1936 British Columbia program of studies provided the most thorough statement of moral education through character development to be found in the curriculum of any province. In the junior high school program, teachers were enjoined "not [to] permit the demands of subject matter to crowd out attention to problems of character." The intent of the British Columbia program was that individual development, while still prized, be subservient to the ideals of state and society through assisting the adolescent to change from an individual outlet to one stressing social responsibility.[89] The tone of the school, reflecting "the outlook and ideals of its staff" was important in this regard. However, there was some inconsistency in a character education that advocated the inculcation of right habits and attitudes while insisting that students be taught to make independent, rational decisions.[90]

Despite the earlier Putman-Weir critique of mental discipline theories, the program implied that even mathematics could contribute to character formation. By teaching rigorous, impersonal logic, and by providing "an opportunity for concentration and perseverance," learning in mathematics could be extended to other fields of life. Science could serve a similar purpose for "the habit of looking for causal connections and basing one's actions upon them should [contribute] ... to character."[91] Later, British Columbia became one of the leading provinces in featuring "guidance" and "counselling" as a means of promoting the traditional moral function of the school. This development which foreshadowed more secular approaches to moral and social education after World War II paradoxically represented a reversion to earlier, more direct methods of moral instruction. As such, it was related to the growth of the mental health movement which will be discussed in Chapter 9.

During World War II, Ontario reverted to a more traditional, explicit moral and religious instruction as part of a wartime "back to the basics" thrust that combined with a new emphasis on imperial patriotism.[92] Sparked by a wartime increase in juvenile delinquency, two weekly one-half hour periods of religious instruction were prescribed in Grades 1 to 6, in addition to the regular opening exercises. Instruction could be given by clergy during school hours, based on a British syllabus recommended by the Inter-Church Committee on Weekday Religious Education. Purportedly "non-sectarian," the program emphasised New Testament studies in the junior grades, and Old Testament studies at the senior level. It aimed to promote both Biblical knowledge and Christian attitudes and behaviour. When a Jewish leader protested this narrowly Christian approach, he was bluntly reminded that "this Government is committed to the support of Christianity." Although school boards had the option of exemption from the program, only forty of 5000 school boards exercised the right.[93]

## Notes to Chapter 8

1 Granatstein, *Mackenzie King*, 52.

2 See R. Stamp, *Schools of Ontario*, 111-2.

3 For accounts of the origins of the groups referred to, particularly the YMCA and YWCA, see Diana Pedersen, "On the Trail" and "Keeping Our Good Girls." See also Murray G. Ross for a history of the YMCA in Canada.

4 See Prang, "The God," 4-6, 16.

5 R. Stamp, "Canadian High Schools," 80.

6 Marsh, 218. See also Coulter, "The Working Young of Edmonton" for a useful account of teenage experience with school and work during the 1920s.

7 Granatstein, *Mackenzie King*, 65-6, 91.

8 See Bissell, *Young Vicent Massey*.

9 See Prang, "Nationalism."

10 Lang, *Education*, 276-7; Ney, "Foreign Film."

11 Lang, "Foreign Magazine," 7, 9.

12 Coats and MacLean, 7.

13 Patterson, "Society and Education," 373.

14 See Goulson, 341-2.

15 S.D. Clark, *Canadian Society*, 37-8.

16 R. Lambert, "Next Steps," 82.

17 Ibid. and R. Lambert, "The National Advisory Council," 4, 10.

18 Phillips, *Development*, 345.

19 Lewis, "Physical Perfection," 154-5; Sheehan, "And What Could," 19-23.

20 Crowley, 1-5, 15.

21 Lyons, "In Pursuit," 29, 73.

22 Ibid., 29, 80, 105.

23 Ibid., 109-10, 155.

24 See G. Pilkington, "History."

25 Currie, 25.

26 See Learned and Sills.

27 Woodhead, *NCCU Proceedings* (1927), 98.

28 McNally, 41-2. On the origin of the CCER see J.C. Miller, *National Government*, 583.

29 Canadian Youth Commission, 5, 15, 26.

30 Patterson, "Society and Education," 366.

31 Angus, 365. See also Hauck, *Some Educational Factors*.

32 Angus, 105-6.

33 See C.E. Phillips, "Study of the United States" and Hauck, "Education." Also CNEA, "A Study of National History Textbooks."

34 MacDougall, viii from introduction to 1973 edition by R.C. Brown.

35 V. Ross, 137.

36 Heap, "New Patterns."

37 See Sheehan, "Social Change," 20-23.

38 Abbott, "Hostile Landscapes." See also R. Stamp, *Schools of Ontario*, 137-8.

39 D. Jones, "Better School Days," 126.

40 Foght, *Survey,* 83.

41 Ibid., 8, 44, 88.

42 J.C. Miller, *Rural Schools,* ix-x, 67.

43 N.S.AR, 1910, 79.

44 Putman and Weir, *Survey,* 236-7.

45 Cited in Lawr and Gidney, *Educating Canadians,* 202-5.

46 N.S.AR, 1940, 40, 83.

47 D. Jones, "Schols and Social Disintegration," 11, 16-7.

48 Alberta Department of Education, *What Is and What Might Be,* 3-5.

49 Argue, 4, 32.

50 Cited in Lawr and Gidney, *Educating Canadians,* 202-3.

51 Conrad, 78.

52 C.E. Phillips, *Development,* 292-3.

53 M. Cameron, *Property Taxation,* 49.

54 R. Stamp, "Vocational Objectives," 255.

55 R. Stamp, *Schools of Ontario,* 115.

56 R. Stamp, "Vocational Objectives," 254.

57 A. Crawford, 56, 61.

58 Fluxgold, *Federal.*

59 Alberta Department of Education, *What Is and What Might Be,* 3, 5, 21.

60 Marsh, 250, 428.

61 James, 73, 77-8.

62 Ibid. 82.

63 *CNEA Proceedings,* 1944, 21.

64 CNEA *Survey,* 1943, 36-7, 45.

65 Ibid., 41.

66 See Lyons, "For St. George" and Barber, "The School."

67 Barber, "The School."

68 N. Sutherland, *Children,* 214.

69 Sandiford, *Comparative,* 431-3.

70 Titley.

71 Hoey, 192.

72 Ibid.

73 Ibid., 194.

74 Ibid., 194-7.

75 See Dahlie, "The Japanese in B.C.," "The Japanese Challenge" Ashworth, *The Forces.*

76 Winks.

77 H. Palmer and Troper, 19-20.

78 Jaenen (1971) cited in Palmer and Troper, 19.

79 See Barman, Chapter 2 and 4 for a discussion of the ideal and its transfer to Canada.

80 Putman and Weir, *Survey*, 148-9.

81 Humphries.

82 Putman and Weir, *Survey*, 148.

83 Parvin, 116-7.

84 CNEA, "Report to the Committee for the Study of Canadian History Textbooks," 6.

85 See Hodgetts, *What Culture* and Trudel and Jain, *Canadian History Textbooks*.

86 Nichols, 320.

87 Van Brummelen, "Shifting Perspectives."

88 B.C. Department of Education, *Program of Studies for the Junior High School, 1927-28*, 5-6, 35.

89 *B.C. Program of Studies for the Junior High School, 1936-7*, 263-66.

90 Labar.

91 Putman and Weir, *Survey*, 259-60.

92 R. Stamp, *Schools of Ontario*, 178-81.

93 Ibid. See also Patterson, "Society and Education," 380. The Hope Report, 125.

# CHAPTER 9

## MEDICALIZING
## THE CURRICULUM,
## 1920-1945

*... social attitudes, shyness and day-dreaming are regarded as matters of importance — probably more so than academic achievement."*
(William Line and J.D. Griffin, 1937)

### Mental Hygiene, Special Education and Mental Testing

As scientific education gathered force during the inter-war period, inter-related developments in mental hygiene, auxiliary or special education, mental testing, child study and guidance reinforced the growing socializing pressures on the school and expanded the non-instructional part of the teacher's role. Conservatives continued to deplore the dilution of the academic function of the school and the overcrowding of the curriculum which they claimed were the consequences of the new trends.

Mental hygiene was associated with the "eugenical movement" and focussed on what was called "the threat of the feebleminded." Before 1920, it was assumed that the causes of feeble-mindedness and mental illness were primarily hereditary. In contrast to the reasoned arguments put forth by other groups in the public health movement, those of the mental hygienists were frequently alarmist and even hysterical in tone.[1] The hereditarian bias of the time was evident in Peter Sandiford's call in 1914 for the limitation of the output of "the defective type." Expressing his concerns in holocaustic tones, Sandiford commented, "We want no lethal chambers but we do want homes where those unfortunates, while passing a calm and happy life, will be prevented from adding defective offspring to the already heavy burdens of normal society."[2]

In 1918, a national mental hygiene movement had emerged, with the organization of the Canadian National Committee for Mental Hygiene (the CNCMH) and the publication of the *Canadian Journal of Mental Hygiene*. Under the leadership of Clarence Hincks, (himself a former mental patient), and Dean C.K. Clarke of the University of Toronto medical faculty, the committee brought together mental hygiene leaders in various provinces. The movement was closely linked with that in the United States. Indeed, no professional movement in the two countries displayed a closer symbiotic relationship across the international boundary in terms of interaction among the principal figures, the common concerns they shared and the funding sources they tapped. In seeking to achieve their aims, groups in both countries gave high priority to work in schools.

The North American mental hygiene movement attracted the support of elites in the political, business and university establishments. In Canada, supporters included the university presidents and medical deans at McGill and Toronto, the premiers of Quebec and Saskatchewan, Lady Eaton and Sir Edward Beatty, the head of the Canadian Pacific Railway who served as chairperson and president of the CNCMH for eighteen years. Using a top-down strategy, these leaders adapted mental hygiene ideas in the service of traditional Canadian values.[3] This elite support, including that of distinguished academic psychologists and medical researchers, belies later accusations by critics such as Hilda Neatby that the Canadian educational establishment had foisted un-Canadian socializing functions on the schools. It would appear, instead, that mental hygiene and related innovations were foisted on an often resistant school system as a result of outside establishment pressure. Thus, in 1920, Clarence Hincks was highly critical of Ontario's slow progress in establishing special classes for mentally deficient children.[4]

Hincks' criticism reflected the continuing preoccupation of Canadian mental hygienists with feeblemindedness. Sutherland has noted how the CNCMH and its affiliates concentrated on four ways of improving the mental health of Canadian children.[5] Since New Canadians were thought to be especially prone to feeble-mindedness, reformers demanded stricter efforts to exclude mentally defective children and adults from the ranks of immigrants. They also wanted feeble-minded and purportedly delinquency-prone youngsters excluded from public schools. These unfortunates were to be segregated, both in their own interest and, more importantly, to prevent the moral contamination and academic retardation of normal pupils. As C.K. Clarke put it in arguing for special classes, "a wise public school board ... will go to no end of trouble to keep its normal children free from sources of contamination."[6] Finally, notes Sutherland, the feeble-minded must not be allowed "to reproduce their kind." In at least two provinces, Alberta and British Columbia, this view resulted in legislation permitting sterilization of so-called defectives.[7]

As early as 1910, special classes were being organized in Toronto for children with physical handicaps and speech defects and for those judged to be mentally deficient or feeble-minded.[8] Although in British Columbia the early emphasis appears to have been more on preventive public health than on schools, Vancouver also organized its first class for subnormal children at this time. Encouraged by the recommendations of the 1919 British Columbia Mental Health Survey, trustees shortly set up a special education staff of sixteen under an American-trained school psychologist. Teachers of "lowgrade feeble-minded children" were sent to the United States for special training. The Vancouver curriculum put special emphasis on manual work, guided by the view that its real value was "not the finished product but the growth of the individual child."[9] A survey of institutions for deaf and delinquent children included a school "where the foreign element is very great." In 1921, custodial care was provided for "lowgrade defectives," leaving the Vancouver schools to concentrate on what was called "the moron problem."[10] In Victoria, the Binet-Simon intelligence test was used to identify "problematic cases" for a special class selected by what a report called "the delicate if sometimes cruel practice of entering those who are unobjectionable in appearances." Within the special class, Montessori methods and materials were used, a system thought admirable for "making the children responsible for the care and order of [the] materials ...."[11]

In 1914, Ontario passed an Auxiliary Classes Act for children unable to cope with the regular curriculum. Later, Dr. Harry Amoss developed detailed categories of the "subnormal" including the "rural subnormal." This group, Amoss implied, had less need of special treatment, since rural children received so much practical education out of school that would serve their later likely vocations.[12] In the early 1920s, the CNCMH estimated that there were 161 classes for subnormal children in operation throughout the country.[13]

During the 1920s, the debate over "nature versus nurture" continued. As "mental hygiene" became redefined by behavioural research, environmental theories gained ascendancy among medical people and scientists, although eugenics as a pseudo-science remained influential in practice. Redefinition led to a modification of attitudes towards the feeble-minded. The belief that the IQ test was a direct and accurate measurement of inherited intelligence was increasingly questioned.[14] New attitudes were reflected in the new faith in the educability of subnormal children. As S.B. Sinclair, Ontario's inspector of "auxiliary classes" put it in 1924, such classes would make subnormal children "law-abiding, helpful, happy citizens with good habits, respect for the law and a willingness to work."[15]

In the early 1940s there were 525 special classes for low ability children throughout Canada, nearly all of which were concentrated in urban areas.[16] By this time, faith in mental measurement and testing as a means of solving all problems of pupil classification seems to have declined somewhat.[17] The fallacious connection between mental retardation and delinquency was increasingly discounted by psychologists. Delinquent behaviour was now sometimes ascribed to a rigid, bookish curriculum.[18] Some attention was now being paid to the gifted. In 1924-25, Dr. C.C. Goldring of Toronto wrote a series of articles in which he pleaded for special education for the "supernormal" whom he defined as those with IQs over 120.[19] However, by the 1940s there were still only four classes for gifted children in Canada, two of which were located in Montreal and two in Saskatoon.[20]

During the inter-war years, a prevailing medical model led to the categorization of special children into three groups: the mentally retarded, the emotionally disturbed, and those with nervous disorders. Chambers sees World War II as a turning point in policy, practices and attitudes towards exceptionality. The need for daycare and the greater contact of mothers with experts and external agencies contributed to this change. A more objective and less prejudiced attitude gradually began to carry over to the treatment of special children in schools.[21]

As the foregoing discussion suggests, the testing movement was closely related to mental hygiene and special education. We noted earlier that the movement in Canada owed much to the influence of Thorndike, whose ex-student, Peter Sandiford, established a testing and research unit at the University of Toronto. The American testing movement had its origins in the work of British and French psychologists, particularly the latter from whom the famous Binet-Simon intelligence test was borrowed and adapted, in the form of the so-called Stanford Revision. By 1910, Lewis Terman had popularized the concept of the Intelligence Quotient (IQ). Shortly, intelligence testing techniques were being applied to achievement testing in most subject areas and to nearly every aspect of educational practice.[22]

Sandiford, although basically an hereditarian, believed, like Thorndike, that human nature was plastic and modifiable, and thus improvable. Greater attention should be given to individual differences which could be identified by tests, thereby enhancing curriculum differentiation.[23] Testing also contributed to the formalization of the curriculum by introducing an aura of efficiency that reinforced conservative, stabilizing influences. It was no accident that testing was the dimension of the new scientific movement that appealed most to Canadians, with their longstanding devotion to examinations as a means of curriculum control. The view of many educators was epitomized in 1923 by Dr. Harry Amoss, when he asserted the need of the school "to test its new material scientifically before processing, just like any manufacturing concern."[24] By this time an interest in the psychological assessment of all children was developing, as scientific or "new type," objective tests, began to influence examination systems and promotion policies in various provinces. This development will be discussed in Chapter 12 with reference to achievement tests. Here, the focus will be on true mental, i.e., intelligence tests.

As we noted in Chapter 5, the first intelligence tests in Canada had been administered in Toronto more than a decade earlier. After the formation of the CNCMH in 1918, tests were used in Ontario, British Columbia and other provinces to identify feeble-minded children. In British Columbia, the Putman-Weir Survey hired Peter Sandiford in 1924 to carry out the first large scale testing of intelligence and achievement in any province. Sandiford ascribed "deep social significance" to differences in intelligence levels among children from different parental occupational backgrounds and racial origins. He concluded that the high test scores of those from professional backgrounds could be explained by the fact that "Intelligence sufficiently high to achieve success in a profession is handed down to the children."[25]

Where racial variations were concerned, Sandiford noted that children of northern European, especially of British origin, rated highest in intelligence. There was little difference in mentality among the British subgroups "although the claim of the Scots to a superior mentality is sustained." Children of Japanese and Chinese origin proved to be superior to the average white population, a result that Sandiford attributed to superior selection among those who migrated to Canada from Asia. Such a selective process, he noted, was a well known phenomenon among immigrants. He did not explain why this phenomenon was not evident among some European groups, whose poor performance, he implied, indicated that they might be a threat to the mental level of British Columbia.[26]

The application of testing and of related medical metaphors to actual curriculum development was illustrated in British Columbia during the 1930s. The 1936-7 Programme of Studies for Senior Secondary Schools suggested that test results might indicate needed changes in content, materials and method.[27] In the British Columbia Junior High School Programme of Studies for the same year, a major purpose of testing was described as "Diagnosis leading to remedial treatment."[28] In Ontario at this time, Sandiford's colleague, William Line, observed that testing had been useful in helping to determine the mental age levels at which various skills and bodies of knowledge could be introduced so that the curriculum could be made "to run more smoothly" and be better fitted to student capacities and to teaching techniques.[29]

## Mental Health for All: Child Study and Guidance

Cohen has described how, in the United States after 1920, the "mental health point of view" resulted in a shift from a curative to a preventive role for mental hygienists, and to the idea of the school's responsibility for children's personality development. The "medicalization" of the curriculum led experts to identify three major sources of school stress requiring rectification: failure which led to feelings of inferiority, truancy, delinquency and to anti-social attitudes; the academic subject-centred curriculum; and disciplinary procedures. To one mental hygienist "the reason for misfit children was a misfit curriculum." Teachers were urged to de-emphasize content and subject matter, and to pay more attention to the child's personality development as opposed to his intellectual development. They were also urged to take the "mental hygiene point of view" towards discipline and children's attendant behaviour problems. Misbehaviour was "not a sin but a symptom" as one mental hygienist put it, requiring treatment rather than punishment.[30]

A therapeutic model of schooling that made the adjustment of personality the chief goal of education also attracted interest in Canada, initially at McGill and the University of Toronto. Later, medical personnel such as Dr. Baruch Silverman, a Montreal psychiatrist, and Dr. Karl Bernhardt of the University of Toronto, both described the rigid academic demands of schooling as a barrier to mental health.[31] Mental hygiene research was supported by the CNCMH research committee through funds from American foundations. In Toronto, W.E. Blatz, William Line and others gradually formed links between the Toronto schools and other agencies. As Canadian reformers, like their American counterparts, began to apply mental hygiene principles to all school children, they exhibited a growing interest in psychological assessment, child development and parent education.[32] All these developments support Sutherland's contention that, by the 1920s, the mental hygienists had placed themselves and their ideas in a very central place in the whole child welfare movement.[33] Inevitably, they saw the school as the most obvious and accessible place to carry out their new self-imposed mandate. In his study of school discipline in Canada over a century, Johnson attributed an improvement in pupil-teacher relations in part to mental hygiene. The decline in the use of corporal punishment, the promotion of extra-curricular activities, and cautious experiments in student self-government assisted "remedial discipline." Nevertheless, teachers remained more concerned with misdemeanours affecting classroom control and with moral transgressions than with undesirable personality traits.[34]

In Toronto during the 1930s, J.D. Griffin and William Line developed a Division of Education and Mental Hygiene within the CNCMH. The primary purpose was to involve schools. The two men published *Mental Hygiene — A Manual for Teachers* in 1937, in collaboration with S.R. Laycock of the University of Saskatchewan. Children who were "shy, seclusive, persistently timid and recessive in their actions" could have such defects remedied through the socializing activities of games, activities and group projects under the direction of capable teachers. Laycock and Line were influenced by British theories derived from their overseas studies under the famous psychologist Charles Spearman, and under Cyril Burt, whose hereditarian theories would later make him infamous.[35]

In 1939, Laycock attributed dislike of school to the fact that "the child is maladjusted to the curriculum."[36] In 1944, he surveyed the mental health climate in 167 classrooms in five provinces, in an attempt "to appraise the degree to which mental hygiene objectives entered into the aims of education in the various provinces, as well as the extent to which mental hygiene principles permeated the curriculum [and] teaching methods ... of the public and high schools." The impact was little apparent, a fact that suggests that, in Canada, mental hygiene was honoured more in theory than in practice. Laycock recommended better teacher training in the principles of mental health.[37]

Earlier, Line had commented on the implications of what he saw as a radical curriculum change with the advent of the "activity program" in

Canada. Citing Peter Sandiford, he observed that psychology had earlier contributed to curriculum reform by suggesting "more effective means and conditions of pedagogy" that saved time and energy in the teaching of both knowledge and skills. The new activity methods which Line optimistically called "the most significant [educational] movement we have ever had in Canada," provided a school environment far more conducive to mental health than any formal curriculum. Such methods enabled teachers, so much more knowledgeable about children than were curriculum policy makers, to treat subject matter not as an end in itself, "but [as] a means to an end — child development."[38]

In 1939, Griffin undertook a demonstration project to encourage thoughtful discussion of human behaviour among senior elementary school children through the use of films and free, non-directive discussion. The fact that no attempt was made to teach the "right answers" or to inculcate particular ethical or moral principles or values was a far cry from traditional Christian moral education, even though the broad objectives were basically similar. The experiment foreshadowed later values education in treating social and moral decisions as tentative and temporary, open to further review and development, rather than as final or absolute. The "Human Relations Class" was a prototype for a similar experiment carried out on a wider scale in the upper middle-class Toronto suburb of Forest Hill Village ("Crestwood Heights") in 1948 by Griffin and J.R. Seeley.[39]

In 1945, a National Committee for School Health Research was organized; it made the mental health of teachers and students an important dimension of its research. A survey of inspectors and principals in all provinces complemented Laycock's classroom survey. While the home was preponderantly blamed for mental health problems, the school was criticized for its large classes, lock-step curriculum, and rigid examination and grading systems. Unsympathetic teachers also contributed to problems. "Generally speaking," the group commented "the teacher still teaches subjects instead of children and thinks of mental health only when overt acts need disciplinary action."[40] Among the curricular changes proposed were compulsory high school courses dealing with marriage, parenthood and related topics.

The pioneer of scientific child study as a distinct endeavour was undoubtedly W.E. Blatz. Through his American-funded longitudinal studies of young children conducted at the Institute for Child Study in Toronto, through teacher and parent education and through his encouragement of research across Canada, Blatz helped child study to form its first formal link with public education. During the 1930s he began to lecture to kindergarten and primary teachers at Toronto Teachers' College.[41] Although Blatz was accused of permissiveness, his main goal was to promote mental health in a humane but structured environment in which social control based on "security theory" was emphasized. Security was defined as "the individual ability to make decisions and accept the consequences."[42] Although there was a Freudian influence in the work of Blatz and his colleagues, arising out of a belief in the crucial importance of the early formative years, Canadian child study appears to have been less influenced by Freudian theory and to have been more behaviouristic and more structured than its American counterpart.[43] Security theory was highly consistent with traditional Canadian moral imperatives.

From its beginnings in Ontario, scientific child study spread to other provinces. S.R. Laycock, who had met C.M. Hincks in Edmonton in 1921, helped to introduce the movement to Western Canada. Later, the Canadian Mental Health Association supported Laycock's salary at the University of Saskatchewan, where he worked with the Saskatoon School Board as a clinical psychologist during the 1930s. There, in addition to his work in mental hygiene discussed above, he organized some of the earliest classes for gifted children in Canada.[44] In Manitoba, the Winnipeg Child Guidance Clinic had its genesis in "psychometrics" in the city's schools in 1925.[45]

The guidance movement in Canada, with its roots in earlier "manners and morals" teaching, was an American innovation closely related to mental hygiene and vocational education. The early mental health surveys in various provinces after 1918 provided data for the development of vocational guidance.[46] Like auxiliary education, guidance was inextricably intertwined with testing. Testing was seen as especially useful in educational guidance as a means of modifying the unrealistic expectations of children and their parents.[47] Educational guidance had strong curricular implications because it became the basis for directing students into various courses and options. E.C. Webster, an industrial psychologist at McGill, saw the need for both educational and vocational guidance to help students resist parental pressure, or at least to assist the home to make wiser decisions.[48] Later, personal guidance became an aspect of Canadian practice. Nearly all the tests and textbooks used in guidance work in Canada were American in origin.

Although vocational guidance was being offered at the Central Technical School in Toronto during the 1920s, the movement developed very little before 1940.[49] In 1943, the Vocational Guidance Centre was established as a sub-division of the Canadian National Committee for Mental Hygiene, and was later incorporated into the Ontario College of Education. The Guidance Branch of the Ontario Department of Education was established in 1944. A year later, the Centre began to publish *The School Guidance Worker*, which in time became a forum for the discussion of curriculum issues. The Centre also distributed tests, forms, information and monographs. Group guidance in Ontario was made compulsory in Grade 9 through a course called Occupations, and became what Phillips later termed "a non-formal subject." According to Stamp, it was a very unpopular course.[50]

Proponents of guidance argued that it should foster individual development, provide exploratory experiences, broaden interests and generally provide accurate educational and occupational information and counselling facilities.[51] That these somewhat utopian aims fell short of achievement was implied by the 1950 Royal Commission on Education, which in the Hope Report expressed disquiet over the naive belief in the universal efficacy of counselling services, and the tendency to transfer to counsellors all the guidance responsibilities of teachers instead of regarding such services as supplementary to those provided by the latter.[52]

During the 1940s, the guidance movement spread across Canada from Ontario, and guidance directors had been appointed in several provinces by the end of the decade. Like its leadership in special education, Ontario's leadership in guidance was remarkable, given the fact that the province lagged behind others in adopting progressive curricular practices during the interwar period. An explanation may lie in the hypothesis that both movements were consistent with the conservative social efficiency ideology of Ontario administrative progressives.

In some respects, British Columbia led Ontario in guidance. By 1943, a weekly guidance period was required in all secondary schools and all large high schools had specialist counsellors.[53] Earlier, in 1936-7, the province had developed one of the most elaborate guidance curricula in the country, based largely on American sources. The junior high school program of studies described the overall aim as "Purposeful Living," which was intended to include happiness, character development, service in the community, correct attitudes in group relationships, orientation to the school program according to abilities and aptitudes, exploration of occupational fields, and the "gainful use of leisure time." According to the program, every effort must be made to correlate the curriculum with life and the local community, in particular with local occupations. The principal must be aware of such matters as why students left school, "the after-school history of withdrawals and graduates," the causes of subject failures and withdrawals, the extent of student leadership and "evidence of bad placement, retardation, over-acceleration."[54]

At the senior high school level, an elaborate handbook identified four dimensions of guidance: educational, moral and social, civic, and vocational, all of which were outlined in considerable detail. The handbook held that moral and social guidance should permeate the curriculum and the whole life of the school, although in the classroom a "moral should not be tacked to every tale." Among the "concrete problems" to be explored were such questions as "What are some of the means adopted by people to acquire popularity?" A study of "social customs of today" included consideration of how best to accept and decline both formal and informal invitations; other topics included table manners, telephone etiquette, deportment at social gatherings, the girl and her escort, the boy as an escort, and boy and girl friendships. Civic guidance covered a broad range of topics from local to world citizenship. Qualities of character and civic leadership were to be learned through activities such as the student council, and school clubs. The guidance class itself should be organized as a club and conducted by means of parliamentary procedure. Vocational guidance included detailed studies of industries and occupations. Recommended activities included an occupational study of a factory or department store and group or individual studies of specific occupations.[55]

The British Columbia guidance program was a remarkably ambitious one which, in the hands of a sympathetic, highly trained teacher, might have been effective. Its effectiveness appears to have been limited by a lack of available time and of qualified teachers. Guidance programs everywhere over the years suffered from becoming academically formalized and abstract and thus removed from the "real world" concerns they were supposed to address; at the same time they were condemned as intellectually sterile, made up of mundane and trivial content. The paradox of this charge was that guidance courses clearly had a rarely realized potential for rigorous intellectual treatment. Subject-oriented teachers lacked the commitment and the competence to enable its principles to permeate their syllabi. Guidance teachers or counsellors were not renaissance men and women and could hardly have been expected to implement a program like that of British Columbia which, if taken seriously, could have constituted most of the curriculum of a school.

In summary, and in the absence of detailed research to date, the impact of therapeutic, mental hygiene approaches in Canadian schools before 1945 seems to have been uneven and indirect. These approaches seem to have had their greatest effect on the development of special education as a more positive view of the educability of those deemed to be both mentally and morally deficient gradually developed. This view reflected a humanitarian impulse, although a social efficiency impulse remained uppermost. Although the mental hygiene movement emphasized the need to broaden educational goals beyond mere intellectual training, its impact on the formalistic curriculum of the typical classroom appears to have been almost nil. Nor does mental hygiene appear to have alleviated punitive disciplinary measures very significantly. Mental hygiene may have spurred the growing secularization of moral education, moving it away from the overt inculcation of traditional Christian moral values. Its chief overall effect may have been to medicalize the professional language of educators as medical metaphors such as symptom, diagnosis, remedial, treatment and similar terms came into use.[56]

## Notes to Chapter 9

1 N. Sutherland, *Children*, 72. The terms "mental hygiene" and "mental health" were often used interchangeably, although the former connoted a psycho-medical approach stressing abnormality focussed as noted, on feeble-mindedness. Later, "mental health" implied a psychological concern for the healthy personality development of all children.

2 Sandiford, "Heredity," 494.

3 T. Richardson, "Mental Hygiene Movement," 10-14.

4 Hincks, address to the Ontario Educational Association, *Toronto Star,* April 1, 1920.

5 N. Sutherland, *Children,* 73-6.

6 C.K. Clarke, 229-31.

7 N Sutherland, *Children,* 75-6.

8 Fleming, III, *Schools,* 363.

9 T. Richardson, "Canadian National Committee," 9-10, 20.

10 N. Sutherland, *Children,* 76.

11 Canadian National Committee for Mental Hygiene (CNCMH), "Mental Hygiene Survey," 21-2.

12 Amoss, 429.

13 N. Sutherland, *Children,* 76.

14 McConnachie, 1, 3, 7.

15 Sinclair, 186.

16 C.E. Phillips, *Development,* 370.

17 Conn.

18 "Editorial Notes — The Non-Academic Child," *The School,* XVIII, no. 8 (April 1930), 603.

19 Goldring, "Wanted," 284.

20 C.E. Phillips, *Development,* 370.

21 Chambers, 2-4.

22 See Cremin, *Transformation,* 186; Selleck, *New Education,* 287.

23 Sandiford, "Heredity," 495.

24 Amoss, 429.

25 See Sandiford's report in Putman and Weir, *Survey,* 456.

26 Ibid. 460-1, 508.

27 *B.C. Program of Studies for Senior Secondary Schools, 1936-7,* 20-1.

28 *B.C. Program of Studies for Junior Secondary Schools, 1936-7,* 18.

29 Line, "Psychology," 661.

30 Cohen, "Mental Hygiene Movement," 124, 130-1.

31 Silverman, 24; Bernhardt, 8.

32 McConnachie, 11-12.

33 Sutherland, *Children,* 70.

34 Johnson, "Changing," 28-31.

35 See Griffin, Line and Laycock, *Mental Hygiene.* A good account of Laycock's work in the mental health movement and of British influences on him and Line will be found in Chernefsky.

36 Laycock, "The Diagnostic Approach," 463.

37 Laycock, "Mental Health Survey."

38 Line, "Psychology," 661-3.

39 Griffin, "Mental Health Canada," 161-4. See also Griffin and Seeley, "Education for Mental Health."

40 A.J. Phiilips, *Some Data*, 15, 11-19.

41 McConnachie, 12. See also Northway, "Child Study in Canada," 27, 32.

42 See Fleming, V, *Supporting Institutions*, 206 and McConnachie, 14.

43 Interview with Jeannette Urbas, former teacher, Institute of Child Study, June 23, 1982. For an explication of Blatz's basic concept see his "Security Theory" (bibliography).

44 Chernefsky.

45 Northway, "Child Study," 20-2.

46 Van Hesteren, 43, 47, 57.

47 Long, 559-60.

48 Webster, 15.

49 Fleming III, *Schools*, 249.

50 Van Hesteren, 155. See also C.E. Phillips, *Development*, 445 and R. Stamp, *Schools of Ontario*, 197.

51 Fleming, III, *Schools*, 250.

52 The Hope Report, 99.

53 King cited in CNEA Proceedings, 1943, 29.

54 B.C. *Program of Studies for the Junior High School*, 1936-7, 270.

55 B.C. *Program of Studies for the Senior High School*, 1936-7, 443, 462-3, 466.

56 See Cohen, "Mental Hygiene Movement."

# CHAPTER 10

## PROGRESSIVE-CONSERVATIVE CHANGE IN THE MAINSTREAM CURRICULUM, 1920-1945

*The new activity or enterprise program implies a new concept of teaching in which book learning and preparation for examinations give place to socialized classroom activities and learning procedures.*

*(Saskatchewan Department of Education, 1940)*

*In our anxiety to get away from the traditional school where the teacher did too much of the thinking for the pupils, we must not allow ourselves to swing to the opposite pole and adopt in its entirety the program of the ultra-progressive school of thought.*

*(Saskatchewan Department of Education, 1941)*

### Rhetoric and Reality in the Elementary Curriculum

After 1920, some curriculum policy-makers, especially in western Canada, began to use the American term "progressive education" as a theoretical label for their reform efforts. Elsewhere, educators continued to use the term "New Education" which had been popularized in Great Britain. According to Selleck, by 1914 British educators had gradually come to define schooling as more than the three Rs, and to view rote learning as less acceptable than in the past. By 1939, concepts such as play, interest and correlation had become part of a uniform set of ideas and procedures that constituted a new intellectual orthodoxy, although British classroom practice was little modified until after World War II.[1]

In North America, progressivism was a loosely applied label, a complex reality that had both liberal and conservative dimensions. Its defining characteristic was change, and the questioning of long established policies and practices.[2] American "administrative progressives" who sought to centralize education under expert leadership in the interests of social efficiency and social control were probably best exemplified in Canada by George M. Weir. The administrative progressives were closely allied with the "educational scientists," of whom Peter Sandiford was the best Canadian example. Both groups shared a conservative social philosophy. The "pedagogical progressives," possibly best represented in Canada by Hubert Newland in Alberta, sought to translate John Dewey's ideas into classroom practice through such means as the "project method" and the "activity curriculum."[3]

In this discussion, the focus will be on curriculum change in the elementary school, with subsequent reference to change at the high school level. Emphasis will be given to the 1930-45 period, which Peter Sandiford described as the era of the first wholesale curriculum revision Canadian educators had ever undertaken.[4] The preceding decade, possibly best described as an interregnum between the pre-1914 New Education thrust and that of the progressives during the 1930s, was one of cautious, sporadic experimentation. Carried out mainly in western Canada and spreading east in a process that was the reverse of that of the New Education, experimentation was accompanied by considerable theoretical ferment as educators attempted to sort out the many ideas and practices that continued to emanate from American and British sources. Much activity was devoted to proselytizing teachers and public and to formulating policy. As in other areas of social policy, a good deal of the effort in western Canada reflected a growing resentment over eastern Canadian domination. This was quite explicit in a statement of one Alberta politician in 1928, when he expressed the hope that needed curriculum change should not be "grey with Ontario dust and heavy with Ontario prejudice" but should "really meet our particular needs in harmony with the progressive ideals now becoming current in the educational world."[5]

Inter-war curriculum ferment may conveniently be dated from Saskatchewan's Foght Report of 1918, discussed in Chapter 7. Foght's appointment illustrated an assumption, common in the western provinces especially, that American expertise and ideas could, with modification, be applied in a Canadian environment that was not thought to be fundamentally different from that of the United States.[6] By 1922, Saskatchewan normal school students were receiving instruction in W.H. Kilpatrick's project method, the most publicized pedagogical innovation of American progressivism during the inter-war years. In Canada it was later known as "enterprise education," forming, with adaptations, the centrepiece of curriculum revision during the 1930s.

Kilpatrick, a disciple and colleague of Dewey at Columbia, had elaborated the project method in 1918 in a monograph of that title. It became possibly the single most influential publication by any progressive educator. He defined a project "as a wholehearted, purposeful activity proceeding in a social environment."[7] The essence of the method was the reorganization of the curriculum into a succession of projects which, by emphasizing "purposeful activity" consonant with the child's own goals, would enhance learning through using Thorndike's concept of positive reinforcement. At the same time, it was intended to serve Dewey's social purpose by creating a school environment more nearly typical of life itself than that of the traditional curriculum. Although Kilpatrick's emphasis on educative intellectual and moral experiences, which was designed to develop character in the interests of group welfare, was fully consistent with Dewey's philosophy, his excessively child-centred stance and his denigration of extrinsic "fixed in advance" subject matter put him at odds with the great philosopher.[8]

Other progressive methods were associated with the Dalton, Winnetka and Unit Mastery Individualized Teaching Plans, which were introduced in Alberta following that province's curriculum revision of 1922. All three plans aimed at individualizing instruction, and had been introduced into the United States by the end of World War I. The Dalton Plan, originating in Massachusetts, was given a five-year trial in Edmonton, beginning in 1924.[9] It used an assignment or contract system under which the pupil worked individually in "subject laboratories" somewhat akin to modern resource centres or working stations. In theory, the entire school could be organized in this way within the traditional timetable and administrative system. In practice, it was used only partially in Alberta as what Sheane called "a challenge to the recitation."[10] Nevertheless, its acceptance in far-off Edmonton was testimony to the rapid spread of innovations at this time.

The Unit Mastery Plan developed by Henry C. Morrison, a leading progressive at the University of Chicago, organized curriculum content and activities into correlated units of instruction aimed at developing skills, content mastery and unified learning experiences. The Winnetka Plan, pioneered by Carleton Washburne in Illinois, was another individualized system in which the curriculum was divided into two parts: the tool subjects or "common essentials" which were individualized, and the "self-expressive" subjects, pursued on a group basis. All three plans were introduced into several other provinces although their overall impact does not appear to have been significant.[11] In Saskatchewan, normal school students were being examined on the new approaches before the end of the 1920s.[12]

Meanwhile, Alberta educators made the most systematic effort to develop a theoretical base that would undergird curriculum change. In G. Fred McNally, Superintendent of Schools and H.C. Newland, a departmental official who had been a founder of the Canadian Teachers' Federation in 1919, this province had two of the nation's leading progressives. Both men were eastern Canadians who had completed their doctorates at Columbia and Chicago respectively. In 1927, Newland founded the Edmonton Education Society, a study group organized for the purpose of discussing the new theories. Two years later, the Calgary Progress Club was established with similar aims.[13] These groups made intensive studies of the writings of the "social reconstructionists" and other American progressives. Social reconstruction in the United States was associated with George S. Counts and other progressives at Columbia University, who argued that the school should take an overtly political stance and promote the building of a new social order. Newland and some socialist-minded educators in Saskatchewan were among the very few Canadian school reformers who advocated this view.[14]

The chief aim of the Edmonton and Calgary groups was to develop true professionalism and professional status and, most importantly, to promote an elite leadership of well-informed and well-qualified educators. Newland and his colleagues aimed subtly to convert the existing leadership, especially in the Department of Education, to the cause of progressive change. In a relatively short time the members themselves assumed positions of leadership and influence in Alberta education and became a highly successful pressure group. In the process, classroom teachers gradually assumed less importance. Thus, while the initial aims were realized, the ideal of professionalizing the entire teaching body was not.[15]

As revealed by Patterson in his analysis of provincial curriculum guides, annual reports, teachers' professional journals and magazines, and interviews with retired teachers, a progressive thrust was evident from coast to coast in the program revisions of the 1930s.[16] Saskatchewan had taken the lead in 1931, with the first formal acceptance by a Canadian provincial authority of the ideas and practices associated with the progressive education movement.[17] Two years earlier, Carleton Washburne had been invited to the province to explain the Winnetka plan and to advise how it could be adapted to Saskatchewan's four thousand one-room rural schools. Subsequently, teachers attended summer schools at Winnetka and tried out Washburne's ideas experimentally. As revision proceeded, broader objectives for schooling were promulgated, including those related to the mental health of all children, which S.R. Laycock had been promoting in the province for several years. In obeisance to Dewey, education was termed "a process of growth and development" having no final stage. The learning of subject matter and skills was declared to be a means to promoting health, social and spare-time activities.[18] In line with the Winnetka scheme and the project method, the Saskatchewan revision individualized certain activities — mainly the teaching of the tool subjects — but used socialized methods, such as group work for creative activities.[19] Patterson concludes that the Saskatchewan effort was more notable in expressing new purposes for schooling than in realizing them in practice. The attempt was tentative, a mixture of old and new, the eclecticism of which gave license to teachers to maintain a tradition of information accumulation and storage.[20]

Progressive ferment in Nova Scotia was promoted by Alexander MacKay's successor, Dr. Henry F. Munro, a graduate of Columbia University in political science. In 1930 he appointed a prestigious, though basically conservative Committee on Studies to review provincial curricula at all levels. In 1935, the Nova Scotia *Handbook to the Course of Study* called for a curriculum that "must be evolving, never static, with social, vocational and avocational aims."[21] The *Journal of Education* for the period was replete with quotations from John Dewey and extracts from Kilpatrick's monograph on the project method. In a direct evocation of the American cardinal principles of education, a revision committee demanded a curriculum that would develop health and character, effective citizenship, worthy home membership and a wise use of leisure time. With some schools giving 600 minutes a week to arithmetic and reading, members of the committee felt that it was impossible to transcend the three Rs in the curriculum. They agreed that these subjects were important, but only as background for the real education of the child. Although the committee recommended an expansion of the elementary curriculum, change was difficult to implement with an untrained teaching force, few of whom grasped progressive theory.[22]

In British Columbia, formal curriculum revision was foreshadowed in 1925 by the proposals of the Putman-Weir Survey. Wood observes that the survey approach and the accompanying testing program previously noted were highly sophisticated new methods of guiding educational policy. As such, both reflected the faith in educational principles and scientific expertise that characterized administrative progressives. The survey was a consciousness-raising exercise, designed to mobilize public support for expert guidance. Putman and Weir made a real effort to tap public opinion and, commendably, saw the value of educating the public in progressive principles while leaving real educational policy-making to the experts. Their report was seen as a means of stocktaking (a business concept) and of establishing the superiority of its authors' viewpoint in the light of their own recognition that education was not yet an exact science.[23]

The Putman-Weir theory of education later came to be exemplified in voluminous curriculum guides that, as noted in Chapter 8, emphasized goals of character and citizenship intended to promote individual initiative, social unity and an ethical community based on Judeo-Christian and liberal-democratic ideals. This updated version of the Ryersonian tradition rejected mental discipline theories that had long been discredited and sought to unify or correlate the old formal subjects by means of the project method, social studies and core curricula. Such traditional goals would be achieved more efficiently than in the past by means of progressive administrative and pedagogical techniques.[24] Despite their advocacy of the project method, Sutherland comments that Putman and Weir's approach treated it so perfunctorily as to give British Columbia teachers little meaningful help in introducing such a radical innovation.[25] In setting forth general objectives such as health, practical efficiency, the cultivation of civic ideals and habits, and common recreational interests, their report pointed to a more educative elementary curriculum, but significantly cited Bonser, an efficiency-minded American curriculum reformer, rather than Kilpatrick and his child-centred ideas. Such sweeping aims were to be achieved by means of a six-year elementary curriculum in which the three Rs would continue to be emphasized and, indeed, if preferred, placed first, with the social objectives "to come incidentally or as by-products."[26] The new elementary school was to be followed by a three-year middle school or junior high school, a proposal that was implemented by 1930. In most provinces by this time the elementary curriculum was encroaching on that of the high school through the offering in Grade 7 of such subjects as algebra and Latin. This trend became one rationale for the six-year elementary school.[27]

With the appointment in 1933 of Weir as British Columbia's Minister of Education and H.B. King, a self-styled progressive, as chief inspector of schools, the revision process was formally launched. (King's views on curriculum-making were noted in Chapter 7.) The social efficiency approach of both men, reflected in their recommendation to the revision committees of the writings of Bobbitt and other American scientific educators, was illustrated by the appearance, in 1936, of three bulletins of more than 200 pages each. There was irony in promoting ostensible autonomy and self-direction for pupils, while imposing detailed prescription on teachers. As befitted the earlier survey, comprehensive statements of philosophy and of aims and objectives — the latter for each subject and sometimes for each unit — were provided. The curriculum should be organized into units, defined as "large comprehensive topics," each built around "some central core of thought or fundamental principle." Subject matter must be unified into "integrated meaningful wholes." About half the instructional time was still devoted to the three Rs, but a move to a more "educative" curriculum was evident in significant time allotments for health, games and exercises, elementary science and the "fine and practical arts," of manual training, domestic science, music and art.[28]

Alberta's major curriculum revisions between 1936 and 1940 have been called the high water mark in the acceptance of progressive education in that province and, indeed, in all of Canada.[29] The first effort was launched in 1936 following the decade of theoretical discussion and limited experimentation noted earlier. In the 1936 curriculum guide, H.C. Newland explained the new enterprise approach:

> The name "enterprise" has been chosen to designate "doing or activity," rather than the familiar "project" because it has a somewhat stricter meaning. An enterprise is a definite undertaking; teachers and pupils agree upon it and tacitly promise to carry it through as agreed. An enterprise is an undertaking chosen, after careful consideration, for its interest and value; carefully planned in advance, carried out according to plan, and brought to a definite conclusion, after which some reckoning of gains is made. An enterprise is not only a carefully organized undertaking in itself, but it is also part of a whole, a definite step in a course designed to cover three years of work. Each enterprise involves planning, the organization of ideas and of materials, and co-operation. Enterprises include both mental and manual work, the collection of information and the practice of skills.[30]

Here and elsewhere in Canada, the British term "enterprise," derived from the famous Hadow Reports of 1926, 1931 and 1933 in Great Britain, was preferred to the American "project method," although the overseas studies in fact drew on progressive sources in the United States.[31] Canadian educators displayed characteristic political sagacity in ascribing progressive ideas to British, rather than American, influences.

Newland explained in an official bulletin that teachers would be given suggestions for constructing enterprises that would "integrate the skills, content and appreciation subjects in social activities and experiences." The suggested activities were to be changed from year to year. A related innovative development was the establishment of two divisions, one for primary grades (1, 2 and 3) and another for junior grades (4, 5 and 6). Grades were no longer to serve as a basis for promotion "but merely as levels of attainment within each division." A pupil might be at the Grade 1 level in reading, Grade 2 in arithmetic and Grade 3 in language. The promotion points were to be at the end of each division. This organization anticipated the modern continuous progress approach.[32]

The enterprise method or "experience education" was most fully adumbrated by Dr. Donalda Dickie of the Calgary Normal School, one of the three experts who had planned the 1936 revision. In 1940, she published *The Enterprise in Theory and Practice*, a comprehensive treatise of more than four hundred pages which was widely cited and quoted in the professional literature across Canada, and was used as a manual in normal schools. In emphasizing the use of language and art as integrating subjects, Dickie cited many American examples of activities and enterprises. Her bibliography included the works of such leading American progressives as Hollis Caswell, W.H. Kilpatrick and Harold Rugg. It also included a useful list of evaluation reports of American progressive experiments.[33]

The theory on which the enterprise was ostensibly based was set out in a long introduction by Dickie's publisher, W.R. Wees, a trained psychologist. Wees attacked "former notions about mind" which treated the students' minds as receptacles, and failed to see them as powers used by the students for some purpose which attracts their interest. School existed, argued Wees, "not to train the mind" but "to educate a child." The teacher's task was, as Herbart had shown, to promote the students' powers of perception through arousing their interest. However, the enterprise as a method was superior to Herbartian pedagogy because, Wees implied, it was more child-centred.[34]

Patterson shows that, even though Alberta led all provinces in its enthusiastic acceptance of progressivism, changes were implemented only cautiously. The use of the enterprise method was voluntary, and the three Rs were still taught as distinct subjects outside the new program.[35] Teachers were, however, expected to experiment with the new pedagogy "by attempting one or two enterprises during the year ...."[36] Earlier, Dickie had indicated that enterprises were to be applied "only to the informational and cultural subjects" and used "only during a part of the day."[37] The skill subjects, or the three Rs, should be taught "by the formal or drill method during part of each day." Alberta inspectors asserted, in 1938, that the "enterprise technique" was in almost universal use, and that 60 per cent of the province's teachers were successful with it.[38] It was said that enterprise education had struck a happy balance between "the extreme subject-matterists and the extreme activists."[39]

At this time, when the revision was at its height, such leading American reformers as Carleton Washburne, Boyd H. Bode, Harold Rugg, Hilda

Taba and Ralph Tyler were invited from the Progressive Education Association to address teachers' conventions in Alberta. Representatives from
Saskatchewan also came to hear them. Many teachers, principals, inspectors and normal school instructors went to study across the border, especially at Columbia University, the mecca of progressive education.[40] Some
Alberta and other western educators belonged to the PEA, and H.C.
Newland was a member of the PEA executive. However, more than a few
Alberta teachers resisted the new approach. One recalled later how many
felt "pressured into some new, vague procedures at the instigation of a
group of theorists." As a result, teachers felt impelled to produce "showy"
projects such as an Indian village or an Inuit igloo. Too often it was the concrete item that became important, with actual learning lost sight of. For
teachers open to the new ideas, there was a lack of materials and facilities,
with the result that they had to depend largely "on what children could
scrounge at home."[41] The problems were summed up later by Sheane:

> The enterprise system called for well-trained, adaptable teachers who
> knew something of child nature and of the laws of teaching. The organi-
> zation required to arrange study materials into teaching units was not
> possible with such inexperienced teachers, nor could they be expected
> to get the most out of such procedures. Because of the quality of the
> teachers, as well as for other reasons, many educators in Alberta
> claimed that the enterprise procedure had not failed because it had
> never been tried in the true sense of the word.[42]

Sheane described the 1940 curriculum revision as a rush job. Public
protest forced the withdrawal of a new report card which discarded grades,
examinations, marks, passing or promotion.[43] The 1940 curriculum guide
emphasized that the curriculum was "a home-grown product" adapted to
Alberta children and schools, and not simply a borrowing from another
system.[44]

The enterprise method was being recommended everywhere in
Canada by this time. In Manitoba, the annual report of the Department of
Education for 1937-38 described a geography unit in a Winnipeg school on
"Transportation in Canada" which became more than a matter of "simply
reading about transportation and reproducing what has been said orally or
in writing." Instead, members of the class searched for historical information on the topic, drawing maps and models of boats and carts. Others
studied railway, water, road and air transportation. The whole class working together was then expected to "assemble models, maps, pictures and
written work of their own," making the whole study "vital and real." The
same report, however, entered a characteristic caveat of Canadian progressives by observing that "life requirements still demand obedience at times
to externally imposed authority and require one to be able to face
unpleasant tasks and conquer difficult situations."[45]

In eastern Canada, the rhetoric of progressive change was featured in
curriculum documents, but even the qualified adoption of new practices

found in the western provinces was less apparent. Thus, despite the genuflections towards the new dispensation noted earlier in Nova Scotia, a 1941 inspector's report in that province described education as "reduced to the study of books by demure pupils sitting at fixed desks" even in activity subjects such as nature study and science. Music and physical education were almost totally neglected and no teachers were making use of available audio-visual aids.[46]

Curriculum discourse and revision were quiescent in Ontario for much of the inter-war period, and there was less apparent systematic adumbration of theory and less conscious planning or proselytizing than took place in Alberta. According to Fleming there was little change in the elementary curriculum in the province between the revisions of 1904 and 1937.[47] However, as noted in Chapter 9, Ontario had taken the lead in what might be called the conservative thrust of progressivism in such fields as mental and achievement testing, "auxiliary" or special education and in guidance and child study. During the 1930s, Ontario teachers' organizations were ahead of the Department of Education in urging progressive change. In 1932, the Ontario Public School Men Teachers' Federation launched a survey which, in co-operation with other groups and with the encouragement of the department, led to a report three years later that recommended far-reaching curriculum revision.[48] The appointment in 1934 of a new Deputy Minister, Duncan McArthur, chairman of the history department at Queen's University, heralded major changes. McArthur criticized a curriculum that aimed solely at imparting information, while neglecting creative work and the development of social consciousness.[49] Three years later, McArthur appointed two progressive educators, Thornton Mustard of the Toronto Normal School staff and Stanley Watson, a school principal, to produce a new course of studies for Grades 1 to 6. The "special indebtedness" to the three Hadow reports in Great Britain was explicitly acknowledged by McArthur in 1937.[50] As noted earlier, Hadow had acknowledged his own debt to American progressives. No doubt Canadian educators were reassured that Hadow, in urging progressive reform, emphasized the need for adequate drill in the three Rs.[51]

A further example of British progressive influence in Ontario at this time was apparent in the establishment of chapters of the New Education Fellowship, called by Stamp "the British Empire equivalent of the PEA."[52] Toronto had the most active chapter among a number that were established in most major Canadian cities during the 1930s.[53] Founded in Great Britain in 1921 by a group of theosophist progressives led by Beatrice Ensor, the NEF soon became an international body that organized a series of conferences during the inter-war years.[54] Following Ensor's Canadian visit in 1929, Canadians began to attend the NEF conferences. Fred Clarke, Professor of Education at McGill, represented Canada on the organizing committee for the 1932 Nice conference. Arthur Lismer, the Group of Seven painter who was already emerging as Canada's leading art educator, presented a paper on "The Course of Art in a Changing World."[55] Canadians provided a link between the NEF and the Progressive Education Association, some, particularly in western Canada, belonging to both. More than 100 were members of the PEA, including several who served on the executive. In 1938, a large international PEA conference was held at Windsor, Ontario, in association with the NEF. The keynote speakers included leading American progressive luminaries such as Carleton Washburne and Harold Rugg. The latter made a nation-wide broadcast on the CBC.[56]

Alberta ideas were influential in the Ontario revision, and H.C. Newland proudly noted that the new curriculum guidelines included wholesale plagiarizing of his own province's program descriptions.[57] The Ontario program specifically recommended the organization of "enterprises," devoting a full chapter to the topic. In 1937-38, C.C. Goldring, superintendent of Toronto schools, claimed that at least 85 per cent of the 2200 public school teachers in Toronto encouraged their classes to undertake enterprises.[58] His cautions against "excessive use" of the method were probably redundant since the evidence is that teachers formalized the enterprise, causing it to fall into disrepute. An overemphasis on tangible results in the form of elaborate projects was a related weakness.[59]

A stronger play orientation seems to have taken hold in the primary grades. The earlier effort to extend kindergarten pedagogy, particularly the ideas of Froebel and Montessori, up into the primary grades had failed. Rather, there had been a reverse downward movement of the three Rs into the kindergarten. In the new program primary children learned manners and morals by example and through songs, games, talks and stories. They studied nature by means of conversations and observation. They participated in vocal music, physical culture, hygiene, art, manual training and sewing sessions.[60] They used Canadianized American readers with clear type, attractive drawings, handsome design and controlled vocabularies. These featured a sanitized, middle-class environment that somewhat attenuated the teaching of the older moral, patriotic cultural heritage. Other changes at the primary level included flexible grading, the combination of grades into divisions, and the streaming of children into different grades in different subjects.

Phillips claims that the "momentous development" epitomized by the Ontario revision of 1937 for a time made elementary education a more dominant interest than secondary education. The major concern of the latter, he noted, was scholarship, and a first concern of the former had rightly become method."[61] Fleming comments that the revision "displayed a highly progressive orientation [which] might have set the schools of Ontario on an entirely new path, had certain circumstances been more propitious." In the 1960s, the authors of the Hall-Dennis Report observed that, except for the strong place of religion in the curriculum, every idea in the 1937 revision anticipated those of enlightened educators later.[62]

As elsewhere, the Ontario revision faced major problems of implementation. Two related problems were the development of the new curriculum within a few months in 1936 on a "crash" basis, and its extreme dependence on two men, Mustard and Watson. Mustard's untimely death in 1939, Watson's departure for war service, and a growing wartime conservatism were other retarding factors. The basic conservative thrust of the revision was revealed by the school inspector who declared that the aim was "to interest the child in his work, so that he wants to do what we want him to do." This view would seem to substantiate Stamp's assertion that the revision focussed on means rather than on ends. Ontario teachers were unable to abandon the patterns by which they themselves had been taught. They could not easily shift from textbook dominance, dictated notes, formal testing, competition, and enforced classroom silence to the use of varied reference materials, continuous assessment, co-operative attitudes and the noisy chatter of enterprise work.[63] Rule comments that Ontario educators characteristically "utilized those aspects of current educational philosophy which best served their needs without truly understanding the basic theoretical concepts."[64]

This survey of the impact of progressive ideas during the 1930s has indicated that the rhetoric and reality of change were far apart. Although progressive ideas permeated the official Canadian educational literature, actual implementation of them was selective, as Patterson's survey demonstrates. He suggests that progressive influence was exaggerated due to the proselytizing language used by reformers, and to the popular criticism voiced by such later critics as Hilda Neatby in the early 1950s. A related factor was the tendency of critics to assume that American criticisms of their schools were equally applicable to Canadian schools. As American progressive ideas were imported into Canada during the 1930s, criticisms of those same ideas flowed across the border through the mass media. These criticisms were taken up by well-intentioned Canadians who assumed that their schools were progressive because they were somewhat different from the schools of their own youth.[65]

Confusion about the impact of progressivism was confounded by the tendency of its defenders to deny that it had had a major impact. In this they were accurate, as Patterson's analysis demonstrates. In fact, as the slow acceptance of mental health cited earlier suggests, it can be argued that the new interwar educational establishment resisted powerful external and other forces, and thereby preserved the traditional academic values of the school. Official documents such as the 1941 Saskatchewan annual report indicated a clear appreciation of the weaknesses of progressive education, and of the need to avoid its extremes in Canada.[66] Be that as it may, what is certain is that problems of implementation were formidable. Not the least of these was the persistence of the rural school problem, and the fact that the progressive thrust was mounted during the exigencies of depression and war. As a consequence, schools lacked resources such as proper libraries, which were indispensable to implementing enterprise education. Large classes and poorly qualified teachers who, as a Manitoba critic put it, were "pedlars of subjects rather than life builders" also hindered progress.[67] Little effort was made to prepare teachers for change, and such in-service efforts as were made were perfunctory. On the other hand, reformers mounted a "hard sell" which provoked negative reactions among teachers. Finally, argues Patterson, the reforms were never given a fair or extensive trial.[68] By the end of World War II a reaction was setting in that portended a conservative tide (to be discussed in Chapter 14).

## Academic Tradition and Social Challenge in the High School

During World War I and its aftermath, demands grew for a more useful, flexible high school curriculum that would provide for more adaptation to local conditions, and for a more adequate general socialization. American influence was evident in frequent references in provincial reports and guidelines to the NEA's cardinal principles of education. The so-called Carnegie Unit, or credit system, was an example of a specific American innovation that attracted attention. Used as a kind of standard accounting or bookkeeping system for high school studies, the plan was first adopted by Alberta in its 1922 curriculum revision. In the United States, a Carnegie Unit was based on the offering of a subject for one class period per day, five days per week through the year, for an annual total of 120 hours of instructional time per subject. Alberta modified the system by using modules of 25-hour units, so that five units represented one Carnegie unit.[69] By the mid-1930s, the western provinces had adopted a similar credit system. In British Columbia, the system assisted the establishment of a flexible curriculum plan of "constants" and electives.

The Carnegie system regularized program scheduling and the use of classroom space for both teachers and students. Fixed blocks of time required more careful planning of units of study and thus assisted curriculum makers in developing the course content of high school subjects. The system was also said to be easily understood by teachers, students and parents. Its disadvantages arose from a rigidity that made curriculum innovation and experimentation difficult.[70] The system put a premium on the quantitative measurement of educational attainment, in terms of time served and textbook pages "covered" while discounting the quality of learning and the needs, interests and abilities of students. It dubiously assumed an equivalence of subjects. A concomitant assumption was that all students could acquire the same amount of learning or subject matter in the same amount of time, a concept antithetical to the modern concept of "mastery learning." On the other hand, the administrative convenience of the Carnegie system was no doubt especially appealing to Canadian educators. The system had little impact in eastern Canada, although the adoption of the credit system in Ontario after 1970 may be seen as a long-term spinoff from it.

During the 1920s, W.F. Dyde, an ex-Canadian at the University of Colorado, conducted the first Canada-wide survey of secondary education.

His study, completed as a doctoral dissertation at Columbia University in 1929, provided a valuable portrait of the high school curriculum during the period, while also suggesting curriculum policy changes to meet the needs of an expanding, more diversified school population. At the outset, Dyde identified a distinctive Canadian system of secondary schools "unified by broadly similar aims, by similar problems and by methods of administration which have much in common." At the provincial level, centralization of control was another prime characteristic. It was a system "in process of democratization" in which the secondary school "had been superimposed upon the elementary school, making a continuous [generally free] system." However, because one third of all high school pupils received secondary instruction in small, rural schools, there was a great inequality of conditions and opportunities in the offering and availability of high school education. Conditions ranged from the well-equipped, well-staffed urban collegiate institutes of Ontario to the rural one-room schools of Nova Scotia where, in 1923, not a single teacher was a university graduate. In Alberta, in 1930, more than 75 per cent of all high schools were one- or two-room institutions.[71]

Dyde concluded that only 36 per cent of Canadian elementary students reached high school. However, although Canada had a lower ratio of secondary attendance than the United States, the ratio was significantly greater than that of any European nation. Moreover, the proportion had increased dramatically by 234 per cent between 1891 and 1923, while the general population was increasing by 82 per cent. Dyde attributed this increase to compulsory attendance laws, to the growth of technical education and, less tangibly, to "the growing [public] conviction that effective citizenship ... [required] more than an elementary education." The Canadian high school by 1923 was "in a period of rapid transition from a highly selective institution to one that is much less selective in character."[72]

Despite progress, serious problems persisted as a result of high failure rates, an excessive number of examinations and the variable quality of instruction. This was illustrated in Manitoba's provincial failure rate of 48 per cent, as compared with a rate of 28 per cent in Winnipeg's collegiate institutes. Another problem was the lack of articulation with the elementary school arising from an "abrupt change in subject matter," illustrated in British Columbia where algebra, geometry and two languages were suddenly confronted. A related problem was an overcrowded curriculum with so much subject matter in a three-year program that in reality should be a four-year one.[73]

The growing scope of the high school curriculum during the 1920s is illustrated by Dyde's survey of enrolments in thirty-two subjects taught in the high schools of Nova Scotia, New Brunswick, Ontario and three western provinces. However, as the accompanying table shows, the traditional subjects were overwhelmingly dominant while the practical subjects ranked low.

Number of Pupils in Publicly Controlled Schools Taking Certain Secondary
Grade Subjects in Six Provinces, 1923

| Subject | No. of Pupils |
| --- | --- |
| 1. English | 86 229 |
| 2. Algebra | 66 291 |
| 3. French | 65 492 |
| 4. History | 64 293 |
| 5. Physical Culture | 57 267 |
| 6. Latin | 56 610 |
| 7. Geometry | 50 367 |
| 8. Arithmetic | 39 944 |
| 9. Geography | 35 617 |
| 10. Art | 29 268 |
| 11. Botany | 24 170 |
| 12. Physics | 23 559 |
| 13. Chemistry | 19 885 |
| 14. Physiography | 13 804 |
| 15. Reading | 10 775 |
| 16. Zoology | 10 437 |
| 17. Elementary Science | 8 167 |
| 18. Manual Training | 7 759 |
| 19. Bookkeeping | 7 201 |
| 20. Household Science | 6 727 |
| 21. Physiology | 4 957 |
| 22. Agriculture | 4 458 |
| 23. Typewriting | 4 041 |
| 24. Stenography | 4 017 |
| 25. Trigonometry | 3 321 |
| 26. Military Drill | 3 220 |
| 27. Business Law, etc. | 2 756 |
| 28. Music | 2 473 |
| 29. German | 2 140 |
| 30. Practical Mathematics | 1 917 |
| 31. Greek | 389 |
| 32. Spanish | 330 |
| Total Sampled | 89 383 |

Source: W.F. Dyde, *Public Secondary Education in Canada* (1929: 186)

Dyde concluded that the backbone of the secondary curriculum was
made up of "five principal branches of study:" English; mathematics
(including arithmetic, algebra and geometry); foreign languages (almost
exclusively Latin and French); the social studies (history and geography);
and science (which embraced physics, chemistry, physiography, botany,

zoology and general science). Although the aesthetic subjects were neglected, art held a high place outside the five backbone branches by virtue of being a required subject for normal school entrance.[74]

Dyde analyzed the relative importance of the backbone branches by weighting them according to the amount of weekly instructional time devoted to each, and by combining the separate elements of mathematics, the sciences and the social studies. This method showed the great predominance of English over any other single subject, and the great importance of French and Latin. Weighting English at 100, the relative importance of the principal branches appeared as follows:

| | |
|---|---:|
| English | 100 |
| Foreign languages | 108 |
| Mathematics | 124 |
| Science | 84 |
| Social studies | 73 |

The results demonstrated, Dyde thought, the continuing value placed by Canadian curriculum policy-makers on "the formal discipline theory of studies" and their disregard of modern psychological research. He concluded that if Canadian secondary schools wanted to take stock of themselves, they would need to make "a close scrutiny of the contribution which present courses in mathematics are making to a liberal education." He questioned the emphasis on foreign languages, to the comparative neglect of the natural sciences and the social studies. He also criticized the low status of the aesthetic subjects, especially music, which was "practically nonexistent." He thought that any consideration of the relative value of studies would depend upon one's concept of educational theory. Mental disciplinarians would find a narrow academic curriculum entirely satisfactory, as would those favouring high selectivity in the secondary school, because they saw such schooling as the privilege of the few rather than the right of the many.[75]

Dyde concluded his study by stating some basic principles that should govern the Canadian high school curriculum. These should include secondary education for all, tailored to the needs of youth through multiple curricula with a common core. To this end, an exploratory, locally controlled junior high school curriculum should be considered, with guidance as a keynote. More attention should be given to determining the educational value of the content of the curriculum.[76]

Dyde's profile of the high school curriculum during the early 1920s may be compared with a survey conducted by the Dominion Bureau of Statistics nearly twenty years later. The DBS study showed that the situation Dyde had described was not enormously different, although full data and a means of weighting similar to what he had used were not available. There appears to have been some expansion in the numbers enrolled in commercial and vocational subjects but the arts remained neglected.[77]

In spite of the formalism and conservatism of the Canadian high school during the inter-war period, Stamp has shown that it was moving in a somewhat more expansive and socializing direction as the majority of Canadian teenagers began to attend for the first time. It gradually acquired some of the custodial functions that the elementary school had acquired earlier. One important consequence was that students came from a wider socioeconomic background than ever before, making the high school "a common meeting ground for the children of all the classes," as one Ontario inspector put it in 1920.[78] No longer was the high school restricted to the children of the elite, even though such students were still overrepresented.

The increase in the high school population resulting from compulsory attendance and the abolition of fees were more symptoms than causes of the change. Vanishing employment opportunities and the desire of parents to extend the education of their children were more powerful reasons. A reduced need for unskilled labour and higher educational demands by employers were secondary causes. Girls in particular were encouraged to stay longer in school, at a time when teenage girls were expected to "do something" after leaving school. "Something" typically meant entering the expanding commercial labour force while awaiting marriage.[79] Increasing numbers of young women began to enroll in the universities. The interwar years were also a period when the "human capital" argument, based on the assumed economic benefits of education, was being proclaimed more insistently.

The new custodial role of the high school reflected the fact that parents had more than economic reasons for keeping their adolescent children in school. The new youth culture noted earlier, with its greater affluence and leisure time and new lifestyles, created new moral concerns among adults during the roaring twenties or Jazz Age. As the social role of the high school expanded into its modern form, extra-curricular activities became more than mere adjuncts to the academic program. By promoting better socialization, such activities as student newspapers, government assemblies and sports enabled students to assume quasi-adult responsibilities and provided real life training situations. Above all, such activities were a means of maintaining control over unruly adolescents that was all the more effective if it could appear to be exerted by the students themselves. The holding of school dances to prevent drinking, the containment of smoking, bad language and vandalism and the regulation of student dress and hair styles complemented regulations regarding attendance, punctuality and homework, all carried out in the name of character development.[80]

Despite an expanding social role, the high schools remained preeminently academic institutions. Modest curricular changes widened the academic base somewhat. This trend developed slowly in the 1920s, but accelerated during the following decade. Even so, one high school principal observed that, as compared with American schools, Canadian curricula still exalted "scholarship and character" as their main aims in contrast to the emphasis on citizenship south of the border.[81] However, one academic critic, J.F. Macdonald, complained that too many students were now following the matriculation course, which was seen as having "a very definite commercial value." High school was no longer regarded as a privilege, and a tradition of hard work was being lost. Macdonald also thought that the concept of a broad liberal education was in danger. Canadians lacked any philosophy of education.[82] To Peter Sandiford, on the other hand, the question was whether secondary schooling was merely a bridge to higher levels, or an integral unit of schooling in its own right.[83]

Although Ontario's 1921 revision promised fewer obligatory subjects and more optional ones, in practice vocational offerings, music and art remained options taken in addition to the matriculation course load. The continuing emphasis on examinations and on matriculation qualifications helped the high schools to maintain an academic emphasis. A significant change in examination policy came with the provision that pupils could be given credit for passing particular subjects, and not required to pass all at once or to repeat the year. In 1920, a single set of examinations in all subjects was established to meet matriculation and graduation diploma require-ments. These replaced separate examinations previously set by the Depart-ment of Education and the University Matriculation Board.[84]

Institutional change, initially in the form of the junior high school, was an attempt both to encourage and accommodate curricular change. As part of the 6-3-3 plan, the junior high school included Grades 7, 8 and 9. The new organization was intended to bridge the gap between the elemen-tary and the traditional high school, and thereby to break down the distinc-tion between the two levels by providing a more continuous curricular experience. Basically, it was intended as an exploratory year where optional subjects and a broader curriculum would be available in a system of partial departmental organization. It was hoped that a less academic emphasis would assist the retention of students and enable them to select future courses wisely, in accordance with their vocational and academic interests and abilities. The system was also intended to reduce retardation and enhance retention through a curriculum better adjusted to pupil needs. By 1935, Alberta and British Columbia had established a 6-3-3 plan province-wide.

British Columbia's junior high school program of 1936-7 stressed that, whether housed in a separate building or not, the curriculum of Grades 7, 8 and 9 should be the same in all schools. What was called "practical arts" (industrial arts and home economics) was made compulsory in all programs. Exploratory curricula designed to develop pupils' interests, apti-tudes and abilities were provided in varied occupational and academic fields, the latter by means of general and survey courses. The program was also intended to provide for individual diagnosis "leading to educational and vocational guidance." An additional cluster of aims included adequate provision for individual differences through the enriched offerings, gradual curriculum differentiation, flexible methods of promotion, provision for varying rates of progress and "vocational training for those who must leave school early." Guidance programs and extra-curricular activities were intended to supplement the curriculum by promoting character and citizenship training as described earlier.[85]

The junior high school was partially adopted in Nova Scotia in the 1930s, but made only limited headway elsewhere in eastern Canada. In Newfoundland, a 1933 report by a British school inspector from Lancashire condemned the dominance of examinations but proposed the substitution of intelligence tests to select, English style, an elite 10 per cent of students deemed capable of absorbing an academic curriculum. A year later, a commission inquiry cited the American cardinal principles but ironically reiterated its support of examinations and the need to cultivate students' memories and powers of concentration.[86]

In Ontario the intermediate school, as the junior high school was termed, gained only limited acceptance. This was due to rivalries between the elementary and secondary teachers' federations, and to the political problem of the grade level to which support of Roman Catholic separate schools should be extended, if the elementary grades were reduced from nine to six. In the event, Ontario policymakers followed a strategy of leaving Grade 9 in the high school but designating it as a "common first year." Under the "McArthur Plan" of 1937, Grade 9 became a transition year, with a wide choice of academic and practical options and by the elimination of Latin (which upset many traditionalists).[87] The McArthur Plan was the most significant change in the Ontario secondary curriculum resulting from the revision of 1937. By this time, the term "grades" was replacing "forms" in the province's high schools.[88]

Another significant organizational change was the establishment of the composite high school which, like the junior high school, also first took root in western Canada. This new institution was intended to overcome the disparity in status and prestige between vocational and academic programs which supposedly arose from establishing them in separate buildings. By housing vocational and university-bound students in the same building, the composite high school would, it was hoped, prove more attractive to the former group than the lower-status vocational schools had been. It would also facilitate the social mixing of a diverse student population. Stamp has described the opening of Western Canada Composite High School in Calgary when the fence between two previously separate technical and academic high schools was removed; the school yearbook took the name "ACATEC." All students were expected to take at least one "shop" course and every subject in the Alberta course of study was offered. In New Brunswick regional high schools became the rural counterparts of composite urban high schools. Although composite high schools were eventually established in most provinces, there is little evidence that even in the progressive western provinces they either reduced the disparity of esteem between academic and vocational programs, or between the students enrolled in each type.[89]

The composite high school had developed in Alberta as a result of the merging in 1935 of senior grade curricula into a single track program made up of a required core of English, social studies and physical education, and a wide variety of options. In this province and in British Columbia, a common program of "cores" and "options," or "constants" and "electives" was established, with a common graduation diploma. In British Columbia, the senior high school curriculum was ostensibly organized into study units. It was recognized that in a system of subject specialization and departmentalization, the correlation of subject matter implied by the unit method would be difficult to attain. Consequently, teachers were reminded of their responsibilities beyond subject matter teaching, especially with regard to character education, high standards of English usage, reading and mental health.[90] In eastern Canada, Ontario established more options at the senior level but still maintained the distinction between matriculation and non-matriculation programs.[91]

There can be no doubt that, as Stamp has commented, the Canadian high school experience in 1939 was significantly different from its 1919 counterpart.[92] Student enrolments had increased notably, although the great majority of Canadian teenagers still did not complete high school. Qualitative change was marked by the more diverse character of the school population *per se*. Together with new social and economic demands, this change increased the socializing role of the schools. Commercial, and other practical studies had been more fully incorporated into the curriculum. More flexible promotion and examination policies had been adopted. Several provinces, led by British Columbia in 1937, had adopted an accreditation system whereby superior schools meeting certain criteria could recommend students for matriculation and graduation without examination.

## Pupil Perspectives on the Inter-war Curriculum

The foregoing account of progressive conservative change in Canadian curricula at both the elementary and secondary levels has suggested how self-declared progressives sought to effect change in Canadian classrooms during the inter-war decades. Inspired by reforming zeal and restrained by ingrained conservatism, they inevitably met with mixed success in achieving their often contradictory goals. One measure of their success or lack of it may be seen in autobiographical accounts of writers who were pupils at the time. Two things are striking about these accounts. Despite drab school environments and meagre resources, the curriculum provided a rich experience which pupils enjoyed. Secondly, that experience was remarkably similar in rural environments as widely separated as Nova Scotia and Saskatchewan.

In a fictional memoir based on his own experience, Ernest Buckler describes the one-room rural school that he attended in Nova Scotia during the 1920s, with its two blackboards, a globe, three maps "chipped with age, walls decorated with nothing but a picture of King George V and a feed calendar and no kindergarten tulips trimming the window panes."[93] Although his class had no crayons "and for some reason all we ever drew was pears," grammar was apparently valuable, when nouns presented a problem that left even the teacher on shaky ground. Reading, however, "was our greatest strength" and even Grade 1 pupils "picked it up as naturally as breathing" — probably, Buckler surmises, because "the stories in their reader had such real interest that they couldn't wait to puzzle them out." Poetry might be turned into prose and systematically analyzed but it "did get under our skins." When the teacher read Gray's "Elegy" aloud, even the class hellions fell silent. In geography, "we could rattle off the capitals of Europe without thinking." In arithmetic in Grade 3, Buckler and his classmates could recite the thirteen times table backward, and were later "captured by the fact that ... anything as smooth as a circle should always be 3.1416 times its diameter." But English history, despite its dull stretches, "was our favourite subject," with its sometimes grisly action, such as smothering little boys, and its glittering personalities, such as Henry VIII and his six wives.

The teacher's main tasks were preparing the high school pupils for the dreaded provincial examinations, and the school as a whole for the "monstrous ordeal" of the inspector's annual visit. The former task led to the criticism that she "put all her time in the higher grades". Pupils could never preguess the inspector's catechism. Thus, if Grade 5 had been drilled on fractions, the inspector might question them on the Wars of the Roses; if Grade 7 had been rehearsed letter-perfect on the Gulf Stream, they might be asked to recite "Abou Ben Adhem." Buckler's account of these ordeals underscores the primary mental discipline role of the school and the absence of the New Education in rural Nova Scotia. He nostalgically concluded that the classroom was a place for the mind and "did as good a job of training as any I've met up with since."

To Fredelle Maynard, a Jewish immigrant girl, the various Prairie schools she attended during the 1920s all seemed alike: brown walls, green window-shades, "alphabet letters marching across the tops of blackboards, a clock, a Union Jack, a photograph of King George V in his coronation robes."[94] Like Buckler, she found English history enthralling, with its orderly progression of "causes, events, [and] results" and its vivid personalities. Her schooling was acquired in the age of drill and memory work when learning, while sometimes fun, was a serious business based on books. Memorization was no doubt overdone, but she was pleased that she learned scenes from Shakespeare and other "memory gems" which became part of her mental furnishings "and ultimately a touchstone of value." Memorization also cultivated a respect for facts, whether of the dates of battles, the digestive juices and their functions or the parts of a flower. Facts, often acquired by copying notes from the blackboard, were rarely used as a basis for informed opinions but "at least we never assumed that it was possible to have valid opinions if we had no facts at all." Although sewing and cooking were thoroughly taught, such "luxury subjects" as music and art were badly taught. In many respects, schooling was "narrow, repressive [and] unimaginative" but again, like Buckler, Maynard enjoyed it "and acquired there a love of learning."

To young British immigrant James M. Minifie, a similar Prairie experience provided a basis for future studies at Oxford and for a later career as one of Canada's leading journalists. Minifie recalled his pilgrimage from a one-room school to Methodist Regina College, where he learned Latin and Greek and acquired a passion for Chaucer. In 1920, further studies at the University of Saskatchewan, then hardly a decade away from unsettled Prairie, introduced Minifie to scholars fresh from Oxford and Dublin, and led him to a Rhodes scholarship.[95]

Almost simultaneously, David Lewis, a Polish Jewish urban immigrant boy in eastern Canada began his own school pilgrimage that enabled him to develop one of the best minds of his generation, and to become one of Canada's leading political figures. Lewis' autobiography describes the ordeal of a twelve year old child unable to understand a word of English, set down in a Grade 1 class in a Montreal elementary school. For a year, he studied Dickens' *Old Curiosity Shop* on his own, with the aid of a dictionary, meanwhile listening carefully to his teacher, whose words he practised orally at home, "reinforcing the lesson with the childish schoolbooks we used in class."[96] By the end of the first year, he had "skipped" into Grade 4 and had acquired a fairly rich vocabulary. Within three years, Lewis entered high school on a scholarship. Like Minifie, he later became a Rhodes scholar. Lewis pays tribute to the warm attention he received from the principal and teachers of his elementary school:

> The principal went out of his way to be kind whenever he met me. He praised my progress, whether deserved or not, and offered to help. Two of my teachers were indefatigable in their support. They often spent time with me after school, during which we concentrated on my pronunciation and speech. This extra tutoring was invaluable and explains the slight lilt in my enunciation which some have thought to be Welsh in origin. My recollection is that there were few, if any, Canadian teachers in our school; they were all "old country" immigrants.[97]

Other pupil perspectives on the inter-war curriculum come from the work of a modern researcher. Sutherland's interviews with adults who were pupils at the time suggest that formalism steadily enlarged in elementary classrooms during the period. His grim picture of the elementary school portrays a drab and unhealthy physical environment; by modern standards the dress of pupils and teachers alike was also drab. School routines within and without the classroom were strictly regimented and minutely regulated by systems of buzzers, bells and often terrifying verbal commands. Such a mode of discipline, together with traditional sanctions such as standing in the corner, writing lines, doing endless arithmetic computations, and the ultimate sanction of corporal punishment, were brought to a peak of effective performance.[98]

The curriculum and teaching methods constituted a simple mode of rote learning based on the times tables, spelling lists, the "Lady of the Lake," capes and bays and Kings and Queens, in a system dominated by the teacher talking and pupils listening. Teaching methods were remarkably consistent from teacher to teacher and subject to subject and, as suggested, were rigidly formal. They entailed endless copying of blackboard notes (often in the form of textbook summaries) and rapt attention to teacher lectures and demonstrations; pupils, with hands on their desks, were expected to "sit up straight and face the front" while chanting drills and reading aloud in sequence from the textbook. It was a system that discouraged independent thought and provided no opportunity to be creative, one "that blamed rather than praised [and] made little effort to build a sense of self-worth." Formal methods were common even in the practical subjects. Science classes were occasionally enlivened by teacher-performed experiments, but these might be written up by a rigid formula, with predetermined conclusions sometimes recorded on the blackboard in advance. Art, music and physical education were made more varied, if only because some children brought their own skills to these classes. Their competence or lack of it made the children look upon these subjects as high or low points in the weekly routine.[99]

Despite the drabness, severity and intellectual torpor described by Sutherland, it would be a mistake to assume that children did not often enjoy their school experience. On the contrary, Sutherland reports that his subjects enjoyed much of it.[100] This confirms the autobiographical accounts already referred to and underscores the ambiguous meaning of the curriculum experience of most students during the inter-war period. Other than the nostalgia which no doubt animated recollections of one of life's most formative experiences, we can only speculate about the reasons for such positive recollections; today they would probably be described as the most deprived of school experiences. One powerful factor was surely the lack of competing sources of knowledge in an information-poor, pre-mass media social milieu, during a period when the curriculum was still defined in terms of traditional lore embodied in textbooks and readers. As a consequence, North American schools in the early twentieth century, although narrow, biased and restrained, served nonetheless in Finkelstein's words as "havens of liberating possibility."[101] It is this function that comes through so clearly in the nostalgic accounts of Buckler, Maynard, Minifie and Lewis. It is probable that most Canadian adults of their generation, whether of rural or urban upbringing, resonate to those accounts.

## Notes to Chapter 10

1 Selleck, *English Primary Education*, 156.

2 Tyack, *One Best System*, 196.

3 The categories are Tyack's, ibid., 127, 197-9.

4 Sandiford, "Curriculum Revision."

5 Cited in Patterson, "Society and Education," 374.

6 Patterson, "Impetus," 176.

7 Cited in Cremin, *Transformation*, 217.

8 Ibid., 217-18.

9 Sheane, 86.

10 Ibid., 86-7.

11 Patterson, "The Experience," 7.

12 Patterson, "Progressive Education: Impetus to Educational Change," 177, citing department of education professional examinations for 1927 and 1928.

13 Oviatt, 72, 75.

14 Canadian academics who were political progressives tended to be conservatives in educational matters if they paid any attention at all to educational policy. However, although the bible of the democratic left, *Social Planning for Canada*, published in 1935, devoted only two pages to education, the authors were critical of the uniformity of public schools that produced standardized students and noted the irony of the fact that private schools did more to encourage self-expression and to train for co-operative living. See League for Social Reconstruction, *Social Planning for Canada*, 35-6.

15 Oviatt, 73, 75, 77.

16 Patterson, "The Experience."

17 Patterson, "Impetus," 180.

18 Ibid., 179.

19 Ibid., 180, citing the *Saskatchewan Public School Curriculum and Teacher's Guide, Grades I-VII*, for 1931, p. 10.

20 Ibid. citing reports of inspectors in Sask. AR for 1932.

21 Nova Scotia, *Handbook to the Course of Study* (1935), iii. On the appointment of the Committee see N.S.AR (1930) xxvi-vii. For details of the Committee's powers, work and recommendations and views on the nature of the curriculum see *Handbook to the Course of Study*, Truro: New Publishing Company, 1935, i-xv.

22 N.S.AR (1935), 83.

23 See Wood, "Hegelian Resolutions," 257-60.

24 Ibid., 265-7.

25 N. Sutherland, "The Triumph," 35.

26 Putman and Weir, *Survey*, 35, 152.

27 Sandiford, "Junior High Schools," 371-3.

28 *B.C. Programme of Studies for Elementary Schools* (1936), 5.

29 Patterson, "Impetus," 189.

30 Alberta, *Programme of Studies for the Elementary School: Grades I-VI, 1936*, 288.

31 See Patterson, "Experience," 19; Stamp, *Schools of Ontario,* 167; Quick, 230; J. Mann, "Progressive Education," 14.

32 Newland, "Official Bulletin," 6.

33 Dickie, *The Enterprise,* 438-9.

34 Ibid. 3-5, 6-7.

35 Patterson, "Impetus," 186-7.

36 Newland, "Official Bulletin," 6.

37 Dickie, "Enterprise Education," 68.

38 Alberta AR, 1938, 61.

39 A.T.A. Magazine, XVII (4), 32.

40 Patterson, "Impetus," 190.

41 Patterson, "Experience," 17.

42 Sheane, 152.

43 Ibid., 128, 138.

44 Patterson, "Experience," 17.

45 Manitoba AR, 1937-8. 112-4.

46 N.S.AR, 1940-1. 53-4.

47 Fleming, III, *Schools,* 119.

48 Rule, 78-9.

49 Stamp, *Schools of Ontario,* 167.

50 See Ontario AR, 1937, 1.

51 Hadow *et al,* 1931, 102-4.

52 R. Stamp, *Schools of Ontario,* 166.

53 Patterson, "Experience," 25.

54 Selleck, *English Primary Education,* 25.

55 Rawson.

56 R. Stamp, *Schools of Ontario,* 170-1. See also Minkler; and Patterson, "Impetus," 189.

57 Ibid., 167.

58 Goldring, "Enterprises," 165-6.

59 Fleming, III, *Schools,* 128-9.

60 Ibid., 120.

61 C.E. Phillips, "The Public School," 186.

62 Cited in Fleming, III, *Schools,* 9-10.

63 R. Stamp, *Schools of Ontario,* 168-9. With reference to the "crash" basis of development of the revision see Ontario AR, 1937, 37.

64 Rule, 89.

65 Patterson, "Experience," 4, citing H.L. Campbell, 48-9.

66 Sask. AR, 1941, 31.

67 Patterson, "Experience," 14, citing *The Western School Journal*, XXXI, December, 1936, 317.

68 Patterson, "Experience," 12-13, 18.

69 P. Baker, 1.

70 Ibid., 4.

71 Dyde, 3-5, 48-9, 52. See also Alberta AR, 1930, 14.

72 Ibid., 70, 73, 75-6, 82.

73 Ibid., 93, 113-5.

74 Ibid., 187.

75 Ibid., 193.

76 Ibid., 223.

77 DBS, Elementary and Secondary Education in Canada, 1942 (data for 1940-1), 34-40.

78 Ontario AR, 1920, 56.

79 R. Stamp, *Schools of Ontario*, 110-1.

80 Ibid., 116-7.

81 Ibid., 201-2. See also R. Stamp, "Canadian High Schools,"

82 J.F. Macdonald, 79, 82.

83 Sandiford, "Junior High Schools," 374.

84 Pullen, 84-7.

85 B.C., *Programme of Studies for the Junior High School, 1936-7*, 5-7.

86 Netten, 30-5.

87 R. Stamp, "Canadian High Schools," 88-90.

88 Disbrowe, 118.

89 R. Stamp, "Canadian High Schools," 90-1.

90 B.C., *Programme of Studies for the Senior High School, 1936-7*, 6-8.

91 R. Stamp, "Canadian High Schools," 90.

92 Ibid., 97.

93 This account is drawn from Buckler, 60-77 with permission.

94 Drawn from Maynard with permission, 119-31.

95 Minifie, 213-9.

96 D. Lewis, 16.

97 Ibid., quoted with permission.

98 N. Sutherland, "Triumph," 5-8, 27-8.

99 Ibid., 10, 12, 16-7.

100 Ibid., 33.

101 Finkelstein, 326.

# CHAPTER 11

## THE OLD SUBJECTS
## IN THE NEW EDUCATION

*A subject ... in school or college is a selection of elements, typically made in identifiable periods, from an enquiry or cultural endeavour which becomes over time an on-going entity in its own right and an institutionalized vehicle for the common endeavours of the school system .... .*

(Ian Westbury, 1980)

### Introduction

In a sense, none of the new subjects of the New Education was new. Sewing, bookkeeping, agriculture and "physical culture" had all had at least a marginal place in the nineteenth century curriculum. What made them new were the new forms they assumed, the new methods by which they were taught, and the new prominence they gained in the curriculum after 1892. It was also true that not all of what are here called the old subjects, (notably the sciences, English literature, foreign languages and social studies) were old, for most of them also had a marginal place in the curriculum before 1892. All these, like the new subjects, changed in form, content and teaching methods.

Possibly the best distinction we can make between old and new is in terms of purpose and status. Certain subjects were seen as contributing to mental discipline or as serving traditional moral and cultural ends, sometimes termed liberal, even though as actually taught they were often far from liberalizing. "Academic" was another common descriptive label that sometimes carried the connotation of the dessicated formalism that the old subjects (and often the new ones) assumed in the classroom. Science, first viewed as an upstart, had gained high status by 1900 as a subject with mental discipline value and practical utility. The arts, sometimes enhanced by the New Education, but often denigrated before and since as "frills," long had an ambiguous status in the curriculum and tended to be seen as marginal subjects in the traditional course of study. With obvious cultural value

— although, as drawing, art began as a practical subject — the arts are here classified with the old subjects.

The status of all these subjects relates to what has been called their "imperialism" in the curriculum. Westbury has suggested that, over time, any subject becomes an institution in the schools, "a structural frame which specifies tasks and meaning contexts within which education takes place." The educative, assessment, teacher training, materials production and examination tasks of school systems, including even the planning of buildings, are to a large extent determined by the demands of subjects. As an institution, a school subject and a discipline are not necessarily the same thing and may be viewed very differently by teachers, university academics and researchers. In the period under discussion here, however, when university dominance of the curriculum was powerful, the approximation between the two was high.[1]

For convenience, the old subjects as described above are here classified into six categories: *English* (including grammar, composition, literature, reading, spelling and writing as well as *French and other languages); mathematics* (including arithmetic); *the sciences* (primarily biology, chemistry and physics); *the social studies* (including history, civics and geography); *the arts* (art, drawing and music). These subjects came to fullest flower in the high school, but aspects of most were also taught in the elementary school. It is as formal secondary studies that the "old" subjects are largely considered below. The emergence of English, mathematics, modern languages and the sciences as matriculation subjects was noted in Chapter 4. Social studies began to come into use as a term in the western provinces about 1920, to describe history, geography and civics at the elementary level. In the high school, history and to a much lesser extent, geography, were taught everywhere as discrete subjects, the former gaining high status as a matriculation subject. Science, formalized in the senior high school as a group of discrete subjects, had little formal place in the elementary curriculum before the 1930s when it began to emerge as general science.

In his profile of the high school curriculum during the 1920s that was discussed in Chapter 10, W.F. Dyde noted several significant variations in subject enrolments among the six provinces. English maintained its high status everywhere; in Ontario physical education ranked second, owing, he thought, to the fact that by 1923 so many high schools in that province were housed in separate buildings with their own gymnasia. Mathematics ranked below foreign languages in Ontario. The outcome of the "Latin debate" in that province was indicated by the fact the nearly 80 per cent of all Ontario high school pupils were still taking Latin in 1923. Alberta gave a high place to history and mathematics and ranked foreign languages comparatively low. Dyde noted that his table gave only a rough picture. Thus, a pupil studying English for five periods a week was equated with one studying geography for only two periods.[2] This and other variations should be borne in mind as we turn to a discussion of content and teaching method in the five major subject areas referred to.

## English, French and Other Languages

For purposes of this discussion English includes reading, spelling and writing, all of which had been established for half a century by 1892. In 1902, John Adams noted the use of alphabetic, phonetic and "look and say" methods in Canadian reading classes.[3] Alexander MacKay asserted in 1914 that the reading class was a literature class "intended to provide a medium for emotional expression." As before, the reader was also a means of teaching spelling, a subject that gradually became more systematized.[4] MacKay, who in 1895 urged spelling reform somewhat along the line of the modern i.t.a. phonetic system, reported in that year that in a survey of one Nova Scotia county he had found 49 per cent of home study time spent on the subject.[5] During the 1920s, Putman and Weir found spelling in British Columbia taught in almost total defiance of psychological principles. Teachers followed aimless procedures, and pupils were unmotivated by any attempt to connect the subject to real life. Time was wasted teaching words already known, or in teaching long or unusual words unlikely ever to be used.[6]

There were serious complaints about standards of English. Professor Dale at McGill University found teachers in training so badly prepared that work had to be done in training that should have been done in the schools. Susan Cameron, also of McGill, described the "bad speech, bad pronunciation and bad grammar" as the chief defect in all students, and referred to a first year course similar to what we would now call "remedial English."[7]

We have seen that, early in the period, readers were essentially a means of forming character through the use of moral and patriotic content. Although this emphasis remained dominant, the goals and methods of teaching gradually broadened. In her 1949 study of Canadian readers, Boyce observed that by 1920 the needs of social efficiency resulted in a greater emphasis on silent reading. Under the influence of psychologists such as Thorndike and Peter Sandiford, reading was "reinvented." Silent reading aimed at training future workers in a commercial and industrial society to follow written instructions efficiently. As well, teachers were enabled to provide more individualized instruction and remediation and to attend more to grading and classroom management. In pioneering the testing movement in Canada, Sandiford greatly influenced the standardized measurement of literacy.[8]

During the inter-war period, as the basic readers became more scientific, the principle of word frequency was used to control the level of difficulty of reading material. By studying the relative frequency and difficulty of words used in large bodies of written material, specialists were able to produce graded materials. In Ontario during the 1940s, readers with controlled vocabularies were recommended by a group of inspectors whose analysis of existing readers had revealed little evidence of a scientific approach. It was suggested that school boards be encouraged to provide at least two different series for each grade.[9] The approach reflected an interest in "functional literacy" which was spurred by wartime demands in the United States for the training of military and industrial workers capable of reading instructions at a fifth or sixth grade level.[10]

During these years, readers became more colourful in style and appearance, even as their content became more bland. As an emphasis on the technical mastery of reading skills developed, ubiquitous Dick and Jane replaced the exotic characters of earlier readers. Readers now portrayed an idealized world of gentle hills and flowing streams and included less story material from great authors.[11] The moral emphasis declined as the content changed from Old World to New World interests, from material dealing with the past to that concerned with the present, from emphasis on the world of the adult to that of the child. Yet, Canadian schools remained textbook schools through the 1940s. In the first six grades the reader was still a basic vehicle through which pupils acquired ideas, inspiration and reading skills.[12]

Where the teaching of writing was concerned, Putman and Weir found an inordinate attention in British Columbia classrooms to learning muscular movements by copying designs, instead of making a straightaway attack at writing words. They commended the writing skills of many pupils who followed the latter approach using the famous MacLean Method of Muscular Movement that had been devised by H.B. MacLean, an ex-Nova Scotian who taught writing at the Vancouver Normal School. Unfortunately, pupil individuality in writing style was inhibited by some zealous teachers who tried to prevent all finger movements.[13] The use of the copy book, the steel pen nib dipped into the desk inkwell and the blotter were classroom rituals from coast to coast throughout most of the period. Writing was thought to promote moral and physical discipline.

Grammar continued to be emphasized in the teaching of English, but Martyn reported that a new *Public School Grammar*, adopted in Ontario in 1899, gave more attention to usage than to the learning of formal definitions. This was a response to the charge of one teacher that the average student was "well stocked with the mere technicalities of English grammar" but had little facility in speaking or writing the first language.[14] However, because the skills of reading and writing were thought to be enhanced by rule-based instruction and by the abstract study of grammatical principles, no formal study would remain more entrenched in the curriculum over the following decades.

In 1920, the *Ontario Public School Grammar and Composition* attempted to simplify the subject, to correlate the teaching of grammar and composition and to reduce the amount of formal grammar taught in the elementary grades. Even so the section of the book devoted to grammar still covered about 130 pages.[15] However, the study of composition now began in Form 1 and the formal study of grammar was deferred to Form 4, a complete reversal of the situation that had been obtained in earlier generations.[16] In an earlier survey of the teaching of composition in Quebec, John Adams had found that, as in Great Britain, the subject was not taught but was instead an exercise in which the pupils were ordered "to write on this or that subject," and expected to tell what they knew rather than to express themselves.[17] This lack of a pedagogy for composition would persist over the following decades.

English literature was taught mostly through readers in the elementary grades, although by the 1920s portions of classic novels, such as *The Mill on the Floss*, and adventure literature by writers such as R.M. Ballantyne were included in the course of study. There was still a strong emphasis on the teaching of literary history and biographical information. The standard English curriculum that would persist for many decades became established at this time in most provinces. Chaucer, Shakespeare, Scott, Wordsworth and Tennyson all came into their own. From Nova Scotia to British Columbia such works as "The Charge of the Light Brigade," "Thanatopsis," "To a Skylark," "The Lotus Eaters," "Essays of Elia," "The Water Babies," "The Merchant of Venice," "Quentin Durward," "The School for Scandal," and Palgrave's "Golden Treasury" became enshrined in the curriculum.[18] Generations of Canadian children were imbued with the traditions of an Old World culture as their teachers carried out Alexander MacKay's injunction that "Choice passages ... be memorized occasionally for recitation with the proper expression."[19] A generation later Fred Clarke remarked on the Canadian practice of testing "even the learning of poetry — memory work as it is often called — by requiring the writing out, with neat handwriting and correct punctuation, of the poem learned." As a result, Clarke observed, "Appeal to the ear is largely overlooked ... "[20]

Canadiana as a term to describe Canadian literature came into use during the 1920s. In 1927, John W. Garvin, an Ontario educator, complained that, apart from an occasional selection, the work of Canadian authors was generally neglected in school readers. Academics showed little respect for the major Canadian poets by then publicly recognized. Garvin wondered whether it was too much to ask that 25 per cent of the space in Ontario readers be devoted to Canadian authors. In 1923, the Canadian Authors' Association enjoined the provincial departments of education to give more attention to meritorious Canadian literature.[21]

Bilingualism and the teaching of English as a second language became serious political and pedagogical issues after 1900, particularly in the Prairie provinces. Controversy focussed on the relative merits of the direct versus the indirect method of teaching. Before World War I, the indirect method, used in bilingual schools, including bilingual normal schools, was favoured by some immigrant groups and by some English-Canadian educators. They pointed out that unilingual English teachers, unable to understand the first language of their pupils, faced serious difficulties in teaching these students English. Opponents of bilingualism favoured the direct method, insisting on the value and efficiency of using unilingual teachers to teach

English directly as the almost exclusive language of the classroom, without the mediation of the pupils' own language. In any event, unilingualism prevailed, as a result of the resurgence of anglo-conformity during World War I.

The bilingual controversy resulted in the first sustained interest in theoretical and practical issues related to teaching English as a second language. In 1913, Norman Fergus Black in Saskatchewan published a pioneering study, *English for the non-English*, which had been his doctoral thesis at the University of Toronto. Black surveyed every provincial department of education, many state departments in the United States, and various authorities overseas. He then directed letters and questionnaires to hundreds of suitably experienced school inspectors, other administrators and teachers. Black concluded that the direct method was the most efficient way of teaching the language to beginners.[22]

The major argument for the direct method was made by J.T.M. Anderson, a Saskatchewan school inspector whose *The Education of the New Canadian* — another Toronto doctoral thesis — became the classic work on "Canada's greatest educational problem" as Anderson sub-titled his book.[23] Drawing considerably on Black's work and on his own, Anderson argued that the direct method is a natural method, similar to that used by children in learning their first language. Drawing also on the new psychological theories outlined in Peter Sandiford's textbook on child development, Anderson urged that language teaching avoid bookishness. It should be practical, utilizing object lessons and outdoor experiences related to the real world of the child.[24] Anderson revealingly described a lesson in which a class of immigrant children sang "Never Let the Old Flag Fall" and "Tipperary." "How many English children," Anderson asked rhetorically, "who sing these patriotic songs can do much better?" He went on in impressive detail to suggest practical teaching methods. Two appendices included examples of language lessons, rhymes and "memory gems."[25]

French was, of course, the dominant first language in Quebec, while elsewhere French and Latin dominated second language instruction. John Adams was surprised to find that French in the anglophone schools of Quebec was no better taught than in Great Britain. Few teachers could speak the language fluently. The "translation" rather than the "natural" method of teaching French was stressed, due to the need in the higher grades to prepare students for examinations.[26] In the 1920s, E.G. Savage, a British exchange inspector, commented that modern language instruction was one of the weakest areas of the Ontario curriculum. Laborious grammatical exercises and little oral teaching or actual reading of texts had given pupils "but a small vocabulary and ... failed to excite their interest in the language."[27] Goldstick's study of modern language instruction confirmed Savage's impressions. By this time, however, 85 per cent of Ontario high school pupils were studying French; enrolments exceeded those in Latin. Improvement was foreshadowed by a notable increase in the number of university graduates entering teaching.[28]

Stamp notes that nearly one-sixth of Ontario high school students were studying German before 1914, but anti-German wartime hysteria caused a precipitous decline in enrolments after that date.[29] In that province and in parts of the West, German was studied by students of that background as well as by students of British background preparing for university programs in modern languages. During these years, Italian and Spanish gained a foothold among the modern languages, although shortages of teachers and textbooks hampered progress.[30]

Many issues concerned with the teaching of modern languages in the 1920s were pinpointed as a result of initiatives undertaken by the Carnegie Corporation of New York. In 1924, a conference in Ottawa brought together the ministers of education, high school teachers, inspectors and administrators and university instructors who agreed to replicate in Canada the Modern Foreign Language Study that had been launched in the United States the previous year. With Carnegie funding and with the advice of the American Council on Education, the study proceeded under the aegis of the National Conference of Canadian Universities. Over the next three years the Canadian Committee on Modern Languages conducted an exhaustive study of modern language teaching, ranging from the elementary to the graduate school. The study included a survey of methods and textbooks, examinations, library facilities, teaching materials, teacher training, and of teacher, pupil and public views of the effectiveness of instruction. The importance of modern languages in Canada for cultural, scientific, commercial and industrial purposes was considered, with particular attention to the teaching of French.[31]

The committee made use of the new psychological testing techniques for carrying out objective surveys. These techniques were said to have made obsolete the old procedure of consulting expert opinion. In the absence of modern instruments for measuring language ability and achievement, the American and Canadian committees had been required to construct tests in all the relevant languages. The result was an extensive testing program comparable to that which Sandiford was then undertaking in British Columbia. An interesting conclusion, at variance with some modern findings, was that high school pupils learned languages much more rapidly and efficiently than younger pupils.[32]

Latin retained a dominant position, particularly in Ontario. The emphasis remained on the mastery of prescribed texts in order to prepare pupils for examinations. British observers such as John Adams, E.G. Savage and Fred Clarke all thought that far too many pupils who could never profit from the subject were forced to take it. In a survey conducted by Leddy during the 1940s, on behalf of the Humanities Research Council of Canada, a decline in Latin enrolments was noted, particularly outside Ontario. The subject was sustained mainly by the entrance requirement of most anglophone universities for two languages other than English, and by the continuing demand for Latin as a compulsory subject for entering medicine. Leddy noted that almost no students studied Greek in Canadian high schools by the 1940s. In general French retained a strong position in the curriculum of anglophone schools. More interesting texts were available and a greater stress on oral language was evident. Quite small numbers of pupils studied Spanish and German. There was a serious lack of trained teachers in both.[33]

Leddy noted that the expansion of the high school population and progressive theories of education had posed a challenge to the traditional humanistic curriculum, in particular to languages. Some critics maintained that ancient and modern languages should not be taught in the high schools at all, and that the objective of English teaching should be utilitarian or functional rather than literary. Yet, despite criticism and ferment, Leddy concluded that there had been surprisingly little outward change in the teaching of languages. In some respects there had been an improvement. Because "functional grammar" had been found to be ineffective, traditional grammar was being restored.[34]

During the 1940s, second language instruction still retained an aristocratic aura, confined as it was outside Quebec to an elite minority of high school students. In that province the matriculation examination had included an oral component since 1922.[35] Elsewhere, the goal of instruction was more cultural than practical; the study of another language was regarded as good for the students, even if they never learned to communicate it. The associated culture was studied for general interest and to relieve monotony, rather than to provide insight into the language. This approach took an essentially outside view of the culture. Nineteenth century theories of mental discipline remained popular, and teaching methods continued to be modelled on the rigid grammar-translation methods used for the study of dead languages.[36] Steinhauer observed that in Ontario the system had made the teacher's lot a relatively happy one. Objectives were clear and unadulterated. The emphasis was on grammatical rules, memorization of vocabularies, idiomatic phrases and illogical exceptions. The medium of instruction was English, and while the acquisition of a reasonable French accent was not penalized, the reaction of one's classmates to such nonconformity was not designed to encourage the student's efforts.[37]

World War II, the founding of the United Nations and the subsequent cold war gave an impetus to the teaching of languages, and to improved methods. This impetus was especially evident in the United States as a result of a serious shortage of qualified speakers of foreign languages among military and diplomatic personnel. With the exception of anglophone Quebec, the new methods, based on psycholinguistic response techniques, spread only slowly into Canada, but did set the stage for new approaches to language teaching during the post-war years. In the United States, special army schools featured small classes, the use of native speakers as models, and constant drill in hearing and speaking the target language. The use of electronic voice production, in particular the tape recorder, enhanced the acceptance of the audio-lingual method of teaching. This method treated language as a vehicle of communication, to be learned by using it, thus making the student an active, rather than a passive learner. Grammar was important, but only in so far as it facilitated the efficient use of the language as a means of communication. An attempt was made to help the student see the relationship between the target language and its parent culture.[38]

## Mathematics

In 1895, Alexander MacKay had urged a reform of weights and measures through the use of the metric system. The school should assist in meeting the challenge of international competition. He urged Ottawa to take action which would force the provinces' hands. He envisaged the schools teaching the metric system to communities and families through the children.[39] Six years later, the Protestant teachers of Quebec expressed a similar view in urging every provincial minister of education and the Federal government to adopt metric measures "as the one and only system to be used."[40] It was an idea whose time had yet to come.

During these years, the decline of arithmetic skills was widely deplored. In 1895, a DEA speaker declared that "Every High School teacher has found abundant evidence of the . . . .lack of accuracy and speed in fundamental calculation." One alleged cause was the decline in the proportion of male teachers, which was said to "have a tendency to affect the interest of the pupils in the more virile parts of the Public School programme . . ." Female teachers who passed their pupils successfully were said to be "the exception to the general rule . . ." Arithmetic suffered from "the growing tendency to introduce the Yankee idea of getting over difficulties by leaving them out." Thus, "complicated fractional expressions," recurring decimals in problems on annuities, and hard algebra problems were being de-emphasized in favour of easy deductions in geometry.[41]

In their 1970 survey of the history of Canadian mathematics, Crawford and his colleagues saw 1894 as a dividing line when "scientism" began to affect the teaching of the subject. Pedagogy began to overshadow content. Provincial isolation began to break down and Canadians became involved in the International Commission on the Teaching of Mathematics, formed in 1911. The report of the Committee of Ten had some influence in Ontario at this time, as applied mathematics entered the curriculum, and as some reduction occurred in the emphasis on Euclidean geometry.[42]

Similar trends occurred in western Canada. Sigurdson reported that by 1930 all students were following a mathematics program leading to university matriculation, even though the numbers going on to higher studies were negligible.[43] Buckles' Alberta study found that by 1912 Euclid was modified by simplifying earlier propositions, omitting some and changing the sequence. New books stressed "intuitive geometry" with graded questions, encouragement of alternative proofs, discouragement of memorization, provision of few proofs and stress on practical applications. In arithmetic however, highly complicated mechanical questions were common, stressing routine application of rules instead of originality. Algebra in Alberta remained fairly constant between 1900 and 1932, but geometry declined in status. The ostensible abandonment of mental discipline and the growing non-selectivity of the high school resulted in a fusion of the various mathematics subjects into "general mathematics." According to Buckles, this innovation was a failure, resulting in a lowering of the average standard of achievement. Heterogeneous grouping also depressed standards, with the university forced to offer remedial courses in mathematics.[44]

Arithmetic remained dominated by the slavish devotion of teachers to ancient methods. So claimed a Saskatchewan school inspector in 1916, in reporting that in no subject was more time wasted to less effect.[45] Putman and Weir in British Columbia were equally critical nearly a decade later. They noted problems on school blackboards that "were of the traditional antiquated type devised by formal disciplinarians," constituting "flat, stale and unprofitable performances with symbols" having "little if any relation to practical needs or situations." Gradgrind instruction, during which pupils copied solutions without explanation or understanding, occupied as much as 100 minutes every morning.[46] Arithmetic slowly declined in the high school curriculum, although mental arithmetic remained important at all levels. In the 1937 Ontario revision of the elementary program, arithmetic suffered a reduced time allotment, losing its pride of place on school timetables. Under the influence of progressive education, an effort was made to give arithmetic greater social and personal relevance through such topics as "Joe Wilson Learns How to Make a Model Glider."[47]

During the inter-war years, classical mathematics retained its dominance. The Canadian Mathematics Congress was formed in 1945. During this decade, the postwar reaction against progressivism led to a new emphasis on arithmetic. In 1950, an Ontario educator, Sonley, charged that progressive educators were averse to drill, with the result that pupils wasted time and were discouraged as a result of their inaccuracies in solving problems. Arithmetic had been watered down to the point that textbooks for Grades 7 and 8 resembled social studies textbooks "with a few fractions thrown in to separate the topics." Another critic, Shuster, speaking at the same meeting and anticipating the unified approach of the later "new math," deplored a compartmentalized approach to the teaching of the various mathematics subjects.[48] Yet, the ablest university-bound high school student of the 1940s followed a regimen little different from that of thirty years before. Although the average elementary school pupil spent a little less time on arithmetic and studied from somewhat less drill-oriented, more colourful textbooks, the program was not significantly different from that followed earlier by earlier generations. Allowing at all levels for a less selective school population, it does not seem that mathematics achievement levels had changed significantly.

## The Sciences

Nature study or rural science was the basis for introducing science content into the elementary curriculum during the New Education. Some science was taught in connection with agriculture, health (physiology and hygiene) and temperance. The hint of later discovery approaches was implicit in Alexander MacKay's view that the aim of science teaching was not the amassing of facts, but the cultivation of a disposition "to inquire at first hand a habit of caution in forming judgements about things."[49] But object lessons in nature study frequently became language lessons, or became formalized, as Putman and Weir noted. A lesson on the loon taught by a Vancouver normal school student that required pupils to point out the bird's features on a blackboard drawing and then to copy a set of notes, resulted in instruction that was *about* nature study rather than a study *of* nature.[50] Yet, as James M. Minifie's experience in a one-room Saskatchewan school demonstrated, an imaginative teacher could inspire students even in the most adverse circumstances. Miss Reaman from Orillia introduced her avid pupil to the Ontario High School botany textbook which he studied all winter, impatiently awaiting spring when, with the help of Spotton's *Canadian Wild Flowers*, he was able to identify specimens gathered by himself and his fellow pupils. For his efforts, he was appointed school botanist. Miss Reaman's subscription to the *Scientific American* was another great contribution to learning in her tiny Prairie schoolhouse.[51]

Hughes' 1964 study of physical science teaching in Alberta provided a national perspective on developments, since that province drew so heavily on Ontario.[52] He saw socio-economic change, changes in school goals, in the nature and size of the school population, in teacher qualifications and supply, and in examinations, university requirements and school organization as all having effects. But, over half a century, curriculum revisions were minor. As a result, the disparity between frontier knowledge and high school content grew. Physics and chemistry remained dominant and general science was slow to take hold.[53] The major goal remained intellectual development on the assumption that practical benefits and applied knowledge would result indirectly. The learning of experimental scientific methods was often hindered by a lack of laboratory facilities, especially in small high schools. Teachers frequently were inadequately trained and classes were large.[54]

In the cities of Alberta, as elsewhere throughout Canada, good facilities increasingly became available. Chemistry began as a descriptive study of elements and compounds; after 1912 such topics as atomic hypothesis, electrolytic dissociation and the molecular theory slowly began to gain ground. In physics the electron theory of matter also gradually took hold. Unfortunately, in neither subject did new experimental laboratory methods have much effect on content in a period when content selection was essentially determined by textbooks. Laboratory work was largely a matter of verifying or illustrating laws already learned rather than true experimentation. Examinations stressed factual results and memorization. However, by the 1920s, chemistry began to go beyond mere description and to incorporate explanations. In spite of later recognition of the "knowledge explosion," of technological change and of science as necessary to effective citizenship, it remained possible to graduate from an Alberta high school without taking a physical science course.[55]

As a new province, Alberta also illustrated the growth of biology and associated life sciences during the period. Biology was often introduced early as an outgrowth of nature study and as an element of general science. Ideally suited to the objectives of progressive education, its content nevertheless remained traditional and discipline-oriented, with an emphasis on memorization and preparation for examinations. While botany, for example, was supposed to stress a practical knowledge of plants, it continued to stress formal classification.[56] The learning of the structure, function and relation of the root, stem, leaves and flowers of typical plants and of the Latin names seems to have persisted for many years. As with elementary science, progressive ideas did have some effect by the 1930s. H.C. Newland, however, saw such effect limited by the inertia of tradition, the "honorific value" of well established subjects, the vested interests of subject teachers themselves, university entrance requirements, and, above all, the tendency of parents to support a *status quo* that they believed provided educational and vocational advantages for their children.[57]

## The Social Studies

Throughout the period, this subject area essentially comprised separate courses in history and geography although, by the 1930s, both were sometimes fused at the elementary level. Elementary social studies was often viewed as the integrating core subject of the progressive curriculum, lending itself particularly to the use of project and enterprise methods. In 1896, George Ross urged that history be taught to younger children "incidentally with the reading lessons" and "conversationally," stressing biography rather than political history.[58] Even such a conservative as John Squair admitted that history and geography had little value "when taught out of books to young children by persons of small culture." He cited an entrance question which he himself could not have answered: "Name four laws passed by the British parliament during the last century that have secured to the English people liberties they formerly did not possess. Give the substance of each of the laws you have named." Such teaching, said Squair, could not help "but created prejudice and benumb intellect."[59]

According to Quick, biography began to find a place in the Ontario curriculum after 1905. Correlation of history with literature, composition, Bible stories, stories of "primitive peoples" and child life in other lands, together with accounts of famous persons were advocated. In 1919, renewed emphasis was given to history *per se* and it was reinstated as a high school entrance examination subject in that year.[60] To H.J. Cody, who became Ontario's minister of education in 1918, history was "the great vehicle of patriotic instruction" in a curriculum that should unabashedly be Protestant Christian, politically conservative, and based on Anglo-Saxon racial superiority.[61] The Ontario Readers, noted earlier, continued in use during the inter-war period, ensuring that Ontario children, like those elsewhere, would remain exposed to a uniform imperial curriculum.[62] The 1915 Ontario teachers' manual on history was a complete curriculum package embodying sample lessons and instructions on the use of the textbook. Teaching methods stressed comparative, "regressive," (working from the present backwards), and concentric approaches. The concentric approach was what would later be termed a "spiral curriculum" and was described as a method of dealing "in ever widening circles with the same topic or event," such as the life of Champlain. Current events were advocated to motivate historical study and to serve as the basis for teaching civics.[63]

The report on the teaching of history and civics in Canadian schools prepared for the National Council of Education in 1923 by members of the University of Toronto history department is interesting chiefly as evidence that academic historians were moving toward a more objective treatment of their discipline. The report caused dismay in the ranks of the Council.[64] A moral function for school history was specifically rejected, although the Toronto group agreed that in providing the material for moral judgements such a function could be an acceptable indirect result. Moral instruction was the proper province of literature and civics rather than history. Nor should history be a medium for teaching patriotism or internationalism. Children needed a realistic view of the world that showed conflict as well as co-operation as ingredients of international relations, although teachers should not dwell on unpleasant aspects of the past more than necessary. Social history might have value, but political history — embodied in institutions and ideas — must have pride of place.[65]

The committee's analysis of the objectives of some provincial curricula implied that there was a danger of history teaching in Canada being prostituted to the service of propaganda. However, there could be no objection to an emphasis on Canadian, British and French history. Where civics was concerned, it was felt that in a population mostly British in origin, there was bound to be something "peculiarly repugnant" in teaching citizenship as a subject. However, the world situation was inevitably making such teaching necessary. Consequently, the report recommended a civics primer "if only as an appendix to a history book." In addition to a civics primer, the committee somewhat inconsistently commended the continuing importance of readers and proposed a "golden book" for elementary schools that would embody "the noblest tradition of the great family of people to which Canada belongs ... " A similar volume was recommended for secondary schools as "a golden book of the British spirit at its truest and noblest ... ."[66]

The National Council report was but one of several efforts to find a common ground for the teaching of Canadian history. The Dominion History Contest sponsored in the 1890s by the DEA, and the CEA study of textbooks in the 1940s, have already been noted. The study in the latter decade by the Canada-United States Committee on Education of the treatment of the respective national histories of each country in the curricula of the other, was another example that attested to a continuing concern for the importance of history in moulding national and international consciousness.[67] In the 1920s, three distinguished Canadian historians expressed the view that something was "radically wrong when so many students in our schools disliked Canadian history."[68] During the interwar years, academic historians were heavily involved in writing textbooks for schools. In 1934, one of their number, Duncan McArthur of Queen's University, became Ontario's deputy minister of education, a post in which he presented the unusual spectacle of a history professor who espoused a progressivist social studies viewpoint. McArthur expressed the view of most provincial policymakers when he declared that the school should counter unrestrained individualism and "create and promote right social attitudes." History was described as "a record of citizenship" and while it should not be used to propagate "certain theories," the subject should demonstrate "the fundamental nature of man as a social being and the interdependence of the welfare of the individual and the well-being of the group."[69]

Geography, much more than history, remained an elementary school subject after 1892, and was little taught at the high school level. Here Canadian trends were influenced by those in the United States, where physical and economic geography became separate and unrelated strands in the curriculum. In that country physical geography or earth science enjoyed short-lived prestige in the high school. Due to the lack of trained teachers and the complete neglect of human geography, the subject was eventually absorbed into general science. Geography in Canadian schools went through a similar cycle and soon died out nearly everywhere except in Ontario. There it retained its hold in the form of a textbook, *Ontario High School Physical Geography* that was also used by several generations of students in a few other provinces. In 1937, physical geography disappeared or became absorbed into courses in economic or commercial geography. The latter had emerged after 1910. Ontario scheduled commercial geography as a required course in the first year of the high school program which emphasized the study of Ontario, Canada and the British Empire, together with a study of selected foreign countries.[70] The subject was eventually absorbed into history or social studies. After 1950, geography slowly revived as a high school subject.

According to Quick, geography texts were often factual compendia, with little emphasis on narrative style, features that made it easier to extract the facts to be tested on the entrance and other examinations.[71] The best known texts produced for use in Ontario and other provinces was a series edited by Professor George W. Cornish of the Ontario College of Education, which provided a systematic or topical "places and products" treatment of commercial geography by commodities. Commerce and transportation were also treated. Studies of the British Empire included standard patriotic sentiments of the day, reflecting a jingoism that Canadians have usually ascribed to American textbooks. London was described as a great city due to "the industry, the thrift ... the sterling business ability ... [and] the honest dealing of its people" while India was said to have "wonderfully improved" under British rule. Although written in Canada ostensibly for Canadian pupils, the book described France as "our neighbour across the channel" with whom, despite earlier bitter struggles, "we have learned to get along on friendly terms."[72]

The low status of geography in the inter-war period was evident in a 1921 survey of textbooks commissioned by the National Council of Education. A.D. Chapman, a British geographer, surveyed seventeen textbooks authorized for use in the nine provinces. Eight of these were written in French by priests untrained in the subject and were of poor quality. Some of those written in English were no better. Chapman deplored the fact that, because each province was a law unto itself, exchanges of teachers and textbooks were discouraged. He equally deplored provincial demands for special editions of books to meet imagined local needs. The two most widely used texts were Ontario products, collectively used in five provinces. To Chapman, the root of the problem was the lack of acceptance of geography as a university discipline, a situation that would plague school geography for another thirty years.[73]

## The Arts

The place of the arts in the curriculum was sometimes featured in discussions at DEA meetings. In 1901, Mrs. F.M.S. Jenkins of Ottawa made a plea for a greater recognition of them, particularly music. She based her argument on Herbert Spencer's definition of education as learning "how to use all our faculties to the best advantage of ourselves and others." Jenkins wondered if the development of imagination, feeling and sentiment was "as much considered ... as the culture of the more purely intellectual faculties."[74]

Gaitskell, in his 1947 survey, took a less than sanguine view of how art had developed in Ontario. Building on the foundations that had been laid in the post-Confederation era, free expression was encouraged in the elementary grades, but the secondary school program remained extremely rigid. The rise of the art schools did enable trained teachers to go beyond the rigidities of linear drawing, and to introduce new media into the classroom. The most significant Ontario trends before 1914 were the control that the technical branch of the department of education gained over art education in the schools, and the influence exerted by professional artists through the art schools. Unique arrangements enabled professional artists produced in these state-supported schools to teach in the public schools as a basic means of livelihood, while pursuing their own artistic work on the side.[75]

The Ontario College of Art, established in 1912, offered courses leading to special teaching certificates. But neither in training nor in teaching — and this was particularly true of the normal schools — were the needs of the child considered. A progressive change began in Ontario in 1937, as art teaching began to move beyond technical training following the efforts of Arthur Lismer, a member of the Group of Seven, who had a special interest in children's art. The criteria of adult art should not be applied to child art, said Lismer. Gaitskell observed that child development rather than art *per se* had become the most important outcome of art education.[76] Artistic appreciation was to be taught indirectly by calling the child's attention to beautiful things, to natural and human phenomena in the environment. The classroom was to be made aesthetically pleasing. Appealing pictures, drawn from the great masterpieces, were to be included in displays.[77]

British Columbia provided an example of how a normal school instructor could greatly influence the subject in schools. Rogers has estimated that W.P. Weston, an English-born and trained art educator at the Vancouver Normal School, trained half the province's new teachers between 1915 and 1946, and influenced many others through summer school instruction. Weston emphasized design and drawing from memory, incorporating his ideas in two teachers' manuals which effectively constituted the elementary school curriculum for many years and were also used in other provinces. As the major shaper of art education in the province for more than three decades, Weston made British ideas of art teaching more influential than the current American theories.[78]

Trowsdale suggests that music found its greatest acceptance in Ontario during the same period.[79] By 1900, half the province's public school pupils were studying the subject, a growth that was assisted by the training of specialist teachers after the founding of the Toronto Conservatory in 1887. The emphasis on method was uppermost; as Cringan said, the question was not now "Shall we teach music in our schools?" but "How shall we teach it?"[80] With the coming of the New Education, stress was put on the value of music as a leisure time "appreciation" subject, an essential part of the education of "the whole child." Ontario's 1904 revision reflected the new notions of self-expression. Songs, taught easily by the now well established tonic sol-fah system, were more important than exercises and note-reading. In music, "Technique should be second to enjoyment and the play spirit should pervade it all."[81] But no real change in the course of study took place, as had occurred in art. Even though music finally became an obligatory subject in 1924, it fared poorly compared with the new subjects, gaining less acceptance than nature study, physical education or art. Small music budgets reflected this low status.[82]

Music could draw the community together and, as the Hamilton Board of Education said in 1920, could promote national identity.[83] However, this ostensible social value of music was still often subordinated to its supposed mental training value.[84] In 1943, "citizenship" was invoked as an objective by the professor of music at Queen's University.[85] Emotional expression and aesthetic value were other justifications. Social and citizenship values were noted in Ontario's 1937 curriculum revision.[86]

Despite its obligatory status during the inter-war period, music was often neglected in rural areas. New controversies over method arose with the advocacy of the progressivist "song method" which posed some challenge to the sol-fah system. As Sir Ernest Macmillan wrote in 1934, "A child should make music before he studies it ... " To Macmillan the chief function of school music, apart from personal leisure values, was that of building future audiences.[87] A major step in Ontario in 1935 was the establishment of a Music Branch under G. Roy Fenwick as first director. For Fenwick, the main aims were aesthetic appreciation, self-appreciation, "a safe outlet for the emotions" and "a leisure-time activity."[88]

In the 1937 curriculum revision, a new music course introduced singing, rhythmic responses and learning to listen as the three basic elements. Creative work (writing simple melodies, making instruments) was to be encouraged, and singing was to develop "the musical sense" through learning national folk songs. Appreciation through listening was important and schools were provided with phonographs and recordings; as well, libraries were to be stocked with books on music. The regulations now prescribed that music be taught every day. For teachers lacking musical ability and training, Fenwick introduced a series of teaching records. He also arranged for the appointment of music supervisors in city and county and district boards.[89]

Despite the progress noted, by 1945 the rationale for music still lacked any coherent and consistent theory. Arguments for it were largely dependent upon the exigencies of the time. Its supporters used generalized statements as arguments, alternately invoking mental discipline and citizenship values that were achieved as well or better by other subjects. This range of values led to a confusion of aims. Although in 1950 the Hope Report confirmed music as an obligatory subject having official approval, it remained suspect and, suggested Trowsdale, this would remain the case until teachers worked out a satisfactory theoretical basis for their subject. Another handicap was that no musicians of stature comparable to Arthur Lismer in art had offered their talents to develop the subject, nor were there books relating the music curriculum to general educational theory and philosophy similar to Dewey's writings on art education.[90]

## Notes to Chapter 11

1 Westbury, 17.

2 Dyde, 187-8, 189, 263.

3 J. Adams, 92.

4 A. MacKay, *Monograph*, 10-11.

5 A. MacKay, "Three Great Reforms," 78-84.

6 Putman and Weir, *Survey*, 139-41.

7 Testimony to RCITTE, 1846, 1910.

8 Boyce; see also de Castell et al, "Defining 'Literacy' in North American Schools," 381-2 and "On Defining Literacy," 9.

9 Parvin, 106.

10 L. Walker, "Progressives," 76.

11 See Sheehan, "Character Training," 80-2 and R. Stamp, *Schools of Ontario*, 168.

12 Boyce, 204.

13 Putman and Weir, *Survey*, 141-5.

14 Martyn, 46, 57.

15 Ibid. 50-1.

16 Ibid. 113-4.

17 J. Adams, 107.

18 A. MacKay, *Monograph*, 27; Langley, 239; Putman and Weir, *Survey*, 304.

19 A. MacKay, "What Is Aimed At," 163.

20 Clarke, "Secondary Education," 567.

21 Garvin, 293-6.

22 Black, *English*.

23 J. Anderson.

24 Ibid. 123-7.

25 Ibid. 254-5.

26 J. Adams, 115-6.

27 Savage, 79.

28 Goldstick, 237-241.

29 R. Stamp, *Schools of Ontario*, 91.

30 Goldstick, 228.

31 American and Canadian Committees on Modern Languages, vii-ix.

32 Ibid., ix, xiii.

33 Leddy, 11-14.

34 Ibid., 3, 4, 6.

35 American and Canadian Committees on Modern Languages, 22.

36 Cipolla, 10; Burnham, 137.

37 Steinhauer, 11.

38 Cipolla, 11-12.

39 A. MacKay, "Three Great Reforms," 74-6.

40 *Educational Record of the Province of Quebec*, 21, (November 1901), 323-4.

41 A. McDougall, 278.

42 D. Crawford, "School Mathematics in Ontario, 1894-1959", 390, 392.

43 Sigurdson, 414.

44 Buckles, 87-9.

45 Sask. AR, 1915, 68.

46 Putman and Weir, *Survey*, 135, 137.

47 Sigurdson, 418.

48 Sonley and Shuster cited in D. Crawford, "School Mathematics in Ontario, 1894-1959," 403-4.

49 MacKay, *Monograph*, 13.

50 Putman and Weir, *Survey*, 160.

51 Minifie, 135-6.

52 W. Hughes, 11.

53 Ibid., 133.

54 Ibid., 142.

55 Ibid., 135-40.

56 J. Belanger, 24.

57 W.L. Hughes, 135, citing Newland.

58 G. Ross, *The School System*, 62-3.

59 Squair, 183.

60 Quick, 179, 182, 185.

61 Cited in R. Stamp, *Schools of Ontario*, 105.

62 Ibid., 93, 105.

63 Minister of Education (Ontario), *History, Ontario Teachers' Manual*, 21-23, 49.

64 Lyons, "In Pursuit," 191.

65 NCE, "Observations," 10.

66 Ibid., 12-13, 17, 19-20, 30.

67 CEA, "A Study of National History Textbooks."

68 G.M. Wrong, Chester W. Martin and W.N. Sage, v.

69 McArthur, 300-302.

70 Tomkins, "School Geography," 8-9.

71 Quick, 153.

72 Cornish, 191, 206, 311.

73 Chapman. The full report was published by the Council as *Report on a Survey of Text Books of Geography Used in Canadian Schools*, Winnipeg 1921.

74 Jenkins, 380.

75 Gaitskell, 19-20.

76 Ibid., 290.

77 Fleming, III, *Schools*, 127.

78 Rogers, "Paint Slinger," 1, 24-7.

79 Trowsdale.

80 Cringan, 309.

81 Trowsdale, citing OEA Music Section Minutes (1921), 99.

82 Trowsdale, 113, 173.

83 Ibid., 95.

84 Ibid., 96-8.

85 Harrison, 394-5.

86 Trowsdale, 101.

87 Macmillan, 90-2.

88 Fenwick, 6.

89 Trowsdale, 193-8.

90 Ibid., 102-4, 114.

# CHAPTER 12

## "PROSAIC SANITY" — PERSPECTIVES ON CURRICULUM CONTROL AND CHANGE IN A NATIONALIZING ERA

*A ... feature of the common countenance of Canadian education is found in the minute prescription of courses of study and textbooks and the meticulous detail of official regulations.*

(Fred Clarke, 1934)

*Canada's security against the plausible superficialities of chaotic and corrosive influences which have worked such mischief elsewhere is to be found ... in the steady ... prosaic sanity which characterizes her people.*

(Fred Clarke, 1935)

During the nineteenth century, limited bureaucracies and the importunities of localism made direct supervision and control of the curriculum difficult. Indirectly, centralized control and uniformity were gradually promoted through textbooks, examinations and teacher training policies. After 1892 these policies were refined and extended and their implementation made more efficient, with the result that, despite the absence of a strong central administrative apparatus, curricular uniformity across each province and among all provinces was considerably enhanced. To be sure, irregular attendance, the high transiency of pupils and teachers, local apathy and the general lack of resources caused the curriculum as experienced by the individual pupil to vary significantly over time and place. Yet these very factors, in particular the lack of resources, also promoted a common experience for all pupils. Economic no less than educational reasons led, for example, to the use of cheap uniform textbooks, dependence on which was reinforced by the meagre background of most teachers. In this chapter, we shall note how, after 1920, as the educational establishment pressed for more "peace and efficiency" in Canadian school systems, an incipient bureaucracy finally emerged that permitted a higher degree of centralized control than had previously been possible.

New Mechanisms of Curriculum Control

Textbooks and Textbook Policy: Towards National Uniformity

Barbara Finkelstein, writing in the United States context, has described the role of the textbook in introducing pupils to "a world of formal discourse" that complemented "the world of conversation" in the community outside the school. As pupils committed textbooks to memory and imitated and reproduced their content, they "were drawn into a world of fixed and contained culture, of orderly structure and sequence." Textbook content was ethnocentric, reflecting a small tolerance for diversity and a narrow range of political and cultural values. Suffused with a kind of pan-Protestant civic morality and moralism, textbooks were models of clarity if not of broadmindedness. Through them, pupils gained "their first systematic experience with a world beyond the confines of family, church and street" and "a first access to information and myth as it had been processed and organized by strangers."[1]

Finkelstein's description of American pedagogy was equally true of Canadian pedagogy, as accounts of their schooling by Ernest Buckler and other writers cited earlier clearly indicate. The essential difference in anglophone Canada was the British ambience of the textbook culture. Textbooks helped to detribalize and deculturalize New Canadian pupils especially, and then to retribalize them into the dominant Anglo-Celtic community. As pupils were introduced through ritual acts of moral and patriotic worship, the textbook-as-curriculum became an agent of civic consciousness.

This role had, of course, been established for decades before 1892. After that date, as George Ross' plea for a national history textbook demonstrated, textbook policy aimed at national as well as at provincial uniformity. In 1906, Robert Pyne, one of Ross' successors as Ontario's minister of education, asked, "Why not try and establish over the whole Dominion a national series of textbooks?" Such a scheme would be economical and would unify Canadians "by including the same loyalty, the same love of home, the same Canadian patriotism throughout the entire Confederation." Pyne's fellow ministers showed varying degrees of support for his plan, but it never materialized.[2]

In practice, however, a high degree of uniformity resulted from the widespread use of Ontario textbooks. In Nova Scotia, Alexander MacKay had been asked by the provincial educational association in 1913 "to consider the possibility of interprovincial co-operation in the preparation of and publication of cheap texts ... " He thought that textbooks in most subjects could be absolutely uniform. Common texts in civics, geography and history could include separate provincial supplements.[3] MacKay's own annual report in the same year recorded that the provincial advisory board had recommended the adoption of a number of Ontario high school textbooks. The Ontario Readers had already been adopted in Nova Scotia's common schools.[4] The report noted the cheapness of the books, resulting from the Ontario government's assumption of royalty, editing, typesetting and plate costs. However, Nova Scotia should not be seen "as parasitic on the larger province of Ontario" and, with the other provinces, should make financial and editorial contributions to textbook production. Five years later, MacKay reported that Nova Scotia education had been "very largely Ontarioized."[5]

In the Prairie provinces, Walker has noted that during the territorial period before 1905, curriculum-making was essentially a process of selecting and prescribing textbooks written or published in Ontario.[6] In his 1918 survey of Canadian urban school systems, W.L. Richardson identified twenty-one textbooks published by the province's education department, with a total of forty-two authorizations in other provinces. Saskatchewan used fifteen Ontario authorized textbooks. The other two Prairie provinces used a total of twelve. Some titles were revised editions of texts originally developed in the western provinces and later published and used in Ontario.[7] Meanwhile, in British Columbia, Superintendent Robinson, expressing a concern still present in Canadian education, described co-operation among the four western provinces in promoting textbook uniformity in order to meet the needs of families constantly moving from province to province.[8]

E.T. White's 1922 study of textbooks in Ontario revealed that regulations governing textbooks were basically similar in most provinces. By this time, textbooks in the core subjects were provided free or at a nominal rental in most provinces, initially on a local option basis. Reliance on detailed regulations was necessitated by limited inspection and supervisory capacity. In Ontario, George Ross and his successors, expanding on the policies initiated by Ryerson, established regulations governing the writing, publishing, pricing, evaluation, selection and distribution of textbooks that were used as a model by other provinces and still form the basis of much contemporary policy. The use of unauthorized textbooks by a teacher could result in suspension and in the witholding by the inspector of the legislative grant to the school board.[9] Under Ross, textbooks were prepared under departmental direction by teachers and professors, using single authors for all texts, except readers for which groups of three authors were used. In establishing strict methods of selection similar to formal systems of evaluation used today, Ross did not hesitate to refer to his regulations as a kind of necessary censorship designed, among other purposes, to ensure sound arrangement and accuracy of subject matter. Trustees and teachers were excluded from the textbook selection process because Ross thought they were incompetent.[10]

Ross' policy encouraged Canadian authorship. Quality and price were carefully controlled. In 1906, Robert Pyne set up a textbook commission to study problems of selection, evaluation, publication and costs. Witnesses from all concerned groups were called, and American and British expertise was consulted. As a result, a policy was established whereby the government prepared its own texts by arranging authorship, making plates, owning copyright and printing by tender. Shortly, Ontario had one textbook per subject. In 1912, a textbook office was established, headed by David Goggin who served as editor and further systematized selection and authorization. The office lasted until 1956 when it was merged with the Curriculum and Textbooks Branch.[11]

Peter Sandiford, writing in 1935, observed that the Canadian passion for uniformity was summed up by the question educators asked: "If the minimum essentials can be determined, what is more natural than to embody them in a group of textbooks to be placed in the hands of each and every pupil?" Canadians thought that a few authorized textbooks could ensure equality of opportunity and social solidarity, and that intellectual salvation could be found between their covers. They studied texts and found that "all too often they restrict their studies too narrowly." School inspection and examinations were directly linked to textbooks. Inspectors policed their use and based their judgements of school achievement upon pupil knowledge of their contents.[12]

According to Parvin, after 1918 Ontario textbooks and pupil knowledge of their contents were increasingly judged by scientific educational criteria. Standardized tests such as the Thorndike-McCall Silent Reading Test were used to examine pupils.[13] Tait claimed later that in the "Old Education," textbooks were used exclusively as an end rather than a means. By contrast, the New Education used textbooks as a means towards the social and educational development of the pupil.[14] Some conservative critics of the New Education believed that more active teaching methods downgraded the use of textbooks.

Ontario regulations gave preference to Canadian and British texts. If neither product was available, an American book could be selected. In such subject areas as science and mathematics, reality often dictated the use of American texts, since no suitable Canadian or British texts could be found. The practice of Canadianizing foreign texts and of provincializing Ontario textbooks authorized in other provinces continued. In 1938, the Alice and Jerry Readers were Canadianized by replacing about half the contents with especially written Canadian and many British narratives and poems. The American flag was replaced by the Union Jack. In the case of some high school textbooks, Canadian spellings, place names and other references were inexpensively welded into duplicates of the American copper electroplates. The contents were almost indistinguishable from the original, but such Canadianized texts were usually printed on poorer, albeit Canadian-manufactured, paper and bound in Canadian cloth of stodgy appearance, with covers of unimaginative Canadian design.[15]

In 1936, the method of preparing books under departmental direction was partly abandoned in Ontario. Selections were made by committees from books submitted by publishers. Alterations or revisions needed to adapt books to curriculum requirements might be made by committees which could also recommend the preparation of an original book written to specification. Seven-year contracts helped to stabilize prices, but by creat-

ing a monopoly also had the effect of freezing the curriculum for the contract period.[16] Authors were typically teachers, often writing in collaboration with university professors who served as co-authors or consultants. By
this time publishers were beginning to develop more sophisticated
editorial, production and design capacities, although some still had no full-
time senior editors or editorial staff. Editorial functions in the largest firms
were often performed by senior executives in their spare time; in the
smaller firms, most if not all of the responsibility for manuscript editing,
production planning, proofreading and sometimes even author liaison
devolved upon the Supervisor of the printing plant.[17]

In testifying before the Hope Commission in Ontario during the late
1940s, publishers took an expansive view of their role. They claimed that,
in addition to providing a service to the school system, they also enhanced
educational thought. They pointed to their close contact with personnel in
the field and to their role in anticipating and giving voice to pedagogical
trends by hiring competent authors to prepare texts consistent with those
trends. Their planning, editing and production staffs rendered an expert
professional service to education. Publishers served as major agents of dissemination, and provided an essential liaison between the creative educator
and the public.[18] During the next two decades, the influence of publishers
as major determinants of the Canadian curriculum would peak.

Before 1950, prices of books in Ontario were kept low by heavy departmental subsidies or by subventions to publishers. In 1943, the costs of supplying books became a legitimate operating cost in the determination of
provincial grants to school boards; by 1950, the provision of free textbooks
had become provincial policy.[19] As in the past, teachers were still required,
under pain of fine or suspension, to use only textbooks authorized or
prescribed by the central authority.[20]

### Examinations and University Policy as Curriculum Control

Textbook and examination policy were closely linked. In 1918, Peter Sandiford described Canadian high schools as "examination-ridden".[21] H.T.J.
Coleman thought that the formal (and formidable) high school entrance
examination, "the greatest evil in our Ontario education," was a source of
misery to parents, teachers and pupils alike. It was part of a Canadian
examination system that made "an unwholesome appeal to the competitive
instincts" and overemphasized intellectual education at the expense of the
emotions and the will.[22] A 1922 Carnegie Foundation study of education
in the Maritime provinces denounced the dominance of examinations and
the resulting merciless selection of pupils. Provincial examinations that
regulated high school admission and subsequent promotion from grade to
grade made the examination "of more importance than the school."[23] In
British Columbia, Putman and Weir, noting the unmodified westward
spread of the Ontario system, deplored the use of examination results as

"the chief criterion of the teacher's success . . . or the most reliable measure of the school's efficiency."[24]

By this time, some modification in high school entrance policy was becoming evident. In 1918, the British Columbia Department of Education had provided for the exemption of designated students from the high school entrance examination on the recommendation of the principal. Later, the examination was abolished and eventually an accreditation system was adopted. Ontario provided for high school entrance by recommendations, but did not finally abolish the entrance examination until 1949. The change may be taken as symbolic of the reduction of the distinction between the elementary and the high school, and of the tacit although cautious acceptance of the latter as a non-selective institution open to all. A few provinces maintained entrance examinations, usually for rural schools, into the 1950s.

University entrance or matriculation examinations proved the most vexing area of examination policy. By the turn of the century, the Ontario universities had largely abandoned separate matriculation examinations in favour of a single provincially-administered one that also served as the "non-professional test" for Second Class teaching certificates. Examinations were set and corrected by a joint examining board of universities and the department in a system free of ministerial or political control. In 1897, George Ross noted that every province had followed Ontario's lead. "All conduct examinations as we do; in fact their regulations are almost a verbatim copy of ours."[25] In 1913, Alexander MacKay called for a single uniform examination system from coast to coast.[26]

Throughout the period, the universities continued to serve as major determinants of school curricula and standards. Matriculation requirements were already essentially the same for all English speaking Canadian universities as early as 1890. The usual requirement was standing in five subjects — classics (including Latin and Greek), mathematics (arithmetic, algebra and geometry), English, history with geography and either a science or a modern language. There was no matriculation examination in Quebec's classical colleges, which students entered at age 12 or 13, in an eight-year program that combined secondary and baccalaureate studies.[27]

W.S. Ellis, Dean of Education at Queen's, deplored a university-oriented examination system that fragmented the curriculum by ignoring "the effect of the whole upon the student's mental training . . . ." Certain subjects were given undue emphasis.[28] The fault, however, did not lie wholly with the universities. In 1921 an Ontario curriculum revision committee had noted that "from lack of anything more suitable," the junior matriculation examination, originally intended for university admission, had "come to be treated very generally as a test of educational fitness for all kinds of positions." Pupils as a result were forced to pursue unsuitable courses of study.[29] When E.G. Savage, a British observer, expressed surprise that the curriculum was not more closely related to rural needs "rather than along the lines set by the universities" he failed to grasp that the curriculum was equally determined by local ambitions and perceptions.[30] Many Ontario farm parents and pupils, like their counterparts elsewhere in Canada, viewed the schools as a means of escape from limited rural employment opportunities. Urban dwellers also refused to be weaned away from the traditional university dominated curriculum and to see their children deprived of opportunities for upward mobility.

Harris observes that undergraduate arts and science programs and the lack of uniformity in admission standards were the two topics of primary interest in discussions at the inter-war meetings of the National Conference of Canadian Universities. Concerns about declining standards and the poor preparation of matriculating students were ascribed to increasing high school enrolments and the development of a stronger vocational emphasis in secondary curricula. For economic and philosophical reasons tradition-oriented Canadian universities were unwilling to accommodate new demands by modifying their academic programs or by adopting the American elective system. They showed little disposition to accept commercial, technical and other optional subjects. If they did not accept or offer a subject, as in the case of geography, it was less likely to be accepted as a school subject.[31]

After 1930, the University of Toronto required senior matriculation (Grade 13) for entrance, a move which created a five-year high school program and greatly increased university dominance of the high schools. As the old freshman year came to be offered in the high schools, junior matriculation, required for entrance to it, became standardized across the province. In other provinces, senior matriculation became an alternative to first year, with the universities and the high schools offering identical first year courses tested by uniform examinations. Following the standardization of junior and senior matriculation curricula and examinations within each province, an essentially equivalent standard became established among all provinces. This equivalence was reinforced by the similarity of university demands in each subject area, together with similar graduation, certification and examination requirements. By 1930, several provinces were granting a general high school graduation diploma in place of the old matriculation diploma. This gave formal recognition to the non-matriculation subjects, although in practice most students still sought to attain the coveted matriculation standard.[32]

In 1936, a CEA committee headed by G. Fred McNally, Alberta's deputy minister of education, reported on high school graduation requirements. The committee concluded that "co-ordination of university admission requirements on the one hand and academic high school programmes on the other is complete." McNally observed that "the universities demand and obtain a thorough grounding in the traditional subjects." These included English literature, English composition, algebra, geometry, chemistry, physics, history, Latin, and French; all of these except the sciences were pursued throughout the entire high school course.[33]Two years later, in a survey of examinations in Canada addressed to an international audience, Ault observed that curriculum revisions had led to some de-emphasis on examinations at the pre-matriculation level and to a greater role for teachers in evaluation. "New type" objective tests were attracting attention, although such innovations were being adopted only slowly and the essay type of examination persisted.[34]

The interest in more objective measures reflected an awareness of the faults of the traditional examination system even among academics. In 1930, W.J. Alexander, a distinguished literary scholar at the University of Toronto, observed that the system was both too centralized and yet only nominally uniform, since there were great oscillations in difficulty from year to year. Examiners were fallible and often out of touch with the work of the schools. Marking standards varied greatly among readers or "sub-examiners." For teachers and pupils, the system was much like a lottery.[35] In the 1940s, James S. Thomson of Queen's University praised a National Conference of Canadian Universities report which had recommended against a Canada-wide entrance requirement. Thomson thought that the diversification of the high school curriculum had been inevitable. However, diversification was requiring the universities to make up deficiencies in entrance requirements by teaching material that had previously been taught in the high schools. In serving a classifying and categorizing function, scientific tests supplemented traditional examinations which continued to provide a gatekeeping function at points of access to the various rungs of the educational ladder, such as high school entrance.[36]

The influence of scientific testing on one area of the curriculum in Canada was illustrated in the 1920s by the survey of modern language instruction noted in Chapter 11. In commending "the scientific or experimental tendency" of an educational world governed by the statistical psychologist, the authors observed that the methods were disparaged in some quarters on the grounds that the higher forms of intellectual or aesthetic activity were said to be too elusive for objective standards of measurement. "Against such an argument it can, however, be urged that everything that can be taught can be measured, and if these higher forms of achievement elude measurement it is only because they are not imparted by scholastic endeavour."[37]

As noted earlier, in the mid-1920s the Putman-Weir Survey in British Columbia hired Peter Sandiford to carry out a scientific testing program. In assessing the intelligence and achievement levels of 17 000 pupils, the commissioners sought to circumvent the problems of traditional examinations which they and others had voiced. Their criticisms focussed on the unscientific nature of testing rather than on examinations *per se*. Objective tests constructed according to scientific principles and "free from ambiguity" were essential to achieve results "more authentic than the mere opinion of schoolmen and administrators." Such tests were preferable to unscientific subjective examinations based on the doctrine of mental discipline. They would help educators to answer a key question, "How well do the pupils ... learn the things which by common agreement they should learn?" By this means, it would be possible "to evaluate as objectively as possible" the quality of teaching in the schools of British Columbia.[38]

Sandiford made extensive use of American tests in the British Columbia assessment. He justified this by claiming that "Our Canadian school systems and our Canadian children are sufficiently similar to those of the United States to enable valuable comparisons to be made with standards already obtained in various parts of the United States."[39] However, American achievement tests in history and geography were unsuitable for use in Canadian schools. Accordingly, special tests were constructed in those subjects. Then, as now, Canadian students performed above American norms on achievement tests in the three Rs. While such results were easily accepted as gratifying evidence of the high quality of British Columbia schooling, retardation and dropout rates much higher than those in American schools probably accounted for the superior Canadian performance. However, neither Sandiford nor Putman and Weir themselves commented on this phenomenon.[40]

Probably the main long-term result of the Putman-Weir testing program was the legitimation of "new type" achievement tests. In 1931, building on his experience in British Columbia, Sandiford launched a major effort to develop more Canadian tests, ironically by means of a grant from the Carnegie Foundation of New York. Developed in the University of Toronto's new Department of Educational Research, which the grant was instrumental in establishing, the so-called Dominion Tests were the first national achievement tests in various Canadian content areas, notably in history and geography. Although there was a growing interest in objective testing, most provinces proceeded cautiously and Canada was relatively free of the testing mania that had developed in the United States. More uniform curricula, more conservative attitudes, centralized textbook policies and province-wide examinations probably qualified the Canadian response to the movement.

Sandiford's work led to the first experimental use of objective tests in Ontario that were designed to deal with the growing volume of junior matriculation examinations in Grade 12. Like his earlier British Columbia tests, the Ontario tests were not standardized but were considered more reliable than traditional examinations, and correlated nearly as well with school marks. As promotion by recommendation came into use in Grade 12 (though not in Grade 13), objective tests were abandoned.[41]

## Teacher Training in the Age of the Normal School

The New Education marked a shift in emphasis in pedagogy from subject to teaching method. In 1898, Thomas Kirkland, the principal of the Toronto Normal School, was happy that knowledge of a subject was no longer all that was required to teach it, but thought that the educational pendulum had swung "too far from the side of no methods at all to nothing but methods." An ignorance of subject matter was "painfully evident" among teachers. Three years later, John Squair complained that there was "too much pedagogy and too little education in the training of teachers," voicing a standard complaint about teacher training that has been heard ever since.[42] Despite an ostensibly more practical emphasis, Newcombe notes that in 1900 Ontario normal school instruction was based almost exclusively on the lecture method and on a total of nine reference works for the entire program. Students were expected to fit all lessons to a Procrustean bed of Herbartian methodology. In a lament still familiar, practice teaching was criticized as an artificial experience.[43]

As the enormous demand for teachers that had arisen during the post-Confederation period continued, policy-makers were pressed to supply teachers in hitherto unprecedented numbers. At the same time, they recognized the equally pressing need to improve the quality of teaching if fundamental educational reform and greater efficiency were to be achieved. The key to both would be found in better teaching methods purveyed through normal school programs. Improved teacher training would also promote traditional goals more efficiently.

During the period before 1920, much teacher training continued to be conducted in union schools or in county model schools and, (as noted in Chapter 8,) the high school remained in many respects a teacher training institution, particularly in western Canada. "Non-professional" subjects included the content to be taught at lower levels; the "professional" subjects included the principles (or "science") of education and pedagogy, (or teaching methods). The lowest, usually third class, certification could be gained in these institutions. Ontario maintained its provncially controlled county model schools in remote, mainly northern areas until as late as 1924. In Nova Scotia at this time, a Class D certificate, the lowest grade, held by 43 per cent of the teaching force in 1921, could be obtained by written examination following the successful completion of two years of high school. Most normal school students arrived with less than a full high school education, many having passed the entrance examination by independent study without ever attending a real high school. Their training was often as brief as three weeks. The annual turnover among Nova Scotia's rural teachers reached 50 per cent.[44]

In western Canada Patterson has noted that socio-economic conditions were a major factor in determining the numbers of teachers trained and the quality of training throughout Alberta's history.[45] In 1914, the 3363 uncertificated persons teaching on permit in the province exceeded the total number of teachers that had been trained in the two provincial normal schools during the preceding decade.[46] War-time conditions, transiency and alternative employment opportunities all worked against quality training.[47]

Nevertheless, by 1920 there had been a clear improvement in both the general education and in the professional training of Canadian teachers over a thirty year period. Thus, while the majority of teachers in Ontario and Saskatchewan had not completed junior matriculation in 1890, by 1920 the reverse was true. Accompanying this trend was the continuing feminization of the teaching force. In 1915, only 256 of Nova Scotia's 2945 teachers were males. In an expanding economy, teaching became less attractive to young men, especially if it demanded higher qualifications. On the other hand, young women were attracted to a traditional occupation that was now gaining professional status. An expanding school population offered secure career opportunities.[48]

Not all educators welcomed feminization, even if it meant that cheaper, more committed and more qualified teachers were obtainable. On his 1913 American tour, J.H. Putman had been struck by the extent of feminization in the United States. Putman proudly claimed that, under him, the Ottawa school system had a higher proportion of well qualified male teachers on its staff than any on the continent. On the other hand, he agreed with his American hosts that, although a better balance between the sexes was healthier, it was preferable to have "a capable womanly woman" in every classroom instead of an unmanly male weakling attracted by low pay![49]

The evolving normal school curriculum included methods courses which encompassed the subject matter of the elementary school curriculum, courses in classroom management and courses in the science of education. Special attention was given to the new subjects. This pattern, described by Patterson for the Calgary Normal School, was typical of the heavy six month programs of Prairie normal schools until the 1940s. Here, as in normal schools in most provinces, academic content beyond the highest grade taught was not considered essential for the teacher.[50] In their textbook- and examination-oriented curricula, in their teaching methods and in their rigidity, narrowness and formalism, the normal schools were in many respects carbon copies of the schools from which their students came, and to which they would return as teachers. It was an effective socializing process for, as Stamp observes of Ontario's normal schools, "the uniformity of the ... curriculum prepared the new teachers to function within a uniform provincial program." Even a generation later little had changed for, in the 1940s and 1950s, Ontario continued to possess "one of the most dictatorial and thoroughly state-controlled systems of teacher training in the western world."[51]

The flavour of teacher training in the 1920s can be captured in the syllabus and student's handbook for the Provincial Normal School in Winnipeg in 1926-27. Students were expected to live in approved boarding houses, subject to staff inspection. Written parental approval was required if students wished to live with friends. Male students were permitted in the girls' lounge "ONLY [sic] when invited for afternoon functions at which members of the staff are present." Two hours of homework were assigned per night. Reading did include the standard new scientific works in education by Thorndike, McMurry, Snedden and others but with a meagrely-educated student body in a crowded program and a repressive atmosphere, we must wonder how effective such exposure was.[52]

Reading the Manitoba handbook illustrates how much the reach of Canadian educators has so often exceeded their grasp. The frustrations of well-meaning reformers promoting curriculum revision in the 1930s can be contrasted with those of earnest, young, mostly female teachers with slender training, who were expected to implement John Dewey's curriculum ideas overnight. By this time, normal school programs had been lengthened. At Calgary, students were incarcerated for nine months, studying twenty subjects in thirty-seven class periods per week. Such programs failed to prepare teachers suited to deal with fundamental educational and social issues.[53]

The limitations of the normal schools and their training inevitably evoked criticism. In 1925, Putman and Weir charged the two British Columbia normal schools with having a concept of teaching "as a trade dependent on definite methods" whereas it should be viewed as a science. Using vitriolic language, the commissioners were critical of poor textbooks and understocked libraries and of an inadequate, bookish curriculum that, relying on lectures and dictated notes, failed to communicate the spirit of the New Education. The students were said to be immature and the staffs ignorant of child psychology and of developments in scientific education, such as tests and measurements.[54] In Protestant Quebec more than a decade later, another survey team that also included Putman criticized normal school training in similar terms.[55]

Despite overcrowding and the severe limitations of facilities and resources, there is evidence that the normal schools were more effective than the critics allowed in preparing their charges to function in school systems that were often even more deprived than the training institutions. Rogers, drawing on the recollections of Vancouver Normal School graduates, demonstrates that students had a strong *esprit de corps* and very warm recollections of their experiences that largely contradicted the criticisms of Putman and Weir. Normal school staff members were well aware of the limitations of their program and were able to improve it after 1925. Students thought that the quality of instruction was high and that training prepared raw young people well for the demanding experience of teaching in one room rural schools. Inevitably, graduates taught "strictly by the curriculum," treating the course of study as a bible. Beginners with slender backgrounds felt, as one graduate recalled, that they needed something "to tell you what to teach and when to teach it and how much you should teach in a year and so on ... " This expertise the Vancouver Normal Schools had amply provided.[56]

The normal schools influenced the curriculum in various ways. They were a prime means of introducing the new subjects, albeit in a sometimes arid and formalistic way. The Ontario teachers' manuals, which were also used in some other provinces, introduced students to the new science of education through acquaintance with the works of McMurry, Thorndike and Dewey, presenting current principles and practices in a Canadian context. Within Ontario, the manuals promoted the uniformity of normal school curricula described by Stamp. As at other levels of the Ontario system, uniformity was also promoted by means of external examinations which for many years were set by the Department of Education from questions submitted by instructors and marked in the normal schools.[57] Although educators such as J.H. Putman of the Ottawa Normal School promoted child study, Herbartian formalism was more popular, especially in the stereotyped lesson plan formats which normal school graduates brought to Ontario classrooms. An indirect influence of the normal schools on the high school curriculum resulted from the gearing of the curriculum to the needs of prospective teachers. In Ontario, Latin lost ground when it was abolished as a pre-requisite for public school teaching in 1904.

At this time, only a miniscule number of Canadian teachers, even at the high school level, were university graduates. In 1921, only 59 of Nova Scotia's teachers held degrees. A common pattern for improving qualifications in most provinces was attendance at normal school followed by part-time studies on the job. Graduates exempted from teacher training by virtue of their academic attainments might undertake voluntary training. With education viewed exclusively as the teaching of content, it was considered insulting to the universities that their graduates should have to undergo further instruction.[58] However, to University of Toronto philosopher, J.G. Hume, "pedagogics" was an important subject that should rank with post-graduate study and could enrich liberal education. It was well recognized overseas and in the United States but was retarded in Canada by the same prejudice that held back the natural and social sciences.[59]

In actuality, Ontario had moved towards obligatory training for high school teaching in 1885 when the specialist teaching certificate was introduced. Prospective teachers were required to write professional examinations following attendance at a "training institute" conducted in a collegiate under the tutelage of the principal and his staff. By 1898 the requirement of an honours degree led the universities to place an increasing emphasis on that degree. Shortly, with the establishment of a full year program for training high school teachers, the universities undertook teacher preparation.[60] After 1920, training was centralized at the Ontario College of Education. However, because the college was effectively controlled by the provincial government, even to the ordering of classroom supplies, it was only nominally a part of the University of Toronto.[61] In due course, training for high school teaching became available at universities in all provinces. A demand grew for more advanced professional training for Canadian educators in order to overcome dependence on American expertise.[62] Such training took the form of degrees in pedagogy, as noted in Chapter 5.

One consequence for the high school of the increasing exposure of teachers to university studies was the emergence of a continuum between the two levels, in the form of a kind of closed circle curriculum. Potential teachers left high school having been subjected to a relatively limited, sequential, developmental curriculum that in history, for example, might typically encompass a sequence from the Stone Age to the twentieth century. At university, they followed a similar curriculum consisting in the era before scholarly specialization of broad, often interrelated, courses that constituted an academic bill of fare at once coherent and comprehensive. As teachers, they returned to the schools to teach a course of study similar to that to which they had by now been twice exposed, at increasing levels of sophistication. Teachers of literature and the sciences followed a similar cycle. The result was a relatively coherent experience to which their successors were less likely to be exposed in a later era of curriculum fragmentation and specialization. By 1940, Canadian teachers at all levels were receiving longer, more systematic training in institutions with higher admission standards than before. Even so, Phillips observes that standards were still low in comparison with those of other western countries.[63]

## Peace and Efficiency in School Administration

In an era of industrial organization and scientific management, Canadian educators sought to systematize and rationalize the structures they had created. Extensive curriculum change and differentiation required that "the managers of Canadian education ... .specify what trustees, teachers and pupils must do, and add modestly to the roles of supervisors to ensure that they did so." In making this comment, Sutherland observes that the supervisory staff of Canadian education did not grow rapidly between the 1880s and the 1920s and barely kept pace with the growth in the system as a whole. Thus, in 1890, Ontario maintained a staff of 81 school inspectors to supervise 9201 teachers, or roughly 113 teachers per inspector; thirty years later, 125 inspectors supervised 15 331 teachers or about 122 teachers each.[64] In 1913, J.C. Miller found that the same low ratios pertained in most other provinces.[65]

Miller himself was in the vanguard of the first generation of educators — G. Fred McNally and H.C. Newland were others — who introduced American scientific management ideas into Canadian school administration. With its resolutely national perspective, Miller's study was the first comprehensive survey of the inspection and supervision needs of Canadian rural schools. Following a discussion of rural education in the United States and several overseas countries, Miller made a close study of Canadian school laws, policies and regulations affecting rural practice. Using the language of scientism, he observed that unless Canada acquired "a more uniform as well as a more adequate and scientific method of reporting upon educational matters," educators could not hope to understand "the real relationship between the raw materials, the process and expenditures and the resulting products ...."[66] Miller's view, noted earlier, of the need for a strong central authority was in conflict with the concomitant need to adapt the curriculum to local conditions. Above all, the rural teacher required guidance which skimpy course outlines, the lack of library facilities, and the absence of adequate supervisory help from principals, supervisors and superintendents made impossible.[67]

Miller's conclusions were based, in large measure, on verbatim responses to a survey questionnaire which he had circulated to school inspectors in all provinces. The results, which provide a fascinating cross-sectional view of Canadian rural classrooms before 1914, make clear how inadequate was supervision in circumstances where inspectors had responsibility for so many teachers. Besides inspecting teachers and pupils, demoting or promoting the latter, and scrutinizing registers and timetables, inspectors were required to assist the teachers with lesson and course planning. They were also expected to teach "illustrative lessons" as a means of disseminating innovations. They conducted "institutes," the chief form of in-service training at the time. In carrying out these manifold duties, the role of inspectors as change agents was limited by their lack of training in the new subjects. The ease with which they were prepared to teach "any model lesson on any subject" made Miller sceptical of illustrative lessons as a form of in-service education. The method probably served less to disseminate the new subjects and methods than to promote Herbartian-style formalized lesson plans.[68]

In a survey of inspectors' reading habits and of literature available to them, which unsurprisingly revealed how little time most had for reading, Miller noted an "almost complete absence of Canadian educational literature." This made Canadian educators almost entirely dependent on American references, a fact that was both "a credit and a matter of regret ... " He thought that there was a serious need for Canadian intellectual leadership in education, especially in educational administration in order to provide scientific analyses and solutions to problems. Miller hoped that British expertise might counteract American influence. He deplored the dearth of Old Country literature but hoped that the growing influx of British teachers would remedy matters.[69]

Measures discussed in Chapter 8 to promote school consolidation and to equalize revenues within each province required expanded provincial and local administrative capacities. Consolidation was initially promoted by the Macdonald-Robertson movement but, except in Manitoba, it was the least successful of the movement's efforts. Miller showed that in Manitoba, consolidation had resulted in a dramatic increase in school attendance. It had also led to an improved teaching force, better school facilities and greater curriculum differentiation, which had made possible the offering of the new subjects and had increased opportunities for secondary schooling.[70] Later, the movement gathered force in other western provinces. In Saskatchewan, "the larger unit of administration" eventually replaced tiny rural school boards in a province where for several decades there were more school trustees than teachers. In British Columbia, Maxwell Cameron noted in his pioneer study of school finance that rural secondary schools offered only minimal curricula unsuited to local needs. His proposals for larger units and for the equalization of revenues across the province led to a consolidation of 650 school boards into 74 by 1945.[71] As noted in Chapter 8, similar national trends resulted in an enhancement of curriculum differentiation and uniformity alike, the former because local school jurisdictions could offer enriched, more varied programs, the latter because rural-urban curricular disparity was reduced.

School consolidation proceeded much more slowly in eastern Canada. In Ontario, higher costs, transportation problems, fears that luxurious schools would spoil children and that larger assemblages of them would encourage epidemics were among the arguments used against the movement. The one-teacher ungraded school long continued to find favour in Ontario, and it was not until the 1960s that effective rural school reorganization became possible.[72] As late as 1964, the province still had 3472 school boards.[73]

Although it has become fashionable to condemn modern central and local bureaucracies as a dead hand on school systems, Sutherland suggests that bureaucracy was probably the only way in which a gradual improvement in the quality of Canadian rural schooling could have been effected before the 1950s. In our own day of better trained teachers, more sophisticated and demanding parents and more self-confident students, close bureaucratic supervision may be less necessary. As bureaucracy slowly developed, it was provincial officials and local school inspectors, especially in rural areas, who prodded school boards into hiring better teachers, paying them better, maintaining decent schools, including sanitary facilities and keeping schools open for moderate lengths of time.[74] These leaders also fought for and obtained province-wide salary scales for teachers and promoted the establishment of teachers' professional organizations. Nothing is more in the Canadian educational tradition (or more in contrast with that of the United States) than the teachers' federation, with its compulsory or "automatic" membership based on provincial legislation, often skillfully engineered by the educational bureaucracy itself. In 1944, George Drew's conservative government in Ontario legitimized the province's teachers' federation, thus giving teachers, as one put it, "the dignity of public recognition of our place in the community."[75]

Before 1920, incipient bureaucracies were taking shape more rapidly in urban than in rural Canada. Stamp has shown how Calgary, in the three decades following 1884, developed an educational ecology indistinguishable from that of any older Ontario city of comparable size.[76] Growth occurred in stages, beginning with a voluntary, private school approach to education and ending in 1914 with a complex urban school system. In 1906, Calgary trustees commissioned Winnipeg School Superintendent Daniel McIntyre to carry out an evaluation of their schools. McIntyre recommended a chief administrator who would be "a leader in everything that would make for the efficiency of the schools," including guiding "the pedagogical reading of the teaching staff." The city's first superintendent was Melville Scott, a native Maritimer and former chemistry professor with a doctorate from Gottingen, Germany, who had taught school briefly in Ontario. Scott was also a self-taught apostle of the New Education; he later co-authored *Public School Methods* with James L. Hughes. As a staunch Victorian Methodist, he symbolized the new breed of administrator who promoted the civilizing and moralizing mission of the public school on the Prairie frontier.[77]

In 1918, five years after Miller's rural survey, the first nationwide survey of urban school administration was undertaken by a Canadian-born American expert, W.L. Richardson, a former manual training superintendent in Toronto.[78] Richardson's exhaustive survey of sixty-three city school systems was modeled on similar American surveys and made use of an extensive scientific questionnaire developed at the University of Chicago, where Richardson had obtained his doctorate under Franklin Bobbitt and Charles Judd. He drew heavily on the emerging literature of scientific management in American school administration and was assisted in his work by Harold O. Rugg, one of the leading American progressives at Columbia University. The survey dealt with such topics as school boards, their constitutions, functions and finances, superintendents and their duties, the qualifications and salaries of teachers, textbooks and supplies, school facilities, and general administration. It also drew on data from every provincial department of education.

Richardson deplored the lack of trained administrators in Canada, particularly of those qualified to supervise teaching, which he deemed their most important function. He advocated scientific methods of appointing and supervising teachers, using interview and observation schedules.[79] From a curricular perspective, the most important section of Richardson's report dealt with textbooks and textbook policy. Richardson's view that "maladjustment of pupils with materials of instruction" was the chief cause of grade retardation was noted earlier. Other topics, discussed from a scientific management point of view, included the most appropriate length for periods of instruction, the need for attractive lunch rooms, the most effective use of the noon hour, the role of medical inspection, and the need for school assembly halls, gymnasia and playgrounds, and effective school janitorial services. The curricular dimensions of most of these topics were often explicitly defined, usually in terms of the effect of the total school environment on learning.

Richardson's survey, like that by Miller, and like such provincial surveys as the Foght study in Saskatchewan, indicated that the professionalization of Canadian school administration and educational theory and practice had clearly begun by 1920. The trend was evident at the local level in Ottawa, where J.H. Putman had been appointed Inspector of Public Schools in 1910. In his 1913 tour of twelve American towns and cities between the Atlantic seaboard and the Midwest, Putman had been impressed with the efficiency of school administration. The superintendent was given wide powers; a lengthy term of office made him "practically a school Caesar." A highly efficient system run on business lines provided freedom and variety. The result, as compared with Ontario's centralized system, was that some American schools were much better than those of Canada, but a great many were worse.[80]

Like Richardson, Putman was impressed with the new American school survey movement and launched a local Ottawa survey before Richardson's nationwide effort was organized. Undertaken by C.E. Mark of the Ottawa Normal School, and completed as a doctoral dissertation in 1918 under Sandiford's supervision at Toronto, the Ottawa survey was a pioneering Canadian effort.[81] It comprised a thorough and systematic documentation of a wide range of data similar to that gathered by Richardson for his sixty-three cities, but in greater depth. Of curricular interest was the information about the characteristics of the teaching staff, including their personalities and "professional spirit and general culture." Personal data for pupils was also gathered, and a survey was made of some subjects of the course of study.

In British Columbia during the 1920s, scientific school administration was promoted by the ubiquitous Norman Fergus Black, a recent arrival from Saskatchewan. Preparatory to organizing a survey of Vancouver and the surrounding school districts of British Columbia's lower Fraser Valley, Black had asked in 1924, "Were the schools really turning out the desired product in a shape easy to be absorbed by the market?"[82] Although less detailed than Mark's Ottawa survey, Black's work also drew heavily on American practice. Published in 1926, the study bore the title, *Peace and Efficiency in School Administration.* Black's analysis was Deweyan in its relatively sophisticated critique of curricular conceptions rooted in mental discipline theory, and in schooling as a preparation for adult life to the neglect of the child's present needs. However, his actual reform proposals were much more in the spirit of such scientific progressives as Thorndike, Franklin Bobbitt and C.H. Judd than in that of Dewey. Thus, Black and his committee emphasized the need for better supervision and inspection as a means of making teaching more efficient, in order to maximize the financial investment in education.[83]

Black advocated the professionalization of administration through the appointment of superintendents who would serve as both business and educational managers, with an emphasis on the latter role. In anticipation of modern administrative theory, Black declared that the "supervising officer should define in concrete terms the goals and standards by which the attainment of pupils and the efficiency of their teachers are to be judged; and, as the leader of his teachers in the matter of professional studies, should help his teachers to familiarity with the best thought and practice bearing upon how their objectives should be reached." He urged maximum local autonomy in a system in which local and provincial authorities shared common goals.[84]

Black conducted his local survey as Putman and Weir were completing their British Columbia provincial survey, which was later termed the most thorough examination of any Canadian school system undertaken to that time.[85] Like Richardson, Putman and Weir advocated specialized, scientific training for those charged with supervising teachers. They emphasized the study of modern educational objectives, "especially as determining curricula and methods of instruction in all schools . . . ." In a vast province where only eighteen inspectors were available to supervise 3200 teachers, administrative expansion was necessary.[86] Putman and Weir made a distinction between supervisory and inspectoral control. The former was concerned with what should be taught, to whom, by whom, how and to what purpose, an emphasis that focussed not on the machinery of education, but on "the character and worth of its products." As such, it constituted a form of control based on "the completest co-operation" between teachers and supervisory staffs. By contrast, inspectoral control was based on "expert knowledge of the conditions and technique of successful and efficient instruction" emphasizing "an impersonal, objective measurement of the results and worth of the school."[87]

Putman and Weir advocated the decentralization of school administration through the appointment of experienced, highly trained local superintendents in the larger centres who would be responsible partly to their school boards but more directly to the government, to whom they would submit detailed annual reports. Under the guise of decentralization, Putman and Weir sought more effective central control by locating agents of provincial authority directly within the local school systems. They proposed that the chief duties of the superintendents should "lie within the walls of the classroom." Each one should be able to give expert advice to teachers, know how to use standardized intelligence and achievement tests, be able to teach illustrative model lessons, give advice regarding retarded children and the physical health of all pupils, and "see that every subject on the programme of studies receives a due proportion of the teacher's time." Finally, said Putman and Weir, the director of education must "supplement the work begun in the normal schools and become a trainer of teachers-in-service." In effect, "He must be an educational efficiency expert."[88]

The Putman-Weir scheme was an advanced bureaucratic model for its time and would ultimately be implemented in British Columbia where, in many respects, it prevails to this day. As a model the scheme constituted a kind of centralized decentralization that became the standard Canadian pattern. After 1950, it helped to actualize an approach to educational administration that MacKinnon claimed later made education unique among government services in Canada.[89] As Fred Clarke pointed out in the 1930s, such a model left Canada with no "free" public opinion in education in press or parliament that could supply enlightened, well-informed and disinterested criticism of policy. More serious, it resulted in a "lack of intelligent backing for sound new departures." On the other hand, Clarke thought that local school boards, with their rigid adherence to the grade system and a misconceived sense of equality, did not use the freedom they had to diversify and enrich the curriculum above the centrally-prescribed minimum. To Clarke, minute prescription and detailed official regulation gave Canadian education a common countenance which its "wrinkles of administrative division" could not hide.[90]

## Perspective: Curriculum Change in a Nationalizing Era

In our discussion of curriculum change during the half century era of nation-building following 1892, we have noted recurrent commentary, controversy and debate to which Canadian and non-Canadian observers alike contributed. The assessments of the former group included some who recorded their experiences as pupils. The latter included a number of distinguished British and American educators who contributed valuable "outside" perspectives on the Canadian curriculum as did "inside" professionals. In this section, the perspectives of both groups will be discussed.

### Outside Views: The Formalism and "Prosaic Sanity" of the Canadian Curriculum

Such external professionals as John Adams, Harold Foght and Fred Clarke collectively brought wide international experience and thoughtful rigour to their commentaries, combining judicious criticism of serious shortcomings with unstinting praise of positive virtues. They often exhibited more awareness of deep-seated problems than did conservative Canadian critics. Thus, they expressed more concern about the serious deficiency of resources, in particular the notable lack of a properly trained teaching force. They were likewise concerned about what they saw as the extreme formalism and centralization of Canadian schooling and curricula, characteristics which domestic critics ignored or saw as virtues. If Canadian educators, ranging from James Cappon in the 1890s to Hilda Neatby in the 1950s, consistently saw a threat to the liberal-classical curriculum and the traditional values it upheld, outsiders such as John Adams in 1902 and A.F.B. Hepburn in 1938 often saw a quite different, opposite problem. The accounts of Quebec Protestant education provided by these Scottish educators in reports thirty-six years apart did not materially differ. Both criticized the bookishness and formalism of curricula.[91]

    Adams and Hepburn, like Fred Clarke, were British observers, visitors from a nation to which Canadian educators looked for a model of rigorous academic schooling. As a consequence, there was unconscious irony in their criticisms of the excessive academicism and formalism of the Canadian curriculum, with its overemphasis on Latin and neglect of subjects such as music and art. Clarke, probably the most astute of all external observers during the period, was particularly critical of the excessive centralization of Canadian schooling, the rigidity of the grade system, the depreciation of teaching, the "standard of the average" and the "ritualization of the school." Although Latin was much overemphasized, Clarke concluded that history, the sciences and mathematics were all well taught in the best schools. The "domination of the average" was a serious problem, evident in the fact that over half of Alberta's students took five or more years to complete a four year course. A further characteristic of Canadian secondary education was the disposition "to think of education in quantitative rather than qualitative terms," a willingness to accept expert detailed prescription from the centre "and the basing of policy on external conditions rather than by inner reflection."[92] Although sound values had enabled Canadians successfully to resist utilitarianism, they were facing problems common to democratic education everywhere. A central problem arising from conservative attitudes in Canada, Clarke thought, was that pupils still suffered under a regime of too much sheer laboriousness, which seriously detracted from genuine intellectual effort.[93] He had identified a problem that Canadian educators ignored in their zeal to curb the excesses of progressivism. While all could agree that intellectual effort entailed hard work, many tended to equate hard work with intellectual effort.

More positively, Clarke saw virtues in Canadian schooling which marked it off from that of the United States, despite outward resemblances. Clarke had no doubt that there was such a thing as Canadian education existing as "a separate and single identity", separate as against the United States; single as against "the jealously-guarded sovereignties of nine distinct provinces." As compared with American education, Canadian practice had faithfully adhered to the principle of a standard curriculum that constituted "a stable scheme of basic studies." "Getting by" was more difficult in Canada, which had not yet succumbed to the evils of "credits" and "units" and other snippet-like approaches to learning that might have undermined the sound liberal tradition on which the Canadian curriculum still rested.[94] The liberality of Canadian courses of study, at least on paper, was impressive, with the result that liberal education was still firmly planted. By avoiding the excesses of countless electives and freak units, and sentimental pandering to the immature impulses and sheer whims of pupils, Clarke thought that Canada had not gone as far as the United States "in breaking up and diluting the great intellectual tradition of western civilization."[95]

E.G. Savage, the English exchange inspector cited earlier, who worked in eastern Ontario in 1925-6, came to conclusions similar to Clarke's. For Savage, contemplating "minute prescription," centralization in the province was complete. An equally complete uniformity of method predominated that stifled creative teaching and tended to make the minimum the norm. Here Savage, like other external critics, could agree with domestic observers that standards were too low, but he tended to give reasons quite opposite from those ascribed to the imputed dangers of excessive liberalization and experimentation. Savage found that, compared with his own country, the province's schools were understaffed and its inspection system inadequate. The best teachers were not as good as England's, nor the worst as bad. Many more were trained, and this meant that the worst English weaknesses were avoided. But Canadian teachers were too concerned with examination results, a factor which made them less creative that their English peers.[96]

Savage deplored the small place accorded art, and the total absence of music in the high schools he visited. Due to costs, manual training and domestic science were taught in only a few schools. On the other hand, the commercial course was widely available, even to pupils who had already matriculated. Latin was taught to far more pupils than could profit from it. There were too many teaching periods, with as many as eleven daily in some schools. Homework was overdone, and since it was often assigned in each teaching period, it was necessarily superficial.[97] In his report, Savage summed up his impressions:

> The Department of Education regulates the subjects to be taken, the length of time for which some them ... may be studied and the year in which they may be studied; it issues syllabuses in each subject and prescribes textbooks which may be used. Finally it examines the product. Little or nothing is left to the initiative of the Principal or of the teachers. All that is necessary is for the teachers, all trained in the same professional school, to follow the syllabus and the textbook, and to see that the facts enshrined therein are known. This is what is, for the most part done. Pupils of the most ordinary intelligence then can scarcely fail to pass ... Unhappily the adventurer electing to stray afield will receive no credit for his adventures and indeed places himself under a handicap by his wanderings.[98]

From 1918 onwards, beginning with Harold Foght in Saskatchewan, American observers voiced criticisms of the Canadian curriculum in terms remarkably similar to those of their overseas counterparts. The 1922 Learned-Sills study of schooling in the Maritime provinces was critical of the formalism of secondary and college teaching while it agreed that the best high school work was impressive, and that college graduates from the region often manifested exemplary achievement when they went on to further studies in the United States. Formalism itself seemed to guarantee a safe, if often mediocre, standard. However, Learned and Sills were critical of the "lean tuition" given by untrained teachers in Nova Scotia's examination-ridden system. Exemplary achievement resulted from a system where pupils had to compensate for defective instruction by self-teaching, which no doubt cultivated enviable habits of initiative and industry, though at the price of failure rates as high as 48 per cent. Only nine secondary schools in the province were doing four full years of work. Learned and Sills concluded that the work in the best of these was impressive. The quality of teaching was excellent, the pupils industrious, and "the effects of hard, accurate, painstaking drill" were everywhere evident. The curriculum was less elaborate and the pupils less spontaneous than in the United States. There was less superficial "smartness" on the part of pupils and less deference to their opinions by teachers. All told, there was "much greater thoroughness, closer thinking, more confident knowledge and more wholesome seriousness on the part of both student and teacher."[99]

The national assessments produced during the 1920s by two former Canadians, W.L. Richardson and W.F. Dyde, further highlighted the formalism and uniformity of the Canadian curriculum. In 1935, William C. Bagley, a leading American dissenter from progressivism, in criticizing the "shocking inefficiency" of his country's schools, averred that Canadian, like Scottish children, were in general so much better prepared in the elementary school subjects that American achievement tests were far too easy for them.[100]

It is probable that external criticism of Canadian formalism, combined with praise of substantial achievement, merely confirmed the view of traditionalists that the curriculum best rested on sound traditional foundations, unsullied by the fashions of progressivism. The essential soundess of what Fred Clarke called the "prosaic sanity" of traditional Canadian practice reinforced the smug complacency of Canadian educators, obscuring for them the likelihood that the best American high schools and elite private colleges provided an academic experience qualitatively superior to any available in Canada. On balance it could be said that if the centralization, uniformity and formalism of the Canadian curriculum led to narrowness and mediocrity at the same time that it ensured a limited measure of solid academic achievement, the bewildering variety of the American curriculum resulted in greater extremes of both weakness and excellence.

## Internal Views: The Traditionalist-Progressive Dichotomy

The previous discussion underscores how much the ongoing curriculum debate in inter-war Canada was cast in a comparative mould, focussed on similarities between and contrasts with American and British theory and practice in particular. Complementing this perspective was one which posed a dichotomy between traditionalism and progressivism that was frequently less than helpful. This was illustrated by the deep ambivalence of progressives that underscored how far they shared the goals of their traditionalist critics. Thus, H.B. King, the British Columbia reformer who worked under Weir in the 1930s, was a member of the Progressive Education Association and viewed himself as a humanitarian innovator. However, from another perspective King was an authoritarian with, in Mann's words, "a narrow statist mind" obsessed with the need for social efficiency and the survival of the status quo.[101]

Traditionalists also displayed ambivalence. Not all idealized formalistic, academic Canadian schooling. John Watson in 1901 condemned a "dead and meaningless" curriculum that comprised "an unorganized collection of miscellaneous information" which took seven or eight years to teach rudiments that could be taught in three years at most.[102] During the 1920s, Thomas Kirkconnell, the successful Ontario headmaster cited earlier, expressed the view that prescription in the province had been pushed "to a fantastic extreme," resulting in a Prussianized system that was "at once one of the most uniformly efficient in the world and one of the most paralyzing to individual initiative in teacher or school." Kirkconnell advocated "a properly socialized secondary school" with more opportunity for the "self-realization" of the average student.[103]

Peter Sandiford, as the leading inter-war Canadian educational theorist, was probably the best example of an educator who combined a traditionalist moralistic stance with a progressive scientific pedagogy. Both perspectives served a highly structured curriculum in a centralized system that the new methods would render more efficient. Sandiford's various comments over a generation led him to conclude that on balance the prescription and formalism of the Canadian curriculum had served the needs of schooling well.[104] (His early 1918 critique was noted in Chapter 7.) Twenty years later, Sandiford surveyed the changes of the 1930s. He observed that although the Canadian curriculum, like Topsy, had simply grown, there had been little radical change in a century. In comparison with the United States, where Teachers College at Columbia University alone had 30 000 revisions on file, the Canadian curriculum had been remarkably stable. Canada was fortunate to have been spared so many frequent upheavals but, since Canadians tended to worship the past, they failed to prepare pupils for a rapidly changing world. "Our education", Sandiford concluded "is retrospective, not prospective."[105]

Sandiford described the revisions that had taken place since 1929 as "competent productions." Some had been produced in a year; others had required several years. Some were relatively brief, like Ontario's 164 pages for Grades 1 to 4, while others were voluminous, like British Columbia's 700 pages covering the same grades. Most compilers claimed that their revisions were tentative, but Sandiford thought that if history was a safe guide, the changes would be the only substantial ones teachers would have to deal with for half a century.[106] In fact, the revisions of the 1930s would stand for about a generation.

In contrast with Patterson's recent evaluation (discussed in Chapter 10) that documents the modest impact of pre-war progressivism, Sandiford's assessment was excessively sanguine. He assumed that learning character and citizenship had become as important as acquiring knowledge. Individual differences were more recognized as dull pupils did "less bookish things" than before, and bright pupils spent more time on handwork. Sandiford was convinced that the school of the future would be a more interesting and a happier place for pupils.[107]

By the time of Sandiford's report, progressivism appears to have become a conventional wisdom in the rhetoric of many segments of the Canadian educational establishment, even at the university level. Such academics as J.S. Thomson, writing in 1941 in the conservative *Dalhousie Review*, praised trends that had brought a healthy breeze of fresh air into schools that were too formalistic, mechanical and examination-ridden. Thomson deplored rote learning and the shameful neglect of art and music. His comments and those of F.C. James reflected the views of some establishment educators who, stepping out of their ivory towers during the period of war-time exigency, confronted some of the realities Canadian educators were facing.[108]

A more conservative view, far removed from such realities, anticipated later disenchantment with progressivism. Carleton Stanley, the president of Dalhousie University, felt that Canadians were too prone to accept American fads and to be seduced by materialism. The emphasis on the new social sciences, on citizenship and on technical education had led educators to abandon the humanities. As a result, it was impossible in some parts of Canada "to find any real content in the whole high school curriculum." To protect children from the "stunning and distracting" forces of the unwholesome "flick," the radio, and "the allegedly 'comic' strip" Stanley advocated the restoration of rural life through the restoration of the rural school. It had been a mistake to urbanize the rural curriculum, treating country children as underprivileged when they were much wiser than bureaucrats seeking to foist radios and movies upon the schools. Their leisure and "blessed state of undistraction" should be left undisturbed.[109]

Hindsight would suggest that the assessments of Sandiford and Thomson, while useful, were far too sanguine, while those of Stanley and other moralist-humanists were serious distortions of what was actually happening in Canadian classrooms. Criticisms by the latter provoked comparatively little controversy during the 1930s when education sparked little general public interest. This situation changed as war-time practical demands and post-war expectations of wider educational opportunities burgeoned. During the inter-war years, as progressivism changed, in Sutherland's words, from a creative social experiment to a single-minded pursuit of its program with solutions to problems applied from diverse sources, a *de facto* national curriculum took shape almost adventitiously.[110] The result was that, by 1945, the resemblances among the provinces in courses of study, textbook, examination and teacher training policies and administrative structures considerably outweighed the differences. The objectives proclaimed in Ontario's 1915 teacher's manual — social control, the diffusion of basic knowledge, social improvement and industrial efficiency — had largely been achieved through ostensibly progressive means that served these unabashed conservative ends.

It could be argued that, as the university ethos was undermined by the corrosive power of modern social and natural science, the school remained the last bastion of Victorian cultural moralism and disciplined intelligence. Intellectually, culturally and morally nearly all Canadian policy-makers before 1945 were Victorian in outlook, the typical products of a Victorian higher education. Many remained influential into the 1950s, at a time when Canadian education was being beseiged at home by social change in the form of mass schooling, cultural diversity and new technological imperatives and abroad by new global tensions. In its schizophrenic orientation, Canadian education began to resemble Canadian politics, in which one of the nation's chief political parties was identified by the contradictory title of progressive-conservative.

A schizophrenic orientation may in part be explained by the fact that progressivism was a many-faceted movement. With respect to Alberta, which served as the cradle of the movement in Canada, Coulter has discussed the limitations of viewing progressivism as an undifferentiated concept. Rather, it appealed to different groups with different goals: to groups seeking to improve rural education; educators seeking pedagogical reform and the professionalization of teaching; and business proponents of vocational education. Applying a conflict model to her analysis of the movement, Coulter concludes that progressivism in its conservative manifestation did not fail, since the centralized control, the testing and streaming procedures and the vocational thrust advocated by the conservative wing of the movement took hold during the 1930s and 1940s.[111] This view is in contrast to the "moderate revisionist" perspective of Patterson who, (as noted in Chapter 10), saw progressivism as a well-intentioned if cautious attempt at curriculum reform that lacked proper policy direction and was never given a fair trial.[112]

## Notes to Chapter 12

1 Finkelstein, 316.

2 *Proceedings of the OEA*, 1906, 98-9.

3 A. MacKay, "Are Any Advantageous Co-ordinations Practicable?" 49-50.

4 N.S.AR, 1913-14, xxii.

5 A. MacKay, "Uniform Textbooks," 56.

6 B. Walker, "The High School Program," 217, 220.

7 W. Richardson, 189.

8 *DEA Proceedings*, 1918, 59-60.

9 E. White, 105.

10 Parvin, 76; G. Ross, *The School System*, 165-7.

11 Parvin, 83-5, 90, 157.

12 Sandiford, "Problems," 563-6.

13 Parvin, 97.

14 Tait, 81.

15 Ontario Royal Commission on Book Publishing, 27-8.

16 Parvin, 106, 109.

17 Ontario Royal Commission on Book Publishing, 29.

18 Briefs to The Hope Commission cited in Parvin, 117-8.

19 Parvin, 111-3.

20 "Textbooks Approved or Recommended for Use in the Elementary and Secondary School," (Ontario), Circular 14, 1951-52.

21 Sandiford, 409-10.

22 Colemen, "Training," 19.

23 Learned and Sills, 6, 9.

24 Putman and Weir, *Survey,* 258-9.

25 G. Ross, *The Policy,* 7.

26 A. MacKay, "Are Any Advantageous Co-ordinations Practicable?", 50.

27 Robin Harris, *History,* 120-1.

28 Ellis, "The University," 62-3.

29 Spence, 37.

30 Savage, 65; Stamp, *Schools of Ontario,* 125.

31 Robin Harris, *History,* 120, 376-7.

32 Ibid., 596.

33 McNally, "Report," 138-40.

34 Ault, 158.

35 Alexander.

36 Thomson, "Matriculation," 43-44.

37 American and Canadian Committees on Modern Languages, xi-xiii.

38 Putman and Weir, *Survey,* 261, 356.

39 Ibid., 437.

40 The persistence of this phenomenon was noted in a 1982 paper by Barbara Holmes. See "Are Canadians Kids Brighter?", unpublished paper, American Educational Research Association, New York, March, 1982.

41 Fleming, V, *Supporting,* 362.

42 Kirkland, 112; Squair, 181.

43 Newcombe, 231.

44 Learned and Sills, 8.

45 Patterson, "History," 192.

46 Chalmers, *Schools,* 32.

47 Patterson, "History," 192, 198.

48 N. Sutherland, *Children,* 167.

49 Wood, "John Harold Putman's 1913 American Tour," 14-5.

50 Patterson, "History," 202.

51 R. Stamp, *Schools of Ontario,* 123, 200.

52 Manitoba Department of Education, Provincial Normal School Student's Handbook, 1926-7, 3-4.

53 Chalmers, *Schools,* 419; Patterson, "History," 202.

54 Putman and Weir, *Survey,* 200-6.

55 Hepburn, 190-1.

56 T. Rogers, "Riding Out," 16.

57 Newcombe, 54, 232.

58 C.E. Phillips, *Development*, 590.

59 Hume, "Pedagogics," 36.

60 Robin Harris, *History*, 179-80.

61 R. Stamp, *Schools of Ontario*, 119.

62 Robin Harris, *History*, 311.

63 C.E. Phillips, *Development*, 581.

64 N. Sutherland, *Children*, 169.

65 J.C. Miller, *Rural Schools*, 151-3. Sutherland points out that Miller's data did not include urban supervisory staffs which were growing more rapidly. However, while not definitive, the data do suggest that the growth of the Canadian educational bureaucracy barely kept pace with the growth in the system as a whole.

66 Ibid., ix-x.

67 Ibid., 76-7.

68 Ibid., 150.

69 Ibid., 184-90.

70 Ibid., 11.

71 M. Cameron, *Report*, 83-87.

72 R. Stamp, *Schools of Ontario*, 72, 126-7.

73 D. Cameron, 31.

74 N. Sutherland, *Children*, 170-1.

75 R. Stamp, *Schools of Ontario*, 180-1.

76 R. Stamp, "The Response."

77 Ibid., 118-9.

78 W. Richardson.

79 Ibid., 157, 166.

80 Wood, "John Harold Putman's 1913 American Tour," 5-6.

81 Mark.

82 N. Black, "School Surveys," 105-7.

83 N. Black, *Peace*, 9, 20-1.

84 Ibid., 9.

85 C. Phillips, *Development*, 263.

86 Putman and Weir, *Survey*, 235, 243.

87 Ibid, 239-40.

88 Ibid., 243-5.

89 MacKinnon.

90 Clarke, "Secondary Education," 563, 567; "Education in Canada," 313.

91 Adams; Hepburn.

92 Clarke, "Secondary Education," 580-1.

93 Clarke, "Education in Canada," 312, 321.

94 Ibid., 309, 316-8.

95 Clarke, "Secondary Education," 563-5.

96 Savage, 35-7, 41-2, 67-8.

97 Ibid., 55-7, 66-7.

98 Ibid., 67-8.

99 Learned and Sills, 9-10.

100 Bagley, 402.

101 J. Mann, "Progressive Education," 152.

102 Watson, 329.

103 Kirkconnell, *Canadian*, 115-6.

104 Sandiford, *Comparative*.

105 Sandiford, "Curriculum Revision," 473-4.

106 Ibid., 474.

107 Ibid., 476-7.

108 Thomson, "The Education," 229; James.

109 Stanley, 385, 388-9.

110 Sutherland, *Children*, 233.

111 Patterson and Coulter, 7-8.

112 Ibid., 1-5.

# PART III

CURRICULUM AND SOCIAL CHANGE,
1945-1980:
CONFLICTING TRENDS IN A
NEW ERA OF MASS EDUCATION

# CHAPTER 13

## CONTEXTS OF CURRICULUM CHANGE, 1945-1980

*In 1945 Canadians had relatively little, hoped for much, but did not really expect it. Surely they never expected exactly what they got.*
*(Robert Bothwell et al, 1981).*

*Education is everybody's business.*
*(Royal Commission on Education in Ontario, 1950).*

*... Canada, without being fully conscious of the fact, is passing through the greatest crisis in its history.*
*(Royal Commission on Bilingualism and Biculturalism, 1965).*

### The Social Context of Curriculum Change

After World War II, widespread fears of unemployment proved unfounded as Canadians, without realizing it, embarked on the greatest surge of prosperity and the greatest diversification of their social, cultural and economic life that they had ever known. Education was central to change, but first it was necessary to expand and renovate school systems and universities that continued to operate at a threadbare pre-war level. This process did not begin in earnest before the mid-1950s. By then, living standards were rising rapidly and most Canadians by the end of the decade were better off than their parents had been in the inter-war period, although the sharing of the new-found prosperity was by no means always fair, just or equitable. By the 1970s, Canadians were spending casually on things their forebears would have thought unattainable luxuries.[1]

### Demographic Trends

The most marked social phenomenon after 1945 was a population explosion fueled by the baby boom and immigration. Unlike previous immigration, the bulk of the post-war influx came to the cities rather than to rural areas. Even more significant in explaining urban growth was an almost unnoticed internal migration from country to city. This latter movement resulted in the gradual breakup of long established cultural islands or marginal out-groups identified by Clark and referred to in Chapter 8. To these could now be added youth. Barriers to social mobility were reduced, and powerful new assimilative forces were released, a process in which schools and universities played a dominant role.[2]

As in the past, natural increase accounted for the greatest proportion of population growth. The war-time and post-war baby boom reached its peak by the late 1950s. This was followed by a significant decline in the birthrate until, by 1976, the number of births had dropped below the population replacement rate. Immigration was also declining by this time, in the face of Canada's growing economic difficulties. Three major trends had marked post-war immigration. Many European immigrants were Roman Catholics, a trend that greatly accelerated the growth of separate schools. Large numbers of skilled workers, professionals, intellectuals, and artists from the middle and upper levels of Eurasian societies reflected a major change in the social origins of immigrants, and did much to encourage an acceptance of multiculturalism.[3] This trend also reduced the urgency to develop needed vocational and technical programs. Finally, the entry after 1960 of large numbers of non-European immigrants from Asia, the Caribbean and Latin America reinforced the need to provide more and better programs in the teaching of English as a second language. Another consequence of this trend was the need for schools to assist the cultural adjustment of these newcomers and to cope with the racial tensions and prejudice that their arrival sometimes provoked. Despite the vast influx of newcomers, the 1981 census indicated that 84 per cent of the total population had been born in Canada, a statistic that had changed little in a century.[4]

In the schools, the population explosion had its most obvious effect in increased enrolments. The coming of mass secondary education was foreshadowed by a 29 per cent increase in high school enrolments between 1950 and 1955. The first wave of the post-war baby boom was most evident in Ontario, where the total school population more than doubled from 663 000 in 1946 to 1 319 000 in 1959. As a second, even larger, baby boom reached school age during the 1960s, spectacular increases in enrolments occurred at all levels across Canada. Elementary enrolments increased from 3.2 million in 1961 to 3.7 million in 1971. Between 1971 and 1976, high school and post-secondary enrolments rose from 1.2 million to 1.9 million in the case of the former, and from 1.7 million to 3 million in the case of the latter. By 1976, falling birthrates were reflected in a decline in the numbers of elementary school children to 3.3 million.[5] Thus, falling school enrolments emerged as a trend almost as suddenly as had the earlier population explosion. By 1980, this decline was being reflected in high school enrolment figures. At the post-secondary level, the entry of the baby boom generation and of more female and part-time students sustained enrolments.

In the period of expansion, a limited supply of well-trained teachers made it sometimes difficult to staff programs which were becoming increasingly numerous and diverse as greater numbers of students with wider ranges of abilities, aptitudes, interests and cultural attributes created new demands for curriculum differentiation. Conversely, the following period of enrolment decline made it more difficult to provide the variety of programs that a still diverse population required. Difficulties were exacerbated by a lower commitment to the support of schooling. This resulted from changing public priorities and a decline in the number of taxpayers with children in school.

## Changing Lifestyles and a Changing Quality of Life

With more than three-quarters of Canadians living in towns and cities by 1976, increasing urbanization underscored the fact that by now the real Canadian scene was a cityscape. The differences between rich and poor were greater and more obvious in Winnipeg than they were across Manitoba. In Toronto and Montreal more diverse cultural groups came into more daily contact than occurred in all the rest of Canada.[6] To the cultural diversity that gave dynamism to the new urban way of life could be added a diversity of activities, jobs, people and neighbourhoods that influenced Canadian lifestyles and work. By the 1970s, the media, especially television, reached into every farm and fishing village, presenting urban points of view, urban landscapes, lifestyles, amenities and events.[7]

The world of work was marked by a decline in rural occupations and in traditional urban blue collar jobs. Service occupations (retailing, finance, government and personal services) became the largest employment sector. The majority of jobs performed by Canadians in 1980 had not existed in 1900. Although one million youth found jobs between 1965 and 1977, youth unemployment was an increasingly serious social problem with which governments tried to cope by creating *ad hoc* stop gap training programs and, more rationally, by creating a burgeoning network of technical schools and junior, community or regional colleges.

The large-scale entry of women, a majority of them married, into the labour force was another social phenomenon of the period. The resulting emergence of the two-income family and of mothers working outside the home had profound consequences for Canadian lifestyles. This trend resulted in greater demands for day care and early childhood educational provision. Larger discretionary family incomes permitted larger investments in the schooling of children. The greater persistence of traditional marriage and family patterns than was popularly supposed was countered by the emergence of single parent families, which became a noticeable feature of Canadian society for the first time;[8] this trend also increased the demand for child care and early childhood schooling. Increasing rates of illegitimate births among Canadian teenage girls evoked calls for more sex education in the curriculum, a demand that reflected the naive but typical North American belief that complex social problems could be alleviated, if not solved, by formal instruction. How far Canadians had liberalized their

views of moral education was illustrated by the fact that, in some purportedly enlightened communities, sex education in schools included instruction in birth control.

Other permissive trends were illustrated by the emergence of the so-
called "drug culture" and of pornography as a growth industry. By 1980,
however, there were signs that, with laws that lowered the drinking age to
eighteen or nineteen in most provinces, many young people were turning
back to alcohol, the traditional solace of their elders. Inevitably, as in the
past, demands arose for school programs to combat alcohol and drug
abuse. The growing acceptance of pornography in most of the media led,
by 1980, to demands for control of material since violence and brutality
towards women and children were sometimes depicted in what was
euphemistically termed "adult entertainment". Some advocates of censorship, unable to reimpose traditional public controls, sought to impose a
mindless control over materials used in school curricula. The continuing
popularity of pornography and the banality of much mass entertainment
made some educators less sanguine than formerly about the assumed
moral and intellectual effects of mass schooling.

All the trends just noted, and others, such as legalized gambling in
the form of lotteries, reflected the decline of traditional religious authority
in Canadian life. In the immediate post-war period, Canada was, like its
American neighbour, still a relatively pious country. Piety was reflected in
the schools in the form of Bible readings, prayers and an increase in formal
religious instruction by 1950. At that time, the churches were still a powerful
force in Canadian life and through the schools were able to enlist the power
of the state to do what they could not achieve themselves.[9]

Ontario's Mackay Report of 1969 recommended the abolition of religious instruction in schools.[10] By this time, church influence had virtually
disappeared from most public school systems. The mainline Protestant
churches were challenged by new, largely evangelical groups such as Pen-
tecostals and Mormons, some of whom established religious-based private
schools or brought pressure to bear for the establishment of public "values
schools." Within both mainline and other church groups, the congregation
remained an important educative influence on many Canadian children.

Sociological studies after World War II focussed on changing patterns
of child-rearing and the status of youth. A study of child-rearing in an
affluent Toronto suburb, "Crestwood Heights" — actually Forest Hill Village
— in the 1950s suggested how much a powerful achievement-oriented ideology of schooling was beginning to assert itself in post-war Canada as secular values of success, health and happiness began slowly to supplant
traditional religious values. The community was literally built around its
schools which were the dominant socializing agency in a setting where
child-rearing was the major industry. The socializing role of the school
increased as it absorbed many leisure-time activities into its programs, making it the centre of the child's life. This socializing role, with its emphasis
on personality development, on social knowledge or *savoir faire* designed to

maintain, or attain, a superior status, and on co-operation, was in some conflict with the academic or achievement values of the school which emphasized competition. Such a welter of conflicting values necessitated a system in which discipline, while more humane than in the past, was no less coercive in serving "the best interests of the child."[11]

Although increasing concern was expressed about the "generation gap," some observers argued that generational conflict resulted from the precocious desire of youth to attain rather than to reject adult status. S.D. Clark maintained that the generation gap had narrowed as compared with earlier periods when young people, living circumscribed lives and confined to primary occupations, were not expected to share in the interests and experience of the adult world. Growing up no longer had any necessary relationship to earning a living. Young people could be part of an adult world even though lacking the means to support themselves.[12] At the same time, the new phenomenon of student part-time employment enabled many adolescents to sustain adult-type lifestyles and even to set the pace for changing fashions among their elders. Hall and Carlton, in their study of an Ontario urban high school during the early 1970s, found that 70 per cent of the students held jobs, with the majority employed more than ten hours per week. The profound social and academic consequences of such employment were implied by teachers who noted that "Many [students] perceive the job as being more significant than school." Preoccupations with jobs, consumption, dating, mating, sociability, and recreation all at times took precedence over academic concerns.[13]

Student employment and increased retention rates made the school itself a more adult, socially heterogeneous environment, less dominated by middle-class values. The new youth sub-culture, with its associated consumption patterns and entertainment values, had been forcefully injected into the environment of the school.[14] Although during the preceding decade a minority of middle-class youth seemed to be moving towards more individualistic, humanistic lifestyles and away from the conventional achievement orientation and traditional career commitment that had been dominant in the 1950s, by 1980 teachers and professors reported a reversion to earlier attitudes.[15] In some respects, students reminded their mentors of the acquiescent youth of the immediate post-war years.

Canadian cultural life remained notably underdeveloped after 1945, apart from the CBC and the National Film Board. At a time when the movie theatre represented the epitome of mass culture, Canadians knew little of the arts and high culture. Most were still "rather poor, extremely busy and more than a little timid" with little time and income for frivolities.[16] During the 1950s, the establishment of the Stratford Festival, the Canadian Ballet Festival, the National Library and the Canada Council gave evidence of a greater national interest in cultural growth.

A major cultural event was the 1951 report of the Royal Commission on the Arts, Letters and Sciences (the Massey Commission). The Commission's terms of reference referred to the desirability of Canadians knowing "as much as possible about their country, its history and traditions, and about their national life and common achievements." The commissioners were emphatically self-conscious in asserting the traditional moral-intellectual basis of Canadian life which they claimed rested on certain habits of mind and convictions which Canadians shared and would never surrender. Specific reference was made to the Loyalist heritage and to the resulting common set of beliefs. Canada had been "sustained through difficult times by the power of this spiritual legacy" which was complemented by the vitality and historical tradition of French Canada. The foundation must be laid for a national tradition of the future.[17]

The Massey Report was culturally an aspect of the powerful nationalizing thrust of the immediate post-war era. In practice its recommendations led to two concrete results of momentous consequence for Canadian cultural and intellectual life: the establishment of the Canada Council and the emergence through federal funding of the universities as central institutions of that life. The commissioners espoused a clear educational philosophy and did not hesitate to state their concerns about the direction of Canadian schooling at all levels, in so doing portending the criticism of progressive education and of American influences that will be discussed in Chapter 14.[18]

During the 1960s, a major cultural explosion became evident with the proliferation of theatres and concert halls, both in the major cities and in many minor ones. It was estimated that attendance at concerts, live theatre, museums, art galleries and similar institutions in a given year exceeded attendance at sporting events. By 1971, the arts were lavishly supported by governments on a per capita scale almost ten times that in the United States, a development that reflected a new public sympathy for and awareness of the arts.[19] The 1981 census revealed that, during the 1970s, the number of libraries in Canada increased by 38 per cent.[20] Here was more heartening testimony to the benefits of popular schooling than that provided by much mass entertainment. Within schools, the cultural explosion was reflected in new facilities for expanded, largely extra-curricular music, drama and fine arts programs.

In no field was the flowering of Canadian culture more evident than in literature, both fiction and non-fiction. The immense popularity of Pierre Berton's books reflected a strong identification with the nation's historical and cultural traditions on the part of an adult population that had been schooled when Canadiana was mostly absent from the curriculum. One of the nation's leading novelists, Margaret Atwood, produced a thematic guide to Canadian literature for schools, significantly entitled *Survival*.[21] The new, though still modest, emphasis on Canadian literature in curricula reflected familiar fears about the assumed external threat to Canadian identity and to traditional moral values now underscored by American domination of publishing and other media, particularly television.

Rapidly changing lifestyles and related increasing affluence, leisure and education, and the increasing consumption of cultural and other goods were reflected in a high level of satisfaction with the quality of life among Canadians in the 1970s, according to a study by Atkinson. Interestingly enough, education ranked at the lowest level of satisfaction among what he called the "major life domains," below marriage, children and friends, and jobs.[22]

## A Federation Under Stress

Despite growing affluence, expanding opportunities, and apparent high levels of individual life satisfaction, there were also high levels of social, economic and political discontent during the period, often evident in expressions of collective dissatisfaction. External military, scientific and industrial threats arising from the cold war and related international crises were a source of continuing national anxiety. Internally, discontent and anxiety focussed on real continuing problems of poverty, disadvantage, regional disparity, racism, and cultural discrimination. By this time, Clark's "cultural islands" were becoming articulate publics, demanding participation in the society. Together with the new overseas immigrants, many were being drawn into the urban middle-class structure.

For most, the opportunities presented were eagerly embraced. For others, whether francophone nationalists, feminists, Native peoples or radical students, social protest took the form of various kinds of dropping out, of seeking separation from the larger society as a paradoxical way of demanding greater participation in it. Clark argued that as various groups sought to join the establishment, the most apparent social change was a diminution rather than an increase in differences among people.[23] Political discontent was most strongly evident in a new upsurge of francophone nationalism, manifested most radically by a separatist movement in Quebec. This upsurge fueled demands among other groups, notably Native peoples and so-called "third force" ethnic minorities. By 1980, "western alienation," sometimes with separatist overtones, had entered the lexicon of political debate.

Nowhere was the demand for greater opportunity more evident than in education, where the high school and university were the locus of a major social revolution, characterized by the phenomenal increase in enrolments already noted. To Clark, however, the real significance of both institutions was their role in reducing social barriers and in becoming the chief melting-pot in post-war Canadian society. They provided opportunities for higher social status at the same time that they functioned as major centres of dissent.[24] Dissent was manifested among many groups of anglophone Canadians over the old question of the Americanization of their economy and culture; their nationalism paralleled that of francophone Canadians.

Quebec's "quiet revolution" was sparked by contradictory francophone attitudes of self-confidence and of fears about cultural survival. For more than a generation industrialization and urbanization had fostered a pent-up demand for reform. Rapid social, cultural, political and economic changes were taking place in a society long noted for its deep seated concern for preserving its unique entity. Nationalism replaced religion as the dominant ideology of Quebecers and the moral fervour previously reserved for maintaining religious integrity focussed on maintaining linguistic integrity.[25] One result was cultural conflict between the linguistic communities, focussed at first largely on the schools. Education was seen as the key to achieving goals of provincial autonomy and economic expansion, both of which demanded a better schooled population. Needed change in clerically dominated schools that were accused of living in the past was legitimized by the proposals of the Parent Royal Commission of 1963-66, undoubtedly the most thoughtful and sophisticated inquiry in Canadian education during the period.[26]

Fears about cultural survival stemmed from a dramatic fall in the Quebec birthrate — itself a symbol of the extent of modernization — by low immigration from francophone countries, and by the strong tendency for immigrants from other countries to assimilate into the anglophone community. To meet the particular threat ostensibly posed to the survival of the French language, successive governments passed various measures during the 1970s. French was made the sole official language of Quebec in 1974, while severe restrictions were placed on admission to English-language schools.[27] Restrictions were extended by Bill 101, which was passed by the separatist Parti Quebecois government elected in 1976.

The initial federal response to the Quebec crisis was the establishment, in 1963, of the Royal Commission of Bilingualism and Biculturalism. Book II of the Commission's report, published in 1968, was entirely devoted to education, and included forty-six recommendations and proposals from many research studies that had been sponsored by the Commission.[28] Some of these had direct curricular implications, to be noted later. One result was a host of bilingual educational initiatives undertaken at federal, provincial and local levels. Concern for shoring up a fragile national identity and Confederation itself sparked efforts to promote Canadian Studies in the curriculum. These efforts will be discussed in Chapter 16.

The consciousness-raising associated with biculturalism had its effect in increasing the self awareness of the Native peoples or "first Canadians" as the B and B Commission termed them. As such they constituted what Allison has called a Fourth World population, conservatively estimated to number more than 600 000 in 1980, following a population explosion that had seen their numbers increase by 40 per cent over twenty years. Of these, 176 000 were school age children, a total greater than the school population of New Brunswick.[29] As noted earlier, federal policy was directed towards Registered (status) Indians on reserves and excluded Metis, Inuit and other "non-reserve" Natives. In 1951, the Indian Act was revised to permit the integration of Registered Indian children into provincial school systems. In 1969, the Northwest Territories assumed responsibility for the education of all Native children. Increasing Native pressure for a strong voice in, if not outright control of, their schools was part of an assertion of a wide range of claims, notably including land claims and their right to maintain their cultural identity. The latter objective could only be achieved through meeting the special schooling needs of Native students. Curriculum reform had met with limited success.

During the B and B Commission hearings, the claims of what came to be called "the other ethnic groups" were strongly asserted. By 1980, these groups collectively outnumbered francophones. In 1971, the federal government formally recognized multi-culturalism by declaring, in Prime Minister Trudeau's words, that Canada was a nation of two official languages but no official culture.[30] Cultural pluralism was asserted to be "the very essence of Canadian society" with the government committed to assist all cultural groups towards full participation in the society; one result was an impetus to multiculturalism in the curriculum, to be discussed in Chapter 16. Some francophones were suspicious of the new policy because it threatened their attempt to achieve a full partnership with anglophones and tended to treat them as simply another ethnic group. "Third force" critics for their part saw multiculturalism as perpetuating their second-class status because it was tied to official bilingualism.[31]

Other sources of tension during the period were associated with poverty, disadvantage, regional disparity, and uneven economic growth. Various federal initiatives to meet these problems included equalization payments to the "have not" provinces, transfer payments to all provinces, and social welfare measures such as an expanded family allowance scheme. These initiatives, in concert with similar provincial initiatives, had significant, if often indirect educational benefits. Brown estimated that in 1977-78 transfer payments to the provinces constituted nearly 22 per cent of all expenditures on education. Between 1965 and 1978, equalization payments helped to reduce the percentage by which the highest-spending province exceeded the lowest-spending province in expenditures on elementary and secondary education from 174 to 54 per cent.[32] However, since the provinces were not obliged to apply the payments to education, federal funds in some cases simply replaced provincial funds and thus added nothing to total school expenditures.[33]

Rural poverty and regional disparity were reflected in the persistence of the long-standing rural school problem, particularly in the more remote areas of Atlantic Canada, Northern Ontario and the Prairie provinces. For both rural and urban areas, Ian Adams and his colleagues in *The Real Poverty Report* described the links between education and affluence as "almost absolute." While the length of schooling of the poor had increased, so had that of the affluent, with the result that the educational gap between them had not been narrowed.[34] The gap was glaringly apparent in a middle-class teacher's account of his futile attempts to teach abandoned and abused Grade 4 children living in a suburban ghetto of high-rises and townhouses in North York, Ontario containing recent immigrants, single parent families, juvenile delinquents and having one of the highest suicide rates in Metropolitan Toronto.[35]

## Education as Everybody's Business

### The Changing Ecology of Schooling

As noted above, post-war circumstances created a new interest and unprecedented demands for education among Canadians who more and more saw schooling as the major means of improved opportunity for their children. Yet, the continuing threadbare condition noted earlier of school systems and universities alike during the decade following 1945 made it impossible to meet the new expectations. Most Canadian children still obtained little more than an elementary education, frequently offered in thousands of drab and spartan one-room schools staffed by ill-trained young teachers. Only a few were able to benefit from elitist academic high school curricula which offered limited opportunities for vocational education. Universities were hard pressed to accommodate the thousands of veterans who flooded into them.

After 1960, the social and educational changes already noted, especially huge enrolment increases and even larger expenditure increases, had major effects on school curricula. Paradoxically, at the very moment of the school's success, the discontents of affluence led some critics to see a decline in its influence. Some radicals even spoke with satisfaction of the "deschooling" of society. Although the home and family were also widely believed to have lost influence, there was abundant evidence that these institutions remained critical — more so, it was suggested, than the school itself — in determining the life chances of the young by providing the educational strategies necessary to school and later career success.[36] Of new elements in the modern educational configuration, none were more obvious than the electronic media, particularly television.

Meanwhile, patterns of schooling were themselves changing from those which confined formal education to schools to those which took place in an increasing variety of institutions catering to a much more varied clientele. Informal education of many kinds had likewise developed rapidly. Patterns changed at both ends of the age scale. Preschool enrolments nearly tripled during the period and although provision still varied in extent and quality across the country, by 1978 more than 90 per cent of five year old children were attending kindergarten.[37] Most provinces had publicly supported kindergartens by this time. Large numbers of children were also enrolled in an estimated 1200 private kindergartens and nursery schools, many of which were licensed by departments of education. Growth in this educational sector reflected the large increase in the number of employed mothers with pre-school children, and the recognition of the crucial importance for learning of the early childhood years.

Thomas pointed out that, because Canada as an immigrant country had always made demands on adults to learn new ways of living, adult education and learning had always been a dominant thread in Canadian history. In the 1930s, adult education had emerged as a self-conscious enterprise. Wartime needs had been met by adults learning things they had never been expected to learn. During the 1960s, it had become increasingly clear that schooling could not meet the lifelong needs of learners. As an enterprise that was essentially voluntary, and less visible and less dependent than schooling on single sources of financial support, adult education was not as affected by the growing budget constraints of the 1970s. During this decade, the number of adults pursuing formal education exceeded the number of children in schools.[38]

## Mass Education and the Expansion of Schooling

After 1945, the new public interest in and demand for education created a crisis mentality that forced politicians to expand schooling. The extent of the crisis and the willingness to meet it were most fully evident in Ontario, where enrolment pressures were greatest. In 1960, the province's Minister of Education, John P. Roberts, told a school trustees' convention with obvious pride that "on the average, one new school or an addition to an existing school has been completed every calendar day for the past ten years." He anticipated that in 1960 a total of 527 new educational units would be constructed.[39]

During the era of explosive growth of the 1960s, mass education came into its own. In its 1976 assessment of Canadian education the Paris-based Organization for Economic Co-operation and Development (OECD) observed that Canada led the industrial nations in the proportion (30.9 per cent) of its population enrolled in fulltime study. With expenditures on education expressed as a proportion of the Gross National Product having doubled during the 1960s, a level had been reached higher than that of any industrial nation, including the United States. It was "an enormous common achievement ... all the more noteworthy in view of very unequal economic, cultural and demographic conditions that produced highly differentiated results in terms of educational development from region to region."[40] The increase in retention rates measured between Grades 2 and 12 was notable between 1961 and 1972, increasing from 35 per cent to 71 per cent.[41] During the 1970s, males began to overtake females in their propensity to complete high school, although the extent of schooling and retention rates continued, as in earlier decades, to be higher among women. Nevertheless, higher level educational and job opportunities still remained restricted for females.

A basic rationale for the expansion of schooling during the period was so-called human capital theory, officially promulgated by the Economic Council of Canada. The theory was based on the assumption that once a high level of physical capital and advanced industrial organization had been achieved, further economic growth would depend mainly on technical innovation, which in turn depended on a highly trained workforce. More education meant more productivity.[42] The theory was initially attractive on grounds of both morality and efficiency for, by promoting greater equality of educational opportunity, social inequalities were reduced and a more effective use of resources was enhanced. Later critics charged that human capital theorists ignored the possibility that higher productivity resulting from more education might reduce the demand for labour and encourage longer school retention as a means of delaying entry to the workforce. Porter claimed that the premise that public education would be a major instrument of social equality had been proved false.[43]

As in the past, various comparisons were made between Canadian and American educational development. During the mid-1960s, the Economic Council, in a study of the relationship between education and economic growth, concluded that the average quality of education was roughly similar in the two countries. One year of education in Canada was approximately the equivalent of one year of education in the United States. In assessing the Canadian rise in educational attainment between 1911 and 1961, based on the assumption that the quality of education had remained about the same over the half century, the study concluded that improvement, measured by years of schooling and average school attendance, had been significant. Yet improvement had been considerably less than that in the United States, with the result that there had been a widening "educational gap" between the two countries, especially at the senior secondary and post-secondary levels. The Council concluded that a lower rate of economic growth and productivity in the Canadian economy was closely related to less educational attainment. This conclusion bore out Porter's claim that the educational system failed to provide an adequately skilled and professional workforce, largely because Canadian education did not "transmit positive values about education to those classes which did not formerly have a high educational level."[44]

Within a decade of the Economic Council study, Canadian educational progress had improved dramatically in relation to that of the United States. This was brought out in Michalos' *North American Social Report*, a remarkable attempt to compare the quality of life in the two countries on a range of dimensions, including education. Michalos showed that with respect to enrolment figures, pupil-teacher ratios, expenditures and other measures, between 1964 and 1974 Canada substantially closed the longstanding educational gap with the United States. From 1969 onward the rate of increase in full time elementary and secondary school enrolment was greater in Canada than in the United States in every year.[45] Michalos recognized that enrolment figures were in themselves "poor surrogate measures of the quality of education." Counting heads was one thing, but counting what goes on inside them, for instance, determining what Canadian students actually learned, was another. For constitutional and political reasons, Canadians had no measures comparable to those provided by the National Assessment of Educational Progress in the United States. Post-secondary enrolments had increased more rapidly in Canada, although the United States still had a significantly higher proportion of its population enrolled at this level and a higher proportion of people holding degrees.[46]

Michalos concluded in summary that "With respect to the general area of education, the quality of life in Canada is higher than that in the United States." In both countries, education improved in more ways than it deteriorated, but improvement had been greater and deterioration less in Canada.[47] Like the OECD assessment, Michalos' analysis indicated that Canada had reached a notable educational "take-off" stage between the mid-1960s and the mid-1970s.

## Expanding Opportunity and Reducing Disparities

Despite notable gains, it was plain by this time that equality of educational opportunity still fell far short of achievement. Students from middle-class families were over-represented in post-secondary institutions, while the children of blue collar workers were under-represented.[48] There was a growing awareness that the social selection process for higher levels of education occurred, not at the point of entry to those levels, but at earlier stages. An Ontario study by Anisef and his associates suggested that the lowering of social, cultural and geographic barriers was probably more important than lowering financial barriers. To this end, the study recommended pre-kindergarten "head start" programs for younger disadvantaged children, and summer enrichment programs for older ones. Other proposed measures included the elimination of stereotyped images of occupational roles from curriculum materials and positive, more systematic efforts to encourage children to proceed to higher education.[49] Other educators advocated "life-long learning" or "recurrent education" as a means of making up for lost opportunities and of providing new ones so that dropouts would no longer be stigmatized, and re-entry into formal education would become possible at any age.[50]

As noted earlier, federal policies had contributed, usually indirectly, to some expansion of educational opportunity. Within the provinces, changes in taxation policy in the form of equalization of tax assessments, together with a major increase in direct provincial support of local jurisdictions, became the chief tools for this purpose. In 1967, under New Brunswick's Equal Opportunity Program, a uniform provincial tax on equally-assessed real property was established. This enabled the province to assume the full cost of a uniform program of elementary and secondary education. A major purpose of the plan was to reduce the disparity between New Brunswick's two linguistic communities and to emphasize the essential unity of the educational norms of both in a modern industrial society.[51]

The New Brunswick plan was a form of what came to be called a "foundation program." Martin and Macdonnell called it "the most prominent plan for educational finance in Canada" during the 1960s. Under it, a province guaranteed a basic uniform schooling provision to all children regardless of where they lived. This was done by paying the difference between the revenues raised by local districts and the cost of a minimum acceptable program. The result was a reduction in intra-provincial disparities but not a full equalization of school provision, since wealthy areas were still able to provide services above the minimum.[52] Variations among provincial foundation programs reflected continuing regional disparities. Such disparities were especially clearly marked in per pupil expenditures which, in 1972, ranged from $586 in the Atlantic provinces to $972 in Ontario.[53] Similar disparities were evident in school retention rates, in capital expenditures, and in teacher training, qualifications, tenure, and salaries.[54]

Despite the persistence of the rural school problem, undeniable progress was evident in the hundreds of new consolidated elementary schools and regional high schools which, by the mid-1970s, were often indistinguishable from their urban equivalents. During the 1960s, Ontario replaced rural school boards with county boards, reducing the number of school sections from 66 245 to 5160 between 1964 and 1968.[55] Over the following decade, Ontario's rural school children gained learning opportunities much more comparable to those of urban children than in the past, although the gap between the two groups remained significant. Disparities also persisted between public and separate school systems in that province.[56]

Outside Ontario an equalization of resources also led to a closer alignment between rural and urban school curricula, and to a reduction of disparities in program provision. Paradoxically, such alignment made programs more similar across each province at the same time that, in matching the diverse offerings of urban schools, those in rural schools became more differentiated. By 1976, throughout Canada the provincial authorities were on average paying two dollars on schools for every one dollar paid by local jurisdictions. In Newfoundland, Prince Edward Island and New Brunswick the provincial authorities were effectively bearing all costs.[57] This was a marked reversal of policy over earlier periods.

Despite such progress, community size was still a factor in retention rates, educational plans, opportunities and accessibility. Students, especially males, from large communities were more likely to finish high school and to continue their studies than those of comparable ability from small communities.[58] Within urban metropolitan areas, disparity was also less evident at this time. To Michael Katz, a radical American school critic, the most striking feature of Ontario education was "the relative lack of wide discrepancies between schools in city and suburb" as compared with the United States.[59]

By this time, educational disparities were being recognized as the result of social and structural conditions largely external to the school. Such conditions were especially apparent with respect to sex and ethnicity. We have noted that females had long outpaced males in school retention rates and in achievement. In particular, girls were more likely to be better readers than boys, and less likely to be in special classes for slow learners. To some educators, schools were in fact feminized institutions that discriminated against boys. On the other hand, while textbooks might lack interest for boys, they reinforced sex role stereotyping among girls by portraying females in restricted home and work roles, thereby contributing to low female expectations.[60] The Royal Commission on the Status of Women recommended that school systems adopt textbooks that portrayed women as well as men in diversified roles and occupations.[61]

Gaskell's analysis indicated that schooling at all levels was only nominally co-educational and that sex segregation continued in classrooms as a function of course enrolment patterns. Thus, school commercial courses catered overwhelmingly to girls and industrial courses to boys. Girls were less likely to take science and mathematics courses beyond the compulsory level. Similar imbalances occurred at the post-secondary level. The real meaning of curriculum organization, suggested Gaskell, was that it began a form of differentiation that continued into the labour market. With more schooling and more marketable skills girls had easier entry to that market than boys, but soon encountered a lower ceiling of opportunity. The placement of the sexes in different school courses meant that their education consisted of different things.[62] This trend continued at the university level, although the 1981 census data revealed a quantum leap in the numbers of female systems analysts, doctors, lawyers and economists. The data also revealed how far women still had to go to achieve educational and vocational equality.[63]

During the early 1960s, the B and B Commission demonstrated marked differences between Canadian ethnic backgrounds and levels of schooling. At the secondary level in Ontario, it was found that dropout rates were much higher for francophone students than for those of British or certain other ethnic origins, such as Jewish and German. Students of Italian origin also had high dropout rates. Disparities were even greater where university education was concerned.[64] By 1980, the various ethnic groups were much more evenly represented in university enrolments, although significant disparities remained.

## Conflicting Policy Trends

The extent to which education by 1960 was seen as "everybody's business" was epitomized by the national conference on education organized in 1958 by the Canadian Teachers' Federation and other groups. Held in Ottawa, the conference drew 850 delegates representing 84 organizations, with a total of three million members.[65] More resources, greater valuing of intellectual achievement and more recognition of the teacher's status were major themes in a conference which, on occasion, featured controversy between traditionalists and progressives regarding the preferred emphases of schooling.

In 1962, the Second Canadian Conference on Education was held in Montreal as a follow-up to the Ottawa meeting. One of many national conferences held during the decade on a host of educational topics, the Montreal meeting attracted 2000 delegates to a vast consciousness-raising exercise that publicized the needs and shortcomings of Canadian education in a period of explosive growth. Background papers, which had a total distribution of 150 000 copies, injected new thinking into topics that included, among others, the aims of education, school finance, teacher professionalism and the impact of technology and the media.[66]

A discussion of educational aims on the opening day of the conference included the progressive views of Phillips and Scarfe, who emphasized a humanistic, activist curriculum aimed at individual and social development. Leddy and de Grandpre, espousing Catholic educational doctrine, were opposed to pragmatic philosophies and advocated a curriculum based on immutable values, a reverence for the past, and the cultivation of reason in an educational environment permeated by a traditional moral outlook. Northrop Frye rejected social adjustment as an aim and saw schooling as an apprenticeship for an ultimate cultural and intellectual education that was a worthy end in itself.[67]

Royal commissions and other official and unofficial inquiries also played a consciousness-raising role during the post-war period. Ontario led the way with the Hope Commission, the 1950 report of which was described by Stevenson as the most comprehensive study of education ever completed in a Canadian province.[68] (its progressive conservative, or conservative progressive, view of school curricula will be discussed in Chapter 14.)

The late 1950s and the early 1960s could be called an era of royal commissions in Canadian education. In 1959 and 1960 alone, no fewer than five commissions, all concerned primarily with elementary and secondary schooling, were reported in Manitoba, Saskatchewan, Alberta, Prince Edward Island and British Columbia. By the end of the following decade, all provinces had examined various levels of schooling or their entire systems; eight studies were concerned exclusively with post-secondary education. During the 1970s, Ontario's Commission on Declining Enrolments was the most comprehensive investigation of that problem carried out in any province, and included a highly sophisticated investigation of the curricular implications of declining enrolments. The same province's royal commission on book publishing dealt largely with educational book publishing, in a study that had considerable curricular significance.[69] Proposals noted earlier for equalizing fiscal resources available for education emanated from official inquiries in several provinces.

In philosophy, the general thrust of the various inquiries ranged from the extreme conservatism of British Columbia's Chant Commission of 1960 to the neo-progressivism of Ontario's 1968 Hall-Dennis and Alberta's 1972 Worth reports.[70] Each was representative of its particular time and milieu, an indication of how, within just over a decade, conflicting trends that in earlier periods would have been manifested over a generation or more, became apparent. Contradictory proposals or minority reports within a particular investigation suggested that commissioners' views sometimes represented less the application of thought-out philosophies or rational solutions, than desperate responses to public and political pressures.

As is often the case with such studies the recommendations of the various inquiries sometimes provided a rationale, if not a rationalization, for changes significantly different from those envisaged by the commissions themselves. Such was the fate of the British Columbia inquiry. Anti-progresssive in orientation, Chant advocated the restoration of intellectual development as the primary function of the school. This goal was defined in terms of acquiring factual knowledge but curriculum reformers interpreted it in terms of Bruner's rather different concept of discovery learning.

Quebec's Parent Report (1963-66) resulted in the appointment, in 1964, of the province's first Minister of Education since 1875, as schools passed from religious to civil control. A new advisory Superior Council of Education blurred the Roman Catholic-Protestant boundary within the dual system, but committees of each faith remained to advise the council on the teaching of religion, morals and other matters. Religious teaching was made voluntary in secondary schools but was routinely taught in elementary schools, although parents could withdraw their children. Co-education was proposed at the secondary level, but with caution "in the light of the moral, pedagogical and economic factors involved."[71]

Parent's recommendations for the reorganization of elementary and secondary schools and their curricula will be discussed subsequently. His proposals for secondary schooling were the most revolutionary of any in his report, and gave Quebec a truly public system at this level for the first time. Five year composite "polyvalent" schools were established to meet the needs of a new and diverse adolescent clientele. The province's famous classical colleges were largely secularized and came under public regulation with generous funding, as did other private schools. By the late 1960s, school retention rates in Quebec were comparable to most in North America. A new post-secondary level was established in 1967 in the form of the CEGEPS (Colleges d'enseignement general et professionnel) which offered pre-university and pre-vocational courses in a system intermediate between the secondary schools and the universities. The result was a unique K-6-5-2(3)-3 pattern of schooling extending from kindergarten through university.

One consequence of the new nationalism was that, although Quebec schools were still officially designated as Catholic or Protestant, in practice they were now divided along linguistic rather than religious lines.[72] At the same time, immersion French and other intensive forms of language instruction were adopted in anglophone curricula. The general curricula of the two solitudes became much more closely aligned than in the past. As elsewhere, a more conservative trend was evident during the 1970s, symbolized by the so-called Green Paper (1977) and a "plan of action". These policy documents pointed to much stronger central control of the curriculum and other matters than had been the case during the heady years of the quiet revolution.[73]

Newfoundland's Warren Commission of 1967 proposed a modernization of the province's school system fully comparable to that under way in

Quebec.[74] Key recommendations, most of which were speedily implemented, including the consolidation of schools (from 230 districts to 36 in 1975), improved school finance and taxation arrangements, the establishment of kindergartens, curriculum revision and expansion and the beginnings of a junior college system. In dealing with the contentious issue of denominational schools, Warren recommended that Newfoundland reduce though not eliminate the religious influence in its school system. In 1968, the offices of denominational superintendents of education were abolished and replaced by unofficial denominational committees, whose advice was restricted to religious matters. Warren's specific curriculum proposals and those of a later 1979 provincial task force will be discussed in later chapters.

In Ontario, the problems of the school population explosion were exacerbated by the uneven distribution of the increase. The shift of enrolment from public to separate schools that resulted from heavy Roman Catholic immigration led the latter to an educational and political maturity that one observer described as the chief overall post-war change in Ontario schooling. A similar shift occurred from rural to urban areas, and from academic to vocational programs. As enrolment and retention rates rose, educational expenditures increased more than nine-fold between 1945 and 1963, while the total provincial population was increasing less than two-fold.[75]

Curriculum change in Ontario during the early 1960s had been portended by the academic reform movement that had originated in the post-Sputnik era following 1957. (Ontario's prominent role in this subject-centered thrust will be discussed in Chapter 14.) Also to be discussed later will be the coincidental major vocational thrust that resulted from the federal Technical and Vocational Training Assistance Act passed in 1960, which led inadvertently to a major transformation of secondary curricula in Ontario and to a lesser extend in other provinces.[76]

Illustrative of the rapid oscillations of the period was the emergence by 1970 of a new child-centred thrust in which Ontario also took the lead, through the work of the Provincial Committee on Aims and Objectives of Education in the Schools of Ontario. Known as the Hall-Dennis inquiry after its joint chairmen, Justice G. Emmett Hall, an eminent jurist and architect of Canada's medicare system, and Lloyd Dennis, an Ontario school administrator, the inquiry was the most publicized, avant-garde of all Canadian post-war reports on education. Its 1968 report, entitled *Living and Learning,* was soon being hailed by some enthusiastic progressives as the most important educational document ever produced in Ontario.[77] In generalizing the province's problems and opportunities to the whole of Canada, the report was consistent with a provincial tradition. The schools must meet the need for a national identity "rooted in the soul of the people".[78]

During the 1960s, administrative reorganization in Ontario was probably more significant than curricular reorganization, and was certainly a *sine qua non* for the latter. As in all provinces, these were the years when a full-blown educational bureaucracy which typically included substantial curriculum policy, development, implementation and evaluation components was finally established. The designation of townships as school areas in 1965, and the subsequent establishment of the county boards noted earlier led to the abolition of the three-member section boards, one of the province's oldest public institutions. Small communities lost control over local school policy and many multi-grade one and two room schools were closed. Within the county boards public (elementary) and high school districts finally amalgamated, with a single board in each case.[79] A reorganization of the department — soon to be called the Ministry — of Education — removed the longstanding dichotomy between elementary and secondary education at the provincial level.

Larger local jurisdictions led to a decentralization that enabled the department's role to shift from that of a regulatory to a support and service role. Guidelines replaced detailed course outlines and provincial inspection ceased entirely. Local jurisdictions acquired impressive curriculum development, implementation and evaluation powers and capacities, including research capacities, although the legal and financial control that remained with the province left the new boards ultimately subordinate to central authority. Moreover, they lacked the local political base that had been available to township and section boards as a means of resisting that authority.[80]

Curriculum-related federal initiatives already noted caused the Department of the Secretary of State to become a *de facto* national Ministry of Education during the period. Federal educational activities were usually cloaked under the guise of cultural activities, as in the case of broadcasting policy, or were disguised to serve national political goals, as in the case of bilingual policy. Initiatives in vocational education ostensibly served economic goals and national labour needs. In most cases, federal incursions into education under whatever guise had notable curricular effects. The new attention given to the teaching of French, and the expansion of vocational curricula were but two examples. Policies and priorities frequently lacked coherence and operated at cross purposes, a result which the 1976 OECD study implied was a consequence of the general lack of an overall national policy in education. A further consequence was that provincial policies and priorities frequently became distorted.[81]

In 1967, the provinces responded to federal incursions by establishing the Council of Ministers of Education, Canada (CMEC). The new body's essentially negative role of containing the federal presence was paralleled by a grudging recognition of the increasing need for national co-ordination in educational policy and related matters. Initially involved in the development of educational television and teacher exchanges, the council increasingly became a conduit of federal funds, supporting university education, bilingual programs in schools and various other activities. It also began in the 1960s to take limited initiatives in Canadian studies and in curriculum co-ordination among the provinces. These initiatives and related federal initiatives, together with the general curricular effects of federal policies referred to above will be examined in later chapters. Also to be examined are the continuing roles of such national voluntary bodies as the Canadian Education Association and the Canadian Teachers' Federation. Finally, two private national inquiries conducted respectively by Hodgetts and Symons into the status and needs of Canadian Studies curricula at the school and post-secondary levels will be considered.[82]

## Notes to Chapter 13

1 Bothwell *et al*, 120, 457.

2 S.D. Clark, 38.

3 Jaenen, "Multiculturalism," 91.

4 V. Ross, "The Way," 4.

5 For demographic trends see Bothwell, 26-33; Organization for Economic Cooperation and Development (OECD), 22-25; Adler and Brusegard, 71-82; Statistics Canada, *Canada's Population.*

6 Simmons and Simmons, 2.

7 Ibid., 7.

8 See Bothwell *et al*, 443.

9 Ibid., 109.

10 See Ontario Department of Education, *Religion Information and Moral Development* (The MacKay Report).

11 This account of the unfolding of a new type of school in the post-war upper middle class suburban culture is based on J. Seeley *et al*, *Crestwood Heights*, 224-276.

12 S.D. Clark, 38-41.

13 Hall and Carlton, 154, 170.

14 Ibid. 91, 170.

15 For a discussion of the shift away from traditional values see Quarter, "Shifting."

16 Bothwell *et al*, 119.

17 Royal Commission on the Arts, Letters and Sciences, xi, 4.

18 Ibid., 15. See Neatby.

19 Bothwell *et al*, 257.

20 V. Ross, "The Way," 18.

21 Atwood, *Survival.*

22 Atkinson, reported in Adler and Brusegard, 277-92.

23 S.D. Clark, 39.

24 Ibid., 41.

25 Magnuson, *Brief History,* 129.

26 Royal Commission of Inquiry on Education in the Province of Quebec, hereinafter referred to as the Parent Commission or the Parent Report.

27 Magnuson, *Brief History* 126-7.

28 See Royal Commission on Bilingualism and Biculturalism. *A Preliminary Report* was published in 1965. Other volumes were published between 1965 and 1971. Book II, *Education*, appeared in 1969.

29 Allison, 105.

30 The Right Hon. P.E. Trudeau, *House of Commons Debates*, October 8, 1971.

31 For conflicting views of multiculturalism, in particular those of Rocher and Lupul see Burnet.

32 W.J. Brown, 159-164.

33 OECD, 94.

34 See Ian Adams *et al*, 216.

35 McLaren.

36 See Note 9, Chapter 5 for a reference to this point for the preceding section of this study.

37 OECD, 200.

38 A. Thomas, 251-7.

39 Cited by John Fraser, 1.

40 OECD, 22, 29, 33.

41 Ibid., 40.

42 See Pike, "Contemporary Directions."

43 Lockhart, 78; Porter, *The Measure*, 242-3.

44 Economic Council of Canada, 73-4; Porter, "Social Change," 126-7.

45 Michalos, 115.

46 Ibid., 98, 95.

47 Ibid., 109-10.

48 Manzer, 188, 192.

49 Anisef *et al*, reported in *University Affairs*, October, 1982, 12. See also their *Pursuit of Equality*.

50 Pike, "Contemporary Directions," 35.

51 Cited in Goulson, 66-7.

52 Martin and Macdonnell, 153, 221.

53 OECD, 51.

54 Martin and Macdonnell, 222-5.

55 D. Cameron, 199-200.

56 Humphreys, "Equality?"

57 OECD, 68-9.

58 Martin and Macdonnell, 231.

59 M. Katz in Myers, *The Failure,* 26.

60 Jane Gaskell "Equal," 174-6.

61 Royal Commission on the Status of Women, 174-5.

62 Jane Gaskell "Equal," 178-81.

63 V. Ross, "The Way," 30.

64 Royal Commission on Bilingualism and Biculturalism, Book II, *Education,* 87-93.

65 Stevenson, "Reaction and Reform," 101.

66 Price.

67 For a discussion of the presentations see Fleming, III, *Schools,* 19-29.

68 Stevenson, "Reaction and Reform," 92.

69 See Ontario, Commission on Declining Enrolments and Ontario, Royal Commission on Book Publishing.

70 See British Columbia, *Report of the Royal Commission on Education* (Chant Report); Ontario, Provincial Committee on Aims and Objectives (report entitled *Living and Learning,* referred to hereinafter as Hall-Dennis); Alberta Commission on Educational Planning (report entitled *A Choice of Futures,* also referred to as the Worth Commission or Worth Report). These and other inquiries will be discussed in subsequent chapters.

71 The Parent Report, 102, 118-21.

72 Magnuson, *Brief History,* 129.

73 Quebec, Ministère de l'Education, *The Schools of Quebec* and *Primary and Secondary Education.*

74 Newfoundland Royal Commission on Education, hereinafter referred to as the Warren Commission.

75 D. Cameron, 68-9, 79.

76 Fleming, III, *Schools.*

77 Ibid. 499.

78 Hall-Dennis, 23.

79 See D. Cameron, 205-7.

80 Ibid. 286-7. For a discussion of the research capacities developed at the local level see B. Levin.

81 For a discussion of the problems referred to here see OECD, 89-103.

82 See Hodgetts, *What Culture?* Symons, *To Know Ourselves.*

# CHAPTER 14

## FROM ACADEMIC REFORM
## TO NEO-PROGRESSIVE CHANGE

*...the school should ... convey to all, insofar as they are capable of receiving it,
the intellectual, cultural and moral training which represents the best in a long
and honourable tradition of Western civilization.*

(Hilda Neatby, 1953)

*...one must accept the modern definition of the curriculum as 'all those activities
in which children engage under the auspices of the school'.*
(The Provincial Committee on Aims and Objectives for Education
in the Schools of Ontario, 1968).

### The Reaction Against Progressivism

Even as the Canadian educational establishment was urging a cautious
vocationally-oriented extension of conservative progressivism, tradition-
minded educators were beginning to question ideas and practices that had
been advocated during the inter-war years. Ontario's Hope Commission of
1950 displayed a characteristic ambivalence. The commissioners defined
two basic philosophical orientations in somewhat oversimplified terms:
"We may think of the traditionalist as one who believes in strict discipline
and the mastering of school subjects and of the progressive as one who
puts emphasis on interest and learning by experience." Although the commissioners presented a fair-minded interpretation of the basis tenets of
Deweyism, in their pose of benevolent tolerance of opposing points of view
they came down more on the traditionalist than on the progressive side. As
a compromise, they suggested a curriculum organization based on a relatively progressive approach in the early years and a traditional one later.[1]

The cautious stance of the Hope Commission no doubt reflected post-
war conservatism. In the early 1950s, W.J. Dunlop, Ontario's Minister of
Education complained that "Too many fads are creeping into education
these days to the exclusion of down-to-earth fundamentals." Only when
"the last shreds of this so-called progressive education are gone," continued
Dunlop, could the schools again produce "loyal, intelligent, right-thinking

and freedom-loving citizens."[2] Similar criticisms were voiced a year later by the federal Massey Commission. With reference to the propensity of Canadian teachers to undertake graduate studies in the United States, Massey asked, "How many Canadians realize that over a large part of Canada the schools are accepting tacit direction from New York that they would not think of taking from Ottawa?" The commissioners were equally concerned about Canadian dependence on American curriculum materials which reflected an emphasis and direction unsuitable for Canadian children. By failing to produce their own materials, Canadians had fallen into a "lazy, even abject imitation" of American educational practices that entailed "an uncritical acceptance of ideas and assumptions alien to our tradition." American textbooks, like the American mass media, were bound to be deleterious because they led to a "weakening of the critical faculties," and "cultural annexation" and retarded the growth of a "wholesome Canadianism."[3] It was a familiar Canadian lament.

The curriculum criticism implied by Massey was most pointedly adumbrated by Neatby's *So Little for the Mind* (1953), a root and branch critique of progressive education which attracted unprecedented public attention. Utilizing mostly official printed sources with the generalizations illustrated "from the personal experiences of teachers in many parts of Canada," Neatby, who had served as a member of the Massey Commission, agreed that the remarkable growth of the system had been good and necessary, reflecting sanguinely that "Canadians have a great traditional respect for education ... ."[4] While the application of modern social science precepts, particularly those of psychology, had been inevitable, even necessary, the resulting "industrialization" of schooling had brought questionable benefits. Nevertheless, Neatby admitted that a more humanitarian, child-centred view of education had had positive value by encouraging an improved school environment and a more active, participative classroom.[5]

Turning to the specific weaknesses of progressivism, Neatby saw an overemphasis on ease, pleasantness and egalitarianism which had resulted in an anti-intellectual, anti-cultural, anti-moral climate in Canadian schools. An overweening bureaucracy of unscholarly experts had uncritically accepted the naturalistic scientific philosophy and pernicious social adjustment doctrines of John Dewey who, Neatby felt, had exerted an "incalculable influence" in Canada. An antipathy to traditional Canadian values was evident in exuberant lists of aims and purposes which were remarkably similar from coast to coast. Expressed in equally similar phraseology which, Neatby implied, was mutually plagiarized or drawn without attribution from American sources, such lists provided evidence of national curricular uniformity, although not in the form of a badly needed Canadian educational philosophy.[6]

For Neatby, the central problem in Canadian education was the neglect of the primary intellectual function of the school. "Character education," "critical thinking," "meaning" and "understanding" had been overemphasized to the detriment of subject matter and intellectual skills. While traditionalists might have unduly separated these processes, progressives had failed to integrate them in an intellectually rigorous way. The problem was most evident in state controlled or approved teacher training, which Neatby saw as the most significant development in modern education. The normal school emphasis on professional knowledge at the expense of liberal education exemplified the same American influences, anti-intellectual tendencies and Deweyan uniformity of thought found in the schools.[7]

Neatby's analysis of provincial courses of study was fair-minded as she acknowledged a commendable retreat from old-fashioned rote learning. The idea of the enterprise — particularly of the unit of work — was sound in principle but questionable in practice. She was critical of the over-emphasis on the immediate and the modern in literature to the neglect of the classics, although she was gratified to note that such poems as Sir Henry Newbolt's *Vitae Lampada* were still being read. The schools provided too many options and the composite high school in particular had been responsible for an erosion of matriculation standards. Music and art, she implied — subjects not formerly seen as essential to the educated person — were overdone.[8]

Neatby was particularly critical of the new methods of evaluation, including objective testing and the use of "recommendation" in place of the former high school entrance examinations. She was ambivalent about how the school should face the challenge of mass education. On the one hand, she thought progressives underestimated the average child. On the other, she saw little reason for the school to exert special efforts to retain the less willing and able. Thus, she ignored or scorned the observations of the Canadian Research Committee on Practical Education. The fact that too many pupils were staying on was evidence, not of public demand, but of the perverse desire of the educational establishment to keep them in school. Her solution to the problems created by progressivism was to restore a humanistic curriculum based on the cultivation of "a vision of greatness" of the type then being advocated by such educators as Sir Richard Livingstone, the famous British classicist, and Robert Hutchins, the American traditionalist. She felt that earlier indirect religious and moral instruction based on Christian principles should be restored to the curriculum.[9]

Although Neatby was accused of being an armchair critic, her cogent criticism of the vacuity that passed for thought throughout much of the Canadian educational establishment struck a responsive chord in an uneasy public faced with the challenge of post-war educational demands. Educators, caught off guard and unaccustomed to public debate, did not always make very credible rejoinders to her arguments.[10] As a result, her analysis helped to set the stage for a gathering North American storm of criticism over the flaccidity of schooling, a storm that would pave the way for a major subject-centred thrust of curriculum reform by the late 1950s. Yet, Neatby's impact was diminished by her disregard of the public mood and of the emerging realities of mass education, and by her failure to address the fundamental problem of providing quality education in a society with limited educational resources but seemingly unlimited expectations.

At a social-philosophical level, Neatby's analysis was the last major idealist-moralist critique of schooling to gain national public attention. Her critique was shared by various fellow moralists, all of whom agreed that the schools had abandoned their traditional primary goal of training the mind and of upholding a social order that valued social restraint and a respect for received wisdom based on disciplined intelligence. Thus, George Grant believed with Neatby in a divine purpose within history and in God-given laws of morality.[11] A.R.M. Lower thought that Canadian schools had lost any unifying spiritual concept and had come to typify the moral anarchy of society.[12] To B.C. Diltz, the controversial dean of the Ontario College of Education, the only answer to the false gods of social science and "educational engineering" lay in the restoration of "organic" education based on a study of great scientific and artistic works expressive of "God's purpose for man."[13] Another critic, Hugh MacLennan, widely regarded as Canada's leading man of letters during the 1950s, took a less explicitly religious perspective in deploring what he called "the rout of the classical tradition." In making social adjustment its chief goal, the school was no longer concerned with disciplining the mind and with seeking to illuminate life. With life itself no longer presented as a coherent experience, there had been a loss of individual and collective self-confidence and of a respect for truth.[14]

A different perspective was supplied by Professor Frank Underhill, another leading Canadian historian, who took part in a unique 1954 Royal Society symposium on education that had been occasioned by the appearance of *So Little for the Mind*. Underhill agreed with Neatby and other intellectual moralists that the root cause of the retreat from traditional values was the false materialism that pervaded society and was reflected in the anti-intellectual nature of schooling. Unlike Neatby, Underhill did not think that Dewey could be blamed for the weaknesses of progressivism. Dewey had been misinterpreted everywhere in North America. Few educators had read or would have been able to understand Dewey's naturalistic secular philosophy; it was hard to imagine any Canadian school administrator ever admitting publicly to being anything but a proper, respectable, God-fearing churchgoer. Dewey was a tough-minded political progressive who had been associated with a program at Teachers' College, Columbia University designed to produce sophisticated teachers as critical of the materialism of American society as were any conservatives. It was unfortunate, suggested Underhill, that the Columbia program had no counterpart in Canada, where there was little awareness of the need to help teachers to confront a society torn by basic value conflicts. For Underhill, the real cause of the intellectual weaknesses of Canadian schooling was a bureaucratic, authoritarian system of administration that left teachers with no scope for decision-making similar to that possessed by academics.[15]

Another perspective on Neatby's analysis was supplied to the Royal Society symposium by N.A.M. MacKenzie, the president of the University of British Columbia who had been a Massey commissioner with Neatby. He cautioned against idealizing the schools of the past, recalling a small Nova Scotia community in which his own sister, fresh out of high school, had taught sixty students in all grades from the first through junior matriculation in a single classroom. A broad view of education was needed in a society which imputed its faults to the schools while placing fresh burdens on them. The universities produced many teachers and thus bore some responsibility for their quality in a system which seriously neglected teacher training and the study of education. MacKenzie did not favour Neatby's elitist approach, specifically opposing ability grouping.[16]

The debates of the 1950s were among the most stimulating that had ever occurred in Canadian education. It was generally agreed that progressivism had brought general improvement but this view was tempered by the thought that something had been inevitably lost. That something, it could be argued, was a static, highly selective system less sustained by cultural and intellectual achievement than its mourners assumed. Sutherland's judgement of the triumph of formalism that persisted into the 1950s seems closest to the mark. The fact was that the structure of Canadian school systems offered no alternative to formalism.[17] This condition reinforced the tendency of the latter day traditionalists and progressives of the 1950s to agree, as their predecessors had, on the time-honoured goals of Canadian schooling, while disagreeing on the means of attaining those goals. Thus, Hilda Neatby put a premium on factual learning divorced from reflective thought, while her opponents made an eclectic, cautious and limited use of little understood progressive theories.

Critiques of the alleged soft pedagogy of progressivism came to a head in 1957 with the Russian launching of Sputnik. Shortly, the Gordon Commission on Canada's Economic Prospects was voicing concerns similar to those being expressed in the United States about the scientific-technological gap between the Soviet Union and North America. As in that country, national shortcomings were laid out at the door of deficient school curricula and related educational neglect. The Commission noted that 80 per cent of pupils entering Grade 1 failed to complete junior matriculation. Gordon joined the Massey Commission in recommending federal support for the universities.[18] In so doing, he reflected a new public awareness of the potential of education for promoting economic growth in the interests of greater individual and collective prosperity, and of improved social welfare and stability.

## Design For Learning: Restoring the Disciplines

Discipline or subject-centered curriculum reform in North America had actually begun before Sputnik. By 1957, new mathematics and science curricula were being introduced experimentally into some Canadian schools. In the United States after that date, further demands quickly led to the most searching reappraisal of schooling that had been seen for half a century. A Harvard psychologist, Jerome Bruner, became the most influential educational theorist since John Dewey. His argument that "any subject can be taught effectively in some intellectually honest form to any child at any stage of development" attracted wide attention.[19]

Unlike Dewey, Bruner and his fellow reformers tended to see the learner as a miniature scientist, with the result that their curricula often embodied the subject matter of the discrete disciplines as represented in the world of the mature scholar rather than in that of the child or adolescent. If intellectual activity was everywhere the same, as Bruner implied, subject matter could be organized in disregard of its suitability for the young student.[20] Nevertheless, Bruner's theory was attractive because it promised to restore academic rigour to schooling and offered a solution to the problem of the knowledge explosion by reducing the complexity and clutter of unlimited quantities of information.[21]

Bruner's theory rested on the assumption that the disciplines had an inherent structure that could be the basis of teaching their most seminal ideas and ways of thinking. To this was added the concept of inquiry or discovery learning. The theory seemed viable when applied to the "hard" sciences, but when applied to the complexity of the social sciences, the "structural revolution" had unforeseen weaknesses. History in particular suffered from a lack of the sequence (except chronological sequence) and coherence characteristic of such subjects as physics or mathematics. Historians were unable to agree on a structure, and many doubted that their subject had one. In any case, Bruner never defined the term precisely and it was used so variously that it seemed like an expression in search of a definition. Some equated structure with the methods of inquiry of the disciplines; to others it was a set of relationships, generalizations, or key concepts. The term "concept" itself also suffered from definitional disability.[22] A related difficulty was the neglect of curriculum coherence and integration that resulted from the emphasis on discrete specialized subject matter.

As Bruner's book, *The Process of Education*, became a manifesto that set the terms of curriculum debate through the 1960s, and as discovery learning became a curriculum slogan, reformers tended to accept as dogmas what Bruner had intended as premises.[23] It was ironical that eminent scientists and mathematicians committed to improving content soon found themselves promoting child-centered "discovery" and other teaching methods that owed much to the despised progressive theories they aimed to supplant. Discovery learning could, in fact, be traced to Dewey's earlier progressive scientific problem-solving method set out in such works as *How We Think* (1910).

Canadian interest in the promises and contradictions of discipline-based curriculum change was epitomized during the 1950s by the emergence of the Ontario Association for Curriculum Development as a voluntary broad-based organization. The Ontario Mathematics Commission was formed as a consortium of classroom teachers, school administrators and university scholars. In 1960-61, a Joint Committee of the University of Toronto and the Toronto Board of Education established study groups to consider curriculum changes in the natural sciences, mathematics, English and social sciences.[24] The committee included some of Canada's most prestigious scholars, together with equal numbers of classroom teachers and faculty of education methods instructors. Despite this ostensible equality, Fleming reported a tendency in the committee for the secondary teachers to defer to the professors and for the elementary teachers to defer to both. This was one reason for the strongly subject-centered approach that permeated the committee's reports and that led some members to advocate subject specialization even in the elementary grades.[25]

In 1962, the Joint Committee published *Design for Learning*, containing proposals for curriculum reform by subcommittees in English, the social sciences and science. The book included an introduction by Northrop Frye, widely recognized as possibly Canada's most eminent scholar. Frye reported that the members of the subcommittees had read *The Process of Education*. Bruner addressed the full committee and, according to Frye, his concept of structure "entered deeply into all the reports." Despite this tribute to Bruner's influence, Frye's account suggested that the Joint Committee had found the new dispensation in some respects less than helpful. When it was not ignored in the reports, "structure" remained undefined. Physics was said to be theoretically coherent because its elementary principles could be explicated, but this was much less true of English and the social sciences. Frye reported that the English subcommittee had gained little help from Bruner's book "beyond a somewhat vague suggestion that tragedy is a central structural principle." Contrary to Bruner's theory about the affinity between the intellectual activity of the child and that of the mature scholar, Frye thought that elementary teaching was "naturally of a strongly deductive cast." The conclusions, generalizations and explanations of the scholar were necessarily presented first and then illustrated by example, observation and experiment.[26]

That not all Canadian educators accepted uncritically the same military and national security imperatives that animated their American counterparts was suggested by Frye's statement that "The kind of vague panic which urges the study of science and foreign languages in order to get to the moon or to uncommitted nations ahead of the communists is ... remote from the educational issues that these reports face." Such goals, like the social goals of progressivism, were unacceptable because "the aim of whatever is introduced into the school curriculum at any level should be educational in the strict and specific sense of the word."[27]

Following Bruner's suggestion of a co-operative Canadian curriculum agency, the Ontario Curriculum Institute was formed in 1963 on the model of the Toronto Joint Committee. The broad mandate of the new body to sponsor an almost unlimited scope of curriculum reform was reflected in the correspondingly broad support of the institute by almost the whole of Ontario's public educational sector. Financial support came from business and industry, private individuals and foundations, including the New York-based Ford Foundation. The increasing complexity of the institute's work led to its replacement in 1966 by the Ontario Institute for Studies in Education, an academic body affiliated with the University of Toronto.[28] This development put Ontario (and Canadian) curriculum studies on a sound graduate studies and research base after 1965, although at the expense, some felt, of the kind of co-operative endeavour that the original body had exemplified in its short life. The rapid growth of the new institute and a large influx of American scholars were seen in some quarters as a mixed blessing.

Subject-centered Bruner-type curriculum reform took root in all provinces during the 1960s. Some of the major developments in the specific subject areas will be discussed in Chapter 18. Watts indicated that in Alberta reforms in mathematics and science teaching were directly modelled on American initiatives.[29] In Newfoundland in 1967, the Warren Commission advocated discovery learning urging that teachers "teach the structure of a subject and (its) strategies of inquiry." The new American courses in high school biology, chemistry and physics should be adapted to the province's matriculation requirements.[30] In Quebec, where Bruner-style reforms in mathematics and science teaching had been pioneered in the anglophone sector, the Parent report urged similar changes in francophone schools. New methodologies in language teaching attracted particular attention. The francophone L'Association Mathematique de Quebec became affiliated with the National Council of Teachers of Mathematics in the United States. At the Council's 1967 meeting in Montreal, a precedent was set when some meetings were conducted entirely in French.[31]

In summary, Canadian curriculum reform efforts tended to be characteristically cautious and derivative. Constitutional constraints prevented national efforts at curriculum reform at the pre-university level similar to those that were mounted in the United States. The provinces, while insisting on their autonomy in educational matters, maintained their tradition of failure to promote research and development. However, as Canadian reformers took over, often holus-bolus, American innovations in mathematics and science teaching, national organizations of school and university teachers were formed that brought a significant national perspective to curriculum change.

By the 1970s, many of the innovations were under attack. The new mathematics were said to have undermined traditional computational skills. There was some reason to doubt that this innovation or those in the sciences had taken wide hold. Hodgetts' 1968 survey of history teaching suggested that teaching in that subject remained tradition- and textbook-bound. Although there was no evidence for other subject areas comparable to that reported by some American researchers, it seemed likely that the forces of curriculum stability were as powerful in Canada as in the United States.

## School and Work: Vocationalizing the Curriculum

The various federal Depression and war-time education-related initiatives described earlier served as a rationale for further initiatives by Ottawa during the post-war period. Between 1945 and 1957, three agreements were negotiated between the federal government and the provinces. The first of these, the ten-year Vocational Schools Assistance Agreement, provided matching funds for secondary vocational training, including the support of courses as low as the Grade 9 level if half the instructional time was devoted to vocational subjects. Later agreements extended these arrangements. Even Quebec's highly autonomy-minded Duplessis regime participated until 1957. After that date Quebec withdrew, apparently as a result of efforts by the federal authorities to exert greater control over the expenditure of its grants.[32] Nevertheless, as compared with its weak response to the Depression, federal response to war-time and post-war vocational needs was relatively decisive and effective. From Ottawa's viewpoint, the constitutional issue was the chief problem and could best be overcome by legislation and action in terms of economic rather than educational need. But by making grants on a population basis, the wealthier, more populous provinces gained disproportionate help. Thus, policy exacerbated rather than alleviated the problem of equal opportunity. In all federal initiatives, the teachers' voice was rarely taken into account.[33]

Meanwhile, independently of federal initiatives, Canadian educators after 1945 tried to provide their own national response to post-war needs. The CNEA Survey of 1943 served as a catalyst for various initiatives that focussed on mental hygiene, school health, Canadian-American relations in education, school textbooks and vocational education, among various concerns. Prior to the formation of the Council of Ministers of Education in 1967, the CNEA, which included deputy ministers and their senior officials, school superintendents and their deputies, university leaders and others, constituted the nearest equivalent to a formal or official Canadian educational establishment. Funding came from provincial grants but specific projects were supported by private, corporate and by Canadian and American foundation grants.

The vocational thrust of the 1943 survey was reinforced by a much more wide-ranging investigation launched by the CNEA in 1948. Undertaken by the CEA-sponsored Canadian Research Committee on Practical Education, the new study constituted a massive investigation of Canadian school leavers, both graduates and dropouts. The committee enlisted the co-operation, services and financial support of provincial departments of education, business, industry, labour and agricultural groups and was made up of twelve members from these groups, half of them provincial educators. Advisory committees were set up in each province to collect provincial data and to examine provincial problems.

Between 1949 and 1951, the committee produced four reports which dealt with a wide range of questions: provisions for practical training in Canadian schools; retardation, wastage and dropping out; methods of retention; and the effectiveness of training in the basic skills and in citizenship as a preparation for living and for earning a living. A large-scale follow-up study of 12 124 graduates and 14 219 dropouts, one of the largest and most representative samples that had been gathered for a research study to that time, was a pioneering effort of its kind in Canada.

The reports showed that the drop-out problem remained serious, varying significantly among provinces and being especially high among rural students and males. Of 100 pupils enrolled in Grade 6 in 1942, only 37.2 per cent were enrolled in Grade 11 five years later. Whereas 49.7 per cent of gainfully employed females age 14 or over had completed 9-12 years of schooling, only 30.2 per cent of males had done so; 11.1 per cent of females possessed thirteen or more years of schooling, but this was true for only 6.3 per cent of males.[34]

In considering the major question of the study, "How well do our schools prepare boys and girls for after-school life?" the committee's second report, published in 1950 under the title *Your Child Leaves School*, focussed on the problem of the dropout. In this first major national expression of concern regarding that phenomenon, an attempt was made to determine why pupils had dropped out, factors connected with dropping out and the occupational or other destinations of both groups following school leaving. Types of curricula available and the characteristics of students enrolled in each were also investigated.[35]

In taking note of such factors as the father's occupation as an indicator of the student's economic status and related educational attainment, the committee displayed an awareness of new social science concepts based on cultural criteria. However, contrary to some studies in our own time, school-related reasons such as lack of interest, lack of ability and the unsuitability of the curriculum were identified as the most important factors related to dropping out. The school needed to improve and adapt its curriculum and to provide better guidance courses. To reduce drop-out rates among boys, teaching must be better attuned to male needs.[36]

Other findings indicated the surprising propensity even of high ability students to drop out; half of all students of average ability did so; the rate for below average students exceeded 80 per cent; one-third of all drop-outs had repeated at least one grade. Employment opportunities and initial wages of dropouts were significantly lower than those of graduates. Employment success was closely related to type of school training.

Although urban students had opportunities to pursue differentiated senior secondary studies in academic, commercial, technical or composite high schools, students in small rural schools often had only the stark option of completing the single program available or of dropping out. A higher proportion of students going to university came from schools with enrolments of over 300 students. Those going to normal schools came from smaller schools, particularly from those with fewer than 100 students. This reflected the fact that teaching continued to have a high attraction for rural girls.[37]

From a sample of four provinces, including the largest, Ontario, the committee identified three types of courses: the academic course (usually college preparatory); the academic course with practical electives (industrial arts, commercial work or home economics) which usually also satisfied college entrance requirements; and the non-college preparatory vocational course which included academic subjects and practical work designed to prepare students for employment. The sample suggested that a more differentiated curriculum was beginning to take hold: about 40 per cent were enrolled in the academic course, 25 per cent in the academic course with practical electives and 35 per cent in the vocational course. In noting that more students of lower ability and economic status were found in vocational courses — although most students in such courses were of average ability — and in noting that academic courses were largely restricted to students from favoured socio-economic backgrounds, the report concluded that "The economic condition of the family appears to be a determining factor in the selection of courses".[38]

In its two final reports, *Two Years After School* and *Better Schooling for Canadian Youth*, both published in 1951, the committee sought "to evaluate and appraise the effectiveness of Canadian educational programs in assisting youth to prepare for work and citizenship." To this end, teachers and principals, pupils, employers and supervisors were surveyed by means of questionnaires.[39] The former students included school leavers, both dropouts and graduates, who had not gone on to further training. In analyzing the questionnaires, the committee showed an awareness of the growing sophistication of educational research. The authors of *Two Years After School* warned that causal relations should not be too easily assumed for "some other factor or factors may be the reason or cause of [an] observed relationship." Thus, the reader was enjoined to proper scepticism about any statement of result. "Moreover," the report added, "interpretations of fact should never be confused with statements of fact."[40]

Possibly the most striking statement in the report — one that confirmed the new concern for economic goals in the curriculum — was that "schooling pays not just in terms of money but in all ways." This view foreshadowed the human capital argument that would provide the rationale for mass education during the 1960s. The report confirmed the committee's earlier findings regarding the employment advantages enjoyed by graduates over drop-outs. More schooling was said to pay in greater job satisfaction, in a greater general "enjoyment of living" and in better citizenship. Finally, by seeking still more education, graduates showed a better appreciation of the value of schooling than their fellows.[41]

To deal with the wastage or dropout problem, which was particularly serious at the junior high school level, the committee urged that teachers be trained in the use of diagnostic tests, in counselling and in the keeping of cumulative records. By these means, they would be able to spot academic laggards, to discover the reason for slow progress and to take appropriate remedial measures. Consideration should be given to the use of specially trained remedial teachers, a proposal that foreshadowed the modern "learning assistance centre." Closer contact between teachers and parents was necessary. "The school should emphasize continually the importance of schooling," even to the point of employing propaganda. Schools should also assist pupils to find suitable jobs and should operate aggressive placement programs in close co-operation with employers. Many of the recommended measures were adopted by a few of the larger city school systems during the 1950s.[42]

In taking a broad view of the socializing responsibility of the school, the committee nevertheless emphasized that the traditional function of the school should be uppermost. In this regard, the committee helped to popularize the term "basic education." While agreeing that the cultural and civic functions of the curriculum were important, the chief emphasis should be on more efficient teaching of the three Rs. Employers were particularly critical of youthful deficiency in the basic skills and of the inability of young employees "to think independently, analyze problems and express thoughts clearly." Although technical training needed more emphasis, "the fundamentals of general education" should take precedence over specific skills. At a time when two-thirds of young women were married by the age of twenty-four, more attention should be given to teaching homemaking skills, with particular reference to child care.[43]

The committee's final report, *Better Schooling for Canadian Youth*, published in September 1951, reiterated various findings and recommendations of the earlier studies. Basic skills rather than specialized vocational skills should be emphasized, in order to overcome the "grave deficiencies" of students in the former. Character training and citizenship were more vital than vocational knowledge. Students should learn the importance of continuing their education beyond school, but university entrance requirements should not dominate the curriculum. The curriculum should comprise a common core with provision for students to take electives adapted to local occupational needs and to transfer easily from one program to another. A recommended elective emphasis on home economics, business education, industrial arts and agriculture represented, in essence, an extension of the pre-war concept of the composite high school. The raising of the school leaving age to sixteen as a common standard across Canada was proposed.[44]

The general goals of the report emphasized (1) the fundamental processes, (2) critical thinking, (3) high standards of behaviour reflecting ideals of service, fair play, duty and responsibility, (4) sound mental and physical health, (5) tolerance and insight into modern social problems, (6) the exploration of the general fields of knowledge, (7) marketable skills, (8) efficient household management and (9) the proper use of leisure time. These objectives bore a remarkable resemblance to the famous cardinal principles referred to earlier which had been part of the North American curriculum lexicon since 1918. While far from radical, the broad character of the list would shortly provide a target for traditionalists who insisted that it diluted the fundamental intellectual responsibility of the school. Yet of the nine objectives, only two were explicitly vocational. Although the stated purpose of the report was to consider "what constitutes a suitable secondary education for students who go directly to employment from school," only one third of the recommendations were directly concerned with vocational education.[45]

In summary, the work of the Canadian Research Committee on Practical Education represented the Canadian educational establishment's effort to come to grips with the new demand for mass secondary education and to confront the dilemma of maintaining academic quality in the face of a growing, less selective school population. By 1950, curriculum revisions in most provinces were in a cautiously vocational direction. But the typical curriculum experienced by the minority who completed high school was still highly academic and ostensibly liberal in character. Yet, the formalism of teaching, with its emphasis on memorization and preparation for passing matriculation examinations, attenuated a reflective approach associated with true liberal education. Obeisance to the liberal ideal was revealed in the committee's emphasis on general, as opposed to specialized, vocational education, on the view that education "should be more inclusive than mere training."[46]

Studies by Downey during the 1960s indicated that Canadians had a less instrumental image of education than Americans and were less concerned that it be vocationally oriented.[47] Taylor, in criticizing the overwhelming academic orientation of Canadian high schools, noted that in 1963 less than 15 per cent of all students were doing vocational work.[48] Nevertheless, attitudes were beginning to change by this time. The result was the greatest ever vocationalizing thrust that, at least temporarily, transformed the high school curriculum, particularly in Ontario. The number of schools with vocational offerings increased significantly, although in 1968 Breton and McDonald reported that half the students in some provinces were still in one-program schools.[49]

The new vocational thrust was largely a consequence of the federal Technical and Vocational Assistance Act of 1960. As the largest federal intervention in Canadian schooling ever undertaken, the act became a classic example of how unintended goals and consequences can give curriculum policy-making a life of its own. Initially designed to combat youth unemployment and to take account of changes in the nation's occupational structure, the act was conceived at a time when the apprenticeship system, with its low wages and dependent relationships, was no longer acceptable to the expanding post-war middle-class. As a consequence it stressed the class-room rather than the work experience.[50] Moreover, although the initial intent had been to focus on technical and vocational training in post- secondary and other institutions outside the public school system, pressures from the provinces, particularly from Ontario, led to a focus on secondary schools.

Over the life (1961-67) of an agreement signed by Ottawa and the provinces, nearly 1.5 billion dollars were spent on capital projects, with Ottawa supplying more than half this amount. All told, 635 vocational wings in composite high schools and full vocational high schools were built, nearly 60 per cent of them in Ontario. During the peak of enrolments, nearly 250 000 students were registered in vocational programs under the plan.[51] Federal support required that facilities be used for courses that were, in the words of the agreement, "given as an integral part of high school education, in which at least one half of the school time is devoted to … courses or subjects designed to prepare students for entry into employment by developing occupational qualifications." Facilities would also be approved for "…courses which provide students with an essential basis for further training after leaving regular high schools … "[52]

In Ontario, the effect of the act in stimulating the development of vocational courses and program enrolments was dramatic. Enrolments increased from nearly 24 per cent of the province's secondary school population in 1960 to more than 46 per cent in 1967. Many of the new facilities had a spillover effect on academic facilities. As Cameron put it, "Without the federal stimulus, the Ontario secondary school course of study would have been developed at a more leisurely pace [and] would also have expressed more fully the educational interests of the province." Because most of the operational costs of the new facilities and programs were a charge on provincial and local budgets, constraints were placed upon the provision of other new programs.[53]

The main curricular result of the scheme in Ontario was a new course of study called the Reorganized Programme, with three basic streams: arts and science, science and technology, and trades, business and commerce. Each stream contained four-and five-year courses. The four-year course, entailing a basic education followed by training on the job, was considered the major innovation. There were also one-and two-year occupational courses for pupils transferred from elementary schools. The components, other than arts and science, were planned in such a way as to meet federal requirements under the capital grant scheme. Preparation for immediate employment and for non-university, post-secondary institutions was to be given at least equal emphasis with preparation for university.[54]

Such at least was the intent. As high schools became composite institutions, provision was made for students to switch from one program to another, and from four-year to five-year courses. In practice this happened infrequently, as the traditional separation between academic and vocational programs remained, leading to the usual academic and social consequences. Middle- and upper-class students were found preponderantly in the university oriented five-year course, and working class and other less advantaged students were found in the four-year course. Moreover, the new vocational programs were an inadequate preparation for skilled employment at a time of continual upgrading of occupational requirements. The situation forced the opening of the province's new Colleges of Applied Arts and Technology in 1967, in order to finish the job.[55]

Despite these limitations, Stamp saw the Reorganized Programme as signalling "the temporary triumph of vocationalism as a central aim of Ontario secondary schooling."[56] It did succeed in boosting retention rates and in diversifying the high school program. Nevertheless, with the termination by Ottawa of the TVTA in 1967, the Reorganized programme was abandoned. In part, abandonment resulted from the adoption of the credit system, to be discussed in Chapter 17. It also reflected a lessening interest in economic goals for schooling in the hedonistic, consumption-oriented society of the late 1960s.[57] Changing trends were consistent with the long-standing anti-vocational bias of Ontario education, with its disregard of the fact that the vast majority of students sought early entry to the labour market. Instead, as one critic put it later, "By and large the secondary school system educates students for more education."[58]

Vocational trends were also apparent in other provinces. Quebec's need to build a public secondary school system for the first time made it possible to construct composite or "polyvalent" schools from the beginning. The Parent Report had been ambivalent about vocationalism. On the one hand, the report argued that vocational and academic curricula should have equal status; on the other hand, Parent thought that pupils in vocational programs should form "a rather restricted scholastic group," constituting no more than 20 per cent of the enrolment. Girls and boys should be channeled into courses appropriate to traditional sex-differentiated occupations.[59] Newfoundland modeled the curricula of its new composite high schools on Ontario's Reorganized Programme and faced similar contradictions.[60] In New Brunswick, unusual success in training vocational teachers enabled the province to enrol one third of all high school students in vocational programs, an emphasis designed to alleviate the province's serious unemployment problem. In Nova Scotia, more vocational facilities were built with federal assistance than in any other Atlantic province. Most of the western provinces used federal funds to add additional wings to existing high schools although some, like Manitoba, built separate vocational high schools. As pioneers of junior and composite high schools and consolidated schools, these provinces had considerable experience with curriculum differentiation. Consequently extensive program reorganization to meet vocational imperatives was less necessary in western Canada.[61]

General issues raised by vocationalizing trends were recurrent subjects for debate among Canadian educators during the period. These issues were the major focus of a conference on secondary education held in 1963. Already, according to Downey, differentiated programs were raising serious questions about the narrowness of vocational curricula and their need to be oriented to the future rather than to the present, and to be undergirded by a strong component of academic studies while also taking account of the role of industry in the educational process.[62] Baker felt that the old idea of the composite high school that provided interdisciplinary enrichment between academic and vocational programs, with a common core for all, had been lost. The notion that the various programs were "separate but equal" was a fiction. Ethical and administrative questions arose from the tendency to allocate students to streams or tracks in the absence of reliable testing and guidance procedures, and in disregard of student and parent wishes. What was needed was a genuine attempt to individualize programs.[63] In 1976, the OECD Examiners offered similar criticisms. Practical courses were too often treated as busy work and provided little basic training of any real value. They seemed a mere appendage, "a basement department" of the academic high school and lacked any theoretical, reflective approach to technology.[64]

By this time, criticisms of vocationalism were being spurred by concerns about economic recession, inflation and unemployment. Calls were heard for a major reassessment of the role of schooling and its relationship to economic growth and work.[65] To Pitman, the real failure of industrial education could be seen in the paradoxical shortage of skilled labour in times of unemployment and in the absence of what he termed a "high-middle level" of technical competence between professional and skilled trades which he called the greatest industrial lack in Canada. In Canada, engineers were used as technologists. Some countries trained one engineer for every five technologists; in Canada the situation was reversed. Schools failed to raise consciousness about the significance of commercial and industrial occupations.[66]

Hall and Carlton reported that students in their inquiry found their first work experience a shock, in that school had not prepared them adequately for sustained tasks carried on at a rapid pace. In this sense they agreed with their employers that school had not prepared them for the real world.[67] The students found a minimal relationship between the skill demands of the workplace and skills learned in schools. This was, in part, a function of the fact that skill demands were minimal in most jobs. Through the use of calculators and computers, for example, bank clerks could function very successfully with no computational skills beyond Grade 6 arithmetic. Writing skills in most service jobs were less relevant than "oral skills" but the latter came down to having a "pleasing personality" an "open manner" and similar psychological traits.[68]

As economic crisis meshed with criticisms of schooling, Career Education was touted as a solution to the problem of the school-work transition. Lazerson and Dunn argued that, as a new name for vocational or industrial education, this solution was a false panacea that made the schools a scapegoat for economic ills. The biggest fallacy was the assumption that unemployment was due to a mismatch between workers and jobs caused by a lack of information and skills. Occupational and social mobility were unlikely to increase as a result of programs that failed to provide the high status, formal credentials so valued by society. On the other hand, segregation and streaming were likely to increase in the schools.[69]

In a later study, Gaskell and Lazerson reported on the transition from school to work by Vancouver working class high school students who had gone directly into the labour market. Most had chosen the same occupations as their parents, entering a sex-segregated labour force which for the girls would be a transition to marriage and motherhood in a traditional family structure. The girls were less critical of their schooling and happier with their jobs than the boys. Both groups, while initially pleased with their first jobs, recognized that schooling had narrowed their opportunities; many wished they had worked harder, made better choices and received better counselling. In their view, school should be more like work, with career and vocational programs, work experience, tighter discipline and less babying. As compared with teachers' evaluations which, although lenient, assumed incompetence or neglect, those of employers were strict but at least implied adult status and responsibility.[70]

## Living and Learning: Neo-Progressive Revival

By the late 1960s, subject-centered and vocationally-oriented curriculum reforms were being superseded by a neo-progressive child-centred and teacher-centred thrust that reflected a new era of decentralization. The teacher-proof curriculum of the preceding decade was superseded, to a degree, by the curriculum-proof teacher. Although discovery learning had strong appeal for them, many progressives welcomed the shift away from Bruner's theories, which had downplayed the importance of the individual learner. As social unrest and youth disaffection grew, Bruner himself announced, "I would be satisfied to declare something of a moratorium on the structure of knowledge and deal with it in the context of the problems that face us."[71]

Child-centred curriculum change soon manifested itself in Quebec in a school system that had been relatively untouched by earlier progressivism. The Parent Report, in recommending "activity methods," revived the Froebelian metaphor of the child as a plant and commended Piaget's stage theory of cognitive development. Withal, the elementary school was seen as needing a relative stability in which the traditional emphases on the three Rs and on moral and religious training would be maintained.[72]

It was in Ontario, in *Living and Learning*, better known as the Hall-Dennis Report, that neo-progressivism came to be epitomized. Although the initial Hall-Dennis mandate had been restricted to the aims and objectives of elementary schooling, the scope was shortly extended to the secondary level. Instead of dealing with educational aims in the usual way, the report devoted attention to issues, ideals, values and opinions relevant to the promotion of learning. It also made many specific suggestions for the improvement of the Ontario school system.[73] In his masterful analysis, Fleming described much of the report as "hortatory and inspirational," assuming the tone of a sermon. When not flawed by cliches and jargon, some sections were "eloquent and even poetic" and the language frequently "clear, forceful and pungent." The report concluded in a more conventional and expository style. Much of it lacked logical organization.[74] To justify its progressive stance, evidence such as that endorsing discovery learning was selectively chosen. Fleming observed insightfully that there was some philosophical inconsistency in Hall-Dennis' advocacy of intrinsic learning motivation under ideal permissive circumstances when the report also advocated the universal mandatory teaching of French and the extension of compulsory attendance beyond the age of sixteen.[75]

The progressive stance of *Living and Learning* was summed up in a preamble entitled "the truth shall make you free." In setting the tone for the rest of the document, the generality of the preamble was consistent with the views of every progressive thinker from Rousseau to Dewey. The result was an expressed optimistic faith in education that was quite typical of the 1960s. Education as the means to truth was described as "the key to open all doors," as the enemy of ignorance, doubt, frustration, poverty and intolerance, as a spur to equality and dignity, and a benefit to every imaginable category of child, including the talented, the physically handicapped, the emotionally disturbed, "the disordered of mind" or the "slow of wit." While praising the Ryersonian system that had served Ontario well for a century, the authors argued that changing social needs required the complete overhaul of inflexible outdated curricula governed by a regimented organization and guided by mistaken aims. It was small wonder that students were alienated, teachers frustrated and parents irate. The solution must be a curriculum with a greater array of learning experiences in a flexible structure minimizing restrictions.[76]

In its emphasis on a greater socializing role for the schools, Hall-Dennis was in the spirit of American progressivism of the 1920s with the siginificant and characteristic Canadian difference that progressive ideology was enshrined in an official government document. Its 258 recommendations emphasized individualization, continuous learning, and maximum flexibility in curriculum facilities and scheduling. Levels, grades and ability grouping, together with distinctions among courses and programs embodied in such terms as "vocational," "technical," "academic," and "commercial," were proscribed, as were traditional subject labels such as history and mathematics. Instead, the curriculum was to be organized around general areas such as environmental studies, humanities and communications. The report avoided recommending a detailed curriculum, opting instead for a general design that emphasized a learning continuum embracing the total K-12 school experience. In implementing such a design, teacher autonomy was essential for as *Living and Learning* insisted:

> The modern curriculum demands that curriculum control be centred in the classroom. In spite of this demand, many teachers find that courses of study, timetables, specific textbooks, standard report cards, system-wide examinations, and many other determinants and controls on the curriculum are prescribed by authorities who cannot possibly understand the program in each classroom for which these factors are prescribed. Until teachers have a large measure of autonomy and a share in policy-making, the modern curriculum cannot be a reality.[77]

The report sold widely and was as widely discussed. Among politicians and the press, response varied from cautious approval to strong enthusiasm. A few dissenters objected to what one journal saw as a "warmed over" revival of John Dewey's philosophy.[78] Among teachers and administrators, those at the elementary level were more positive than those at the secondary level who maintained a strong subject orientation. Others criticized Hall-Dennis' permissiveness, obsession with change, disregard of unchanging human nature and a failure to appreciate the new flexibility of the secondary school.[79] To Phillips, probably the leading Ontario old style progressive, the reception accorded the report indicated that Canadian reformers were less on the defensive by 1970 than were their American counterparts.[80]

Various university academics responded critically to *Living and Learning*. Carl Bereiter, an educational researcher, was critical of the advocacy of idealistic but unachievable educational goals, which he distinguished from learning goals, or "the basics." The former would condemn children to failure and disillusionment. Criteria of success or failure would not be eliminated but simply made less explicit because parents and teachers would still hold normative expectations of learning goals that children should achieve.[81]

The most direct attack on Hall-Dennis was mounted by James Daly in a booklet entitled "Education or Molasses?". Daly like his fellow historian, Hilda Neatby, fifteen years before, attacked what he saw as the naive progressivism of a report that had little conception of real children. His criticisms were by no means entirely negative but he argued that if the report were viewed as a whole, as its authors desired, it was a bad one with some good in it.[82] Daly's reaction was summed up in these words:

> It reads like a badly written sermon of the new lay theocracy, the progressively-oriented educrats. Like most bad sermons, it is full of truisms mixed with outlandish assertions, good sense tumbled together with bathos and shallow moralism. One mark of poor thinking and bad writing is the failure to distinguish between stirring eloquence and pompous pretension. In the Report, no cliche is forgotten, no platitude overlooked. Relentlessly the verbal molasses pours out.[83]

Like Neatby, Daly's demand for the restoration of liberal, intellectually rigorous humanistic learning to the curriculum seemed equated in his mind with the restoration of old-fashioned mental and physical discipline that suggested a continuing faith in the moral efficacy of traditional sanctions. Thus, he praised the little red schoolhouse of nostalgic memory where "there was competition among the boys to see who could take the most [corporal] punishment."[84]

Daly and other critics had no more immediate success than Neatby before them in countering trends that reflected the Canadian public's ongoing commitment to mass education in a society that many saw as increasingly permissive. However, it was the general thrust of Hall-Dennis rather than its specific proposals that was most influential. The individualization of learning that it advocated served as a rationale for the adoption of the credit system in Ontario's high schools, which abolished fixed structured programs in favour of individualized timetables and programs that ignored grade barriers and streams. In keeping with the spirit of the new system, the Ontario Department of Education moved towards the decentralization previously described. Decentralization was marked by the greatest relaxation of bureaucratic control, though no apparent diminution in the number of bureaucrats, since Ryerson had established the system more than a century before.

Relaxed control resulted from what Hall and Carlton called a "largely unnoticed shift" that had occurred in the form of an "extraordinary response and adaptation of the educational institutions and their personnel to demands for change." In their view, the emergence of education, "with very little effort ... as the largest single industry in the province" and of innovation had led to indiscriminate expansion and to a consequent serious dilution of the curriculum and academic standards.[85] However, the real problems associated with the shift lay outside the schools and were not basically pedagogical or internal. The difficulty was that the response of the schools had been reactive.

> ... the educational philosophies of the later sixties were retrospective rather than prospective. They were adaptations to changes in society that were rapidly pressing the school into an altered role. The new pedagogy quite literally was an accommodation to the little understood pressures that built up around the schools.[86]

Decentralization had seen the replacement of the former detailed course of study by "guidelines" viewed by teachers, reported Hall and Carlton, as so general "that you could get by the whole year without teaching anything substantial."[87] For experienced teachers this was often no problem and proved liberating in the best sense. Neophytes and less committed teachers spoke of "a non-existent course of study," particularly at the Grade 9 and 10 levels. Curriculum differentiation and teacher autonomy, together with a diversity of teaching methods, had led to a minimal degree of consistency and continuity in learning.

Outside Ontario, neo-progressivism was most strongly evident in western Canada. The British Columbia Teachers' Federation produced its own report, *Involvement — The Key to Better Schools,* which reflected the same progressive spirit as *Living and Learning.*[88] In Alberta, the Worth Commission study was likewise written from a neo-progressive futuristic perspective, echoing such fashionably counter-cultural notions as "self-actualization" and the disappearance of work, both to be achieved by a bloodless, neutral technology apparently situated, as one critic suggested, outside time or society. Apart from the occasional use of high-blown metaphor ("the educational skyline is already ablaze with neon offerings ... ") Worth appropriately expressed most of his ideas in the neutral language of social science.[89] Over 15 000 copies of the report were sold in Alberta, and many more to other parts of Canada and to every American state. A "Reader's Companion" to Worth was distributed to every household in the province and elicited hundreds of briefs and responses and extensive media coverage. The report provided some sanction for the province's ill-fated thrust into values education (to be noted in Chapter 16).

It was probable, as Hall and Carlton suggested, that the spirt of the times, reflected in the social ferment and permissiveness of the 1965-1975 decade, was as much responsible for neo-progressive change in all provinces as any inquiries or policy proposals made by educators. Increased teacher professionalism and militancy, themselves a product of a better educated teaching force than in the past, spurred decentralization. On the other hand, the Canadian tradition of centralization remained, serving both as a brake on precipitate change and as a spur to innovation in Ontario where, with official endorsement, neo-progressive ideas became more firmly rooted and resistant to attack even when they became less popular.[90]

In the absence of Canada-wide or even province-wide longitudinal data, the impact of neo-progressivism and the validity of claims and counter-claims regarding its effects on achievement were hard to confirm. As will be noted later, assessment programs in the late 1970s which largely superseded traditional external examinations — British Columbia's ambitious effort was possibly the best example — did not indicate any serious decline in standards. Even so, as the Hall-Carlton analysis indicated, uneven performance among a much more heterogeneous school population than any known in the past was often attributed to neo-progressive innovation and fueled a growing back to basics movement which will be examined in Chapter 15. The virtual abolition of province-wide examinations, and with it the abandonment of any external measures of selection for post-secondary study during the 1970s, moves which made Canada unique among western nations, probably represented the major change during the period. At the elementary level, the sector most open to neo-progressive change, even severe critics conceded that many classrooms carried on in the traditional manner.[91] Neither in Ontario nor in Alberta, the provinces where the rhetoric of innovation was most loudly proclaimed, were most proposals in advance of those of the 1930s.

## Notes to Chapter 14

1 *Hope Report,* 12. See also Fleming III, *Schools,* 15.

2 See R. Stamp, *Schools of Ontario,* 193.

3 Royal Commission on the Arts, Letters and Sciences, 15-6.

4 Neatby, *So Little,* xi.

5 Ibid., 5-9, See also W.G. Hardy.

6 Ibid., 13-17, 27, 31-6.

7 Ibid., 43-5, 71, 89.

8 Ibid., 146, 172, 204-6.

9 Ibid., 231, 307, 326-32.

10 Stevenson, "Reaction and Reform," 99.

11 G.P. Grant, "Adult Education," 5.

12 Lower, "Education," 5-6.

13 Cited in *Canadian Federation for the Humanities,* 4.

14 MacLennan.

15 Underhill, 17-22.

16 N. MacKenzie, 35-8.

17 N. Sutherland, "The Triumph," 35.

18 Canada, Royal Commission on Canada's Economic Prospects, 447.

19 Bruner, *Process,* 14.

20 D. and L. Tanner, *Curriculum Development,* 12-3.

21 K. Osborne, 4.

22 Ibid, 7, 9.

23 D. Tanner, *Secondary Curriculum,* 41.

24 Burnham, v-vi.

25 Fleming, *Preoccupation,* 194.

26 Frye, 8-10.

27 Ibid.

28 For an account of these developments see Fleming, V, *Supporting,* 177-86.

29 Watts, 6-7.

30 Newfoundland Royal Commission, I, 145, 178.

31 Potvin, 365.

32 Fluxgold, 71-4.

33 Ibid., 109, 113-4.

34 Canadian Research Committee on Practical Education (CRCPE), "Practical Education," 12, 40-2.

35 CRCPE, *Your Child.*

36 Ibid., 18-24, 35.

37 Ibid., 28, 37-8, 61.

38 Ibid., 61, 78.

39 CRCPE, "Two Years," 1, 41.

40 Ibid., 49.

41 Ibid., 5, 8.

42 Ibid., 11-14.

43 Ibid., 16-7, 20, 25-6, 29.

44 CRCPE, "Better Schooling" 15, 19-25.

45 Ibid., 5.

46 Ibid., 6.

47 Downey, "A Canadian Image," 213-4. See also the study of Manitoba high school students by Sharp *et al.*

48 T. Taylor, 9.

49 Cited in Martin and Macdonnell, 270.

50 Bothwell *et al*, 259.

51 Young and Machinski, 9(2), Summer (1973), 23-5.

52 D. Cameron, 166.

53 Ibid., 163, 177.

54 Ibid., 168.

55 R. Stamp, "Government and Education," 480-2.

56 R. Stamp, *Schools of Ontario*, 205.

57 This view is a basic theme in Hall and Carlton.

58 John Fraser, 155.

59 Quebec Royal Commission (Parent Report), Vol. III Part Two, 169, 176-7.

60 Newfoundland Royal Commission, I, 146-7.

61 The account of developments in various provinces is taken from Stringer.

62 Downey, "Secondary Education," 6-7.

63 H. Baker, 14-16.

64 OECD, 32-3.

65 See Lazerson and Dunn, "Schools and the Work Crisis."

66 Pitman, 12.

67 Hall and Carlton, 31.

68 Ibid., 178-79.

69 Lazerson and Dunn, "School," 296-9.

70 Jane Gaskell and Marvin Lazerson, "Between School and Work."

71 Bruner, "The Process of Education Revisited," 21.

72 Quebec Royal Commission (Parent Report), Vol. III Part Two, 5, 7, 13.

73 Fleming, III, *Schools*, 499.

74 Ibid., 501.

75 Ibid., 511.

76 Ontario, Provincial Committee on Aims and Objectives, 9-10, 15.

77 Ibid., 136.

78 Fleming, III, *Schools*, 554-9.

79 Ibid., 563-5.

80 Ibid., citing C.E. Phillips.

81 In Crittenden, 62-70. For a later similar criticism see Mark Holmes, "A Critique."

82 Daly, 1.

83 Ibid., 5.

84 Ibid., 12.

85 Hall and Carlton, 15-16.

86 Ibid., 260.

87 Ibid., 56.

88 British Columbia Teachers Federation.

89 See C.J. Bullock for a cogent critique of the Worth Report.

90 See M. Holmes, "Progress," 424.

91 Ibid., 423, 427.

# CHAPTER 15

## NEO-CONSERVATIVE CHANGE: OLD REACTIONS AND NEW AMBIGUITIES

*There are some things which everyone needs to know and should be able to do. The core curriculum is the selection, organization and prescription of this material which must be taught to every student.*
*(British Columbia Ministry of Education, 1976).*

## Curriculum Development as a Pseudo-Science: Trends and Critiques

### Systematic Curriculum Making and Applied Research

During the two decades following 1960, Canadian educators probably gave more self-conscious attention to systematic curriculum development than had ever occurred in the past. In 1977, Milburn examined the various forms that the Canadian curriculum had assumed. He identified a number of approaches: disciplined study based on subjects derived from the academic disciplines, an approach of which Bruner's structural model had been a variant; child-centered schooling; and "democratic," "reformist," "social reconstructionist" and emancipatory curricula. In practice, Canadian curriculum developers had become involved at a second or implementation level "one step removed from discussion of first principles..." As a result, the curriculum development task had become largely technical.[1] Many teachers were not trained to discuss first principles, and were thus at a disadvantage when these surfaced in public discussion. A technical concept of curriculum development, whether based on psychological models such as behavioral objectives or the associated familiar Tyler model, had the effect of inhibiting teachers and the public alike from engaging in an open discussion of issues.[2] In the development process itself, even agreement on the inclusion of particular subject matter might mask intense disagreement on the curricular approach or orientation appropriate to a given course or curriculum.[3]

A number of issues identified by Milburn were implied in our earlier discussion of Bruner-style academic reform. Tanner, writing of the American experience, was critical of the lack of research to support the enthusiastic claims made by the academic reformers. Such evaluation as was carried out tended to focus on measuring the amount and rate of learning factual material in disregard of other outcomes, such as theoretical understanding and problem solving ability, which were claimed as special objectives of the new curricula. Tanner cited a psychologist, Ausubel, who concluded that research evidence did not support the claims made for discovery learning. A false dichotomy was posed between receptive and discovery learning and between deductive and inductive methods. Either type of learning could be rote or meaningful, depending on the conditions under which it occurred; either method could involve inquiry and discovery even though the teaching strategies used were essentially different.[4]

Although Canadian curriculum developers hopped on the Bruner bandwagon, Frye's comments (cited earlier) indicated that they were not entirely uncritical.[5] Pratt observed that behavioural trends in pedagogy had shifted during the early 1960s from the question "What should students learn?" to "How should intended learnings be stated?"[6] An attempt was made to develop congruency among objectives at classroom, school, district and provincial levels in the interests of efficiency and accountability. Much behaviorally oriented pedagogy owed its origins to the influence of Bloom's well-known *Taxonomy of Educational Objectives*. Based on a classification of goals in terms of overt behavior, Bloom's work came to be cited in many curricula in North America. According to one Canadian critic, MacLeod, its influence was enormous because, in promising to make curriculum development truly scientific and to provide precision in determining what should be taught, Bloom sanctioned a shift from long range goals to goals defined in terms of immediate behaviour. Moulding character and providing lessons on which students could reflect later in life were not considered worthwhile objectives.[7]

However, Milburn's analysis indicated that the behavioural approach had foundered on the rock of teacher resistance. Humanists rejected the notion that the only learning that takes place is that which can be observed and measured. This was the view taken by Moss, a Canadian teacher of English who thought that in seeking to rescue his subject from the incoherence of child-centered progressivists, the proponents of behavioural objectives and systems analysis had effectively emasculated it. Moss advocated a subject-centred organization based on Bruner's notion of teaching the discipline at the highest and broadest level.[8]

As American curriculum models became accepted, and as the language of behavioural science came to permeate Canadian policy documents, indigenous development was characteristically neglected as revealed by the pitifully small resources devoted to it by provincial and local jurisdictions. Pratt observed that Canadian work had been almost totally derivative in such major areas of interest as mastery learning, school effectiveness, open classrooms, behavioral objectives and other curriculum panaceas.[9] By 1980, as it became increasingly apparent internationally that the best intentions and best laid plans of developers provided no guarantee of curriculum change, implementation came to be perceived as the central problem of development. Canadian theorists and practitioners such as Fullan took a lead in meeting this problem, which will be discussed in Chapter 19.[10]

By this time, there was evidence of more interest in and of more resources being directed to applied curriculum research in provincial and local jurisdictions throughout Canada. One reason for this was the growing number of highly trained administrators and researchers at these levels. Levin described in some detail the place of the school district research unit and its capacity to contribute to a much closer relationship between educational research and practice. Such units, of which there were at least thirty in Canadian school systems in 1974, were blessed as a result of curriculum decentralization, with impressive research capacities. They served a valuable interpretive and catalytic function by providing liaison between external investigators and school systems.[11] Particular attention was given to assessment and evaluation as most ministries, local jurisdictions and other agencies sought to evaluate their curricula in response to public and political demands for greater accountability.

At the provincial level, assessments of a quite sophisticated character were carried out after the mid-1970s. Those in British Columbia and New Brunswick were notable examples. Such assessments constituted a form of applied curriculum research, frequently yielding data that provided opportunities for further, more basic, research. The lack of national assessments or what might be called meta-assessments to provide a pan-Canadian perspective on school achievement has been noted. Thus, the national impact of American projects that were incorporated into Canadian mathematics and science curricula during the 1960s was mostly unknown.

On an international level, Canadian curriculum developers, in addition to their recognized achievements in implementation, had taken a lead in such fields as second language teaching. Pratt suggested that they had unique opportunities for development related to the needs of specific populations such as Native peoples. Distance education was an emerging field in which Canada, by virtue of its geography and technical expertise, could make unique contributions. Canadians were also in a position to draw on expertise available from the United States, Great Britain and Australia and thereby to produce a critical and creative synthesis of international curriculum practice. No longer should Canada's middle position simply make her a target of international cultural and curricular imperialism.[12]

## Renewed Curriculum Criticism

If Canadian curriculum policy-makers and practitioners avoided discussion of first principles and ultimate goals during the 1960-80 decades, humanist scholars and radical critics had no such inhibitions. The views of George

Grant, Northrop Frye and James Daly have already been noted. Their critique, essentially a continuation of that advanced earlier by Hilda Neatby, was in a Canadian moralistic tradition that had, however, lost most of its authority in the new pluralistic society. During the 1960s, Grant extended his earlier analysis to the university curriculum. He observed that in pursuing their main purpose of producing personnel for a technological society, Canadian universities had developed a curriculum aimed at the mastery of human and non-human nature. In the natural sciences, the motive of wonder had been subordinated by the motive of power. Value free social science, with its concept that good and bad were simply subjective preferences, had been elevated to the status of a public religion. The humanities had likewise assumed the status of non-evaluative disciplines, and become highly research-oriented, covering themselves with "the mantle of science and Protestant busyness." English was characterized by the "Shakespeare industry." History had developed a vast apparatus of scholarship, the very existence of which was paradoxical in an age that increasingly believed that little could be learned from past human experience. Philosophy had become concerned with the analysis of language, methods and thought and had abandoned its historic interest in questions about what was true, beautiful and good.[13]

Robertson Davies, another leading Canadian man of letters, writing in 1964 for an American audience, took a more sanguine view than that taken by his fellow humanists. He thought that critics ignored the recency of universal education, which was still an unproven experiment working on the most intractable and varied sort of raw material. We would be forced by experience, argued Davies, to realize that no single system of education could suit all children. Some needed training so radically different from anything previously known that it could not be called education in the modern sense at all. He thought that the Canadian school system was still basically sound and secure. The greatest weakness of the curriculum was its failure to promote an intelligent use and understanding of language. The Canadian curriculum should aim at producing a nation of people who knew what they were saying and what was being said to them.[14]

On the radical side, various analysts during the period shared with humanist-conservatives many criticisms of technological imperatives in the curriculum. Probably the best known of such critics was an American expatriate sociologist, Edgar Friedenberg. Another radical critic, George Martell, had helped to establish *This Magazine is About Schools* (later *This Magazine*) which came to be recognized as one of the most acutely analytical of the various periodicals devoted to schooling to appear in North America in the late 1960s.[15] Friedenberg and Martell differed in their perspectives, with Martell more overtly political in his analysis. Neither shared the essentially moralistic perspectives of the humanist critics. Like the latter, the radicals deplored curricula that afforded little if any opportunity for meaningful social and philosophical analysis. John Porter, a critic on the moderate left, disagreed with the humanist and radical view that Canadian schools and universities were too attuned to social needs. If anything, he seemed to wish that this might be true. To Porter, the academic elitism of the Canadian curriculum was the major problem.[16]

Another critic, Marshall McLuhan, was less easily classified than others mentioned. Himself classically trained, McLuhan's offbeat analyses, focussed largely on the impact of the electronic media on schooling and learning, made him an international media celebrity in his own right.[17] Sometimes viewed as a counter-cultural guru or as an iconoclastic social radical, McLuhan's public image — itself exemplifying the "cool" ambiguity that his own enigmatic theories posited as basic to media success — masked an academic conservatism that was in the tradition of Canadian cultural moralism. The critic of print-oriented culture, whose work was paradoxically disseminated mainly through best selling books, appeared to favour a bookish curriculum more than his image implied.

By the late 1970s, professional curriculum theorists, many of them voicing criticisms similar to those advanced by humanist and other critics from outside the field, were gaining international recognition. Van Manen and Aoki at the University of Alberta advanced the concept of an emancipatory curriculum. It was described by the former as designed to produce attitudes, understandings and competencies "which genuinely are directed towards self-determination and autonomous decision making," a concept far beyond what Van Manen called the "core basics," of the three Rs.[18]

Egan, a curriculum scholar at Simon Fraser University, attracted international attention with his critique of the dominance of psychological theories in education, which he argued had few, if any, implications for practice. He was particularly critical of Piaget's stage theory, which he thought rested excessively on a notion of cognitive processes that ignored how children in practice tried to make sense of their world. Egan argued that the sense-making process was revealed in children's initial interest in mythic portrayals, an interest derived from fundamental human emotions such as love and fear. This premise served as a basis for Egan's own theory of educational development.[19]

Scholars such as Daniels, Coombs and Werner at the University of British Columbia focussed variously on such questions as the role of ordinary language in curriculum theory and practice, which they suggested had more salience than externally derived technical languages and theories. These scholars were also interested in curriculum criticism and theories of change.[20] Connelly, Roberts and other scholars at the Ontario Institute for Studies in Education were interested in various deliberative and philosophical models of curriculum research. The OISE scholars gave a high place to the professional role of the teacher as a partner with academic specialists, curriculum theorists and others in development. On this view, curriculum reform was a theory-practice problem involving the practical uses of knowledge. What Connelly called "logistic" views of curriculum reform too often discredited the practical knowledge of practitioners.[21]

Meanwhile, two other scholars, Bereiter, a psychologist at OISE and

Barrow, a British philosopher based temporarily at the University of Western Ontario, were making proposals for a dramatic revision of the schooling process in response to radical critiques. Bereiter recommended a curriculum based on a sharp distinction between skill training or "the teaching of performance" and child care, the latter using the informal model of the British infant school. Barrow proposed a compulsory common core curriculum emphasizing health, moral values, literacy and numeracy. Like Bereiter's plan, this essential training curriculum would take up no more than half the school day, with other educational responsibilities relegated to informal environments not necessarily located in schools at all.[22]

Most of these scholars were linked to international networks which extended into the United States, Great Britain, Australia, Israel, Germany and Sweden. The premier international journal in the field, *Curriculum Inquiry*, was based at OISE. The critical approaches advanced by the new breed of Canadian curriculum scholars had raised the levels of awareness of teachers and administrators regarding theoretical and practical issues. If a reflective consideration of first principles was still lacking, as Milburn claimed, some Canadian teachers were nevertheless becoming intellectually excited by curriculum debate and controversy for the first time.

## Conflict, Constraint and Narrowing Horizons after 1975

### Back to the Basics

The economic constraints that had led to demands for more career-oriented schooling by the late 1970s also led to more restricted budgets which, together with declining school enrolments, resulted in a less expansive, more restrained and pessimistic outlook among educators, following fifteen years of unprecedented growth. Changing public priorities and wider social concerns were associated with pollution, the renewed threat of nuclear war and the new economic challenges posed by high technology and intensified foreign commercial competition. The economic and commercial challenge was as old as Confederation; the nuclear threat dated from the 1950s. As in that decade, general concern focussed on the demand for a more rigorous school regimen epitomized by the slogan "back to basics;" this was accompanied by a demand for the "recentralization" of authority in curriculum and other policy matters.

Rapid oscillations in perceived social needs and public demands made it difficult to think of curriculum change in terms of such conventional categories as "traditional," "progressive," "child-centered" or "subject-centered." Thus, concern for restoring the "basics" was paralleled by concern regarding sexism and racism and the special needs of children categorized as minority, disadvantaged and exceptional. All the issues noted cut across ideological and philosophical boundaries. Neo-conservatives and neo-progressives alike could agree that the schools must deal more effectively with racism and exceptionality. The bewildering scope, variety and complexity of curriculum issues transcended any simple focus on the assumed need for greater academic rigour or on the general welfare of the child.

Much controversy regarding the basics and the associated concept of literacy focussed on the very definition of these terms. As Milburn commented, the back to basics movement seemed to take on a different image, depending on the curriculum context against which it was examined. He saw the term as an over-simplified slogan that gathered under its wing as many anti-intellectuals as those interested in thoughtful debate.[23] Not everyone agreed that competence in the basic skills had declined. Nor was there agreement over the extent, nature and cause of decline and of the remedy for it. As Hall and Carlton observed, the concept of the basics or basic skills was "disarmingly simple" but in practice far from so. Thus, mathematics and writing skills did not have a separate existence of their own but were embedded in a milieu which for the student included, among many elements, the inclination (or otherwise) to "strive for high standards when these may be ignored by those around him (parents, journalists, advertisers, teachers, politicians)...." Skill levels could not be defined arbitrarily in advance but must be related to the fit "between skill proficiencies and the situational demands of both employment and academic settings."[24]

In the employment setting, the minimal relationship between the skill demands of the workplace and skills learned in school and the minimal skill demands of most jobs was noted earlier. In the school setting, Hall and Carlton concluded that skills were discounted in the traditional subject areas of the curriculum. Although mathematics instruction had probably been upgraded in the senior high school, in English such subjects as "theatre arts" and similar oral-oriented courses had displaced the teaching of writing skills. For those advocating a traditional liberal education as a path to skill competence, there was a seeming paradox:

> The belief of parents that youngsters enrolled in English courses were learning to read and write more skilfully was frequently unfounded. Even where literature remained as the focus of study, the approach was often content or idea-oriented, leading back to social, moral, economic or political issues rather than to an enhanced appreciation of style or structure.[25]

Other problems related to the lack of emphasis on skills across the curriculum at the high school level, where the responsibility was seen as belonging almost exclusively to the English and mathematics teachers. There was a serious lack of articulation between the elementary and secondary levels. Where the reaction of pupils was concerned, Hall and Carlton reported that elementary students enjoyed school and saw learning the three Rs as the basic task. However, variations in emphasis and approach across classrooms made their own development "appear to them as a sequence of very different experiences with particular teachers." Elementary teachers, the most bewildered of any group by the basics debate, felt that they were coping adequately with the problem in the face of wholesale curriculum innovation and home and media influences that undermined academic standards.[26]

The reaction of secondary school students and teachers will be considered in Chapter 17. At the post-secondary level, Hall and Carlton claimed that students and their instructors had adjusted, like their counterparts at other levels, to the changed milieu. Although university students were critical of the failure of the schools to provide skills, they had learned to minimize their reading and to substitute oral communication for written work. This adjustment was abetted by their instructors who utilized the lecture system and demanded limited reading, usually based on a core text; little writing was demanded and objective tests were widely used. Hall and Carlton observed that adjustment or adaptation was a response at all levels, not only to outside pressures, but was also a response, albeit inadequate, to what came to be known as the "knowledge explosion" — to the cultural shift towards a technical and scientific mode.[27] As they put it,

> The capabilities now in demand depart from the heritage of literacy and humanist skills; they are predominantly oral, quantitative or schematic. Utility takes precedence over convention or aesthetic value, and the vernacular adapts readily to the new media.[28]

Another perspective on the basic skills-literacy debate was supplied by de Castell and her colleagues. In the elementary grades during the postwar years, reading and writing skills had become divorced from traditional literary contexts that provided moral codes, social values and cultural knowledge. "Functional literacy" stressing "communication skills" was now taught by methods that had originally been developed to assist the understanding of simple military instructions. Reading became scientifically dissected into teachable and testable sub-skills taught by means of packaged instructional systems such as the famous SRA kits. Teaching was guided by medical and managerial metaphors, embodied in such terminology as diagnosis, prescription, treatment, checking up. The serious study of literature was deferred to the secondary grades. With a premium now placed on bland, culturally neutral, insignificant content designed to enhance pedagogy, Canadian content was neglected.[29]

The new emphasis on the three Rs created divisions and alliances within and across the ranks of conservative traditionalists, liberal progressives and radical educators alike. Some traditionalists, espousing a narrow functional view of literacy, took the technocratic competency-based approach to teaching reading described above. To this they often added an emphasis on so-called life or consumer skills which became requirements in several provincial high school curricula. Other traditionalists became enamoured of teaching the basics through old-fashioned drill methods intended to restore mental and moral discipline based on the Judeo-

Christian ethic. Disciplinary methods sometimes included corporal punishment, which was reinstituted in some local jurisdictions. Still other conservatives as anti-vocational proponents of high culture saw the basics in terms of the need to restore traditional cultural content to the curriculum.

For their part, progressive, liberal and radical educators, concerned with improving the life chances of the young, sometimes favoured the cognitive skill-related curricula demanded by conservative technocrats. Other liberals and radicals shared with heritage-minded conservatives an opposition to any behavioural-based curriculum reform that failed to promote reflective thinking or to teach substantive content. However, the nature of such content also aroused controversy. To some Christian fundamentalists and political conservatives, subject matter should reflect their own religious and cultural values. To nationalists, a cultural historical heritage emphasis required more Canadian content in the curriculum. Other Canadian Studies enthusiasts saw the need for a contemporary focus on public issues. Supporters of the arts saw their subjects as basic, arguing that "visual literacy" attained through the cultivation of aesthetic skills, judgement and appreciation were fundamental to becoming an educated person.

The foregoing by no means exhausted the list of what many saw as basics in the curriculum. Thus, paradoxically, a movement that seemed to call for a narrowing of the curriculum seemed in practice to result in a demand for broadening it. As British Columbia's Deputy Minister commented in 1980, special interest advocacy groups were constantly pressuring his department to add to the curriculum in the interest of what they deemed to be essential skills or knowledge.[30] Hall and Carlton noted the same phenomenon in Ontario, where the "growing use of the school as a proselytizing agency" had led to an invasion of

> all sorts of "worthy" outsiders, including safety organizations, humane societies, agricultural, labour, occupational, craft, philanthropic, conservationist, humanist or cultural groups which afford a steady source of visits, films, assemblies, trips, or activities if they have not already contributed to some area of the regular curriculum. This enrichment has serious practical consequences for the school's effort to confer basic skills.[31]

Many educators argued that research evidence provided no warrant for the view that competence in the basic skills had declined. Their argument was supported by results of various provincial assessments of achievement in the subject areas during the late 1970s.[32] It was unclear that public opinion was as critical of the schools as some asserted. This seemed to be confirmed by national and Ontario surveys which showed a higher level of general satisfaction with public education than media controversy suggested. The fact that persons with children in school had the most favourable views seemed particularly significant.[33] Defenders of the schools constantly pointed to mass schooling as a major factor in explaining variability in standards and achievement. Related to this factor was the vastly changed socio-economic and ethnic composition of the school population.

These factors were emphasized in Ontario's 1977 Interface Study, which had been designed to assess the academic transition of students from secondary school to college and university. In addressing concerns that basic skills in English and mathematics had declined at the secondary-post-secondary "interface," and that this decline, together with variations in marking standards among secondary schools, had hindered university admissions decisions, the study noted serious problems of comparability between student generations and among contemporary schools. Apart from the fact that even educators of the same generation had difficulty in agreeing on what should be tested, students of the late 1970s constituted a very different slice of the population than did their predecessors. Finding comparable measures of language and mathematics skills across generations was nearly impossible. It was likewise difficult to determine generational differences in instructional practices such as the teaching time available, the teaching methods used, the structure of the curriculum and, in the case of English teaching, language usage in the various media.[34]

Of particular importance to the interface investigators was the question of the relative usefulness of teacher assigned marks vis-à-vis examination marks as a basis for university admission and student placement in programs. In what was possibly the major finding of the study, it was concluded that "the marks assigned by teachers in 1975 correlate as highly with unversity performance as did departmental examination results in 1956 or 1967." School to school variations in marking standards were a serious problem, however. The problem was compounded by probable variations in university marking standards, curricula and teaching methods. Indeed, there was some irony, the study implied, in university tolerance of such variation in the name of an academic freedom professors were not willing to accord teachers. One consequence was that a given university course might, by pure happenstance, build more directly on school course content than another.[35]

Two national studies seemed to bear out the interface implication that the crisis in academic standards had been exaggerated. In a 1976 survey of English teaching in Canadian universities, academics admitted that the top 10 or 15 per cent of entering students were "every bit as good as they had ever been."[36] A 1978 national survey of academic achievement in the senior high school, sponsored by the Canadian Education Association, was particularly valuable for its documentation of many local studies of achievement that had been conducted in most provinces. Chief educational officers across the country felt that science and second language performance had improved; mathematics and social studies remained about the same; in language and literature most felt there had been a decline. In general, the respondents expressed more satisfaction than dissatisfaction with standards of achievement in the traditional academic subjects.[37]

As indicated earlier, the response of the educational establishment to the literacy crisis took the form of recentralization and the institution of core curricula. In most provinces, measures, often expressed in remarkably similar language, took the form of attempts to define the school's purposes more precisely and narrowly and to reduce its socializing functions. In 1976, British Columbia's Minister of Education claimed that citizens were demanding that the government "take a more positive role in defining what should be taught in our schools and in assessing the results of that teaching."[38] In the same year, Ontario's minister, Thomas Wells, declared, "We are going to take a much firmer grasp on what is actually being taught in the elementary and secondary schools of the province."[39] Alberta's Harder Report of 1977 suggested that "the objectives of education ... be confined to what the schools can do," with free options reduced and content more clearly defined and carefully sequenced.[40] Quebec's 1979 "Plan of Action" reiterated the need for "defining the main obectives of the school system and of selecting the means whereby the quality of education throughout Quebec may be ensured." Curriculum uniformity must be restored in a system where materials had replaced courses of instruction.[41]

"Core curriculum" became the most common term in the lexicon of recentralization. As such, it was afflicted with ambiguities as difficult as those already noted for "the basics" and "literacy." Historically, American progressives had used the term to denote a body of integrated subject matter, typically drawn from the social studies and the language arts, that served as a core around which other subjects and related activities could be organized. Hughes observed in 1982 that in Canada, while the language of curriculum debate was no more consistent than elsewhere, the notions of general education, core curriculum, common core and common curricula were all closely linked. While there was a danger that the curriculum could become overly prescriptive, the objectives and content of the core programs that were mandated across the country during the late 1970s were relatively broad. Most consisted of modest lists of general objectives that left teachers with considerable flexibility as regards what could be taught and what could be accepted as appropriate standards of achievement.[42]

British Columbia and Ontario took the lead in 1976 in implementing core curricula. A 1977 policy guide in the Pacific province mandated three levels of curriculum: that which must be taught, for example, the skills and knowledge deemed fundamental to the education of all students; that which should be taught; and that which might be taught.[43] The new policy was accompanied by the Provincial Learning Assessment Program, a testing program covering the major subject areas. Like similar programs in other provinces, this effort was much broader than the minimum competency testing programs that swept across the United States during the 1970s. The British Columbia assessment tested a wider range of objectives and thus seemed less likely to restrict the range of what was taught or to lower the standards of attainment of abler students.[48]

In Ontario, Wells took a similarly liberal view of the basics and confessed to some hesitancy in using the term, for he realized that "it begs philosophical debate as to its true meaning." But "recognizing that a broad interpretation is essential," he quickly acknowledged that the basics went well beyond the three Rs, even though many citizens were thinking in terms of the latter. As actually prescribed, the Ontario core curriculum was defined in general terms in the form of high school credit requirements in English, mathematics, science and Canadian studies (typically history and geography). Wells disclaimed any intention of restoring a "definitive lock-step curriculum" made up of "detailed and prescriptive courses of study."[45]

A 1979 Newfoundland report on curriculum reorganization acknowledged the influence of British Columbia's core curriculum guide but restated provincial educational aims in much more sophisticated form, expressed in terms of the primary, secondary and tertiary responsibilities of the school. Primary responsibilities were those for which schools were established and for which they should supply a complete program. Secondary responsibilities were shared with other social institutions. Tertiary responsibilities were those for which other institutions had primary responsibility with the school restricted to a supporting role. Some objectives served to identify the content of the curriculum and were discipline-based; others, less content-specific, for instance, critical thinking, must be realized across the curriculum. A third category required behavior exemplifying certain values and attitudes on the part of teachers and the school administration.[46]

The results of neo-conservative curriculum change in Canada were apparent to a British observer in 1980, who commented that curriculum guidelines showed similarities among the provinces as authorities tightened their control. Rowan's analysis was based on the Council of Ministers' Student Transfer Guide to Secondary Education, which had been developed ostensibly to assist students and parents transferring between schools in different provinces. The guide also, however, reflected a growing feeling that some national thinking ought to be going on about what students were expected to learn. Rowan observed that, as the provinces restored central control over the curriculum, teachers seemed to be objecting less than might have been expected. She attributed this to the fact that their federations were able to take an active part in developing the new guidelines, and that in practice teachers were free to disregard them. In addition, teachers had found curriculum development work very demanding of time and effort. Some were grateful to be relieved of a task for which they had not been trained.[47]

## Declining Enrolments and the Shrinking Curriculum

The phenomenon of declining enrolments was another constraint imposed on the curriculum during the late 1970s. The lack of readiness of educators to face such an exigency despite the accumulating evidence of demographic data over a decade was hardly designed to enhance confidence in the sophistication of modern educational planning. Still preoccupied with the pressures of the long post-war baby boom, it was understandable that a shift from an expanding to a contracting situation had proved disconcerting. Shortly, ministries, school trustee organizations, and teachers' federation groups in most provinces began to study the new phenomenon and its various implications. Of such studies, those undertaken by Ontario's Commission on Declining Enrolment (CODE) in 1978-79 and by the Newfoundland Task Force on Curriculum Reorganization referred to above were the most sophisticated.

The Ontario study was the only one that gave sustained and systematic attention to the curricular implications of declining enrolments. Connelly and Enns, as leaders of the commission's curriculum task force, reported on their studies of all 193 school boards in Ontario as well as on surveys of more than 2000 teachers. They concluded that declining enrolments, together with financial constraints and more conservative public attitudes towards education, were having a pervasive influence on the curriculum. The elementary schools appeared to be adjusting more readily to the new circumstances than were secondary schools with their curricular and organizational specialization.[48]

The foregoing general conclusions resulted from the task force's attempt to answer three questions: Do declining school enrolments negatively influence the curriculum? If so, in what ways? What can be done about it? In seeking answers to these questions, the investigators observed that curriculum issues seemed to be derived from other issues — demography itself, finance, facilities and staff — discussed in the literature on declining enrolments. Not everyone agreed that declining enrolments do affect the curriculum. During decline the other issues noted, especially that of staff, had more salience than curriculum issues which "tend to remain below the surface until school closure becomes an issue."[49]

The commission concluded, echoing the unsurprising view of the Ontario Teachers' Federation, that staff reductions would have profound curricular effects if program cutbacks occurred one by one as teachers were lost. Through surveys of teachers and administrators, an overall provincial picture of the effects was obtained. In the absence of detailed local studies which time constraints prevented, no view of local effects was possible. In this circumstance, the investigators hypothesized that in a decentralized system such as Ontario had developed since 1950, local effects of decline had probably been much stronger than overall provincial effects. If the expansion of the 1960s had helped to induce an exploding curriculum, then decline would logically contribute to a "shrinking curriculum." However, decline itself should not be viewed as the only variable. Rather, it interacted as noted with other forces, including economic exigency and social conservatism.

Most school boards reported or anticipated negative effects in most subject areas. In elementary schools special programs and their specialized personnel were particularly affected. The rank order of expected effects on elementary subject areas from most to least was creative arts, language arts, mathematics, sciences and social sciences. In secondary schools the rank order was official languages, general and multidisciplinary studies, business studies, social sciences, creative arts and other languages. At this level, fears of the effects of decline focussed on the attenuation of ability grouping and on the likely reduced diversity of course offerings. At both levels, the basic skills as a curricular goal constituted a powerful factor in perceptions of appropriate "decline policy." Thus, 96 per cent of elementary teachers indicated they would close a school rather than give up the arithmetic program whereas only 25 percent would choose closure over jettisoning drama. Among secondary teachers, mathematics had the highest priority and "other languages" the lowest.[50]

The task force rejected the idea of an overall detailed provincial policy for dealing with the curricular effects of decline as inappropriate to a decentralized, diverse system. A major concern had to do with the effects on long established policy principles, such as the recognition of the child's individuality, equality of opportunity and shared decision-making regarding curriculum purposes and content. The short term effects on these policies were seen as limited, but long term effects were viewed as much more serious. Declining enrolments were unlikely to have any impact on the social, cultural and intellectual diversity of the school population, for example. But a more restricted curriculum resulting from decline could have a serious effect on opportunities available to that population — for example on opportunities to learn appropriate second languages.[51]

In formulating recommendations, the curriculum task force proposed policies that stressed student commonalities and curriculum priorities. These policies should encompass an "expected minimum range" of curriculum opportunities for all children cast ultimately in the form of a "foundations program." Such a program should be developed according to criteria of individual choice; retention of local involvement and responsibility; public acceptance based on careful specification and debate and a slow introduction "within a known timeline;" a required core program "not reflect[ing] prejudice nor particular ideologies;" and principles of continuity throughout the K-13 curriculum.[52]

Considerable attention was devoted to curriculum resources. The era of expansion had permitted a large increase in resources including widespread teacher involvement in the writing of local curriculum materials, a policy that had contributed strongly to professional development. As a compromise between those administrators who favoured a reversion to the centralized authorization of commercially produced materials and those who wished to retain local curriculum resources and services, the curriculum task force proposed a plan for the establishment of one or more curriculum material development centres. The plan would take account of experience elsewhere in small countries where centres provided for joint collaboration among publishers, academics, school people and government officials in a system involving "the thoughtful development and testing of trial materials." If pursued in Ontario, "the professional development potential for participating teachers [should] be exercised."[53]

## Notes to Chapter 15

1 Milburn, "Forms," 192-8.

2 See Tyler.

3 Milburn, "Forms," 206.

4 D. Tanner, *Secondary Curriculum,* 24-7.

5 Frye, 8.

6 Pratt, "Humanistic Goals."

7 MacLeod.

8 Moss, 18-9.

9 Pratt, "Curriculum Design in Canada."

10 See Fullan, *Meaning.*

11 Levin, 10-12. See also Deisach, *School Board Research Units in Canada.*

12 Pratt, "Curriculum Design in Canada," 4.

13 G.P. Grant, "University Curriculum," 48-54.

14 Davies, 141-4.

15 See also Martell, *The Politics of the Canadian Public School.*

16 See Porter, *The Measure* and Porter *et al, Stations and Callings.*

17 McLuhan.

18 Cited in Milburn, "Forms," 202.

19 See Egan.

20 See, for example, Daniels and Coombs, "The Concept of Curriculum."

21 See, for example, Connelly, "The Functions of Curriculum Development." The appearance in 1980 of a handbook on curriculum planning for classroom teachers by Connelly and two colleagues was an interesting example of an attempt to relate curriculum theory and practice. See Connelly *et al, Curriculum Planning.* At Queen's University in the same year David Pratt produced the first comprehensive book on curriculum design by a Canadian. It was shortly being widely reviewed and used in North America. See Pratt, *Curriculum Design and Development.*

22 Bereiter; Barrow. See also Covert.

23 Milburn, "Forms," 199.

24 Hall and Carlton, 2-3.

25 Ibid., 127.

26 Ibid., 21.

27 Ibid., 250.

28 Ibid., 261.

29 See de Castell *et al,* "Declining Literacy in North American Schools," 383-6.

30 Cited by Turner, 22 from interview with R.J. Carter.

31 Hall and Carlton, 59.

32 See Bognar; Foulds; A. Murray; Traub *et al.*

33 See Goldsborough; CEA, *Results of a Gallup Poll;* Livingstone.

34 Traub *et al,* 24.

35 Ibid., 28-9.

36 Priestley and Kerpneck, 19.

37 Nyberg and Lee, 58-9.

38 Cited in A. Hughes, "Curriculum," 22.

39 Ibid.

40 Ibid., 23.

41 Quebec, Ministere de l'Education, *Schools of Quebec,* 86-7.

42 A. Hughes "Which Way," 586.

43 B.C. Ministry of Education, *What Should Our Children Be Learning?*

44 For a critique of the competency testing movement in the United States see D.P. and L.B. Resnick.

45 Wells, 4-6.

46 Newfoundland Department of Education, *Report of the Sub-Committee on Curriculum Organization,* 2-5.

47 Patricia Rowan, "Comparing the Cores," *Times Educational Supplement,* July 18, 1980.

48 Connelly and Enns, "Shrinking Curriculum," 277-304.

49 Ibid., 278.

50 Ibid., 282-3.

51 Ibid., 286.

52 Ibid., 288-9.

53 Ibid., 297-98.

# CHAPTER 16

## CANADIAN STUDIES, CULTURAL PLURALISM AND MORAL EDUCATION IN THE CURRICULUM

*. . . the quality of civic education in any nation is an important factor in molding that nation's future.*

*(A.B. Hodgetts, 1968)*

*People of all races, religions and cultures represented in Canada should be shown as contributors to Canada's development, whether by virtue of good citizenship or through special achievements.*

*(Ontario Ministry of Education, 1981)*

*The study of values should be an essential part of the total educational process. Values are too complex to be considered as a separate course and must be an integral part of all programs since teachers express their own values to their students in a multitude of ways.*

*(Nova Scotia Public School Programs, 1980)*

### What Culture? What Heritage? Canadianizing the Curriculum

#### Canadian Studies and Political Socialization

Concern about Canadian identity in the curriculum was recurrent for the century following Confederation. During the post-war era of self-confident national expansion and explosive educational growth, such concern was muted as Canadians became less preoccupied with expressing national fervour than with expanding a school system suddenly required to serve the interests of upward mobility. Yet, fervour was not far below the surface, as the greatest expression of national feeling in Canadian history would reveal at Expo in 1967. Five years later, the *Toronto Star* commented editorially in words that uncannily echoed nineteenth century concern:

American textbooks ... can be an effective and insidious instrument for Americanizing the thinking of young Canadians at the most impressionable period of their lives. They can instil the idea that the United States is the centre of the world; that its foreign policy is always right and it opponents have always been wrong; that its ways of doing things are the most advanced and efficient on the globe ...[1]

Unique among celebrations of the centennial of Confederation was the $150 000 National History Project, funded and launched in 1965 by the Board of Governors of Trinity College School, a private institution for boys located at Port Hope, Ontario. Directed by A. B. Hodgetts, a history master at the school, the project was an assessment of civic education, that is, of the influence of formal instruction in developing the feelings and attitudes of young Canadians towards their country and its problems and in teaching the knowledge on which those attitudes were presumably based. The aim was to generate interest and concern, to encourage further investigation, and to urge that the provinces work together in the mutual cause of national awareness and understanding. This aim rested on the belief that the study of Canada and its problems "should and could be one of the most vital subjects taught in our schools and ... could become a much more effective instrument ... in the fostering of understanding among [our] people ..."[2]

The National History Project was privately sponsored because it had been felt that a study free of the political implications of the British North America Act could report more frankly on the teaching of Canadian Studies than one financed by governments. However, Hodgetts established liaison with and gained the approval of the Canadian Education Association and later of the Council of Ministers of Education. In 1968, his study culminated in a report, *What Culture? What Heritage?* published in cooperation with the Ontario Institute for Studies in Education. This report, the publication of which may conveniently mark the birth of the formal Canadian Studies movement, made publishing history in Canadian education as a best seller that appealed to professional educators, the media, academics and a broad spectrum of the general public. With data drawn from interviews, questionnaires, student essays, curricula, courses of study, textbooks and other literature and visits to 847 classrooms in all provinces and in both official language communities, the study was the largest and most comprehensive ever made of the teaching of any subject area in Canadian schools. As such, it was a pioneer study of political socialization in the classroom based on firsthand observation.

Focussing on Canadian studies, defined as history, social studies and civics, Hodgetts' account of stifling teaching methods and boredom and apathy evident in so many classrooms belied both the harsh criticism of those who had characterized the schools as glorified play pens, and the optimism of those who had assumed that Canadian classrooms were exciting centres of creative learning. He found that courses of study, with the notable exception of Quebec, tended to be identical. Textbooks offered only bland consensus interpretations of Canadian realities. Much of the content was antiquated and useless. Recent history was neglected; after 1931 Canadian Studies seemed to peter out as courses became amalgams of British, American and European history. In the great majority of anglophone classrooms, the emphasis was almost exclusively on political and constitutional history, on what one pupil called "nice, neat little Acts of Parliament" to the almost total exclusion of economic, social and cultural history. Many pupils expressed an active dislike for Canadian Studies, and more than a few indicated a preference for American history, about which they often claimed to be more knowledgeable.

Lack of teaching skill and of a basic knowledge of Canadian content by teachers was a prime cause, in Hodgetts' view, of the parlous state of the field. He portrayed drab classrooms dominated by "chalk and talk," textbook recitation methods in which teaching aids and supplementary materials were either lacking or unused. The assignment and lecture methods were the most commonly used approaches, entailing mere recitals of the textbook and minimal discussion or other student participation. Such discussion as did occur was often "aimless chit-chat." The much-vaunted inquiry or discovery method, when used at all, often degenerated into mindless or factless discussion led by teachers untrained in it or espousing the dogma "It doesn't matter what you teach."[3] On the rare occasions when current events were discussed, a world affairs viewpoint dominated, to the detriment of Canadian topics, which Hodgetts thought many teachers deliberately shunned.[4] More positively, about 20 per cent of the classrooms featured good teaching about Canadian affairs, conducted by teachers on a dialogue basis using the inquiry method. Students in these classes were interested and well informed, and were exposed to a wide range of opposing and controversial interpretations through lessons in which critical thinking skills, together with high level oral and written expressison, were cultivated.[5]

Hodgetts was highly critical of administrators (principals, inspectors and consultants) who, overly concerned with "administrivia," did little to support Canadian Studies, and sometimes frankly disdained the field. A major conclusion of his study was that all the weaknesses he observed in the schools were found in the universities and training institutions. Faculties of education, often preoccupied with fussy methodologies, neglected reflective or analytical approaches to subject matter and ignored the social and political contexts of education, while doing little to train student teachers in inquiry methods and discussion techniques. Teaching in faculties of arts was dominated by textbook and lecture methods used by instructors who, when not purveying a set view of the Canadian past, espoused a skepticism and relativism that probably reinforced the mindless liberalism of many would-be teachers. Some academics showed a disdain for the schools and for the problems of teachers, if not for teaching itself.[6]

Hodgetts' investigation anticipated a growing international interest in political learning or socialization, such as in what and how adults and children learn about their respective societies. Considerable controversy existed regarding the relative influence of various agencies — family and home, church, the media, the peer group and the school — in developing political knowledge, skills, beliefs, attitudes and values. As in Canada, studies in nations such as the United States, Great Britain and Germany revealed startling political and historical ignorance among both students and adults. Such findings in nations with significantly different school systems suggested to some researchers that there might be common explanatory factors operating that lay outside the influence of the school.[7]

Among non-school factors, the family and the electronic media were seen as especially significant influences. Some social scientists believed that attitudes towards parental authority transferred to political authority and to the political system as a whole. School factors were thought to include the "hidden curriculum" of the school's authority structure. The teacher as a beneficent image of social authority and universal classroom norms of ostensible equality and fair treatment for all might serve as a positive political model. Conversely, the school's encouragement of uniformity of behaviour might be inimical to the democractic process. Grade and streaming patterns, testing, desk arrangements and grading systems might also influence the child's perception of role, hierarchy, status and decision-making in the larger society.[8]

In Canada, considerable attention was given to the influence of the electronic media in promoting a sense of national community. A 1974 study of a sample of 810 Ontario students aged ten to twenty-three indicated that television was the major source of political information by a wide margin, far outranking teachers, who also ranked behind the home, newspapers and magazines.[9] Other studies of the political socialization of Canadian children and youth stressed a social cleavage, as opposed to a consensus or equilibrium view of society. History teaching in Canada seemed to be, as Hodgetts' study showed, a divisive rather than a binding force in contrast to the role of that subject in other societies. There was evidence that, while elementary school children had common and positive perceptions of Canada, in adolescence these perceptions began to diverge. Cleavages between anglophone and francophone youth became so wide that their political learning was described by one social scientist as "socialization into discord" and as reflecting in the words of another researcher "emergent sectionalism."[10]

These findings were confirmed by research ranging from Alberta to Cape Breton, which suggested that as they grew older, Canadian young people became more aware of and more positive towards their provincial and regional "civic cultures" and, in some cases, less positive towards Canada as a national community.[11] Richert's research indicated that francophone elementary school children were less inclined than anglophone children to identify Canada as their country, and that both groups had a weaker sense of national identity than American children of similar age.

Ontario youth were an exception, as far as political alienation was concerned.[12] Harvey and his associates concluded that their sample of 1955 high school students in that province possessed a nationalistic outlook of almost xenophobic proportions.[13]

Higgins and other researchers came up with surprising findings that Canadian children were not highly Americanized, and that the Queen was viewed highly favourably as a political symbol by anglophone and francophone children alike. It was hypothesized that positive affection for the Crown as a formal role in the Canadian political system might transfer in later years to the regime or the political community. A major conclusion was that after Grade 1, affection for and evaluation of political roles combine to create a broad picture of the structure of political authority in Canada.[14]

None of the studies referred to took much explicit note of the role of the school in political socialization. In 1970, a B and B Commission study of textbooks by Trudel and Jain concluded that there were two mutually exclusive Canadian historical traditions representative of the two linguistic communities. Francophone and anglophone textbook authors were said to inhabit "two different worlds" with the result that Canadian history was taught "not from the national stand-point but from the provincial." A common school history was needed if further national schism was to be averted.[15] Four years later, Richert confirmed these conclusions by demonstrating that francophone and anglophone children identified overwhelmingly with heroes and historical symbols of their own culture, and with different periods of Canadian history, the former with the pre-1760 era and the latter with the post-1760 era.[16]

The Trudel-Jain study of textbooks was but one of many that attested to a growing realization of the power of curriculum materials as socializing agents. Hodgetts' report had earlier found most textbooks inadequate on most counts; as noted, teachers tended to adhere slavishly to them. In a 1971 study, *Teaching Prejudice*, conducted on behalf of the Ontario Human Rights Commission, McDiarmid and Pratt examined 143 textbooks for evidence of bias and prejudice. They found these characteristics to be pervasive. Pratt's later study of social studies textbooks reported that most portrayed a homogeneous image of society, biased towards middle-class and Anglo-Saxon cultural values, while conveying a negative image of other groups. Class and other social cleavages were absent and consensus interpretations were the norm.[17]

Political socialization research seemed to suggest that, in Canada, civic education was necessarily a tentative curricular enterprise. Despite this fact, and the inconclusive nature of many findings, the research suggested possibilities for broader objectives for Canadian Studies curricula. While the school could not be expected to solve society's problems, few probably disagreed with Hodgetts that, despite its limitations, it could do much more than was being done to promote national understanding and civic awareness.

## Upgrading Canadian Studies in the Curriculum

The main recommendation of Hodgetts' study had been that a Canadian Studies Consortium be established in the form of an interprovincial network of regional centres involving persons from every level of education. Following the assistance of the Ontario Institute for Studies in Education and with the blessing of the Council of Ministers of Education, the Canada Studies Foundation was formed in March, 1970 as a politically independent organization, with Hodgetts as Director and Walter Gordon, the leading Canadian nationalist of the time, as board Chairman. The purpose was to develop an intensive, privately funded experimental five-year program of interprovincial curriculum development that would demonstrate the possibilities of long-range funding by governments.[18] Although most of the nearly three million dollars raised between 1970 and 1975 was from the private sector, substantial support was also obtained from the Canada Council and the federal Department of the Secretary of State.

The emphasis of the Foundation's work was on broad programs at the elementary and secondary school levels that were designed to encourage interdisciplinary course content, innovative teaching methods "and the kind of intellectual skills, attitudes and value systems that civilized living; in a country like Canada requires."[19] The term "Canada Studies" in preference to "Canadian Studies" in the name of the organization was deliberately intended to convey a national, Canada-wide perspective, to be encouraged by the co-operative development, use and exchange of curriculum materials on an inter-provincial basis through a network of educators across the country. The concept of "continuing Canadian concerns" was adopted as an organizing principle for curriculum development. "Continuing" implied the historical perspective deemed necessary for an understanding of contemporary issues; "concerns" implied questions significant to the quality of Canadian civic life. The intent was that questions and inquiry issues relevant to "continuing Canadian concerns" should be based on the essential characteristics of Canadian society, — its bilingual, culturally diverse, regional, vast, exposed, northern, industrialized, urbanized, democratic and federal nature.

The teacher-based strategy adopted by the foundation in its first, 1970-75, phase resulted in fifty teacher teams totalling about 250 members in three major project groups that collectively spanned all ten provinces. By 1975, dissemination activities had directly exposed some 4000 teachers across Canada to Canadian Studies curriculum development through regional and national conferences and workshops. Activities entailed a cooperative process of vertical interaction among educators — teachers, administrators, university and community personnel — from various levels and among their organizations, teachers' federations, local school systems, departments of education and universities. Horizontal interaction was promoted across regional and provincial boundaries. The foundations's resources had a multiplying effect in the form of cash, time, facilities and services provided by these groups, and of teacher commitment to curriculum development work far beyond the call of ordinary duty. Although social studies predominated, such subject areas as art, science and literature were also represented in project work. Political considerations dictated a strategy of "seeding" or supplementing existing curricula in preference to developing totally new curricula. The foundation was the only national curriculum endeavour in Canada on a scale comparable to those in the United States and Great Britain during the period.[20]

Despite its achievements, documented by an independent evaluation that was itself a unique Canadian endeavour, the foundation exhibited various weaknesses, some of them endemic to curriculum development in a complex national milieu and others endemic to curriculum development in general.[21] Weaknesses arising from regionalism were inadvertently fostered by the foundation's deliberate policy of decentralization and project autonomy. This policy inhibited horizontal interaction and reinforced the tendency towards differing perceptions of objectives on the part of various participating groups that are a common feature of curriculum development. Hodgetts' own statement that his investigation had had two separate but closely interrelated areas of concern — one the national interest, the other purely pedagogical — contributed to differing perceptions.[22] Teacher preoccupation with pedagogical concerns, with the process of curriculum development and with purely local studies seemed to relegate "continuing Canadian concerns" to the background. However, mutual professional interests shared through horizontal interaction became the means of developing a greater pan-Canadian awareness.[23]

An initial aim of the foundation had been to remedy the serious dearth of Canadian Studies materials to which Hodgetts had drawn attention. This priority was reduced as it became apparent that a comprehensive packaged publishing program would be too costly, and would be counter to the preferred decentralized field-based development strategy that had been adopted. Commercial and non-commercial products by teacher teams did fill some curricular gaps, but their production served more importantly to meet the felt professional development needs of their teacher-authors. This confirmed the Ford Foundation experience in the United States.[24] Carswell and Aoki respectively documented the foundation's general impact on teacher growth and on curriculum theory and practice, while Robert and Allard discussed the impact from a francophone perspective.[25]

During the 1975-78 period, the foundation received joint federal-provincial funding through the Department of the Secretary of State and the Council of Ministers of Education, Canada. Following the withdrawal of Council support, a federally-funded third phase was launched, with emphasis on the development of a common "pan-Canadian" framework designed to study Canada as a totality through a public issues approach that de-emphasized purely historical studies. A framework embodying this approach appeared in 1978 under the title *Teaching Canada for the 80s*.[26] The new more centralized thrust entailed the development of teaching guides and exemplary student materials through university-based centres.

In a 1976 general assessment of Canadian Studies, Gallagher noted a continuing lack of sensitivity to the field in colleges and universities — "the major sources of supply for Canadian schools" — as revealed by the Symons Report in 1975. Many students did not have the opportunity to study contemporary Canada as a totality. Regardless of what curriculum guides might state, curricula still had a strong local or regional bias. A corresponding emphasis on world studies meant that a curious lacuna existed in terms of any national perspective. Canadian cultural studies (literature, music, art) were nowhere required, although there had been a real increase in the teaching of these and of interdisciplinary studies. In the social studies there was substantially more content than Hodgetts had found a decade earlier. The media and the publishing industry were giving greater emphasis to Canadian content than formerly.[27]

Other developments during the decade saw Ontario establish two compulsory credits in Canadian Studies for high school graduation in 1973; Nova Scotia followed suit four years later. Canadian Studies goals stressing knowledge of the cultural heritage were prominent in British Columbia's core curriculum promulgated in 1976. During these years, Alberta launched a program to develop materials across the twelve grades. The program tended to stress Alberta Studies rather than Canada Studies. Similar parochialism was evident in the Prince Edward Island curriculum, in which students examined Confederation and Canadian economic development from a perspective that was literally insular.

Another interesting effort during the period was the Canadian Public Issues Program, developed at the Ontario Institute for Studies in Education and modeled, in part, on a similar Harvard project.[28] In anticipating the values education programs which shortly developed, the public issues approach aimed to promote social understanding through the active discussion of major social conflicts. Much attention was given to methods of analyzing issues, teaching discussion skills and helping students to dissect controversy. The program included units on Quebec, foreign ownership, strikes, women, and Native survival. In the process, Canadian Studies became more interdisciplinary and thematic. Curricula necessarily included historical background and contexts, but a reverse chronology was used, by which contemporary issues were first examined and their historical origins and development traced.[29]

As social tensions increased, the certainty that historical study had traditionally offered decreased. Osborne commented that uncertainty was even evident in textbook titles. Previously, titles had formally proclaimed Canada's success: *Building the Canadian Nation; The Romance of Canada; Colony to Nation.* By the late 1960s the fanfare was muted, as revealed in more neutral, less triumphant and less assertive titles: *Challenge and Survival; The Canadian Experience; In Search of Canada.* The last-named book, attractive and popular, contained large doses of social science, public issues and values education.[30] There was a sporadic but spotty growth of new courses and programs in social history, labour history, women's studies, multicultural studies and in political and sociological studies.

Canadian Studies in the schools were enhanced by the growth of national organizations among teachers of social studies, English, art, science and other subject areas. No longer did Canadian teachers have to hold national breakfast meetings at conventions in Texas. Journals such as *The English Quarterly* and *The History and Social Science Teacher* provided national forums in various subject areas. After 1978, the Council of Ministers of Education took some useful initiatives through exchanges of materials and curriculum guides in various subject areas, but the traditional Canadian preference for bureaucratic and administrative solutions to educational problems and the continuing failure to address truly national goals did not lead to any optimism that effective, truly country-wide curriculum efforts in Canadian Studies would continue.

Federal support of the Canada Studies Foundation after 1978 was part of a new program established by the Secretary of State in the form of a cultural initiative aimed at both the school and post-secondary levels. The program had been influenced by the Symons report, *To Know Ourselves* (1975) which conveyed the findings of the Commission on Canadian Studies that had been established by the Association of Universities and Colleges of Canada in 1972. Headed by T.H.B. Symons, a noted scholar in Canadian history, the study arose out of a widely expressed concern "for more attention to Canadian circumstances in the curriculum of the country's universities."[31] Symons was as critical of the failure of post-secondary institutions to meet their responsibilities to Canadian society as Hodgetts had been with respect to the similar failure of the schools nearly a decade before. Symons proposed a stronger emphasis on Canadian Studies in the education of teachers. He recommended research on Canadian Studies curriculum development, together with an emphasis on increased communication and consultation among those interested in the field at all levels of the educational system, from the primary grades to postgraduate programs.[32]

# Whose Culture? Whose Heritage? Cultural Pluralism and the Curriculum

## The Dilemmas of Cultural Pluralism

The Canadian Studies movement was both a reflection of and an attempt to resolve the growing tensions in Canadian society after 1960 that were discussed earlier. In most cases, the school was seen as a prime agent for resolving tensions. As a result, myriad programs and various forms of bilingual, bicultural and multicultural education began to flourish. Multicultural education in particular defied definition and precise use. As a result it was open to interpretations as diverse as those of the various groups and interests who voiced claims to a place in the curriculum. Jaenen, a leading scholar in the field, noted how "mutilated multiculturalism" caused multicultural education to be perceived in various contradictory ways: through rhetorical cliches about cultural survival as an alternative to the supposed American melting pot; "as a mosaic or patchwork of folklorish characteristics or contributions" within the framework of the dominant culture; "in a cosmopolitan context as the Canadian extension of international cultures;" "as a transitory immigrant phenomenon which will dissipate as the forces of assimilation inevitably do their work;" "as a permanent feature of the Canadian landscape . . . ."[33]

The suspicions of francophones and of third force ethnic groups regarding multiculturalism as a policy were noted in Chapter 13. To a mainstream anglophone critic, John Porter, multiculturalism was based on a magnification of cultural differences that served to perpetuate the anglophone monopoly of elite privilege in Canadian society.[34] Burnet saw multiculturalism as a policy as a necessary supplement to bilingualism. With the establishment of the B and B Commission in 1963, Canadians had begun to accustom themselves to a new model of their society.[35] In Book IV of its report, the commission had recommended that the languages and related cultural features and contributions of "the other ethnic groups" be incorporated as options in school programs.[36] In 1972, a Ministry of State for Multiculturalism was established, in order "to promote creative encounters and interchange among all Canadian cultural groups in the interest of national unity." Soon a wide range of activities was being promoted, ranging from folk festivals and related activities that sometimes confirmed ethnic stereotypes, to serious scholarship. Most provinces began to promote multiculturalism in the curriculum, but not always without controversy.

Reviewing multiculturalism and its development through the 1970s, McLeod conceded that progress had been made. However, anglophone Canadians still tended to regard multiculturalism as a policy for immigrants and "ethnics" while francophones, seeking equality of status for themselves, remained preoccupied with bilingualism. McLeod saw what he called ethnic specific and problem-oriented approaches to multicultural education as inadequate. The traditional Hebrew after-hours parochial school exemplified the former approach. Problem-oriented multicultural education was exemplified by such programs as teaching English as a second language (ESL). An assimilative approach concentrated on language instruction while neglecting cultural instruction that could have assisted adjustment to the majority society. Anti-discrimination programs, usually crisis-oriented, short-lived and intermittent, were another aspect of problem-oriented multicultural education.[37]

McLeod favoured a cultural-intercultural approach that focussed on developing capabilities to enable people to live in a pluralistic society. The defining characteristics of this approach were an ability to transcend one's own culture while retaining a secure sense of individual and group identity, and a knowledge of other cultures such that the individual could behave and act capably within more than one. Cultural-intercultural education, based on a realistic appraisal of Canadian society, was ideally designed to promote multiculturalism as an ethic that would pervade the entire school system. McLeod admitted that implementing such an approach would be difficult because it would require a reexamination of the assumptions of education.[38]

Wilson, citing an Ontario poll that showed 43 per cent of the respondents favouring more emphasis on "the culture held in common by most Canadians" and less emphasis in the curriculum on minority cultures, thought that there was danger of a backlash if the schools moved too far ahead of public opinion and tried to solve problems that were the responsibility of society. In a society that gave only lip-service to multiculturalism and continued to restrict upward mobility to traditional groups, there was a further danger that multicultural programs might restrict the opportunities of children enrolled in them.[39] More optimistically, Berry cited surveys in the late 1970s that revealed a general, if moderate acceptance of cultural diversity, and positive attitudes towards immigrants and ethnic groups on the part of Canadian adults and schoolchildren alike. Those living in ethnically mixed neighbourhoods or with experience of other regions of Canada, and those of higher educational and occupational status had the most positive attitudes. Support for a diverse Canada did not seem to undercut social cohesion or national unity. Overall, concluded Berry, there was a fund of goodwill among Canadians towards cultural diversity.[40]

Few provinces by 1980 had adopted a comprehensive policy on multicultural education. Saskatchewan's Multicultural Act of 1979 was a model for all provinces in its intent to assist individuals and groups "to learn about the nature of their cultural heritage and ... about the contributions of other multicultural groups in the province." The act approved the right of every group "to retain its distinctive group identity and to develop its relevant language and its traditional arts and sciences without political or social impediment ...[41] " Other provinces were cautiously moving in a similar direction by 1980.

## Bilingualism and Biculturalism in the Curriculum

Measures within Quebec to protect the French language and to restrict the use of English had particular salience for schooling. After 1974, entrance to English schools was restricted to those possessing a working knowledge of English. Proficiency tests in that language were required for those whose first language was not English, a measure aimed not only at non-anglophone immigrants but at the many francophone children — estimated at 75 000 in 1974 — whose parents desired English proficiency for their offspring. To be sure, francophone schools continued to teach English as a second language. The 1981 census revealed that 98 per cent of Quebec francophones studied English in high school, compared with 33 per cent of Ontario anglophones who studied French.[42]

After the election of the separatist Parti Quebecois government in

1976, admission to English schools was restricted to children attending a Quebec school or who had an anglophone parent living in the province at the time the act was passed. Those who had received English schooling in Quebec or who had learning disabilities were also exempted from the regulations.[43] The anglophone community was particularly outraged by the fact that the new restrictions applied not only to immigrant children but to those born in other provinces, a measure that was later declared unconstitutional by the courts in a 1984 decision that invoked the so-called "Canada Clause" of the new constitution. Some Roman Catholic immigrant groups tried to defy the new law. As a result of language legislation, anglophone out-migration and declining birthrates, enrolments in English-speaking schools were severely reduced by 1980. The forced entry of non-francophone, non-anglophone immigrant children ("allophones") into francophone schools had the effect of reducing the cultural homogeneity of those schools.

Many Quebec anglophones responded positively to the new language regime by making significant efforts to improve the deficient second language French instruction in their schools.[44] The first and most successful French immersion programs in Canada evolved from initiatives taken in 1965 by two internationally known McGill University scholars, Dr. Wilder Penfield, famous for his work on the brain and language, and Dr. Wallace Lambert, who had worked on the social psychology of bilingualism. From this beginning and as a result of the unprecedented 1969 federal decision to implement B and B Commission proposals to assist the provinces in meeting the extra costs of second language instruction, the immersion phenomenon spread across Canada to become one of the largest scale educational innovations of the century. As such it attracted international attention and was described by one American researcher as probably the most successful language teaching program ever devised.[45]

Stern observed that a French immersion class was not primarily a language class. It was a class in which subjects other than French, such as mathematics, history or art were presented in French. French immersion was teaching *in* French, not teaching *of* French. Immersion might assume various forms: early, middle or late, according to the age or grade level at which it was presented; partial immersion referred to classes in which both official languages were used as the media of instruction for part of the school day. Conventional "core French" instruction might be supplemented by "extended French" in which the language was used as the medium of teaching one subject.[46]

Second language teaching programs constituted a unique endeavour in federal-provincial co-operation in education that was relatively free of the conflict that often featured other endeavours. Far from objecting to federal subsidy for language instruction, the provinces on occasion demanded that it be increased. This demand reflected a notable increase in the provision to francophones of schooling in their own language. In 1977, the provincial premiers agreed to provide instruction in both official languages wherever numbers warranted, a policy that was subsequently monitored by the

Council of Ministers of Education. New Brunswick, following a B and B Commission recommendation, declared itself a bilingual province in 1969 and established a dual system of education on the old Quebec model. Ontario, while refusing to go as far, did promote, through regulation, a very significant expansion of francophone education during these years. In western Canada, where anti-francophone prejudice was probably deepest, Alberta and Saskatchewan passed legislation in the late seventies that permitted French and other languages to be used as languages of instruction. In these and other western provinces, schools sometimes had difficulty in keeping up with the demand for immersion French classes.

A particularly innovative federal-provincial effort was the second-language monitor program by which university students, teaching in provinces other than their own, assisted second language instruction in their first language. Travel and exchange programs, conferences, seminars and curriculum development were other initiatives that helped to promote bicultural, as distinct from purely bilingual instruction. This policy was consistent with the B and B Commission recommendation that English and French be taught, not as foreign languages, "but with an emphasis on the Canadian milieu in which these languages are used."[47] In 1977, the Canadian Association of Immersion Teachers was formed at a conference in Ottawa attended by over 1000 teachers and administrators. It was estimated that by 1980 some 75 000 young people were enrolled in immersion programs or had had an immersion background in their schooling.[48]

Stern credited parents rather than professional educators with the impetus for immersion and other innovative programs.[49] Voluntary organizations such as Canadian Parents for French were part of an impressive national consciousness-raising effort that was on the whole unmarked by the rancour that often attended the promotion of official bilingualism in spheres other than schooling. The "school option" to bilingualism proved much more viable than the sometimes counterproductive effort to teach middle-aged anglophone civil servants to acquire facility in French.

Unlike many curriculum innovations, immersion programs and second language programs were generally subject to extensive and rigorous research, sometimes of a longitudinal nature. Stern saw the endeavour as unusual in the long-term co-operation among researchers, administrators and teachers that the immersion approach engendered. He credited the research reports coming out of initial Quebec experiments with influencing the spread of the immersion concept outside that province.[50] Summing up research and evaluation studies of French immersion programs, Lapkin and Swain concluded that students from a majority language group, regardless of ability levels, can be taught a second language with no long-term negative effects on first-language development or on content learning. At the same time, students became highly proficient in the target language. Immersion students were much more appreciative of cultural diversity than were other students.[51] Krashen hypothesized that the subject matter class might be even better than the language class for language acquisition.[52]

The Canadian immersion experience was not viewed entirely positively by all researchers. Stern and Bibeau both observed that its very success in appealing to elite anglophone groups was a source of difficulty in evaluating the achievement. Although immersion increased anglophone awareness of the French fact, it did not necessarily increase contacts with or improve attitudes towards francophones.[53] There was some evidence of later language regression on the part of early immersion students.[54] Bibeau was especially critical of claims that immersion graduates were equal to francophones in language facility. This was manifestly false but as Krashen pointed out, the immersion class should not be expected to produce students capable of speaking at native levels. It had succeeded in producing "intermediates" who could use the language for real communication with its speakers.[55]

## Multiculturalism in the Curriculum

Multiculturalism followed closely behind bilingualism and biculturalism as a new curriculum initiative after 1970, as a greater though still modest emphasis was put on "third force" cultures. The teaching of English as a second language (ESL) became a growth industry in such school systems as Vancouver, where as much as 40 per cent of total enrolment in some years consisted of students for whom English was not their first language. By 1972, nearly 400 000 Canadian children came from such homes.[56] Four years later, the Toronto Board of Education defined a New Canadian student as one "who may be unable to achieve academic success with regular programs because his or her language, dialect or culture is different from that of the school system."[57]

Increasingly, second language teaching had a cultural as well as a linguistic basis, as the effort was made to introduce students to the dominant heritage in ways that would relate positively to their own heritage and assist their integration into Canadian society. Ashworth found that teachers tended to view problems of cultural adjustment as much more serious than those concerned with language, or even with academic progress. Yet language skills received twice as much emphasis as that given to field trips and other means of acquainting children with the Canadian way of life. A related problem was the tendency of ESL programs to treat all immigrant children pretty much the same, even though children from Eastern cultures faced adjustments different from those faced by immigrants of European origin.[58]

Problems of school adjustment of New Canadian children were highlighted in Lambert's comparative study of child-rearing values held by Canadian-born and educated teachers from both language groups and those held by immigrant parents. Teachers were more permissive than working class immigrant parents. Some teachers reinforced parental sex biases, while others countered them. Thus, francophone teachers, generally more lenient with aggressive boys as compared with aggressive girls, reinforced the Japanese parental bias, while countering the permissive bias of Greek parents towards female aggressiveness. Lambert and his colleagues concluded that school was usually a pleasant experience for immigrant children in that teachers tended to be more permissive than parents. In some cases, however, they had higher expectations of pupils, which possibly served as a corrective to too much parent attention or favouritism directed to one sex over another.[59]

Ashworth described three types of ESL programs: reception classes that entailed a gradual integration of students into regular classes; cultural integration, entailing learning English in the regular classroom; and withdrawal classes entailing intensive ESL teaching accompanied by integration into the regular classroom. These approaches gave rise to a number of issues facing ESL teachers and administrators, which Ashworth summed up in the form of several questions. She asked whether "new" Canadians should be separated from "old" Canadians. Should retention of first languages be encouraged and should teaching be through the medium of those languages? Should the value systems and customs of immigrants give way to those of the host community? Should different ethnic groups be treated differently?[60]

A 1977 survey of ethnicity within Canadian social studies curricula conducted by Werner and his colleagues found considerable bias by omission.[61] The Native peoples and the British and French were the cultures predominantly portrayed in curricula. However, Native groups, and some others, such as the Hutterites, were characteristically perceived as exotic. There was a tendency to view all ethnic minorities as problem groups. Though supposedly the beneficiaries of the paternalistic policies of the two dominant cultures, the minorities were often perceived as outsiders in conflict with the majority groups.

The Werner survey referred to four approaches that seemed to dominate curricula in multicultural and ethnic studies. The first of these was the *museum approach*, whereby a group was studied in terms of isolated, exotic details that lacked any context and led to no conceptual understanding. The *heritage approach* stressed charter group dominance and was, as indicated, ethnocentric and paternalistic in its approach. The *disciplines approach* was pursued mainly through the use of history. Finally, the least used but potentially the most promising was the *interdisciplinary approach*, which sought to apply social science concepts, to consider conflicting interpretations and to treat value issues.

The survey made it clear how much development was needed before cultural diversity could become an ethic that permeated the curriculum. Nevertheless, considerable progress had been made at both the provincial and local levels, as accounts by McLeod and Wilson indicated.[52] Saskatchewan's legislation has been mentioned. In a remarkable about-face, Quebec granted the Montreal Greek community status as an "associate system," using a trilingual curriculum, with French as the normal language of instruction. Greek was taught as a heritage language. Other ethnic groups in Montreal received similar privileges.[63] Multiculturalism was officially supported in the Maritime provinces but implementation was limited. Ontario established a high school history course entitled "Canada's Multicultural Heritage."

McLeod described impressive local efforts in Winnipeg and Toronto.[64] Toronto, with Canada's largest and most diverse multicultural milieu, probably went further than any urban school system in recognizing cultural pluralism. Multicultural content was proposed for all subject areas. Bilingual and bicultural programs were instituted for teaching "ancestral languages" and, for West Indian children, English as a Second Dialect (ESD). In 1977 Ontario inaugurated a Heritage Languages Program, which within three years was enrolling more than 76 000 public and separate school pupils in forty-four different language programs ranging from Albanian to Urdu. By 1980, an estimated 250 000 children across Canada were studying a non-official language, usually on an after school basis in schools, churches and homes. Funding came from community, local school board, provincial and federal sources, as well as from some foreign governments such as those of Japan, Greece and Portugal, which sometimes even provided textbooks and educational consultants.[65]

Foreign support added to the controversy that developed in Ontario over the question of teaching heritage languages. Some critics charged that such teaching could balkanize Canada, undermine national identity, divert funds from more valid school needs and create citizens unable to cope in any language.[66] By contrast, heritage language teaching provoked little opposition in western Canada. Alberta probably went farthest, with its inauguration in 1974 of a Ukrainian-English bilingual immersion program in Edmonton's public and separate schools. Wilson reported in 1981 that ten bilingual public schools were in operation in the city. Of these, five were Ukrainian, three were Jewish and two were German; there were also three Ukrainian bilingual separate schools.[67]

An increasing aspect of multicultural education by 1980 was the attempt to counter prejudice, discrimination and outright racism. As racism became a significant social issue, curricular responses took the form of programs designed to foster more positive attitudes towards ethnic groups. Multicultural programs such as some of those already described began to incorporate content and teaching strategies designed to enhance interracial understanding. Human rights education was also introduced into the curriculum in some cases. Extensive efforts were made to counter bias in curriculum materials. The McDiarmid-Pratt study of textbook bias has already been noted. Similar studies were carried out in other provinces. Following a major 1974 analysis of textbooks, the Nova Scotia Human Rights Commission recommended the removal of biased books and the addition of new ones containing more material and positive content on minorities, particularly blacks and Indians. In this way, the curriculum would "present a true picture of all people who make up this Canadian nation."[68]

Several provinces set up regular review procedures for screening all books authorized in their curricula. In 1977, an Ontario ministerial advisory committee developed guidelines to assist authors and publishers to avoid bias and prejudice in the preparation of learning materials. The resulting publication, *Race, Religion and Culture in Ontario School Materials*, was probably the most sophisticated document of its kind in the country, and in Pratt's opinion virtually ensured the elimination of racial, ethnic, cultural and religious bias in future Ontario textbooks.[69] Four basic principles were proposed as a framework for developing learning materials representing racial, religious and cultural minorities. Materials should promote student self-worth, reflect Canadian diversity fully and accurately, facilitate mutual awareness, understanding and appreciation and recognize human interdependence and the universality of human experience. The responsibilities of authors, publishers, illustrators and editors were defined. Suggestions for language usage and illustrations were made. The guideline concluded with a twenty-seven item checklist for the evaluation of racial, religious and cultural bias in textbooks.[70]

As a result of changing attitudes and the various initiatives described, considerable progress was made during the 1970s in producing textbooks that were on the whole less biased, more scholarly, more inclined to use primary sources, less sententious and more prepared to devote considerably more space to minorities and their treatment in Canadian society. Thus, in a comparative analysis of Ontario textbooks published before 1967 and some between 1977 and 1980, Pratt found that, whereas in the earlier period seven of the ten terms most frequently used to describe Indians were negative, by 1980 seven were positive.[71]

Issues related to racism, like those related to sexism and to emerging new issues such as "ageism" (portrayal of the elderly) and "handicappism," underscored the pressures faced by textbook authors. Where multiculturalism was concerned, questions endemic to all textbook analysis were especially sensitive. Should the world be presented as it is or as we might wish it to be? Whereas episodes of prejudice and intolerance in the history of the majority culture were now to be taught candidly and critically on the basis of absolute moral judgments, authors were very reluctant to pass judgments on negative aspects of other cultures lest they be charged with bias. Thus, the treatment of women and various minorities in Third World cultures were glossed over or omitted in a manner once standard in Canadian domestic history. Pratt suggested that Canadian educators needed to develop a clear, consistent, explicit and defensible set of values, abandoning the tendency to make absolute moral judgments on Canadian history and society while being morally relativist in treating all other cultures.[72]

A CEA national survey of multiculturalism at the provincial and local levels emphasized the need for research as a basis for policy in dealing with racism in the classroom. Kehoe, the leading Canadian researcher on this topic, reported that few assessments were made to determine the main causes of prejudice. There was an urgent need to identify successful and unsuccessful approaches in the classroom. The assumption that knowledge changes attitudes, that simply providing information about an ethnic group has value, was misplaced. Since there is no evidence that students necessarily identify with victims or become morally concerned by portrayals of injustice, the emphasis on historical bad news may be equally misplaced. Emphasis should be put on the positive achievements of minority groups and cultural similarities rather than on exotic and bizarre differences; information should be presented from an insider's point of view. The survey reported a number of endeavours in local jurisdictions such as Scarborough, Ontario where encouraging success in combatting racism had been achieved through programs that embodied research-based principles of the type described by Kehoe.[73]

Although the Native peoples were an obvious dimension of multiculturalism, as the first Canadians they were viewed apart from other ethnic groups, a stance that recognized their *a priori* cultural distinctiveness, while also perpetuating paternalistic attitudes towards them. The mere fact that the Native people remained largely non-urbanized, with considerable numbers still living in remote areas, no doubt contributed to perceptions and curriculum policies different from those applied to other minorities. There was, however, a similarity in policies revealed in tentative efforts to stress this diverse minority's cultural heritage in its own and in majority curricula. In the latter case, the First Canadians typically disappeared from social studies textbooks shortly after the explorers and settlers arrived on the scene, reappearing, Renaud noted, "in a semi-negative light when the school program [dealt] with Riel and the opening of the Prairies."[74]

As with other minorities, it was slowly recognized that maintenance of Native cultural identity required special schooling provisions. The provincialization of Native education noted earlier had clear benefits arising from the administration of policy by experienced educational personnel who were able to promote innovative measures designed to improve the quality of schooling. The B and B Commission noted that provincialization was being accompanied by the development of kindergarten and other new programs to meet Native cultural and linguistic problems and to assist the preparation of youth for work in the majority society.[75] Between 1945 and 1962 the Prairie provinces took steps to establish the first local Native school systems. By the 1970s, about 60 per cent of Native children were attending provincial schools. During the decade the Native Indian Brotherhood began to exert pressure to slow the pace of provincialization in the interest of promoting band-operated and locally controlled federal schools.[76] Band-operated schools had been established in several provinces in which Native languages were taught and sometimes used as languages of instruction. Native curriculum developers assisted in the preparation of materials emphasizing local cultures and value systems relevant to their communities. Ontario prepared curriculum documents on Native peoples for all grade levels for use in teaching both Native and majority students.

A major difficulty in Native education was the lack of trained Native teachers. As Allison suggested, it was difficult to see how Caucasian teachers, ignorant of Native culture, could comprehend the economic realities of working a trap line in the northern forests; or how children helping on the line could comprehend the teacher's confident use of words and concepts based on the comfortable suburban life of Dick, Jane and their non-working dog, Spot.[77] In reviewing the seventeen Native Indian teacher education programs across the country in 1980. More reported that 600 students were enrolled in specialized training programs. The number of Native teachers had risen dramatically, but was still a miniscule proportion of the total teaching force. Jaenen saw a weakness in teacher education programs related to multicultural education generally, that resulted from a failure to provide needed curriculum development and implementation skills. At the same time, curriculum guidelines tended to emphasize educational theory and strategies, to the neglect of content and of needed historical and sociological insights.[78]

Where the Inuit were concerned, the Honigmanns noted that in the school system of Frobisher Bay the curriculum was related neither to their traditional role on the land nor their newly found career in town. Non-Native teachers, teaching in non-Native language, used curricula oriented to southern Canada.[79] The Mackenzie Pipeline Inquiry or so-called Berger Commission of 1977, in supporting the right to self-determination for northern Natives, emphasized the right of parents to educate their children for the purpose of transmitting and preserving their language and culture.[80] Robinson reported that some progress had been made in this direction by 1980 through the development of locally published curriculum guides and teaching materials. The territorial educational system had moved from entire reliance on southern Canadian curricula to a middle ground position of combining selected southern with locally developed resources. In so doing, ideas from Greenlandic, Scandinavian, Soviet and Maori New Zealand curricula, among others, had been used. Local topics studied included permafrost and oil and gas. An adaptation of a British Nuffield science unit in astronomy, "Looking at the Sky," was based on a study of circumpolar constellations.[81] Such emphases would be strengthened if a 1982 report by the territorial legislative assembly's Special Committee on Education that recommended decentralization of the school system was adopted.[82]

## Old and New Morality in the Curriculum

### Values Shifts: Moral and Religious Education in the Early Post-war Years

Ontario's initiative in re-emphasizing religious instruction during the 1940s was followed by several other provinces. How far traditional moral aims were still accepted in Ontario as late as 1950 was revealed when the Hope Royal Commission in that year cited the goals of the Programme of Studies for Grades 7 and 8, to the effect that the social purposes of the school implied the existence of standards of behaviour "generally agreed upon ... [and derived] from the ethics of the Christian religion and the principles of democratic living."[83] The commissioners singled out two cardinal virtues which they identified as beyond dispute: honesty and Christian love. As Fleming remarked, apparently Jewish love or Buddhist love would not do.[84] These virtues, viewed as absolute truths, together with other virtues, habits, customs and conventions, were to be taught by precept and example and inculcated by the school because they were essential to the preservation of society. The school must insist that children learn "to live in the way that society approves and not in a way that will certainly be to [their] disadvantage ... ." Thus, the school would carry out its mandate to educate as defined by the *Oxford Concise Dictionary:* "to give intellectual and moral training." The commissioners made no apology for emphasizing "moral training," for the evil wrought in the world in the recent past "by sharp intellects unsupported by moral foundations" was too obvious.[85]

Similar sentiments were expressed in 1958, in a brief prepared by the Saskatchewan General Advisory Committee on Education for submission to the Canadian Conference on Education. In identifying a dominant Canadian set of values and beliefs to which it was thought most Canadians would subscribe, the brief gave first place to "A belief in a Creator and Father of mankind in order to provide a spiritual foundation for living and a deep regard for the dignity and sanctity of life." Other values included a belief in human perfectibility and in the work-success ethic.[86]

Yet, as the Crestwood Heights study noted earlier revealed, moral education was beginning to lose its religious content. Religious education was now purveyed through a weakened vocabulary of religion that embodied vague recommendations against aggression and in favour of love and sympathy so qualified as to be "scarcely considered as behavioural guides." The trend was illustrated by the kindergarten phrase "to give thanks for a lovely day," directed "to some not too clearly defined 'source of good' in the universe."[87]

Despite ambiguity, a good deal of religious activity was still found in Crestwood Heights schools in the form of traditional classroom observances, celebrations on public occasions such as school concerts, and the major Christian holidays. In part, this was because, in deference to the minority who still saw the curriculum as including a religious component, the school must not be seen as a "godless" institution. Thus, although formally exempted from the provincial requirement of religious instruction, schools in Crestwood Heights continued to promote a much diluted nondenominational Protestantism. In promoting adherence to the emerging value-system of health, happiness and success, the school had to pay some deference to traditional values "without jeopardizing clear transmission of the new ideology."[88] In these early post-war years, a pragmatic middle-class social consensus was reflected in the superficial complementarity of the two value systems, which enabled mainstream Canadian society to make a relatively smooth transition from primarily religious to primarily secular values.

## Values Education: Morality in a New Key

Reporting in 1969, Ontario's Committee on Religious Education in the Public Schools, the so-called MacKay Committee, surveyed the state of religious education in the province and elsewhere in Canada. Ontario, Quebec and Newfoundland required a systematic study of the Scriptures. Ontario based its religious education on a comprehensive series of teachers' guides. Some provinces made no provision for religious education, and others maintained it on an optional basis. With respect to religious exercises, the situation across Canada was more uniform. The opening or closing of the school day with a Bible reading, sometimes accompanied by a prayer, was either mandatory or permissive. No province required that a child be present for devotional exercises against the wishes of his or her parents.[89]

The Committee noted that all provinces still expected the school to have a comprehensive responsibility for ethical and character education, and the teacher to be a moral exemplar and didactic moral tutor. According to the Ontario Public School Act, the teacher was required "to inculcate by precept and example respect for religion and the principles of Christian morality and the highest regard for truth, justice, loyalty, love of country, humanity, benevolence, sobriety, industry, frugality, purity, temperance and all other virtues."

By 1969, a variety of factors was causing Canadian educators to reconsider curriculum policy with respect to religious education. The further secularization of society and the corresponding decline of traditional religious authority were accompanied by a growing religious pluralism that was reflected in the presence of large non-Christian religious groups in classrooms, together with children of atheists and agnostics. Changing moral standards regarding sexual and other attitudes and behaviour made teachers less willing and able to serve as traditional moral role models; some regarded the imposition of such a role as an infringement of their professional autonomy and personal rights. Others, such as the young draft-avoiding American teacher employed in a Newfoundland outport, served as the missionaries of a new secular humanism that in its self-absorption and dogmatic commitment to anti-traditional values of democracy, equality and sexual fulfilment constituted a world view as uncritically advocated as the hierarchical Christian world view that it replaced.[90]

Religious observance in classrooms was often perfunctory and, despite provincial legislation, was in many cases probably not being carried out at all by 1970. The MacKay Committee recommended the removal of religious instruction from the Ontario curriculum. School opening exercises should retain the National Anthem and a prayer, but should basically be "inspirational and dedicational" rather than confessional. Through a program of "incidental teaching and study," religious information stressing respect for all religions should be made an essential objective from Grades K through 13. An optional formal course on world religions should be offered in the senior secondary grades. Character building should pervade every curricular and extra-curricular activity through a program "carefully planned and administered incidentally throughout the whole school spectrum." The focus of such a program should include ethics, social attitudes and moral values and principles.[91]

On the face of it, this sounded like old-fashioned indirect moral instruction, shorn of its religious overtones. In practice, the approach was intended to emphasize moral education for the purpose of stimulating the student's capacity to make value judgments and moral decisions. Indoctrination in any specific set of beliefs and the imposition of moral precepts as a means of character development were to be avoided. The Committee recommended moral values education (MVE) based on Kohlberg's well-known theory of moral reasoning which used Piaget-style stages of moral development. The teacher should no longer be a moralizer but a helper of children in moving from one stage of development to another. In doing so, use should be made of realistic anecdotes and stories involving genuine moral conflicts, or dilemmas, which children could discuss and reflect upon before choosing alternative courses of action. Patronizing adult moral cliches and "moralizing tales" which were, in fact, lacking moral and literary merit, should be strictly avoided.[92]

Not surprisingly, the MacKay proposals evoked controversy, much of it foreshadowing the criticism which would soon engulf the new values education movement. Church leaders had predictable reservations, although they seemed to agree that the strongly Protestant orientation of the existing program could no longer be justified. To Cragg it was naive to suppose that moral reasoning was a practical basis for moral education. There was, in Hare's view, an inconsistency in making the highly dubious claim that religious commitment was incompatible with "true" education. Ryan argued that MacKay's relativism, ostensibly in opposition to indoctrination, was itself a form of indoctrination, just as the claim that all values are relative was itself a value claim. Complete freedom to choose ignored the possibility that students might make a choice, for instance Nazism which was incompatible with democratic liberalism. It also ignored the likelihood that if the school and the home failed to inculcate values, other agencies, such as the media, would do so.[93]

In practice, moral values education took three forms. These included the Cognitive Moral Development (or moral reasoning) approach described above associated with Kohlberg at Harvard, the related Reflective Approach associated with Beck, and the Moral Education Project at the Ontario Institute for Studies in Education. The work of the latter project and that of the Association for Values Education Research at the University of British Columbia constituted the most intensive research-based efforts in the country, and attracted national and international attention. A third approach, Values Clarification, was the most popular and most controversial. It was criticized by proponents of the other approaches to values education and by proponents of traditional Christian-based moral education.

Values Clarification was criticized because it typically ignored decisions that involved conflicts between values. Too often its purportedly Deweyan problem-solving techniques relied on memorization and were thus anti-educational. Although the Values Clarification method had worth in encouraging students to become aware of their own values, its failure to distinguish between moral and non-moral questions, and a tendency to reduce all questions to mere matters of opinion and taste without requiring students to justify their own values were serious weaknesses. Simulation and role-playing exercises that might require children to make hypothetical life and death decisions affecting their peers were condemned as too far removed from reality, too emotionally freighted and potentially destructive of students' self-concepts.[94]

Other approaches to values education assumed that there was, or could be, a recognized right or wrong, and that rational moral principles and rules could and should be taught. In using Piaget's stage theory of child development, Kohlberg had posited six stages of moral growth achievable by systematic teaching, as described above. The method was criticized for its sometimes weak pedagogy, reflected in inappropriate age-topic matches. The idealism of its ultimate goal, whereby the student would reach an autonomous stage of moral action based on such self-chosen ethical principles as the Golden Rule, could not be gainsaid. By contrast, Beck's Reflective Approach was criticized on the ground that it failed to establish criteria for moral reflection and ignored the intrinsic value of moral ideals.[95] Some critics claimed that it also ignored youth need for some absolutes, the absence of which led to an interest in bizarre religious and other cults. Nevertheless, Beck's *The Reflective Approach to Values Education* achieved a circulation of 5000 copies in Ontario and was recommended to other provinces by the Council of Ministers of Education.

Teaching strategies derived from the three forms of moral values education were incorporated into such subjects as guidance and counselling, English, social studies, and health and physical education. This last subject area sometimes served as a vehicle for sex education, using Values Clarification techniques. Curriculum guidelines that recommended morally neutral discussion of a full range of heterosexual activities aroused predictable opposition while also suggesting how far the Canadian curriculum was moving beyond the advocacy of traditional moral norms.[96] Harper observed that research provided little basis for assuming that sexual values and behaviour could be changed by classroom instruction. In any case, the question of whose values would be taught was central. The difficulty of distinguishing information from values lent complexity to the whole enterprise.[97] Another critic, Wright, commented on the failure of Alberta's values-based social studies curriculum to differentiate types of values — economic, prudential, moral and aesthetic — that had distinctive standards, rules and principles. Students were given little guidance in evaluating their principles as a means of arriving at morally mature autonomous decisions.

No real help was given "in discovering whether or not an argument is logically consistent."[98]

In a survey of provincial policies regarding moral values education, Cochrane and Williams attempted to determine the extent of official policy and to appraise how far such policy was reflected in practice. Using a wide definition of the field, they reported that all provinces except Prince Edward Island had some published policy or statement on some aspect of it. No province required teacher training and most showed little interest in evaluating curricula in moral values education. Apathy resulted from ignorance of theory and literature, fear of political and religious controversy and public confusion, indifference and disagreement. Policy-makers themselves had confused and inconsistent concepts about the nature and justification of the field.[99] Daniels and Oliver agreed that little real values education was going on in Canadian schools. Taped classroom discussions in some British Columbia schools revealed that teachers rarely capitalized on opportunities to inject value issues into the curriculum.[100]

Cochrane and Williams reported a tenuous relationship between curriculum policy statements and school practice. In fact, Gow asserted that the relationship between practice and educational aims as stated in public school acts was totally contradictory. Thus, Ontario's act retained an emphasis on traditional moral indoctrination. Retention of the old aims meant that official policy and values education practice were in fundamental conflict. This led to protests, and in some cases to court action, by parents who complained, with some legal justification, that what they called secular humanism was being imposed contrary to officially promulgated traditional Christian ethics.[101]

Gow, following a religious orientation, argued that there were core moral precepts, "timeless moral principles," acceptable to the religious and non-religious alike, that could serve as the basis for a defensible values-based curriculum. Daniels and Oliver implied, from a non-religious perspective, their own belief that such a core might exist. The issue for them was one of means, dependent upon whether a truly reflective moral reasoning approach could be used.[102] Ontario commissioned a guideline intended to identify universally accepted personal and social values that, transcending religion and race in the classroom, should be taught to elementary school pupils.[103] Alberta took a similar tack. Some critics claimed that such policies represented a capitulation to religious fundamentalists; to the latter, on the other hand, God was still excluded from the curriculum.

## Values Schools and Family Choice

Values schools were distinguished from values education as described above by the fact that they were explicitly designed to inculcate community norms, usually those of a specific religious community. Such schools constituted a social setting in which desired values were explicitly and frequently stated, and in which teachers were selected to be typical role models for the students who if conformers were rewarded, and if nonconformers were punished. Values schools were co-ordinated with the home and the church to make all mutually supportive. To their critics, these schools did not constitute true values education because they failed to promote reflection and understanding and denied student choice.[104]

Although most values schools were private or independent, some groups brought pressure to bear on public jurisdictions to accommodate their demands, a trend that sometimes promoted political, religious and community conflict. This trend reflected the phenomenon of "family choice" in schooling that was very much in the Canadian tradition.[105] Church and state, far from being separated in Canada, had long been partners. Religious observance was not prohibited as in the American curriculum; on the contrary it had traditionally been required.

During this period the tradition described above was extended, as British Columbia, through its 1977 Independent Schools Support Act, began to provide public support to both denominational and secular private schools.[106] Private school enrolments across Canada increased by more than 40 per cent between 1971 and 1978, although in 1978 more than 96 per cent of Canadian children still attended public schools. Not all private schools were values schools in the strict sense, but most reflected parental dissatisfaction with the public schools. For conservative parents, the breakdown of the old tacit consensus based on non-denominational Protestant values meant that the moral stance of the school was no longer consistent with their own. There was some irony in the fact that conservative parents and radical "free" schoolers alike sometimes accused the public schools of preparing students to fit mindlessly into a consumer society. A related irony was that the different types of alternative schools favoured by both groups embodied many features of the ideal progressive public school. The traditional elite private school, whose supporters often criticized the alleged "frills" of the public schools, sometimes offered a smorgasbord of extracurricular activities which public schools could not easily match.

One Alberta educator, Peter Bargen, wondered why, if alternatives were available in public school academic and multicultural programs, they should not be available in moral and religious education. To some critics, however, the teaching of what might be called heritage religions was even more divisive than the teaching of heritage languages. Nevertheless, Bargen insisted that, even though his proposal would admittedly undermine the concept of the neighbourhood school and have serious implications for school governance, public schools could and should reflect the broadly based value positions of a pluralistic society. As it was, the fiction of neutrality served as a highly efficient mechanism of indoctrination, forcing the schools "to conduct catechism classes in moral relativism."[107]

Other conservative Christians agreed with the need for a pluralistic approach to religion in the curriculum, claiming that the lack of public agreement on religion as an area of belief was no grounds for its exclusion. Thiessen and Wilson argued that there was a similar lack of agreement and of tests for determining the validity of value and factual claims with respect to sex education, capitalism and Marxism. The argument had some validity but was nevertheless fallacious, for when theories such as capitalism and Marxism were studied in schools it was usually agreed, at least in principle, that they should be studied objectively. This was an approach unlikely to be taken by conservative Christians in studying their own theories. The case was underscored by controversies over the teaching of creationism in science curricula.[108]

Fears that religiously-based and other types of private schools might foster intolerance and divisiveness were undermined by the findings of Erickson and his colleagues that students in British Columbia's independent schools were significantly less prejudiced towards minority groups than were their public school counterparts. Erickson, an American researcher, had been funded by the U.S. Congress to study the effects of public funding on British Columbia private schools in order to provide guidance to policy-makers in his own country.[109] His conclusion paralleled an earlier finding by Cooper that Newfoundland's denominational school system — the prime example of religious pluralism in Canadian public education — did not lead to religious intolerance or social divisiveness.[110]

Values schools grew apace after 1970, largely in the western provinces. By 1980, all four provinces recognized private schools for purposes of funding provided on varying scales. Variation was based on the degree to which the schools met standards of teacher certification, followed provincial curricula, were subject to public inspection and provincial examinations, and conformed with public school building standards. Alberta had the most comprehensive policy, one which required ministry approval for the operation of all schools. Some were public values schools. As a result of a key court case based on the freedom of religion clause of the Alberta Bill of Rights, the province had been required to recognize the right of parents to send their children to a Mennonite private school even though its teachers lacked provincial certification.[111]

As values schools gained greater public recognition and funding and were expected to accede to various measures of public control, issues arose with respect to their curricular freedom. Seventh Day Adventist Schools and those affiliated with the Society of Christian Schools — the latter consisting of about one hundred institutions concentrated mainly in British Columbia and Ontario — drew many of their curriculum materials from their American parent organizations.[112] Such materials did not meet Canadian content regulations, a fact which created tensions, particularly in Ontario where Christian and other private schools were required to submit to inspection and to meet core curriculum requirements in order to be accredited for high school graduation purposes. Christian educators did not object to provincial requirements, but demanded freedom to determine the grade levels and curricular contexts in which guidelines could be used.[113] Some also demanded more serious discussion of philosophical and pedagogical issues in the interest of countering a centralizing uniformity that was seen as antithetical to quality education and cultural diversity.[114]

Public funding and curriculum control of private schools increasingly blurred the distinction between the public and private sectors. Within the public sector, the existence of separate schools and school systems parallel to public institutions had long constituted official recognition of what were in many respects *de facto* values schools. Martin and Macdonell saw the ten provincial school jurisdictions as comprising five different kinds of systems according to the recognition of religious denominational rights. Newfoundland and Quebec had long had public values schools in the form of denominational and "confessional" schools.[115] Newfoundland identified the understanding and practice of universal Christian principles, and the development and practice of moral values as a major secondary responsibility of its schools, with the church and the family having primary responsibility. Although Quebec sought to abolish "confessionality" in its school system, public opposition prevented this.

Alberta went farthest during the 1970s in permitting the establishment of religiously based schools within its public system. A remarkable development occurred with the funding of the Talmud Torah School by the Edmonton Public School District; all of its work except certain special cultural out-of-school activities was publicly supported.[116] This development raised little controversy, but in neighbouring Saskatchewan civil libertarians and members of the local Muslim community objected when the Regina Public School Board, acting on provisions of the Saskatchewan Public School Act of 1979, which had entrenched Bible readings in the schools, voted by a 4-3 margin to "encourage" teachers to carry out provincial policy by conducting school prayers.[117] Such controversies suggested that, as in the past, Canadians could not avoid confronting the moral imperatives of schooling.

## Notes to Chapter 16

1 *Toronto Star,* May 30, 1972, 6.

2 Hodgetts, *What Culture?,* 1.

3 Ibid., 41-7, 50-2.

4 Ibid., 93.

5 Ibid., 53-6.

6 Ibid., 94, 104.

7 See, for example, National Assessment of Educational Progress (U.S.A.), *Changes in Political Knowledge and Attitudes* Denver, 1978; Stradling, Robert, *The Political Awareness of the School Leaver,* London: The Hansard Society, 1977; Peter Borowsky, "What Are German School-Children Learning About Hitler?", *The History and Social Science Teacher,* 14, no.2 (Winter, 1979), 113-118.

8 For a discussion of major issues in political socialization research from a Canadian perspective see Zureik and Pike, Volume I, 3-56. See also Tomkins, "Political Socialization" and Pammett and Whittington.

9 Belovari *et al.*

10 Johnstone; Lamy.

11 Skogstad; Ullman.

12 Richert, "Canadian."

13 T.G. Harvey *et al.*

14 Higgins; Whittington.

15 Trudel and Jain, 15, 133.

16 Richert, "Impact."

17 McDiarmid and Pratt, *Teaching Prejudice*; Pratt, "The Social Role."

18 Tomkins, "Canada Studies Foundation," 7.

19 Canada Studies Foundation, *Annual Report*, 1971, 6-7.

20 Tomkins, "Canada Studies Foundation."

21 See Duckworth.

22 Hodgetts, "What Culture?," 15.

23 Bernier *et al, External Evaluation.*

24 Tomkins, "Canada Studies Foundation," 15.

25 See Aoki, Carswell and Allard. See also Robert, "Les Conditions" and "Perspectives Nouvelles." R.M Anderson and B. Robert *Reflections* contains useful firsthand accounts of the experiences of teachers in the Foundation's work.

26 Hodgetts and Gallagher, *Teaching Canada.*

27 Gallagher, "Canadianizing."

28 See Bourne and Eisenberg.

29 Ibid., 7. See also Osborne, 22.

30 Osborne, 25-6.

31 Symons, *To Know,* 2.

32 Ibid., 130, 134, 197.

33 Jaenen, "Mutilated," 79.

34 Cited in Burnet, 207-8.

35 Ibid., 206.

36 Palmer and Troper observe that the Commission argued that the concept of ethnic group could not be delimited to ethnic origin, "biological affiliation" and ancestry or to the ritual, language or visible artifacts associated with a particular group. While ethnic identity may be manifested by such attributes, the ethnic group creates its own symbols of identity; the symbols do not create the ethnic group. An ethnic group is an ethnic group because individuals within it identify with the group and are generally recognized by non-members as being

members of the group. This concept of the ethnic group has considerable implications for treating multiculturalism in schools.

37 K. McLeod, "Multicultural Education," 13-18.

38 Ibid., 18-9.

39 J.D. Wilson, "Multicultural Programmes," 72-3.

40 Berry, 103, 106.

41 Jaenen, "Multiculturalism," 85.

42 V. Ross, "The Way," 24.

43 Magnuson, *Brief History,* 128-9, 142.

44 Genesee, 25.

45 See Lapkin and Swain, 53; Krashen, 61.

46 Stern, "Immersion Phenomenon," 4.

47 B and B Commission, Book II, *Education,* 202.

48 Stern, "Immersion Schools," 5.

49 Ibid., 4.

50 Ibid., 4, 6.

51 Lapkin and Swain, 52-3.

52 Krashen, 62.

53 Stern, "Immersion Phenomenon," 5; Bibeau, 45.

54 Bibeau, 45-6.

55 Krashen, 62.

56 Ashworth, *Immigrant Children,* 206.

57 K. McLeod, "Multiculturalism," 43.

58 Ashworth, "Results," 87-8.

59 W. Lambert et al, 382, 385.

60 Ashworth, "Results," 85-6, 93-4.

61 Werner *et al, Whose Culture?*

62 K. McLeod, "Multiculturalism"; J.D. Wilson, "Multicultural Programmes."

63 Canada, House of Commons, *Equality Now,* 114-5.

64 K. McLeod, "Multiculturalism," 42-3.

65 *MacLean's Magazine,* January 18, 1982, 46-7.

66 Ibid.

67 J.D. Wilson, "Multicultural Programmes," 67.

68 N.S. Human Rights Commission.

69 Pratt, "Bias in Textbooks," 155.

70 Ontario Ministry of Education, *Race, Religion and Culture* 12, 16-7.

71 Pratt, "Bias in Textbooks," 155-8.

72 Ibid., 158-64.

73 Roe, 38; Kehoe, "Achieving Goals."

74 Renaud, 35-6.

75 B and B Commission, Book II, *Education,* 128.

76 Allison, 106-9.

77 Ibid., 110.

78 See More, 32; Jaenen, "Mutilated," 86. For a useful survey of Native education see Canada, Department of Indian Affairs and Northern Development, *Indian Conditions — A Survey,* Ottawa, 1980.

79 Cited in Martin and Macdonell, 239-40.

80 Mackenzie Valley Pipeline Inquiry.

81 Robinson, "Curriculum," 222-4.

82 Northwest Territories Legislative Council.

83 The Hope Report, 124.

84 Ibid 27; Fleming, III, *Schools,* 14.

85 Fleming, III, *Schools,* 27, 29-30.

86 Janzen, 50-3.

87 Seeley *et al, Crestwood Heights,* 239-43.

88 Ibid.

89 Ontario Department of Education, *Religious Information,* 15-6.

90 See Sawyer. See also review by Anne Roche of this autobiographical account of teaching in an outport near Gander, *Books in Canada,* no.1, (January, 1980), 10-11.

91 Ontario Department, *Religious Information,* 93-5.

92 Ibid., 63.

93 Cragg; Hare, 17-18; W. Ryan, 21-2.

94 Daniels and Oliver, "Values Education," 223-5.

95 For a critique of Kohlberg, Beck and other approaches to values education see Gow, 59-73.

96 Ibid., 97, 102-4.

97 See R.J. Clark *et al, Issues,* 59-61.

98 Wright in Connors *et al,* 116-7.

99 Cochrane and Williams, 1-5, 10-13.

100 Daniels and Oliver, "Values Education," 213.

101 See Cochrane and Williams, 6; Gow, 141.

102 Daniels and Oliver, "Values Education," 228.

103 See *Toronto Globe and Mail,* November 21, 1981.

104 Daniels and Oliver, "Values Education," 223-4.

105 Lazerson and J.D. Wilson, "Historical," 98.

106 Ibid., 105.

107 Bargen, 13, 16, 19.

108 Thiessen and L.G.R. Wilson.

109 Erickson *et al*, 12, 19.

110 Cooper cited in Martin and Macdonell, 236.

111 J.D. Wilson, "Religion," 106.

112 Ibid., 109.

113 Simon, 2.

114 Guldemond, 4.

115 Martin and Macdonell, 159.

116 Personal communication to the author from E.K. Hawkesworth, Deputy Minister of Education, Alberta, April 1, 1981.

117 *MacLean's Magazine,* February 23, 1981, 31.

# CHAPTER 17

# THE ELEMENTARY
# AND THE HIGH SCHOOL
# IN A NEW ERA

*... the curricular and pedagogical arrangements of the elementary school have an important role to play in the elimination of deficits and the achievement of equality of educational opportunity.*

*(OECD, 1976)*

*[The] adaptation of the [Ontario high] schools has been a smooth and orderly process, in tune not only with the interests of students, but also with the interests of the politicians, the economists and the public ...*

*(O. Hall and R. Carlton, 1977)*

The modest elementary school revision of the 1930s continued into the post-war period. At the high school level, academic aims remained dominant, with scholarship and character stressed; this was in contrast to the social aims of the American high school. According to Stamp, wartime and post-war circumstances in Ontario led to a more conservative environment that, by the 1950s, bore more resemblance to the environment of the 1920s than to that of the depression decade.[1]

During the twenty years following 1960, a new curriculum lexicon appeared. It featured such terms as language experience, the integrated day, continuous progress, cuisenaire rods, new math, discovery learning, inquiry methods, immersion French, second language English, Nuffield science, values education, multi-media packages, Kodaly music, computer literacy, family life education, pre-schooling, team teaching, non-grading and open area classrooms. Innovations occurred within the frameworks of provincial educational systems that increasingly possessed a common structural pattern. As the accompanying chart shows, excluding kindergarten, seven provinces defined elementary schooling in terms of six grades; British Columbia utilized a seven grade system and Ontario and Prince Edward Island eight grades.[2] Increasingly, at all levels the structures had become more similar. All provinces except New Brunswick and Prince Edward Island had free public kindergartens by 1980. Except in Quebec and

Newfoundland, high school graduation occurred at the end of Grade 12. In Ontario Grade 13 was a unique honour graduation year. Newfoundland planned to extend secondary schooling to Grade 12 and Ontario considered the phasing out of Grade 13 during the 1980s.

## The Changing Elementary School

### Early Childhood Education

Pre-school and kindergarten education constituted one level at which there was significant development during the 1940s. E.J.M. Church's 1950 nation-wide survey showed that 70 per cent of the institutions he identified had been established following the outbreak of war, as a response to war-time conditions. Nursery schools and day nurseries were mostly under private auspices. Kindergartens, mostly publicly supported, were intended to serve a broad range of objectives, covering physical and social skills, habits of order, regularity and neatness, co-operative and responsible attitudes, and broadening children's awareness and appreciation of their environment through observations and investigation. Particular attention was given to "articulation," or readiness for formal instruction. Additionally, the development of personality was emphasized through free and spontaneous expressive activities utilizing language, music and rhythmic instruction. Daily activities included music, rhythms, language or discussions, stories and handwork. Most programs included free play and rest periods, medical inspection, dramatizations, individual and group routines and outdoor play.[3]

To ensure "articulation" in preparation for entry to the primary grades, some provinces prescribed definite areas of learning corresponding to those of elementary curricula. Ontario identified seven areas: health, safety and physical development; English; social studies and citizenship; natural sciences; arithmetic; music; arts and crafts. Although these divisions were formal, the teaching was largely indirect and informal, Church claimed. Nevertheless, the pattern suggested how, as noted earlier, formalism extended into the lower grades, in contrast to the hopes of reformers who had expected to see Froebelianism extended upward. It also suggested that the orderly routines of Blatz's "security theory" had more influence on Canadian preschool education than Freudian or other "free" pedagogy.[4] Corbett's 1967 Ontario study confirmed the emphasis on formalistic readiness in kindergarten programs, which was combined with a Froebelian bias that had, however, lost its metaphysical dimension based on God-man-nature unity and harmony. Corbett reported that the kindergarten retained its role as the initial mediator between the home and the school. The OECD Examiners expressed concern that many kindergarten teachers were not well enough trained for their special tasks, and that upgrading programs were much needed.[5]

**Comparison of Provincial Organization of Grades**

| | 1 | 2 | 3 | 4 | 5 | 6 | 7 | 8 | 9 | 10 | 11 | 12 | 13 | YEAR OF STUDY |
|---|---|---|---|---|---|---|---|---|---|---|---|---|---|---|
| K | ELEMENTARY | | | | | | SECONDARY<br>Junior \| Senior<br>High \| High | | | | | | | BRITISH COLUMBIA |
| K | ELEMENTARY | | | | | | SECONDARY<br>Junior High \| Senior High | | | | | | | ALBERTA |
| K | ELEMENTARY<br>Division 1 \| Division 2 | | | | | | SECONDARY<br>Division 3 \| Division 4 | | | | | | | SASKATCHEWAN |
| K | ELEMENTARY | | | | | | SECONDARY<br>Junior High \| Senior High | | | | | | | MANITOBA |
| K | ELEMENTARY | | | | | | | SECONDARY | | | | | | ONTARIO |
| K | ELEMENTARY | | | | | | SECONDARY | | | | | | | QUEBEC |
| | ELEMENTARY | | | | | | SECONDARY<br>Junior High \| Senior High | | | | | | | NEW BRUNSWICK |
| Pr | ELEMENTARY | | | | | | SECONDARY<br>Junior High \| Senior High | | | | | | | NOVA SCOTIA |
| | ELEMENTARY | | | | | | | SECONDARY | | | | | | PRINCE EDWARD ISLAND |
| K | ELEMENTARY | | | | | | SECONDARY | | | | | | | NEWFOUNDLAND |

K – Kindergarten
Pr – Primary
Source: T.E. Giles. Used with permission.

As noted in Chapter 13, preschool enrolments burgeoned after 1960. The increasing emphasis on an educational component in programs was especially aimed at providing a head start for the disadvantaged. In 1973, Ryan reported various stimulation programs designed to provide visual, tactile and auditory stimulation for disadvantaged infants. One project included the study of teaching techniques and the development of curriculum guides and materials for infants aged up to thirty months. In 1970, the Canadian Welfare Council had sampled 491 programs in day nurseries, nursery schools and private kindergartens. Although basically performing a parenting function, staff in all these facilities were assuming more formal educational roles despite their frequently inadequate qualifications. Ryan noted a concern in some quarters about an overemphasis on academic and intellectual development, to the neglect of social and emotional development. Evaluation, including longitudinal assessment, was badly needed.[6]

## The Open and Closed Classroom

A cautious obeisance to progressive principles in the elementary school of the 1940s was evident in the recognition in Ontario's Hope Report of 1950 of the trend to the education of "the whole child." The report proposed various measures to modify the undesirable "single, uniform, strictly graded curriculum." For all pupils there should be a minimum core of skills and knowledge "to be attainable with reasonable success . . . ." This would be augmented by what was called "a supplement" for pupils of average ability, an "enriched supplement" for the above average and "special educational treatment" for the "markedly atypical," — the seriously below average.[7]

A year before the Hope Report appeared, Ontario's Minister of Education, Dana Porter, introduced the Porter Plan. It embraced a two-divisional (primary and junior) six grade system. A new intermediate division (Grades 7, 8 and 9) continued to recognize the first two of these grades as elementary, in recognition of the fact that, constitutionally, Roman Catholics had the right to tax support for the first eight years of separate schooling. The new divisions were curricular rather than administrative or structural, and thus defused potential political-religious conflict.[8]

After 1950, a new minister, W.J. Dunlop, advanced the anti-progressive line referred to earlier. Dunlop attacked fads that encouraged "self-expression and day dreaming" and that "were slowly giving the taxpayer the impression that he was contributing to psychological laboratories rather than schools." Yet, how little progressive ideas had penetrated Ontario classrooms, apart from a few suburban communities such as "Crestwood Heights," and how far a nineteenth century ethos continued to pervade rural classrooms during these years, was apparent in an approving account that an American writer, John Keats, gave of his children's experience in a two-room rural school in eastern Ontario in 1953-55.[9]

Keats found the contrast with the humane, luxurious, consolidated school his children attended in Maryland to be striking. The atmosphere of Rockport school with its four red-brick walls and two small rooms with interior decoration painted by the parents themselves was spartan. The pupils sat at fixed rows of desks in classrooms totally lacking modern facilities and learning aids. The setting was remarkably like that of Ernest Buckler's Nova Scotia school of the 1920s described in Chapter 10. Boys and girls entered in lines by separate doors, remaining standing in line while the teacher bade them good morning. Keats' children were amazed to see a pupil struck by a leather switch for having botched her lesson. The school was like a drill field where the children were paraded at command, taught by rote methods and required to do homework. Such a regimen was unknown in progressive Maryland, but to Keats the Rockport school was far more effective in teaching solid information and in developing competence in the three Rs, particularly in essay writing. An itinerant music teacher also taught the pupils to read music and sing songs. Keats reported, after a return visit to Rockport in 1963, that schooling had remained virtually unchanged in a decade.

Keats' account confirms Stamp's observation that, for most Ontario post-war elementary school pupils, the school experience was similar to that of their parents. Urban children attended classes in schools that, apart from their larger size and facilities such as libraries and gymnasia, were very similar to that of Rockport. Silent, totally teacher-directed classes in which marks came in carefully worked-out percentages seemed a far cry from those that had been envisioned by reformers hardly more than a decade before. After eight or nine years in such a carefully monitored environment, successful pupils were recommended by their principals for entrance into high school.[10]

Despite the persisting formalism and moralism of the elementary school, secular, socializing, humanizing influences were becoming evident by 1950. Seeley and Sim described the "Human Relations Classes" which they conducted as a part of their Forest Hill experiment in suburban Toronto and reported in *Crestwood Heights*. Based on a free discussion method, the classes were not intended to provide "thinly disguised Sunday School lessons." Neither the teacher nor the school was to have a previously determined objective or goal to be achieved by the end of the teaching period. One result of this group-directed experience was that visitors to the classes were "at first somewhat dismayed by the seemingly chaotic nature of some of the discussions." Those who stayed on for several sessions were usually impressed, claimed the authors, by the "clear, critical thinking" which began to emerge.[11]

The mental hygiene view of education that brought mental health and schooling together in the interest of personality and character development was disseminated by a training program that involved thirty-five teachers from all provinces.[12] To be sure, the schools of Forest Hill Village in which the program had been conducted were far from typical of the period, but their ethos was a harbinger of the change that would gradually come to most Canadian elementary schools after 1960. The earlier formalism noted by Sutherland would be attenuated, though by no means entirely lost, while the harsh discipline would be considerably modified. The shift of the ethos of the school was becoming apparent in school buildings and facilities. As the authors of *Crestwood Heights* put it, "Where the old type of school was a monument to the efficacy of learning in a puritanically ugly environment, the new school stressed social learning in an atmosphere of lightness, colour and accepted, self-conscious modernity." While most children still attended old type schools in the 1950s, new buildings constructed to accommodate the post-war baby boom were far brighter, better equipped and more luxurious.[13] Appropriately enough for children being trained for an emerging consumer society, new suburban schools increasingly resembled shopping centres.

By the mid-1950s, the reaction against progressivism was leading to the subject-centred curriculum reform discussed in Chapter 14. Although emphasis was initially placed on secondary reform, the new math focussed on change in the elementary curriculum. The activity tradition of the elementary school made it, at least in theory, more amenable to the new "discovery" teaching. Less public dissatisfaction with elementary schooling, together with a curriculum that was more developmentally and less academically oriented also probably enhanced receptivity to change.

Probably the most publicized innovation in the elementary school after 1960 was the open area (or open plan) classroom. An innovation launched without prior research, it was later justified, not usually very convincingly, on the basis of *ex post facto* research. A shift to open-plan construction had begun in Canadian schools in 1966; by 1968 most boards had some form of open plan in their new schools. A variety of open plans, some combined with traditional closed classrooms, were identified in a 1973 CEA survey. The largest open area described included fourteen classes in a completely open space.[14]

Many virtues, mostly social rather than intellectual, were claimed for the open area approach. These included informal personal relations and more interaction among pupils; more self-discipline and independence; and more learning opportunities arising from greater teacher co-operation, exposure to specialist and resource people and more individual attention. Critics pointed to less flexibility and more distractions than had been anticipated. Characteristic of most innovations, the system was based on the questionable assumption that all children would benefit equally from it. Teachers made little effort to develop common goals, and there was rarely sufficient time for consultation and co-operative planning. Very little was known about the extent and effectiveness of team teaching. Critics were especially vocal about the lack of evaluation studies.[15] On the crucial question of academic achievement, a 1977 Ontario study indicated that traditional classrooms were more effective than open classrooms in disadvantaged neighbourhoods.[16] However, other studies in Ontario and in Alberta indicated general teacher satisfaction with the approach.

The era of royal commissions and other inquiries cited earlier paved the way for curriculum change in the elementary schools throughout the period. In British Columbia, the 1961 Chant Report assumed an anti-progressive stance in questioning the over-emphasis on the doctrine of interest. In place of a multiplicity of aims, Chant posited intellectual development as "the primary or general aim" of British Columbia's schools. Intellectual development, interpreted as the acquisition of factual knowledge, would be restored to British Columbia schools through a reorganization of the curriculum into three categories: the "central subjects", of the three Rs; the "inner subjects", of social studies, science and languages other than English; and the "outer subjects," of art, music, physical education, home economics, industrial arts, commercial subjects, agriculture and drama. The kind of intellectual development that Chant advocated was very different from discovery-oriented curriculum reform that emphasized independent thinking.[17]

In eastern Canada, reports by Parent in Quebec and Warren in Newfoundland reflected the need of both provinces to modernize their nineteenth century elementary curricula. Parent's recommendation of a system of nursery schools and kindergartens resulted in a sixfold increase in kindergarten enrolment by 1968. As a result of revised notions of child rearing in Quebec, preschooling was now accepted as a supplement to the family's role rather than as an encroachment on it.[18] Parent proposed two cycles of co-educational elementary schooling "conceived in accordance with the spirit, the principles and the techniques of the activist (that is, active experience) school."[19]

Warren recommended a system of kindergartens followed by a six year two-cycle plan similar to that of Quebec. His forty-three recommendations emphasized Brunerian principles, skill development, physical education and good health habits, and a broad cultural bill of fare that included such subjects as children's literature, art, music and French. Warren recognized that such an expanded curriculum would require a variety of teaching materials, new pedagogies and a major upgrading of a teaching force that on average possessed no more than a high school education.[20]

In Ontario, the Hall-Dennis inquiry made its greatest impact at the elementary school level. Phillips' visits to classrooms nearly a decade after the publication of *Living and Learning* convinced him that the curriculum was by then far removed from the course content and authorized textbooks of earlier times. He described Cherokee Public School in North York, an open area, friendly, relaxed informal school with large murals on the walls that had been painted by Indian artists as the pupils watched. "The library was as informal as could be, with not only books but live creatures, includ-, ing two boa constrictors." A former student had written Phillips to describe the elementary school in which he directed library research, taught French daily, along with volleyball and a recorder group and also conducted numerous field trips. Although mathematics, spelling and grammar seemed to be going out of style, he reported that "I sneak [them] in daily." This teacher observed that "The hard part is attending the thousands of meetings — we are never given time to implement the ideas."[21]

Phillips was reporting a new flexibility that partly reflected a more relaxed moral outlook among Canadians in a more permissive and pluralistic society. The same outlook could be detected in Alberta's Worth Report, which was somewhat reminiscent of that province's 1930s progressivism. The new outlook was illustrated by Ontario's 1975 statement of elementary school goals summarized in *The Formative Years*, a document that was backed up by a longer, 111-page statement, *Education in the Primary and Junior Divisions*.[22] Neither publication gave any lists of solid content, but described learning experiences ostensibly designed to permit mastery of the three Rs. Ontario's "approach to curriculum" was based on careful planning designed to meet pupil needs through a "cyclic review process" involving not only administrators and teachers, but thousands of Ontario citizens whose views were solicited through discussions, surveys and briefs. Phillips commented that it was no wonder that twenty-five professionals were required in the Ministry's Curriculum Branch. "To produce, understand or interpret material of this kind is no job for one human being."[23]

Despite the commitment to change, an equal commitment to stability was evident in Ontario's curriculum documents. Of eighteen pages of statements in *The Formative Years* detailing what children were to master, eleven were devoted to the three Rs. Most traditional subject areas were recognizable. More contemporary were such headings as "values," "decision-making" and "Canadian studies."

The same continuing commitment to stability was evident in other provinces by the late 1970s. Quebec's 1979 "Plan of Action" emphasized the definition and reinforcement of "terminal educational objectives" and "the consolidation of things learned" together with evaluation at the end of each cycle "by means of appropriate instruments." The weekly time to be devoted to each subject was specified. By 1980 in Nova Scotia, seventy per cent of the allotted time in the primary grades was devoted to language arts and mathematics.[24]

There was some paradox in the co-existence of "permissive" elementary schools and the burgeoning "back to basics" movement. The latter trend sparked a new interest in teaching behaviour that focussed on improving classroom management, on the more efficient use of lesson time, or "time on task," and on the improvement of basic teaching skills. Positive change was most evident in the acceptance of the concept of continuous progress which had contributed to the virtual disappearance of grade and age retardation as universal promotion, or what some critics called "social promotion" became the norm. Here was the clearest and most easily documented change of any during the period. After 1970, various urban school boards across Canada established a number of alternative elementary schools, several of which featured co-operative curriculum planning by parents and teachers. Most such schools espoused distinctive philosophies that permitted curricular emphases varying from the three Rs to the fine arts.

The best summation of elementary school trends was provided by the OECD Examiners in 1976. They praised the new flexibility of curricula. The Examiners were particularly impressed with the primary level, Grades 1 to 3 in most provinces, although they felt that possibly too many approaches were being tried with too little evaluation. Classrooms were characterized by a friendly relaxed atmosphere that encouraged individual initiative and co-operation. They praised the individualism of programs while pointing out that if such programs were based on "incompletely understood instruments" there was a danger of building in irreversible forms of selection and ability and streaming. Many teachers had not yet come to terms with the new approaches and many parents could not see why their children needed more than the basic skills.[25]

## The Changing High School

### Conflicting Trends in the Curriculum

Since the turn of the century, the Canadian high school had been the focus of debate and controversy arising from concerns about what its central purposes should be. Since 1900, the high school continued to affirm its academic tradition, while bowing stiffly to the importunities of vocational demands, progressive impulses and the new social challenges posed by expanding enrolments. After 1950, explosive expansion conflicted with new academic pressures engendered by the cold war. At this time, there emerged a youth sub-culture of unique dress and hair styles: ducktail haircuts, white bobby socks, loafers and pony-tails. By now, television was beginning to make a significant impact. Yet youth were charged with being apathetic, unadventurous and conformist, characteristics that were also evident in classrooms where teaching remained based on traditional methods of recitation, memorization and frequent testing.[26]

Criticisms of the high school curriculum received by a Manitoba Legislative Committee in 1945 centred around problems of equality of opportunity and relevance to life. Yet differentiation had not been successful for, despite the provision of options, the academic tradition reigned supreme "even in the face of a persistent demand for a more realistic and more relevant program." Despite criticisms, the influence of academic tradition was understandable, the committee felt. It conferred status. The matriculation course, "traditionally academic and remote as it may be" continued to hold sway because it demanded something of value — "an attitude of mind, a quality of spirit or determination, of willingness to work, however uncongenial the task may be." For the employer, the course acted as a sieve which made high school graduates preferable to students "who have not been able to make the grade." For teachers, the matriculation course with its "orderly and progressive" subjects formed a "definite synthesis" that told them exactly what to teach and enabled them easily to test the success of their efforts. As an alternative to the matriculation course, the committee recommended a modest degree of differentiation "not [to] be carried too far" by means of a "common core" of studies similar to that already established in Alberta and British Columbia.[27]

In Ontario during the 1940s, a notable high school trend was the organization of district high schools which replaced the old continuation schools. Thus did rural teenagers begin to share the high school experience of their urban friends. The yellow school bus, which became ubiquitous in all the provinces during the 1950s, symbolized the urbanization of the rural school. Administered separately from elementary schools in new high school districts, the new schools, each accommodating 300 to 400 pupils, brought better educational opportunity to rural pupils through the broader curricula and better facilities available in modern buildings. As they began shortly to serve three quarters of Southern Ontario's rural areas, school attendance increased at double the rate of that of urban areas, even though the rural population was declining.[28] Another factor that promoted increased enrolments in Ontario and most other provinces by 1950 was the abolition of high school fees.

Ontario's Hope Commission of 1950 echoed the same academic conservatism of the Manitoba Legislative Committee noted above. The Commission proposed no earth-shaking changes in the high school program.

While the "experience concept" was appropriate to the early elementary grades, beyond that level "the teacher and pupil have little time for thinking of life situations ... and must address themselves for most of the day to the study of subject matter organized in separate categories." The traditional subjects emphasizing definite facts and values "should receive increasing emphasis through the school and should occupy nearly all the time of students after approximately the age of sixteen."[29]

In 1949, a year before the Hope Commission reported, the Porter Plan organized the Ontario curriculum on the basis of four divisions that it still maintains, primary (Grades 1 to 3), junior (4 to 6), intermediate (7 to 10) and senior (11 to 13). The high school entrance examination was abolished. The new intermediate division, designed to reduce the sharp separation between elementary and secondary education, provided terminal courses for students leaving high school at age sixteen. An intermediate diploma had been established for these students a decade earlier. Both steps were a recognition of the increasing diversity and holding power of the high school and of the needs of those adolescents who, while staying in school longer, were still enrolling in less academic programs and leaving before graduation to enter the labour force. The trend was evident nationally although most pupils — 75 per cent in Ontario — still dropped out.

An interesting feature of the Porter Plan was the encouragement of voluntary local responsibility for curriculum development which foreshadowed more ambitious efforts twenty years later. For the first time in Ontario's history, local administrators and teachers were to have control over course content in order to meet local needs. The ideal, as one teacher leader put it, was that no longer would a few subject-matter experts meeting briefly in Toronto construct courses of study for miners' children in Red Lake. Through an elaborate system of committees in every subject area, more than 1200 revised courses were developed by 1952. Yet, despite initial enthusiastic teacher response, the plan proved short-lived due to the opposition of W.J. Dunlop, the new Minister of Education, lack of sufficient support by the department, inadequate local consultation and the general haste with which it had been implemented.[30] Fleming thought that the plan failed because local needs did not vary greatly from one part of Ontario to another. Decentralized curriculum development was less valuable for producing new courses than for improving the skills of teachers.[31]

A 1950 survey of the Ontario senior secondary curriculum indicated that English, mathematics and foreign languages, including Latin, continued to dominate Grade 12 and 13 offerings, although science had improved its status as had Grade 12 history.[32] In Atlantic Canada, Newfoundland essentially lacked a true high school system outside St. John's. The entry of the province into Confederation in 1949 led to a broadening of high school curricula in the early 1950s and to the establishment of regional high schools as a result of federal assistance for vocational education.[33] Nova Scotia and New Brunswick also established regional high schools in rural areas on the model of the composite high schools established elsewhere. New Brunswick and Prince Edward Island established twelve-grade school systems on a 6-3-3 plan.[34] Curricula in all these provinces remained prescriptive but some revisions of high school curricula were attempted.

Protestant Quebec was not dissimilar from other provinces. On the Catholic side the classical colleges were an outstanding example of a persisting nineteenth century classical curriculum.[35] A breakthrough had been made in the 1950s when high schools were permitted to offer the classical course,[36] but secondary education remained essentially confined to the colleges, which continued to be the training ground for the Quebec social and political elite.

For the 1935-45 decade, high school curriculum change in the western provinces continued the trends noted earlier. Although university matriculation courses continued to dominate, the integration of academic and practical subjects proceeded more successfully in these provinces than anywhere else. In British Columbia, for example, practical electives had equal status with academic offerings, which enabled matriculants to include them as options in their programs. Continuing its emphasis on character education and social adjustment, in 1950 the province introduced a course in "effective living" (later called "health and personal development") that combined elements of health, physical education, guidance, mental health and sex education, this last disguised as "home and family living."[37]

Despite the various national studies that had been launched to consider social and individual needs engendered by the Depression and World War II, the immediate post-war period proved to be one of comparative curriculum stability. The expansion of formal guidance services was one of the few significant innovations. Canadian schooling at all levels remained notably non-experimental. Although Hilda Neatby's *So Little for the Mind* stimulated a vigorous public debate on the merits of progressivism which paralleled a similar debate in the United States, serious policy alternatives were lacking.[38] There were no counterparts in Canada to such studies as *Education for All American Youth* (1944), *General Education in a Free Society* (The Harvard Report, 1945) and James B. Conant's *The American High School Today* (1959) which influenced curriculum policy in the United States. These studies did attract some attention in Canada, but were less influential than Bruner's *The Process of Education*.

As Canadian educators cautiously began for the first time to face up to the phenomenon of mass education during the 1950s, growing pressures for curriculum change caused some to hark back to a pre-war golden age. There was some irony in the fact that, although such critics as Neatby condemned the alleged academic slackness of the high schools of the 1950s, that decade would itself later be seen during the turbulent decades to follow as a golden age of student docility, curriculum stability and scholastic rigour. After 1960, conflicts of purpose were exacerbated in the high school. As in the elementary school, permissiveness and conservatism coexisted uneasily. Conflicts were underscored by the retention and expansion of the high school's most widely acknowledged traditional role, that of university preparation, and the growth of a stronger vocational role. Despite the growth of vocationalism, a growing custodial role paradoxically served the purpose of delaying student entry into an overcrowded labour market. Finally, many now expected the high school's traditional moral role to be filled by values education.

Writing in the early 1960s, Downey saw the Canadian high school as characterized by a state of ferment rarely witnessed before. Unfortunately, innovations often lacked any conceptual framework, relatedness and purpose, characteristics which probably contributed to their short life.[39] As "streams" and "tracks" had become the norm in curricula, and as programs became vocationalized and specialized, the concept of a general education for all was lost.[40] General education became an ambiguous term. In its classical liberal sense general education was seen as appropriate for the able but not for the less able student. As applied to specific courses, such as general mathematics, or to programs, it acquired connotations of academic inferiority.[41]

In no province during the period were contrary pressures and dilemmas more apparent than in Ontario. Academic curriculum reform, vocationalism and neo-progressive change all made a major impact. Administrative reorganization led to a reduction in the traditional separation of elementary and secondary curricula as both types of school came under single county school boards. The adoption of the credit system, whereby students could accumulate freely chosen course credits in place of former prescribed programs of courses, brought Ontario into line with the western provinces and contributed to a high degree of organizational uniformity across Canada. Individualized programs made possible by the system and by computer technology permitted students in effect to construct their own courses of study. In Grades 12 and 13, they could select a combined total of thirty-three credits, with the sole requirement that three courses be selected from each of four designated areas: communications, social sciences, pure and applied sciences, and arts. All courses were offered at five levels of difficulty, ranging from remedial to advanced. No longer did students have to repeat courses already passed. A failed course could be repeated at a different level.[42]

Despite fears that students would choose soft options, a degree of essentialism was retained in the new system. Enrolments remained steady in English and mathematics and increased in the sciences, although some decline occurred in history and languages. Post-secondary admission requirements remained prime determinants of course choices, although the universities were forced to modify their entrance criteria and to depend more on individual schools to define readiness for advanced study. The high school became more developmentally-oriented, acquiring, at least temporarily, some of the characteristics of the elementary school.[43]

The merits and limitations of the new dispensation could be seen in the flexible system of interdisciplinary, work-study and independent-learning courses used in York County's *avant garde* Thornlea High School. Highly motivated students were able to dig deeply into their work, while others skipped classes with abandon. Students could be seen at any time of the day in their carpeted lounge studying, playing cards, strumming guitars or chatting. To some teachers such permissiveness reduced standards, while to others the reverse was true. One high school principal complained that the system had changed his role from that of an educational leader to "being the manager of a supermarket."[44] Other critics charged that instructional time had been reduced, flexibility of choice was offset by inflexible timetabling, students lost the security of a "homeroom," the value of a high school diploma had been debased, guidance counsellors were overworked, students were alienated, and teachers felt insecure.[45]

Hall and Carlton confirmed the apprehension of many critics and threw considerable light on the impact of curriculum change in Ontario's high schools. The school had adapted to a more heterogeneous, affluent clientele by means of an exploding curriculum characterized by course marketing and similar consumption styles. As students became arbiters of the curriculum, subject or course enrolments emerged as important new controls. At the same time social and personal development goals became as important as academic goals. The phenomenon of part-time student employment led to startling changes in students' academic workloads and attitudes. Again the school reacted to change by adapting to it with a reduction in homework, a policy consistent with the changing work ethic in society.[46]

Hall and Carlton reported that some high school teachers were disillusioned by the permissiveness of the new system, blaming the elementary schools and the universities for academic decline. The latter had diluted their standards and lowered student expectations. Nevertheless, teachers viewed their best students as competent as ever. Students, for their part, were highly critical of the radical inconsistency in the values and practices of the teaching to which they were exposed, especially in language instruction. Spelling, writing and grammar skills were virtually ignored by some teachers but emphasized by others. To the students, learning and remedial provisions appeared to have been the school's most successful response to the "basic skills" crisis. They did not always appreciate the anti-establishment views of some teachers and guidance counsellors whose non-directive stance implied a disparagement of academic competence.[47]

Changes similar to those in Ontario were occurring in the other provinces. In Quebec, the old classical colleges that did not become CEGEPS became secondary schools. The gradual loss of autonomy of the colleges, and curriculum changes that heralded the decline of a classical course of study that dated from the establishment of the famous Jesuit College de Quebec in 1635 marked a major stage in the modernization of Quebec education. The resulting trauma was indicated by a 1963 statement of the Federation des Colleges classiques. Noting that the ancient languages had been at the root of Quebec's classical curriculum, the Federation insisted that *"given the Latin origin of our people and the necessity to fight for our cultural survival"* [emphasis in original], it was necessary "for the active elite of the French-Canadian nation to remain in contact with Latin ... or with one or the other of the ancient languages."[48] In the event, an attempt was made in the new "polyvalent" (composite) high schools to maintain a curriculum balance consistent with the province's humanistic tradition. The Parent Report recommended a tripartite organization of arts of expression, the natural and social sciences and "the overall training of the individual" through practical studies and physical, moral, civic and religious education. Grades 7 and 8 became a two-year exploratory cycle followed by a more specialized one covering Grades 9, 10 and 11. As in Ontario, individualization required decentralization; inspection was "an obsolete function" and should be replaced by local supervision. Guidance was a cornerstone of the new system. Provincial examinations were retained, although in modified form.[49]

In Newfoundland in the 1960s, the Warren Commission, utilizing British terminology of an "O" level curriculum for average and below average students and an "A" level matriculation program for abler students, proposed three types of program. A basic program containing English, history, mathematics and science courses was proposed for all students; restricted options emphasizing languages and the sciences and required prerequisite study should be open to academically inclined students; open options including home economics, music, art, and industrial arts should be offered to others. A terminal program ending in Grade 10 or 11 was also recommended.[50] In 1979, a task force study recommended a credit system and two-year course sequences at the senior level, which was shortly extended to Grade 12.[51]

By 1980 Nova Scotia had adopted a credit system. As in Newfoundland, curricula were organized according to the presumed ability and probable destination of students. Two cycles of high schooling included a junior high school with standard and "adjusted" programs, the latter designed for students "with somewhat limited demonstrated ability to handle abstract learning." At the senior high school level, High School Completion, i.e., academic and secondary vocational programs were established, the latter offered in regional vocational schools.[52]

In western Canada, high school curriculum change took an initial conservative direction under the Chant proposals in British Columbia. Chant's concept of "central", "inner" and "outer" subjects noted earlier for the elementary curriculum was more applicable to the high school.[53] Concurrent with Bruner-like curriculum change, six types of high school program were identified: Academic-Technical (for university-bound students), Commercial, Industrial, Community Services, Visual and Performing Arts, and Occupational. British Columbia maintained the highest secondary school graduation rate of any province but, like others, it was far from free of dropout problems and of elitist distinctions among programs.

Elsewhere in western Canada, by the late 1960s, Hall-Dennis style curriculum change was evident in some quarters. A Regina composite high school similar to Toronto's Thornlea High School was described by an ecstatic Toronto columnist as "the brightest flower among Canada's secondary schools." Interestingly enough, this avant-garde institution which stressed team teaching, continuous progress, "steadily increasing student freedom" and the downplaying of examinations was under the control of the Roman Catholic Separate School Board. The board's director had become enamoured of innovation as a result of visits to similar institutions in Nova Scotia, Florida, Nevada and California.[54] Like its Ontario counterpart, the Regina school was far from representative of Canadian institutions, most of which remained structured and relatively tightly controlled. On balance, more relaxed attitudes rather than radical changes *per se* characterized Canadian high schools during the 1960s.

The OECD report indicated that Canadian secondary schools had developed some good models, but that these had been poorly disseminated. In comparison with some other nations, comprehensive secondary schooling was relatively well accepted in Canada. The examiners were critical of large impersonal high schools in which excessive and premature specialization caused students to commute among subject-based departments as early as the age of twelve. They were also critical of variations in graduation standards and grade standards among the provinces, which exacerbated the difficulty of establishing equivalence on a national scale.[55]

## The High School and the Renewed Search for Purpose

Many critics deplored the lack of curriculum uniformity consequent upon decentralization to which they attributed the alleged decline in high school standards. Others claimed that university-bound students were still gaining a traditional academic preparation.[56] Research by Nyberg and Lee, commissioned by the CEA in 1978 and stimulated in part by declining Scholastic Aptitude (SAT) scores in the United States, reported mixed views by school administrators of academic standards in Canadian high schools. In the absence of any national measures, the study had been forced to draw on provincial and local research.[57]

The facilitation of student transfer among the provinces had long been an argument advanced for national curricular uniformity. The Council of Ministers' Secondary School Transfer Guide, published during the late 1970s, was designed to ensure that the educational development of students moving from province to province would be as continuous as possible. Course descriptions for all provinces were provided in English, French, social studies, mathematics and science. This useful compendium indicated the terminology, course system, credit requirements, examinations and grading practices, patterns of school and curriculum organization and high school graduation requirements of every province. Fairly detailed course comparison information was provided which indicated a significant degree of uniformity in various subject areas.[58]

While some critics deplored a lack of uniformity, others criticized the lack of diversity. The latter was exemplified by the absence of specialized secondary institutions apart from commercial and vocational high schools of often dubious prestige. The typical comprehensive, all purpose, multi-program North American high school found its epitome in Canada, which had nothing comparable to such elite institutions as New York's Bronx High School of Science or specialized American schools for the arts. By the late 1970s, greater diversity was becoming apparent, spurred in part by concern about the education of the gifted. The Earl Haig Secondary School for the Arts in North York, Ontario, was one of the most notable specialized institutions in the country. Together with the Claude Watson School of the Arts, an elementary institution, it offered artistic training in dramatic and visual arts and in music and dance to selected students in conjunction with a balanced academic program that extended from Grades 4 through 13. Taught by highly talented teacher specialists, the curriculum also provided exposure to professionals in the visual and performing arts and took advantage of the wealth of cultural opportunities in Metropolitan Toronto through visits to galleries, concerts and theatrical performances.[59] By 1980, two more similar schools were being planned in Metropolitan Toronto. At this time, upwards of twenty schools, most of them public institutions, in six provinces were offering or planning to offer the International Baccalaureate Program. Based in the schools of several nations, the program offered a culturally enriched highly academic curriculum to selected senior high school students.[60]

A related trend to diversity could be seen in the growth of so-called alternative schools, most of which were small units or mini-schools located within or attached to regular public secondary schools. A 1982 survey in the United States that included Canadian schools identified 2500 alternative schools across North America and concluded that, despite a conservative trend, the alternative movement was alive and well.[61] Thirty-seven Canadian schools were identified, of which twenty-one were located in Vancouver and the balance in Ontario, mostly in Metropolitan Toronto. Alternatives ranged from schools for students with learning, emotional or other adjustment problems to those for the academically and artistically talented or for those seeking to acquire a second language facility. The survey did not include religiously oriented so-called values schools such as those within Alberta's public school system discussed in Chapter 16.

By this time, general concerns about the high school and its curriculum were being expressed across North America, many of them reminiscent of those that had been voiced during the Sputnik era a generation earlier. Proposals for change ranged from those calling for greater individualization of curricula to others calling for the restoration of uniformity to a system in which individualization was said to reign supreme and in which a traditional general educational function had been subverted. To some critics, instructional practices had changed little since 1900. Teachers went about their business in roughly similar ways and classrooms had changed only slowly over time. This view was not necessarily contradicted by the claim that as inconsistent reforms had accumulated side by side, programs and curricula grew increasingly incoherent.[62]

How far any of these generalizations applied to Canadian high schools was difficult to determine, but trends similar to those south of the border were clearly discernible. Hodgetts' investigation of Canadian Studies and a later study of science education by the Science Council of Canada suggested that teachers continued to follow traditional instructional practices.[63] This conclusion seemed to be confirmed by evidence of the widely acknowledged failure of subject-centred curriculum reform that has been noted. A growing problem by the mid-1970s was the tendency of the specialized admission requirements of university science and professional faculties to reduce the opportunity of a general education for able, no less than for lower ability, students. There was some irony in complaints by universities about the alleged illiteracy and ignorance of entering students when their own entrance requirements were encouraging highly career-oriented students to give less emphasis to the traditional cultural subjects in favour of the "hard" sciences, mathematics and pre-professional subjects.

As in the United States, all the trends noted were leading to calls for remedial action by the late 1970s. In that country, a plethora of national studies of high schooling was shortly launched, most of them with foundation and corporate support. The lack of a tradition of such support, together with familiar constitutional obstacles, inhibited similar efforts in Canada, apart from the OECD study. At the provincial level, Ontario's Secondary Education Review Project (SERP), launched in 1980, was the most ambitious effort of its kind that had been seen in any province for some years. The study was established to consider how Ontario schools could best prepare students for the world of work, to assess the credit system and to respond to concerns about standards and discipline. The thousands of submissions to the Project indicated that the people of Ontario wanted coherence and practicality in school programs, excellence and consistency in standards, a stronger sense of responsibility to the public, and greater quality control in program, instruction and student achievement.[64]

Stressing that educational goals and curricula should be compatible, the SERP study set out thirteen goals that bore considerable resemblance to the American seven cardinal principles formulated sixty-two years earlier. To achieve these goals, a basic common core of academic subjects should be offered together with life skills. The latter included such topics as nutrition, fitness, human relations, resource management, career planning, parenting, computer literacy and personal law, all to be woven into the curriculum. This wide range illustrated the difficulty of striking a balance between a stronger, more rigorously defined educative, academic role and an increased socializing role for the high schools, both of which were being demanded by critics. In keeping with Ontario tradition, the SERP study struck a national note by stressing the need to foster interprovincial relationships by means of a greater degree of co-operation in curriculum policy matters among the provinces, to be achieved through the Council of Ministers of Education. The increasing interprovincial mobility of students was said to require a greater degree of compatibility among curricula. An increased sharing of curriculum materials was necessary in order to foster a sense of Canadian identity.[65]

## Old and New Dilemmas: Guidance, Exceptionality, Educational Media

### Guidance and Counselling in a New Era

Longstanding concerns about the mental health of children were carried over into the post-war period, as revealed in the report of the National Committee for School Health Research noted in Chapter 9. By the 1960s mental health *per se* seems to have become a less overt concern among educators as the credit system and the individualization of programs put a premium on guidance. The counsellor increasingly became a curriculum mentor to students in the selection of courses, thereby exerting a significant potential influence on the shape of the program in each individual school. The development of new programs gave counsellors a greater role in curriculum planning. A survey of *The School Guidance Worker*, the premier Canadian publication in the field, revealed a number of perennial or recurrent issues along with some new ones.[66] Defining the field and its purposes, and determining the appropriate role and training of the guidance teacher or school counsellor were persisting concerns. The increasing complexity of the educational system, of the economy and of the world of work, together with social changes and shifting values, had greatly increased the need for counselling. Vocational guidance, once the essence of the field, waxed and waned through the period. Educational guidance, designed to assist students to select suitable high school and post-secondary programs, remained the basic function throughout the 1970s.

The question of the relative emphasis to be given to individual or group guidance excited controversy. Parmenter favoured group guidance as a time-tabled subject. His list of proposed course topics suggested the wide scope that many saw for guidance and counselling. The list included orientation to the school itself, personal and social adjustment, the use of leisure, planning for the future, exploring occupations and industries, and studying about educational opportunities. To Parmenter it was apparent that such a list included content and aims, both skill and attitudinal, that made the subject as important as any in the curriculum.[67]

A major aim of some counselling programs was to help students learn more effectively through teaching study skills. Some questioned the efficacy of attempting to do so in isolation from an academic context. Critics deplored the tendency to transfer all counselling duties to the guidance counsellor; such duties, they maintained, should be regarded as a special service supplementing rather than supplanting the work of the classroom teacher. Defenders of the special approach pointed to the almost total lack of training of classroom teachers in counselling. A recurring problem arose from the tendency of some guidance teachers to follow a philosophical orientation different from that of classroom teachers. The latter tended to stress academic achievement while counsellors emphasized human development.

In elementary schools the stress in guidance and counselling was on personal development, with particular reference to emphasizing the transition to high school. At both levels, the old emphasis on mental health was sometimes retained, although some recognized the danger of the counsellor assuming a psychiatric role. Personal counselling in group guidance sometimes became a form of teaching directed at the solution of students' personal problems. Here there was an attendant danger that "pop" psychology and "pop" sociology might be encouraged. Friesen favoured the serious study of these disciplines to assist students' understanding of their own and society's problems.[68]

Daniels noted the moral values dimension to the counsellor's role. Since counsellors inevitably and frequently were in situations where they must engage in normative reasoning, training in such reasoning was essential, particularly in dealing with such topics as "personal development" and "family life." The many value issues masked by these topics constituted a hidden curriculum in which issues were often treated as mere matters of opinion not open to reasonable discussion. Counsellors had a moral responsibility to deal with normative issues in a rational way.[69]

## Exceptionality

In a period when disadvantage and limited opportunity were of increasing concern to policy-makers, particular attention was focussed on children deemed exceptional or special. This heterogeneous minority, estimated to number one million, or 12 per cent of the total child population by 1970, was defined by its common characteristic of a need for special educational services. As such, its numbers cut across all social groups and classes. As "exceptionality" became a new term in the lexicon of schooling, policy initiatives were undertaken in all provinces through legislation, funding, facilities and programs to a degree unmatched in other areas of concern. These initiatives, like those related to economic and cultural disadvantage, reflected a new moral imperative in Canadian schooling that contrasted encouragingly with the negative, frequently harsh morality of the past.

Over forty years there had been a shift from a medical to an educational model in dealing with exceptional children. Thus, the medical term "aphasic" was replaced by the more neutral descriptive term "learning disabled." The concept of exceptionality, originating in recognition of the physically handicapped and the feeble-minded, had broadened as such categories as the mentally retarded and the emotionally disturbed came to be more clearly defined. The poor achievement of seemingly normal children led to new categories of social disadvantage and cultural alienation. Later, the English language deficiencies of immigrant children sometimes led to their categorization as exceptional.[70] As a concern for cognitive development came to be complemented by a concern for social development and for the right of all children to a common school experience, the integration or mainstreaming of exceptional children in regular classrooms gradually became official policy. Mainstreaming became a controversial issue with potentially revolutionary implications for the curriculum, teaching methods, the organization of the regular classroom and the training and work of teachers.

Most of the issues referred to were considered in the 1970 report of the Commission on Emotional and Learning Disorders in Children (CELDIC), a body formed in 1966 as part of a united national effort funded by private foundations and by federal and provincial grants. In deploring divided jurisdictions, policies, responsibilities, practices and services related to exceptionality, the commission noted the tendency to view the special child as a problem whose total nature was ignored. All children should be educated to their full potential.[71] The exceptional child was defined as one "who requires special attention in the school system if he is to achieve his optimum development," a perspective that avoided any connotation associated with deviation from the normal.[72]

The report noted serious problems arising from the lack of universally accepted definitions of categories of exceptional children and of learning disorders. Diagnostic labels such as the mentally retarded and the emotionally disturbed, like the tests used to identify such categories, had obvious value, but even more obvious limitations. Teaching expectations based on tests taken as a true and permanent measure of a child's capacity resulted in instruction geared to the measure rather than to the child.[73]

The CELDIC study was critical of single track, centralized, prescriptive curricula that fell far short of meeting the needs of all children. There should be less emphasis put on prescribed bodies of subject matter. A related problem was slavish adherence to the printed word and failure to utilize other media.[74] Kendall judged that in the future the school would need to become less preoccupied with a narrow band of traditional academic skills and more concerned with the whole range of cognitive, affective, social and adaptive behaviors.[75]

By the early 1970s, there was a greater acceptance of mainstreaming, a greater flexibility in organizational arrangements and more attention to exceptionality in teacher education programs. Some provinces, notably Saskatchewan, were now making special education services mandatory. Headstart and similar preschool programs for exceptional children were being established. Alberta began to deploy teams of itinerant specialists in remote areas of the province.

Mandatory provision was extended in Ontario legislation in 1980 that defined exceptionality in the following terms:

> (an) 'exceptional pupil' means a pupil whose behavioral, communication, intellectual (including the intellectually gifted), physical or multiple exceptionalities are such that he or she is considered by a board committee to need placement in a special education program.[76]

In that year, Bill 82 mandated universal access of all Ontario's school age pupils to a publicly supported education regardless of special needs. Bill 82, modelled partly on U.S. Public Law 94-142, was the most sweeping legislation in Canada. Regulations included special curriculum support documents to supplement basic guidelines and programs. Parents or guardians were to be involved in the assessment, identification and placement of exceptional pupils. A particular feature of the bill was the mandatory provision of enriched programs, acceleration and other services for gifted children on the same basis as those for other exceptional children. As with other categories of exceptionality, there were debates over the relative merits of mainstreaming and segregation of the gifted. A 1980 CEA survey revealed that approximately 13 500 gifted children were being served across Canada through a variety of special arrangements that varied unevenly between rural and urban areas and between provinces.[77]

## Old and New Media

For educators, the impact of the media had to be considered from two perspectives. After 1960 the enormous informal educative influence of television in many respects superseded the influence of the home and the school. There were also formal educative possibilities within the school itself. The impact of radio and film in classrooms reached a peak during the 1950s, before the advent of television. School broadcasts (discussed in Chapter 8) ceased nationally by 1981. Films retained a place in classrooms, mainly through the productions of the National Film Board. In 1950-51, almost five million children saw NFB films in their classrooms, through the co-operation of the provincial departments of education.[78] Used on a borrow or rental basis, these films, like radio broadcasts, were linked to school curricula and served the need for Canadian content. Published guides and the work of educational liaison officers, some of them former teachers, enhanced the use of NFB films. The work of these officers continues; the guides have been replaced by a newsletter circulated to 30 000 teachers, which includes curricular suggestions for the use of films.[79]

To Marshall McLuhan, Canada's international media guru, the informal educative influence of television provided a rich sensory environment for children that contrasted with the puny and undernourished environment of the school in which archaic social and moral patterns were perpetuated.[80] Other critics attributed the illiteracy of students largely to the debased "public language" of the media. Television offered the most expertly prepared visual elements, while the auditory elements consisted of language that was too often inartistic, slovenly, unfocussed and inaccurate.[81] As an example of the measures available to commercial television, an American book-length account of the production of a single thirty-second commercial indicated an expenditure of time, talent and funds greater than what would be available throughout the average classroom teacher's entire career.[82]

Few facts were better known and documented than the extent of exposure of North American children to television, which was said to occupy their waking time more than any other activity, including school. A 1978 survey of 20 000 New Brunswick students conducted "to gather information thought to be relevant to student writing ability" indicated that the majority of students in Grades 5 and 8 in that province spent more time in front of the television screen than in the classroom.[83] In view of educators' rhetoric about the school's mission to promote "critical thinking," there was some irony in the failure to promote discriminating viewing of televised entertainment. By 1980, some school systems, such as that of Scarborough, Ontario, were inaugurating programs in "media literacy" for children and "television awareness training" for parents.[84]

Where the school use of the new media was concerned, Fleming characterized the attitude of some educators as one of Luddite resistance and fear. Excessively attached to verbalization and determined to maintain humanistic values, they downgraded the value of "gadgets." At another, more positive extreme, other educators saw the new media as radically transforming teaching and learning for the better. Fleming categorized educational media into two types: those that simply supplied information in some auditory or visual form, and those that provided for a direct response on the part of the learner. Radio, slides, films, and television fell into the first category. The telephone, the programmed text, the teaching machine, tapes, language laboratories and computer assisted instruction fell into the second category.[85] Some of these media were incorporated into school libraries, which often came to be known as "resource centres." The growth of libraries, the appointment of qualified school librarians and growing links between classroom and library provided for an enrichment of the formal curriculum that was one of the more encouraging developments of the period.[86]

Less encouraging was the evidence supplied by Hodgetts to the effect that, while most teachers had access to most of the new media, only the overhead projector received significant use and then only as a substitute for the blackboard. Other media were used "simply [as] a relaxed, passive diversion from regular classes." The Hall-Dennis Committee reported that audio-visual aids in Ontario schools were "employed in a narrow didactic manner." Teachers offered as excuses the amount of time required to set up equipment, the inconvenience of fitting radio and television programs into the timetable, the unsuitability of particular programs for particular age groups, the need to cover the required courses of study, and the pressure of examinations.[87]

During the early 1960s, much faith was pinned on programmed learning and teaching machines. The approach was based on a plausible psychological theory; it was practical, easily understood and produced tangible, measurable results. It focussed attention on the organization and analysis of content, and had the potential to free teachers to be more creative. Yet, the approach failed because school systems neglected in-service training of teachers and left the development of programs to commercial producers who lacked access to classrooms.[88] Part of the problem may have been the attempt to apply an abstract psychological theory. One Canadian supporter of the method observed, with reference to F.B. Skinner's celebrated success in teaching pigeons to play ping pong, that "hungry pigeons could not be equated [in motivational terms] with overfed children." A related problem was the use of American programs, often unsuited to Canadian curricula. No development in Canadian education, Fleming thought, was more influenced by American trends.[89]

The television set became ubiquitous in schools during the period, but how much and how effectively educational television (ETV) was used was a moot point. What Fleming called a "school-teacherish reaction" to the medium was epitomized by treating television as a means of extending the image of the teacher to more classrooms, with more children sitting at desks. School telecasts were most effective when curriculum-based guides were provided and when they were combined carefully with other activities in a total learning situation.[90]

In 1961, the CBC began a twice weekly schedule of Canadian School Telecasts in co-operation with the National Advisory Council on School Broadcasting. The first telecasts were in Nova Scotia, in the form of twenty minute segments on physics and chemistry that were designed to be integrated into the regular class period as a means of improving poor pupil performance in those subjects. Most telecasts were aimed at the intermediate grades and covered most subjects of the curriculum. Later, an agreement was signed between the CBC and the Council of Ministers of Education whereby the former provided free facilities and the latter paid all direct programming costs. The CMEC also publicized programs among schools and provided needed teaching aids. By 1980, the Canadian School Telecasts were broadcasting for half an hour, twice a week. These national telecasts were supplemented by thrice weekly provincial broadcasts, sponsored and often produced by departments of education using free CBC facilities. All told, 1000 hours annually were available for school telecasts. The policies described reduced federal-provincial jurisdictional disputes which revolved around Ottawa's determination to maintain its prerogative to strengthen national cultural links, and the determination of provincial bureaucrats who saw their control of program content as a natural extension of their longstanding power to control textbook and other formal curriculum content.[91]

Computer applications in education (CAE) as a media innovation found their first use in Ontario in the individualization of student timetables and for student record keeping, thereby assisting the implementation of the credit system and indirectly influencing curriculum change. Early computer-assisted instruction (CAI) appeared to have drill and tutorial assistance functions, but made limited impact. By 1980, the microcomputer was invading classrooms. The Prairie provinces and Ontario were in the lead in a development that many thought vital to future Canadian prosperity. The new medium, with its potential for social, economic and cultural impact, was one with which elementary school children were likely to be more familiar than were their teachers. A much earlier teaching of keyboard skills than had ever been envisaged in the past seemed a likely necessity.

To be sure, at least one American expert was skeptical about the practical need for computer literacy.[92] Another, noting that CAE appeared to be mundane, speculated that the innovation might suffer the fate of educational television. More positively, CAE seemed to be a grassroots movement promoted by teachers, rather than a deliberate outcome of educational policy. As such, computers were the only instruments of high technology frequently found in some schools. Relatively modest costs and the potential for easily adapting software to curricular needs were positive features in their acceptance. A lack of programs and of criteria for developing them, together with the need for a vast program of teacher training, were serious problems.[93] One critic, Lorimer, noted the shortage of programs based on Canadian life and society, a consequence of typical Canadian dependence on the products of multinational publishers. Standardized courseware promoted a curricular uniformity that belied the possibility of individualized learning that was claimed for computer assisted teaching.[94] Ontario began to evaluate courseware in terms consistent with longstanding textbook evaluation policy, a measure that promised to promote Canadianization. As middle-class homes and schools acquired computers, some critics expressed fears that the social and intellectual gap between advantaged and disadvantaged students could be widened.

## Notes to Chapter 17

1 R. Stamp, *Schools of Ontario*, 193.

2 Giles, 243.

3 Church, 37-8.

4 Ibid.

5 Corbett, 10-14, OECD, 167.

6 T. Ryan, 196-8, 202-3, 217-9.

7 Hope Report, 34, 78.

8 R. Stamp, *Schools of Ontario*, 190-1.

9 Dunlop cited in ibid., 193; Keats.

10 R. Stamp, *Schools of Ontario*, 194.

11 Seeley and Sim, *Crestwood Heights*, 102-112.

12 Griffin and Seeley, "Education," 17.

13 Seeley and Sim, *Crestwood Heights*, 246-9.

14 CEA, *Open-Area Schools*, 25.

15 Ibid., 15, 20-1.

16 Traub *et al*, *Openness in Schools*.

17 British Columbia, *Report of the Royal Commission*, 17-18, 320, 353.

18 Magnuson, *Brief History*, 115.

19 Quebec, *Report of the Royal Commission*, Vol.III, Part Two, 5, 20.

20 Newfoundland, *Report of the Royal Commission* Vol.I.

21 C.E. Phillips, "The Public School," 287-90.

22 Ontario, *Formative Years; Education in the Primary and Junior Divisions*.

23 C.E. Phillips, "The Public School," 227.

24 Quebec Ministère, *Schools of Quebec*, 125; Nova Scotia *Public School Programs*, 1979-80, 11.

25 OECD, 41-42, 167.

26 R. Stamp, *Schools of Ontario*, 196.

27 Manitoba Legislative Assembly, 38.

28 R. Stamp, *Schools of Ontario*, 195.

29 Hope Report, 34.

30 Pullen, 102, 106, 156, 212.

31 Fleming, III, *Schools*, 136.

32 Ontario AR, 1950, 151.

33 Newfoundland AR, 1951, 26.

34 Pullen, 33-5.

35 Ibid., 37.

36 Magnuson, *Brief History*, 98.

37 Pullen, 44.

38 In the United States the attack on progressivism was led by a conservative historian, Arthur Bestor. Both of his best-selling books, *Educational Wastelands* (1953) and *The Restoration of Learning* (1955), were widely read in Canada.

39 Downey, "Secondary Education," 1-2.

40 H. Baker, 14-5.

41 Downey, ''Secondary Education,'' 6.

42 Fleming, *Preoccupation*, 210-1.

43 R. Stamp, *Schools of Ontario*, 222; C.E. Phillips, ''The Public School,'' 221.

44 R. Stamp, *Schools of Ontario*, 223.

45 Ibid., 246.

46 Hall and Carlton, 91, 170-1, 269.

47 Ibid., 22-5, 114.

48 Lamontagne, 149.

49 Parent Commission, Vol.III, Part Two, 16-7, 249.

50 Newfoundland Royal Commission, Vol.I, 166.

51 Crocker and Riggs, 100-2, 131-2.

52 Nova Scotia, *Public School Programs 1980-1*, 12, 17.

53 British Columbia Royal Commission (Chant Report).

54 Zwicker, ''The Most Up-to-Date High School,'' *The Globe Magazine*, January 7, 1967.

55 OECD, 32, 46, 109, 206.

56 R. Stamp *Schools of Ontario*, 246-7.

57 Nyberg and Lee.

58 CMEC, *Secondary Education*.

59 Letter to the author from Mr. Carl Hogg, Curriculum Co-ordinator, North York Board of Education, December 12, 1982; description of Earl Haig program in *Education Ontario*, Newsletter, Ontario Ministry of Education, September, 1982.

60 International Baccalaureate Office, *Bulletin No.15* (October 1979).

61 Raywid.

62 For discussions of historical trends and contemporary concerns regarding curriculum and instruction in American high schools see James and Tyack, ''Learning from Past Efforts''; see also Cuban, Cusick.

63 See Orpwood *et al.*

64 Ontario Ministry of Education, *Secondary Education Review Project* (SERP), 1.

65 Ibid., 3-4, 13.

66 Carried out by Jean Mann, May, 1983.

67 Parmenter, 3-5.

68 Interview with Professor John Friesen, Department of Counselling Psychology, University of British Columbia, April 7, 1983.

69 Daniels, ''Moral Education and Counsellor Education,'' 13-4.

70 See Chambers.

71 Commission on Emotional and Learning Disorders in Children (CELDIC), 2-3, 9-10.

72 Ibid., 139.

73 Ibid., 480-2.

74 Ibid., 109, 479.

75 Kendall, "Developmental," 35.

76 Ontario Ministry of Education, *A Guide to Bill 82* (1980).

77 CEA, *The Gifted and Talented Student*.

78 Marjorie McKay, 81. See also Lysyshyn.

79 Swan, 11-12.

80 McLuhan. The media master presented these views to the Hall-Dennis Committee. See R. Stamp, *Schools of Ontario*, 227.

81 Priestley and Kerpneck, 13-4.

82 Arlen.

83 New Brunswick Department of Education, *Evaluation* (Newsletter, April 1979), 2.

84 Toronto Globe and Mail, June 21, 1980, 1-2.

85 Fleming, III, *Schools*, 310-2.

86 In 1982, Ontario produced a comprehensive guideline for the use of the library resource centre in the curriculum. The publication highlighted the responsibilities of teachers and teacher-librarians for curriculum development using a "resource-based learning" approach. It also emphasized the responsibility of administrators to supply curriculum support services related to library resource centres.

87 Hodgetts, 61. See also Hall-Dennis, 15.

88 Fleming, *Preoccupation*, 197-8.

89 Fleming, III, *Schools*, 318, 326.

90 Fleming, *Preoccupation*, 199; III, *Schools*, 332.

91 For a discussion of school television policy see Fleming, *Preoccupation* 200-4; Swan, 3-5; and Rosen.

92 See "The Myth of Computer Literacy," *Harpers* (August, 1983), 23.

93 Myron Atkin cited in *Networking, B.C.*, 1, no.2, (May, 1984), Newsletter of the Centre for the Study of Curriculum and Instruction, U.B.C. See same source for an account by Gloet of computer use in Vancouver schools.

94 Lorimer, 107-8.

# CHAPTER 18

## PROFILES OF
## THE SUBJECT AREAS,
## 1945-1980

*... a subject in the schools is an institution in the schools, a structural frame which specifies tasks and meaning contexts within which education takes place.*
(Ian Westbury, 1980)

During the 1950s the subject areas remained relatively stable, apart from the tentative curriculum reforms in mathematics and science programs already noted. The explosion of the curriculum that took place after 1960 was manifested most obviously in the form of courses such as theatre arts, data processing, world religions, film making, urban studies, family life education, computer studies, consumer fundamentals, Boolean algebra, motion geometry and forest ecology, to name but a few titles that would have fallen strangely on the ears of earlier curriculum developers. Difficulties of classification were illustrated by courses in consumer studies, which might logically find a home in subject areas as diverse as home economics, mathematics, social studies or business education. In Prince Edward Island a course entitled Home Management in Practice turned out to be an offering in mathematics that comprised a review of the fundamentals of arithmetic and algebra applied to banking and retail problems.[1] Such classifications reflected the ambiguities of a curriculum era afflicted with new problems of purpose and focus.

The surveys of provincial curricula that were launched by the Council of Ministers of Education during the late 1970s, together with the growth of national organizations in the subject areas on a scale never seen before were evidence of continuing nationalizing imperatives in the curriculum. The council surveys had been undertaken "in response to a concern for closer co-ordination and co-operation in the development of curriculum."[2] Related aims were to estimate the level of commonality among the provinces and to predict the future level.[3] The following discussion focusses descriptively on change and attempted change, as well as on the ongoing traditional imperatives in each major subject area.

## English, French and Other Languages

English in the elementary and junior high school grades was often called language arts, a descriptive term that included reading, spelling, oral and written language, and literature. In the senior grades in some provinces communications replaced English as a descriptive label. Such offerings as theatre arts, film study and film making, corrective reading, language in work situations, and personal writing were sometimes subsumed under "communications arts." Composition was now taught under such labels as writing skills and written expression. English as a second language enjoyed a boom during the period, as we have seen.

Old controversies over the teaching of English continued to flourish. Knowledge of grammar was still associated with writing ability, although rule-based teaching did diminish temporarily. Questions about the integration of English with other subjects, the separation of composition and literature, the appropriate sequence of skills and content, and the value of disciplinary vis-à-vis student-centred approaches were other issues that remained current. A new interest in linguistics forced teachers to question the validity of studying the language as though it obeyed rigid rules. A related interest in semantics weakened the concept of a single standard of "good" English.

Canadian teachers of English were influenced by both British and American approaches, and by controversies associated with each. They tended to favour the British approach which, as presented at the famous Dartmouth Conference held in New Hampshire in 1966, emphasized language activities suited to later adult life.[4] British delegates questioned the American emphasis on Bruner's discipline-centred approach, asserting that "It is literature not literary criticism which is the subject." A unitary approach was advocated as a counter to the separation of instruction into isolated segments of composition, literature, drama, speech and language. In urging this approach, the Toronto Joint Committee emphasized that students should spend more time practising writing than in listening to advice on how to write. Young children could be introduced to great literature through listening to good stories, a method that was described as "not a passive response but a kind of imaginative basic training . . . ." Descriptive grammar which tells how language is constructed should be applied to living rather than contrived or artificial language. Normative grammar which tells how people ought to read and write "should emanate from the active usage of the society of educated speakers and writers."[5]

In Saskatchewan, Robinson later noted the influence of British ideas through the work of John Dixon, who traced the growth of English teaching from an earlier stage that emphasized skills and initial literacy to an emphasis on the cultural heritage and, in the modern period, on personal growth. Robinson described a final stage of "languaging" whereby the pupil would be able to gain power over language. Old fashioned "composition" should be superseded by "the writing process," a method akin to that used by the professional writer. The method, drawn from American experiments, involved a pre-writing stage of discovering a topic, discussing, reading, listening, observing and recalling, culminating in planning; the writing stage entailed revision, editing and rewriting; a final stage of post-writing led to response and evaluation.[6]

Some teachers of English literature recognized that the expansion of the high school population, the demise of provincial examinations, the rise of the credit system, the new media and the advent of the paperback had greatly changed the context of teaching. To the consternation of traditionalists, classics and masterpieces were now downplayed, although Shakespeare and Shaw remained relevant. Contemporary works such as *The Catcher in the Rye* and *The Lord of the Flies* that dealt with themes supposedly more appealing to modern teenagers now had a larger place. Progressives sometimes ignored the evidence from the popularity of science fiction and medieval epics in books and film that young people were not necessarily always enamoured of presentism. In more avant garde classrooms, dissection of literary works gave way to discussions of ideas and characters, to performance, to individual library-based work and to the study and use of the media through making class newspapers, tape recordings and short films.[7]

During the 1960s, the genre remained a basic mode of organizing the curriculum although, as Northrop Frye observed, it did not meet Bruner's criteria of structure very satisfactorily.[8] University instructors deplored their students' ignorance of the various genres and their inability to distinguish a sonnet from an ode. Students were likewise said to be ignorant of great literary names and of common terms of criticism such as *denouement*.[9] To Moss, an Ontario English teacher, the move from a discipline to the British personal growth theory had resulted in an English curriculum lacking any rational guiding framework, intellectual structure or coherent pedagogy. The shapeless busy work of an "activities curriculum" and the stultifying procedures of a behavioral model were equally to be avoided.[10]

By the 1970s, Canadian literature was gaining a significant place in some curricula. In *Survival*, her thematic guide for high schools, Margaret Atwood likened Canlit to a map, "a geography of the mind" that gave Canadians a shared knowledge of who they were and where they had been.[11] Harker reported that Canadian students were not always enchanted by their literature, sometimes viewing it as "the monotonous succession of poverty-stricken farmers on snow-swept prairies, death, gloom and defeatism."[12] By this time, the organization of the Canadian Council of Teachers of English and a thriving publication, *The English Quarterly*, were providing national forums for teachers that had never been available in the past. Dictionaries of Canadianisms and Canadian English were introduced into some school programs.[13]

A surprising finding of the 1972 Survey of Canadian English, conducted among more than 14 000 Grade 9 Canadian-born English speakers, was that young people, rather than busily coining new expressions, were preserving and probably even renewing older forms of speech. The investigators were concerned that teaching could destroy these forms if too much emphasis was given to conformity with the artificial norms of a society unaware of its heritage and uncertain of its future. Textbooks should be based on Canadian English and imported language textbooks should not be tolerated.[14]

Among various provincial surveys of student achievement and instructional practices in English language and reading carried out in the late 1970s, those in New Brunswick and British Columbia were particularly notable, if only for their large scale. In 1978, writing skills in both provinces were surveyed.[15] The New Brunswick survey included all students in Grades 5, 8 and 10. In general, writing skills in the province were described as satisfactory. British Columbia writing achievement, particularly at the senior level, was less satisfactory. Increased responsibility for writing skills by teachers in all subject areas was recommended. A 1980 reading survey of 100 000 pupils in Grades 4, 8 and 12 was the most detailed and thorough one of its kind in any province during the period. In general, reading achievement was reported as satisfactory. A concentrated effort was recommended to improve the reading skills of secondary students.

The Council of Ministers' survey of English and language arts programs across the provinces provided a portrait of the curriculum in 1979. A "fairly high level of agreement" on goals was reported. Most curriculum guides had been developed within a similar philosophical framework. Some very basic differences existed, but these were largely a matter of interpretation and application. The level of commonality was greatest in the early years and "progressively harder to observe in the senior grades." This was attributed to the influence of publishers' language arts programs at the former level where basal reading series were remarkably similar across the country; specialization caused less uniformity at the latter level. Although integration remained a goal, a new set of categories (oral language, writing, reading, listening, speaking, viewing, doing, literature, media) was replacing the traditional divisions of composition, grammar and literature. With the near disappearance of formal grammar in the elementary grades and the de-emphasis on the mechanics of writing, pupils now learned to write by writing. Spelling was taught in the context of reading and writing rather than as two separate subjects, although spellers were still widely used. At higher grade levels, objectives in terms of skills, content and concepts were broadly similar, with variations most evident in widely varying specific content and teaching emphases and in the materials used.[16]

The boom in French as both a first and second language and in English as a second language was noted in Chapter 16. However, the cause of bilingualism in the high schools was not advanced by university policies that relaxed language requirements for admission purposes. Other modern languages, notably Spanish and German, remained relatively popular but Canadians in general eschewed language study. The ancient languages almost disappeared from the curriculum, although Latin retained a foothold in a few schools and by 1980 was showing signs of a modest revival. The teaching of so-called heritage languages was also noted in Chapter 16.

The shift in teaching both official languages and other modern languages was marked by an interest in practical as compared with traditional cultural aims. The new audio-lingual approach was enhanced by the use of the tape recorder and other electronic devices. During the 1940s, the anglophone schools of Quebec led the way in reforming language teaching by putting a stronger emphasis on oral French. Everywhere over the next two decades the Direct Method of teaching French gradually took hold. As new texts, materials and teaching aids in the form of detailed, carefully programmed teachers' manuals, wall charts, flash cards, slides, tapes and tests became more common, the ideal classroom became a language laboratory. For teachers used to reliance on a mastery of grammar as their chief stock in trade, the change was sometimes traumatic. New skills of oral fluency and acceptable pronunciation were now required, together with a knowledge of phonetics, of idioms and of French and Quebecois culture. A few adherents of the old grammar-translation regime waged guerilla war against the new order, in part by reliance on traditional testing procedures which enabled them and their students to survive.[17]

As teachers found themselves producing back-up materials for the written parts of courses and still conjugating verbs or lecturing on the agreement of the past participle, they found that, theorists to the contrary, a second language was not learned simply by osmosis. For students, the pattern drills of a system in which habit formation through overlearning and constant repetition was the goal were often as stultifying as the translation methods required in traditional language learning. The language laboratory with its booths was thought to reduce the embarrassment felt by young people in attempting to learn a language. Yet the isolation of booths introduced an element of artificiality to language study by negating the possibility of natural communication between human beings which is the essence of such study. Nevertheless, students did apparently acquire a greater oral facility than in the past as the audio-lingual approach came into use in all provinces by the early 1970s.[18]

While Spanish and German remained the most popular non-official languages, little attention was given to Asian languages, even in British Columbia where Canada's growing trade links with the Pacific world were most obvious. Nor was much attention given to Russian, even after the launching of Sputnik in 1957. Whereas the number of American schools teaching Russian increased from sixteen to more than 1000 in seven years, Burnham reported that by 1967 only nine Ontario schools taught the language, usually by antiquated methods that neglected listening and speaking skills.[19]

## Mathematics and Business Education

The "new mathematics," at the cutting edge of curricular change by 1960, reached its peak during the following decade. The new emphasis on inter-relationships among mathematical ideas and on teaching understanding was consistent with advances in applied mathematics related to the growth of industrial automation and computer technology.[20] Mathematics, long the handmaiden of the physical sciences, became essential to the solution of problems in the social sciences, industry and commerce. In the 1970s, computer studies and metrication, although having applications across the curriculum, had their base in mathematics.

The new mathematics included many new topics and the introduction of traditional topics at earlier ages. Program aims included the development of the concept of a set or collection of objects from which the concept of number was derived, leading to a study of the number system and its oper-ations and laws; a second aim was to make the language of mathematics precise, distinguishing between number and symbol, for example, "one" as a concept and 1 as a symbol or name for the number; thirdly, there was an attempt to give old ideas and tools new uses or emphases, as in the case of trigonometry, which now provided knowledge essential for the electrical and electronics engineer.

During the 1950s, the Ontario Mathematics Commission took the lead in promoting collaborative efforts involving the Ontario Teachers' Federation, the universities and departmental personnel. Mathematics reform set the pace for a new openness in curriculum matters, to the con-sternation of some members of the department and to the surprise of non-governmental groups. Openness was evident in consultations with more than 1000 mathematics teachers, and in the participation of more than 200 schools in field trials of new teaching materials between 1959 and 1966.[21] The Commission's work also paved the way for that of the Toronto Joint Committee and the Ontario Curriculum Institute. Its members took part in a national seminar convened by the Canadian Teachers' Federation in 1960 that involved sixty representatives from all provinces and from all levels and aspects of mathematics education. Seven years later, at a second seminar, the Canadian Association of Teachers of Mathematics was formed. Although there were significant divergences among the provinces in offer-ings, there was a tendency, particularly in Ontario, British Columbia and New Brunswick, for university preparatory courses to follow the proposals of the Mathematics Commission of the College Entrance Examination Board in the United States.[22]

During these years, links that had been established between Canadian and American mathematics educators were strengthened. The Mathematics Council of the Alberta Teachers Association, formed in 1961, became one of the first Canadian affiliates of the National Council for the Teaching of Mathematics. Later, the American organization held its national meeting in Montreal, where some sessions were conducted in French.

Shortly, some American textbooks were translated into French.[23] Most provinces used American textbooks, suitably Canadianized and, after 1970, metricated. These were usually based on the work of the School Mathematics Study Group (SMSG), the most popular of the American curriculum projects in Canada.

By 1968, criticism of the new approach was surfacing. Some critics claimed that, as a result of the abandonment of drill, innovative methods had led to a loss of traditional computational skills by pupils. Mathematics, it was said, was becoming too abstract. Defenders claimed that traditional skills were not downgraded and that any decline was probably a result of an erroneous belief by teachers that computational competence was no longer necessary.[24] The most positive development was the introduction of the metric system, especially in elementary schools where it was claimed as a particularly successful example of curriculum innovation. The schools were, in fact, well ahead of the public in accepting metrication, although many teachers continued to use non-metric measures even when these no longer appeared in textbooks. Between 1974 and 1979, 400 000 copies of a Metric Style Guide produced by the Council of Ministers of Education were distributed to all teachers in Canada and found markets in the United States and Australia. A handbook on teaching methods and implementation in various subject areas had also been produced.[25]

Apart from metrication, Robitaille thought that the new mathematics had been more talked about than implemented. He doubted that basic skills had declined; competency tests were not introduced into Canada and there seemed less criticism of mathematics teaching than in the United States. Robitaille's survey of 3000 British Columbia teachers gave no evidence that the new methods were widespread. Total group instruction and teacher explanation predominated. Teachers preferred textbooks that stressed skills development and drill exercises over the development of concepts and principles. The typical mathematics lesson entailed ten minutes of marking homework, fifteen minutes to present a new lesson and twenty-five minutes of seatwork.[26] The stability of the mathematics curriculum over a century was revealed by Phillips' comparative study of Canadian textbooks. The content of those used in the 1950-70 period was remarkably similar to that of the 1850-70 period, although the modern textbooks were more colorful, more fully illustrated and contained more varied exercises.[27]

Although national assessments of mathematics achievement were lacking, notable provincial assessments were carried out in New Brunswick and British Columbia during the 1970s. The 1977 assessment in the latter province tested 100 000 pupils in Grades 4, 8 and 12. Characteristically, Canadian mathematics educators were dependent on American research but it was difficult to interpret data, for example, on female achievement in mathematics among francophones in Trois Rivières on the basis of data collected for black females in Biloxi, Mississippi. Low ratios of female to male students in senior classes and generally lower levels of performance by girls were increasingly recognized as serious problems. These were thought to be related to a shortage of female mathematics teachers and a consequent lack of role models for girls.[28] A 1976 Science Council of Canada study reported a generally deplorable attitude to mathematics throughout society. Some bright students thrived on a subject that was a kind of mental yoga; for many others, mathematics was deeply frustrating and irrelevant.[29]

The survey of provincial mathematics curricula conducted in 1978-79 by the Council of Ministers of Education revealed mixed trends. A new conservatism was evident in the emphasis on the basic skills, a trend that was reinforced by the need for students to master decimals in learning the metric system. Number skills were now being stressed as high as Grade 9. At this and earlier levels, textbooks, now largely Canadian published, took an integrated approach to mathematics. It was claimed that in the elementary grades there was now less emphasis on abstractions, precise definitions and terminology and more stress on audiovisual aids, and hands on experience with manipulable materials. At the senior high school level, there were major differences among the provinces over an integrated approach, for instance, over whether algebra and geometry should be integrated or taught independently. Geometry had apparently declined but algebra was probably as entrenched as ever among the ablest students.[30]

All provinces appeared to offer a traditional rigorous academic bill of fare at the senior level, usually in the form of a three-year program for university-bound students which was sometimes supplemented by enriched courses for potential specialists. For non-specialists not going into science and mathematics, programs were often unsuitable. Studies by Beltzner and O'Reilly indicated that the proportions of able Canadian students pursuing "hard" mathematics was as high as in most nations.[31] For students not bound for university, general mathematics, purportedly less theoretical and more practical, stressed mastery of fundamental skills and useful applications in the business or industrial world. The diversity of mathematics offerings was revealed in Prince Edward Island, which offered eighteen senior courses with titles ranging from traditional Algebra and Geometry to Mathematics in Life, Consumer and Career Math., Vocational Mathematics and Home Management in Practice.[32]

## Business Education

Expanded business education programs included marketing, accounting, data processing, consumer economics and law that were ostensibly available to all students but that, in practice, were usually confined to students in non-academic commercial streams. In the traditional commercial subjects of typing, shorthand and bookkeeping, the schools lagged as much as a generation behind offices in introducing such new equipment as electric typewriters and, later, word processors. However, the gap began to narrow with the adoption of teaching innovations such as simulations, model offices, school stores, work experience and co-operative education involving links between schools and employers. Although they agreed that the field had a legitimate vocational emphasis, business educators did not see their function as that of job training. Programs, as alternatives to academic studies, should create an awareness of vocational options and contribute to the self-esteem of students too often stigmatized as slow learners or failures. Business education programs had been reasonably successful as among the few in schools that led directly to fairly high level employment.[33]

## The Science Curriculum

Hughes' comment that in Alberta there was little enthusiasm for innovation in science teaching until the late 1950s could be extended to all provinces. By 1959 the cold war imperatives that had spurred reforms in the United States were revealed in Alberta's Cameron Royal Commission comment that "Nothing less than national security, not to mention our standard of living, depend upon extensive and intensive science education."[34] British Columbia's Chant Commission, in urging curriculum reform "in the light of world conditions," emphasized the need for intellectual development that would give a better understanding of science through content more closely related to pure science.[35]

Ontario curriculum reformers, such as the members of the Toronto Joint Committee, were critical of the confusion of aims in science teaching. Progressive child-centred pedagogy was said to have downplayed the importance of formal study and the amassing of an ordered body of scientific information. An appeal to the child's natural instincts disregarded the fact that the scientific study of nature was an activity that appealed rather to humankind's unique intellectual faculties. Ontario reformers agreed with British and American views that science teaching should emphasize "the scientific attitude" and be closer to what science really was.[36]

It was soon apparent that science curriculum reform was time-consuming and costly. Support by the National Science Foundation for the development of the Chemical Bond Approach (CBA) textbook in the United States had extended over six years at a cost of 1.3 million dollars. The Biological Sciences Curriculum Study (BSCS), also funded from the NSF, and the Nuffield Science Project in Great Britain were even more costly. In the absence of public or private funds, Canadian science educators leaned heavily on these external developments.[37] So-called Nuffield Science from Great Britain was particularly influential in the elementary grades, where it encouraged the jettisoning of textbooks in favour of kits of materials, experimental methods and open-ended teaching. However, many elementary teachers with limited training in science were uncomfortable without the security of a textbook. By 1970, teachers were being encouraged to make more use of the textbook to discuss and consolidate the concepts to be learned while maintaining some of the earlier activity approach. This approach was exemplified by the STEM (Space, Time, Energy, Matter) program which came into use in all provinces.[38]

By the mid-1970s, nearly all students in elementary and junior high school grades were studying science. At the latter level, general science expanded, earth and space science were introduced, and laboratories were installed on a wide scale as a more experimental approach was taken. However, it was at the senior high school level in chemistry, physics and biology that the most far-reaching and lasting changes probably occurred, heavily influenced by American ideas.

In chemistry, the Chemical Bond Approach (CBA) and the Chemical Education Materials Study (CHEM Study) both stressed the discovery method, experimental approaches and theory rather than description. Of the two, the more practical laboratory-oriented two-year CHEM Study course first introduced in Saskatchewan in 1964 proved more popular. By 1967 more than half of Saskatchewan's Grade 11 and 12 students were taking the program, and by 1968 most provinces had adopted it. In Quebec the program was translated into French. University chemists and other professionals working through the Chemical Institute of Canada took an interest in school chemistry and forged links with teachers through in-service conferences, workshops, industrial visits, teaching aids, newsletters and similar means, to a degree probably unmatched by any other disciplinary group. CHEM Study stimulated an upgrading of other chemistry curricula and encouraged the first of several Canadian-authored textbooks.[39]

Despite these gains, studies by Even in Ontario and Nasr in British Columbia indicated that achievement in chemistry still seemed oriented to the recall of factual knowledge. Materials were not always used as intended. Many teachers found the discovery approach too time-consuming, frustrating and difficult. In adapting and modifying the CHEM Study program, teachers often ignored its developers' objectives but displayed a greater awareness of classroom realities.[40]

Canadian physicists took part in the work of the Physical Sciences Study Committee (PSSC) in the United States which Hart, a Carleton University scientist, described as "a carefully integrated program of laboratory exercises and films controlled by the textbook." Basically, the program was an enriched one taught by selected, specially trained teachers to selected students.[41] As with chemistry, university academics such as Hart played a prominent role in physics reform. In British Columbia, physicists responded to cold war imperatives related to the alleged shortage of scientific labour by urging an increase in the quality and number of physics teachers in order to increase the enrolment of able students studying the discipline at university. Many teachers sided with their university colleagues in defining physics even more abstractly than in the past and in restricting enrolments to the ablest students. Other teachers, however, emphasized the social and applicative aspects of physics, an approach designed to appeal to a wider range of students and not, coincidentally, to increase enrolments. These conflicting views supported Goodson's view that curriculum reform typically involves competition for status, territory and resources among contending interest groups.[42]

In the event, PSSC physics prevailed in most provinces confirming the high status the subject had long enjoyed as a mathematical, abstract, university-oriented discipline. In the process, the abstraction of the new physics led to a decline in enrolments, which was countered through alternative textbooks that enabled PSSC to be adapted to regular physics classes. In the late 1970s, a less specialized American alternative, Harvard Project Physics, was imported into Canada.[43] As with most of the new curricula, few attempts were made objectively to evaluate claims made for the advantages of the PSSC approach. As Tanner pointed out in the United States, claims rested mainly on the testimonials of the developers themselves and a few users. The neglect of objective evaluation paradoxically contradicted the very spirit of science that the new physics was supposed to promote.[44]

Most students in North American schools studied biology. Dale, a Canadian biologist, described school biology as quite literally "a cut and dried subject." He cited Farley Mowat's puzzlement as a one-time student of the subject that the science of life was mainly concerned with dead animal matter. Courses had long purveyed unrelated facts about plants and animals, laced with elementary generalizations dogmatically presented. Students successfully passed matriculation examinations on the basis of memorizing teacher dictated notes in the form of summaries of textbooks.[45]

To overcome the weaknesses noted, Canadian university and high school teachers collaborated in designing new courses and materials based on the Biological Sciences Curriculum Study organized in the United States in 1959. Using approaches similar to those employed in the new chemistry and physics curricula, the BSCS program was produced in "Blue," "Green," and "Yellow" versions, that respectively emphasized a life development, behavioural ecological and reproductive evolutionary approach. The "Yellow" version was the most widely used in Canada. All versions highlighted methods of collecting data and made use of living organisms in the laboratory, where half the allotted time for the course was to be spent. By the late 1960s, the new biology had been implemented in most provinces and some Canadian textbooks had been prepared.[46]

By 1980, a social-moral issue was surfacing in biology and other science curricula arising from demands by some religious groups that "creationism" be taught on an equal basis with evolution. The Creation Science Association of Canada, under the leadership of a science teacher and with the support of some parents, persuaded school boards in several provinces to require the teaching of both theories, ostensibly to ensure that students gained a more sceptical view of Darwinism. Unfortunately, in opposing creationism as an unsupported, unscientific theory, some evolutionists did not always assist their valid case by paradoxically upholding an outmoded concept of evolutionary theory with religious-like fervour.

Province-wide assessment programs in the late 1970s included assessments of science teaching. The largest of these, conducted in British Columbia in 1978, tested student achievement and attitudes towards science and scientists, and perceptions of teaching methods. As reported by Hobbs and Erickson, there was a tendency, especially in the senior grades, for boys to outrank girls in performance levels, although this was not true with respect to process and scientific literacy goals. Lecturing and note-taking were commonly used teaching methods at the high school level, while elementary science teaching seemed more attuned to the new methods.[47]

A Council of Ministers 1978-79 survey of curricula across Canada confirmed the trends that have been discussed above. The survey also confirmed that a more applicative trend was taking hold. There was considerable diversity at the senior high school level, where 130 courses were offered, most of them emphasizing biology, chemistry and physics. Some provinces offered interdisciplinary courses or offered several levels of the same course. Most offered general courses for lower ability students or for those not planning to pursue science any further. Some offered enriched or advanced courses. The survey identified a high level of agreement on the goals of science teaching, although there were some variations of emphasis across the country between content and process goals. Many provinces continued to define their programs in terms of a published textbook. There was a high degree of commonality of content, albeit that particular topics might be taught in different grades. Since some teachers taught process-oriented programs by traditional methods while others used an activity approach with a traditional textbook, an authorized program might bear little resemblance to the teaching approach used in a particular classroom.[48]

The CMEC Survey was shortly complemented by the Science Education Study (SES) launched in 1980 by the Science Council of Canada with the approval of the Council of Ministers. Focussed primarily on elementary and secondary school curricula, the project was the largest and potentially the most significant national curriculum inquiry since Hodgetts' investigation of Canadian Studies. Proposed by James Page, an historian, the SES was inspired by the Symons Commission on Canadian Studies, which had deplored the neglect of a Canadian dimension in science teaching.[49]

The final report of the study, significantly entitled *Science for Every Student: Educating Canadians for Tomorrow's World*, was preceded by an analysis of provincial guidelines and curricula that revealed a high degree of similarity among programs in all jurisdictions.[50] A background paper accompanying the final report revealed that, except in the early school years, textbooks were the preponderant basis of instruction. There was a general lack of a Canadian perspective in textbooks, particularly of Canadian science and technology and its history and impact on society. The northern character of Canada and the lifestyles and activities of Canadians as these relate to science and technology were neglected, as was information about career possibilities in the field. Textbooks gave scant attention to issues of social significance, to moral values issues such as the ethics of genetic engineering or whale hunting, or to the political dimensions of problems such as nuclear waste disposal. Although the textbooks conformed broadly with the aims of ministry guidelines, most suggested experiments were highly structured and, like the laboratory manuals used in senior grades, provided limited scope for inquiry learning. Students in the elementary grades were receiving only a token education in science.[51]

Canada's 98 000 science teachers, most of them non-specialist elementary teachers, were described as enthusiastic, although not always adequately trained. An 8:1 ratio of male to female teachers was a serious problem, exacerbated by the fact that most saw no need to give special attention to the needs of girls in order to overcome the low participation of women in the scientific professions. Teachers were divided as regards the relative importance of teaching content vis-à-vis stressing the social significance and the nature of science. Although Science and Society objectives were rated high, teaching an awareness of science as it is practiced in Canada was not. In general, personal growth objectives were stressed at lower levels and content objectives in higher grades. The practical applications of science were rated high at all levels, though often ignored in practice.[52]

## The Social Studies

Margaret Atwood's amusing account of the ethnocentric and imperial European-oriented social studies curriculum that she experienced as a pupil in the early 1950s is reminiscent of Fredelle Maynard's experience a generation earlier.[53] Atwood sang "Rule Britannia" and drew pictures of the Union Jack "under teachers who believed in the Empire." She learned the kings of England and the explorers. The kings were fun because "they were red, blue and purple" but the explorers, "once they hit Canada and got into the woods" were tedious. She learned very little about Louis Riel, W.L. MacKenzie and Quebec "except that they all lost." In high school Atwood studied the Ancient Egyptians, the Greeks and Romans, Medieval Europe, the Elizabethan Age and the American Civil War and emerged "knowing quite a lot about pyramids, Henry VIII, Hitler, serfs, Winston Churchill, the cotton gin and F.D.R."

Subject-centred curriculum reform initially had little effect on the social studies. Bruner's theory had limited application to the field, especially to history. His own *Man: A Course of Study*, a widely acclaimed although controversial interdisciplinary curriculum for the elementary grades, was one of several attempts to teach a general understanding of human society using concepts from all the social sciences. Edwin Fenton's Social Studies Program for Able High School Students which used a cultural-historical approach, and the Harvard Public Issues Project were other popular American interdisciplinary projects. The High School Geography Project was discipline-based. Canadian moves to interdisciplinary studies were slower than those in the United States. Bruner's curriculum attracted only limited attention, even though *Man: A Course of Study* was based largely on the famous National Film Board production on the Netselik Inuit. Some Canadian teachers were attracted to Fenton's work and to the High School Geography Project. As noted in Chapter 16, the Harvard project provided the model for the Canadian Public Issues Project.

Initial Canadian reform was probably more experimental than its American counterpart in the use of area, local and sample studies, together with large scale maps and air photographs in geography and documents or primary sources in history, approaches that owed something to British influences. As the popular British-produced Jackdaw kits were introduced into some classrooms, Canadian history teachers were pioneering in North America in the use of the primary source method by producing their own discovery-type materials.[54] British influences were most evident in geography, a subject that, due to its low status in the universities before 1950, remained, except in Ontario, confined to the elementary school.[55] Soon, however, geography took root at higher levels and became a matriculation subject, gaining in another decade a status equal to that of history. The arrival in 1951 of N.V. Scarfe as Dean of Education at the University of Manitoba brought the leading world figure in geographic education to Canada from Great Britain. A year earlier Scarfe had chaired a notable UNESCO international symposium at Montreal, where some Canadian geographers were introduced to new ideas for teaching the subject in schools.[56] In 1952, Scarfe became chairman of another international group charged with investigating the status of geography in various countries, including Canada. Too often, Scarfe found, it was taught inadequately in Canada "as a minor portion of social studies," especially in western Canada. In eastern Canada it had more status as a separate subject with a sound "physical basis."[57]

Scarfe advocated a form of discovery learning which long pre-dated Bruner in British school geography. He and other British geographers later introduced British texts adapted for Canadian use. In due course, indigenous discovery-type texts were produced by Canadians.[58] By the 1970s, the growth of university geography in most provinces had contributed to the growth of school geography. Urban and cultural geography in provincial curricula complemented traditional descriptive regional geography and enriched systematic geography which had previously been dominated by studies of "physical elements."

American approaches in the form of the new social studies, exemplified by Alberta's values-based curriculum, took strongest hold in western Canada. To Milburn, Canadian social studies was not bursting with creative energy during this period. An emphasis on crises and themes and on the methods and structures of disciplines did not necessarily prepare informed and responsive citizens any better than had earlier litanies of facts and eras.[59] As we noted in Chapter 16, social studies was central to the new emphasis on Canadian Studies and multicultural studies. History lost much of its former status and by the 1970s historians themselves no longer contributed significantly to the writing of school textbooks. Within the discipline excessive specialization and quantitative and other techniques had undermined the traditional grand, if unduly romantic, sweep of historical, literary narrative.[60]

The analyses of textbooks undertaken by Trudel and Jain, by Pratt and McDiarmid and by Hodgetts were mentioned in Chapter 16. A unique nationwide analysis of textbooks and related curriculum documents was undertaken by Walsh during the early 1960s. He identified three dominant interpretations. "Catholic histories," popular in Quebec, glorified the Christian ideal that had been best realized in medieval Europe before secularism and materialism were seen to have hastened the decline of civilization. "Progress histories," reflecting an American view, portrayed a beneficent progression of events that was belied by the realities described and oversimplified in the confines of the textbooks. "Histories of limited interpretation," while also subject to the limitations of compression, were more accurate, scholarly and balanced, more circumspect in their judgements and more cautious in their generalizations.[61]

Not surprisingly, the rise of the new social studies evoked criticism from professional historians. To Hertzmann, the Alberta curriculum of the 1960s betrayed an ignorance of the nature of history, and by mixing the social science disciplines it invited incoherence and chaos. Skills and attitudes were the natural results of good teaching and not the by-products of lists of false or misleading "understandings." Current events were best learned by students on their own from the media.[62] In Ontario, academic historians were similarly critical of such indoctrinative goals as "appreciation," which appeared in curriculum guidelines during the 1970s. They objected to the notion that content should be subordinated to objectives and not be seen as important for its own sake. Facts and dates used to enhance attitudes and understandings were said to result in a whimsical selection of historical content, as illustrated by a guideline that treated the opening up of the West in the 1880s before studying Confederation.[63]

As in other subject areas, there was some reason to doubt that the new dispensation had taken hold. Osborne thought that, despite all the ferment, most classrooms remained untouched and lessons proceeded much as they always had.[64] Hodgetts' survey found that only a handful of teachers used inquiry methods.[65] Downey's 1975 assessment of the Alberta values curriculum revealed that not more than 20 per cent of Alberta's teachers were using a values approach.[66] Milburn's doubts that citizenship objectives were being promoted any more effectively have been noted. On the positive side, the emergence of a national community of social studies educators was evident in the organization of the Canadian Association for the Social Studies, the Canada Studies Foundation and the Canadian Foundation for Economic Education. *The History and Social Science Teacher,* with 4000 subscribers, was arguably the best and certainly one of the most widely read national teachers' journal in any subject field.

Social studies as a term remained confined to the elementary level, except in western Canada where it also served an umbrella function to describe separate subjects, mainly geography and history, at the high school level. In the elementary grades, social studies generally failed to fulfill its earlier promise to integrate the curriculum except in a few primary level curricula. The traditional disciplines retained a stronger hold in eastern Canada. However, after 1970 there was convergence among the eastern and western provinces in values education, multicultural and Canadian Studies. The introduction of new subjects and more interdisciplinary approaches was reflected in Ontario's establishment of courses with such titles as World Religions, Man in Society, Politics, and Urban Studies. In some provinces occasional elective courses in labour and women's history were offered.

A 1979-80 survey by the Council of Ministers described the major goal of the social studies as being "to provide students with the knowledge, skills, values and thought processes which will enable them to participate effectively and responsibly in the ever-changing environment of their community, their country and their world." This ambitious approach was said to stress inquiry and discovery by students rather than passive reception of knowledge or memorization of facts. There was now thought to be a better balance between knowledge, skills and aims, and between local, provincial, national and international topics. Attempts to eliminate bias from textbooks, to emphasize values education, to provide materials appropriate to exceptional children, to Native students and members of immigrant and other minority groups were under way in all provinces.[67]

At the primary level, broad interprovincial commonality was revealed in studies of family, neighbourhood and community using an "expanding horizons" approach. At the intermediate level, the focus shifted to communities in other times and places. The Native peoples, explorers and early Canadian settlements were time-honoured topics, but local and provincial studies were gaining acceptance by the mid-1970s. The greatest variations among provinces were at the junior high school level.[68]

At the senior level, Canadian content tended to dominate, sometimes taught from a comparative perspective and usually from a disciplinary one. Economics, geography and history were the dominant disciplines at this level. A Canadian economics course was being offered in every province except Manitoba. Geography was taught in six provinces. History offered the greatest variety of courses, although it was now an optional subject taken by only a minority of students through high school graduation. Canadian history still tended to be offered from a chronological centralist perspective. World history courses were still Europe-centred, although more attention was being given to non-western cultures by 1980; a course in modern world problems was offered in four provinces. Surprisingly little attention was given to the study of the United States in most curricula. Political science was offered in five provinces, law in six, and sociology, psychology, religious studies, anthropology and philosophy were only offered in one or two provinces.[69]

## The Arts: Visual, Performing and Practical

These areas of the curriculum included various long-established subjects such as art (now often called fine arts), music, industrial arts (formerly manual training), home economics (formerly domestic science) and physical education. Most had broadened considerably. Fine art might now sometimes include pottery and sculpture as well as traditional drawing and painting. Dance might be taught as part of physical education and be occasionally linked with music. Drama or theatre arts, together with the speech arts of elocution, public speaking and debating might be included in the language arts of English curriculum but, like dance, were more often part of the extra-curricular programs of schools. Burnham noted that the objectives of all the creative arts included the promotion of aesthetic attitudes,"art for art's sake"; a satisfying outlet for pupils' feelings and emotions; and activities to develop creativity and a worthy use of leisure time.[70]

### Art

In the case of art, the lofty aims described by Burnham had been advanced by progressive educators during the 1930s. During the early post-war years they fell far short of realization. Blanche Snell, an Ontario educator, thought that the low status of art and the limited qualifications of teachers meant that future Canadian citizens were being deprived of the opportunity to cultivate aesthetic sensibilities. She cited an outstanding Quebec art teacher, G. Paige Pinneo, to the effect that children in home economics and industrial arts classes gained no introduction to design nor any chance to develop any awareness of line or form. Commercial designers faced an undiscriminating public whose art training was usually limited to elementary or junior high school classes taught by instructors with degrees in other subjects and two or three summer courses in arts and crafts at best. Snell's survey of provincial curricula showed that before 1950 art was rarely accepted for matriculation purposes.[71]

During the 1950s, the organization of the Canadian Society for Education Through Art and its sponsorship of a comprehensive national survey of the field were positive developments. The survey reported encouragingly that by 1960 at the elementary level increasing emphasis was being given to free expression and experimentation, as the broad educational and developmental value of art came to be better recognized. As marks and grades fell into disfavour, evaluation was carried out in terms of the child's growth rather than in the assessment of a product. At the high school level more emphasis was placed on the development of skill and taste. In the senior grades, however, where art was usually an option taken by a minority of often non-academic students, limited attention was given to practical work, and the emphasis was on art appreciation and history, using a formalized approach. Much more continuity and consistency in the art curriculum from kindergarten through Grade 12 was recommended.[72]

After 1960, the art curriculum continued to be plagued by such familiar problems as poorly trained teachers, lack of proper facilities, limited or inflexible scheduling in schools, the status of the subject as a frill or outer subject, and its general non-acceptance for university admission purposes. This rejection by the universities was paradoxical in the light of the vast expansion of fine and performing arts programs that had occurred in their own curricula. The net result was to give art a marginal place in the high school curriculum. However, Canadian art educators began to draw on American art projects, both those based on behavioural psychometric methods and those emphasizing a broader teaching of appreciation using expensive multi-media packages. The costs of both approaches caused them to have limited impact in Canada. British Columbia made use of the Ohio Curriculum Guides during the early 1970s. As a neo-progressive curriculum shift they enabled art as expression and as a means to developing creativity to gain more credence.[73]

During the late 1970s, there was a shift back to more formal teaching and skill development. The continuing low status of art and a lack of financial support for it was paradoxical during a period of tremendous public cultural boom in Canada. One encouraging development in some programs was the use of the *Artist in the Schools*, an approach which, originating in the United States, hired artists to teach and to work on their own projects in the school, enabling pupils to learn about art and artists through direct observation.[74]

## Music

This subject probably had more support than art as an accepted part of the general education of students. The publicity value of performing bands, orchestras and choirs, and the wide popularity of competitions and festivals caused musical performance to rival athletic performance in schools. The social importance of music in teenagers' lives also affected its role in the schools. School programs received an enormous boost when music teachers recognized the legitimacy of jazz and rock. The subject became one of the few areas of the curriculum in which there was a positive response to student interests and knowledge. At the same time, music educators did not ignore their obligation to introduce students to the written music of the past.[75]

Burnham reported that music teachers felt that, while listening was important for appreciation and enjoyment, these goals could only be realized through vocal or instrumental performance.[76] In the elementary grades singing was stressed, with more attention given to choral and orchestral work at later stages. Jazz ensembles, concert bands and choral groups all flourished. The two most influential developments were the introduction of the Orff method from Austria and the Kodaly method from Hungary. Both methods emphasized the creation of children's music, with a stress on participation and music making, incorporating movement, folk melodies and instruments such as the xylophone, bells and the ukelele. The Kodaly method, with its vocal emphasis, was particularly relevant to Canada because the tonic sol-fah system was already established and accepted.[77]

Despite progress, music, like art, faced problems of finding a place in an overcrowded curriculum. Disagreements existed over such issues as the relative merits of choral and instrumental music, what constituted good or bad music, the most appropriate teacher training, the relationship between mere entertainment and the acquisition of performance skills, and competition and the importance of creative work in developing musicianship in children. Music, said the critics, could no longer be justified by confusing appeals to non-musical criteria such as the promotion of social skills and citizenship.[78]

## Industrial Arts

Problems of purpose, status, definition and terminology that had plagued the early manual training movement were evident in industrial arts (or industrial education as it was now sometimes called). A continuing issue was that of the role of the subject in general education vis-à-vis a utilitarian vocational role. Downey observed in 1963 that narrow craft-oriented programs ignored the need to apply basic knowledge from academic subjects to the technological imperatives of modern industrial society.[79] More than a decade later, Gradwell commented that the very term industrial arts had an obsolescent ring. Industry and technology and their links with science could not be adequately portrayed as experiences in woodworking, metalworking and drafting.[80]

By the late 1970s, wider objectives were being proclaimed for the field. The Alberta curriculum described industrial education as providing "a continuum of experience starting with exploratory experiences ... in the elementary and junior high school, expanding in the high school to the development of skills in career fields and culminating in on-the-job experience." Manitoba and Saskatchewan guidelines described industrial arts in similar terms, but stressed a general educational and cultural function that would familiarize students with the social and economic phenomena of the technological world.[81]

Separate industrial arts curricula of the kind popular during the New Education era largely disappeared from the elementary school as some elements were incorporated in mainstream subjects or as part of life skills courses. In the junior high school grades, a common pattern by 1980 was the provision of exploratory experiences using modules based on various major fields of study, such as drafting, electricity, metalwork and woodwork. In the senior high school, career-preparation and the pursuit of a vocational area in depth were common patterns that sometimes entailed work-study programs and articulation with apprenticeship schemes and post-secondary vocational curricula. So-called occupational programs for non-academic slow learning students featured most curricula.

## Home Economics

This subject had aesthetic, scientific, practical and moral objectives, all inherited from its origins in domestic science. Some curricula included attention to the aesthetics of interior design and the furnishing of homes with discriminating taste. Family studies and studies of nutrition linked home economics to the social and physical sciences, thus giving the subject a broader educational function. The use of sociological concepts in home economics classes, though infrequent, had the potential for promoting intellectual understanding. A family studies emphasis was related to values education, pursued through such topics as divorce and its causes, and family planning, although these predictably controversial topics, if treated at all, were more often pursued in other subject areas. Nutrition and consumer studies included consideration of "junk" and "fast" foods and consumer protection laws. In general, family studies stressed the quality of life in a changing environment.[82]

Although the emphases noted were ostensibly moving home economics beyond, if not away from, the teaching of traditional cooking, sewing and household management skills, these traditional elements remained significant in the curricula of most provinces. An emerging trend during the 1970s was the enrolment of both boys and girls in home economics and industrial arts programs, with results that would have surprised and possibly dismayed earlier school promoters. Boys could proudly display cakes they had baked in home economics classes and girls could display bookcases made in woodworking classes.

## Health and Physical Education

In 1945, the CEA and the Canadian Public Health Association launched the first full-scale survey of health conditions and the teaching of health in Canadian schools through the National Committee for School Health Research. More than 90 per cent of elementary and 70 per cent of high schools were surveyed. The survey examined school physical environments in great detail but gave its major attention to the teaching of health, nutrition (food rules) and physical education. Where health teaching was concerned, the Junior Red Cross was credited with being the major positive factor in instruction. General health and cleanliness were found to be the chief emphasis in classrooms. Few teachers had much training in teaching the subject and unsatisfactory factual rote methods predominated as in the past. During the 1950s health and physical education gained importance, arising from an increased awareness of physical fitness influenced by

American cold war concerns for preparedness.[83] After 1960, greater affluence and leisure and the growth of an ideology of individual self-fulfilment led to a broader view of fitness, as the focus of physical education shifted from a militaristic orientation, mass calisthenics and aggressive team sports to a focus on sports to be pursued throughout life. Students were now introduced to a variety of both individual and team sports and were taught life skills for individual development.

Despite these trends, by the 1970s educators and members of the medical profession were concerned about the lack of fitness of Canadian children, a condition that many attributed to the decline of self-generated play resulting from television viewing, the example of adult sedentary behaviour and the growth of competitive adult organized sport such as "pee-wee" hockey and Little League baseball that excluded many.[84] The 1979 British Columbia Physical Education Assessment reported a "disturbingly high incidence of overweight students."[85] Such findings led the Canadian Medical Association to pressure departments of education to expand programs and to allot more time to physical education in schools. Although the subject ranked after English as the one most likely to be compulsory in Canadian schools, a 1973 Saskatchewan study reported that no other country devoted so little scheduled time to physical education. Thus, in the elementary grades Canadian schools allotted but one hour per week to the subject, as compared with five hours per week in France, a nation noted for the academic bias of its curriculum.[86]

Interesting new developments included movement education, which emphasized agility, strength, cooperation and safety. An individual or group might be directed to cross an area, keeping as close to the floor as possible without the use of the limbs or by using only certain limbs. Rarely was a class engaged in drill or calisthenics in unison. Games continued to play an important role in programs, often as culminating activities in physical education classes. Coeducational classes became the norm in many schools. Regular classes were now often held outdoors. Aquatic sports and outdoor activities (cycling, jogging, skiing) were occasionally incorporated in curricula during the 1960s.[87] Inter-school athletic competition remained important in Canadian high schools for its value in promoting school spirit and good public relations, although there was little of the hoopla associated with such competition in the United States. Friesen found that in Canada, as compared with the United States, students valued academic achievement more than athletic achievement.[88]

A long tradition of a national community of interest and of federal support remained evident in physical education during this period. In 1980, the Canadian Association for Health, Physical Education, and Recreation (CAPHER), founded in 1933 and thus one of the older national subject associations, obtained support from a federal agency, Fitness Canada, for the publication of the Basic Skills Series, a set of teachers' guides. Based on modern principles of curriculum planning, these detailed systematic guides had originally been developed within the Calgary Board of Education.

Disseminated throughout Alberta and other provinces, such titles as *K-3 Games* were an interesting example of how local curriculum development could contribute to common national curriculum objectives and practices.[89]

A 1977 survey by Deisach revealed that physical education and health curricula had the main responsibility for family life education, a term often used as a euphemism for sex education in order to deflect public controversy. Family life was to be taught across the curriculum, to enhance student understanding of personal development and family living and to avoid its treatment as a pernicious form of humanism. There was little objection to teaching essential knowledge about sex and interpersonal relationships *per se*. In practice, family life education was taught in only a minority of schools, mainly in larger urban districts.[90]

In a 1971 survey, Elkin reported that controversy centred on what information should be taught and by whom and how programs should be administered.[91] A naive view of the socializing power of the curriculum was shared both by those who feared that sex education would encourage promiscuity and experimentation and by those who hoped that it would reduce abortion, venereal disease, marital breakdown and teenage pregnancy while encouraging positive, responsible attitudes towards sex. Harper's doubts about the validity and efficacy of sex education were noted in Chapter 16.

## Notes to Chapter 18

1 CMEC, *Secondary Education*, 77.

2 CMEC, *Mathematics*, 1.

3 CMEC, *English*, 1.

4 For an account of the Dartmouth Conference and international attempts at English language reform see D. Tanner, *Secondary*, 251.

5 Frye, 10.

6 S.D. Robinson, "Changes;" "English Curriculum."

7 Linehan, 11-13.

8 Frye, 22.

9 Priestley, 37.

10 Moss, 15-20, 24.

11 Atwood, *Survival*, 18-19.

12 Harker, 6.

13 These included *A Dictionary of Canadianisms* (Toronto: Gage, 1967), *Dictionary of Canadian English: The Beginning Dictionary* (Toronto: Gage, 1962) and *Dictionary of Canadian English: The Senior Dictionary* (Toronto: Gage, 1967).

14 Scargill and Warkentyne, 103, 105.

15 See B. Roberts; British Columbia Ministry of Education, *Language, B.C.* (1976); *Assessment of Written Expression* (1978); *Reading Assessment* (1980).

16 CMEC, *English*, 2, 6.

17 Steinhauer, 11-12.

18 Fleming, III, *Schools*, 329; McConnell, 46-9.

19 Burnham, 181-2.

20 Ibid., 95.

21 Kinlin 6-7.

22 See D. Crawford, "Rethinking," 429 ff. and Horne.

23 Potvin, 365-7.

24 Boyko, 92-4.

25 *Liaison* (CMEC newsletter), 6 no.2 (July,1981); 4 no.1 (February,1979).

26 Interview, Prof. Robitaille, U.B.C., May 12, 1981; see also Robitaille and Sherrill, "Achievement Results" and "Teaching of Mathematics."

27 Gary Phillips, 109.

28 See Robitaille and Sherrill, "Achievement Results;" Sherrill, "Mathematics Education Research."

29 Beltzner *et al.*

30 CMEC, *Mathematics*.

31 Beltzner *et al*; O'Reilly.

32 CMEC, *Mathematics*, 22-3.

33 Interview, Prof. Shirley Wong, U.B.C., June 12, 1981.

34 W. Hughes, 145; Alberta, Royal Commission on Education (Cameron Commission, 1959), 111-2.

35 British Columbia, Royal Commission on Education (Chant Commission), 1, 255, 313.

36 Fleming III, *Schools*, 210-8.

37 Burnham, 67.

38 CMEC, *Science Curricula*, 3.

39 Warrington and Newbold, 162-4. An early successful Canadian text that exemplified the "new" chemistry was S. Madras and G.G. Hall, *Basic Modern Chemistry* (Toronto: McGraw Hill, 1963).

40 Even; Nasr.

41 Hart, 33.

42 Goodson. For an account of developments in physics in British Columbia see P.J. Gaskell and Rowell, "Physics" and "Changing School Subjects."

43 CMEC, *Science Curricula*, 6.

44 D. Tanner, *Secondary Curriculum*, 39, 91.

45 H. Dale, 42.

46 Ibid.

47 Hobbs and Erickson. See also British Columbia Ministry of Education, *Science Assessment*.

48 CMEC, *Science Curricula*, 6-9.

49 Symons, *To Know Ourselves*, 162. See also Page, *A Canadian Context*.

50 Science Education Study, *Bulletin* (June, 1981), 3.

51 Orpwood and Souque, 11-14.

52 Ibid., 17.

53 Atwood, "Nationalism," 10-11.

54 See for example N. Sutherland and Deyell, *Making Canadian History* (Toronto: Gage, 1966).

55 See L.D. Stamp, 21-5.

56 See N. Scarfe, *Handbook*.

57 International Geographical Union. See also Scarfe, "Teaching Geography."

58 See for example Tomkins, Tomkins and Hills, *Canada: A Regional Geography* (Toronto; Gage, 1962); Scarfe, Tomkins and Tomkins, *A New Geography of Canada* (Toronto: Gage, 1963) and Doreen M. Tomkins, *Discovering Our Land* (Toronto: Gage, 1966).

59 Milburn, "The Social Studies," 206, 216, 219.

60 Osborne, 26, 28.

61 Walsh. See also Milburn, *Teaching History*, 129-133.

62 Hertzman. See also Milburn, *Teaching History*, 124-8.

63 *Toronto Globe and Mail*, September 6, 1977.

64 Osborne, 13.

65 Hodgetts, *What Culture?*, 56.

66 Downey, *The Social Studies*.

67 CMEC, *Social Studies*, 4-5.

68 Ibid., 6.

69 Ibid.

70 Burnham 210. For a useful later survey of provincial curricula in the arts see CMEC, *Arts* (1983).

71 Cited in Forbes, 48-50. See also Snell.

72 Eason, 9-12, 35-6.

73 Interview, Prof. Jim Gray, U.B.C. June 14, 1981.

74 Ibid.

75 Burnham, 216.

76 Ibid.

77 Kalman *et al*, 852.

78 Ibid.

79 Downey, "Secondary," 6-7.

80 Gradwell.

81 Western Canadian Industrial Education Invitational Conference (1982).

82 Interview, Prof. Susan Parrish, U.B.C., June 17, 1981; Susan Parrish-Connell, "International Home Economics," 6.

83 CEA, "A Health Survey," 10-15, 41-5, 52-3, 56, 65.

84 Bailey, 10-12.

85 British Columbia Ministry of Education, *Assessment of Physical Education*, 1-2.

86 Saskatchewan Department of Education, Report of the Saskatchewan Advisory Committee on Physical Education.

87 Interview, Profs. Alex Carre and Peter Moody, U.B.C., June 21, 1981.

88 D. Friesen, 49-52.

89 CAPHER. Information regarding dissemination supplied by Mr. Don Williams, Calgary Public School Board.

90 Deisach.

91 Cited in Shymko, 51.

# CHAPTER 19

## CONTROLLING AND MAKING THE CURRICULUM: PERSPECTIVES ON THE POLICY PROCESS

*The educational system is the largest instrument in the modern state for telling people what to do.*

(Frank MacKinnon, 1960)

*The practical arguments in support of uniformity of practice across Canada are so obvious that they do not need stating ...*

(Newfoundland Department of Education, 1978)

### Old and New Mechanisms of Curriculum Control

#### Textbook and Materials Policies

Few areas of policy and practice saw more ferment over the period than that of textbooks and related curricular materials. Throughout the 1950s, policy remained much as it had been for the best part of a century. Departments of Education, through their selection processes and criteria, largely controlled the writing and publication of textbooks and through regulations strictly guided their selection and use. The single authorized textbook in each subject area remained the norm and the major determinant of the curriculum; its content still provided the basis for preparing tests and examinations. In the mid-1960s, Hodgetts reported that nearly 90 per cent of the classes he observed "unquestioningly followed the gray, consensus version of the textbook ... " with its "ready-made verdicts." Recitation of textbook content was a preferred teaching mode.[1]

Some trends towards liberalization of textbook policy became evident by 1950. Following the suggestions of Ontario's Hope Commission, which noted that the single textbook was inadequate for adapting teaching to local needs, Ontario moved from a policy of single authorization to the multiple authorization of series of textbooks adapted to different levels.[2] A year later, the province instituted a system of stimulation grants on a per-pupil basis which made Circular 14 a list of virtually free approved books available to school boards. The use of multiple texts was thought to be especially necessary for teaching reading in order to reduce pupil failure.

In advancing more liberal views, the Hope Commission reiterated the Ontario conviction of the indispensable role of the textbook in learning. Views about its contribution to the economy of both teaching and learning, its role as a guide to content and course organization, and its use as a supplement to instruction were remarkably similar to those that had been advanced in the Ryerson era.[3] Over the following twenty years, the liberalization and decentralization of textbook policy became the norm in most provinces. Whereas in 1949 Ontario's Circular 14 had included 101 titles supplied by sixteen publishing houses, in 1979 there were 2182 titles supplied by 104 publishers.[4] Curriculum differentiation, the credit system and a more diverse school population had created a demand for more varied teaching materials. Booklets, paperbacks and multi-media kits were used to supplement and sometimes to replace the textbook. However, multiple authorizations of textbooks for a given course often meant only that similar topics were covered in a similar order in similar ways.

Publishers, faced with fragmented and shrinking markets, felt constrained to adhere more closely to curriculum guidelines. More sophisticated methods of market research were often necessary in order to determine the nature of the actual curriculum and of resource needs. In 1970, the problems of the publishing industry prompted a major Ontario royal commission study. The study noted that textbook sales were the greatest source of revenue for the industry and that without them Canadian publishing would not be able to survive. The fact that upwards of 40 per cent of all students in the country were domiciled in the province meant that Canadian texts were, in practice, Ontario texts. The role of publishers in influencing the curriculum was said to go beyond the provision of materials to meet provincial guidelines. The publisher's representative, typically a former teacher, was the main point of contact with schools in promoting a firm's products. Representatives became quite directly involved in curriculum policy and in selection processes through monitoring program changes, through maintaining contact with provincial officials and curriculum committees, and through promoting their products by means of exhibits, free materials and workshops for school staffs.[5]

Selection committees included representatives from all levels of the educational structure, as well as from related organizations such as teachers' federations and outside interest groups. New Brunswick's 1970-1 Directory of Provincial Curriculum Sub-Committees listed forty-nine committees covering fifty-one subjects and involving about 300 people. Increasingly, local school boards gained the power to select and prescribe materials. By 1972, Alberta, Manitoba and Newfoundland had granted legislative authority for this purpose. Alberta policy provided that materials could be prescribed by board resolution, with a copy of each item to be forwarded to the Department of Education. School boards were enjoined to use a variety of approaches, textbooks and supplementary materials. The textbook had value in giving organizational structure to content and in providing for concept and skill development, but it was not to constitute the course of study, because its pedagogy was often too didactic.[6]

A 1978 Ontario study by Kormos indicated that teachers rated their own and other locally produced materials as a major resource in overcoming the inadequacies of commercial materials.[7] New computer, copying and duplicating technologies were helpful to teachers in creating their own materials and in individualizing the curriculum. Local jurisdictions such as North York in Ontario had highly sophisticated policies and methods for the development, testing and implementation of local materials by teacher authors on a contract basis to meet needs in such areas as multiculturalism, Canadian Studies, women's studies and values education.[8]

The historic concern for preserving a Canadian publishing industry and for maintaining a Canadian perspective in materials was reinforced by the growing influence of multi-national, mainly American publishers. Some multi-national publishers produced exemplary Canadian (or Canadianized) materials. In some subject areas such as science, materials originally developed by federally funded American projects were adopted by Canadian school systems, with the ironical result that the United States government indirectly had more influence on curriculum change than did the Canadian government. To meet the multi-national challenge, most provinces during the 1970s began to encourage or require Canadian authorship and publication of curriculum materials. This policy was reinforced by purchasing regulations in most provinces, and by various forms of federal assistance to Canadian publishers. In Ontario in 1972, Circular 15, *Canadian Curriculum Materials*, a consolidated catalogue of books and media, was issued to parallel Circular 14. Non-Canadian texts could be listed only when suitable Canadian texts were not available, as in the case of some used for teaching modern languages.[9] In 1975, Ontario introduced a Learning Materials Development Plan designed to encourage the development of Canadian materials in specific curricular areas where markets were too limited to permit profitable development.

The trends described, the use by the provinces of similar systematic selection and evaluation procedures and provincial requirements that materials conform with curriculum guidelines reflected a high degree of policy uniformity across Canada. By this time, the four western provinces were using the New York based EPIE (Educational Product Information Exchange) system as a means of evaluating and selecting materials. Teachers and other personnel were systematically trained in the use of this analysis scheme. Readability and an emphasis on skill development had become important selection criteria in all provinces. Similar skill sequences and recommended instructional practices made for national uniformity. As the Council of Ministers' subject surveys and transfer guide illustrated, there was a growing uniformity in content goals.

External demands for a voice in textbook policy led to the increasing bureaucratization and politicization of the selection process. Conservatives, liberals and radicals alike demanded the exclusion of materials and topics deemed controversial, obscene, sexist or racist. Thus, *The Diviners* was attacked by religious fundamentalists for its alleged obscenity and *Huckleberry Finn* by human rights liberals for its alleged racism.[10] Human rights legislation in several provinces had considerable influence on textbook policy and selection, and thereby became an instrument of curriculum control.

Policy-makers and teachers were frequently at a loss in dealing with pressure groups who sought to influence the selection of materials. Some groups became adept at what Boyd, writing in the United States context, called "the politics of controversy," whereby the process of simply making a program controversial might cause officials and publishers to back off from it.[11] Few groups seemed to trust teachers or students to deal rationally with controversial material in ways that might create valuable learning opportunities. Selection was not always easily distinguishable from censorship. In the absence of judicial protection such as that afforded under the United States Bill of Rights, Canadians had only *ad hoc* defences against censorship.

New concerns for eliminating bias resulted in selection and evaluation procedures that were, in some respects, stricter than those of the past. Thus, in selecting materials for inclusion in Ontario's Circular 14, evaluations considered bias, congruence with curriculum guidelines, accuracy, objectivity, Canadian salience, readability, the quality and use of illustrations, and general technical quality.[12] The Vancouver School Board was in the vanguard in Canada in adopting carefully thought out selection and reconsideration or "challenge" policies dealing with materials. The emphasis was on the right to read, listen and view. The major criterion for judging material was to be its appropriateness "for its intended educational use."[13]

In addition to external groups that sought to control curriculum content, there were voluntary, public, and corporate agencies that produced their own materials, which they sought to inject into school programs. Voluntary agencies included the United Nations Association, the Canadian Cancer Foundation and groups seeking to combat drug, alcohol and tobacco addiction. The work of such bodies as the Canada Studies Foundation and the Canadian Foundation for Economic Education has been described. Public agencies included many of the estimated sixty-six federal government departments and agencies involved in education, such as External Affairs, the National Museums of Canada, the CBC, and the Department of Agriculture.[14] Anderson noted that three Ontario ministries, Environment, Health and Agriculture, annually distributed several million pieces of literature as well as posters, films and similar materials, many directed to schools. In British Columbia in 1980, the Deputy Minister of Education speculated that other ministries were collectively spending more money on curriculum development than was his own.[15] In some cases, their efforts entailed fully developed curriculum packages including evaluation, teacher training and implementation procedures.

Corporate agencies such as the Canadian Forestry Association supplied large quantities of materials to schools. British Columbia Hydro provided an energy program made up of lesson aids and total curriculum packages created by teacher-authors for use in all grades. Critics such as Beattie and Gaskell raised serious questions about the objectivity of such materials. Others felt that, as long as materials reflected a balanced perspective and were used to promote skills of critical inquiry, they could enrich the curriculum in significant ways. In a period of budget restraint it seemed likely that attractive, well-organized, often free packages of corporate-produced materials would become more popular. There was a clear need to document the extent and impact of such materials and for teachers to make professional judgments about their worth.[16]

The new conservative mood of the late 1970s led to greater curriculum control through control of materials. Quebec's plan of action was critical of the virtual abandonment of textbooks, which had left students without any systematic guide to learning and parents and trustees without one of their main points of reference for judging the schools. Other materials were ill adapted to schools and handouts had been used excessively. The textbook ensured that prescribed course topics were actually taught. It demonstrated appropriate teaching methods. The written word remained significant "even in this age of electronics." The new policy provided that each textbook must be approved "from the moral and religious point of view" by the Catholic or Protestant Committee of the Superior Council of Education.[17] In Nova Scotia, most submissions to the Walker Commission recommended increased funding of classroom supplies but many were critical of the frequency of textbook changes, of the lack of a core text available to every student and the unreasonably high number of courses available at some schools.[18]

## Evaluation, Assessment and New School-University Relationships

Increasing enrolments, incipient mass secondary education, a greater diversity of course offerings, and continuing teacher transiency resulted in disparities in achievement that led, during the 1950s, to a renewed interest in testing as a means of restoring uniform standards. In Ontario, Grade 13 objective tests of the type used during the inter-war years were revived by the Atkinson Study of Utilization of Student Resources. The study had the prestige sponsorship of A.J. Ketchum, the headmaster of Trinity College School, Sidney Smith, the president of the University of Toronto and R.W.B. Jackson, the head of a group of Ontario College of Education researchers. These men hoped that more objective ability-achievement measures would prove more effective for university admission purposes than traditional examinations, which put too much emphasis on cramming, conformity and learning isolated facts.[19]

The program used slightly modified versions of achievement tests developed by the United States College Entrance Examination Board (CEEB) together with the Scholastic Aptitude Test (SAT) and College Ability Tests, administered by the Educational Testing Service in Princeton, New Jersey. In the event, objective test scores did not prove to be better than the old examination system as a basis for university admission.[20] However, they continued in partial use in Grade 13 and were shortly administered in Grade 12 to all students seeking the Ontario Secondary School Graduation Diploma. A modified SAT (SAT Ontario or SATO) was developed, and provincial achievement tests in English, French, and Chemistry were prepared.[21]

The Atkinson Study maintained a five-year follow-up of participant success at university, other institutions, and employment, using achievement records and ratings from employers. It was followed by the larger Carnegie Study of Identification and Utilization of Talent in High School and College which, involving 120 000 Ontario students in Grades 7 through 9, was a project on a scale unprecedented in Canada. The Carnegie Study was primarily confined to an appraisal of later in-school achievement. In Fleming's view, the main outcome of both studies was the development of the tests themselves.[22]

A prime difficulty in maintaining uniformity in achievement and common university admission standards was the growing diversity of curricula and entrance requirements within the higher institutions. Specific requirements for admission to particular faculties and programs meant that the schools were no longer able to provide a common sequential background of preparation useful for further studies. H.L. Campbell thought that the only solution would be for universities to accept students of good ability regardless of specific background. By offering beginning or preparatory courses required in specific programs, students would not have to make premature choices of subjects. Students from smaller schools where all prerequisites could not be offered would not be unfairly penalized.[23]

Problems of school-university articulation were examined in 1951 by a joint committee set up by the CEA and the NCCU. The committee's report reiterated now familiar concerns about the disparity between legitimate university academic needs and the requirement that the school system stress the citizenship needs of a diverse high school population. The universities had more clear-cut goals, but had to meet conflicting pressures between demands for greater academic rigour on the one hand and more flexible entrance requirements on the other.[24] This conclusion attested to the problems beginning to face Canadian policy-makers as they entered the era of mass education.

Manning's 1954 study provided a useful summary of examination policies across Canada in the first post-war decade.[25] By this time, four provinces were recommending their best students for high school graduation without writing external departmental examinations. In general, the trend was towards making promotions more and more the responsibility of local school authorities. Examination policy was usually the responsibility of boards or committees that included full-time departmental officials, university and teacher representatives, and, in the cases of Newfoundland and Quebec, members of the clergy. The actual administration of examinations in most provinces was under departmental officials who were usually linked with or responsible to the curriculum division. Generally, persons selected to set examination papers were university professors, departmental officials or practising teachers.[26]

In 1950, failure rates among the provinces and from year to year within each province varied greatly, but were high everywhere by later standards. In junior matriculation algebra, failure rates in five provinces analysed by Manning ranged from 17.6 per cent in Nova Scotia to 51.5 per cent in New-foundland. Similar variations were reported in other subjects. In Nova Scotia the failure rate in chemistry varied from 28.3 per cent in 1949 to 47.8 per cent in 1950.[27] These data suggest that unscientific examination procedures continued to exert a capricious influence on the evaluation of student achievement, with sometimes drastic effects on the life chances and future opportunities of the young.

By 1950, high failure rates also reflected the increase in the numbers of students of low or mediocre ability who were staying in school. Manning's study suggested that academic requirements would have to be broadened to accommodate a more diverse school population. This should be done openly, Manning thought, by simplifying curriculum and diploma requirements, thereby meeting the needs of the average student more realistically. This would be less detrimental to effective education than lowering standards in the traditional academic subjects. Passing these subjects had already been made easier, he claimed, by using fewer difficult and more stereotyped questions. Memorized answers, credit for vague, indefinite or partial answers, and lower penalties for inaccurate language usage and calculation had attenuated standards.[28]

In 1960, the determination of standards remained firmly in the hands of the universities. All students in a province wrote the same examinations administered by the schools and the Department of Education. Essentially the same number of papers passed at the same minimum grade was required in all provinces and there was, in Harris' words, "remarkably little difference in the standards represented by matriculation from one end of Canada to the other." By varying the difficulty of questions it was possible to identify the best candidates for university admission.[29]

Despite such a high degree of uniformity, there was a strong demand by this time for common entrance requirements to the universities. At the NCCU meeting in 1961, it was argued that a common standard was needed because Canada was now "a nation rather than a group of provinces." Much greater mobility among the provinces was leading to a disruption of children's educational programs. As a result, it was proposed that a national testing program be established using CEEB-type tests to be administered by a Canadian body in liaison with the CEEB.[30]

Not everyone shared NCCU concerns about selection and examination standards. Public concerns mounted over what many saw as unduly restrictive university admissions policies. A senior Ontario government official, J.R. McCarthy, commented in 1964 that universities could not continue to evade their responsibilities by raising already high admission requirements. Pride of tradition should not be used to perpetuate outmoded practices.[31] Standardization was increasingly questioned as a distortion of the educational process and of the curriculum. Much testing was said to be irrelevant and redundant, retained largely for the mystique associated with it. As a result, teachers made little use of test results in their teaching and curriculum planning.[32]

In the event, two contradictory trends became evident during the early 1960s: on the one hand the demand for more uniform examination and selection systems, and on the other the demand for the abolition of province-wide testing and the substitution of local assessment. In Ontario, the twin response took the form of a shift to province-wide objective examinations and a gradual devolution of the examination function to the schools. A Grade 13 program was introduced, modeled on and largely made up of items from the CEEB tests. Developed by a new testing organization, the Ontario Admission to College and University (OACU), the program became the prototype for a national effort launched in 1969 by the Ottawa-based Service for Admission to College and University (SACU). The SACU effort proved abortive although, for a brief period, SACU tests were used across Canada and for a time it appeared that a Canadian equivalent to the CEEB might develop. Before long, 100 000 anglophone and francophone students were writing SACU tests at major centres across Canada. Many universities required the test scores for admission, usually in combination with the student's record.[33]

However, despite a unique and promising initiative that brought together representatives from universities and colleges and all departments of education, and used committees of teachers, civil servants and university experts to develop tests, SACU faced serious problems from the start. Its credibility was impaired by the use of first language French and English achievement tests and a Canadian Scholastic Aptitude Test (CSAT) modeled on CEEB tests. This had been done on the specious assumption of a similarity between Canadian and American students and institutions.[34] The tests could not be tailored to separate provincial curricula and, while useful in monitoring educational standards, were not able to shape standards as traditional provincial examinations had done. Even their major function as a university admission screen was attenuated by the suspicion that the universities, although they had led the demand for uniform tests, relied more on school records than on test scores. Moreover, SACU had failed to promote its program effectively or to provide follow-up research and information on the predictive value of its tests.[35] In addition, at a time of growing Canadian regionalism and of decentralization of educational policy, the time was not ripe for a national testing program. As a result, by 1972 limited use was being made of the system.

By this time it was evident that the new tests were less effective predictors of university success than had been hoped. The result was a devolution of the examination function to the schools; this began in Ontario in 1965 when school assessments were included as part of the evaluation process for the first time. Departmental examination results were supplemented by internal records of school achievement, which were used as a basis for granting tentative early university admission. In 1968, Grade 13 departmental examinations were abolished.[36] The new policy received wide support from administrators, teachers, press and public. The generally favourable reaction was underscored by support from traditional quarters such as the prestigious Trinity College School, whose headmaster declared that "the cancellation of ... external examinations is the most important step that Ontario has taken since the introduction of compulsory education ..."[37] Gradually, external examinations were abolished in most other provinces.

In the new system, principals became responsible for recommending students to the ministry for their high school diplomas. Teachers, using student class performance and various instruments of their choice, now felt sufficiently professional to assume full responsibility for evaluation. Some critics pointed to a serious problem in eliminating external evaluation entirely. Public examinations satisfied a criterion of fairness better than any other because justice was done and was seen to be done. In placing an impossible responsibility on principals and teachers, Canada had moved from what had been one of the most examination-ridden educational systems in the world to one in which large-scale uniform examinations were no longer the norm.[38]

By the late 1970s, the new conservative mood in Canadian education was leading to demands for the restoration of some type of uniform assessment. The universities were facing serious difficulties in assessing the knowledge possessed by incoming students, a situation that had serious implications for their own course and curriculum planning. Difficulties were exacerbated by the growing curricular permissiveness of the universities themselves, as in their cafeteria-style offerings they emulated the high schools. Academic freedom had come to mean that the university teacher had absolute power to determine the texts and instructional practices used and the methods of evaluating students.[39]

The initial response of policy makers to the new demands was to establish elaborate assessment programs such as those in British Columbia and New Brunswick referred to earlier. The new programs entailed periodic testing of sample populations of students at designated grade levels and in various subject areas. In addition, goals, course materials and instructional practices were evaluated. The view of teachers, parents, employers, school boards, clergy, universities and students themselves were solicited on the efficacy of curricular offerings. In effect, such programs constituted a monitoring system designed to appraise standards, to assess student achievement and to provide a basis for curriculum development and renewal. Holmes called them a form of "dipsticking." He thought that the system had the advantage of showing where strengths and weaknesses lay, at comparatively little cost. Its great weakness was that it did not provide direct information to the student, the school, the board or the ministry.[40]

Like the previous objective testing programs, the new assessment programs sometimes drew fire as a result of their use of American testing instruments. Thus, New Brunswick's provincial Evaluation Branch, established in 1975 as part of the most ambitious assessment effort in Atlantic Canada, drew on American criterion-referenced tests developed by the Westinghouse Learning Corporation and made performance comparisons between New Brunswick and American students.[41] Some critics expressed concern about the bias content of American tests, reflected in such questions as "From what country did America declare her independence in 1776?" To meet this problem, resort was made to the Canadianization of tests. In doing so, test developers failed to address the problem of cultural bias in Canadian tests. Largely trained in the United States and familiar with American testing methods, they tended to ignore those differences between their own and American society that influenced test performance.[42]

Nova Scotia's assessment program comprised domain-referenced Tests in High School Achievement that were intended to supplement local assessment and designed to demonstrate student competence in five major fields of learning that formed the core of Nova Scotia education.[43] British Columbia developed the most extensive provincial assessment program in Canada. The major question addressed by the program was: To what extent are all students achieving the basic objectives of the public school system? Formerly, an important question had been: What percentage of students should be admitted to higher levels of schooling? In judging assessment results, Mussio and Greer thought that a distinction must be made between norms and standards. It was no doubt satisfying to know that British Columbia students were above American norms in mathematics and science. However, in a system now accountable for the education of all students, this satisfaction was misplaced if large numbers of young adults were entering the job market lacking important skills, notwithstanding that teaching might be better than in some past time or in some other jurisdiction.[44]

Although Alberta took a similar comprehensive view of assessment, Ontario took a different approach, with the setting up in 1976 of the Ontario Instrument Assessment Pool, which was based on a curriculum-oriented approach to evaluation. The intent was to provide a wide range of instruments drawn from a pool of existing and new measures related to the goals and objectives of Ontario education, and developed co-operatively by the Ministry of Education, school boards, teachers' organizations and subject groups, administrators and faculties of education. Banks of test items would allow teachers to select items geared to the objectives being assessed and to topics outlined in official guidelines. In addition, the Pool suggested methods for conducting consistent classroom observations and structured interviews. It also included methods and reference materials to assess student growth in listening, speaking, writing, music and art, and in affective areas concerned with attitudes, self-image, moral development and self-discipline. By 1978, curriculum-oriented instruments were under development for intermediate grade level use in English, Geography, History and Mathematics and for elementary level second language French.[45]

The direct curricular effects of the assessment programs described were problematical. Most provided for follow-up revision at the provincial and local levels in the form of updating curriculum guides and materials to meet the deficits and needs that the assessments had indicated. Sustained follow-up at the local level was a costly and time-consuming process that most ministries seemed to leave to local discretion. Assessment programs undoubtedly served a political function by demonstrating that ministries had a concern for maintaining some degree of uniformity of standards. Goble observed that, although one government had gone so far as to acknowledge that allegations of slipping standards had been disproved by its own research, because the allegations were widely believed they had to be treated as though they were valid.[46] In some cases, assessments appeared to have a direct impact on curriculum policy. Thus, Downey's 1975 assessment of the values-based Alberta social studies curriculum became a basis for revising that curriculum three years later.

The CEA study of academic achievement at the senior high school level, which Nyberg and Lee had conducted in 1978, indicated general satisfaction with academic standards. Local evaluation policies were surveyed, by means of questionnaires to chief education officers. Final examinations were still in widespread use, but were now typically constructed by groups of teachers for use throughout a school or school system, usually within the framework of local or provincial policy. Final grades were determined by combining scores on these examinations with work done by students during the school year. Despite their general satisfaction with achievement standards, the chief education officers favoured more uniform standards across local school systems and individual provinces.[47]

In 1978, Ontario hosted a Cross-Canada Dialogue on Evaluation which brought together thirty-two educators from eight provinces who were interested in evaluation. Ontario officials agreed to co-ordinate the preparation of an inventory of materials and resources used for evaluation in the various provinces. The inventory was intended to facilitate bilateral discussions about possible sharing and joint development of evaluation practices in the future.[48] The approach was parallel to similar interprovincial sharing of curriculum materials and guidelines which the Council of Ministers of Education was promoting on a voluntary basis.

By this time the universities, faced by restricted budgets and by the chaos that some claimed had resulted from the abolition of external testing, were stiffening their admission requirements. In 1980 Douglas Kenny, the president of the University of British Columbia stated that by increasing its admission standards, "the university meant to ensure that the high schools had a solid program."[49] Shortly, the University of Toronto followed the U.B.C. lead when its faculty of arts and science voted to disallow a range of commercial and technological studies as acceptable for admission, and to restrict allowable credit in such areas as dramatic and visual arts, family and interdisciplinary studies, and physical education and health.[50] Students were constrained to emphasize the hard sciences, English and mathematics to the detriment of preparation in the cultural subjects, a trend that undermined the traditional liberal educational function of the high school and contributed to a narrowing of the curriculum. Students were reinforced in their conviction that vocational, cultural and recreational subjects were not worthy studies. By this time the restoration of university entrance and province-wide testing was being mooted in several jurisdictions.

## Teacher Training and Teacher Education

By the mid 1940s war-time and post-war demands for teachers caused a significant decline in the extremely modest standards of teacher training and certification that had been slowly and painfully developed over half a century. How far the established system prevailed into the 1950s was suggested by Keats, the American suburbanite cited in Chapter 17. In describing his children's experience in a two-room rural school in Ontario, he noted that both teachers "seemed to follow instruction manuals that told them what they must tell the children and how to do so ... ." Keats thought that this rigid pattern of instruction, "designed to be impervious to the worst effort of the world's most incompetent teacher" had nevertheless given his children a sound schooling.[51]

The period was noteworthy for the fact that the training and education of teachers finally came under the jurisdiction of the universities. The process had begun in Alberta in 1946 when the normal schools ceased to operate and a Bachelor of Education program was established. However, it was not until thirty years later that all provinces required a university degree as a minimum basis for certification. In recommending that teacher training be accorded university status, a 1949 CEA survey on the status of the teaching profession in Canada warned that undue academicism should not be allowed to inhibit an understanding of the ever-broadening and more varied responsibilities of the schools. It was proposed that professional standards "be sufficiently uniform among the provinces to facilitate the acceptance of certificates by all provincial authorities with a minimum of additional training." Low entrance requirements designed to overcome the severe post-war teacher shortage were said to attract transients, who soon left for higher paying, higher status occupations.[52]

With regard to the content of teacher training, the report urged an emphasis on general education at both the secondary and university levels in preference to traditional disciplinary matriculation and undergraduate competence; social understanding, aesthetic appreciation and non-academic personal and social skills and qualities were more important. In teacher training *per se*, overloaded classroom schedules should be reduced and more attention given to studies of a "broad professional character to develop a sound philosophy of education." Too few teachers were acquiring knowledge of the many valid findings concerning learning, methods and curricula that were available from what the study called "the developing science of education."[53] By 1974, Ontario, the last major bastion of the normal school, finally made a university degree mandatory for all teachers. By 1980, only one normal school, the Nova Scotia Teachers' College, remained in Canada. The crux of the change had been the effort to put the training of elementary teachers on a par with that of secondary teachers, a task not easily achieved.

In 1977, Calam described how developments during the period had given rise to a baffling mosaic of degrees, programs, certificates, diplomas, summer offerings, emergency measures, internships, credits and institutes. Here was a concept of the teaching profession that defied analysis.[54] By 1980, Ontario had reduced its thirty-nine different kinds of certificates to one which still, however, required detailed explanatory footnotes. Whereas formerly teacher training had been the term used to denote the preparation process that led to certification or licensing, increasingly teacher education came into use as a collective term to describe the combined academic, professional and practical elements of programs. Since in theory, prospective teachers now acquired their content background in the academic component taken in faculties of arts and science, training in methods and other courses no longer gave as much emphasis to what had in the normal schools sometimes been called professionalized subject matter. Content and method were now sharply separated.

Some critics charged that the new programs were not necessarily a better basis for developing effective classroom practice than the old narrow, formalistic programs of nostalgic memory. The academic independence that the university teaching model exemplified for instructors and the lack of official governmental supervision that had prevailed formerly diminished congruence between school and teacher training curricula. More positively, the requirement of a university degree meant that teachers now had a broader, deeper and ostensibly more liberal education. It could be said that teachers were now better educated, although not necessarily better trained.

Most high school teachers continued to be prepared under so-called consecutive programs, i.e., by means of an arts or science degree followed by a year of professional training. Undoubtedly the new so-called concurrent Bachelor of Education programs that combined academic study and professional training made their greatest contribution by upgrading elementary teaching. Whereas in 1960-61, only 25.7 per cent of Canadian teachers outside Quebec held university degrees, by 1978-79 this proportion had increased to 72.7 per cent.[55] There were still serious disparities among provinces however, and in some rural areas as many as half of all teachers still lacked degrees in 1980. Disparagement of professional training to the contrary, the problems of the schools invariably led to demands for more training that would enable teachers to meet ever expanding needs. The exploding curriculum of the schools, it seemed, required an exploding curriculum in teacher education. Calam observed that briefs presented to a British Columbia inquiry proposed mandatory courses that taken together amounted to a six-year program beyond a degree.[56]

In the light of a diversity of certificates and requirements, there was some paradox in the monotonous similarity among programs from province to province. Within the new university setting, efforts after 1960 to break the monotony were based on various competing models or images of the teacher that were reflected in competing program models. Most persistent was what Macdonald termed the omnicapable model of the warm, personable, intelligent, knowledgeable, articulate, patient, efficient, gentle teacher who assumed the role of a kind of secular priest. Calam described this and other competing models.[57] In practice, the structure of traditional programs remained. A limited application of new approaches misled some educators to conclude that one method of training teachers was as good as the next; it was a view often justified by the proclamation of the jejune truism that there was no one best method. Dissatisfaction and confusion reflected the sense that teacher education had little positive impact on the school curriculum.

The major attempt to counter dissatisfaction took the form of extended school-based experiences designed to capitalize on student perception of practice teaching as the one useful component of their training. During the 1960s, Simon Fraser University adopted a form of internship that attracted national attention. In principle, a more realistic school experience better integrated with course work and an improvement of school-university communication were clear gains. In practice, research suggested that the student teacher was more easily socialized to the instructional task in conventional ways.[58]

In a period when the central role of the teacher in curriculum development was increasingly recognized, it was surprising that pre-service programs still gave so little systematic attention to the study of curriculum theory and practice and to issues such as those involved in the selection and evaluation of learning materials. A number of the most valuable curriculum innovations of the period were sometimes introduced to schools through integrated programs in bilingual, multicultural, second language and special education teacher training of the type noted earlier. Foundations faculty and other instructors made a particular contribution in heeding Symons' demand for more Canadian content in teacher education curricula through a greater attention to Canadian educational issues.[59]

By 1980, a growing interest across Canada in research on teaching was being touted as a means of bringing greater rigour and coherence to teacher education programs. Some educators were critical of an approach that they felt overstressed clinical supervision as a training method and emphasized narrow skill development in teaching the basic subjects of the curriculum. Others, however, pointed to the need to improve the simple efficiency of teaching which, from the research evidence, functioned at a low level. A new concern for bringing system and order to teaching was reminiscent of earlier Herbartianism, although the researchers concerned often seemed unaware of their historical debt.

## Managing the Curriculum: Administrative Control and Implementation

During the 1950s, systems of inspection, supervision, school administration and finance matured, and broader curriculum goals attracted interest as the CEA studies of practical education indicated. Gradually, teachers, educational experts and laypersons were brought into the curriculum building-process, as H.L. Campbell termed it.[60] In practice, this meant cautious modification of centrally developed curricula directed by superintendents responsible to the central authority. More democratic teacher-directed development of the type exemplified by Ontario's Porter Plan proved abortive. Phillips argued that provincially prescribed programs were not seriously restrictive, since the best teachers disregarded them and most others were glad to have their duties clearly defined. There was reason to believe that teachers had more freedom under the dictates of a tolerant central authority at a distance than under a local superintendent zealous for the success of a program "democractically" contrived.[61]

Pullen described how curriculum revision was organized in the various provinces during the 1950s. Nearly all provinces by this time had curriculum directors. A common pattern consisted of general or curriculum advisory committees under which specific committees, including subject committees, functioned with responsibility for drawing up courses, recommending textbooks and the like. Both types of committee included teachers or their federation representatives, university faculty, department officials and sometimes laypersons.[62]

In 1952, possibly the most ambitious national endeavour in Canadian education since the Macdonald-Robertson movement a half century earlier was launched, in the form of the CEA-Kellogg Project in Educational Leadership. Funded by means of a $266 000 grant from the Michigan-based Kellogg Foundation and matched by comparable Canadian resources, the project involved 644 people during its five-year life, including half of Canada's 700 school superintendents and inspectors. Others involved included Ministers of Education or Deputy Ministers, university faculty members and a few teachers and trustees.[63]

The major purpose of the project included the inter-communication of ideas and practices among the various Canadian regions through building up a fund of knowledge and materials on school supervision and administration in Canada. In order to encourage practical solutions to problems encountered at the local level, the project sought to promote the development of training programs for school executives. In the nationalizing milieu of the St. Laurent years, it was not surprising that increased national understanding was seen as the major overall purpose of the project.[64]

The building up of a fund of knowledge based on Canadian experience on which administrators could draw included knowledge about curriculum policy and curriculum development. This was partly achieved by the core activity of the project, the annual interprovincial CEA University of Alberta Short Course, an event which continues on a self-supporting basis. Over a thirty-year period, a large majority of anglophone Canadian superintendents and many of their senior assistants, together with many francophone officials, gained unique opportunities to share ideas and experiences with their colleagues across the country, thereby obtaining and contributing to a national perspective on education. In addition, national organizations of superintendents and inspectors and of educational faculty members were established. Of special significance was a new national graduate program in educational administration and supervision which was based at the University of Alberta and initially funded by the Kellogg Foundation.[65] Thus, the CEA-Kellogg Project helped to promote common structures and practices that gave considerable uniformity to the increasing control which Canadian administrators sought to maintain in a rationalized bureaucratic system.

Despite oscillations between subject-, child- and society-centred curriculum change after 1960, and shifting trends between centralization and decentralization of authority, the Canadian tradition of administrative control remained alive and well. While textbook and examination policies became more permissive, and while teachers asserted a new professional autonomy with some success, administrators now sought to control classroom practice by more extensive and sophisticated supervisory techniques. Rapid growth and greater affluence led to a marked expansion of supervisory personnel and to a greater organizational complexity, marked by greater bureaucratization and professionalization of administration.

Traditionally, curriculum policy and its implementation had been an aspect of general administration. In Ontario the establishment between 1965 and 1976 of separate Curriculum Development and Curriculum Services branches, and their later unification into a single Curriculum Branch, were a recognition that policy in the area had become increasingly important and that school programs were constantly changing or developing. Complexity was illustrated by the existence of committees that revised guidelines or developed new ones, and others that interpreted them for classroom teachers. Phillips commented half-facetiously that "by abandoning the practice of issuing courses of study in definite or cut-and-dried form, by delegating final responsibility for curriculum to local authorities and teachers, and by issuing guidelines open to continued discussion and reconsideration, the central authority could hope to keep everyone busy and content and so ensure further curriculum development."[66]

As ministries expanded their policy and planning functions, they devolved their inspectoral and supervisory functions to the local level. Ontario however, interposed nine regional offices between the two levels as outposts of the central authority, intended to serve a liaison function between the ministry and school boards. The complement of the Niagara Regional Office included twenty-five professionals plus support staff. Each school board within the region had its own supervisory roster.[67] In British Columbia, the Prince George School District illustrated the supervisory capability and highly trained leadership of a remote modest-sized urban-rural school district. This Curriculum Services Department comprised twenty-three personnel operating within four branches that resembled a miniature ministry of education. A statement of guiding principles reflected a high level of technical and conceptual expertise.[68]

Guidelines and directives now emanated profusely from both levels of the curriculum hierarchy. Provincial guidelines might be used directly by teachers in small local jurisdictions, but in larger county boards and urban districts with a full complement of supervisors, consultants, co-ordinators and other administrative personnel, so-called second-generation guidelines were produced. In either case, the resulting outlines or resource documents might be upwards of 200 pages in length. Such compendia were reminiscent of the detailed courses of study of preceding generations.

The role of teachers in curriculum development waxed and waned during the 1970s. Friesen and Holdaway, analyzing what they called the curriculum debate in Canadian education, distinguished between curriculum development and the planning of instructional programs. They argued that curriculum development was a provincial activity that should involve teachers, departmental staff and outside experts. Instructional planning, more related to teachers' classroom competence, was best carried out at the local level within the guidelines of externally developed curricula. Some teachers demanded the abolition of department directives and sought the right to decide what should be taught; they disregarded the insecurity and extra work this would mean for themselves and the repetitive learning and lack of adequate content knowledge for students that would result. Friesen and Holdaway pointed out that teachers had wide discretion in interpreting provincial curricula. Even when they used the same textbook, teachers placed significantly different emphases on different aspects of content. Although such freedom was desirable, there was still a need for centrally co-ordinated provincial leadership.[69]

The attempt of provincial authorities during the late 1970s to make guidelines more comprehensive yet still flexible represented an effort to establish a new balance between centralized and decentralized curriculum development. Ontario's Minister of Education, Thomas Wells, called it "adjusting the pendulum." Guidelines were developed by writing teams of ministry officials and teachers; advisory-review committees of teachers provided input to the writing process and helped to validate guidelines. Wells took pains to deny that the new approach meant an abandonment of local curriculum development. Guidelines would be more substantive and helpful than before, but there was no intention to write detailed prescriptive courses of study.[70]

The initiatives described were accompanied by a boom in in-service education and professional development programs across Canada through conferences, workshops and courses offered by hundreds of agencies, including ministries, faculties of education, teachers' federations and school districts. Fullan was critical of poorly integrated efforts in which any connection between in-service training and curriculum implementation was often non-existent. Provincial curriculum guidelines were providing a common focal point within each province for many groups to develop more concrete in-service programs as the relationship between staff development and curriculum implementation became more evident. Fullan predicted that guidelines would motivate in-service activities increasingly in the future.[71]

As administrators slowly came to realize that knowing and controlling what transpired behind the classroom door was the most problematical of issues, implementation became a new buzz word in the curriculum lexicon. Experience showed that there was frequently a great discrepancy between reported and actual use, for instance, between what an innovation was supposed to be and what actually happened in the classroom. Evaluators typically took the use of curriculum materials for proof of change, but this ignored many questions, including whether or not the materials were being used in accordance with the objectives of the developers.[72] Thus, inquiry-based materials intended to promote discovery learning might be used didactically, thereby undermining the objectives they had been designed to achieve. Some research indicated that teachers continued to ignore precisely stated objectives and systematic curriculum planning *per se*.[73]

A major consideration in curriculum implementation was role or behavioural change that might be required of the teacher. Fullan noted that bringing about role change was very complex; he cited the example of a set of 1978 Ontario Ministry guidelines produced for intermediate grades (7 to 10) English. The guidelines were analyzed in terms of stated or implied teaching strategies, of which 261 were identified in the first sixty pages of the document. Most of these required both role and behavioural change on the part of the teacher. Other studies identified elementary schools where as many as one hundred or more innovations might be introduced within a school year. Such data suggested that, while teachers were often castigated for their failure to be innovative, they might well perform their best curriculum service by their resistance to indiscriminate change. Fullan also reported that, even when curricula were locally developed by teachers on site, they suffered the same implementation problems when disseminated to other teachers as those produced externally.[74]

A national survey by Fullan reported common implementation problems across the provinces. Although guidelines now specified learning outcomes and defined content more precisely, they were rarely couched in terms for immediate and practical use. Teaching strategies and activities were poorly developed and integrated. Evaluation typically focussed on outcomes, but unsatisfactory outcomes merely indicated that there was a problem without providing any guidance in meeting it. The instructional and learning activities that linked objectives and outcomes were often ignored and complex problems were glossed over in the rush to produce an end product. Governments faced a dilemma; in encouraging widespread debate over abstract goals, policy decisions were delayed and discussions bogged down while the practical changes at stake were ignored. By the time of adoption a new guideline might be discredited.[75]

Further problems arose from the failure to realize that a curriculum guideline was not an intact curriculum ready for use. Many teachers did not use guidelines, and derived curricula from locally developed materials, from textbooks and similar sources, few of which matched guidelines. To overcome this problem, some ministries began to commission textbooks closely matched to guidelines. Another key issue was whether implementation should be carried out by means of what Fullan called a fidelity approach, whereby practice should closely exemplify ministry policy, or by means of a mutual adaptation approach that could provide for a flexible interpretation of curricula attuned to local needs. Governments needed to realize that, while legally responsible for insuring compliance with policies, there were limits to what could be accomplished through regulation. Fullan thought that more energy should be spent in developing local capacity to implement, with less emphasis by ministries on their regulatory and bureaucratic role that often entailed enormous paperwork, reporting and costs.[76]

## Who Makes the Curriculum? A National Perspective

### Rational and Irrational Curriculum Policy-Making

The need to justify policies and to recognize the teachers' central role in curriculum development meant that administrators were faced with serious predicaments. In the years of relative stability and goal consensus before 1960, policy-making was a hierarchical process, with conflict contained and resolved within organizations. Senior administrators were authorities and experts, able to direct and shape the course of the system. The politics of education was thought to be non-existent; custom and habit were influential in the making of policy.[77]

During the 1960s, policy-makers began to pin faith on administrative models and various techniques in the form of sophisticated information systems, social forecasting and cost-effectiveness methods. They believed that the future could be shaped according to some rational plan. Rationality increasingly came to be equated with models and tidy linear systems, exemplified in the case of curriculum policy by the use of Bloom's Taxonomy,

Tyler's famous rationale, behavioural objectives and the like. Curriculum documents became sprinkled with esoteric charts that were often disregarded in practice. To one critic, such charts resembled Leonardo da Vinci's plans for building aircraft, and were about as functional.[78]

Confidence that problems could be solved by careful analyses and rational methods was undermined by the precipitate expansion of the 1960s. At the same time, traditional administrative authority declined as students, teachers and parents became much more involved in governance and policy-making through well organized interest groups. The emergence of educational politics and participation undermined a purely rational approach. By the early 1970s, the educational environment had become much less supportive.[79]

Housego described an influence system that caused interest group politics to determine policy decisions affecting curricula and schools. In most provinces this system was made up of the executives of the provincial teachers' and trustees' associations and senior ministry officials. Policy issues were resolved as a result of compromise among these interest groups; only recommendations on which they achieved consensus went to provincial cabinets and legislatures for ratification.[80]

Ricker and Stapleton were sceptical of the interest group thesis.[81] Interest groups were not necessarily powerful simply because they were consulted. While they had a very real capacity to resist change, groups could be co-opted as well as consulted meaningfully, and could be used to legitimize policy as well as to help formulate it. Policy-making was often more a matter of elite accommodation than of pluralistic bargaining. The granting of minority religious or linguistic rights was an example. Within ministries, as Stapleton's analysis of the adoption of the credit system in Ontario revealed, the policy process was a matter of negotiation between contending internal interest groups in an organization much less unified or monolithic than was commonly assumed. In the Ontario case, such internal negotiation was more important than that with external interest groups which were only perfunctorily consulted.[82]

Elitist policy-making often represented *ad hoc* responses to demands generated by broad public concern and pressure. Such was the case with the establishment of mandatory Canadian Studies requirements in various provinces. Van Manen has described how the $8 387 000 Alberta Heritage Resources Project was launched in 1977 when Premier Lougheed wrote to the Director of Curriculum.[83] The promulgation of core curricula in various provinces during the late 1970s was another example of *ad hoc* political responses to a perceived public demand or crisis. Thus, the imposition of Canadian Studies requirements took the form of broad and general directives sometimes accompanied by demands for immediate remedial action for which teachers were frequently ill-prepared. Overloaded curricula based on objectives that often seemed to be at cross purposes led to compromises and to curriculum development by accretion, or by what some called "incrementalism" that belied a rational planning process.

## Inter-provincial and Federal Curriculum Policy Influences

Collectively, the provinces played a national curriculum role through the Council of Ministers, which became a major inter-provincial forum for senior bureaucrats. When established in 1967 the Council described itself as "an inter-provincial educational agency set up for co-ordination, information and liaison purposes operating at the inter-provincial, provincial-federal and international levels . . . ."[84] It also described itself as the official channel for decisions affecting Canada-wide policy. Yet none of its decisions was binding on any province. Statements made by the council were to be considered a unanimous position unless minority statements were filed.[85]

The ambiguous constitutional and political status of the council led to ambivalence on its part about its national function and about the need for national goals in Canadian education. On the one hand, a national function was strongly and exclusively asserted and the OECD charge that Canada lacked national educational goals was vigorously denied.[86] On the other hand, it was claimed that it was unnecessary to develop national policies since there were no unfulfilled national needs that required such policies. A large measure of common objectives, structures, programs and services among unique provincial systems, together with federal support programs, was said to reveal goals shared by both levels of government.

The council's role in co-ordinating educational television, in promoting bilingual programs and the use of the metric system, and its initiatives in Canadian Studies and other curriculum endeavours probably influenced provincial policies and priorities.[87] In 1978 the Ministers observed that all provinces, despite inevitable differences in curriculum policy resulting from regional diversity, were interested "in identifying common elements in curriculum, sharing information systematically and in increasing the co-ordination of their curriculum-related activities." Policy recommendations, co-operation and information sharing in curriculum and other matters were the responsibility of task forces and committees of provincial civil servants. The process was illustrated by the comparative surveys of provincial curricula in the major subject areas which, as noted earlier, highlighted commonalities that exemplified the trend "towards accenting the teaching of common and basic elements . . . ."[88] The surveys were widely distributed to curriculum developers, subject consultants and curriculum committee members in each province. The CMEC Secondary School Transfer Guide was another initiative with national implications.

The council's Curriculum Committee, made up of the provincial curriculum directors, exhibited great interest in common approaches to policy matters. They regularly exchanged information regarding revisions and learning materials, provincial evaluations and general curriculum issues and policy developments. Particular attention was focussed on the possibilities of common textbook evaluation policies and on greater co-operation in the provision of suitable learning materials. The committee devoted considerable time to such matters of common concern as the educational uses of computers, the role of the arts in education, career education and the impact of declining enrolments.[89]

The federal role in education was even more ambiguous and confusing than that of the Council of Ministers. This largely reflected the policy relations between the two levels of government, which a member of the OECD examining team later described as akin to "sex as it used to be in times of prudery. You do it but you do not talk about it, and even if you should allude to it, you never use the right words."[90] A considerable federal presence in educational policy was tolerated as long as nobody called it such, and as long as there were no overt strings attached to money coming from Ottawa. In urging that the Council of Ministers be developed into a national forum for policy development, the OECD examiners suggested that the federal government become involved in a systematic and open manner in discussing educational matters that transcended provincial boundaries, possibly by means of formal federal representation.[91]

Following the designation by the federal cabinet in 1973 of the Department of the Secretary of State as the agency responsible for federal policies and programs relating to education, most initiatives undertaken by Ottawa were pursued in consultation with the council. By 1980 the Secretary of State was serving as the federal point of contact in negotiations. The department's major responsibility had been the administration of fiscal transfers in support of post-secondary education. Gradually, this responsibility widened as Ottawa's direct curricular influence became apparent in its support of vocational, bilingual, Native education and Canadian Studies programs. Thus, federal support of bilingual programs in British Columbia caused the number of elementary grade pupils studying French to quadruple during the 1970s.[92] Here was an example of how federal educational policy, never identified as such, could affect and alter provincial priorities. Less formally, many federal educational activities which influenced the curriculum were subsumed under the label of "culture" through such agencies as the National Gallery, the Canada Council, the CBC, and the National Film Board. These and many other departments and agencies aimed a variety of materials at classrooms. Since many such activities did not come under the aegis of the Secretary of State, there was no co-ordinating mechanism for them, with the result that their impact was often contradictory and ineffective.[93]

A revealing provincial view of curriculum policy as a national concern was evident in a survey of national needs and possibilities undertaken in 1980 by Mussio, British Columbia's curriculum director. Mussio advocated "some form of nationally accepted core curriculum" through inter-provincial co-operation in order to meet the needs of the estimated 100 000 children who moved among the provinces annually. All children had a right to a common quality education reflecting "the values and attitudes consistent with the economic, cultural and social well-being of the country." A series of common curriculum models in the basic subject areas could be developed to guide program development in each province and to assist publishers to produce common textbooks for a national market. Common approaches to testing and evaluation could assist the establishment of national norms and standards and reduce dependence on American tests, which were defining the standards and priorities of Canadian schools. There was a need to document the progress of learning in the country as a whole in terms of common knowledge, skills and attitudes in the same way that the progress of the economy was charted.[94]

## Quasi-public, Voluntary and Private Influences

Many organizations of a quasi-public, private and often voluntary character that sought to influence the curriculum during the period have been noted. The absence of effective mechanisms for official policy co-ordination at the national level gave non-governmental organizations a special importance. In the past such groups as the CEA and the Canadian Teachers' Federation had collaborated with each other and with provincial and federal authorities on initiatives of national significance in such areas as educational broadcasting and health and vocational education. With the advent of the Council of Ministers such collaboration ended, as advisory committees that had included all these interests were replaced by committees of civil servants that met in private and issued no public reports.

Nevertheless, voluntary agencies continued to play a role in curricular matters. In some cases, they were funded partly or largely by governments, and directly or indirectly served the interests of government policy. Thus, the CEA in co-operation with other voluntary organizations and the Ministries of Education had sponsored the Nyberg-Lee survey of high school evaluation policies and achievement standards referred to earlier. In most cases, the efforts of voluntary agencies to influence curricula were subtle and indirect. Such was Roald's conclusion with respect to the Canada Studies Foundation and the Canadian Foundation for Economic Education (CFEE).[95] Limited resources and the likely negative consequences of overt political pressure led each to seek acceptance of its ideas in school systems by means of such low profile activities as workshops, materials development and curriculum projects. In the case of the Canada Studies Foundation, the support of the Council of Ministers proved short-lived; the Council did not appreciate what it perceived as a usurpation of its prerogatives by an unofficial group whose objective of promoting teacher-based national projects was incompatible with its own emphasis on curriculum development within provincial guidelines.

Other organizations of a quasi-public, voluntary or private character included university groups, trustees' and teachers' organizations and subject associations. Although universities retained considerable influence on the curriculum because of their power to set admission standards, in general academics had a less direct impact on development than in the past. Teachers' federations, usually through their provincial subject specialist organizations, had a direct input to curriculum policy-making, by virtue of their representation on provincial committees. Less formally, they sought to influence the curriculum through their own professional development programs, "lesson aids" services, and media campaigns on curriculum. National organizations of subject matter specialists such as the Canadian Association of Science Educators and the Canadian Council of Teachers of English were active through conferences, journals and newsletters but appeared to have only indirect influence.

Still less direct in influence were such national groups as the Canadian Society for the Study of Education, organized in 1972. Together with its affiliate, the Canadian Association of Curriculum Studies, the organization brought together university researchers and members from the public educational sectors who, through publications such as *The Canadian Journal of Education*, conferences and workshops attempted to influence curriculum policy. Less formal organizations proliferated as curriculum interest groups during the period. Thus, alarmed by the declining status of the fine arts in the curriculum consequent upon the re-emphasis on the "basics," the Canadian Conference on the Arts in 1978 sponsored a National Inquiry into Arts and Education in Canada by means of a series of provincial task forces.[96]

## Students, Teachers and Parents as Interest Groups

Throughout the period, teachers, parents and students demanded a larger role in formulating educational policy and in making educational decisions. Student demands centred on a more "relevant" curriculum, more student choice in programs and student representation in policy-making. Martin and Macdonell observed that there had been a general neglect in Canada of research on the schooling experience from the student point of view. By 1980 a few researchers were investigating student views of ability grouping, the aims of education, homework and school discipline.[97] Some provincial assessments solicited student opinion on the efficacy of curricula and on possible directions for change.

During the 1970s the self-image, expectations and attitudes of teachers were undergoing changes as they shifted away from a professional, social service model towards a trade union one that embodied greater autonomy. As with students, a lack of opportunity to participate in policy-making contributed to teacher dissatisfaction. Little research had yet been done in Canada on the teacher's role in curriculum development.[98] The OECD report was critical of a bureaucratic structure that reflected an industrial organization of education and inhibited any broad participation by teachers in decision-making.[99]

Compulsory membership in teachers' federations, long established in Canada, laid a basis for collective bargaining. It became linked to the ideology of trade unionism in the 1970s and led, in some cases, to bitter strikes. As relationships between teachers and governments and school boards became adversarial, public and press became critical of what they saw as the unprofessional behaviour of teachers. Teacher militancy increasingly focussed on working conditions, an issue that had high curricular salience. A 1980 strike by Calgary teachers that focussed on preparation time during the day attracted national attention and brought the issue to the fore. A commission report that ended the strike without resolving the issue concluded that teachers had a right to a voice in factors that determined the climate of their work, such as the number of students taught, the number of contact hours, and the time spent on non-instructional tasks.[100] School trustees and government officials felt otherwise, fearing that bargaining over such matters would pre-empt their policy-making function, destroy professionalism, and undermine public control of education.[101] In Ontario, Hennessy proposed that collective bargaining, which he believed had profoundly negative consequences, should be replaced by politically independent machinery to determine salaries and benefits on a provincial basis. Working conditions should be determined at the community level through school governing boards that would replace county school boards, and be made up of equal numbers of trustees and teachers with full power to determine the curriculum and manage the schools. A somewhat similar radical proposal had been made by MacKinnon earlier.[102]

Parent power became a phenomenon during the period, and was advocated in a book called *About Schools*,[103] that attracted national attention. The Parent-Teacher or Home and School movement had long existed, but its genteel approach was now replaced by demands for real involvement in decision-making. In some communities, parent councils became *de facto* governing bodies that forced school boards to heed local demands. School boundaries when not abolished entirely became much more flexible. This trend, together with alternative schools, gave some reality to the concept of family choice. American-style suits against schools and teachers had not yet appeared in Canada but the new emphasis on individual rights made such moves more probable.[104]

Everybody, it seemed, had an interest in the development of the curriculum. Various policies, programs and projects were developed. The struggle to identify and implement the goals continued.

## Notes to Chapter 19

1 Hodgetts, *What Culture?*, 24, 26-7, 45.

2 Hope Report, 148.

3 Ibid., 149.

4 James Fraser.

5 Totton, 275-6, 285. See the Report of the Ontario Royal Commission on Book Publishing, pp. 168-218, for a detailed discussion of educational publishing in Ontario and Canada.

6 Barrett, 332, 337-9.

7 Kormos.

8 Carl Hogg, North York Board of Education cited in Anderson and Tomkins, *Understanding Materials*, 40-1.

9 James Fraser.

10 For a discussion of textbook censorship problems in Canada see Judith Dick, "North of '49" and "Not in Our Schools" and articles by Stuewe, Brewer, Callwood and Findley.

11 Boyd, 15-6.

12 James Fraser.

13 Vancouver Board of School Trustees, *Selection of Learning Resources*.

14 Anderson and Tomkins, *Understanding*, 57-8.

15 Cited in Turner.

16 Ayres in Anderson and Tomkins, *Understanding*, 59-60. See also Beattie, including papers by Beattie and Gaskell.

17 Quebec Ministère de l'Education, *Schools of Quebec*, 102-6.

18 Nova Scotia Department of Education, *Report on Public School Financing*, 16.

19 Fleming, *Preoccupation*, 191.

20 Ibid., 192.

21 Fleming, V, *Supporting*, 364.

22 Ibid., 202-4.

23 H.L. Campbell, 87, 89-90.

24 Ibid., 54.

25 Manning.

26 Ibid., 186-7.

27 Ibid., 206.

28 Manning, 239.

29 R. Harris and Pilkington, "Curriculum Trends," 115.

30 Johns, "Proposal," 78-9.

31 Editorial, *School Progress*, 33, no.3 (March,1964), 29.

32 J.C. Mackenzie, 5, 8.

33 Fleming, V, *Supporting*, 382-3.

34 See H.A. Elliott for a statement of this assumption.

35 Gretsinger, 14-15.

36 Fleming, *Supporting*, 328-9, 344.

37 Cited in ibid., 345-6.

38 M. Holmes, "Progress," 429.

39 Robin Harris and Pilkington, "Curriculum Trends," 116; Priestly and Kerpneck, 52.

40 M. Holmes, "Testing," 9.

41 New Brunswick Department of Education, *Provincial Testing*, 90.

42 See Barbara Holmes.

43 Nova Scotia Department of Education, *Guide to Nova Scotia Achievement Tests*, 1.

44 Mussio and Greer, 27-8.

45 Penny, 6-7, 10. See also Ontario Ministry of Education, *Ontario Assessment Instrument Pool*.

46 Goble in *The Kappan* 63, no. 10 (June, 1982), 700.

47 Nyberg and Lee, 6-7.

48 Reported in *Evaluation New Brunswick*, Newsletter, Evaluation Branch, New Brunswick Department of Education, April 1979, 2.

49 *The Vancouver Sun*, February 2, 1980.

50 *The Toronto Globe and Mail*, January 6, 1981.

51 Keats, 36, 39.

52 CEA, *Recommendations Concerning the Status of the Teaching Profession*.

53 Ibid., 26, 119.

54 Calam, "Diversity," 130-1.

55 Chamberlin, 52.

56 Calam, "Diversity," 136.

57 Ibid., 138. See also John Macdonald, 41.

58 Ibid., 142 citing Pierce.

59 See Symons, *To Know Ourselves*, 59.

60 H.L. Campbell, 103.

61 C.E. Phillips, "Education," 298.

62 Pullen, 45-52.

63 CEA, *Five Years*, 3-4; see also CEA, "A Project."

64 CEA, *Five Years*, 9-10.

65 Ibid., 5.

66 C.E. Phillips, "The Public School," 225.

67 Ibid., 217.

68 Prince George, BC School District, *Curricular Services Department*, 1982.

69 D. Friesen and Holdaway, 30-1, 33.

70 Wells, 3, 6.

71 Fullan, "School-Focussed In-Service Education," 22, 61.

72 Fullan, "Conceptualizing," 40-1.

73 Oberg.

74 Fullan, "Conceptualizing," 46, 49.

75 Fullan, *Meaning,* 242-3, 246-8.

76 Ibid., 243-4, 251.

77 Housego, "Administration," 382.

78 MacLeod.

79 Housego, "Administration," 383-4.

80 Housego, "Pluralist Politics," 14-5.

81 Ricker; Stapleton.

82 Stapleton, 39-44.

83 Van Manen *et al* in Werner, *Curriculum Canada,* 118-20.

84 Cited in Bergen "Council of Ministers," 11.

85 Bergen, "Perspectives," 1.

86 OECD, 149.

87 Bergen, "Council of Ministers," 11.

88 *Liaison* (CMEC Newsletter) 3 no.5 (December, 1978),2.

89 Ibid.

90 Hamm-Brucher, 47.

91 OECD, 89, 98.

92 Hargrave, 27 citing Manley-Casimir, "Schooling."

93 Ibid., 24, 26.

94 Mussio, 12-13, 15.

95 Roald.

96 Canadian Conference of the Arts.

97 Martin and Macdonell, 72, 92-4.

98 Ibid., 111, 117.

99 OECD, 106.

100 Kratzman.

101 Goble in *The Kappan* 63, no.6 (Febuary, 1982), 414.

102 Hennessy; MacKinnon.

103 R. Stamp, *About Schools.*

104 Henchey, "Alternatives," 236; "Pressures," 151.

# EPILOGUE

Writing of the American context during the late 1970s, Boyd observed that "If there is one proposition about curriculum politics that is clear, it is that the school curriculum becomes an issue in communities and societies that are undergoing significant change."[1] His observation was equally applicable to Canada during a period of massive post-war social and economic transformation. This transformation led to a new common way of life that was at once more culturally diverse, more cosmopolitan, more homogeneous and more varied than in the past.[2] Monolithic anglo-conformity and traditional Protestant middle-class morality no longer represented required norms in a secularized pluralistic society. Yet paradoxically, despite diversity, regional differences and cultural conflict, Canadians were more alike in 1980 than they had been in 1945. Even as the nation became more decentralized and less integrated, its people became more homogeneous. Thus anglophones and francophones increasingly shared similar outlooks and lifestyles.

All these changes were reflected in schools and in their curricula. As with general social change, the transformation was so rapid and so extensive that Canadians could be forgiven for not understanding its magnitude, and for not easily grasping how much their school systems had changed since their own youth. A questioning of long established anglo-conformity and Christian morality was reflected in the curriculum in ways ranging from multicultural programs to values education. The teaching of imperial patriotism was superseded by the teaching of an often ill-defined Canadian identity suffused with a greater appreciation of the Canadian mosaic. A narrow academic curriculum with limited choice was replaced by a broader, more diverse, more vocationalized yet more personalized curriculum with a bewildering choice of options. The concept of a common liberal secondary education was attenuated as curricula were adjusted to meet the demand for the mass schooling of a student body that, in terms of social origins, ethnic background and academic ability, was far more diverse than ever before. Administratively, as decision-making was devolved to the local level, as detailed provincial courses of study were replaced by guidelines, and as the single prescribed textbook and province-wide examinations were mostly discarded, the concept of a common curriculum was further attenuated. On the surface, the curriculum and curriculum policy seemed fragmented, disjointed and incoherent from a national or even from a provincial standpoint.

Yet below the surface, nationalizing imperatives were operating as in the past. If Canadians had fewer illusions about and lower expectations of their schools by 1980, there was still a strong tendency to see education as a panacea for social, cultural, economic, political and moral ills. If Canada was, as often described, a unity in diversity, the same could be said of

Canadian curriculum. While the classroom experience of Canadian children in the 1970s was probably a less common one than that of the meagre and briefer regimen of the 1930s, it seemed unwise to underestimate the extent of commonality. Indeed, the routinized sameness of that experience was one of the major charges directed at the school by many of its critics. Similar Canadian Studies, bilingual, second language and multi-cultural goals were featured in curriculum guidelines from coast to coast. The old Judeo-Christian ethic of loving one's neighbour still existed, albeit in secularized form. Celebrating the virtues of cultural diversity and abhorring the evils of racism became a new moral norm, as universally and authoritatively inculcated as any in the past. Concern for the needs of exceptional children also represented a new moral norm. Less positive and more problematical was the growing emphasis on "credentialism" whereby grades, tests, scores and degrees had become essential passports to employment and further education. This trend re-enforced the formalistic, bureaucratic structure of schooling. Critics pointed to a new educational underclass barred by deficiencies in formal education from full participation in a diploma-ridden society.

The Council of Ministers, the creation of which was a tacit recognition of national imperatives, made efforts to align provincial textbook and evaluation policies that promoted national perspectives. Even a cursory examination of textbook authorizations indicated that, despite the much greater variety of teaching materials now available, there remained a high degree of common textbook use, at least in the core subjects. Through nationalizing initiatives, provincial policy-makers acting collectively were able to demonstrate their Canadianism by extending their very Canadian penchant for curriculum uniformity beyond their individual jurisdictional boundaries. Similar university admission policies, academic programs and standards were aspects of a national system of higher education that retained a number of common and distinctive features; these encouraged a significant common curricular response on the part of school systems necessarily sensitive to university expectations. The growth of an integrated national economy created a demand for national education designed to produce scientists, technicians, managers and other professionals for both the private and greatly expanded public sectors. Federal funding of teaching and research at the post-secondary level and, more surreptitiously, the funding of vocational and cultural programs at lower levels was necessary to meet these needs. These initiatives belied the myth of federal non-involvement in education.

As in the past, the Canadian curriculum was still powerfully influenced by international forces. Critics and commentators continued to compare Canadian schooling with that of the United States, Great Britain, the Soviet Union and Japan. The most common cross-national comparison was with the United States, as in the Michalos study cited earlier.[3]

Schooling norms in Canada over this period appeared to have more closely approached those of the United States. Nothing better illustrated the massive transformation in public schooling after 1960 than Michalos' conclusion that the quality of Canadian education by the mid-1970s exceeded that of American education. Whether or not this was true, it seemed that Canadian education had become more Americanized than ever. In another sense, however, it had become less Americanized, as a national context took shape that enabled Canadians to develop their own solutions to their own problems.

Michalos' study was complemented by that of the OECD. The OECD report praised an enormous common quantitative achievement, but observed that progress could be seen only partly in statistics. All across Canada, a series of profound qualitative changes in curricula, school organization and government and educational expectations occurred. In general, the most important development over two decades was the systematic building of comprehensive provincial school systems, most notably in Quebec.[4]

The educational system had changed from following a basically selective principle of operation to one of trying to aid young people to develop their knowledge and skills in ways that differed according to their needs and capacities. The examiners were convinced that the results were much better than in many European countries. Yet much remained to be done, if the needs of the under-privileged and economically disadvantaged, notably those of Native peoples, were to be met adequately. Especially serious was the relative failure to make the curriculum more practical. The examiners were also critical of the failure of Canadian schools to do more to develop the artistic talents of students; music and art still tended to be treated as frills in the curriculum.[5]

Overriding all these limitations was the failure to define educational goals relevant to a vision of the national interest. To the OECD, Canada could no longer pursue a policy of predominantly unplanned development, nor ignore a careful consideration of the social and intellectual role of education in the society. There was an unwillingness or inability to think deeply about and to discuss thoroughly a range of alternatives to existing practice. This was related to the lack of fundamental research, one of the weakest areas of the Canadian educational system. More positively, the reaction against progressive trends was less sharp than in some other countries, even though distinctly present. Despite a more uncertain and conservative policy climate by the mid-1970s and a relative decline in the enthusiasm and resources that had characterized the preceding decade, a reasonably optimistic but much more realistic view of future tasks and possibilities remained.[6]

At a time when schooling and education were seen as panaceas for all social problems, it was not surprising that considerable effort was made to prescribe for or to predict the future of schools and their curricula. Some saw the need for schools to revert to a traditional curriculum in a conservation-oriented society of scarcity and lowered expectations requiring an inculcation of such values as respect for authority, industriousness, thrift and social responsibility. Other prophets, reflecting a belief in the twentieth century religion of progress and in the perfectibility of human-kind through education, saw a benign self-actualizing society emerging in which a vision of maximum curricular choice in the service of individual fulfilment and social betterment would be realized. Beyond such scenarios were those that predicted the disappearance of traditional schools and teachers altogether.

Responsible scholars who made it their business to try to assist the educational policy process rarely espoused any particular scenario for the future, and prudently focussed on attempting to lay out the possibili-ties. A host of global problems — the population explosion, food shortages, environmental deterioration, energy shortages, disparities between rich and poor nations, political instability, international violence and the ever-present threat of nuclear holocaust — all had salience for curriculum planners. However, if addressed at all in schools, they were rarely addressed effectively.

By 1980 an echo of the earlier baby boom seemed likely to increase schooling demands. Competition for resources became severe as other public priorities began to take precedence over education. The new milieu raised urgent questions about methods of funding, new linkages between education and work, alternative approaches to credentialism and the general need for retraining in a learning society. All these trends seemed likely to influence curriculum policy.[7]

Concern increasingly focussed on economic disarray, illustrated by chronic unemployment, declining industries and an alleged national failure to maintain pace with international competition. Bleak scenarios were painted of vast future populations condemned to enforced long-term lei-sure. Optimists pointed to past technological change that had not, as had been predicted, led to permanent unemployment. A failure to meet the demands of a high tech society, epitomized by the Japanese challenge, had by 1980 created an alarm that was reminiscent of the post-Sputnik Soviet challenge a generation earlier. Critics pointed to the need to take advantage of high technology in the educational process *per se.* As regards the impact of computer applications on curricula and classrooms, the jury was still out in 1980. Henchey suggested that if multi-national corporations increased their monopoly of the preparation of sophisticated, teacher-proof learning materials, the function of the teacher might be reduced to that of a pedagog-ical technician.[8]

Pratt, in focussing specifically on educational needs that were neglected in the Canadian curriculum, doubted that educators could con-tinue to tinker any longer with the Victorian curriculum. In a process that was essentially political, rational arguments for change were of little avail. This suggested that curriculum questions had some kind of deep psychic significance. A possible explanation was that people who felt that they had been relatively successful in life, the middle-class who were the most vocal critics of the schools, ascribed their success in part to their education.

Accordingly, they sought an education for their children as similar as possible to what they had experienced a generation earlier. Support for curriculum change would suggest that their own schooling had in some sense been deficient. Hence their continued devotion to fractions and Euclidean theorems, Shakespeare learned by rote, predicates and subordinate clauses, lists of historical dates and outline maps of Europe.[9]

Pratt posited a range of needs — survival, social, aesthetic, philosophical (relating to the need for meaning) and psychological (relating to the need for children to develop positive self-concepts). All of these needs were largely neglected in the curriculum. Education everywhere had always been the most important factor contributing to health and longevity, and Pratt thought that this was likely to remain the case. Curriculum developers could not continue to neglect such survival needs as the teaching of personal health care, the study of foreign policy, peace strategies and conflict resolution. Nor could an occupational focus be neglected when the evidence was that, next to family and friends, jobs were the most important means of meeting social needs, since individual identity was in large part made up of one's formal contribution to society. As a consequence of the neglect of aesthetic needs, young children's interests in nearly all artistic genres — singing, dancing, acting, painting, drawing, modelling and storytelling — tended to atrophy after they entered school. Similarly, children entered school with positive self-concepts arising out of their success in mastering such skills as walking, talking and many others, all acquired from intrinsic motivation. Relying on extrinsic motivation, and emphasizing failure, schooling lowered the self-esteem of many children. The belief that triumph over failure and adversity promoted achievement and developed character was fallacious, for nothing succeeded like success and nothing failed like failure.[10]

Pratt's reiteration of concerns relating to the liberal *vis-à-vis* the practical in the curriculum, and indeed to the very meaning of these terms, and to the socializing *vis-à-vis* the educating role of schools, had engaged policymakers for more than a century. Throughout that period, the basic structure of schooling, curricula and teaching had remained remarkably stable. If Pratt's utopian goals of enhancing meaning and a more positive self-concept were to be met, educators in the future would have to mediate the conflicting demands of stability and change more constructively than they had done in the past.

## Notes to Epilogue

1 Boyd, 12

2 Bothwell *et al*, 460.

3 Michalos.

4 OECD, 30.

5 Ibid., 35-6, 39.

6 Ibid., 36-37, 101, 144.

7 Stevenson, "Educational Policy," 273-4.

8 Henchey, "Pressures," 156-8.

9 Pratt, 32-3.

10 Ibid., 24-8.

# Bibliography

Abbot, John, "Hostile Landscapes and the Spectre of Illiteracy: Devising Retrieval Systems for 'Sequestered' Children in Northern Ontario," 181-194 in *An Imperfect Past: Education and Society in Canadian History*. Ed. J.D. Wilson. Vancouver: Centre for the Study of Curriculum and Instruction, U.B.C., 1984.

Adams, Ian, W. Cameron, B. Hill and P. Penz, eds., *The Real Poverty Report*. Edmonton : Hurtig, 1971.

Adams, John, *The Protestant School System of the Province of Quebec*. Montreal: E.M. Renouf, 1902.

Adler, H.J. and D.A. Brusegard, *Perspectives Canada III*. Ottawa: Minister of Supplies and Services, 1980. (Published for Statistics Canada.)

Alberta Commission on Educational Planning, *A Future of Choices: A Choice of Futures*. The Worth Report. Edmonton: Queen's Printer, 1972.

Alberta Department of Education, *What Is and What Might Be in Rural Education in Alberta*. Edmonton: The Department, Department of Education, 1935.

Alberta Department of Education, *Report of the Royal Commission on Education*. The Cameron Report. Edmonton: Queen's Printer, 1959.

Alberta Education, *Alberta Education and Diploma Requirements: A Discussion Paper Prepared for the Curriculum Policies Board*. The Harder Report. Edmonton, 1977.

Alberta Education, *Curriculum Development for Alberta Education*. 1977. Edmonton: Alberta Curriculum Branch of the Department of Education.

Alexander, W.J., "Province-wide Examinations in Secondary Schools," *NCCU Proceedings 1930*: 81-88.

Allard, Michel, "Une réalité: Un groupe de recherche bilingue," *Canadian Journal of Education*, 2, no. 1, (1977), 43-48.

Allen, Richard, *The Social Passion: Religion and Social Reform in Canada, 1914-28*. Toronto: University of Toronto Press, 1973.

Allison, Derek J., "Fourth World Education in Canada," *Journal of Canadian Studies* 18, no.3 (Autumn 1983), 102-118.

Althouse, J.G., *The Structure and Aims of Canadian Education*. Toronto: Gage, 1949.

American and Canadian Committees on Modern Languages, *Modern Language Instruction in Canada*, Volume II. Toronto : University of Toronto Press, 1928.

Amoss, Harry, "The Abnormal Pupil," *OEA Proceedings 1923*: 418-429.

Anderson, J.T.M., *The Education of the New-Canadian: A Treatise on Canada's Greatest Educational Problem*. London and Toronto: Dent, 1918.

Anderson, R.M., "The Need for Order in External Influences on Curriculum Making: Provincial and Federal Influences from Outside the Official Educational Sector," 100-112 in *Curriculum Canada II: Curriculum Policy and Curriculum Development*. Ed. J.J. Bernier and G.S. Tomkins. Vancouver: Centre for the Study of Curriculum and Instruction, U.B.C., 1980.

Anderson, R.M. and B.A. Robert, *Reflections Concerning the Canada Studies Foundation: An Internal Evaluation of Eight Years of Activity*. Toronto: Canada Studies Foundation, 1979.

Anderson, R.M. and G.S. Tomkins, *Understanding Materials: The Role of Materials in Curriculum Development*. Vancouver: Centre For the Study of Curriculum and Instruction, 1981.

Angus, Henry, *Canada and Her Great Neighbour*. Toronto: Ryerson Press, 1938.

Anisef, Paul, Norman Okihiro and Carl James, *The Pursuit of Equality: Evaluating and Monitoring Accessibility to Postsecondary Education in Ontario*. Toronto: Ontario Ministry of Colleges and Universities, 1982.

Aoki, Tetsuo, "Theoretic Dimensions of Curriculum: Reflections From a Micro-perspective," *Canadian Journal of Education* 2, no.1 (1977), 49-56.

Argue, K.F., *Wealth, Children and Education in Canada*. Ottawa: CTF, 1945.

Arlen, Michael, *Thirty Seconds*. New York: Farrar, Strauss and Giroux, 1980.

Armour, Leslie and Elizabeth Trott, *The Faces of Reason: An Essay on Philosophy and Culture in English Canada 1850-1950*. Waterloo: Wilfred Laurier University Press, 1981.

Armstrong, F.H., H.A. Stevenson and J.D. Wilson, eds., *Aspects of Nineteenth Century Ontario*. Toronto: University of Toronto Press, 1974.

Arnold, Matthew, *Culture and Anarchy*. London: Smith Elder, 1882.

Ashworth, Mary, *Immigrant Children and Canadian Schools*. Toronto: McClelland and Stewart, 1975.

———, "Results and Issues from a National Survey of ESL Programs," 84-94 in *Education of Immigrant Students: Issues and Answers*. Ed. A. Wolfgang. Toronto: OISE, 1975.

———, *The Forces Which Shaped Them: A History of the Education of Minority Group Children in British Columbia*. Vancouver: New Star Books, 1979.

Atlantic Institute of Education, *A Guide to Public Education in Nova Scotia*. Halifax: The Institute, 1980.

Atwood, Margaret, "Nationalism, Limbo and the Canadian Club," *Saturday Night*, (January 1971), 10-11.

———, *Survival: A Thematic Guide to Canadian Literature*. Toronto: Anansi, 1973.

Audet, Louis-Philippe and Armand Gauthier, *Le Systeme Scolaire au Quebec*. Montreal: Beauchemin, 1967.

Audet, Louis-Philippe, "Attempts to Develop a School System for Lower Canada:1760-1840," 145-167 in *Canadian Education – A History*. Ed. J.D. Wilson *et al.* Scarborough: Prentice-Hall, 1970.

———, "Education in Canada East and Quebec, 1840-1875," 167-189 in *Canada Education – A History*. Ed. J.D. Wilson et al. Scarborough: Prentice Hall, 1970.

———, "Society and Education in New France," 70-85 in *Canadian Education – A History*. Ed. J.D. Wilson et al. Scarborough: Prentice Hall, 1970.

Ault, A.E. "Examinations in Canada," 154-71 in *The Yearbook of Education for 1938*. Ed. H.V. Usill. London: Evans Brothers, 1938.

Bagley, William C., "Is Subject Matter Obsolete?" *Educational Administration and Supervision*, XXI,no. 6 (September 1935), 401-12.

Bailey, Alan W., "The Professional Preparation of Teachers for the Schools of the Province of New Brunswick, 1784 to 1964." Unpublished doctoral thesis, Toronto: University of Toronto press, 1964.

Bailey, D. "Physical Activity Vital for All Children," *Proceedings Canadian Intramural Recreation Association*, (1979), 10-12.

Baker, Harold S., "Changing Purposes and Programmes of the Canadian High School," 11-24 in *The Canadian Secondary School: An Appraisal and a Forecast*. Ed. L.W. Downey and L.R. Godwin. Toronto: Gage, 1963.

Baker, Peter, *The Carnegie Unit: Pros, Cons and Alternatives*. Edmonton: Alberta Education, 1980.

Barber, Marilyn, "Canadianization Through the Schools of the Prairie Provinces Before World War I: The Attitudes and Aims of the English Speaking Majority," 281-94 in *Ethnic Canadians: Culture and Education*. Ed. M.L. Kovacs. Regina: Canadian Plains Research Centre, 1978.

———, "The School in the Community: Rural Saskatchewan in the 1920s." Unpublished paper, Vancouver: The Canadian Historical Association, 1983.

Bargen, P.F., "Family Choice, Schooling and the Public Interest," Unpublished paper, Vancouver, 1980.

Barman, Jean, *Growing up British in British Columbia: Boys in Private School*. Vancouver: University of British Columbia Press, 1984.

Barrett, F.L., "Textbook Selection in the Other Canadian Provinces,": 331-343 in *Background Papers*, Ontario Royal Commission on Book Publishing. Toronto: Queen's Printer, 1972.

Barrow, R., *The Canadian Curriculum: A Personal View*. London: The University of Western Ontario, 1979.

Belanger, Jennifer, "Changes in Senior High School Life Sciences Program in Alberta, 1905-1978," in *Alberta Science Education Journal* 18, no.2, (April 1980), 24-36.

Bell, Walter N., *The Development of the Ontario High School*. Toronto: University of Toronto Press, 1918.

Belovari, S. et al, "Political Orientation of Students in Southern Ontario," *History and Social Science Teacher* 11, no. 1 (Winter 1976), 33-42.

Beltzner, Klaus P., A. John Coleman, Gordon D. Edwards, *Mathematical Sciences in Canada*, Science Council of Canada, Background Study no. 37, July 1976. Oshawa: Maracle Press, 1976.

Berard, Robert, "History, Religion and Moral Education in Canada 1880-1920." Unpublished paper, Toronto, 1982.

Bereiter, C., *Must We Educate?*. Englewood Cliffs, N.J.: Prentice Hall, 1973.

Bergen, John J., "Perceptions of the Council of Ministers of Education," *The Canadian Administrator* 26, no. 8 (May 1971), 1-6

_____, "Council of Ministers of Education in Canada: At a Political Juncture?" 9-18 in *The Politics of Canadian Education*. Ed. J.A. Wallin. Edmonton: Canadian Society for the Study of Education, 1972.

Berger, Carol, *The Sense of Power: Studies in the Ideas of Canadian Imperialism, 1867-1914*. Toronto: University of Toronto Press, 1970

_____, *Science, God and Nature in Victorian Canada*. Toronto: University of Toronto Press, 1983.

Bernhardt, Karl S., "A Mental Hygiene Approach to Education," *Canadian Education* III, no.2 (March 1948), 7-23.

Bernier, J.J., E. Duckworth, A. Lecuyer and N. Sutherland, *External Evaluation of the Canada Studies Foundation*. Toronto: The Foundation, 1975.

Bernier, J.J. and G.S. Tomkins, eds., *Curriculum Canada II: Curriculum Policy and Curriculum Development*. Vancouver: Centre for the Study of Curriculum and Instruction, University of British Columbia, 1980.

Berry, John W., "Mulitcultural Attitudes and Education," 103-113 in *Multiculturalism in Canada – Social and Educational Perspectives*. Ed. R.J. Samuda et al. Toronto: Allyn and Bacon, 1984.

Bibeau, Gilles, "No Easy Road to Bilingualism" *Language and Society* 12 (Winter 1984), 44-47.

Binkley, David, "John Dewey in Ontario," *Past and Present*. Waterloo: University of Waterloo, (October 1983), 6-7.

Birchard, Isaac James, "Flashback," in *Education*(6), Toronto: Gage Ltd., 1967, 93-99.

Bissell, Claude, *The Young Vincent Massey*. Toronto: University of Toronto Press, 1981.

Black, N.F., "English for the Non-English." Unpublished doctoral thesis, University of Toronto, 1913.

_____, "School Surveys," *The B.C. Teacher* III, no.5 (January 1924), 105-107.

_____, *Peace and Efficiency in School Administration*. Toronto: Dent, 1926.

Blatz, W.E., "Security," *The School* XXIX, no.6 (February 1941), 499-503.

_____, *Understanding the Young Child*. Toronto: Clarke Irwin, 1944.

Blishen, Bernard, ed., *Canadian Society: Sociological Perspectives*. 3rd edition. Toronto: Macmillan, 1968.

Bliss, Michael, "Pure Books on Avoided Subjects: Pre-Freudian Sexual Ideas in Canada," 89-108 in *Canadian Historical Association Historical Papers, 1970*. Ed. J. Atherton et al. Ottawa: The Association, 1970.

_____, *A Living Profit*. Toronto: McClelland and Stewart, 1974.

Bobbitt, Franklin W., *The Curriculum*. Boston: Houghton Mifflin, 1918.

_____, *How To Make a Curriculum*. Boston: Houghton Mifflin, 1924.

Bognar, Carl, "Back to the Basics – An Introductory Survey," *Interchange*. 7, no.4 (1976-77), 1-2.

Bothwell, Robert, Ian Drummond and John English, *Canada Since 1945: Power, Politics and Provincialism*. Toronto: University of Toronto Press, 1981.

Boulianne, Réal, "The Royal Institution for the Advancement of Learning, 1820-1829." Unpublished doctoral thesis, McGill University, 1970.

Bourinot, J.G., *Our Intellectual Strengths and Weaknesses*. Montreal, 1893. Reprinted, Toronto: University of Toronto Press, 1973.

Bourne, Paula and John A. Eisenberg, "The Canadian Public Issues Program," *Orbit* 30 (December 1975), 16-18.

_____, *Social Issues in the Curriculum: Theory, Practice and Evaluation*. Toronto: OISE, 1978.

Boyce, Eleanor, "Canadian Readers Since 1846: A Study of Their Merits and Weaknesses as Instruments of Education," Unpublished doctoral thesis, University of Manitoba, 1949.

Boyd, William L., "The Politics of Curriculum Change and Stability," *Educational Researcher* 8, no.2 (February 1979), 12-18.

Boyko, Michael, "The History and Development of Mathematics Instruction in the Elementary Schools of Ontario 1960-1973." Unpublished magistral thesis, University of Toronto, 1974.

Boyle, David, "The Natural Sciences in the Public Schools," *OTA Proceedings 1880*, 36-45.

Boylen, J.C. et al, *Toronto Normal School*. Toronto: School of Graphic Arts, 1947.

Brauner, C.J., *American Educational Theory*. Englewood Cliffs, N.J.: Prentice Hall, 1964.

Breton, Raymond, "Academic Stratification in Secondary Schools and the Educational Plans of Students," *The Canadian Review of Sociology and Anthropology* 7, no.1 (1970), 17-34.

Breton, Raymond and John C. McDonald, "Occupational Preferences of Canadian High School Students," 268-94 in *Canadian Society – Sociological Perspectives*. Ed. B. Blishen et al. Toronto: Macmillan, 1968.

Breton, Raymond, John McDonald and Stephen Rieter, *Social and Academic Factors in the Career Decisions of Canadian Youth*. Ottawa: Information Canada, 1972.

Brewer, Barry F., "Licence, not Freedom," *Books in Canada* 8, no.8 (October 1979), 8-9.

Brewin, M.J., "The Establishment of an Industrial Education System in Ontario." Unpublished magistral thesis, OISE, 1967.

British Columbia, *Report of the Royal Commission of Education*. The Chant Report. Victoria, 1960.

British Columbia Department of Education, *Courses of Study for the Public, High and Normal Schools of British Columbia*. Victoria: King's Printer, 1920.

British Columbia Ministry of Education, *What Should Our Children Be Learning? Goals of the Core Curriculum*. Victoria: The Ministry, November, 1976.

British Columbia Ministry of Education, *Language, B.C. An Assessment in the English Language Arts: A Pilot Study*. Victoria: The Ministry, 1976.

British Columbia Ministry of Education, *British Columbia Social Studies Assessment – Summary Report, 1977*. Victoria: The Ministry, 1977.

British Columbia Ministry of Education, *British Columbia Science Assessment: Summary Report*. Victoria: The Ministry, 1978.

British Columbia Ministry of Education, *British Columbia Assessment of Written Expression 1978, Summary Report*. Victoria: The Ministry, 1978.

British Columbia Ministry of Education, *British Columbia Assessment of Physical Education, 1979, Summary Report*. Victoria, The Ministry, 1979.

British Columbia Ministry of Education, *British Columbia Reading Assessment 1980, Summary Report*. Victoria, The Ministry, 1980.

British Columbia Teachers Federation, *Involvement: The Key to Better Schools, Report of the Commission on Education*. Vancouver: BCTF, 1968.

Brockman, Lois, John Whiteley and John Zubek, eds., *Child Development: Selected Readings*. Toronto: McClelland and Stewart, 1973.

Brown, James A., "Children's Development of Concepts Related to Country and Nationality: A Canadian Perspective," *Canadian Journal of Education* 5, no.3 (1980), 55-65.

Brown, Robert Craig and Ramsay Cook, *Canada 1896-1921, A Nation Transformed*. Toronto: McClelland and Stewart, 1974.

Brown, Wilfred J., *Education Finance in Canada – A CTF Report*. Ottawa: CTF, 1981.

Bruneau, William, "Opportunism and Altruism in Official Moral Education, 1880-1939: The Examples of France and Canada." Unpublished paper, Vancouver: University of British Columbia, 1983.

Bruner, Jerome S., *The Process of Education*. New York: Vintage Books, 1960.

————, "The Process of Education Revisited," *Phi Delta Kappan* LIII, no.1 (September 1971), 18-21.

Bryce, George, "The Canadianization of Western Canada," *Proceedings and Transactions of the Royal Society of Canada*, IV, 3rd series (September, 1910), xxvii-lvi.

Bryce, R.C., "The Technical and Vocational Training Assistance Act of 1961-67: An Historical Summary and Documentary Analysis." Unpublished doctoral thesis, University of Alberta, 1970.

Buckler, Ernest, *Oxbells and Fireflies*. New York: Alfred Knopf, 1968.

Buckles, Irene, "The Evaluation of the Mathematics Program in Alberta High Schools." Unpublished magistral thesis, University of Alberta, 1956.

Bullock, C.J., "The Futility of Changeless Change: The Worth Report, Progressivism and Canadian Education," 307-18 in *Reading, Writing and Riches*. Ed. R.W. Nelsen and D.A. Nock. Kitchener: Dumont Press, 1978.

Burnet, Jean, "The Policy of Multiculturalism within a Bilingual Framework," 205-14 in *Education of Immigrant Students: Issues and Answers*. Ed. A. Wolfgang. Toronto: OISE, 1975.

Burnham, Brian, ed., *New Designs for Learning: Highlights of the Ontario Curriculum Institute, 1963-1966*. Toronto: University of Toronto Press, 1967.

Burwash, Nathaniel, "National Education," DEA Proceedings, 1904, 43-49.

Byrne, Neill and J. Quarter, eds., *Must Schools Fail? The Growing Debate in Canadian Education*. Toronto: McClelland and Stewart, 1972.

Calam, John, "Diversity and Despair in the Education of Teachers," 129-146 in *Precepts, Policy and Process*. Ed. H.A. Stevenson and J.D. Wilson. London, Ont.: Alexander Blake Associates, 1977.

_____, "Culture and Credentials: A Note on Late Nineteenth Century Teacher Certification in British Columbia," *B.C. Historical News* 14, no.1 (Fall 1980), 12-15.

_____, "Teaching the Teachers: Establishment and Early Years of the B.C. Provincial Normal Schools," *B.C. Studies* 61 (Spring 1984), 31-63.

Calam, John, ed., *The Study of Education : Canada, 1982*. Vancouver: CSSE, 1982.

Calkin, J.B., *Notes on Education: A Practical Work on Method and School Management*. Truro, N.S.: D.H. Smith and Co., 1888.

Callwood, June, "Reason, not Passion," *Books in Canada* 8, no.9 (November 1979), 6-7.

Calnan, D.M., "Postponed Progress: Coburg Common Schools, 1850-1871" in *Victorian Coburg* Ed. J. Petryshyn, Belleville: Mika, 1976.

Cameron, Agnes Deans, "Parent and Teacher," *DEA Proceedings*, (1904), 240-244.

Cameron, David M., *Schools for Ontario: Policy Making, Administration and Finance in the 1960s*. Toronto: University of Toronto Press, 1972.

Cameron, Maxwell D. *Property Taxation and School Finance in Canada*. Toronto: Canadian Education Association, 1945.

_____, *Report of the Commission of Inquiry into Educational Finance*. Victoria: King's Printer, 1945.

Campbell, H.L. *Curriculum Trends in Canadian Education*. Toronto: Gage, 1952.

Canada, Department of Indian Affairs and Northern Development, *Indian Conditions: A Survey*, Ottawa, 1980.

Canada, Department of Labour, "Purpose and Objectives of Commercial Education": *Vocational Education* no.17 (September 1926), 1-3.

Canada, Department of Labour, *Proceedings of the Recent National Conference on Technical Education*. Bulletin no.2. Ottawa, 1927.

Canada, Department of Labour, "History of Vocational Education in Canada," *Vocational Education* no.28 (August 1928).

Canada, Department of Labour, *The Employment of Children and Young Persons in Canada*. Ottawa: King's Printer, 1930.

Canada, Department of Labour, *Vocational Education in Canada 1949*. Ottawa, 1949.

Canada, House of Commons, *Equality Now*, Proceedings of the Special Committee on Participation of Visible Minorities in Canadian Society. Ottawa: Queen's Printer, 1984.

Canada, Royal Commission on Industrial Training and Technical Education, *Report of the Commissioners*, Parts I-IV, Ottawa: King's Printer, 1913.

Canada, Royal Commission on the Arts, Letters and Sciences, *Report*. The Massey Report. Ottawa: King's Printer, 1951.

Canada, Royal Commission on Canada's Economic Prospects, *Final Report*. The Gordon Commission. Ottawa: Queen's Printer, 1958.

Canada, Royal Commission on Bilingualism and Biculturalism, *Preliminary Report*. Ottawa: Queen's Printer, 1965.

Canada, Royal Commission on Bilingualism and Biculturalism, *Book I: The Official Languages*. Ottawa: Queen's Printer, 1969.

Canada, Royal Commission on Bilingualism and Biculturalism, *Book II: Education*. Ottawa: Queen's Printer, 1969.

Canada, Royal Commission on Bilingualism and Biculturalism, *Book III: The World of Work*. Ottawa: Queen's Printer, 1969.

Canada, Royal Commission on Bilingualism and Biculturalism, *Book IV: The Cultural Contribution of Other Ethnic Groups*. Ottawa: Queen's Printer, 1969.

Canada, Royal Commission on the Status of Women in Canada, *Report*. Ottawa: Minister of Supply and Services Canada, 1970.

Canada and Newfoundland Education Association, *Textbooks in Social Studies in the Dominion of Canada and Their Relation to National Ideals*. Toronto: The Association, 1941.

Canada and Newfoundland Education Association, *Proceedings*, 1943.

Canada and Newfoundland Education Association, *Report of the Survey Committee to Ascertain the Chief Educational Needs of the Dominion of Canada*. Toronto: The Association, 1943.

Canada and Newfoundland Education Association, *Proceedings*, 1944.

Canada and Newfoundland Education Association, "The Canada-United States Committee on Education," in *Canadian Education* 1, no.1 (October 1945), 44-47.

Canada and Newfoundland Education Association, "Report of the Committee for the Study of Canadian History Textbooks," *Canadian Education* 1, no.1 (October 1945), 3-34.

Canadian Association for Health, Physical Education and Recreation, *K-3 Games*, Basic Skills Series. Ottawa: CAPHER, 1980.

Canadian Association of Mathematics Teachers, *Mathematics in Canadian Schools*. Ottawa: CTF, 1967.

Canadian Conference of the Arts, *Reports of the National Inquiry into Arts and Education in Canada*. Ottawa: CCA, 1977-79.

Canadian Conference on Children 1960, *Reading Habits and Preferences of Canadian Children*. Winnipeg: Manitoba Library Commission, 1960.

Canadian Council on Children and Youth, *Admittance Restricted: The Child as Citizen in Canada*. Toronto: The Council, 1978.

Canadian Education Association, "A Health Survey of Canadian Schools," 1945-6. Report No.1 of the National Committee for School Health Research. *Canadian Education* II, no.2 (Jan., Feb., Mar. 1947).

Canadian Education Association, "A Study of National History Textbooks Used in the Schools of Canada and the United States," *Canadian Education* II, no.3 (April, May, June 1947), 3-92.

Canadian Education Association, *Recommendations Concerning the Status of the Teaching Profession – A Report*. Toronto: The Association, 1949.

Canadian Education Association, "A Project in Leadership," *Canadian Education* VII, no.2 (March 1952), 3-8.

Canadian Education Association, "Five Years in Retrospect: Final Report of the CEA-Kellogg Project in Educational Leadership," *Canadian Education* XII, no.2 (March 1957), 3-29.

Canadian Education Association, *Open-area Schools: Report of a CEA Study*. Toronto: The Association, 1973.

Canadian Education Association, *Results of a Gallup Poll of Public Opinion in Canada about Public Involvement in Education Decision*. Toronto: 1979.

Canadian Education Association, *The Gifted and Talented Student in Canada: Results of a CEA Survey*. Toronto: CEA, 1980.

Canadian Federation for the Humanities, *Humanities Research Council of Canada/Canadian Federation of the Humanities, 1943-1983: A Short History*. Ottawa: The Federation, 1983.

Canadian National Committee for Mental Hygiene, "Mental Hygiene Survey, Province of British Columbia," *Canadian Journal of Mental Hygiene* II (1920), 14-29.

Canadian Research Committee on Practical Education, "Practical Education in Canadian Schools," Report #1, *Canadian Education* IV, no.2 (March 1949), 3-79.

Canadian Research Committee on Practical Education, *Your Child Leaves School*. Toronto: C.R.C.P.E., 1950.

Canadian Research Committee on Practical Education, "Two Years After School," *Canadian Education* VI, no.2 (March 1951), 1-147.

Canadian Research Committee on Practical Education, "Better Schooling for Canadian Youth," *Canadian Education* VI, no.4 (September 1951), 9-30.

Canadian Teachers' Federation, *Federal Direct and Indirect Involvement in Canadian Education*. 1973.

Canadian Youth Commission, *Youth Challenges the Educators*. Toronto: Ryerson Press, 1946.

Cappon, James, "Literature for the Young: Notes on the High School Reader," *Queen's Quarterly* I, no.1 (July 1893), 27-39.

_____, "Is Ontario to Abandon Classical Education?" *Queen's Quarterly* XII, no.2 (October 1904), 190-206.

_____, "Sir William Macdonald and Agricultural Education," *Queen's Quarterly* II, no.3 (January 1905), 315-22.

Carlton, R.A., "Popular Images of the School," 36-53 in *Education, Change and Society: A Sociology of Canadian Education*, Ed. R.A. Carlton et al. Toronto: Gage, 1977.

Carlton, R.A., L.A. Colley and N.J. McKinnon, eds., *Education, Change and Society: A Sociology of Canadian Education*. Toronto: Gage, 1977.

Carswell, Ronald J.B., "Teacher Development as an Outcome of Canadian Studies Curriculum Development," *Canadian Journal of Education* 2, no.1 (1977), 35-42.

Carter, Bruce M., "James L. Hughes and the Gospel of Education." Unpublished doctoral thesis, University of Toronto, 1966.

Cartwright, Ethel, "Physical Education and its Place in the School," *DEA Proceedings* 1913. 109-123.

Chaiton, A. and N. McDonald, eds., *Canadian Schools and Canadian Identity*. Toronto: Gage, 1976.

Chalmers, J.W., *Schools of the Foothills Province: the Story of Public Education in Alberta*. Toronto: University of Toronto Press, 1967.

Chamberlin, Richard J., *Too Few Apples: Meeting the Challenge of Declining Enrolments and Teacher Redundancy in Canada*. Toronto: CEA, 1980.

Chambers, J., "A Retrospective View of Special Education," 2-10 in *The Exceptional Child in Canadian Education*. Ed. G. Kysela. Edmonton: CSSE, 1980.

Chapman, A.D., "The Position of Geography in Canada," *The Geographical Teacher* XI, (Spring 1921), 52-54.

Charyk, John C., *The Little White Schoolhouse*. Saskatoon: Prairie Books, 1968.

_____, *Those Bittersweet School Days*. Saskatoon: Western Producer Prairie Books, 1977.

Chernefsky, M. "A Touch of Laycock." Unpublished magistral thesis, University of Saskatchewan, 1978.

Child, A.H., "The Ryerson Tradition in Western Canada," 279-301 in *Egerton Ryerson and His Times*. Ed. N. McDonald and A. Chaiton. Toronto: Macmillan, 1978.

Choquette R., J. Wolforth and M. Villemure, *Canadian Geographical Education*. Ottawa: University of Ottawa Press, 1980.

Church, E.J.M., "An Evaluation of Preschool Institutions in Canada ," *Canadian Education* no.3 (June 1950), 14-46.

Cipolla, J.F., "A Decade of Transition: From the Traditional to the Audiolingual," *Nova Scotia Journal of Education* 21, no.1 (Fall 1971), 10-13.

Clark, R.J., R.D. Gidney and G. Milburn, *Issues in Secondary Schooling*. London, Ontario: Faculty of Education, University of Western Ontario, 1983.

Clark, S.D., *The Developing Canadian Community*. Toronto: University of Toronto Press, 1962.

_____, *Canadian Society in Historical Perspective*. Toronto: McGraw-Hill Ryerson, 1975.

Clarke, C.K., "Junvenile Delinquency and Mental Defect," *Canadian Journal of Mental Hygiene* 2, no.3 (April-October 1920), 228-32.

Clarke, Fred, "Secondary Education in Canada," 557-605 in *The Yearbook of Education For 1934* ed. Lord Eustace Perry. London: Evans Brothers, 1934.

——, "Education in Canada – an Impression," *Queen's Quarterly* XLII, no.3 (Autumn 1935), 309-21.

Clement, W.H.P., *History of the Dominion of Canada*. Toronto: Copp Clark, 1897.

Clifton, Rodney A., "Factors Which Affect the Education of Canadian Indian Students," 183-203 in *Education, Change, and Society: A Sociology of Canadian Education* ed. R.A. Carlton et al. Toronto: Gage, 1977.

Coats, R.H. and M.C. MacLean, *The American-born in Canada*. Toronto: Ryerson Press, 1943.

Cochrane, Don and David Williams, "The Stances of Provincial Ministries of Education Towards Values/Moral Education in Public Schools," *Canadian Journal of Education* 3, no.4 (1978), 1-14.

Cochrane, D.B. and Martin Schiralli, eds., *Philosophy of Education : Canadian Perspectives.* Toronto: Collier Macmillan, 1982.

Cochrane, Honora M., ed., *Centennial Story: The Board of Education for the City of Toronto 1850-1950*. Toronto: Nelson, 1950.

Cockrell, Richard, *Thoughts on the Education of Youth*. Toronto: Bibliographical Society of Canada, 1949. (Reprinted from 1795).

Cohen, Sol, "The Mental Hygiene Movement, The Development of Personality and the School: The Medicalization of American Education," *History of Education Quarterly* 23, no.2 (Summer 1983), 123-149.

Coleman, H.T.J., "Training for the New Citizenship," *Queen's Quarterly* 27, no.1 (July 1919), 12-21.

Commission on Emotional and Learning Disorders, *One Million Children*. The CELDIC Report. Toronto: Leonard Crainford, 1970.

Conn, Henry, "Measuring Aptitude for School Work," *The School* XIX, no.8 (April 1931), 717-20; XIX, no.9 (May 1931), 824-27; XIX, no.10 (June 1931), 939-42.

Connelly, F. Michael, "The Functions of Curriculum Development," *Interchange* III, nos. 2-3 (1972), 161-177.

Connelly, F.M., A.R. Dukacz and Frank Quinlan, eds., *Curriculum Planning for the Classroom.* Toronto: OISE, 1980.

Connelly, F. Michael and Robin Enns, "The Shrinking Curriculum: Priniciples, Problems and Solutions," *Curriculum Inquiry* 9, no.4 (Winter 1979), 277-304.

Connors, Bryan, Ian Wright, Kerry Geddes and John Grant, "Reform or Reaction? The New Social Studies in Alberta," *The History and Social Science Teacher* 15, no.2 (Winter 1980), 115-8.

Conrad, Arthur, "Educational Development in Nova Scotia Under Henry Fraser Munro." Unpublished magistral thesis, St. Mary's University, 1960.

Cooper, G.A., "Some Differential Effects of Denominational Schooling in Newfoundland on the Beliefs and Behaviours of Students." Unpublished doctoral thesis, University of Toronto, 1972, 157-180.

Copp, Terry, "The Condition of the Working Class in Montreal, 1847-1920," *Canadian Historical Association: Annual Papers (1972)*. Ottawa, 1972.

——, *The Anatomy of Poverty: The Condition of the Working Class in Montreal 1897-1929*. Toronto: McClelland and Stewart, 1974.

Corbett, Barbara E., "The Public School Kindergarten in Ontario, 1883-1967 – A Study of the Froebelian Origins, History and Educational Theory and Practice of the Kindergarten in Ontario." Unpublished doctoral thesis, University of Toronto, 1968.

Cornish, George W., *Canadian Geography for Juniors*. British Columbia Edition. Toronto: Dent, 1928.

Cosentino, Frank and Maxwell Howell, *A History of Physical Education in Canada*. Toronto: General, 1971.

Coulter, Rebecca, "The Working Young of Edmonton, 1921-1931," 143-59 in *Childhood and Family in Canadian History* ed. Joy Parr. Toronto: McClelland and Stewart, 1982.

Council of Ministers of Education, Canada, *Analysis of Science Curricula in the Provinces.* Toronto: The Council, 1981.

Council of Ministers of Education, Canada, *English Language Arts: A Survey of Provincial Curricula at the Elementary and Secondary Levels*. Toronto: The Council, 1981.

Council of Ministers of Education, Canada, *Mathematics: A Survey of Provincial Curricula at the Elementary and Secondary levels.* Toronto: The Council, 1981.

Council of Ministers of Education, Canada, *Secondary Education in Canada: A Student Transfer Guide.* 3rd edition. Toronto: The Council, 1981.

Council of Ministers of Education, Canada, *Social Studies: A Survey of Provincial Curricula at the Elementary and Secondary Levels.* Toronto: The Council, 1982.

Council of Ministers of Education, Canada, *Arts: A Survey of Provincial Curricula at the Elementary and Secondary Levels.* Toronto: The Council, 1983.

Covert, James R., "A Structural Case for Curriculum Reform," 72-82 in *The Study of Education: Canada, 1982* ed. John Calam. Vancouver: CSSE, 1982.

Craddock, Sonia, "Canadian Children's Literature in the Elementary School: An Historical Perspective and Contemporary Rationale." Unpublished paper, Vancouver: University of British Columbia, 1978.

Cragg, A. Wesley, "Moral Education in the Schools," in *Canadian Journal of Education* 4, no.1 (1979), 28-38.

Crawford, A.W., "The Progress and Development of Secondary Vocational Education in Canada," *CEA Proceedings 1927*, 51-66.

Crawford, D., "Developments in School Mathematics in Canada: A Survey," *Canadian Education and Research Digest*, no.4 (December 1964), 306-319.

_____, "Rethinking School Mathematics: 1959-Present," 426-50 in *A History of Mathematics Education in the United States and Canada.* Washington, D.C.: National Council of Teachers of Mathematics, 1970.

_____, "School Mathematics in Ontario, 1763-1894: From Settlement to System," 371-89 in *A History of Mathematics Education in the United States and Canada.* Washington, D.C.: National Council of Teachers of Mathematics, 1970.

_____, "School Mathematics in Ontario, 1894-1959: Expansion and Moderate Reform," 385-411 in *A History of Mathematics Education in the United States and Canada.* Washington, D.C.: National Council of Teachers of Mathematics, 1970.

Cremin, Lawrence, *The Transformation of the School.* New York: Vintage Books, 1961.

_____, *Public Education.* New York: Basic Books, 1976.

_____, *American Education: The National Experience, 1783-1876.* New York: Harper and Row, 1980.

Cringan, A., "Methods in Teaching Music," *OEA Proceedings, 1900*, 309-12.

Crittenden, Brian, ed., *Means and Ends in Education: Comments on Living and Learning.* Toronto: OISE, 1969.

Croal, A.G. "The History of the Teaching of Science in Ontario, Canada, 1800-1900." Unpublished doctoral thesis, University of Toronto, 1933.

Crocker, R.K. and F.R. Riggs, *Improving the Quality of Education: Challenge and Opportunity, Final Report, Task Force on Education.* St. John's Newfoundland: Department of Education, 1979.

Crowley, T.A., "The Early Home and School (Parent-Teacher) Movement in Canada: Progressive Education and Populist Response." Unpublished paper, Guelph, 1982.

Cuban, Larry, "Persistent Instruction: The High School Classroom, 1900-1980," *The Kappan* 64, no.2 (October 1982), 113-8.

Cummings, H.R. and W.T. MacSkimming, *The City of Ottawa Public Schools: A Brief History.* Ottawa: Board of Education, 1971.

Currie, Sir Arthur, "Is Canadian Education Fulfilling its Purpose?," *NCCU Proceedings 1927*, 22-31.

Curtis, Bruce, "Schoolbooks and the Myth of Curricular Republicanism: The State and the Curriculum in Canada West, 1820-1850," *Social History* XVI, no.32 (November 1983), 305-330.

_____, "The Speller Expelled: 'Useful Knowledge' and the Politics of Literacy in Canada West." Unpublished paper, McMaster University, 1982.

_____, "Preconditions of the Canadian State: Educational Reform and the Construction of a Public in Upper Canada, 1837-1846," *Studies in Political Economy* 10 (Spring 1983), 99-121.

Cusick, Philip, "An Rx for our High Schools," *Character*, 22, no.7 (May 1981), 1-3.

Dahlie, Jorgen, "The Japanese in B.C.: Lost Opportunity? Some Aspects of the Education of Minorities," *B.C. Studies* 8 (Winter 1970-1971), 3-16.

———, "The Japanese Challenge to Public Schools in Society in British Columbia," *Journal of Ethnic Studies* 3, no.1 (Spring 1974), 10-24.

Dale, Hugh M, "Reviving the Life Sciences," *School Progress* 34, no.3 (March 1965), 42-44.

Dale, John, *Education and Life.* Proceeding of the National Council of Education Conference Toronto 1923. Toronto: Oxford University Press, 1924.

Daly, James, *Education or Molasses: A Critical Look at the Hall-Dennis Report.* Ancaster: Cromlech, 1969.

Daniels, Leroi and Charlotte Oliver, "Values Education In Canada: An Introduction and Current Assessment," 213-30 in *Precepts, Policy and Process: Perspectives on Contemporary Canadian Education* eds., H.A. Stevenson and J.D. Wilson. London, Ont.: Alexander Blake Associates, 1977.

Daniels, L.B., "Moral Education and Counsellor Education," *The School Guidance Worker* 31, no.2 (November-December 1975), 11-18.

Daniels, L.B. and J.R. Coombs, "The Concept of Curriculum," 251-8 in *Philosophy of Education: Canadian Perspectives* ed. D.B. Cochrane and Martin Schiralli. Toronto: Collier Macmillan, 1982.

Danylewycz, Marta, Nadia Falmy-Eid and Nicole Thivièrge, "L'ensiegnement menager et les 'home economics' au Quebec et en Ontario au debut du 20e siècle: une analyse compareé," 67-119 in *An Imperfect Past* ed. J.D. Wilson. Vancouver: Centre for the Study of Curriculum and Instruction, University of British Columbia, 1984.

Davies, Robertson, "Educating for the Future," *The Atlantic Monthly* 214, no.5 (November 1964), 140-4.

Dawson, C.A., and E.R. Younge, *Pioneering in the Prairie Provinces: The Social Side of the Settlement Process.* Toronto: MacMillan, 1940.

de Castell, Suzanne and Alan Luke, "Defining Literacy in North American Schools: Social and Historical Conditions and Consequences," *Journal of Curriculum Studies* 15, no.4 (October-December 1983), 373-390.

de Castell, Suzanne, Alan Luke and David MacLennan. "On Defining Literacy," *Canadian Journal of Education* 6, no.3 (1981), 7-18.

Deisach, D., *School Board Research Units in Canada.* Toronto: CEA, 1974.

———, *Family Life Education in Canadian Schools.* Toronto: CEA, 1977.

Dick, Judith, "North of 49: Schools and Controversial Books in Canada," *Phi Delta Kappan* 63, no.7 (March 1982), 448-9.

———, *Not in Our Schools: School Book Censorship in Canada – a Discussion Guide.* Ottawa: Canadian Libraries Association, 1982.

Dickie, Donalda, "Enterprise Education," *Nova Scotia Journal of Education* IX, no.1 (January 1938), 68.

———, *The Enterprise in Theory and Practice.* Toronto: Gage, 1940.

Disbrowe, Harold, *A Schoolman's Odyssey.* London: University of Western Ontario, 1984.

Dominion Bureau of Statistics, *The Organization and Administration of Public Education in Canada.* Ottawa: King's Printer, 1921.

Dominion Bureau of Statistics, *Illiteracy and School Attendance in Canada.* Ottawa: King's Printer, 1926.

Dominion Bureau of Statistics, *Elementary and Secondary Education in Canada, 1938-40.* Ottawa: King's Printer, 1942.

Dominion Bureau of Statistics, *Elementary and Secondary Education in Canada, 1940-42.* Ottawa: King's Printer, 1944.

Dorotich, Daniel, ed., *Education and Canadian Multiculturalism: Some Problems and Some Solutions.* Saskatoon: CSSE, 1981.

Downey, L.W. and L.R. Godwin, eds., *The Canadian Secondary School: An Appraisal and a Forecast.* Toronto: Gage, 1963.

Downey, Lawrence W., "Secondary Education: A Perspective," 1-10 in *The Canadian Secondary School* ed. L.W. Downey and L. Ruth Godwin. Toronto: Macmillan, 1963.

_____, "A Canadian Image of Education," 213-214 in *Canadian Society : Sociological Perspectives* ed. B. Blishen et al. Toronto: Macmillan, 1968.

Downey, L. and Associates, *The Social Studies in Alberta – 1975*. Edmonton: L. Downey Research Associates, 1975.

d'Oyley, Vincent, *Black Presence in Multi-ethnic Canada*. Vancouver : Center for the Study of Curriculum and Instruction, University of British Columbia, 1982.

Duckworth, Eleanor, "Assessing the Canada Studies Foundation, Phase I: An Approach to a National Evaluation," *Canadian Journal of Education* 2, no.1 (1977), 27-34.

Dukhan, H., "The Development of the Junior High School and the Senior High School in Metropolitan Toronto." Unpublished magistral thesis, University of Toronto, 1959.

Dunn, Timothy, "Work, Class and Education: Vocationalism in British Columbia's Public Schools, 1900-1929." Unpublished magistral thesis, University of British Columbia, 1978.

_____, "Teaching the Meaning of Work: Vocational Education in British Columbia," 236-56 in *Shaping the Schools of the Canadian West* ed. D.C. Jones et al. Calgary: Detselig, 1979.

_____, "Vocationalism and its Promoters in British Columbia, 1900-1929," *Journal of Educational Thought* 14, no.2 (August 1980), 92-107.

_____, "The Rise of Mass Public Schooling in British Columbia, 1900-1929," 21-51 in *Schooling and Society in 20th Century British Columbia* ed. D.C. Jones et al. Calgary: Detselig, 1984.

Dupuis, N.F., "The Conservative and the Liberal in Education," *Queen's Quarterly* 9, no.2 (October 1901), 119-125.

Dyde, W.F., *Public Secondary Education in Canada*. New York: Columbia University, Teachers College Press, 1929.

Eason, M.F., "A Study to Discover the Sources of Influences Underlying Art Education in Canada." Unpublished doctoral thesis, Pennsylvania State University, 1955.

_____, "Opportunities for Art Education in Canada." Unpublished paper prepared for the Canadian Conference on Children. Toronto, 1960.

Eccles, W.G., "A Belated Review of Harold Adams Innis, *The Fur Trade in Canada.*," *The Canadian Historical Review* LX, no.4 (December 1979), 419-441.

Economic Council of Canada, *Towards Sustained and Balanced Economic Growth*. Second Annual Review. Ottawa: Queen's Printer, 1965.

Egan, Kieran, *Educational Development*. New York: Oxford University Press, 1979.

Eggleston, John, *The Sociology of the School Curriculum*. London: Routledge and Kegan Paul, 1977.

Elliott, H.A., "The Validity of SACU Tests," *SACU Bulletin* no.2 (1968).

Ellis, W.S., "The Making of a Curriculum," *The Educational Monthly of Canada* (September 1903), 296-300.

_____, "The University and the Schools," *Queen's Quarterly* 19, no.1 (July 1911), 61-66.

Elson, Ruth M., *Guardians of Tradition: American Schoolbooks of the Nineteenth Century*. Lincoln, Nebraska: University of Nebraska Press, 1964.

Emberley, Jean, *Children in Canada*. Hamilton: McMaster University Press, 1978.

Emery, J.W., *The Library, the School and the Child*. Toronto: Macmillan, 1917.

Erickson, Donald A., Lloyd MacDonald and Michael E. Manley-Casimir, *Characteristics and Relationships in Public and Independent Schools (Summary)*. Interim Report as an Aspect of COFIS – A Study of Consequences of Founding Independent Schools in British Columbia. Vancouver: Educational Research Institute of British Columbia, February, 1979.

Esson, Henry, *Strictures in the Present Method of Teaching the English Language and Suggestions for its Improvement*. Toronto, 1852.

Even, Alexander, *Changes in Academic Achievement Patterns in Grade 12 Chemistry, 1964-1972*. Toronto, Ont.: OISE, 1976.

Fair, Myrtle, *I Remember the One-Room School*. Cheltenham, Ont.: Boston Mills Press, 1979.

Falardeau, J.C., "Leon Gerin: His Life and Work," 59-75 in *French-Canadian Thinkers of the 19th and 20th Centuries* ed. Laurier Lapierre. Montreal: McGill University Press, 1966.

Farquar, R. and I. Housego, *Canadian and Comparative Educational Administration*. Vancouver: Centre for Continuing Education, 1980.

Fenwick, Roy, "Music in the School," *The Educational Courier* 6, no.6 (December 1935), 6.

Fergusson, Charles B., *The Inauguration of the Free School System in Nova Scotia*. Halifax: Public Archives of Nova Scotia, 1964.

Findley, Timothy, "Better Dead than Read? An Opposing View," *Books in Canada* 7, no.10 (December 1978), 3-4.

Finkelstein, Barbara, "Private Conflicts in Public Schools: The Sabotage of Educative Possibilities," *Phi Delta Kappan* 62, no.1 (January 1981), 326-328.

Fiorino, Albert F., "Philosophical Roots of Egerton Ryerson's Idea of Education as Elaborated in His Writings Preceding and Including the Report of 1846." Unpublished doctoral thesis, University of Toronto, 1975.

———, "The Moral Education of Egerton Ryerson's Idea of Education," 59-80 in *Egerton Ryerson and His Times* ed. N. McDonald and A. Chaiton. Toronto: Macmillan, 1978.

Firestone, O.J., *Industry and Education: A Century of Canadian Development*. Ottawa: University of Ottawa, 1969.

Fitch, J.H., "A Century of Educational Progress in New Brunswick, 1800 to 1900." Unpublished doctoral thesis, University of Toronto, 1930.

Fleming, William G., *Education: Ontario's Preoccupation*. Toronto: University of Toronto Press, 1972.

———, *The Expansion of the Educational System*. Ontario's Educative Society, Vol.I. Toronto: University of Toronto Press, 1971.

———, *The Administrative Structure*. Ontario's Educative Society Vol.II. Toronto: University of Toronto Press, 1971.

———, *Schools, Pupils, and Teachers*. Ontario's Educative Society, Vol. III. Toronto, University of Toronto Press, 1972.

———, *Supporting Institutions and Services*. Ontario's Educative Society, Vol. V. Toronto, University of Toronto Press, 1972.

———, *Significant Developments in Local School Systems*. Ontario's Educative Society, Vol. VI. Toronto, University of Toronto Press, 1972.

———, *Educational Contributions of Associations*. Ontario's Educative Society, Vol. VII. Toronto: University of Toronto Press, 1972.

Fluxgold, Howard, *Federal Financial Support for Secondary Education and its Effect on Ontario, 1900-1972*. Toronto: Ontario Teachers' Federation, 1972.

Flynn, Louis J., *At School in Kingston, 1850-1873*. Kingston: Roman Catholic Separate School Board, 1973.

Foght, Harold W., *The School System of Ontario with Special Reference to the Rural Schools*. Washington, D.C.: U.S. Bureau of Education, 1915.

———, *A Survey of Education in the Province of Saskatchewan, Canada*. Regina: King's Printer, 1918.

Forbes, John Allison, "Art Education: Its Cultural Basis, Its Development and Its Application in Alberta Schools." Unpublished magistral thesis, University of Alberta, 1951.

Forrester, Alexander, *The Teachers' Textbook*. Halifax: A. and W. McKinley, 1867.

Foulds, Jim, "You Can't Go Home Again," *Interchange* 7, no.4 (1976-1977), 10-12.

Fox, W.A., "School Readers as an Educational Force," *Queen's Quarterly* XXXIX, no.4 (November 1932), 688-703.

Fraser, James A., "The Circular 14 Story – Approved Textbooks in Ontario," *Orbit* 10, no.4 (October 1979), 8-9.

Fraser, John, *Education in Peel Secondary Schools*. Mississauga, The Peel Board of Education, 1979.

Frégault, Guy, *Canadian Society in the French Regime*. Ottawa: CHA, 1956.

Friesen, David, "Academic – Athletic Popularity Syndrome in the Canadian High School Society (1967)," *Adolescence* III, no.9 (Spring 1968), 39-52.

Friesen, David and E.A. Holdaway, "The Curriculum Debate in Canadian Education," *Education Canada* XIII, no.1 (March 1973), 30-33.

Frye, Northrop, ed., *Design for Learning*. Toronto: University of Toronto Press, 1962.

Fullan, Michael, "Conceptualizing Problems of Curriculum Implementation," 40-50 in *Curriculum Canada: Perceptions, Practices, Prospects*. Ed. W. Werner. Vancouver: Centre for the Study of Curriculum and Instruction, University of British Columbia, 1979.

_____, "School – Focused In-service Education in Canada." Unpublished paper prepared for Centre for Educational Research and Innovation, (OECD), 1979.

_____, *The Meaning of Educational Change*. Toronto: OISE, 1982.

Gaffield, Chad, "Schooling, the Economy and Rural Society in Nineteenth Century Ontario," 69-92 in *Childhood and Family in Canadian History* ed. Joy Parr. Toronto: McClelland and Stewart, 1982.

Gagan, David and Herbert Mays, "Historical Demography and Canadian Social History: Families and Land in Peel County, Ontario," *Canadian Historical Review* XIV, no.1 (March 1973), 27-47.

Gaitskell, C.D., *Art Education in the Province of Ontario*. Toronto: Ryerson Press, 1948.

Gallagher, Paul, "Canadianizing the Curriculum," *Contact* 26 (September 1976), 1-6.

Garvin, John W., "Canadian Literature and the Ontario School Readers," *OEA Preceedings* 1927: 292-296.

Gaskell, Jane, "Equal Educational Opportunity for Women," 173-196 in *Canadian Education in the 1980s* ed. J. Donald Wilson. Calgary: Detselig, 1981.

Gaskell, Jane and Marvin Lazerson, "Between School and Work: Perspectives of Working Class Youth," 197-211 in *Canadian Education in the 1980s*. Ed. J.D. Wilson. Calgary: Detselig, 1981.

Gaskell, P.J. and Patricia M. Rowell, "Physics for the Physicist: A Contextual Study of Curriculum Revision." Unpublished paper, New Orleans/Vancouver, April, 1984.

_____, "Changing School Subjects: The Case of Physics in British Columbia, 1958-1964." Unpublished paper: Guelph/Vancouver, June, 1984.

Gear, James L. "Factors Influencing the Development of Government Sponsored Physical Fitness Programmes in Canada from 1850-1972," *Canadian Journal of History of Sport and Physical Education* IV, no.2 (December, 1973), 1-25.

Genesee, Fred, "French Immersion Programs," 25-38 in *Bilingualism and Multiculturalism in Canadian Education* ed. S. Shapson et al. Vancouver: University of British Columbia, Centre for the Study of Curriculum and Instruction, 1982.

Gidney, R.D., "The Reverend Robert Murray: Ontario's First Superintendent of Schools," *Ontario History* 63, no.4 (December 1971), 191-204.

_____, "Upper Canadian Public Opinion and Common School Improvement in the 1830s," *Social History* V, no.9 (April 1972), 48-60.

_____, "Elementary Education in Upper Canada: A Reassessment," 13-21 in *Education and Social Change: Themes from Ontario's Past* ed. Paul Mattingly and M.B. Katz. New York: New York University Press, 1975.

Gidney, R.D. and D.A. Lawr, "The Development of an Administrative System for the Public Schools: The First Stage, 1841-50," 160-183 in *Egerton Ryerson and His Times* ed. Neil McDonald and Alf Chaiton. Toronto: Macmillan, 1978.

_____, "Egerton Ryerson and the Origins of the Ontario Secondary School," *The Canadian Historical Review* LX, no.4 (December 1979), 443-465.

_____, "Bureaucracy vs. Community? The Origins of Bureaucratic Procedure in the Upper Canadian School System," *Journal of Social History* 13, no.3 (Spring 1980), 438-57.

Giles, T.E., *Educational Administration in Canada*. Calgary: Detselig, 1982.

Gillett, Margaret, *We Walked Very Warily: A History of Women at McGill*. Montreal: Eden Press, 1981.

Goldring, C.C., "Wanted: An Investment in Canadian Brains," *The School* XIII, no.4 (December 1924), 283-5; XIII, no.5 (January 1925), 367-70; XIII, no.6 (February 1925), 471-4.

_____, "Enterprises in Toronto Schools," *CNEA Proceedings*, 1938, 164-6.

Goldsborough, Harriet, "Notes on Canadian Education," *The Kappan* 61, no.5 (January 1980), 355, 361.

Goldstick, Isidore, *Modern Languages in the Ontario High School – A Historical Study*. Toronto: University of Toronto Press, 1928.

Gonick, Fay, "Social Values in Manitoba Education, 1910-1930." Unpublished magistral thesis, University of Manitoba, 1974.

Goodlad, John, *A Place Called School*. Toronto: McGraw-Hill Ryerson, 1984.

Goodson, Ivor, "Subjects for Study: Aspects of a Social History of Curriculum," in *Journal of Curriculum Studies* 15, no.4, (October-December 1983), 391-408.

Gordon, C.W., "Moral and Spiritual Lessons of the War for Canadian Education," 3-7 in *Report of the National Conference on Character Education in Relation to Canadian Citizenship*. Winnipeg: National Council of Education, 1919.

_____, *Postscript to Adventure: The Autobiography of Ralph Connor*. New York: Farrar and Rinehart Inc., 1938.

Gosselin, Amedée, "Education in Canada Under the French Regime," 323-97 in *Canada and Its Provinces* Vol. XVI ed. A. Shortt and A.G. Doughty. Toronto: Glasgow Brook and Co. 1914.

Goulson, Cary F., *A Source Book of Royal Commissions and Other Major Governmental Inquiries in Canadian Education 1787-1978*. Toronto: University of Toronto Press, 1981.

Gow, Kathleen, *Yes, Virginia: There is a Right and Wrong*. Toronto: John Wiley and Sons, 1980.

Gradwell, John B., "Secondary School Technology Programs," *Canadian Vocational Association Journal* 10, no.1 (May 1974), 38-41.

Graff, Harvey, *The Literacy Myth*. New York: Academic, 1979.

Granatstein, J.L., *MacKenzie King: His Life and World*. Toronto: McGraw-Hill Ryerson, 1977.

Granatstein, J.L., Irving Abella, David Bercuson et al., *Twentieth Century Canada*. Toronto: McGraw-Hill Ryerson, 1983.

Grant, George, "Adult Education in the Expanding Economy," *Food for Thought* 15, no.1 (September-October 1954), 4-10.

_____, "The University Curriculum," 47-68 in *The University Game* ed. H. Adelman and D. Lee. Toronto: Anansi, 1968.

Gray, Ann Margaret, "Continuity in Change: The Effects on Girls of Coeducational Secondary Schooling in Ontario, 1860-1910." Unpublished magistral thesis, University of Toronto, 1979.

Green, G.H.E., "The Development of the Curriculum in the Elementary Schools of British Columbia Prior to 1936." Unpublished magistral thesis, University of Toronto, 1938.

_____, "The Development of the Curriculum in the Secondary Schools of British Columbia." Unpublished doctoral thesis, University of Toronto, 1944.

Gretsinger, Al, "SACU – Alive but Not Well?," *The School Guidance Worker* 28, no.4 (March-April 1973), 13-15.

Griffin, John D., "Mental Health – Canada: The Chronicle of a National Voluntary Movement – The Canadian Mental Health Association, 1918-1980." Unpublished manuscript, Toronto, 1981.

Griffin, J.D., W. Line and S. Laycock, *Mental Hygiene – A Manual for Teachers*. Toronto: Gage, 1937.

Griffin, J.D. and J.R. Seeley, "Education for Mental Health: An Experiment," *Canadian Education* VII, no.3 (June 1952), 15-25.

Grubb, W. Norton and Marvin Lazerson, "Vocational Education in American Schooling," *Inequality in Education* no.16 (March 1974), 5-18.

Guillet, Edwin C., *In the Cause of Education: Centennial History of the Ontario Educational Association 1861-1960*. Toronto: University of Toronto Press, 1960.

Guldemond, A., Letter, *Curriculum Connnections* 12, (Winter, 1979), 4.

Hackett, Gerald T., "The History of Public Education for Retarded Children in the Province of Ontario, 1867-1964." Unpublished doctoral thesis, University of Toronto, 1969.

Hadow, W.H. et al., *The Primary School*. London: His Majesty's Stationery Office, 1931.

Hall, Oswald and Richard Carlton, *Basic Skills at School and Work: The Study of Albertown*. Toronto: Ontario Economic Council, 1977.

Halpenny, J. and Lilian B. Ireland, *How To Be Healthy*. Toronto: Gage, 1911.

Hamilton, W.B., "Society and Schools in New Brunswick and Prince Edward Island," 106-125 in *Canadian Education: A History* ed. J.D. Wilson, R.M. Stamp and L.P.Audet. Scarborough: Prentice-Hall, 1970.

_____, "Society and Schools in Newfoundland," 126-44 in *Canadian Education: A History* ed. J.D. Wilson, R.M. Stamp and L.D. Audet. Scarborough: Prentice-Hall, 1970.

_____, "Society and Schools in Nova Scotia," 86-105 in *Canadian Education : A History* ed. J.D. Wilson, R.M. Stamp and L.P. Audet. Scarborough: Prentice-Hall, 1970.

_____, "Thomas McCulloch, Advocate of Non-sectarian Education," 21-37 in *Profiles of Canadian Educators* ed. R.S. Patterson, J.W. Chalmers, J.W. Friesen. Toronto: D.C. Heath, 1974.

Hamm-Brucher, Hildegard, "Canadian Education: A View from Abroad," 45-52 in *Canadian Education in the 1980s* ed. J.D. Wilson. Calgary: Detselig, 1981.

Hardy, John S., "Training Third Class Teachers: A Study of the Ontario County Model School System, 1877-1907." Unpublished doctoral thesis, University of Toronto, 1981.

Hardy, W.G., *Education in Alberta*. Calgary: Calgary Herald, 1954.

Hare, William, "The MacKay Report on Religious Education," *Teacher Education* (Spring 1971), 16-23.

Hargrave, Susan, "Federal Intervention in Canadian Education," 23-33 in *Federal-Provincial Relations: Education Canada* ed. J.W.G. Ivany and M.C. Manley-Casimir. Toronto: OISE, 1981.

Harker, W. John, "Teaching Canadian Literature: an Evaluation." Unpublished paper, CSSE, Montreal, 1980.

Harris, Cole, "Of Poverty and Helplessness in Petite Nation," *Canadian Historical Review* LII, no.1 (March 1971), 23-50.

Harris, Robin S., *A History of Higher Education in Canada 1660-1960*. Toronto: University of Toronto Press, 1976.

Harris, Robin S. and G.R. Pilkington, "Curriculum Trends in Canadian English Language Universities Since 1960," 111-121 in *The Curriculum in Canada in Historical Perspective* ed. G.S. Tomkins. Vancouver: CSSE, 1979.

Harrison, F.L., "Music in Education for Democracy," *The School* XIII, no.5 (January 1943), 394-7.

Hart, John., "Is the P.S.S.C. Course Suitable for Canadian High Schools?" *School Progress* 33, no.3 (March 1964), 33-35, 50-51.

Harvey, D.C., *A Documentary Study of Early Educational Policy in Nova Scotia*. Halifax: Public Archives of Nova Scotia, 1937.

Harvey, T.G. et al., "Nationalist Sentiment Among Canadian Adolescents: The Prevalence and Social Correlates of Nationalistic Feelings," 232-62 in *Values in Canadian Society*, Vol. I. ed., E. Zureik and R.M. Pike. Toronto: McClelland and Stewart, 1975.

Hauck, Arthur A., *Some Educational Factors Affecting Relations Between Canada and the United States*. Easton, Pa.: The Author, 1932.

_____, "Education and Canadian-United States Relations," *Social Education* IX, no.2 (February 1945), 67-70.

Heap, Ruby, "New Patterns in Quebec Education: La Ligue de l'Enseignement 1902." Unpublished paper, Montreal, 1982.

_____, "The Rural School Movement in Quebec, 1900-1921." Unpublished paper, Montreal, 1984.

Heise, B.W., *New Horizon's for Canada's Children*. Proceedings of the Canadian Conference on Children, 1960. Toronto: University of Toronto Press, 1961.

Henchey, Norman, "Pressures for Professional Autonomy and Public Controls," 147-160 in *Precepts, Policy and Process* ed. H.A. Stevenson and J.D. Wilson. London, Ont.: Alexander Blake Associates, 1977.

_____, "Alternatives to Decay: Prospects for the Teaching Profession in the Eighties," 233-250 in *Canadian Education in the Eighties* ed., J.D. Wilson. Calgary: Detselig, 1981.

Henley, Richard, "The Canadianization of Nova Scotians 1878-1896." Unpublished paper, Halifax, June 1981.

_____, "The New Education in Nova Scotia." Unpublished paper, Halifax, 1982.

Hennessy, Peter, *Schools in Jeopardy*. Toronto: McClelland and Stewart, 1979.

Hepburn, W.A.F., *Report of the Protestant Education Survey*. Quebec, 1938.

Herner, S.S., "Uniformity of Text-books," *OEA Proceedings, 1881*, 102-108.

Hertzmann, Lewis, "The Sad Demise of History: Social Studies in the Alberta Schools," *Dalhousie Review* XLIII, no.4 (1963), 515-522.

Heyman, R., R. Stamp and D. Lawson, *Studies in Educational Change.* Toronto: Holt Rinehart Winston, 1972.

Higgins, Donald, "The Political Americanization of Canadian Children," 251-264 in *Foundations of Political Culture: Political Socialization in Canada* ed. J Pammett and M.Whittington. Toronto: Macmillan, 1975.

Hobart, Charles W., "Eskimo Education in the Canadian Arctic," *The Canadian Review of Sociology and Anthropology* 7, no.1 (1970), 49-69.

Hobbs, E.D., and Gaalen L. Erickson, "Results of the 1978 British Columbia Science Assessment," *Canadian Journal of Education* 5, no.2 (1980), 63-80.

Hodgetts, A.B., *What Culture? What Heritage? A Study of Civic Education in Canada.* Toronto: OISE, 1968.

Hodgetts, A.B. and P. Gallagher, *Teaching Canada for the 80s.* Toronto: OISE, 1978.

Hodgins, J.G., *Geography and History of British North America.* Toronto: Maclear and Co., 1857.

————, *Early Lessons in General Geography.* Montreal: John Lovell, 1864.

————, *Documentary History of Education in Upper Canada 1790-1876.* 28 vols. Toronto: Warwick Bros. and Rutter, 1894-1910.

————, *The Establishment of Schools and Colleges in Ontario 1792-1910.* 3 Vols. Toronto: King's Printer, 1910.

Hoey, R.A., "Canada: Education of Indians and Eskimos," 189-97 in *The Yearbook of Education* 1949 ed. J.A. Lauwerys and N. Hans. London: Evans Brothers, 1949.

Holmes, Barbara, "Are Canadian Kids Brighter?" Unpublished paper, American Educational Research Association, New York, March 1982.

Holmes, Mark, "A Critique of New-progressive Trends in Canadian Education," *Interchange* 2 (1971), 63-80.

————, "Testing in Canada – Whose Responsibility?" *The School Guidance Worker* 32, no.4 (March-April 1977), 5-10.

————, "Progress or Progessive Decline – A Response to Howard Russell," *Curriculum Inquiry* 12, no.4 (Winter 1982), 419-432.

Hood, Hugh, *A New Athens.* Toronto: Oberon Press, 1977.

Hoodless, Adelaide, *Public School Domestic Science.* Toronto: Copp Clark, 1898.

————, *Report to the Minister of Education, Ontario, on Trade Schools in Relation to Elementary Education.* Toronto, 1909.

Hopkins, J. Castell, ed., *Canada: An Encyclopedia of the Country.* Toronto: Linscott Publishing Co., 1898.

Horne, Edgar, "A Comparative Study of College Preparatory Curricula in Canada in 1964-65." Unpublished doctoral thesis, University of Illinois, 1966.

Housego, Ian, "Pluralist Politics and Educational Decision-making," 13-23 in *School Boards and the Political Fact* ed., Peter J. Cistone. Toronto: OISE, 1972.

————, "Administration and Policy-making in Education: The Contemporary Predicament," 380-90 in *Canadian and Comparative Educational Administration* ed. R. Farquar and I Housego. Vancouver: Centre for Continuing Education, 1980.

Houston, C.J. and W.J. Smyth, "Transferred Loyalties: Orangeism in the United States and Ontario," *The American Review of Canadian Studies* XIV, no.2 (Summer 1984), 193-212.

Houston, Susan, "Politics, Schools and Social Change in Upper Canada," 28-56 in *Education and Social Change: Themes from Ontario's Past* ed. P. Mattingly and M.B. Katz. New York: New York University Press, 1975.

————, "Victorian Origins of Juvenile Delinquency: A Canadian Experience," 83-109 in *Education and Social Change: Themes from Ontario's Past* ed. Paul Mattingly and M.B. Katz. New York: New York University Press, 1975.

Hughes, Andrew S., "Curriculum 1980: The Centralization of Authority," 21-30 in *Curriculum Canada II: Curriculum Policy and Curriculum Development* ed. J.J. Bernier and G.S. Tomkins. Vancouver: Centre for the Study of Curriculum and Instruction, University of British Columbia, 1980.

_____, "Which Way General Education?" *Educational Leadership* 39, no.8 (May 1982), 585-587.

Hughes, James L., "The Kindergarten, a National System of Education," *DEA Proceedings* 1892, 266-72.

_____, "The Relationship of the Kindergarten to the Public School System," *NEA Journal of Proceedings and Addresses* 1894, 483-89.

Hughes, James L. et al., *Public School Methods*, Vol.3. Toronto: School Methods Company, 1908.

Hughes, Walter L., "A Study of the Development of the Secondary School Physical Science Program in Alberta." Unpublished magistral thesis, University of Alberta, 1964.

Hume, J.G., "Moral Training in Public Schools," *DEA Proceedings 1898*, 233-4.

_____, "Pedagogics as a University Subject," *DEA Proceedings 1898*, 33-45.

Humphreys, Edward H., "Equality? The Rural-Urban Disparity in Ontario Elementary Schools," *Education Canada* II, no.1 (March 1971), 34-39.

Humphries, C.W., "The Banning of a Book in British Columbia," *B.C. Studies* (Winter 1968-69), 1-12.

Innis, Hugh R., *Bilingualism and Biculturalism*. Toronto: McClelland and Stewart, 1973.

Institut Fur Didaktik der Mathematik der Universitat Bielefeld, *Comparative Studies of Mathematics Curricula – Change and Stability 1960-1980*. Bielefeld: der Universitat, 1980.

International Geographical Union, *Report of the Commission on the Teaching of Geography in Schools*. Chicago: Denoyer Geppert, 1956.

Ivany, J. W., George and Michael E. Manley-Casimir, ed. *Federal-Provincial Relations: Education Canada*. Toronto: OISE, 1981.

Jaenen, Cornelius, *The Role of the Church in New France*. Toronto: McGraw-Hill Ryerson, 1976.

_____, "Multiculturalism and Public Education," 77-96 in *Precepts, Policy and Process: Perspectives on Contemporary Canadian Education* ed. H.A. Stevenson and J.D. Wilson. London, Ont.: Alexander Blake Associates, 1977.

_____, "Mutilated Multiculturalism," 79-96 in *Canadian Education in the 1980s* ed., J. Donald Wilson. Calgary: Detselig, 1981.

_____, "Education for Francisation: The Case of New France in the Seventeenth Century." Unpublished paper, Ottawa, 1983.

Jain, Genevieve, "Trois Generations de Nationalisme dans les ecoles du Quebec et de l'Ontario 1867-1914," Canadian Historical Association, unpublished paper, Montreal, 1972.

_____, "Nationalism and Educational Politics in Ontario and Quebec 1867-1914," 38-56 in *Canadian Schools and Canadian Identity* ed. A. Chaiton and N. McDonald. Toronto: Gage, 1977.

James, F.C., "The Role of Education in Postwar Reconstruction," *Canada and Newfoundland Education Association Proceedings 1942*, 19-83.

James, Thomas and Daniel Tyack, "Learning from Past Effects to Reform the High School," *Phi Delta Kappan* 64, no.6 (February 1983), 400-6.

Janzen, Henry, *Curriculum Change in a Canadian Context*. Toronto: Gage, 1970.

Jarrell, Richard A., "Science as Culture in Victorian Toronto," *Atkinson Review of Canadian Studies* 1, no.1 (Fall 1983), 5-12.

Jenkins, F.M.S., "The Educational Value of Music," *DEA Proceedings 1901*, 380-5.

Johns, W.H., "Proposal Concerning Common Entrance Requirements for Canadian Universities," *NCCU Proceedings 1961*, 78-9.

_____, "Committee on Common Entrance Requirements Report," *NCCU Proceedings 1962*, 101-4.

Johnson, F. Henry, "Changing Conceptions of Discipline and Pupil-Teacher Relations in Canadian Schools," *Canadian Education* VII, no.3 (June 1952), 26-36.

_____, "Changing Conceptions of Discipline and Pupil-Teacher Relations in Canadian Schools." Unpublished doctoral thesis, University of Toronto, 1952.

_____, *A History of Public Education in British Columbia*. Vancouver: University of British Columbia, Publications Centre, 1964.

_____, *A Brief History of Canadian Education*. Toronto: McGraw-Hill, 1968.

_____, "The Ryersonian Influence on the Public School System of British Columbia," *B.C. Studies* 10 (1971), 26-34.

Johnston, A.J.B., "Education and Female Literacy at Eighteenth Century Louisbourg: The Work of the Soeurs de la Congregation de Notre Dame," 44-66 in *An Imperfect Past* ed., J.D. Wilson. Vancouver: Centre for the Study of Curriculum and Instruction, University of British Columbia, 1984.

Johnstone, John C., *Young People's Images of Canadian Society: An Opinion Survey of Canadian Youth 13-20 Years of Age*. Royal Commission on Bilingualism and Biculturalism, Staff Study No.2. Ottawa: Queen's Printer, 1969.

Jones, David C., " 'We Cannot Allow It to be Run by Those Who do not Understand Education' – Agricultural Schooling in the Twenties," *B.C. Studies* 39 (Autumn 1978), 30-60.

_____, "Agriculture, the Land and Education." Unpublished doctoral thesis, University of British Columbia, 1978.

_____, "Schools and Social Disintegration in the Alberta Dry Belt of the Twenties," *The Prairie Forum* 3, no.1 (1978), 1-19.

_____, " 'The Little Mound of Earth': The Fate of School Agriculture," 85-94 in *The Curriculum in Canada in Historical Perspective* ed., G.S. Tomkins. Vancouver: CSSE, 1979.

_____, "Creating Rural Minded Teachers: The British Columbian Experience, 1914-1924," 155-176 in *Shaping the Schools of the Canadian West* ed. D.C. Jones, N.M. Sheehan and R.M. Stamp. Calgary: Detselig, 1979.

_____, "The Strategy of Rural Enlightenment: Consolidation in Chilliwack, B.C., 1919-20," 136-51 in *Shaping the Schools of the Canadian West* ed. D.C. Jones, N.M. Sheehan and R.M. Stamp. Calgary: Detselig, 1979.

_____, "The Zeitgeist of Western Settlement: Education and the Myth of the Land," 53-70 in *Schooling and Society in Twentieth Century British Columbia* ed. J.D. Wilson and D.C. Jones. Calgary: Detselig, 1980.

_____, "Better School Days in Saskatchewan and the Perils of Educational Reform," *The Journal of Educational Thought* 14, no.2 (August 1980), 125-137.

Jones, D.C. and Timothy Dunn, "All of Us Common People and Education in the Depression," *Canadian Journal of Education* 5, no.4 (1980), 23-40.

Jones, David C., Nancy M. Sheehan and Robert M. Stamp, ed. *Shaping the Schools of the Canadian West*. Calgary: Detselig, 1979.

Jones, D.C., N. Sheehan, R.M. Stamp and N. McDonald, *Approaches to Educational History – Monographs in Education V.* Winnipeg: University of Manitoba, 1981.

Joy, Richard, *Languages in Conflict*. Toronto: McClelland and Stewart, 1972.

Judge, Harry G., "The English Public School: History and Society," *History of Education Quarterly* 22, no.4 (Winter 1982), 513-524.

Kalman, J., G. Potvin and L. Winters, *An Encyclopedia of Music in Canada*. Toronto: University of Toronto Press, 1981.

Katz, Joseph, *Society, Schools, and Progress in Canada*. Toronto: Pergamon Press, 1969.

Katz, Joseph, ed., *Canadian Education Today*. Toronto: McGraw-Hill, 1956.

_____, ed., *Elementary Education in Canada*. Toronto: McGraw-Hill, 1961.

Katz, Michael B., "Who Went to School?" *History of Education Quarterly* XII, no.3 (Fall 1972), 432-454.

_____, "The People of a Canadian City, 1851-52," *Canadian Historical Review* LIII, no.4 (December 1972), 402-426.

_____, "Class, Bureaucracy and Schools," 15-28 in *The Failure of Educational Reform in Canada* ed., D Myers. Toronto: McClelland and Stewart, 1975, 15-28.

_____, *The People of Hamilton, Canada West: Family and Class in a Mid-Nineteenth Century City*. Cambridge, Mass.: Harvard University Press, 1976.

Katz, M.B., and Ian Davey, "Youth and Early Industrialization in a Canadian City," 581-611 in *Turning Points in the History and Sociology of the Family* ed., John Demos. Chicago: University of Chicago Press, 1978.

Kazipedes, A.C., ed., *The Teaching of Values in Canadian Education*. Edmonton: CSSE, 1975.

Kealey, Greg, *Canada Investigates Industrialism: The Royal Commission on the Relations of Labour and Capital, 1889*. Toronto: University of Toronto Press, 1973.

Keats, John, "To the Little Red (Canadian) School House," *Maclean's*, November 16, 1963: 25, 34-39.

Kehoe, J.W., *Handbook for Enhancing the Multicultural Climate of the School*. Vancouver: Western Educational Development Group, 1984.

————, *Achieving Cultural Diversity in Canadian Schools*. Cornwall: Vesta Publications, 1984.

————, "Achieving Goals of Multicultural Education in the Classroom," 139-153 in *Multiculturalism in Canada – Social and Educational Perspectives* ed., R.J. Samuda et al. Toronto: Allyn and Bacon, 1984.

Kendall, David, "Developmental Processes and Educational Programs for Exceptional Children," 13-41 in *The Exceptional Child in Canadian Education* ed., G. Kysela. Edmonton: CSSE, 1980.

Ketchum, Anthony, "The Most Perfect System: Official Policy in the First Century of Ontario's Government Secondary Schools and its Impact on Students Between 1871 and 1910." Unpublished doctoral thesis, University of Toronto, 1979.

King, A.J.C., "Ethnicity and School Adjustment," *Canadian Review of Sociology and Anthropology* 5, no.2 (May 1968), 84-91.

King, H.B., *School Finance in British Columbia*. Victoria: King's Printer, 1935.

Kinlin, J.F., "Eight Years in Mathematics with the Department of Education." *Ontario Mathematics Commission Proceedings* (March 1966), 3-10.

Kirkconnell, Watson, *A Canadian Headmaster*. Toronto: Clarke, Irwin and Co. Ltd., 1935.

Kirkconnell, W. and A.S.P. Woodhouse, ed. *The Humanities in Canada*. Ottawa: Humanities Research Council, 1947.

Kirkland, Thomas, "Some Characteristics and Tendencies of Modern Education and Their Remedies," *DEA Minutes and Proceedings 1898*, 108-114.

Klinck, Carl F., ed., *Literary History of Canada: Canadian Literature in English*, Second Edition, 2 vols. Toronto: University of Toronto Press, 1976.

Kormos, Jim, "Educator and Publisher Perceptions of Quality Curriculum and Instructional Materials During Declining School Enrolments." Unpublished paper, Toronto, 1978. Prepared for the Commission on Declining Enrolments in Ontario.

Kovacs, Martin L., *Ethnic Canadians: Culture and Education*. Regina: Canadian Plains Centre, 1978.

Kraslen, Stephen D., "Immersion: Why It Works and What It Has Taught Us," *Language and Society* 12 (Winter 1984), 61-64.

Kratzmann Arthur, *A System in Conflict*. Undated. No publisher, Calgary, 1981.

Krug, Edward A., *The Shaping of the American High School*. New York: Harper and Row, 1964.

Kysela, G., ed., *The Exceptional Child in Canadian Education*. Edmonton: CSSE, 1980.

Labar, Carol, "Character Development and the Curriculum Between the Wars: The B.C. Case." Unpublished Paper, Vancouver, B.C., 1981.

Laird, Sinclair, "The Meaning of Experimental Education," *The School* II, no.5 (January 1914), 293-7.

Lajeunesse, Marcel, "Espoirs et Illusions d'une Reforme Scolaire au Quebec du XIXe Siecle," *Culture* 31 (June 1970), 149-59.

Lambert, R.S., "Next Steps in Canadian School Broadcasting," *Proceedings, Canada and Newfoundland Education Association*, 1943, 81-85.

————, "The National Advisory Council on School Broadcasting," *Canadian Education* VII, no.3 (June 1952), 3-14.

————, *School Broadcasting in Canada*. Toronto: University of Toronto Press, 1963.

Lambert, W.E., J.Hamers and F. Smith, *Child Rearing Values: A Cross-National Study*. New York: Praeger, 1979.

Lamontagne, Jacques, "The Rise and Fall of Classical Education in Quebec: A Systematic Analysis", 139-158 in *Education Change and Society: A Sociology of Canadian Education* ed. R.A. Carlton et al. Toronto: Gage, 1977.

Lamy, Paul, "Political Socialization of French and English Canadian Youth: Socialization into Discord," 263-80 in *Values in Canadian Society*, Vol.1 ed. E. Zureik and R.M. Pike. Toronto: McClelland and Stewart, 1975.

Landon, Fred, *Western Ontario and the American Frontier*. Toronto: McClelland and Stewart, 1967.

Lang, S.E., *Education and Leisure*. Proceedings of the Education conference, Victoria, 1929. Toronto: Dent, 1930.

_____, "Canada and the Foreign Magazine," National Council of Education, (n.d.)

Langley, G.J, "The Programme of Study Authorized for Use in the North-West Territories to 1905 and the Province of Saskatchewan to 1931 and the Textbooks Prescribed in Connection Therewith." Unpublished magistral thesis, University of Saskatchewan, 1944.

Lapkin, Sharon and Merrill Swain, "Research Update," *Language and Society 12* (Winter 1984), 48-54.

Lapp, Donald A., "The Schools of Kingston: Their First One Hundred and Fifty Years." Unpublished magistral thesis, Queen's University, 1937.

Lauwerys, J.A., *The Purposes of Education: Results of a CEA Survey*. Toronto: CEA, 1973.

Lawr, Douglas A., "The Development of Agricultural Education in Ontario, 1870-1910." Unpublished doctoral thesis, University of Toronto, 1972.

Lawr, D.A. and R.D. Gidney, ed., *Educating Canadians: A Documentary History of Public Education*. Toronto: Van Nostrand Rheinhold, 1973.

Lawr, D.A. and R.D. Gidney, "Who Ran the Schools? Local Influence on Educational Policy in Nineteenth Century Ontario," *Ontario History* LXXII, no.3 (September 1980), 131-143.

Laycock, S.R., "The Diagnostic Approach to Problems of Pupil Adjustment," *The School* XXVII, no.6, (February, 1939), 461-68.

_____, "A Mental Health Survey of Canadian Schools." Unpublished manuscript, Saskatoon, 1944.

_____, *Special Education in Canada*. Toronto: Gage, 1963.

Lazerson, Marvin and Timothy Dunn, "Schools and the Work Crisis: Vocationalism in Canada Education," 285-304 in *Precepts, Policy and Process: Perspectives on Contemporary Canadian Education* ed. Hugh A. Stevenson and J. Donald Wilson. London, Ont.: Alexander Blake Associates, 1977.

Lazerson, M. and J.D. Wilson, "Historical and Constitutional Perspectives on Family Choice in Schooling: The Canadian Case," 1-22 in *Family Choice in Schooling: Issues and Dilemmas* ed. M. Manley-Casimir. Lexington, Mass.: Lexington Books, 1982.

Lazerte, M.E. and D. Lortie, "Articulation of High Schools and Universities," *Canadian Education* VIII, no.1 (December 1952), 48-54.

Leacock, Stephen "Literature and Education in America," *University Magazine* VIII, no.6, (February 1909), 3-17.

_____, "The Apology of a Professor," *University Magazine* IX, no.2 (April 1910), 176-181.

_____, "The University and Business," *University Magazine* XII, no.4, (December 1913), 540-549.

League for Social Reconstruction, *Social Planning for Canada*. Toronto: Nelson, 1935.

Leake, Albert, *Instructional Education: Its Problems, Methods and Dangers*. Boston: Houghton Mifflin, 1913.

Learned, William S. and Kenneth C.M. Sills, *Education in the Maritime Provinces, Bulletin No.16* New York: Carnegie Foundation, 1922.

Leddy, J.F., "The Place of the Humanities in Secondary Education" 1-16 in *The Humanities in Canada* ed. W. Kirkconnell et al. Ottawa: Humanities Research Council of Canada, 1947.

Leithwood, K. and A.S. Hughes, eds., *Curriculum Canada III: Curriculum Research and Development and Critical Student Outcomes*. Vancouver: Centre for the Study of Curriculum and Instruction, U.B.C., 1981.

Lenskyj, Helen, "Femininity First: Sport and Physical Education for Ontario Girls, 1890-1930," *Canadian Journal of The History of Sport* XIII, no.2 (December 1982), 4-17.

Levin, Benjamin, "Research and Practice: The Place of the School District Research Unit," 9-15 in *The Study of Education 1982* ed. John Calam. Vancouver: CSSE, 1982.

Lewis, David, *The Good Fight: Political Memoirs, 1909-58*. Toronto: Macmillan, 1981.

Lewis, Norah, "Advising the Parents: Child Rearing During The Interwar Years." Unpublished doctoral thesis, University of British Columbia, 1980.

_____, "Physical Perfection for Spiritual Welfare: Health Care for the Urban Child, 1900-1949," 135-166 in *Studies in Childhood History: A Canadian History* ed. P.T. Rooke and R.L. Schnell. Calgary: Detselig, 1982.

_____, "Creating the Little Machine: Child Rearing in British Columbia 1919 to 1939," *BC Studies* 56 (Winter 1982-83), 44.

_____, " 'No Baby – No Nation': Mother Education, A Federal Concern, 1921 to 1979" Unpublished paper, Vancouver, 1983.

Light, Beth, and Alison Prentice eds., *Pioneer and Gentlewomen in British North America, 1713-1867.* Toronto: New Hogtown Press, 1980.

Line, William, "Psychology and The New Deal in Education," *The School* XXVIII, no.8 (April 1938), 660-7.

Linehan, Donal, "The New English," *Journal of Education* 5 (Winter 1973-74), 11-13.

Livesay, D.L., "The PSSC High-School Program in Canada," *Physics Canada* 17, no.5 (Winter 1961), 23-28.

Livingstone, David W., *Public Attitudes Towards Education in Ontario in 1978.* Toronto: OISE, 1978.

Lockhart, Alexander, "Educational Policy Development in Canada: A Critique of the Past and a Case for the Future," 76-88 in *Education, Change and Society* ed. R.A. Carlton et al. Toronto: Gage, 1977.

Londerville, John, "The Schools of Peterborough: Their First Hundred Years." Unpublished magistral thesis, Queen's University, 1942.

Long, John, "Intelligence Testing", *The School* XXV, nos. 6,7 (February 1937), 463-6; (March 1937), 557-61.

Lorimer, Rowland M., *The Nation in the Schools: Wanted – A Canadian Education.* Toronto: OISE, 1984.

Love, James H., "Cultural Survival and Social Control: The Development of a Curriculum for Upper Canada's Common Schools in 1840," *Social History* XV, no.10, (November 1982), 357-382.

Lower, Arthur R.M., *Colony to Nation, A History of Canada.* Toronto: Longmans, Green, 1947.

_____, "Education in a Growing Canada," 1-13 in *Canadian Education Today* ed. J. Katz. Toronto: McGraw Hill, 1956.

_____, *Canadians in the Making.* Toronto: Longmans, 1958.

Lucas, Sir Charles, *Lord Durham's Report on the Affairs of British North America.* 3 vols. Oxford: Clarendon Press, 1912.

Lupul, Manoly R., "Education in Western Canada Before 1873," 241-64 in *Canadian Education: A History* ed. J.D. Wilson et al. Scarborough: Prentice Hall, 1970.

_____, "Educational Crises in the New Dominion to 1917," 266-89 in *Canadian Education: A History*, ed. J.D. Wilson et al. Scarborough: Prentice Hall, 1970.

_____, "The Portrayal of Canada's 'Other' Peoples in Senior High School and Social Studies Textbooks in Alberta, 1905 to the Present," *The Alberta Journal of Educational Research* XXII, no.1 (March 1976), 1-33.

Lyons, John, "In Pursuit of an Ideal: A History of the National Council of Education." Unpublished doctoral dissertation, University of Alberta, 1980.

_____, "For St. George and Canada: The Fellowship of the Maple Leaf and Education in the Prairies, 1919-1929," 195-215 in *An Imperfect Past: Education and Society in Canadian History* ed. J. Donald Wilson. Vancouver: Centre for the Study of Curriculum and Instruction, 1984.

Lysyshyn, James, *A Brief History of the National Film Board of Canada.* Montreal: NFB, 1971.

McArthur, Duncan, "Education for Citizenship," *Canadian School Journal* XIII, no.2 (October 1935), 299-302.

McConnachie, Kathleen, "The Canadian Mental Hygiene and Eugenics Movements in the Interwar Years" Unpublished paper, Toronto, October, 1983.

McConnell, Robert, "Currents in Contemporary Moderns Teaching," *Canadian Modern Language Review* XXX, no.1 (October 1973), 46-51.

McDiarmid, G. ed., *From Quantitative to Qualitative Change in Ontario Education: A Festschrift for R.W.B. Jackson.* Symposium Series 16. Toronto: OISE, 1976.

McDiarmid, Garnet and David Pratt, *Teaching Prejudice: A Content Analysis of Social Studies Textbooks Authorized for Use in Ontario.* Toronto: OISE, 1971.

Macdonald, J.F., "Is the Present High School Curriculum in Canada Adequate to the General Needs: The Bearing of this on the University." NCCU Proceedings (1932), 76-81.

MacDonald, John, *The Discernible Teacher.* Ottawa: CTF, 1970.

McDonald, Neil, "Canadian Nationalism and Northwest Schools 1884-1905," 59-87 in *Canadian Schools and Canadian Identity* ed. R. Chaiton and N. McDonald. Toronto: Gage, 1976.

_____, "Egerton Ryerson and the School as an Agent of Political Socialization," 81-106 in *Egerton Ryerson and His Times* ed. N. McDonald and R. Chaiton. Toronto: MacMillan, 1978.

_____, "Political Socialization in Ontario Schools 1867-1914." Unpublished paper, Calgary, February 1980.

_____, "Canadian Nationalism and Education, 1867-1914." Unpublished doctoral thesis, University of Toronto, 1981.

McDonald, Neil and A. Chaiton, eds., *Egerton Ryerson and His Times.* Toronto: Macmillan, 1978.

McDougall, A.H., "Has Mathematical Education in the Province of Ontario Declined in Recent Years?" *Mathematical Physical Association Proceedings 1895* (OEA), 276-279.

MacDougall, John, *Rural Life in Canada: Its Trends and Tasks.* Toronto: Westminster, 1913. (Reprinted 1973 in University of Toronto Press Social History Series)

MacGregor, Ronald N., *Canadian Art Education in the 80s* Edmonton: Canadian Society for Education Through Art, 1980.

MacKay, Alexander, "School Preparation for Industrial Pursuits," *DEA Proceedings 1892:* 241-9.

_____, "The True Purpose and Function of the High School," *DEA Proceedings 1892:* 63-77.

_____, "Three Great Reforms – How May We Hasten Them?" *DEA Proceedings 1895:* 74-91.

_____, *Dominion Education Association Proceedings 1898:* XXXV-XXXIV (On Empire Day).

_____, "Moral Instruction and Training in the Public Schools of Canada," 282-98 in *Moral Instruction and Training in Schools* ed. M.E. Sadler. London: Longmans Green, 1908.

_____, "What is Aimed at as an Elementary Education in Public Schools of Nova Scotia," *DEA Proceedings 1909:* 160-8.

_____, "Are Any Advantageous Co-ordinations Practicable Between the Educational Systems of the Provinces?" *DEA Proceedings 1913:* 49-56.

_____, "Dominion School Texts," *The School,* I, no.6 (February 1913), 378-81.

_____, *Monograph on the Curricula of the Public Schools of Nova Scotia.* Halifax: King's Printer (Commissioner of Public Works and Mines), 1914.

_____, "Uniform Textbooks for Canadian Schools," *CEA Proceedings 1918:* 55-69.

McKay, Marjorie, *History of the National Film Board.* Montreal: NFB, 1964.

MacKenzie, J.C., "What's Happening in Testing Today," *The School Guidance Worker* 27, no.4 (March-April 1972), 5-9.

MacKenzie, N.A.M., "First Principles," *Transactions of the Royal Society of Canada* XLVIII, Series III, Sections 1 and 2, 1954: 35-40.

MacKenzie, William, "External Influences on Manual Training in Canada to 1910." Unpublished paper, Vancouver, April 1984.

MacKenzie Valley Pipeline Inquiry, *Northern Frontier, Northern Homeland.* (Report of the Inquiry, also known as the Berger Report). Ottawa: Ministry of Supplies and Services, 1977.

McKillop, A.B., *A Disciplined Intelligence.* Montreal: McGill-Queen's University Press, 1979.

MacKinnon, Frank, *The Politics of Education.* Toronto: University of Toronto Press, 1960.

McLaren, Peter, *Cries from the Corridor: the New Suburban Ghettos.* Agincourt, Ont: Methuen Publications, 1980.

MacLennan, Hugh, "The Rout of the Classical Tradition," Horizon VIII, no.2 (November 1960), 17-25.

McLeod, Keith A., "Education and the Assimilation of the New Canadians in the North-West Territories and Saskatchewan 1885-1934." Unpublished doctoral thesis, University of Toronto, 1975.

_____, "A Short History of the Immigrant Student as 'New Canadian'," 19-31 in *Education of Immigrant Students, Issues and Answers* ed. Aaron Wolfgang. Toronto: OISE, 1975.

———, "Politics, Schools and the French Language," 59-83 in *Shaping the Schools of the Canadian West* ed. D.C. Jones, N.M. Sheehan and R.M. Stamp. Calgary: Detselig, 1979.

———, "Multicultural Education: A Decade of Development," 12-26 in *Education and Canadian Multiculturalism* ed. D. Dorotich. Saskatoon: CSSE, 1981.

———, "Multiculturalism and Multicultural Education: Policy and Practice," 30-49 in *Multiculturalism in Canada – Social and Educational Perspectives* ed. R.J. Samuda et al. Toronto: Allyn and Bacon, 1984.

MacLeod, R.C., "History in Canadian Schools," Report to the CHA, *Canadian Historical Review* LXIII, no.4 (December 1982), 573-585.

McLuhan, Marshall, "Education in the Electronic Age," 515-31 in *The Best of Times/The Worst of Times: Contemporary Issues in Canadian Education* ed. H.A. Stevenson et al. Toronto: Holt, Rinehart and Winston, 1972.

McMenomy, Lorne, "A History of Secondary Education in Saskatchewan." Unpublished magistral thesis, University of Saskatchewan, 1946.

Macmillan, Sir Ernest, "School Life and Music," *OEA Proceedings 1934:* 89-93.

McNally, G. Fred, "Curricula For Canadian High Schools," *CEA Proceedings 1934:* 134-148.

———, "Report on High School Graduation Requirements," *CEA Proceedings 1936:* 137-143.

———, "Some Highlights in the History of the Association," *Canadian Education* VII, no.1 (December 1951), 39-46.

MacNaughton, Katherine F.C., *The Development of The Theory and Practice of Education in New Brunswick 1784-1900.* Fredericton: University of New Brunswick, 1947.

Magnuson, Roger, *A Brief History of Quebec Education.* Montreal: Harvest House, 1980.

Magsino, R. and J. Baksh, eds. *The Aims and Functions of Schooling: A Focus on Newfoundland Education.* St. John's: Faculty of Education, Memorial University of Newfoundland, 1980.

Mainwaring, Mary, "An Historical Survey of the Roles of Provincial Examinations in the Ontario Educational System During Their First Fifty Years of Operation, 1875-1926." Unpublished magistral thesis, University of Ottawa, 1980.

Manitoba Department of Education, *Provincial Normal School Student's Handbook, 1926-27.* Winnipeg, 1926.

Manitoba Legislative Assembly, *Report of the Special Select Committee of the Manitobal Legislative Assembly on Education.* Winnipeg: King's Printer, 1945.

Manley-Casimir, M.E., "Schooling in a Federal State," *Education Canada* 20, no.1 (Spring 1980), 4-10.

Manley-Casimir, M.E., ed., *Family Choice in Schooling: Issues and Dilemmas.* Lexington, Mass.: Lexington Books, 1982.

Mann, George, "Alberta Normal Schools: A Descriptive Study of Their Development, 1905-1945." Unpublished magistral thesis, University of Alberta, 1961.

Mann, Jean, "Progressive Education and the Depression." Unpublished magistral thesis, University of British Columbia, 1978.

———, "G.M. Weir and H.B. King: Progressive Education or Education for the Progressive State," 91-118 in *Schooling and Society in 20th Century British Columbia.* Ed. J.D. Wilson and D.C. Jones. Calgary: Detselig, 1980.

Manning, W.G., "Department of Education Examinations in the Schools of the Canadian Provinces." Unpublished magistral thesis, University of Saskatchewan, 1954.

Manzer, Ronald, *Canada: A Socio-Political Report.* Toronto: McGraw-Hill Ryerson Ltd., 1974.

Mark, C.E., *The Public Schools of Ottawa: A Survey.* Ottawa: Pattison Printers, 1918.

Marling, Alexander, *A Brief History of Public and High School Textbooks Authorized for the Province of Ontario, 1846-1889.* Toronto: Warwick and Sons, 1890.

Marsh, L.C., *Canadians In and Out of Work.* Toronto: Oxford University Press, 1940.

Martell, George, ed., *The Politics of the Canadian Public School.* Toronto: James Lewis and Samuel, 1974.

Martin, W.B.W. and A.J. Macdonnell, *Canadian Education: A Sociological Analysis.* 2nd edition. Scarborough: Prentice-Hall, 1982.

Martyn, H.G., *Grammar in Elementary Schools.* Toronto: Ryerson Press, 1932.

Masemann, Vandra L., "Multicultural Programs in Toronto Schools," *Interchange* 9, no.1 (1978-79), 29-46.

Massey, Vincent, "Primary Education in Ontario," *The University Magazine* 10, no.3, (1911), 495-503.

Mattingly, P. and M.B. Katz, ed. *Education and Social Change: Themes from Ontario's Past*. New York: New York University Press, 1975.

Maynard, Fredelle, *Raisins and Almonds*. Markham, Ont.: Paperjacks Ltd., 1973.

Merchant, F.W., "The Ontario Examination System." Unpublished doctoral thesis, University of Toronto, 1903.

Meyer, John W., David Tyack, Joane Nagel and Audri Gordon, "Public Education as Nation Building in America: Enrollments and Bureaucratization in the American States, 1870-1930," *American Journal of Sociology* Vol.85, no.3 (November 1979), 591-613.

Michalos, Alex C., *North American Social Report: Volume III, Science, Education and Recreation*. Boston: D. Reidel, 1981.

Milburn, Geoffrey, *Teaching History in Canada*. Toronto: McGraw-Hill Ryerson, 1972.

_____, "The Social Studies Curriculum in Canada: A Survey of the Published Literature in the Last Decade," *The Journal of Education Thought* 10, no.3 (1976), 214-24.

_____, "Forms of Curriculum: Theory and Practice," 191-212, in Hugh A. Stevenson and J. Donald, *Precepts, Policy and Process: Perspectives on Contemporary Canadian Education* ed. H.A. Stevenson and J.D. Wilson, London, Ont.: Alexander Blake Associates, 1977.

Milburn, G. and J. Herbert, ed. *National Consciousness and the Curriculum: The Canadian Case*. Toronto: OISE, 1975.

Millar, John, *The Educational System of the Province of Ontario*. Toronto: Warwick and Sons, 1893.

Miller, Albert H., "The Theory and Practice of Education in Ontario in the 1860s." Unpublished doctoral thesis, University of British Columbia, 1968.

Miller, J.C., *Rural Schools in Canada: Their Organization, Administration and Supervision*. New York: Columbia University, Teachers' College Press, 1913.

_____, *National Government and Education in Federated Democracies: Dominion of Canada*. Pennsylvania: Science Press Printing Company, 1940.

Minifie, James M., *Homesteader: A Prairie Boyhood Recalled*. Toronto: MacMillan, 1972.

Minkler, Frederick, "The Progressive Education Conferences at Hamilton and Windsor," *The School* (Secondary Edition), (January 1939), 378-383.

Moffett, Samuel, *The Americanization of Canada*. Toronto: University of Toronto Press, 1973. (Originally published in New York, 1907).

Moogk, Peter, "Manual Education and Economic Life in New France," 125-68 in *Facets of Education in the Eighteenth Century* ed. James Leith. New York: Oxford, 1977.

_____, "Les Petits Sauvages: The Children of Eighteenth Century New France," 17-43 in *Childhood and Family in Canadian History* ed. Joy Parr. Toronto: McClelland and Stewart, 1982.

More, Arthur J., "Native Indian Education in Canada," *Education Canada* 20, no.1 (Spring 1980), 32-40.

Morrison, A.B, "Curriculum Construction," 75-95 in *Canadian Education Today*, ed. J. Katz. Toronto: McGraw-Hill, 1956.

Morrison, T.R., "Reform As Social Tracking: The Case of Industrial Education in Ontario, 1870-1900," *The Journal of Educational Thought* VIII, no.2 (August 1974), 76-110.

Morrison, T. and A. Burton, eds. *Options: Reforms and Alternatives for Canadian Education*. Toronto: Holt Rinehart Winston, 1973.

Morrow, Den, "The Strathcona Trust in Ontario, 1911-1939," *Canadian Journal of History of Sport and Physical Education* VIII, no.1 (May 1977), 72-90.

Morton, A.S. and C. Martin, *History of Prairie Settlement and Dominion Lands Policy*, Toronto: MacMillan, 1938.

Moss, Peter D., "The Subject-Centred Curriculum: Last Chance or Lost Cause?" *English Quarterly* 4, no.1 (Spring 1971), 18-27.

Mott, Morris, "One Solution to the Urban Crisis: Manly Sports in Winnipeg, 1900-1914." Unpublished paper, CHA, Winnipeg, 1981.

Murray, Alan, "The Literacy Debate: Sharing the Facts," *Interchange* 7, no.1 (1976-77), 19-23.

Murray, Walter, "Public Schools and Ethical Culture," *The Educational Review*, X, no.3 (August 1896), 51-56.

_____, "Teaching Versus Preaching," *The Educational Review* XV, no.4 (February 1902), 186.

Mussio, Jerry J., "The School Curriculum: A National Concern," *Educational Canada* 20, no.1 (Spring 1980), 11-15.

Mussio, Jerry J., and R. Nancy Greer, "The British Columbia Assessment Program: An Overview," *Canadian Journal of Education* 5, no.4 (1980), 22-40.

Myers, Douglas, ed., *The Failure of Educational Reform in Canada*. Toronto: McClelland and Stewart, 1975.

Naegele, Kaspar D., "Children in Canada – Present and Past," 18-29 in *New Horizon for Canada's Children* ed. B.W. Heise. Toronto: University of Toronto Press, 1961.

Nasr, Gamal El Din Ibrahim, "The Implementation of CHEM Study in British Columbia Secondary Schools: A Survey." Unpublished magistral thesis, University of British Columbia, 1977.

National Council of Education, *Report of the National Conference on Character Education in Relation to Canadian Citizenship*. Winnipeg: The Council, 1919.

National Council of Education, *Report on A Survey of Text Books of Geography Used in Canadian Schools*. Winnipeg: The Council, 1921.

National Council of Education, *Observations of the Teaching of History and Civics in Primary and Secondary Schools of Canada*. Toronto: The Council, 1921-3.

National Council of Teachers of Mathematics, *A History of Mathematics Education in the United States and Canada*. Washington, D.C.: N.C.T.M., 1970.

National Education Association (U.S.A.), Commission on the Reorganization of Secondary Education, *Cardinal Principles of Secondary Education*, United States Bureau of Education, Bulletin no.35. Washington, D.C. Government Printing Office, 1918.

Nay, Marshall A., "Alberta's Developing Patterns in Science Education," *SCAT Bulletin* 7, no.1 (December 1967), 25-40.

Neatby, Hilda, *So Little for the Mind: An Indictment of Canadian Education*. Toronto: Clarke Irwin, 1953.

_____, *Quebec: The Revolutionary Age, 1760-1791*. Toronto: McClelland and Stewart, 1966.

Nelsen, Randle W. and David A. Nock ed. *Reading, Writing and Riches*. Kitchener, Ont.: Between the Lines, 1978.

Nesbitt, W.C., "The Development of the Saint John School System to 1871." Unpublished magistral thesis, University of New Brunswick, 1970.

Netter, John W., "Aims of Education in Newfoundland," 23-40 in *The Aims and Functions of Schooling: A Focus on Newfoundland* ed. R. Masigno and I. Baksh. St. Johns: Memorial University, 1980.

New Brunswick Department of Education (Evaluation Branch), *Provincial Testing and Evaluation Programs 1977-8*. Fredericton N.B.: The Branch, Spring, 1977.

Newcombe, Erwin E., "The Development of Elementary School Teacher Education in Ontario Since 1900." Unpublished doctoral thesis, University of Toronto, 1965.

Newfoundland Department of Education, *Report of the Sub-Committee on Curriculum Reorganization*. St. John's: The Department, 1979.

Newfoundland Royal Commission on Education, *Report of the Royal Commission on Education and Youth*, 2 vols. St. John's, 1967.

Newland, H.C., "Official Bulletin – Department of Education – The New Elementary and The New Intermediate Programme," *The A.T.A. Magazine*, (May 1936), 6-7.

Ney, Frederick J., *Canada and the Foreign Film*. Winnipeg: National Council of Education, n.d.

Nichols, E.W., "The Little White Schoolhouse," *Dalhousie Review* V, no.3 (1925-26), 311-23.

Northway, M.L., "Child Study in Canada: A Casual History," 11-46 in *Child Development: Selected Readings*, ed. L. Brockman et al. Toronto: McClelland and Stewart, 1973.

Northway, M.L. ed., *Twenty-five Years of Child Study*. Toronto: University of Toronto Press, 1951.

Northwest Territories Legislative Council, *Learning: Tradition and Change in the Northwest Territories*. Yellowknife: The Council, 1982.

Nova Scotia Department of Education, *Guide to Nova Scotia Achievement Tests, Level Three*. Halifax: The Department, 1978.

Nova Scotia Department of Education, *Public School Programs, 1979-80*. Halifax: The Department, 1979.

Nova Scotia Department of Education, *Public School Programs, 1980-81, 1981-82*. Halifax: The Department, 1980.

Nova Scotia Department of Education, *Report on Public School Financing*. The Walker Report. Halifax: The Department, 1982.

Nova Scotia Human Rights Commission, "General Statements of Major Findings: Textbook Analysis," 191-8 in *Publishing for Canadian Classrooms* ed. Paul Robinson. Halifax: Canadian Learning Materials Centre, 1981. Also published as *Textbook Analysis: Nova Scotia*. Halifax: Queen's Printer, 1981.

Nyberg, Verner R. and B. Lee, *Evaluation Academic Achievement in the Last Three Years of Secondary School in Canada*. Toronto: CEA, 1978.

Oberg, Antoinette, "Implications of Curriculum Decisions by Teachers for Curriculum Making," 54-65 in *Curriculum Canada II: Curriculum Policy and Curriculum Development* ed. J.J. Bernier and G.S. Tomkins. Vancouver: Centre for the Study of Curriculum and Instruction, University of British Columbia, 1980.

Oliver, Edmund H., *The Country School in New English Speaking Communities in Saskatchewan*. Regina: Saskatchewan Public Education League, 1915.

Ontario Department of Education, *Text-book Commission Report, 1907*. Toronto: King's Printer, 1907.

Ontario Department of Education, *History, Ontario Teachers' Manual*. Toronto: Copp Clarke, 1915.

Ontario Department of Education, *History of Education, Ontario Teachers Manual*. Toronto: United Press, 1915.

Ontario Department of Education, *School Management, Ontario Teachers Manual*. Toronto: Ryerson Press, 1915.

Ontario Department of Education, *The Science of Education, Ontario Teachers Manual*. Toronto: The Department, 1915.

Ontario Department of Education, *Religious Information and Moral Development. The Report of the Committee on Religious Education in the Public Schools of the Province of Ontario*. The MacKay Report. Toronto: The Department of Education, 1969.

Ontario Ministry of Education, *The Formative Years*. Toronto: The Ministry, 1975.

Ontario Ministry of Education, *Education in the Primary and Junior Division*. Toronto: The Ministry, 1976.

Ontario Ministry of Education, *Implication of Declining Enrolment for the Schools of Ontario: A Statement of Effects and Solutions*. Toronto: The Commission on Declining Enrolments, 1978.

Ontario Ministry of Education, *Ontario Assessment Instrument Pool – A General Introduction*. Ontario: The Ministry, 1980.

Ontario Ministry of Education, *Issues and Directions: The Response to the Final Draft of the Commission on Declining Enrolments in Ontario*. Toronto: The Ministry, 1980.

Ontario Ministry of Education, *Report of the Secondary Education Review Project*. Toronto: The Ministry, 1981.

Ontario Ministry of Education, *Secondary Education Review Project – A Discussion Paper*. Toronto: The Ministry, 1981.

Ontario Ministry of Education, *Race, Religion and Culture in Ontario School Materials: Suggestions for Authors and Publishers*. Toronto: The Ministry, 1981.

Ontario Ministry of Education, *Partners in Action: The Library Resource Centre in the School Curriculum*. Toronto: The Ministry, 1982.

Ontario Ministry of Education, *The Renewal of Secondary Education in Ontario: Responses to the Report of the Secondary Education Review Project*. Toronto: The Ministry, 1982.

Ontario Provincial Committee on Aims and Objectives in the Schools of Ontario, *Report: Living and Learning* The Hall-Dennis Report. Toronto: Queen's Printer, 1968.

Ontario Royal Commission on Book Publishing, *Background Papers.* Toronto: Queen's Printer, 1972.

Ontario Royal Commission on Book Publishing, *Canadian Publishers and Canadian Publishing.* Toronto: Queen's Printer, 1973.

Ontario, Royal Commission on Education in Ontario, *Report* The Hope Report. Toronto: King's Printer, 1950.

O'Reilly, Robert R., "Attitudes of Secondary Students Concerning the Nature of Mathematics, Mathematics Teaching and Learning Related to Achievement," *Canadian Journal of Education* 5, no.3 (1980), 76-86.

Organization for Economic Co-operation and Development (OECD), *External Examinaters' Report on Educational Policy in Canada.* Paris: UNESCO, 1975.

Orpwood, Graham W.F. and Jean-Pascal Souque, *Science Education in Canadian Schools* Summary of Background Study 52. Ottawa: Science Council of Canada, 1984.

Osborne, Kenneth, "To the Schools We Must Look for Good Canadians: Developments in the Teaching of History Since 1960." Unpublished paper. Vancouver: CHA, 1983.

Oster, John, "The Image of the Teacher in Canadian Prairie Fiction." Unpublished doctoral thesis, University of Alberta, 1972.

Ostry, Sylvia, *Canadian Higher Education in the 70s.* Ottawa: Information Canada, 1970.

Ouellet, Fernand, "L'enseignment primaire: responsabilité des Eglise ou des etats (1801-1836)?," 241-258 in *Ecole et Societé au Quebéc* ed. P. Belanger and G. Rocher. Montreal: Editions HMH, 1970.

Oviatt, Patricia E., "The Educational Contributions of H.C. Newland." Unpublished magistral thesis, University of Alberta, 1970.

Page, James, *A Canadian Context for Science Education.* Ottawa: Science Council of Canada, 1979.

_____, *Reflections on the Symons Report: The State of Canadian Studies in 1980.* Ottawa: Secretary of State, 1980.

Palmer, Harold and H. Troper, "Canadian Ethnic Studies: Historical Perspectives and Contemporary Implications," *Interchange* 4, no.4 (1973) 15-23.

Pammett, Jon and Michael Whittington, *Foundations of Political Culture: Political Socialization in Canada.* Toronto: MacMillan, 1975.

Park, Julian, *The Culture of Contemporary Canada.* Ithaca, N.Y.: Cornell University Press, 1957.

Parmenter, M.D., "Group Work Related To Guidance," *School Guidance Worker* 21, no.4 (January 1966), 1-8.

Parr, Joy, *Labouring Children: British Immigrant Apprentices to Canada, 1869-1924.* Montreal: McGill-Queen's Press, 1978.

_____, ed., *Childhood and Family in Canadian History.* Toronto: McClelland and Stewart, 1982.

Parrish-Connell, Susan, "International Home Economics: Home Economics in Canada." Unpublished Paper, Bangkok, 1982.

Parsons, J., G. Milburn and M. van Manen ed. *A Canadian Social Studies.* Edmonton: Faculty of Education, University of Alberta, 1983.

Parvin, Viola, *Authorization of Textbooks for the Schools of Ontario, 1846-1950.* Toronto: University of Toronto Press, 1965.

Pascoe, C.F., *Two Hundred Years of the S.P.G. – An Historical Account of the Society for the Promotion of the Gospel in Foreign Parts, 1701-1900,* 2 vols. London: The Society, 1901.

Patterson, Robert S., "The Establishment of Progressive Education in Alberta." Unpublished doctoral thesis, Michigan State University, 1968.

_____, "Society and Education During the Wars and Their Interlude," 360-84 in *Canadian Education: A History* ed. J.D. Wilson, R.M. Stamp, and L.P. Audet. Scarborough: Prentice-Hall, 1970.

_____, "Hubert C. Newland: Theorist of Progressive Education," 289-307 in *Profiles of Canadian Educators* ed. R.S. Patterson et al. Toronto: D.C. Heath, 1974.

_____, "A History of Teacher Education in Alberta," 192-210 in *Shaping the Schools of the Canadian West,* ed. D.C. Jones, N.M. Sheehan and R.M. Stamp. Calgary: Detselig, 1979.

———, "Progressive Education: Impetus to Educational Change in Alberta and Saskatchewan." 173-198 in *The New Provinces: Alberta and Saskatchewan, 1905-1980.* Ed. Howard Palmer and Donald Smith. Vancouver: Tantalus Research Limited, 1980.

———, "Progressive Education: The Experience of English Speaking Canadians 1930-1945." Unpublished paper, Edmonton, Febuary 1982.

Patterson, Robert, J. Chalmers and John Friesen, ed. *Profiles of Canadian Educators.* Toronto: D.C. Heath, 1974.

Patterson, Robert and Rebecca Coulter, "Reconsidering Progressive Education in Alberta." Unpublished paper, Edmonton, 1983.

Pavey, E.J., "James Wilson Robertson: Public Servant and Educator." Unpublished magistral thesis, University of British Columbia, 1971.

Pedersen, Diana, " 'Keeping Our Good Girls Good': The Young Women's Christian Association of Canada, 1870-1920." Unpublished magistral thesis, Carleton University, 1981.

———, " 'On the Trail of the Great Quest': The YMCA and the Launching of Canadian Girls in Training." Unpublished paper, CHA, Ottawa, 1982.

Penny, Douglas A., "Provincial Evaluation Policy and the Ontario Instrument Assessment Pool," *The School Guidance Worker* 34, no.4 (March-April 1979), 5-10.

Phillips, A.J., *Some Data on Mental Health Problems in Schools,* Report no.2, National Committee for School Health Research. Toronto: 1948.

———, "A Five-Year Program in School Health Research," *Canadian Education* V no.3 (June 1950), 3-13.

Phillips, C.E. "The Teaching of English in Ontario." Unpublished doctoral thesis, University of Toronto, 1935.

———, "A Study of the United States in Canadian Schools," *Social Education* IX, no.2 (February 1945) 71-72.

———, "Education," 293-326 in *The Culture of Contemporary Canada* ed. Julian Park. Ithaca, N.Y.: Cornell University Press, 1957.

———, *The Development of Education in Canada.* Toronto: Gage, 1957.

———, "The Public School in Ontario." Unpublished manuscript, Toronto, 1978.

Phillips, Gary W., "A Comparative Analysis of Nineteenth and Twentieth Century Mathematics Textbooks." Unpublished M.Ed. paper, Vancouver, University of British Columbia, 1974.

Pike, Robert, "Equality of Educational Opportunity: Dilemmas and Policy Options," *Interchange* 9, no.2 (1978-9), 30-39.

———, "Contemporary Directions and Issues in Education: A Sociologist's View of the Last Twenty Years," 27-46 in *Canadian Education in the 1980s* ed. J. Donald Wilson. Calgary: Detselig, 1981.

Pilkington, Gwendoline, "A History of the National Conference on Canadian Universities, 1911-61." Unpublished doctoral thesis, University of Toronto, 1974.

Pitman, Walter, "Unrealistic Hopes and Missed Opportunities – The 60s in Canadian Education," 17-26 in *Canadian Education in the 80s* ed. J Donald Wilson. Calgary: Detselig, 1981.

Porter, John, "Social Change and the Aims and Problems of Education in Canada," *McGill Journal of Education* I, no.2 (Fall 1966), 125-30.

———, *The Measure of Canadian Society – Education, Equality and Opportunity.* Toronto: Gage, 1979.

Porter, John, Marian Porter and Bernard Blishen, *Stations and Callings: Making It Through the Schools.* Toronto: Methuen, 1982.

Potrebenko, Helen, *No Streets of Gold: A Social History of Ukrainians in Alberta.* Vancouver: New Star Books, 1977.

Potvin, D.J., "Mathematics Education in French Speaking Canada," 353-70 in *A History of Mathematics Education in the United States And Canada.* Washington, D.C.: National Council of Teachers of Mathematics, 1970.

Prang, Margaret, "Nationalism in Canada's First Century," *Canadian Historical Association Historical Papers,* 1968. Ottawa: The Association, 1968.

_____, "The Girl God Would Have Me Be: The Canadian Girls in Training, 1915-1939." Unpublished paper, Vancouver, 1983.

Pratt, David, "The Social Role of School Textbooks in Canada," 100-25 in *Socialization and Values in Canadian Society* Vol.I ed. E. Zureik and R. Pike. Toronto: McClelland and Stewart, 1975.

_____, "Humanistic Goals and Behavioural Objectives: Towards a Synthesis," *Journal of Curriculum Studies* VIII, no.4 (May 1976): 15-25.

_____, *Curriculum: Design and Development*. New York: Harcourt Brace Jovanovich, 1980.

_____, "Curriculum Design in Canada." Unpublished paper, Vancouver, 1981.

_____, "Curriculum for the 21st Century," 21-36 in *Curriculum Canada III: Curriculum Research and Development and Critical Student Outcomes* ed. K. Leithwood and A.S. Hughes. Vancouver: Centre for the Study of Curriculum and Instruction, 1981.

_____, "Bias in Textbooks: Progress and Problems," 154-166 in *Multiculturalism in Canada-Social and Educational Perspectives* ed. R.J. Samuda et al. Toronto: Allyn and Bacon, 1984.

Prentice, Alison, *The School Promoters: Education and Social Class in Mid-Nineteenth Century Upper Canada*. Toronto: McClelland and Stewart, 1975.

_____, "The Feminization of Teaching," 49-65 in *The Neglected Majority: Essays in Canadian Women's History* ed. Susan Mann Trofimenkoff and Alison Prentice. Toronto: McClelland and Stewart, 1977.

Prentice, Alison and Susan Houston ed. *Family and Schooling in Nineteenth Century Canada*. Toronto: Oxford University Press, 1975.

Price, Fred W., ed., *The Second Canadian Conference on Education: A Report*. Toronto: University of Toronto Press, 1965.

Priestley, F.E.L. and H.I. Kerpneck, *Report of Commission on Undergraduate Studies in English in Canadian Universities*. Toronto: The Association of Canadian University Teachers of English, 1976.

Pullen, Harry, "A Study of the Secondary School Curriculum Change in Canada With Special Emphasis on an Ontario Experiment." Unpublished doctoral thesis, University of Toronto, 1955.

Putman, J.H., "Shortening the Elementary School Course," *Queen's Quarterly* XXVII, no.4 (April/May/June 1920), 398-408.

_____, *Fifty Years at School: An Educationist Looks at Life*. Toronto: Clarke Irwin, 1938.

Putman, J.H. and G.M. Weir, *Survey of the School System* (British Columbia). Victoria: King's Printer, 1925.

Quarter, Jack, "Shifting Ideologies among Youth in Canada," 119-36 in *From Quantitative to Qualitative Change in Ontario Education* ed. G. McDiarmid. Toronto: OISE, 1976.

Quebec Ministère de l'Education, *Primary and Secondary Education in Quebec (Green Paper)*. Quebec, Le Ministère, 1978.

Quebec Ministère de l'Education, *The Schools of Quebec: Policy Statement and Plan of Action*. Quebec: Le Ministère, 1979.

Quebec Report of the Royal Commission of Inquiry on Education in the Province of Quebec *The Parent Report*, 5 vols. Quebec: The Commission, 1963-66.

Quick, Edson G., "The Development of Geography and History Curricula in the Elementary Schools of Ontario, 1846-1966." Unpublished doctoral thesis, University of Toronto, 1967.

Rasporich, A.W. and H.C. Klassen, ed. *Frontier Calgary: Town, City and Region, 1875-1914*. Calgary: McClelland and Stewart West, 1975.

Rawson, W.T.R., ed., *Report of the Sixth World Conference, New Education Fellowship, 1932*. London: New Education Fellowship, 1932.

Raywid, Mary Anne, "Schools of Choice: Their Current and Future Prospects," *Phi Delta Kappan* 64, no.10 (June 1983), 684-688.

Redmond, Gerald, "Diffusion in the Dominion: Muscular Christianity in Canada to 1914." Unpublished paper, 1982.

Renaud, A., *Education and the First Canadians*. Toronto: Gage, 1971.

Resnick, Daniel P. and Lauren B., "Improving Educational Standards in American Schools," *Phi Delta Kappan* 65, no.3 (November 1983), 178-80.

Richardson, Theresa, "The Canadian National Committee for Mental Hygiene, 1918-1940: British Columbia as a Case Study in the Dissemination of Ideas in Educational Policy." Unpublished paper, Vancouver, University of British Columbia, April 1984.

_____, "The Mental Hygiene Movement in the United States and Canada: A Comparative Analysis of Policy, Production and Promotion." Unpublished paper, Vancouver, University of British Columbia, April 1984.

Richardson, W.L., *Administration of Schools in the Cities of the Dominion of Canada*. Toronto: Dent, 1921.

Richert, J.P., "Canadian National Identity: An Empirical Study," *American Review of Canadian Studies* IV, no.1 (Spring 1974), 89-99.

_____,"The Impact of Ethnicity on the Perception of Heroes and Historical Symbols," *Canadian Review of Sociology and Anthropology* VIII (May 1974), 159-63.

Ricker, Eric, "The Influence of Interest Groups: A Reassessment," 131-41 in *What's So Canadian about Canadian Educational Administration?* ed. R.G. Townsend and S.B. Lawton. Toronto: OISE, 1981.

Rioux, Marcel and Y. Martin, ed. *French-Canadian Society Vol. I.* Toronto: McClelland and Stewart, 1964.

Ritchie, E., "The Best Collegiate Education for Women," *DEA Proceeding(1898)*, 118-129.

Roald, J.B., "Private Sector Influences on Curriculum Making: The Case of Educational Foundations As Interest Groups," 120-6 in *Curriculum Canada II: Curriculum Policy and Curriculum Development* ed. J.J. Bernier and G.S. Tomkins. Vancouver: Centre for the Study of Curriculum and Instruction, University of British Columbia, 1980.

Robert, Benoît, "Les conditions préables dans le devéloppement des études du Canada," *Canadian Journal of Education* 2, no.1 (1977), 17-26.

Robert, B.A. et al, *Perspectives Nouvelles en Enseignment du Canada.* Toronto: Canada Studies Foundation, 1979.

Roberts, Bryan, *The 1978 New Brunswick Writing Assessment Program: An Introductory Report.* Fredericton, N.B.: Evaluation Branch, Department of Education, 1979.

Robertson, J.W., "Professor Cappon's Article in Queen's Quarterly, January 1905," *Queen's Quarterly* 12, no.4 (April 1905) 420-4.

Robins, S.P., "The Desirability of Dominion Registration of Trained Teachers," *DEA Proceedings 1901*, 53-7.

Robinson, Paul, "Curriculum and Materials Development in the Northwest Territories," 221-8 in *Publishing for Canadian Classrooms* ed. Paul Robinson. Halifax: Canadian Learning Materials, 1981.

Robinson, Paul, ed., *Publishing for Canadian Classrooms.* Halifax: Canadian Learning Materials, 1981.

Robinson, Samuel D., "Changes in the Teaching of Writing: One Teacher's Response," *Skylark* 18, no.3 (1983), 1-4.

_____, "The English Curriculum in the Future Tense: Implication for the Curriculum and Instruction Review Committee (Saskatchewan)," *Skylark* 19, no.4 (1983), 1-5.

Robitaille, D.F. and J.M. Sherrill, "Achievement Results in the B.C. Mathematics Assessment," *Canadian Journal of Education* 4, no.1 (1979), 39-53.

_____, "The Teaching of Mathematics in British Columbia," *Canadian Journal of Education* 5, no.1 (1980), 14-26.

Rocher, Guy and P. Belanger, eds. *Ecole et Société au Québec: Eléments d'une Sociologie de l'Education.* Montreal: Editions HMH, 1970.

Roe, Michael, *Multiculturalism, Racism and the Classroom.* Toronto: CEA, 1982.

Rogers, Tony, "Riding Out the Storm: the Normal Schools and the Putman and Weir Survey of the School System." Unpublished paper, Vancouver, 1982.

_____, "The Paint Slinger: Six Feet of Smile: A Study of W.P. Weston." Unpublished paper, Vancouver, 1983.

Ronish, Donna, "Canadian Universities and Higher Education for Women, 1869-1875: British and American Influences." Unpublished paper, Montreal, 1983.

Rooke, Patricia T. and R.L. Schnell, "The King's Children in English Canada: A Psychohistorical Study of Abandonment, Rejection and Colonial Response, 1869-1930," *Journal of Psychohistory* 8, no.4 (Spring 1981), 387-420.

_____, "Child Welfare in English Canada, 1920-1948," *Social Service Review* 55, no.3 (September 1981), 484-506.

Rooke, Patricia and R.L. Schnell, eds., *Studies in Childhood History: A Canadian Perspective.* Calgary: Detselig, 1982.

Rosen, Earl, ed., *Educational Television, Canada: The Development and State of ETV.* Toronto: Burns and MacEachern, 1967.

Ross, George W., *The School System of Ontario (Canada) Its History and Distinctive Features* (International Education Series #38). New York: D. Appleton and Co., 1896.

_____, The Policy of the Education Department. Toronto: Warwick, 1897.

_____, "Education in Ontario Since Confederation," 174-9 in *Canada, An Encyclopedia of the Country,* Vol.III ed. J. Castell Hopkins. Toronto: Linscott Publishing Co., 1898.

Ross, Murray J., *The Y.M.C.A. in Canada: The Chronicle of a Century.* Toronto: Ryerson, 1951.

Ross, Val, "The Way We Are," *Maclean's.* (July 4), 1983, 18-32.

Ross, Vincent, "Evolution de l'ideologie scolaire officielle dans les manuels de pedagogie quebecois," 127-158 in *Values in Canadian Society,* Vol.I ed. E. Zureik and R. Pike. Toronto: McClelland and Stewart, 1975.

Rowan, Patricia, "Comparing the Cores," *The Times Educational Supplement.* no.3344 (July 18, 1980), 30.

Rowe, Frederick W., *Education and Culture in Newfoundland.* Toronto: McGraw-Hill Ryerson, 1977.

Royce, Marion V., "Arguments Over the Education of Girls – Their Admission to Grammar Schools in This Province," *Ontario History* LXVII, no.1 (March 1975), 2-13.

Rule, J.W., "Innovation and Experimentation in Ontario's Public and Secondary Schools." Unpublished magistral thesis, University of Western Ontario, 1979.

Rutherford, Paul, "The New Nationality, 1864-1895: A Study of the National Aims and Ideas of English Canada in the Late Nineteenth Century." Unpublished doctoral thesis, University of Toronto, 1973.

_____, *Saving the Canadian City: The First Phase 1880-1920.* Toronto: University of Toronto Press, 1974.

_____, "The People's Press: The Emergence of the New Journalism in Canada 1869-99," *Canadian Historical Review* LVI, no.2 (June 1975), 169-191.

_____, "Tomorrow's Metropolis: The Urban Reform Movement in Canada," 368-92 in *The Canadian City: Essays in Urban History* ed. G. Stelter and A. Artibise. Toronto: McClelland and Stewart, 1977.

_____, *A Victorian Authority: The Daily Press in Late 19th Century Canada.* Toronto: University of Toronto Press, 1982.

Rutter, Michael et al, *Fifteen Thousand Hours: Secondary Schools and Their Effects on Children.* Cambridge, Mass.: Harvard University Press, 1979.

Ryan, Thomas J., *Poverty and the Child.* Toronto: McGraw Hill, 1972.

Ryan, William L., "*Liberalism, Values and the Mackay Report,*" Teacher Education (Spring 1973), 21-26.

Ryerson, Egerton, *Report on a System of Public Elementary Instruction for Upper Canada.* Montreal: Lovell and Gibson, 1847.

_____, "The Importance of Education to a Manufacturing and Free People," *Journal of Education of Upper Canada* October, 1848, 300.

_____, *First Lessons in Christian Morals for Canadian Families and Schools.* Toronto: Copp Clark, 1871.

_____, *First Lessons on Agriculture.* Toronto: Copp Clark, 1871.

Sadler, M.E., *Moral Instruction and Training in Schools,* 2 vols. London: Longman's Green, 1908.

Samuda, Ronald J., John W. Berry and Michel Laferriere, eds. *Multiculturalism in Canada-Social and Educational Perspectives.* Toronto: Allyn and Brown, 1984.

Sandiford, Peter, "On the Making of Lesson Plans," *The School* II, no.2 (October 1913), 128-31.

―――, "Heredity and Education," *The School* II, no.8 (April 1914), 491-4.

―――, *Comparative Education.* Toronto: Dent, 1918.

―――, "Junior High Schools and Junior Colleges on the Reorganization of Secondary Education," *Queen's Quarterly* XXXIX, no.4 (April-June 1927), 367-383.

―――, "Problems of Canadian Education," *The School* XXIII, no.7 (March 1935), 563-8; XXIII, no.8 (April 1935), 654-9.

―――, "Curriculum Revision in Canada," *The School* XXVI, no.6 (February 1938), 472-477.

Sangster, John Herbert, *Elementary Arithmetic in Decimal Currency.* Montreal: John Lovell, 1860.

Saskatchewan Department of Education, *Report of the Saskatchewan Advisory Committee on Physical Education*, Regina, August 1973.

Saskatchewan Department of Education, *Rural Education: Options for the 80s.* Regina, 1981.

Saskatchewan Department of Education, *Special Education: A Manual of Legislation, Regulations, Policies and Guidelines*, 1981.

Saskatchewan Educational Commission, *Report*, 1915.

Savage, E.G., *Secondary Education in Ontario.* London: Her Majesty's Stationery Office, 1928.

Sawyer, Don, *Tomorrow Is School And I'm Sick To Heart Thinking About It.* Vancouver: Douglas and McIntyre, 1979.

Scarfe, Janet C., "Stephen Leacock's Perception of the University." Unpublished magistral thesis, University of Toronto, 1976.

―――, "Letters and Affection: The Recruitment and Responsibilities of Academics in English-speaking Universities in British North America in the Mid-Nineteenth Century." Unpublished doctoral thesis, University of Toronto, 1981.

Scarfe, N.V., *A Handbook of Suggestions on the Teaching of Geography.* Utrecht: UNESCO, 1951.

―――, "The Teaching of Geography in Canada," *The Canadian Geographer* V (1955), 1-8.

Scargill, H. and H. Warkentyne, "The Survey of Canadian English: A Report," *The English Quarterly* 5, no.3 (Fall 1972), 39-46.

Schubert, William H., *Curriculum Books: The First Eighty Years.* Lanham, MD: University Press of America, 1980.

Science Council of Canada, *Science for Every Student: Educating Canadians for Tomorrow's World.* Ottawa: The Council, 1984.

Scott, A. Melville, "What is Aimed at as an Elementary Education in the Public Schools of Alberta," *DEA Proceedings 1909*, 180-183.

Scott, William, "What Child Study Has Done for the Teaching World," *DEA Proceedings 1901*, 282-90.

Sealy, Nancillien, "Language Conflict and Schools in New Brunswick," 305-15 in *Ethnic Canadians: Culture and Education* ed. Martin L. Kovacs. Regina: Plains Research Centre, 1978.

Seath, John, *Education for Industrial Purposes, A Report by John Seath* (Report to the Ontario Department of Education). Toronto: King's Printer, 1911.

Seeley, J.R., R.A. Sim and E.W. Loosley, *Crestwood Heights: A Study of the Culture of Suburban Life.* Toronto: University of Toronto Press, 1956.

Selleck, R.J.W., *The New Education*, 1870-1914. London: Pitman, 1968.

―――, *English Primary Education and the Progressives, 1914-1939.* London: Routledge and Kegan Paul, 1972.

Semple, Stuart, "John Seath's Concept of Vocational Education in the School System of Ontario, 1884-1911." Unpublished magistral thesis, University of Toronto, 1964.

Seth, James, "Psychology in Its Relation to the Art of Teaching," *DEA Proceeding 1892*, 145-50.

Shack, Sybil, *Armed With a Primer.* Toronto: McClelland and Stewart, 1965.

Shapson, Stanley, Vincent d'Oyley, and Anne Lloyd, *Bilingualism and Multiculturalism in Canadian Education.* Vancouver: Centre for the Study of Curriculum and Instruction, University of British Columbia, 1982.

Sharon, Donna, *Communications and Information Technologies in Canadian Elementary and Secondary Schools.* Toronto: The Ontario Educational Communication Authority, 1984.

Sharp, Emmit and G.A. Kristjanson, *Manitoba High School Students and Drop-outs*. Manitoba: Department of Agriculture, 1967.

Sheane, G.K., "The History and Development of the Elementary School in Alberta." Unpublished doctoral thesis, University of Toronto, 1948.

Sheehan, Nancy, "The Social Aims of Selected English Canadian Educators, 1896-1914." Unpublished magistral thesis, University of Calgary, 1971.

_____, "Alexander H. MacKay: Social and Educational Reformer," 253-270 in *Profiles of Canadian Educators* ed. R.S. Patterson et al. Toronto: D.C. Heath, 1973.

_____, "Social Change and Educational Innovation in Nova Scotia, 1892-1914," *Nova Scotia Journal of Education* 1, no.1 (Fall 1973), 20-23.

_____, "Character Training and the Cultural Heritage: An Historical Comparison of Elementary School Readers," 77-84 in *The Curriculum in Canada in Historical Perspective* ed. G.S. Tomkins. Vancouver: CSSE, 1979.

_____, "Indoctrination: Moral Education in the Early Prairie School House," 222-235 in *Shaping the Schools of the Canadian West* ed. D.C. Jones et al. Calgary: Detselig, 1979.

_____, "Temperance, Education and the WCTU in Alberta, 1905-1930," *The Journal of Educational Thought* 14, no.2 (August 1980), 108-124.

_____, "Social Change, The WCTU and the Curriculum, A Canadian Comparison." Unpublished paper, Calgary, 1982.

_____, "External Input to Curriculum Policy-Making: Temperance in Nova Scotia Schools – 1880-1930." Unpublished paper, Calgary, 1982.

_____, " 'And What Could Little Children Do?' Saskatchewan, the World War and the Junior Red Cross Movement." Unpublished paper, Calgary, 1983.

_____, "The IODE, the Schools and World War I," *History of Education Review* 13, no.1 (1984), 29-43.

_____, "The WCTU and Educational Strategies on the Canadian Prairies," *History of Educational Quarterly* 24, no.1 (Spring 1984), 101-119.

_____, "National Pressure Groups and Provincial Curriculum Policy: Temperance in Nova Scotia Schools, 1880-1930," *Canadian Journal of Education* 9, no.1 (Winter 1984), 73-88.

Sherrill, James, "Mathematical Education Research in Canada." Unpublished paper, Vancouver, 1981.

Shortt, S.E.D., *The Search for an Ideal: Six Canadian Intellectuals and their Convictions in an Age of Transition, 1890-1930*. Toronto: University of Toronto Press, 1976.

Shutt, Greta, *The High Schools of Guelph*. Toronto: University of Toronto Press, 1961.

Shymko, D.L., "Quo Vadis? Family Life Education in Canada: Past, Present and Future." *Canadian Home Economics Journal* 28, no.1 (January 1978), 48-53.

Siegfried, André, *The Race Question in Canada*. Toronto: McClelland and Stewart, 1966.

Sigurdson, S.E., "Mathematics Education in Western Canada," 412-25 in *A History of Mathematics Education in the United States and Canada*. Washington, D.C.: National Council of Teachers of Mathematics, 1970.

Silcox, S., "The Time Factor and the Course of Study," *The School* I, no.1 (September 1912), 28-36.

Silver, Harold, *Education as History*. London: Methuen, 1983.

Silverman, Baruch, "Some Aspects of the Mental Hygiene of Childhood," *The Teachers' Magazine* XII, no.50 (February 1930), 22-26.

Simmons, James and R. Simmons, *Urban Canada*. Toronto: Copp Clark, 1969.

Simon, Roger, "Impact of Provincial Curriculum Policy on Public Alternative and Private Independent Schools," *Curriculum Connections* 11 (Autumn 1978), 3-4.

Sinclair, S.B., "The Selection of Pupils for Auxiliary Classes," *The School* XIII, no.3 (November 1924) 184-9.

Sizer, Theodore, *Secondary Schools at the Turn of the Century*. New Haven: Yale University Press, 1964.

Skogstad, G., "Adolescent Political Alienation," 185-208 in *Socialization and Values in Canadian Society* Vol.I ed. E. Zureik and R. Pike. Toronto: McClelland and Stewart, 1975.

Smith, Alan, "Metaphor and Nationality in North America," *Canadian Historical Review* LI, no.3 (September 1970), 247-275.

———, "American Culture and the Concept of Mission in Nineteenth Century English Canada," *Canadian Historical Association Papers,* 1971, 169-182.

———, "American Culture and the English Canadian Mind at the End of the Nineteenth Century," *Journal of Popular Culture* IV, no.4 (Spring 1971), 1045-51.

———, "Old Ontario and the Emergence of a National Frame of Mind," 194-217 in *Aspects of Nineteenth Century Ontario* ed. F.H. Armstrong et al. Toronto: University of Toronto Press, 1974.

———, "The Continental Dimension in the Evolution of the Canadian Mind," *International Journal* XXXI, no.3 (Summer 1976), 443-469.

———, "The Myth of the Self-made Man in Canada, 1850-1914," *Canadian Historical Review* LIX, no.2 (1978), 190-219.

Snell Blanche, "Art – The Cinderella of the School Curriculum," *Canadian Art* III, no.3 (April-May 1946), 125-7.

Society for the Propagation of the Gospel, *Classified Digest of the Records of the SPG, 1701-1792.* London: The Society, 1896.

Spence, Ruth Elizabeth, *Education as Growth: The Significance for the Schools of Ontario.* Toronto: no publisher, 1925.

Spencer, Herbert, *Education: Intellectual, Moral and Physical.* New York: D. Appleton and Company, 1882.

Squair, John, "Entrance Requirements to High School and Universities," *DEA Proceedings 1901,* 178-188.

Stamp, L.D., *Geography in Canadian Universities: A Report to the Canadian Social Science Research Council.* Ottawa: The Council, 1951.

Stamp, R.M., "The Campaign for Technical Education in Ontario, 1876-1914." Unpublished doctoral thesis, University of Western Ontario, 1970.

———, "Government and Education in Post-War Canada," 444-70 in *Canadian Education: A History* ed. J.D. Wilson et al. Scarborough: Prentice-Hall, 1970.

———, "Vocational Objectives in Canadian Education: An Historical Overview," 241-63 in *Canadian Higher Education in the Seventies* ed. Sylvia Ostry. Ottawa: Information Canada, 1972.

———, "James L. Hughes, Proponent of the New Education," 192-212 in *Profiles of Canadian Educators* ed. R.S. Patterson et al. Toronto: D.C. Heath, 1974.

———, "John Seath: Advocate of Vocational Preparation," 233-252 in *Profiles of Canadian Educators* ed. R.S. Patterson et al. Toronto: D.C. Heath, 1974.

———, *About Schools: What Every Canadian Parent Should Know.* Toronto: New Press, 1975.

———, "The Response to Urban Growth: The Bureaucratization of Public Education in Calgary, 1884-1914," 153-168 in *Frontier Calgary* ed. R.W. Rasporich and H. Klassen. Calgary: McClelland and Stewart West, 1975.

———, *School Days: A Century of Memories.* Calgary: Board of Education, 1975.

———, "Technical Education, the National Policy and Federal – Provincial Relations in Education, 1899-1919," *Canadian Historical Review* LII, no.4 (December 1976), 404-423.

———, "Canadian Education and the National Identity," 30-7 in *Canadian Schools and Canadian Identity* ed. A. Chaiton and N. McDonald. Toronto: Gage, 1977.

———, "Empire Day in the Training of Young Imperialists," 100-11 in *Canadian Schools and Canadian Identity* ed. A. Chaiton and N. McDonald. Toronto: Gage, 1977.

———, "Canadian High Schools in the 1920s and 1930s: The Social Challenge to the Academic Tradition," 76-94 in *Historical Papers.* London, Ont.: CHA, 1978.

———, "Ontario at Philadelphia: The Centennial Exposition of 1876," 302-317 in *Egerton Ryerson and His Times* ed. N. McDonald and A. Chaiton. Toronto: Macmillan, 1978.

———, *Schools of Ontario, 1876-1976.* Toronto: University of Toronto Press, 1982.

Stanley, Carleton, "Too Much Trust in 'Civics'," 382-91 in *The Yearbook of Education 1940* ed. F.H. Spencer. London: Evans Brothers, 1940.

Stapleton, John J., "The Department of Education as a Policy-Maker: The Case of the Credit System in Ontario," 39-46 in *The Politics of Canadian Education* ed. J.A. Wallin. Edmonton: CSSE, 1977.

Statistics Canada, *Canada's Population: Demographic Perspectives*. Ottawa: Ministry of Supply and Resources, 1979.

Steinhauer, David, "The Old Order Changeth." *Canadian Modern Language Review* XV, no.2 (Winter 1959), 11-13.

Stern, H.H., "Immersion Schools and Language Learning," *Language and Society* (Spring/Summer 1981), 3-6.

_____, "The Immersion Phenomenon", *Language and Society* 12 (Winter 1984), 4-7.

Stern, H.H., ed., "The Immersion Phenomenon," Special Issue, *Language and Society* 12, (Winter 1984). Ottawa: Commissioner of Official Languages, 1984.

Stevenson, Hugh A., "Reaction and Reform," 95-110 in *The Curriculum in Canada in Historical Perspective* ed. G.S. Tomkins. Vancouver: CSSE, 1979.

_____, "Educational Policy and the Future," 269-281 in *Canadian Education in the 80s* ed. J.D. Wilson. Calgary: Detselig, 1981.

_____, "The Federal Presence in Canadian Education, 1939-1980," 3-22 in *Federal – Provincial Relations: Education Canada* ed. J.W.G. Ivany and M.E. Manley-Casimir. Toronto: OISE, 1981.

Stevenson, H.A., R.M. Stamp and J.D. Wilson, ed. *The Best of Times, The Worst of Times: Contemporary Issues in Canadian Education*. Toronto: Holt, Rinehart and Winston, 1972.

Stevenson, Hugh A. and J.D. Wilson, eds. *Precepts, Policy and Process: Perspectives on Contemporary Canadian Education*. London, Ont.: Alexander Blake Associates, 1977.

Stewart, F.K. *Interprovincial Co-operation in Education: The Story of the Canadian Education Association*. Toronto: Gage, 1957.

Stock, Marie, "Modern Language Teaching in Upper Canada a Century Ago," *Canadian Modern Language Review* XVI, no.4 (Summer 1960), 5-8.

Stratton, R.W., "The Position of Classical Study in the High Schools of Ontario," *DEA Proceedings* 1892, 178-87.

Stringer, Judith A., "Survey of Vocational Trends in Canadian Curricula." Unpublished paper, Vancouver, 1981.

Strong-Boag, Veronica, *The Parliament of Women: The National Council of Women of Canada, 1893-1929*. Ottawa: National Museum of Man, Mercury Series, 1976.

_____, "Intruders in the Nursery: Childcare Professionals Reshape the Years One to Five, 1920-1940," 160-178 in *Childhood and Family in Canadian History* ed. Joy Parr. Toronto: McClelland and Stewart, 1982.

Stubbs, Gordon, "The Role of Egerton Ryerson in the Development of Public Library Services in Ontario." Unpublished magistral thesis, University of British Columbia, 1960.

Stuewe, Paul, "Better Dead than Read?," *Books in Canada* 7, no.8 (October 1978), 3-5.

Sutherland, G.R., *The Development of Industrial Arts in Nova Scotia*. Halifax: Nova Scotia Department of Education, 1969.

Sutherland, Neil, *Children in English-Canadian Society: Framing the Twentieth Century Consensus* 2nd edition. Toronto: University of Toronto Press, 1978.

_____, "The 'New' Education in Anglophone Canada: "Modernization' Transforms the Curriculum," 49-60 in *The Curriculum in Canada in Historical Perspective* ed. G.S. Tomkins. Vancouver: CSSE, 1979.

_____, "The Triumph of 'Formalism': *Elementary Schooling in Vancouver from the 1920s to the 1960s*. B.C. Studies. University of British Columbia Press, Spring 1986.

Sutherland, N. and Edith Deyell, *Making Canadian History*, 2 vols. Toronto: Gage, 1966, 1967.

Swan, Susan, *Educational Activities of the Canadian Broadcasting Corporation and the National Film Board of Canada*. Toronto: Ontario Educational Communication Authority, 1984.

Symons, T.H.B., *To Know Ourselves: The Report of the Commission on Canadian Studies*, 2 vols. Ottawa: Association of Universities and Colleges of Canada, 1975.

Symons, T.H.B. and James E. Page, *Some Questions of Balance: Human Resources, Higher Education and Canadian Studies, Volume III of To Know Ourselves: The Report of the Commission of Canadian Studies*. Ottawa: Association of Universities and Colleges of Canada, 1984.

Tait, G.E., "A History of Art Education in the Elementary Schools of Ontario." Unpublished doctoral thesis, University of Toronto, 1957.

Tanner, Daniel, *Secondary Curriculum: Theory and Development*. New York: Macmillan, 1971.

Tanner, Daniel and Laurel N. Tanner, *Curriculum Development: Theory into Practice*. New York: Macmillan, 1975.

Taylor, Stanley, "Changes in Biology in Ontario High Schools, 1871-1978." Unpublished paper, Vancouver, 1982.

Taylor, T., "Professionally Geared High School Programs Constitute a Luxury Canada Cannot Afford," *Canadian Vocational Association Journal* 2, no.3 (Winter 1967), 8-13.

Thiessen, Elmer J. and L.G. Roy Wilson, "Curriculum in the Church-State Controversy: Are the Mennonites Justified in Rejecting the Public School Curriculum?," *INFORM* 3, no.1 (January 1981), unnumbered.

Thomas, Alan M., "Education: Reformation and Renewal in the 80s," 251-68 in *Canadian Education in the 1980s* ed. J.D. Wilson. Calgary: Detselig, 1981.

Thomas, Jane, "The Emergence of Domestic Science in Vancouver Schools: 1905-1925." Unpublished paper, Vancouver, 1984.

Thompson, Henry P., *Into All Lands: The History of the Society for the Propagation of the Gospel in Foreign Parts 1701-1705*. London: Society for the Promotion of Christian Knowledge, 1951.

Thomson, J.S., "The New Education has come to Canada . . . ." *Dalhousie Review* XXI, no.2 (July 1941), 224-231.

———, "Matriculation," *NCCU Proceedings 1947*, 43.

Titley, Brian, "Duncan Campbell Scott and Indian Educational Policy", 141-153 in *An Imperfect Past: Education and Society in Canadian History* ed. J.D. Wilson. Vancouver: Centre for the Study of Curriculum and Instruction, U.B.C., 1984.

Tomkins, George S., "Some Aspects of American Influence on Canadian Educational Thought and Practice." Unpublished magistral thesis, McGill University, 1952.

———, "Education and the Canadian Constitution," *The Teachers' Magazine* (Quebec) XXXIX, no.196 (April 1959), 7-10.

———, "Canadian Education and the Development of a National Consciousness," 6-28 in *Canadian Schools and Canadian Identity* ed. A. Chaiton and Neil McDonald. Toronto: Gage, 1976.

———, "The Canada Studies Foundation: A Canadian Approach to Curriculum Intervention." *Canadian Journal of Education* 2, no.1 (1977), 5-16.

———, "Political Socialization Research and Canadian Studies," *Canadian Journal of Education* 2, no.1 (1977), 83-91.

———, "Towards a History of Curriculum Development in Canada," 1-17 in *The Curriculum in Canada in Historical Perspective* ed. George S. Tomkins. Vancouver: CSSE, 1979.

———, "School Geography in Canada: An Historical Perspective," 3-17 in *Canadian Geographical Education* ed. R. Choquette et al. Ottawa: University of Ottawa Press, 1980.

———, "Foreign Influences on Curriculum and Curriculum Policy Making in Canada: Some Impressions in Historical and Contemporary Perspectives," *Curriculum Inquiry* II, no.2 (1981), 157-166.

———, "The Social Studies in Canada," 12-30 in *A Canadian Social Studies* ed. J. Parsons et al. Edmonton: Faculty of Education, University of Alberta, 1983.

Tomkins, George S., ed., *The Curriculum in Canada in Historical Perspective*. Vancouver: CSSE, 1979.

Totton, S.J., "The Marketing of Educational Books in Canada," 270-311 in *Background Papers* Ontario Royal Commission on Book Publishing. Toronto: Queen's Printer, 1972.

Townsend, R.G. and S.B. Lawton, ed. *What's So Canadian About Canadian Educational Administration – Essays on the Canadian Tradition in School Management*. Toronto: OISE, 1981.

Traub, Ross E., Carla Wolfe, Richard G. Wolfe and Howard Russell, "Interface Project II and Ontario Review of Educational Policy," *Interchange* 2, no.4 (1976-77), 24-31.

Traub, Ross, Joel Weiss and Charles Fisher, *Openness in Schools*. Toronto: OISE, 1977.

Trofimenkoff, Susan and Alison Prentice, ed. *The Neglected Majority*. Toronto: McClelland and Stewart, 1977.

Trowsdale, Cameron, "A History of Public School Music in Ontario.". Unpublished doctoral thesis, Toronto: University of Toronto, 1962.

Trudel, Marcel and Genevieve Jain, *Canadian History Textbooks: A Comparative Study.* Royal Commission on Bilingualism and Biculturalism, Staff Study No.5. Ottawa: Queen's Printer, 1970.

Turner, Judith, "The Community and the Curriculum," *The B.C. Teacher* 60, no.1, (September-October 1980), 21-3.

Tyack, David, *The One Best System: A History of American Urban Education.* Cambridge, Mass.: Harvard University Press, 1976.

Tyack, David, Michael Kirst and Elizabeth Hansot, "Educational Reform: Retrospect and Prospect," *Teachers College Record* 81, no.3 (Spring 1980), 253-269.

Tyler, Ralph W., *Basic Principles of Curriculum and Instruction.* Chicago: University of Chicago Press, 1949.

Ullman, Stephen, "Nationalism and Regionalism in the Political Socialization of Cape Breton Whites and Indians," *The American Review of Canadian Studies* V, no.1 (1975), 66-97.

Underhill, Frank H., "So Little for the Mind: Comments and Queries," 15-23 in *Transactions of the Royal Society of Canada* XLVII (June 1954), Series III.

Urquhart, M.C. and K.A.H. Buckley, ed. *Historical Statistics of Canada.* Toronto: Macmillan, 1965.

Van Brummelen, Harro, "Textbook Policies in British Columbia: The Imposition of Uniformity Through Benevolence." Unpublished paper, Vancouver, B.C., December, 1982.

_____, "Shifting Perspectives: Early British Columbia Textbooks from 1872 to 1925," *B.C. Studies* 60 (Winter 1983-84), 3-27.

Vancouver Board of School Trustees, *Selection of Learning Resources: A Policy Statement.* Vancouver: Vancouver School Board, 1978.

Van Hesteren, F.N., "Foundations of the Guidance Movement in Canada." Unpublished doctoral thesis, University of Alberta, 1971.

Van Manen, M. and L. Stewart, ed. *Curriculum Policy-making in Alberta Education.* Edmonton: Faculty of Education, University of Alberta, 1978.

Verma, Dhirenda, "Technical-Vocational Education in Nova Scotia within the Context of Social, Economic and Political Change, 1880-1975." Unpublished doctoral thesis, Atlantic Institute of Education, 1978.

Vernon, F., "Some Aspects of the Development of Public Education in the City of St. Catharines." Unpublished magistral thesis, University of Toronto, 1960.

Vertinsky, Patricia, "Education for Sexual Morality: Moral Reform and the Regulation of American Morality of the Nineteenth Century." Unpublished doctoral thesis, Faculty of Education, University of British Columbia, 1982.

Waite, P.B., "Sir Oliver Mowat's Canada: Reflections on an Un-Victorian Society," 12-32 in *Oliver Mowat's Ontario* ed., D. Swainson. Toronto: Macmillan, 1972.

Waites, K.A., *The First Fifty Years: Vancouver High Schools, 1890-1940.* Vancouver: Board of School Trustees, 1942.

Walker, B.E., "Public Secondary Education in Alberta: Organization and Curriculum, 1889-1951." Unpublished doctoral dissertation, Stanford University, 1955.

_____, "The High School Program in Alberta During the Territorial Period, 1889-1905," 211-221 in *Shaping the Schools of the Canadian West* ed. D.C. Jones et al. Calgary: Detselig, 1979.

Walker, Laurence, "Progressives and Conservatives in Reading Education: A Response to Margaret Hunsberger." 73-84 in *School Subject Research and Curriculum/Instruction Theory, Curriculum Canada V* ed. D. Roberts. Vancouver: Centre for the Study of Curriculum and Instruction, University of British Columbia, 1981.

_____, " 'More a Torment Than a Benefit': English Grammar in Nova Scotia Schools in the Nineteenth Century." Unpublished paper, Halifax, 1984.

Wallin, J.H.A., ed., *The Politics of Canadian Education* Edmonton: CSSE, 1977.

Walsh Gerald, "A Survey of Philosophies of History in Canadian High Schools," *Canadian Journal of History and Social Science* 2, no.3 (1966-67), 8-14.

Wangerin, Walter M., "A Descriptive Study of the Minimum Requirements for Graduation from Secondary Education in the Provinces of Canada in 1958." Unpublished doctoral thesis, University of Alberta, 1959.

Warrington, C.J. and B.T. Newbold, "Chemical Canada: Past and Present." Ottawa: The Chemical Institute of Canada, 1970.

Watson, John, "The University and the Schools," *Queen's Quarterly* VIII, no.4 (April 1901), 322-340.

Watts, Morrison, *Curriculum Building Procedures in Alberta*. Edmonton: Department of Education, 1965.

Webster, E.C., *Guidance for the High School Pupil: A Study of Secondary Schools in Quebec*. Montreal: McGill Social Research Services, 1938.

Weinstein, Pauline, "An Analysis of Methodology in the Teaching of Arithmetic Concepts as Reflected in Textbooks Used in Canadian Schools Prior to 1890." Unpublished doctoral thesis, University of Oregon, 1973.

Wells, Thomas L., "Adjusting the Pendulum," *Interchange* 7, no.4 (1976-1977), 3-6.

Werner, Walter, ed., *Curriculum Canada: Perceptions, Practices, Prospects*. Vancouver: Centre for the Study of Curriculum and Instruction, 1979.

Werner, W., B. Connors, T. Aoki, and J. Dahlie, *Whose Culture? Whose Heritage?*. Vancouver: Centre for the Study of Curriculum and Instruction, University of British Columbia, 1977.

West, J. Thomas, "Physical Fitness, Sport and the Federal Government, 1909 to 1954," *Canadian Journal of History of Sport and Physical Education* IV, no.1 (December 1973), 26-42.

Westbury, Ian, "Change and Stability in the Curriculum: An Overview of the Question," 12-36 in *Comparative Studies of Mathematics Curricula Change and Stability 1960-80*. Bielefeld: Institut fur Didaktik der Mathematic der Universitat Bielefeld, 1980.

Western Canadian Industrial Education Invitational Conference, *Sharing in the 80s and Beyond* (*Proceedings*) Edmonton, 1982.

Wetherell, J.E., "Conservatism and Reform in Education Methods," *Ontario Teachers' Association Proceedings 1886*, 85-88.

White, E.T., *Public School Textbooks in Ontario*. London: The Chas. Chapman Co., 1922.

White, J.F., "The Function of the Public School in Character Formation," 59-63 in National Council of Education *Report of the National Conference on Character Education in Relation to Canadian Citizenship*. Winnipeg, 1919.

White, O.E., "The History of Practical Education Courses in Canadian Secondary Schools." Unpublished magistral thesis, McGill University, 1951.

Whittington, Michael S., "Children and the Monarchy: Canadian Perceptions of the Queen," 240-250 in *Foundations of Political Culture: Political Socialization in Canada*, ed. J. Pammett and M. Whittington. Toronto: Macmillan, 1975.

Willoughby, Jeremiah, *Progress of Education in Nova Scotia During Fifty Years*. Halifax: Nova Scotia Printing Company, 1884.

Wilson, J. Donald, "Education in Upper Canada: Sixty Years of Change," 190-213 in *Canadian Education: A History* ed. J.D. Wilson et al. Scarborough: Prentice-Hall, 1970.

———, "The Ryerson Years in Canada West," 214-64 in *Canadian Education: a History* ed. J.D. Wilson et al. Scarborough: Prentice-Hall, 1970.

———, "Religion and Education: The Other Side of Pluralism," 97-113 in *Canadian Education in the 1980s* ed., J.D. Wilson. Calgary: Detselig, 1981.

———, "Multicultural Programmes in Canadian Education," 62-77 in *Multiculturalism in Canada – Social and Educational Perspectives* ed. R.J. Samuda et al. Toronto: Allyn and Bacon, 1984.

———, "Cockrell, Richard," *Dictionary of Canadian Biography*, Toronto: University of Toronto Press, forthcoming.

Wilson, J. Donald, ed., *Canadian Education in the 1980s*. Calgary: Detselig, 1981.

———, *An Imperfect Past: Education and Society in Canadian History*. Vancouver: Centre for the Study of Curriculum and Instruction, University of British Columbia, 1984.

Wilson, J. Donald and David C. Jones, eds. *Schooling and Society in 20th Century British Columbia*. Alberta: Detselig, 1980.

Wilson, J.D., R.M. Stamp and L.P. Audet, ed. *Canadian Education: A History.* Scarborough: Prentice-Hall, 1970.

Wilson, Susan W., "Social Factors in the Historical Development of Domestic Science." Unpublished paper, Vancouver, 1981.

Wilson, William, *Daniel McIntyre and the Winnipeg Schools.* Winnipeg: University of Manitoba Press, 1981.

Winks, Robin, *Blacks in Canada.* Montreal: McGill – Queen's University Press, 1970.

_____, "Negro School Segregation in Ontario and Nova Scotia," *Canadian Historical Review* XLVIII, no.2 (June 1969), 164-91.

Wirth, Arthur G., *Education in the Technological Society, The Vocational-Liberal Studies Controversy in the Early Twentieth Century.* Scranton: Intext Educational Publishers, 1972.

Wolfgang, Aaron, ed., *Education of Immigrant Students: Issues and Answers.* Toronto: OISE, 1975.

Wood, B. Anne. "Hegelian Resolutions in the New Education Movement: The 1925 Putman-Weir Report," *Dalhousie Review* 62, no.2 (Summer 1982), 254-277.

_____, "John Harold Putman's 1913 American Tour," *Vitae Scholasticae* 2, no.1 (Spring 1983), 35-59.

_____, "In Defense of Froebel: Ontario's 1913 Rejection of the Montessori System." Unpublished paper, Halifax, June, 1984.

_____, "Ontario's Kindergarten-Primary Movement: Utilitarianism Subverts Idealism," *Journal of the Midwest History of Education Society* 12, 1984, 94-107.

_____, *Idealism Subverted: The Making of a Progressive Educator.* Montreal: McGill-Queen's Press, 1985.

Wrong, G.M., C. Martin and W.N. Sage, *The Story of Canada.* Toronto: Ryerson, 1929.

Young, D.R. and A.Y. Machinski, "An Historical Survey of Vocational Education in Canada," *Canadian Vocational Association Journal* 8, no.3 (Fall 1972), 10-12, 28; 8, no.4 (Winter 1972-3), 4-5, 18-25; 9, no.1 (Spring 1973), 18-22, 33; 9, no.2 (Summer 1973), 22-34.

Zureik, Elia and Robert M. Pike, ed. *Socialization and Values in Canadian Society,* 2 vols. Toronto: McClelland and Stewart, 1975.

# INDEX

DATE DUE